THE CORRESPONDENCE OF
Alexander Pope

ALEXANDER POPE

*From the painting by Sir Godfrey Kneller, now in the Collection of
the Earl of Crawford and Balcares*

THE

CORRESPONDENCE

OF

Alexander Pope

EDITED BY

GEORGE SHERBURN

VOLUME III
1729–1735

OXFORD

AT THE CLARENDON PRESS

1956

Oxford University Press, Amen House, London E.C. 4

GLASGOW NEW YORK TORONTO MELBOURNE WELLINGTON
BOMBAY CALCUTTA MADRAS KARACHI CAPE TOWN IBADAN

———

PRINTED IN GREAT BRITAIN

CONTENTS

VOLUME III

The Painting of Alexander Pope, by Sir Godfrey
Kneller, now in the Collection of the Earl of
Crawford and Balcarres   *Frontispiece*

LETTERS 1729–1735   *p.* 1

UNDATABLE LETTERS   *p.* 515

This year started with alarms concerning the extreme illnesses of Gay and of Mrs. Pope and with worries over the publication of *The Dunciad Variorum*. Pope's use of his noble friends in securing *The Dunciad* from piracies and his use of Lord Oxford's library for deposits there of his letters are among the striking developments of the year. Once *The Dunciad* was out and approved at Court (where, on account of *Polly*, Gay was disapproved of), Pope went to work collecting materials for a final volume of Swift–Pope Miscellanies; but this went slowly, and Motte the publisher proved troublesome with regard to finances. The publication by Pope of the rare second volume of Wycherley's *Posthumous Works* quickened the poet's interest in his own letters, the return of which he had requested from various correspondents. In letters to Caryll his disparagement of Teresa Blount becomes overt and he states definitely that he himself plans never to marry. His friendship with David Mallet emerges towards the end of the year when he begins to aid in getting Mallet's *Eurydice* accepted at Drury Lane.

---

†POPE *to* GAY[1]   [1728/9]

1735

Dear Gay,—No words can tell you the great concern I feel for you; I assure you it was not, and is not lessen'd, by the immediate apprehension I have now every day lain under of losing my Mother. Be assur'd, no Duty less than that, should have kept me one day from attending your condition: I would come and take a room by you at *Hampstead*, to be with you daily, were she not still in danger of death. I have constantly had particular accounts of you from the Doctor, which have not ceas'd to alarm me yet. God preserve your life, and restore your health. I really beg it for my own sake, for I feel I love you more than I thought, in health, tho' I always lov'd you a great deal. If I am so unfortunate as to bury my poor Mother, and yet have the good fortune to have my prayers heard for you, I hope we may live most of our remaining days together. If, as I believe, the air of a better clime as the Southern Part of *France* may be thought useful for your recovery, thither I would go with you infallibly; and it is very probable we might get the Dean with us, who is in that abandon'd state already in which I shall shortly be, as to other Cares and Duties. Dear *Gay* be as chearful as your Sufferings will permit: God is a better friend than a Court: Even any honest man is a better. I promise you

[1] Towards the end of 1728 and in Jan. 1729 Gay was ill of fever, asthma, and pleurisy. At times his life was despaired of. Mrs. Pope was ill at much the same time.

my entire friendship in all events, heartily praying for your recovery. |
Your, &c.

Do not write, if you are ever so able: The Doctor tells me all.

†POPE *to* GAY   [1728/9]

1735

I faithfully assure you, in the midst of that melancholy with which
I have been so long encompassed, in an hourly Expectation almost of
my Mother's death; there was no circumstance that render'd it more
insupportable to me, than that I could not leave her to see you. Your
own present Escape from so imminent danger, I pray God may prove
less precarious than my poor Mother's can be; whose Life at her age
can at best be but a short Reprieve, or a longer Dying. But I fear, even
that is more than God will please to grant me; for, these two days
past, her most dangerous Symptoms are returned upon her; and unless
there be a sudden change, I must in a few days, if not in a few Hours,
be depriv'd of her. In the afflicting Prospect before me, I know nothing
that can so much alleviate it as the View now given me (Heaven grant
it may encrease) of your recovery. In the sincerity of my heart, I am
excessively concern'd, not to be able to pay you, dear *Gay*, any part
of the debt I very gratefully remember I owe you, on a like sad
occasion, when you was here comforting me in her last great Illness.
May your health augment as fast as I fear it pleases God hers must
decline: I believe that would be very fast——may the Life that is
added to you be past in good fortune and tranquility, rather of your
own giving to your self, than from any Expectations or Trust in others.
——May you and I live together, without wishing more felicity or
acquisitions than Friendship can give and receive without obligations
to Greatness——God keep you, and three or four more of those I
have known so long, that I may have something worth the surviving
my Mother. Adieu, dear *Gay*, and believe me (while you live and while
I live) | Your, &c.

As I told you in my last letter, I repeat it in this: Do not think of
writing to me. The Doctor, Mrs. *Howard*, and Mrs. *Blount*, give me
daily accounts of you.

†POPE *to* GAY   [1728/9]

1735
                                                        Sunday Night.

I truly rejoyc'd to see your hand-writing, tho' I fear'd the trouble it
might give you. I wish I had not known that you are still so excessively weak. Every day for a week past I had hopes of being able in

a day or two more to see you. But my poor Mother advances not at all, gains no strength, and seems but upon the whole to wait for the next cold Day to throw her into a Diarrhœa that must, if it return, carry her off. This being daily to be fear'd, makes me not dare to go a day from her, lest that should prove to be her Last. God send you a speedy recovery, and such a total one as at your time of Life may be expected. You need not call the few words I writ to you either kind, or good; That was, and is, nothing. But whatever I have in my Nature of Kindness, I really have for you, and whatever Good I could do, I wou'd among the very first be glad to do to you. In your circumstance the old Roman farewell is proper. *Vive! memor nostri.* | Your, &c.

I send you a very kind letter of Mr. *Digby*[1] between whom and me two letters have pass'd concerning you.

‡POPE *to* GAY[2]   [1728/9]

1735

I am glad to hear of the progress of your recovery, and the oftner I hear it the better, when it becomes easy to you to give it me. I so well remember the Consolation you were to me in my Mother's former Illness, that it doubles my Concern at this time not to be able to be with you, or you able to be with me. Had I lost her, I wou'd have been no where else but with you during your confinement. I have now past five weeks without once going from home, and without any company but for three or four of the days. Friends rarely stretch their kindness so far as ten miles. My Lord *Bolingbroke* and Mr. *Bethel* have not forgotten to visit me: the rest (except Mrs. *Blount* once) were contented to send messages. I never pass'd so melancholy a time, and now Mr. *Congreve*'s death touches me nearly. It is twenty years that I have known him. Every year carries away something dear with it, till we outlive all tenderness, and become wretched Individuals again as we begun. Adieu! This is my Birth-day, and this is my Reflection upon it.

> With added Days if life give nothing new,
> But, like a Sieve, let ev'ry Pleasure thro';
> Some Joy still lost, as each vain Year runs o'er,
> And all we gain, some sad Reflection more!

---

[1] Pope's friend the Hon. Robert Digby had died in 1726, but apparently there was some correspondence, not known to be preserved, with Robert's older brother, Edward.

[2] This letter almost certainly involves conflation of two letters or the addition to a letter written shortly after Congreve's death (19 Jan. 1728/9) of the verses and the sentence introducing the verses. The letter does not seem to have been written on 21 May (Pope's birthday) in spite of the last sentence, and the verses were written at least as early as 1724. See Ault, *New Light*, pp. 202–5.

Is this a Birth-day?—'Tis alas too clear,
'Tis but the Funeral of the former Year.
                              I am Yours, &c.

*POPE *to* THE EARL OF BURLINGTON[1]   [1728/9]

Chatsworth

My Lord,—After many unforseen delays the Printers have got within
two sheets of the book, & I chuse rather to send the papers thus, than
defer too long the material point in which your Lordship's friendship
is to procure me Mr Fazakerley's opinion. The whole Question is
only this: If there be any thing in these sheets (for the other two can
have nothing of that sort) which an Action may be grounded upon?
and if there be, which those things are? that Mr F. would mark or
alter them in this Copy. The time of publication pressing, I could wish
he read them as soon as possible. Your Lordship needs not even name
me as any way concern'd in that publication, which Mr F. will
observe is guarded against by the manner in which it is publish'd, but
the apprehension is only, lest if the Printer & Publisher be found, any
such Action could be brought; for we would be safe even against this.

It would be impertinent, my Lord, to make you an Excuse, for
a thing you had the goodness to ingage in of your own motive; there
is only room for thanks, which are sincerely payd you, with all the
Regard & Esteem imaginable, by | My Lord | Your long-oblig'd & |
Your ever oblig'd Servant | A. Pope.

I beg my Lady Burlington's Patronage of the Ass & the Dunciad,
me and my burden.

*POPE *to* THE EARL OF BURLINGTON[2]   [1728/9]

Chatsworth

My Lord,—I need not tell what your Lordship must know, that I
am greatly obliged by you. I hope my Lady Burlington is as well as you
can wish or expect, of whose state of health I find the messenger can
give no acct.

Indeed I could be glad of the Decisive opinion of Mr Fazakerly, it
will otherwise be impracticable to publish the thing before Mr. G's.[3]

---

1 This letter must antedate 10 Apr. when *The Dunciad Variorum* was published. Pope is
now sending all but the last two (innocent) sheets of the volume to be submitted to the
inspection of the distinguished lawyer, Nicholas Fazakerley. See Pope to Burlington, 23
Dec. 1728.

2 Concern over possible libels in *The Dunciad* as well as over the healths of Lady Burlington
and Mrs. Pope places this letter early in 1729.

3 Pope was meticulous in timing his publications. If 'Mr. G' is Gay, the reference is to
Polly, which appeared actually a fortnight before the first quarto *Dunciad*. This *Dunciad* bore

and I am grown more Prudent than ever, the less I think others so. I was just going to ask your Lordship's friendly advice on a point I think material, when my Lord Duke of Roxburgh came: If I could see you to morrow, (without too just a fear of being unseasonably troublesome while Lady Burlington remains confined) I should tell you my prudential doubts & schemes at large, which possibly might defer the whole matter. But I will not be so importunate unless your Lordship allows me expresly, by sending for me again in the morning.

My Mother (to whom you did so much honour yesterday in your obliging account of her, & today in enquiring after her) is not so ill as to be insensible of it, and begs your acceptance of her Services.

I can't express with what real respect & sincere Sentiments I am | My Lord, | Your most Obligd, most Obedient | & affectionate Servant | A. Pope.

I heartily wish my Lady's timely recovery agst Wednesday sennt.

POPE *to* FORTESCUE   [*January* 1728/9]
1797 (Polwhele, i. 323)

Wednesday.

The very melancholy situation I have been in from the very day you begun the journey to Devonshire,[1] made me not willing to break the enjoyment and peace of your domestic satisfactions in your family there; and poor Mr. Gay's great danger added to my concern. My mother still keeps her bed, and I fear is very unlikely to rise again; the distemper which probably will finish all her decays, holds upon her, and does not yield to any remedies; the most is an interval from pain into weakness and slumbers. God knows when I shall see you or any body; in the mean time I thank you for many offices of your friendship, and beg you will continue to assist my sister's affairs; I presume Essington is now in town,[2] and would send you his account, if demanded. Mrs. Blount has charged me with many speeches to be made you upon your care in her annuity. But I am unable to say, or almost do any thing, my own spirits are so sunk. I wish you sincerely joy of what I am told is given you,[3] and shall always make it my wish to

the imprint of 'A. Dod', and it appeared on 10 Apr. Gilliver (who may well be 'Mr. G') put his name to quarto *Dunciads* first advertised on 17 Apr. See Griffith, Nos. 211–17. Pope is inclined to prudence. Possibly he thought Gay imprudent with regard to *Polly*. Gilliver was, one imagines, fully as prudent as Pope. We shall hear more of his prudence later.

[1] Fortescue has returned from a visit in Devonshire, possibly for the Christmas season. Gay's great danger seems to be in the past tense, but Mrs. Pope is still very ill. These details fit January of 1729.

[2] Essington evidently owed Mrs. Rackett money, and for the next few years will try to avoid payment.

[3] In December it had been announced that Fortescue was appointed Solicitor-General to H.R.H. Prince Frederick. Pope may be uncertain about this, or more likely has a rumour of added benefits due for Fortescue.

Heaven for you. *Det vitam, det opes, æquam animam tibi ipse parabis.*
Your very faithful servant, | A. Pope.

Pray make my compliments to Mr. Horace Walpole,[1] whom I
would have waited on with my thanks, but for this confinement on
account of my mother.

Address: To Wm. Fortescue, esq. at his house in Bell-yard, near Lincoln's
Inn.

POPE *to* MRS. RACKETT   [1728/9]

Ushaw College
                                                      Thursday night

Dear Sister,—I have been agen with Mr Fortescue. He desires you
first to tell me, Whether you took out Letters of Administration, on
Mr Rackets death? It will be necessary too to send the Mortgage
Deeds to Mr Fortescue. He says you cannot Divide the Sum from
the Principal, whatever the mony be you take up; but the *whole* must
be made over, in Trust, & then a Declaration of Trust again given to
you, to repay you & be accountable for as much as is the Remainder
of it. In this case, if you do not care to make it over to Mr *Jervas*,
you may do it to *me*, & I'll take up the mony on *my own account*, & let
the Security pass between you & me only. Send me your Answer to
Lord Oxfords to morrow. Yours ever, A. Pope

POPE *to* FORTESCUE[2]   [1728/9]

Harvard University

You see by the inclosed my Sister is in an Alarum: I suppose occasiond
by a meer mistake of Mr Cruse's Clark;[3] or by her own too much
Haste in running to administer before him. I beg You will cause that
mistake forthwith to be removed, that she may, without loss of time,
proceed with full Powers.

I must intreat your vigilance as to her Great Affair, that it may be
done with all convenient Speed: It seems Cruwys says there is some
difference in the account as kept by Mr Racket & by the other Party

---

[1] Sir Robert's brother. The cause for thanks is obscure. Conceivably it may be the Avignon
abbey secured by Pope's intervention for Father Southcote. Since Horatio Walpole was
closely allied with Cardinal Fleury he may deserve credit not given him by either Spence or
Ruffhead.

[2] The date is quite uncertain. Pope's brother-in-law, Charles Rackett, had died in 1728,
and letters of administration had been granted to the poet's sister, the widow, on 7 Nov.
1728. Thereafter for some time her affairs were in or near litigation.

[3] Mr. Cruse is Mrs. Rackett's lawyer, mentioned below as Cruwys. He is possibly Samuel
Cruwys, called to the bench in the Inner Temple in 1737. A family of this name came from
Devonshire, as did Fortescue.

in the chancery Suit. If you please to have a meeting with Mr Essington & examine His account of what has been pay'd into his hands, it will be the readyest way & is very necessary.

I am glad you had not the mortification of seeing the Country, this sad & gloomy day. I heartily wish my self with you. Adieu dear Sir. I hope better luck next Sunday. Till then | Vive memor nostri:¹ | who am always | Dear Sir, | Your true friend | & obliged faithful Servant, | A. Pope

My Mother sends you her hearty Services.

Address: To | William Fortescue Esqr at | his house in | Bellyard

POPE *to* FORTESCUE²   [1728/9?]

1797 (Polwhele, i. 323–4)

I first thank you for your kind visit, and hope you are not the worse for the cold day. I find by the inclosed that there must be more money somewhere to be found of my sister's affair. For the principal sum was 1700*l.* beside interest, and, as I understand no part of the principal ever was paid, I therefore beg you to cause enquiry to be speedily made of Mr. Thurston, the master in chancery. Pray ought you not to require a sight of Essington's books themselves, where the account was kept, if his extract prove not satisfactory? The question my sister asks about one Abbot I cannot answer, unless you find it in the writings and papers she sent you. I have troubled you with the parcel for New England. For all your kindnesses I thank you cordially, and am, with sincere esteem, your faithful friend and servant, | A. Pope

My mother is rather worse than better.

Address: To Wm. Fortescue, esq. in Bell-yard, near Lincoln's Inn, London.

POPE *to* THE EARL OF OXFORD³   [6 *January* 1728/9]

Longleat Portland Papers, xii

Janu: 6. 1728/9

My Lord,—It is not to be exprest how sensible I am of your Goodness in sending so often, & interesting yourself in all my Concerns, especi-

---

¹ An echo of Horace, *Carmina*, iii. xxvii. 14.
² 'The parcel for New England' as well as Mrs. Rackett's troubles with Essington help to date the letter. Pope has received the letter of the Rev. Mather Byles (25 Nov. 1728) and is sending him the promised parcel of his *Works* or, more likely, of the *Odyssey*. See Byles's letter of 1736 (iv. 16).
³ The date in the superscription is in Lord Oxford's hand. The endorsement on the cover is that of a secretary.

ally in one of so tender a nature as this. Indeed my poor Mother
continues in a most uncertain, dangerous way, hard to discover if more
of Decay, or of Disease? She was 2 days seemingly mending, now as ill
again as ever. She has not once rose out of bed in sixteen days. I bad my
Servant this morning leave this account at your door: I am very much
sunk my self, & know not when I can hope to see you? There's no
possibility of quitting her for a day, or else I had been with my poor
friend Gay. God preserve him; if he dies he will not leave an honester
Heart behind him in this kingdom. I am troubled still about Cook, (as
the smallest triffles will affect one in a Spleenatic weak condition.)
So I've been acquitting my Conscience about him to Mr Westley, to
whom I beg your Lordship to transmit this. I entreat you, if this Illness of my Mother lasts, to give me One day, & bring him with you
that I may thank him. It will be great charity, & therfore you will do
it. My Lady Oxford will be assured of my sense of her kind Enquiries,
& believe no man can be with sincerer affection & esteem than I,
My Lord | Your ever faithfull | obliged Servant. | A. Pope.

Address: To the Right Honorable | the Earl of Oxford.
Endorsement: Mr Pope / Jan 6. 1728

POPE *to* BENJAMIN MOTTE[1]   [14 *January* 1728/9]
The Pierpont Morgan Library
                                                          Jan. 14. 1728/9.
Sir,—Your Letter pretty much surprizes me. What I accorded to
you as a *Free Gift*, you seem to take as a Condition of an Agreement
which was made long before. And what I gave upon My *Word*, you
seem unwilling to have no further *Security* for. I shall certainly keep
it; & that is your Security; & be assurd I will give you no other; nor
shall I think you much deserved a Goodnaturd Concession given upon
Honour, if you dared not Trust it? As to the *Note* I ask'd of you, even
to ask *that* was a Concession; for the *Mony* is due, & hath been some
time—I am quite indifferent as to the time of printing the third
volume,[2] nor do I know what bulk it will make till the Dean is consulted: So that when ever You have Perform'd your part of what *Is a
Covenant*, & *past*; it will be time enough to make demands of my performance of what is but a *Voluntary kindness* in mine, &, *to come*. Once
more I assure you I will do it; & I will do it without being bound any
way but by my Word. I am Sr. Yours A. Pope

That you may not Mistake me; I mean thus. When you have paid

---

[1] The date is in the hand of Motte, not of Pope. The letter concerns Motte's failure to
perform his parts of the agreement for the three volumes of *Miscellanies*, made first on 29
Mar. 1727, and finall settled 1 July 1729. See *Gent. Mag.* xliv (1855), 363.
[2] The third volume, so called, was the fourth to be published. It appeared in Oct. 1732.

the 100ll, either to Mr Gay or me, Or given him or me a Note for it
for value recd: as then the Agreement for the former Vols. will be
made good, I will give you a full discharge, & give you a Title to the
other volume for 25ll (to which you shall have liberty, on my Word,
to add the Poem.¹) If you don't understand this, you are very blind
to my good will to you, which I assure you is very great.

Address: To | Mr Motte, Bookseller, | at Temple Barr | Fleetstreet. | London.
Postmark: 14/IA

THE EARL OF OXFORD *to* POPE   20 *January* 1728/9

Longleat Portland Papers, xii
                                    Dover Street. Janu: 20: 1728|9.

Sir,—I was in hopes to have seen you before this by your kind letter
& message, but I am affraid it is neither so well as you would wish
with your good mother and consequently it is but indifferent with
yourself.

I obeyed your request & sent your letter to mr Westley,² but upon
consideration when I saw him last I forbid him to show the letter, the
reasons I will tell you when I see you, I belive you will not dislike
them. Westley has not been able to see *cooke* I suppose he is at hide
& not to be found, I was glad of it for my own reasons.

poor honest Gay recovers. but congreve is gone.³

my Wife desires her compliments & good Wishes to mrs pope & to
yourself I join in with my wishes for you both I am with true re-
spect and esteem | Sir | Your most | affectionate & most | humble
Servant | Oxford.

POPE *to* THE EARL OF OXFORD⁴   [21 *January* 1728/9]

Longleat Portland Papers, xii
                                         Jan. 21. 1728/9

My Lord,—I am in truth in a very melancoly situation: My Mother
not mending, but lying in so languishing a state, & under such daily
danger of going away at once, as the Diarrhœa & Fever returns, (which
is never quite off, half a day certain.) Conversation with her I can
have none, for at best she lyes dozing; Yet leave her a day I cannot,
lest that day should prove her last.

I am greatly obligd to you for stopping a Letter you had objections

---

¹ Probably *The Dunciad*, which had at a last moment been displaced in vol. iii by the *Peri
Bathous*.   ² For this letter to Wesley see vol. v.
³ Congreve had died in London on 19 Jan.
⁴ In the superscription the date is in Lord Oxford's hand. The endorsement is that of a
secretary.

to (I dare say for good reasons)   I wish extremely to see your Lordship, & will, the first day possible. Mr Congreves death was to me sudden, & strook me thorough. You know the Value I bore him & a long 20 years friendship—God keep you My Lord & all yours! I am truly sensible of all the proofs of your great Goodness, & ever faithfully My Lady's & Your Lordships | obliged & most humble Servant | A. Pope

Address: To the Rt. Hon. the Earl | of Oxford.

Endorsement: Mr Pope | Jan 21. 1728/9

POPE *to* THE EARL OF OXFORD[1]   [30 *January* 1728/9]

Longleat Portland Papers, xii

Janu. 30: 1728/9

My Lord,—I often think, when I write you these short, insignificant Letters, how very imperfectly, or rather with what Nothingness (to use a good puritan Expression) they show the real great Esteem I bear you, & the Sense I feel of your Lordships constant favors on all occasions. The truth is, at this particular Time I feel them doubly, when I want a Prop to rest my Mind upon, almost every hour, when I see nothing here but sickness, & hear of nothing from abroad but the danger or death of my Friends.

It will be great charity, my Lord, if a finer day than ordinary should dawn at this season, if you would fill your coach with one or two such as you should like for four or five hours, and dine here on Mutton and a broild chicken. I fancy Mr Lewis might attend you, or Mr Westley would think me a grateful man for contriving him This reward for the strange Company I've once or twice ingagd him in. I beg to know if this be feasible. You see I presume much, but I have some reason, for I love you much. I am my Lady Oxfords and your Lordships ever | faithfull Servant | A. Pope.

Address: To the Rt. Hon. the Earl of | Oxford, in Dover street | Piccadilly | London.

Endorsement: Mr Pope | Jan 30, 1728/9

THE EARL OF OXFORD *to* POPE   30 *January* 1728/9

Longleat Portland Papers, xii

Janu: 30: 1728|9

Sir,—I am obliged to you for giving your self the trouble to write   I am allways pleased to hear from you and of you and shall with great

---

[1] In the superscription the date is in Lord Oxford's hand. The endorsement is by a secretary.

pleasure wait upon you when it is convenient   if munday be a proper
day I will come and bring Friend Lewis and Westley if he can come
if not some good man in his room. I desire we may dine at one o clock
that we may not be in the Dark for I hate works of Darkness. Ld
Dupplin and Wooton[1] went to see Gay, and found him fine & well and
took the Air with him. I belive this piece of News would be very
agreable to you.

If the day I have named should be improper pray let me know and I
will come some other day.

you are often in my thoughts and if it would ease you I feel for you,
if the prayers of a Heretick woud do you any good you have them   I
am with true respect and esteem | your most affectionate | humble
Servant | Oxford

my Wife is your humble Servt.

POPE *to* THE EARL OF OXFORD   [31 *January* 1728/9]

Longleat Portland Papers, xii

Janu: 31: 1728/9.

My Lord,—According to the kind Indulgence you give me, why may
not I ask to see you rather on Sunday, (when Westley will have no
Schoolbusiness)   It happens that Munday is the only day that may be
less convenient, (for my Mother is to do a Christian duty that day at
which I attend, & I would wish when your Lordship can come, it may
be as Early as possible, the days being much too short for your Com-
pany. I am with great sincerity | My Lord | Ever yours. | A. Pope

My Lady Oxford & Lady Margaret have me always for their
Servant.

Address: To | the Rt. Hon. the Earl of | Oxford. | Doverstreet.

POPE *to* FORTESCUE   [1728/9]

The Pierpont Morgan Library

Im forc'd to write to you on this red-lind paper, for I've not a sheet in
the house beside. I sent Bowry to ask you when I might hope to see
you? I really want it, for I am very near sunk in melancholy, having
been full 6 weeks here,[2] attending a very melancholy Care. I would
otherwise have tryd to fix a day to meet you at Sir R. W's (with His

---

[1] Viscount Dupplin was the nephew of Lord Oxford. John Wootton, the painter, was a
friend of Gay's: he designed most of the plates for Gay's *Fables* (1727).

[2] His mother's illness had begun in December. See Pope to Oxford, 6 Jan., for statements
as to the duration of her illness. Pope is vague on such matters.

permission, and your Co-adjutor-ship) I have particular reason to desire to know a thing, which I believe He will tell me if you ask it,
Who was Author of a Book calld *an Essay on the Taste and writings
of this age*,[1] dedicated to him? & a Libel upon Me. I formerly sent it
to Sir R. by you (as I think.) Pray ask him, & assure him of my respect-
full Services. I am Ever | Dear Sir | Yours. | A. Pope.

[Se]nd me some paper: tis all [I] get, by you men in place.

POPE *to* THE EARL OF OXFORD[2]   [1 *February* 1728/9]

Longleat Portland Papers, xii

Febr 1: 1728/9.

My Lord,—Excuse the hurry & illbreeding of this Scrap of paper, I
will with joy expect you on Tuesday.

Your Lordships most | sincere obligd Servant | A. Pope.

If you would drink good wine, pray bring just 2 bottles with you
for I have but 2 in the house.

Address: Lord Oxford.

Endorsement: Mr Pope | Feb. 1. 1728/9

||POPE *to* CARYLL[3]   3 *February* 1728/9

Add. 28618

Twickenham Feb 3d 1728/9

I assure you I am glad of your letter; and have long wanted nothing
but the permission you now give me, to be plain and unreserved upon
this head, ⌜upon which⌝ I wrote ⌜actually a letter⌝ to you long[4] since;
but a friend of yours and mine was of opinion, it was taking too much
upon me, and more than I could be entitled to by long[5] acquaintance

---

[1] This pamphlet of fifty-odd pages was published by J. Roberts about the end of May
1728. It was dedicated to Walpole and was (so the titlepage said) 'By a Gentleman of C—st
C—h, Oxon.' Pope had evidently sent it (so he thought) some time ago to Sir Robert. Hence
the letter is, with proper doubts, placed during the period when *The Dunciad Variorum* was
in final stages of preparation. The pamphlet is there listed, with no author mentioned, p. 94
(quarto edition).

[2] The date in the superscription is in Lord Oxford's hand. The endorsement is made by a
secretary. Pope writes on a Saturday.

[3] In his editions of 1737–42 Pope printed this letter as 'To Mr. C—.' In all his printed
texts the letter was dated 2 Sept. 1732. It may easily appear shocking that Pope should print
accusations of uncharitableness in this letter and not print his later letter (16 Feb.), in which
he admitted that the accusation was a mistake; but the shifting of the date and the suppression
of Caryll's identity preclude any very bad effects in publishing the letter.

Pope's omissions are as usual placed in half-brackets, and his other revisions for publication
are here indicated. Once printed his text underwent only few and unimportant revisions.

[4] you long] you concerning it long *1737–42*.

[5] by long] by the mere merit of long *1737–42*.

or[1] ⌐the mere merit of¬ good will. ⌐I vow to God,¬ I have not a thing in my heart relating to any friend, which I would not, in my own nature, declare to all mankind. The truth is what you guess: I could not ⌐much¬ esteem your conduct, to an object of misery so near you as Mrs Cope;[2] and I have often hinted it to your self. The truth is I cannot yet esteem it, for any reason I am able to see. But this I promise, I ⌐fully¬ acquit you as far as your own mind acquits you: I have now no farther cause;[3] for the unhappy lady gives me now no farther pain. She is no longer an object either of yours or of my compassion; ⌐and¬ the hardships done her, ⌐by whomsoever,¬ are lodged in the hands of God, nor has any man more to do in't, but[4] the persons concerned in occasioning them.

⌐As to my small assistance, I never dreamt of repayment; so the true sorrow you express for my being a *loser* is misplaced. Indeed, I was a little shocked at one circumstance, that some of your Sussex acquaintance declared: *That you remitted me ten pounds a year for her* (which you know was not true; but I don't impute this report to you). The only thing I am now concerned at is, that (for want of some abler or richer friend to her) I myself stand engaged to Abbé Southcote[5] for 20ll. toward his charges for surgeons and necessaries in her last illness: which is all I think my self a *loser* by; because it does her no good.

⌐In regard to Mrs Patty Blount, what I told you in her vindication, of her case, was no more than a justice she deserves, and which ought to be done her to everybody; so that it was no particular application to yourself, nor could be the ground of any resentment in my part. And indeed I'm not only unable to judge whether her relations would or would not, do her service? but whether she herself would accept it from them? Because she has declined it from those who had some merit and much desire to render it her, persons of the first power and friends of the sincerest inclinations; so that her regards for the mother and sister are even superior to yours.¬

Now[6] for the interruption of our correspondence; I am sorry you seem to put the test of my friendship upon that ⌐issue of my writing as formerly,¬ because it is what I am disqualified from towards all my

---

[1] or] and *1737–42.*

[2] Mrs Cope] Mrs. —— *1737–42.* (Mrs. Cope had died 12 May 1728.)

[3] Cause, for] cause of complaint, for *1737–42.*

[4] do in't, but] do in them except *1737–42.*

[5] In condemning Pope for his reproaches to Caryll, Elwin quotes from a letter by Mrs. Cope's brother to our Caryll (8 June 1728; found in Add. MS. 28228, f. 277) as saying, 'You did more for her in her illness than anyone of her kindred or friends as she herself said not long before she died—and if you did not do more, you had (without doubt) good reasons for it.' Caryll had sent £25 a year to Mrs. Cope; apparently others than Pope thought that possibly he might have done more. The fact that Pope, no kin to the lady, is being asked to defray surgeon's bills indicates that something was wrong.

[6] Now for] As for *1737–42.*

other acquaintance, with whom I hold no such correspondence.[1] I'll name you a few obstacles[2] which I can't surmount: want of health, want of time, want of eyes,[3] and one yet stronger than all:[4] I write not upon the terms of other ⌈honest⌉ men; and[5] however glad I might be of expressing my respects,[6] opening my mind, or venting my concerns to my private friends, I dare not,[7] while there are Curlls in the world. If you please to reflect either on the impertinence of weak admirers, the malice of low enemies, the avarice of mercenary booksellers, or the silly curiosity of people in general, you'll confess I've small reason to indulge correspondences (in which too I want materials, as I live altogether out of town, and have entirely abstracted my mind (I hope) to better things),[8] unless my friends would ⌈do (as indeed some have been prevailed upon, and as you know I have many years desired you would do)⌉ send me back those forfeitures of my discretion, commit to my justice what I trusted only to their indulgence, and return me at the year's end those trifling letters, which can be to them but a day's amusement, but to me may prove a discredit to posterity.[9]

I come now to a particular you complain of ⌈as to writing. I am not to my knowledge 2 or 3 letters in your debt. I never received but one, which was to tell me just after your kind visit here that you were safe arrived at home. Nor did I receive any *request* from you; only that (if I remember right) Mrs Blount told me once, you had a desire to *know something*⌉ *about some party-papers*,[10] *and their writers*, which I could not tell[11] you, because I never was, or will be privy to such things.[12] And if by accident I had known a thing, thro' my acquaintance with any of the writers, which they concealed;[13] I should certainly never be the reporter of it.

For my waiting on you at Ladyholt,[14] I have often wished it. It was my compliance to a superior duty that hindered me, and one which you are too good a Christian to wish I should have broken. I have never but once left my mother (at her great age) for more than a week,[15] ⌈when I was driven, for my own preservation, to Bath last

---

[1] with whom . . . correspondence] with whom I cannot hold any frequent commerce. *1737–42.*   [2] a few obstacles] the obstacles *1737–42.*
[3] want of eyes] want of good eyes *1737–42.*
[4] than all] than them all *1737–42.*   [5] men; and] Men. For *1737–42.*
[6] respects] respect *1737–42.*   [7] I dare not] I hardly dare *1737–42.*
[8] things) unless my friends] things than common news. I wish my friends *1737–42.*
[9] discredit to posterity.] discredit as lasting and extensive, as the aforesaid weak admirers, mean enemies, mercenary scriblers, or curious simpletons, can make it. *1737–42.*
[10] you complain of . . . about some party papers] you complain of, my not answering your question about some party papers *1737–42.*
[11] writers. . . . tell] authors. This indeed I could not tell *1737–42.*
[12] such things] such papers *1737–42.*
[13] accident . . . concealed;] accident thro' my acquaintance with any of the writers, I had known a thing they conceal'd; *1737–42.*   [14] Ladyholt] your country house *1737–42.*
[15] broken . . . week,] broken, having never ventur'd to leave my mother (at her great Age) for more than a week, which is too little for such a journey. *1737–42.*

season. Then I assure you I had a merit you do not know of; for I did my utmost to make you in my way home, and had accomplished it, had not my Lord Scarborow's¹ design of going then to Sussex been put off.⌐

Upon the whole, I must acquit myself of any act or thought ⌐or guilt,⌐ in prejudice to the regard I owe you as so long and obliging an acquaintance and correspondent. I am sure I have all the good wishes for yourself and whole² family that become a friend. There is ⌐nothing,⌐ no accident, ⌐no action,⌐ that can happen for your credit⌐, or happiness,⌐ which I should³ not be ready to extol, or to rejoyce in ⌐sincerely.⌐ And therefore I beg you to be assured I am, in disposition and will, tho not so much as I would be in testimonies, or proofs,⁴ | your ⌐very affectionate, obliged | and real servant | A: P:⌐

⌐My mother keeps her bed still, notwithstanding the good account you have had of her amendment and recovery.⌐

†SWIFT *to* POPE⁵   13 *February* 1728/9

1740

Dublin, Feb. 13, 1728.

I liv'd very easily in the country: Sir A.⁶ is a man of sense, and a scholar, has a good voice, and my Lady a better; she is perfectly well bred, and desirous to improve her understanding, which is very good, but cultivated too much like a fine Lady. She was my pupil there, and severely chid when she read wrong; with that, and walking and making twenty little amusing improvements, and writing family verses of mirth by way of libels on my Lady, my time past very well and in very great order; infinitely better than here, where I see no creature but my servants and my old Presbyterian house-keeper, denying myself to every body till I shall recover my ears.

The account of another Lord Lieutenant was only in a common news-paper, when I was in the country, and if it should have happen'd to be true, I would have desired to have had access to him as the situation I am in requires. But this renews the grief for the death of our friend Mr. Congreve, whom I loved from my youth, and who surely besides his other talents, was a very agreeable companion. He had the misfortune to squander away a very good constitution in his younger days; and I think a man of sense and merit like him, is bound in con-

---

¹ The estate of Stanstead, which adjoined Ladyholt, belonged to the Earl of Scarborough.
² whole] your *1737–42*.
³ your credit . . . which I should] your advantage, and no action that can redound to your credit, which I should *1737–42*.
⁴ proofs, | your] writing, Yours &c. *1737–42*.
⁵ This is Swift's reply to Pope's letter of 12 Nov. 1728. Is it a fragment only?
⁶ Sir A.] Sir Arthur Acheson *1741 Dab.*

science to preserve his health for the sake of his friends, as well as of himself. Upon his own account I could not much desire the continuance of his life, under so much pain, and so many infirmities. Years have not yet hardened me, and I have an addition of weight on my spirits since we lost him, tho' I saw him so seldom; and possibly if he had liv'd on should never have seen him more. I do not only wish as you ask me, that I was unacquainted with any deserving person, but almost, that I never had a friend. Here is an ingenious good-humour'd Physician,[1] a fine gentleman, an excellent scholar, easy in his fortunes, kind to every body, hath abundance of friends, entertains them often and liberally, they pass the evening with him at cards, with plenty of good meat and wine, eight or a dozen together; he loves them all, and they him; he has twenty of these at command; if one of them dies, it is no more than poor Tom! he gets another, or takes up with the rest, and is no more mov'd than at the loss of his cat; he offends no body, is easy with every body—is not this the true happy man? I was describing him to my Lady A—,[2] who knows him too, but she hates him mortally by my character, and will not drink his health: I would give half my fortune for the same temper, and yet I cannot say I love it, for I do not love my Lord[3] who is much of the Doctor's nature. I hear Mr. Gay's second Opera[4] which you mention, is forbid, and then he will be once more fit to be advised, and reject your advice. Adieu.

POPE *to* THE EARL OF OXFORD[5]   [14 *February* 1728/9]

Longleat Portland Papers, xii

Feb: 14: 1728/9.

My Lord,—I have indeed been ill, tho I knew you Good, & therfore would not tell you. But I am better, & hope soon to prove it by waiting on you.

My Mother mends as to Health, but her illness has greatly affected her Memory: I wish it goe no farther.

I beg my Lady Oxford to know me for her very grateful Servant.

Among a thousand things I take (and ought to take) kindly of you; or (to speak in a Style more proportiond, my Lord, to your Lordship & me) that I look upon as a great honour; I must mention what you were pleasd at parting last, to tell me, That you would come again. Pray good my Lord & my Friend, do: If I don't see you in four days.

---

[1] Dr. Helsham.—1741 *Dab*. Ball (iv. 59 n.) tells us that he was a Professor of Natural and Experimental Philosophy in Dublin.
[2] Lady A—] Lady Acheson *1741 Dab*.
[3] Lord who] Lord —— who *1741–2*. Curll (1741*Lc*) adds a footnote 'Bolingbroke'.
[4] *Polly*.—1741 Dab, Lc.
[5] The superscribed date is in Lord Oxford's hand; the endorsement in that of a secretary.

I am with thorough Esteem & gratitude, wishing you all Good things, My Lord, | Yours Ever. | A: Pope.

Address: To the Rt. Honble | the Earl of Oxford.

Endorsement: Mr Pope | Feb 14. 1728/9

THE EARL OF OXFORD *to* POPE   14 *February* 1728/9

Longleat Portland Papers, xii

Dover Street: Feb: 14. 1728/9.

Sir,—I beg your pardon for not sending you the papers I promised you[1] but they were not in my own power till two days since. I have sent you Ballads Two, epigrams Two, intelligencers five.—these last I must desire you will restore to me.

I am sorry to hear that you yourself have been ill. it is very hard when you are setting so great an example of Filial piety and carrying that Duty to so great a height you should be afflicted in your body, as well as your mind. God Almighty comfort you, and support you, for he only can   I have seen Gay at my House he looks well, he is at present very busie.[2]

I am with true | respect and esteem | your most affectionate | humble Servant. | Oxford.

My Wife sends her compliments to you. I can only say this I wish for what ever you do

Address: For. | Alexander Pope esqr.

POPE *to* CARYLL[3]   16 *February* [1728/9]

Add. 28618

Twitnam Feb 16.

I assure you once more, it is an ease to my mind, and a contentment to receive your letter. Nor was I so defective as to you it might seem, in not beginning in this matter. I had actually written, and directed you, a long letter upon the whole, but was prevented merely by another's judgment, which judgment, too, was meant in respect and tenderness for you. I wish to God I had been (according to my own

---

[1] Pope is presumably collecting materials for the volume of *Miscellanies* ultimately published in 1732. *The Intelligencer* was a weekly essay published in Dublin and written by Swift and Dr. Sheridan. It began 11 May 1728 and ran to 20 numbers, the last of which is dated 1729.

[2] Busy, doubtless, with the subscription for *Polly*, his suppressed opera, which was published 25 Mar. 1729.

[3] Through presumably a printer's error Elwin dated this letter 6 Feb. The transcript reads 16.

nature) the person active in this, and I give you with reluctance the merit herein of doing a friend's part.

As to the lady now dead, I have had the most positive assurances from one that could not be mistaken (unless wilfully so) that she had no such assistance as what you now tell me from your hands of 20ll a year. That was the sum I sent her myself constantly upon an assurance that nobody else did so much, or near so much, ever since her brother's misfortune in the Mississippi. You will therefore be so just as to acquit me of any hard suspicion of your conduct that was my own, or chargeable upon me, since it was upon assurances and positive informations that I thought you unkind, and Abbé S: yet makes a demand upon me for her last necessities, which I am sure implies *no other* defrayed them.

The request you bring into my mind of Mr Englefield's picture,[1] was what I found *utterly impossible*, and I dare engage would be so to the best painter in Europe after so many years elapsed since his death. The two sets of Homer's *Odyssey* have ever been at your service for those places, but I knew not how to convey 'em, and you shall have them when ever you will, most gladly. The *Iliad* in 4⁰ is not to be procured but by great accident. I have wanted a set these two years, and the only one I could hear of, Lintot had the conscience to ask 10ll. for.

I am seriously obliged for your kind consent to return me those letters, to prevent a mischief I am daily afraid of. The sets of Homer shall be left at Mr Jervas's, for your messenger at the same time. Indeed, sir, I have all the inclinations of a sincere well-wisher and friend to you and your family, a just sense of the long continuance of your good opinion and favour toward me, and a hearty desire any way in my power to show that sense of it. Tho' you say you are going into Essex, I would not defer saying thus much, and particularly thanking you for this renewal of your friendship, for which you shall find me never ungrateful to the degree it deserves from me, who am truly and with respect | Dear sir | Your most affectionate obliged | Friend and servant | A: P:

The Verses on Mrs Patty had not been printed,[2] but that one puppy of our sex took 'em to himself as author, and another simpleton of her sex pretended they were addressed to herself. I never thought of show-

---

[1] It seems possible that Caryll, knowing Pope's intimate acquaintance with the Englefields, wished him to paint from memory a likeness of Henry Englefield (d. 1720).

[2] On the verses to Mrs. Patty, see Ault, *New Light*, pp. 195–206. They had circulated in MS., had been printed in 1724 in newspapers, and had been gathered into the Pope–Swift *Miscellanies*, the 'last' volume. The puppy was James Moore-Smythe, who had 'borrowed' six lines for use in his play, *The Rival Modes* (1727), and the simpleton was probably Judith Cowper, to whom Pope had sent the lines (in June 1723) in a letter which certainly did not apply the lines to Miss Cowper, but perhaps left the door open for such an application.

ing 'em to any body, but her; nor she (it seems) being better content to merit praises and good wishes than to boast of 'em. But indeed they are such as I am not ashamed of, as I'm sure they are very true and very warm.

I should be very glad to meet you at your return, either in town or here, if my mother's recovery permit. She is better at present.

I shall soon have a small parcel[1] to send you, if I know where to leave it, to be conveyed safe?

POPE *to* THE EARL OF OXFORD[2]   [20 *February* 1728/9]

Longleat Portland Papers, xii

Thursday. | Feb: 20: 1728/9

My Lord,—I hoped to have found a Daily Watch unnecessary to my Mother before now, & to have had 2 or 3 days to pay my acknowledgments in town to a Friend or two, especially to your Lordship. I find I must be absent but one day, & in it hope to meet with you at leisure the hour I can call, tho uncertain when, as yet. It shall be my First Visit, I assure you My Lord.—I return the Intelligencers, with that one which may well be calld An Intelligencer Extraordinary (in the modern style:) writ no doubt by some Wagg, & printed surreptitiously. I am with the utmost regard My Lord | Your most Obliged obedient | faithful Servant | A. Pope.

Address: To | The Rt. Hon. the Earl | of Oxford.
Endorsement: Mr Pope | Thursday Feb 20. 1728/9

GAY *to* POPE[3]   [*Feb.–March* 1728/9]

1745 (Ayre)

Dear Mr. Pope,—My Melancholy increases, and every Hour threatens me with some Return of my Distemper; nay, I think I may rather say I have it on me. Not the divine Looks, the kind Favours and Expressions of the divine Dutchess, who hereafter shall be in Place of a Queen to me, (nay, she shall be my Queen) nor the inexpressible Goodness of the Duke, can in the least chear me. The Drawing-Room

---

[1] Very likely *The Dunciad Variorum*, first placed on sale 10 Apr. 1729. Caryll might get an advance copy.

[2] Pope dated the letter merely 'Thursday'. The specific date is in Lord Oxford's hand, and the endorsement in that of a secretary.

[3] The letter seems to have been written shortly after 1 Mar., on which date the Duchess of Queensberry because of her energetic solicitation of subscribers to *Polly* was forbidden the Court. The letter was first printed in William Ayre's *Memoirs of Pope*, ii (1745), 117–18. How Ayre (or Curll, his probable publisher?) got hold of the letter is unknown, but the letter seems to be genuine. In 1745 no letters concerning Gay's illness were in print, and a forger would hardly be likely to recall such a detail as this 'distemper'.

no more receives Light from those two Stars. There is now what
Milton says is in Hell, Darkness visible.—O that I had never known
what a Court was! Dear *Pope*, what a barren Soil (to me so) have I
been striving to produce something out of! Why did I not take your
Advice before my writing Fables for the Duke, not to write them?
Or rather, to write them for some young Nobleman? It is my very
hard Fate, I must get nothing, write for them or against them. I
find myself in such a strange Confusion and Depression of Spirits, that
I have not Strength even to make my Will; though I perceive, by
many Warnings, I have no continuing City here. I begin to look upon
myself as one already dead; and desire, my dear Mr. *Pope*, (whom I
love as my own Soul) if you survive me, (as you certainly will) that
you will, if a Stone should mark the Place of my Grave, see these
Words put on it:

> Life is a Jest, and all Things show it;
> I thought so once, but now I know it.

With what more you may think proper.

If any Body should ask, how I could communicate this after Death?
Let it be known, it is not meant so, but my present Sentiment in Life.
What the Bearer brings besides this Letter, should I die without a
Will, (which I am the likelier to do, as the Law will settle my small
Estate much as I should myself) let it remain with you, as it has long
done with me, a Remembrance of a dead Friend: But there is none
like you, living or dead.

I am, dear Mr. Pope, | Your's &c. John Gay.

*POPE to THE COUNTESS OF BURLINGTON[1]   [1729]

Chatsworth

If my Lady Burlington cares to be troubled with the Weight of Mr
Pope, and his Dunciad, her Ladyships Coach will carry them all to
day to Chiswick: and they may wait upon her, and ask Blessing of the
Ass their Grandmother there, about one or two a clock.

Twitnam, Sunday, past 9.

SWIFT to POPE   6 *March* 1728/9

1765 (Deane Swift)

March 6th, 1728–9.

Sir,—If I am not a good correspondent, I have bad health; and that
is as good. I passed eight months in the country, with sir *Arthur* and

---

[1] *The Dunciad Variorum* with its 'ass' frontispiece was presented to the King at Court
on 12 Mar. 1729. One assumes that Lady Burlington, a member of the Household and con-
fidante of Pope, would see an advance copy. Sundays close to the day of presentation would
be 2 or 9 Mar.

my lady *Acheson*, and had at least half a dozen returns of my giddiness and deafness, which lasted me about three weeks a piece, and, among other inconveniencies, hindred me from visiting my chapter and punishing enormities, but did not save me the charges of a visitation-dinner. This disorder neither hinders my sleeping, nor much my walking, yet is the most mortifying malady I can suffer. I have been just a month in town, and have just got rid of it in a fortnight: and, when it is on me, I have neither spirits to write, or read, or think, or eat. But I drink as much as I like; which is a resource you cannot fly to when you are ill. And I like it as little as you: but I can bear a pint better than you can a spoonful. You were very kind in your care for Mr *Whalley*; but, I hope, you remembered, that *Daniel*[1] is a damnable poet, and consequently a public enemy to mankind. But I despise the lords decree, which is a jest upon common sense: for, what did it signify to the merits of the cause, whether *George* the Old, or the Young, were on the throne?

No: I intended to pass last winter in *England*, but my health said No: and I did design to live a gentleman, and, as *Sancho's* wife said, to go in my coach to court. I know not whether you are in earnest to come hither in spring: if not, pray God you may never be in jest. Dr. *Delany* shall attend you at *Chester*, and your apartment is ready; and I have a most excellent chaise, and about sixteen dozen of the best cyder in the world; and you shall command the town and kingdom, and *digito monstrari*, &c. And, when I cannot hear, you shall have choice of the best people we can afford, to hear you, and nurses enough; and your apartment is on the sunny side.

The next paragraph strikes me dumb. You say I am to blame, if I refuse the opportunity of going with my lady *Bolingbroke* to *Aix-la-Chapelle*. I must tell you, that a foreign language is mortal to a deaf man. I must have good ears to catch up the words of so nimble a tongued race as the *French*, having been a dozen years without conversing among them. Mr. *Gay* is a scandal to all lusty young fellows with healthy countenance; and, I think, he is not intemperate in a physical sense. I am told he has an asthma, which is a disease I commiserate more than deafness, because it will not leave a man quiet either sleeping or waking. I hope he does not intend to print his Opera[2] before it is acted; for I defy all your subscriptions to amount to 800*l.* And yet, I believe, he lost as much more for want of human prudence.

[1] The Primate (Lindsay) had given the Rev. Nathaniel Whalley the rectory of Armagh, but the Government, claiming the right of presentation, gave the living to Richard Daniel (who had published some verses), who was also Dean of Armagh. The papers were drawn just at the time of the death of George I, and when the Lords ruled on the matter apparently Dean Daniel was victorious. See Ball, iv. 46 and 60.

[2] The Second Part of the *Beggar's Opera.*—1765 (i.e. *Polly*). *The Beggar's Opera* had brought Gay at least £800.

I told you some time ago, that I was dwindled to a writer of libels on the lady of the family where I lived, and upon myself; but they never went further: and my lady *Acheson* made me give her up all the foul copies, and never gave the fair ones out of her hands, or suffered them to be copied. They were sometimes shewn to intimate friends, to occasion mirth, and that was all. So that I am vexed at your thinking I had any hand in what could come to your eyes. I have some confused notion of seeing a paper called *Sir Ralph the Patriot*,[1] but am sure it was bad or indifferent; and, as to the *Lady at Quadrille*,[2] I never heard of it. Perhaps it may be the same with a paper of verses called, *The Journal of a Dublin Lady*, which I writ at Sir *Arthur Acheson's*; and, leaving out what concerned the family, I sent it to be printed in a paper which doctor *Sheridan* had engaged in, called, *The Intelligencer*, of which he made but sorry work, and then dropt it. But the verses were printed by themselves, and most horridly mangled in the press, and were very mediocre in themselves; but did well enough in the manner I mentioned, of a family-jest. I do sincerely assure you, that my frequent old disorder, and the scene where I am, and the humour I am in, and some other reasons which time hath shewn, and will shew more if I live; have lowered my small talents with a vengeance, and cooled my disposition to put them in use. I want only to be rich, for I am hard to be pleased; and, for want of riches, people grow every day less solicitious to please me. Therefore I keep humble company, who are happy to come where they can get a bottle of wine without paying for it. I give my vicar a supper, and his wife a shilling, to play with me an hour at back-gammon once a fortnight. To all people of quality, and especially of titles, I am not within; or, at least, am deaf a week or two after I am well. But, on *Sunday* evenings, it costs me six bottles of wine to people whom I cannot keep out. Pray, come over in *April*, if it be only to convince you that I tell no lies, and the journey will be certainly for your health. Mrs. *Brent*, my house-keeper, famous in print for digging out the great bottle,[3] says she will be your nurse; and the best physicians we have shall attend you without fees: although, I believe, you will have no occasion but to converse with one or two of them to make them proud.

Your letter came but last post, and you see my punctuality. I am

---

[1] Under title of 'The Progress of Patriotism, a Tale' this item was printed in *The Country Journal: or, the Craftsman* of 3 Aug. 1728, and was reprinted in *The Intelligencer*, No. 12. Apparently (?) not by Swift, it was precisely the sort of political piece that Pope ruled out as contents of the *Miscellanies*, vol. iii (1732).

[2] Swift is probably right in assuming that Pope is talking of the poem by Swift that became known as *The Journal of a Modern Lady*. Swift may have sent the poem to *The Intelligencer*, but it was published separately as an octavo pamphlet. See *Poems* (ed. Williams), pp. 443-53.

[3] The reference is to Swift's poem 'Stella's Birth-Day. A Great Bottle of Wine, long buried, being that Day dug up.' See *Poems* (ed. Williams), pp. 740-3.

unlucky at every thing I send to *England*. Two bottles of usquebagh were broken. Well, my humble service to my lord *Bolingbroke*, lord *Bathurst*, lord *Masham*, and his lady my dear friend, and Mr. *Pultney*, and the doctor, and Mr. *Lewis*, and our sickly friend *Gay*, and my lady *Bolingbroke*; and very much to *Patty*,[1] who I hope will learn to love the world less, before the world leaves off to love her. I am much concerned to hear of my lord *Peterborow* being ill. I am exceedingly his servant, and pray God recover his health. As for your courtier Mrs. *Howard*, and her Mistress, I have nothing to say, but that they have neither memory nor manners; else I should have some mark of the former from the latter, which I was promised above two years ago: but, since I made them a present, it would be mean to remind them. I am told poor Mrs. *Pope* is ill: Pray God preserve her to you, or raise you up as useful a friend.

This letter is an answer to Mr. *Ford*, whose hand I mistook for yours, having not heard from him this twelve-month. Therefore you are not to stare; and it must not be lost, for it talks to you only.

Again, forgive my blunders: for, reading the letter by candle-light, and not dreaming of a letter from Mr. *Ford*, I thought it must be yours, because it talks of our friends.

The letter talks of *Gay*, and Mr. *Whalley*, and lord *Bolingbroke*, which made me conclude it must be yours: so all the answering part must go for nothing.

POPE *to* BENJAMIN MOTTE[2]   8 *March* 1728/9

The Pierpont Morgan Library

March 8. 1728/9

Sir,—I've received a letter from the Dean, who desires I would send to you to send the balance of your account to the Widow Hyde in Dames Street Dublin, & she will pay it. As to our account I am concernd I spoke a passionate word or two to you the other day; the truth is I thought myself very ill us'd in your complaining of me to Mr Lewis, & I was also provokd at finding from him (sometime before) how you had been as backward with the Dean's Note. It looks a little insensible of the Goodwill, which I'm sure both He & I bore you; & there could be no Shadow of an Excuse on any pretence of *That Book's* not selling, which had so extraordinary a Run. I desire therefore that you will tell me by a line, when I may draw upon you for the rest of the fifty (i e 35ll.) and intreat you to put me no more out

---

[1] Martha Blount.

[2] The date is not certainly in Pope's hand, but it is contemporary—presumably Motte's entry. Pope tore away the bottom of the sheet and rewrote the final sentence in the left-hand margin.

of Countenance to Mr Gay, (as I had been before by you to the Dr) but that you'l send me a Note of fifty payable to Him on demand. Upon which I will finish our whole account and observe punctually what I promisd you after, which till then you have no right to claim as it is no way due, but an Act of Free good-will. | Your h: Servant | A. P.

FENTON *to* BROOME   12 *March* [1728/9]

Elwin-Courthope, viii. 153

Easthampstead Park, March 12, [1729].

The reason, dear Broome, and a true one I solemnly assure you it is, why I have so long neglected to write was because I had lost your letter which contained your directions how to send to Pulham, so that if you had omitted the postscript in your last, I must still have deferred writing till I had inquired you out at London. I am now, and for some weeks have been, confined to my chamber by the gout, which I look upon to be an annual tribute which I must pay till the lease of my tenement expires. However I hope to be well enough to see you this summer, which I shall be able to give you a certainer account of after I have talked with Lord Gower,[1] from whom I received a message about a fortnight since that he wanted to see me in town to settle matters before he went into the country. In your next pray inform me how I shall send you Waller,[2] which I think will be published before Easter. I see in the prints that your friend young Thurston[3] has entertained the world with a Miscellany, but I have never seen it. I grow very incurious about our modern belles-lettres. Those old fellows of Greece and Rome have got such a scurvy trick of discovering new beauties every time one reads them that they mostly engross the little time that I spare to poetry.

> Singula de nobis anni prædantur euntes;
> Eripuere jocos, Venerem, convivia, ludum;
> Tendunt extorquere poemata.[4]

But Dr. Broome has seven years good before he can repeat these verses with a just grace, and therefore let me know what your muse is about.

Honest Gay is printing his contraband play[5] by subscription, by which he will make an ample equivalent for its not being acted, if some few of the quality will follow the junior Duchess of Marl-

---

[1] Fenton had agreed to become tutor to Lord Gower's son.—Elwin.
[2] In this year Fenton brought out his admirable quarto edition of Waller.
[3] Mr. Joseph Thurston in 1729 published a volume of *Poems on Several Occasions*.
[4] Horace, *Epistles*, ii. ii. 55–57.   [5] *Polly*.

borough's example, who has subscribed 100*l.* I have never heard anything of or from Pope since I wrote last. I see by the preface to
Themistocles[1] that Tom Southerne is still alive and plays the he bawd
as formerly for the muses. Believe me to be ever, with sincere esteem,
your affectionate humble servant.

POPE *to* THE EARL OF OXFORD [*March* 1728/9]

Longleat Portland Papers, xii

My Lord,—If this finds your Lordship at home, pray be pleasd to tell
me what number of books[2] exactly the Binder sent to you? The inclosed
Letter I have at last procured.[3] I am Ever | Your Lordships most
faith|ful Servant | A. Pope.

Address: To the Rt. Hon: the Earl | of Oxford.
Endorsement: Mr Pope | March 1728/9

POPE *to* THE EARL OF OXFORD[4] [*March* 1728/9]

Longleat Portland Papers, xii

[Mar. 1729]

My Lord,—In great haste, for a very material reason,[5] I desire you
to keep lockd up & send not one of the Dunciads to any body till I
have the honor to see you again in 3 or 4 days.
　I am My Lord | Your most faith-|ful Servant | A. Pope.

Address: To | My Lord Oxford | These
Endorsement: Mr Pope | March 1728/9

POPE *to* THE EARL OF OXFORD [13 *March* 1728/9]

Longleat Portland Papers, xii

March. 13: 1728/9.

My Lord,—You are now at full liberty to publish all my faults &

---

[1] Samuel Madden's *Themistocles* had run for a week in February, and was immediately
published. At the end of his Preface Madden acknowledges the aid of Southerne's 'warm
declarations and hearty zeal' in recommending the play.

[2] Bound copies of *The Dunciad Variorum* are in Dover Street waiting distribution by Lord
Oxford. See the next letter.

[3] Possibly a letter from Fazakerly about *The Dunciad?*

[4] The date is, in the superscription, modern; in the endorsement the hand of the secretary. The address is not Pope's hand.

[5] Elwin thought the 'material reason' was Pope's desire to cancel a passage. This might
well be, but that purpose would have required Lord Oxford to return all copies. The present
assumption is rather that Pope sent Oxford copies before the presentation at Court was
arranged (i.e. before 12 Mar.), and he now wishes the copies to remain undistributed until
after that event. Consider the letter that immediately follows.

Enormities; The King & Queen had the book yesterday by the hands of Sir R. W.¹ so that your Lordship may let me fly, (as Ennius hath it)

Vivus per ora virum.
Volat Irrevocabile Dunciad.²

I am with extreme affection, but with great Esteem & respect | Your Lordships faithful | Servant | A. Pope.

Just gone to Twitnam.

Address: To the Rt. Hon. the | Earl of Oxford.
Endorsement: Mr. Pope | March 13. 1728/9

POPE *to* THE EARL OF OXFORD³   *27 March* [1729]

Longleat Portland Papers, xii

March 27th

My Lord,—I am every day wishing to converse with you, tho I almost fear I do it too often, that is, every time I am in town, & often (of late) at odd hours, perhaps unseasonable ones. I have but one way to remedy it, which is, if you will make me what the Romans calld Amicus Omnium horarum, by allowing me when I come next to lodge with you; & then, by the privilege of a Domestic, your Lordship may send me out of your room at any hour that you would be better imployed. If this Proposal be (as you were lately so good as to tell me) not inconvenient, whenever you will prove it by an Overt Act I will believe it, namely whatever day you can pass at Twit'nam, you shall carry me home with you.

I beg your Lordship to send about 20 books to Cambrige,⁴ but by no means to be given to any Bookseller, but disposd of as by your own Order at 6s. by any honest Gentleman or Head of a House. If

¹ Savage in his *Collection of Pieces . . . published on Occasion of the Dunciad* (1732), p. vi, remarked, 'On the 12th of *March*, 1729, at *St. James's*, that poem was presented to the KING and QUEEN (who had before been pleased to read it) by the Right Honourable Sir *Robert Walpole*: And some Days after, the whole Impression was taken and dispersed by several Noblemen and Persons of the first Distinction.' It was probably upon reading of *The Dunciad* of 1728 that the King is said to have called Mr. Pope 'a very honest man'. The variorum *Dunciad* was in a sense considered by Pope as a response to a request from the King for clarification of the poem. See Pope to Lord Oxford, 17 June 1728.

² In Cicero, *Tusculan Disputations*, I. xv. 34.

³ The secretary's endorsement, which places the letter in 1727, is so clearly wrong that it leads one to suspect that these secretarial endorsements are all late and without much, if any, authority. The second paragraph of the letter clearly concerns the marketing of *The Dunciad Variorum*, which sold for 6s. 6d.

⁴ This paragraph shows well Pope's amazing gift for getting services even from noble friends. Clearly his intimacy with the Digby family continued after the death of his friend Robert Digby in 1726. Within six weeks after this letter the Viscountess Scudamore died of smallpox.

you send to Mr Digby's at Lady Scudamores house in Pall mall, he will deliver 'em to your order.

To apologize to your Lordship for so many Liberties as you have indulgd me, would be to distrust your very goodness that incouragd them. I'll only say therefore what follows in a plain & necessary consequence to them, that I am with constant sense & truth, | My Lord | Your most obligd | obedient & faith|ful Servant | A. Pope.

My Mothers & my own Services attend Lady Oxford & Lady Margaret.

Endorsement: Mr Pope March 27. 1727

POPE *to* BENJAMIN MOTTE   *28 March* 1729

Dawson's Book Shop (1938)

Mr Motte,—I hope you have done as I have desird so often, to Mr Gay.[1] You have now had time enough to determine on the matter I left to your Choice. however in the meantime pray pay Ten pound to the Bearer, which he wants, and place it on account for part of your debt. We will settle the rest as soon as you please.

Your affect. Servant | A. Pope.

March 28th | 1729.

[On verso] pray send me the Iliad from Mr Graham.[2]

Address: To Mr Motte.

†SWIFT *to* BOLINGBROKE *and* POPE[3]   *5 April* 1729

1740
                                        Dublin, April 5, 1729.

I do not think it could be possible for me to hear better news than that of your getting over your scurvy suit,[4] which always hung as a dead weight on my heart; I hated it in all its circumstances, as it affected your fortune and quiet, and in a situation of life that must make it every way vexatious. And as I am infinitely obliged to you for the justice you do me in supposing your affairs do at least concern me as much as my own; so I would never have pardoned your omitting it. But before I go on, I cannot forbear mentioning what I read last summer in a newspaper, that you were writing the history of your own

---

[1] See Pope to Motte, 8 Mar. 1728/9.

[2] Possibly Motte as well as Caryll (see to Caryll, 16 Feb. 1728-9) has been told that Pope is hoping to pick up a quarto *Iliad*.

[3] The editions of 1741-2 contain no significant textual revisions. The Dublin editions translate the Latin phrases in footnotes.

[4] The suit concerned the first Lady Bolingbroke's property.—Ball.

times. I suppose such a report might arise from what was not secret among your friends, of your intention to write another kind of history; which you often promis'd Mr. Pope and me to do:[1] I know he desires it very much, and I am sure I desire nothing more, for the honour and love I bear you, and the perfect knowledge I have of your publick virtue. My Lord, I have no other notion of Oeconomy than that it is the parent of Liberty and ease, and I am not the only friend you have who hath chid you in his heart for the neglect of it, tho' not with his mouth, as I have done. For there is a silly error in the world, even among friends otherwise very good, not to intermeddle with mens affairs in such nice matters. And my Lord, I have made a maxim, that should be writ in letters of diamonds, That a wise man ought to have Mony in his head, but not in his heart. Pray my Lord enquire whether your Prototype, my Lord Digby, after the Restoration when he was at Bristol, did not take some care of his fortune, notwithstanding that quotation I once sent you out of his speech to the H. of Commons?[2] In my conscience, I believe Fortune like other drabbs, values a man gradually less for every year he lives. I have demonstration for it; because if I play at piquet for six-pence with a man or woman two years younger than myself, I always lose; and there is a young girl of twenty who never fails of winning my money at Backgammon, though she is a bungler, and the game be Ecclesiastic. As to the publick, I confess nothing could cure my itch of medling with it but these frequent returns of deafness, which have hindred me from passing last winter in London; yet I cannot but consider the perfidiousness of some people who I thought when I was last there, upon a change that happened, were the most impudent in forgetting their professions that I have ever known.[3] Pray will you please to take your pen and blot me out that political maxim from whatever book it is in: that *Res nolunt diu male administrari*; the commonness makes me not know who is the author, but sure he must be some Modern.

I am sorry for Lady Bolingbroke's ill health; but I protest I never knew a very deserving person of that sex, who had not too much reason to complain of ill health. I never wake without finding life a more insignificant thing than it was the day before: which is one great advantage I get by living in this country, where there is nothing I shall be sorry to lose; but my greatest misery is recollecting the scene of twenty years past, and then all on a sudden dropping into the present. I re-

---

[1] The annotations of Elwin and Ball call this project 'A history of the Tory administrations in Queen Anne's reign'. Writing to Swift (2 Aug. 1731) Bolingbroke comments on the project 'about which you say, you and Pope have often teased me'; and describes the scope of the history—which he did not write. See iii. 212–13.

[2] See Bolingbroke to Swift, 1 Jan. 1721/2, in Ball, iii. 109–13, esp. p. 111 and notes 8 and 9.

[3] Swift's spleen is probably directed against the failure of Queen Caroline and the Court to provide decently for Gay.

member when I was a little boy, I felt a great fish at the end of my line which I drew up almost on the ground, but it dropt in, and the disappointment vexes me to this very day, and I believe it was the type of all my future disappointments. I should be asham'd to say this to you, if you had not a spirit fitter to bear your own misfortunes, than I have to think of them. Is there patience left to reflect by what qualities wealth and greatness are got, and by what qualities they are lost? I have read my friend Congreve's verses to Lord Cobham, which end with a vile and false moral,[1] and I remember is not in Horace to Tibullus, which he imitates, "that all times are equally virtuous and vicious" wherein he differs from all Poets, Philosophers, and Christians that ever writ. It is more probable that there may be an equal quantity of virtues always in the world, but sometimes there may be a peck of it in Asia, and hardly a thimble-full in Europe. But if there be no virtue, there is abundance of sincerity; for I will venture all I am worth, that there is not one humane creature in power who will not be modest enough to confess that he proceeds wholly upon a principle of Corruption, I say this because I have a scheme in spite of your notions, to govern England upon the principles of Virtue, and when the nation is ripe for it, I desire you will send for me. I have learn'd this by living like a Hermit, by which I am got backwards about nineteen hundred years in the Æra of the world, and begin to wonder at the wickedness of men. I dine alone upon half a dish of meat, mix water with my wine, walk ten miles a day, and read Baronius. *Hic explicit Epistola ad Dom.* Bolingbroke, & *incipit ad amicum Pope.*

Having finished my Letter to Aristippus,[2] I now begin to you. I was in great pain about Mrs. Pope, having heard from others that she was in a very dangerous way, which made me think it unseasonable to trouble you. I am ashamed to tell you, that when I was very young I had more desire to be famous than ever since; and fame, like all things else in this life, grows with me every day more a trifle. But you who are so much younger, although you want that health you deserve, yet your spirits are as vigorous as if your body were sounder. I hate a crowd where I have not an easy place to see and be seen. A great Library always makes me melancholy, where the best Author is as much squeezed, and as obscure, as a Porter at a Coronation. In my own little library, I value the compilements of Grævius and Gronovius,[3]

---

[1] Congreve's 'Letter to Viscount Cobham' ends with the couplet:

> Believe it, Men have ever been the same,
> And all the Golden Age, is but a Dream.

[2] i.e. to the philosopher. Aristippus was a favourite of Bolingbroke's.

[3] These two Dutch scholars, authors respectively of *Thesaurus Antiquitatum Romanorum* (12 v., fol.) and of *Thesaurus Græcarum Antiquitatum* (12 v., fol.), among other works, are ironically commended for their magnificent appearance. One recalls Swift's opinions of such men expressed in his *Battle of the Books*.

which make thirty-one volumes in folio (and were given me by my Lord Bolingbroke) more than all my books besides; because whoever comes into my closet, casts his eyes immediately upon them, and will not vouchsafe to look upon Plato or Xenophon. I tell you it is almost incredible how Opinions change by the decline or decay of spirits, and I will further tell you, that all my endeavours from a boy to distinguish my self, were only for want of a great Title and Fortune, that I might be used like a Lord by those who have an opinion of my parts; whether right or wrong, it is no great matter; and so the reputation of wit or great learning does the office of a blue riband, or of a coach and six horses. To be remembred for ever on the account of our friendship, is what would exceedingly please me, but yet I never lov'd to make a visit, or be seen walking with my betters, because they get all the eyes and civilities from me. I no sooner writ this than I corrected my self, and remember'd Sir Fulk Grevil's Epitaph, "Here lies, &c. who was friend to Sir Philip Sidney." And therefore I most heartily thank you for your desire that I would record our friendship in verse,[1] which if I can succeed in, I will never desire to write one more line in poetry while I live. You must present my humble service to Mrs. Pope, and let her know I pray for her continuance in the world, for her own reason, that she may live to take care of you.

POPE *to* CARYLL   8 *April* 1729

Add. 28618

It is a real pleasure to me that you take so well (as in truth I meant it) the letter I lately wrote you. But it is a vexation to me, (and fell out just at a juncture when of all things I wished nothing unlucky should fall out) that I received not yours till a full fortnight after its date. My poor mother's memory has suffered extremely by her late illness, and it happening that I was from home when yours came, it seems she had put it up with design to keep for me, and then totally forgot it. I found it by chance among linen 2 days ago. I sent immediately to know Mr Mackenzie's chambers,[2] but I conclude he is gone before this out of town. I shall hear tomorrow. If so, I can only leave the books (*Odyssey* and all) at Mr Jervas's, till you send for 'em, unless you will direct them to some other hand.

By the way, those books have laid there this month, but I suppose

---

[1] Pope had dedicated *The Dunciad* to Swift, and he now wishes a verse compliment from Swift in return. Ultimately his desire for a memorial of their friendship led him to the edition of the Swift–Pope correspondence.

[2] Mackenzie, a relative of Lady Mary Caryll, evidently was to receive books for Caryll. Mackenzie had chambers in Gray's Inn. He was secretly married to Lady Carrington, on whose estate Mrs. Rackett had an annuity of £55 per annum. See Pope to Mrs. Rackett, 9 July 1729 and BM. Add. MS. 28238, f. 25.

you have not had the *Odyss*: because your last mentions it not; and I
being scarce ever in town, I've not seen Jervas these 4 months. The
other book is written (all but the poem) by 2 or 3 of my friends,[1] and
a droll book it is. They have the art to make trifles agreeable; and you'll
not be at a loss to guess the authors. It would have been a sort of curiosity, had it reached your hands a week ago, for the publishers had not
then permitted any to be sold, but only dispersed by some lords of theirs
and my acquaintance, of whom I procured yours. But I understand
that now the booksellers have got 'em by the consent of Lord Bathurst.

I thank you for the letters, which I read all over.[2] I thank you too
for your friendly care about 'em, which I discover from your enclosure
that covers 'em. Indeed, the fear of rascally booksellers makes me
willing to secure such private things as many letters must necessarily
contain, from appearing in public. But that I have long born you a true
regard, is what I am not, nor ever shall be ashamed of; and as a proof
of it, I desire you will accept of as many back again, as fall not under
that apprehension above said. You may look upon this as a second deed
of gift in friendship, to confirm and ratify the first writings.

I wish yourself better health, your whole family an happy Easter,
Mrs Caryll all felicity, the fair lady your scribe[3] everything she wishes
to herself: and am | Dear sir | Your very affectionate and | most humble
servant | A: P.

April 8th. 1729.

POPE *to* THE EARL OF OXFORD[4]   [18 *April* 1729]
Longleat Portland Papers, xii

April. 18 1729.

My Lord,—I did not think so very soon to trouble you with a Letter:
But so it is, that the Gentlemen of the Dunciad intend to be vexatious
to the Bookseller & threaten to bring an action of I can't tell how many
thousands against him. It is judgd by the Learned in Law, that if three
or four of those Noblemen who honour me with their friendship

---

[1] More than once Pope averred that the notes and apparatus of *The Dunciad Variorum*
were by friends of his. Pope still evaded legal responsibility as author of the poem, and sought
to protect himself and Gilliver, his bookseller, by having the poem dispersed by Lord Oxford,
Lord Bathurst, the Hon. Edward Digby, *et al.* The endeavour was perhaps to protect copyright as well as to avoid libel suits. Presently Gilliver will refuse to bring out a second edition
without further protection, and the three noble lords (Oxford, Bathurst, Burlington) will
sign a sort of conveyance of property to Gilliver. See the Twickenham edition of *The Dunciad*
(ed. J. R. Sutherland), pp. xxviii–xxix.

[2] After two years of urging Caryll at last has returned Pope's letters. He evidently in his
covering letter told Pope that Miss Catherine Caryll, his daughter, had transcribed the letters
before returning them.

[3] Catherine Caryll served as amanuensis because of Caryll's gout.

[4] The date is not in Pope's hand, nor is it surely Lord Oxford's. The endorsement is in
the usual secretary's hand.

would avow it so openly as to suffer their Names to be set to a Certificate of the nature of the inclosed, it would screen the poor man from their Insults. If your Lordship will let it be transcribd fair, & allow yours to be subscribd with those of Lord Burlington, Lord Bathurst & one or 2 more, I need not say it will both oblige & honour me vastly. I beg a Line in answer, I cannot say how much I am Ever

My Lord your obligd affect: Servant A. Pope

Whereas a Clamor hath been raisd by certain Persons, and Threats uttered, against the Publisher or Publishers of the Poem call'd the *Dunciad* with notes Variorum &c. We whose names are underwritten do declare ourselves to have been the Publishers and Dispersers thereof, and that the same was deliverd out and vended by our Immediate direction.

Address: To the Rt. Hon. the | Earl of Oxford.

Endorsement: Mr Pope | April 18. 1729

POPE *to* BENJAMIN MOTTE[1]   8 *May* [1729]

The Pierpont Morgan Library

May the 8th

Sir,—Being so constantly taken up, when I am in town, I have been twice or thrice disappointed of signing what you desired. Upon reading carefully the Copy of the agreement. I think (to express both our purposes) This following will be proper to be the Form, which you may write (if you approve it) on the back of the agreement and if you'l send it me per bearer, or when you please, I will return it to you signed. | I am always | your affect: Servant.

I Alex. Pope hereby acknowledge that I and the other persons mentiond in this agreement have receivd full Satisfaction for the same, and that Mr Motte hath the Entire title & Property of the three Volumes of Dr. Swifts & our Miscellanies, now printed. But it is between us agreed, in consideration of 25 pounds which I Benjamin M. hereby acknowledge to be payd to me by Mr Pope that if Mr Pope or Dr Swift shall publish any Other Volume or Volumes of Miscellanies beside the 3 abovesaid the right & sole property of such additional Volume remains wholly Their own, any thing in these articles to the contrary notwithstanding. Witness our hands, A P.
this   of   in the year,   B. M.

Address: To | Mr Motte.

[1] The year is added to the rest of the date, but by a modern hand. The year seems correct since the letter fits in with other letters and agreements with Motte of this year. See *Gent. Mag.* xliv (1855), 364, for the agreement signed 1 July 1729 by Pope and Motte.

POPE *to* FORTESCUE[1]   [15 *May* 1729?]

The Pierpont Morgan Library

Thursday

I was one day in town, but could not find you in the Evening. I have
been ill, but nothing would make me better than the Sight of a Friend.
Several of mine are ill also: I hope You will hold up, to comfort me.
I must beg you to inform me carefully, & to bid your Clerk also mind
it, when ever Mr Roberts comes to Town, (the person whose annuity
Mrs Blount purchasd) that She may have his Life Ensurd, which it
seems can't be done but when He is present. This is a Very material
point, to Her, & She intreats you to give me the first notice. Mr White
told Mr Bethel, he would be in town soon.

I must also desire you to let me have a Copy from Mr Cruwys of
Abbot's Account what moneys he paid to Mr Essington &c. Next
Sunday I am ingaged, Any other day I am at your Service wholly, as
I am Entirely Dear Sir & affectionately | Your Friend. | A. Pope.

Address: To Wm. Fortescue Esqr | in Bell Yard near Lincolns | Inn fields. |
London.

Postmark: 16/MA

POPE *to* THE EARL OF OXFORD[2]   [16 *May* 1729]

Longleat Portland Papers, xii

May. 16. 1729.

My Lord,—I propos'd to have challeng'd your kind promise this
week, of passing a day at Twitenham: But I have found my Mother
much worse, & been not without alarms about her, from sudden fits
of Extream short breath which yet continue.

I see a Book with a Curious Cutt calld Pope Alexrs Supremacy[3] &c.
4°. In it are 3 or 4 things so false & scandalous that I think I know the
Authors, and they are of a Rank to merit Detection. I therfore beg
your Lordship to send a Careful hand to buy the Book of Lintot, (who
must not be known to come from you) & to enter down the day of the
month. I would fain have it bought of him, himself. The book is writ

---

[1] The date is deduced from the blurred postmark and from the fact that the 15th was
'Thursday'.

[2] The date is in Lord Oxford's hand; the endorsement in that of a secretary.

[3] *Pope Alexander's Supremacy and Infallibility examin'd; And the Errors of Scriblerus and
his Man William Detected. With the Effigies of his Holiness and his Prime Minister* . . . was
published, according to *The Monthly Chronicle*, 13 May 1729. The authors have been thought
to be Thomas Burnet, youngest son of the bishop, George Duckett, presently to be made
Commissioner of Excise, and John Dennis, who seems strangely described as 'a person who
has great obligations to me'. The cut was offensive—Pope's head joined to the body of a
monkey. His prime minister was an ass. His man William, mentioned in the title-page,
would be William Cleland, whose name was signed to the prefatory 'Letter to the Publisher'.

by Burnet, & a Person who has great obligations to me, & the Cut is done by Ducket. I would fain come at the proof of this, for Reasons of a Very High Nature.

Let the same Man, after he has the book, go to Roberts the Publisher[1] in Warwick lane and threaten him, unless he declares the author; Or any other method your Lordship can judge best.

I will not beg pardon for this, but take all to that account which I can never repay, but by being for life | My Lord | Your most obliged | most faithfull | Servant | A. Pope.

I hope Lady Oxford recovers of her complaint, & is well.

Endorsement: Mr Pope | May 16. 1729.

POPE *to* MRS. HOWARD[2]   [*May* 1729]

Yale University

Madam,—The first word I heard of this vexatious thing was on Saturday at 3 a clock. I went to Lord Ilays[3] by 5, thinking he might be in the country as usual, on Saturday. Next morning I was ingagd to Lord Burlington at Chiswick, from whence I sent you my letter: I was obligd to go on by water to London, to see a Sick friend, & returnd not home till last night late. I then found your letter which gave me, besides the Uneasiness I partake with you an additional one, in finding you seem to dislike the word or two I spoke to the Steward. It was no more than to express my Surprize, after his having been satisfyd fully with your paying 30s a year for the 2 acres, wherever they lay (and if I remember right you have a Receit from him for the last years rent to that purpose) that Mrs Vernon should take this course without giving any notice. Whereas its certain from what Pigot told me, that The Trustees for the charity could no way legally pretend to an *Ejectment* unless the Rent were stopt by the Tenant, which was not here the case: and could therfore be only Mrs Vernons act & deed. In this I am since confirmd by your Servant, Saffold, who says when the men came to measure, they brought one Parsons with them the

---

[1] James Roberts, at this time and earlier the publisher of attacks on Pope, became the publisher of his letters in 1735 and 1737.

[2] The date is taken from the contemporary endorsement.

[3] Lord Islay, afterwards Duke of Argyll, as trustee for Mrs. Howard (whose husband was still living), bought the grounds of Marble Hill in several small lots, from John Gray, Esq., Robert Parsons, and Thomas Vernon, gents. One lot of two acres and of uncertain position was held under a charity, and the lease was assigned to Lord Islay by Mr. Vernon, whose widow seems to have attempted to exercise some rights over it, and Mrs. Howard no doubt disapproved of a proposition which she understood Pope to have made that she should rent it, as that would be an admission that the land in question had not been included in the original assignment.—Croker–Elwin. [*Islay* = elsewhere *Ilay*.]

Churchwarden, whom they told, they did this *only for the Satisfaction of Mrs Vernon.*

I should fancy the Trustees might be influenced from the Dean of Pauls, or some proper person, to take no Ejectment while the Rent is continued, or to take any security for the Value of the 2 acres, or Exchange them: Since Their whole business is but to see the charity paid on. And if they do not prosecute the matter, Mrs Vernon sure cannot in her own name, for shame. The Fact is, that these 2 acres, in the Lease, which I remember to have read some years since, are said to lye *between Capt. Grays ground & the West Side* (toward the Alehouse) So that it may be anywhere among those grounds behind the Horsechestnuts, for any thing said in the Writings. The Old mans Evidence is all they have for it.

What you seem to disapprove, as of my speaking to your Steward *for you to rent it*, is a mistake, for it was not *My* Proposal, but *His*; and I was so far from entring into it readily, that I told him I thought the proceeding very extraordinary: and would not so much as propose it to you, but whatever he had to say about renting either the whole or part, he might write to you, or Mrs Vernon might write to you, themselves.

They expect Capt. Gray every day here. As soon as he comes, I will see him. I hope I need not tell you how much I detest dirty doings in general, and how much I partake in being vext at any that affect You in particular, that is in other words how much I would deserve to be | Your most reall | humble Servant, | A. Pope.

My Mother is but in a bad state of health, nor I in a good one. I would wait on you at any time; I wish it could be to any purpose.

Endorsement: Mr Pope to Mrs | Howard. May | 1729

POPE *to* CARYLL   30 *May* 1729

Add. 28618

May 30. 1729.

I am first to give you very sincere thanks for your kind visit, and double thanks for its being so well *timed*, to remove in the best manner the little shadow of misconstruction between us. I assure you I had, and have thought, and shall think often of your estimable proceeding in this affair. How many men of less sense and less friendship had taken quite another turn than I see by pleasing experience you can be capable of? I protest I never twice in my life have found my own sincerity succeed so well; and I beg your pardon for doubting, but I was not without some doubt of it, herein. I am now glad you questioned, glad I disguised nothing, glad we were both in the right, nay not sorry if

I was a little otherwise since it has occasioned the knowledge of that dependence which I ought and am to have on your friendship and temper.[1] I hope this will find you and your whole family in that perfect health I wish them; in perfect harmony and all other happiness I am sure it will. Whatsoever you can give yourselves by *virtue*, you will; let but *Fortune* do her part in the rest.

You will laugh sometimes when you read the notes to the *Dunciad*, and sometimes you will despise too heartily to laugh (there is such an edifying mixture of roguery in the authors satirised there). The poem itself will bear a second reading, or (to express myself more justly and modestly) will be better borne at the second than first reading, and that's all I shall say of it. My friends who took so much pains to comment upon it, must come off with the public as they can. All I wish to have your opinion of in relation to their part, is as to the morality and justifiable design in the undertaking, for of what is honest or honorable no man is a better judge.

Adieu, till I hear from you. Be assured, dear sir, I am at all times, glad to do so; and will at some times tell you so; but if not so frequently as really I wish, impute it charitably. Forgot you never can be, esteemed you ever will be, and loved and wished well you ever must be, by | Dear sir | your affectionate obliged | Friend and servant. | A: P:

My mother is as you saw her, and your servant. I made your compliment to Mr Pulteney. The Lady *Sola*,[2] at Petersham, I wish were *Sola* still; for since her mother came home, she has used her in a manner I dare not relate. I found her all in tears, and the family in an uproar.

I am this day going into Essex,[3] from whence, God willing, I return by Saturday next.

DR. ARBUTHNOT *to* SWIFT[4]   9 *June* 1729

Add. 4805

[In part:]

Your freinds whom you mention in yours are well; Mr Gay is re-turnd from Scotland,[5] & has recoverd his strength by his journey. Mr

---

[1] Pope is here absolving Caryll with regard to his charities to Mrs. Cope.

[2] Teresa Blount. The family had a small house in Petersham, as well as a house in London.
—Elwin.

[3] It is not clear whether this visit of one week was to Down Hall (the Earl of Oxford) or to Leighs (the Duchess of Buckingham) or to some friend such as John Morley or Mr. and Mrs. Knight.

[4] The entire letter is printed by Ball in iv. 86. The part given here supplies important details concerning *The Dunciad*.

[5] *The Universal Spectator* for 26 Apr. says that the Duke of Queensberry set out on Thursday [the 24th] 'with a splendid Equipage for Scotland'. Gay evidently went with him.

Pope is well. he had gott an injunction in chancery against the printers who had pyrated his dunciad; it was dissolv'd again because the printer could not prove any property nor did the Author appear.[1] that is not Mr Gays case for he has own'd his book. Mr Poulteny gives you his service. They are all better than my self, for I am now so bad of a constant convulsion in my heart, that I am like to expire sometimes We have no news that I know of. . .

FENTON *to* BROOME   24 *June* [1729]

Elwin–Courthope, viii. 154

Easthampstead Park, June 24, [1729].

Dear Broome,—Your last letter came to this place soon after I was gone to London, from whence I am but just returned, where I shall spend some weeks, but am in hopes of seeing you about Michaelmas; for Lord Gower's son will continue at Westminster till next spring. While I was in town I was very busy in planting my nephew in poor Mr. Harrison's chambers,[2] which he bought of his executors. He is supposed to have left about 16,000*l.* to his brother's son.

You never sent me word how I should send Waller to you, which I beg to know by the next post, having left orders with Mr. Tonson to lay one by for you.

I saw our friend Pope twice when I was at London. He inquired after your welfare, but said that you had dropped correspondence by not answering his last letter. The war is carried on against him furiously in pictures and libels; and I heard of nobody but Savage and Cleland who have yet drawn their pens in his defence.[3] He told me that for the future he intended to write nothing but epistles in Horace's manner,[4] in which I question not but he will succeed very well.

What is your reverence employed about? Your friends in Middlesex, particularly Mr. Blount, complain that you are too sparing of your prose, and excuse your neglect of writing upon no other account than that you are engaged with the muses nine. When I was in town I

---

[1] Gay's judgement is reported in *The Universal Spectator* for 14 June as recently granted. Pope, less fortunate, now proceeded to persuade Lords Burlington, Bathurst, and Oxford to put their signatures to a document assigning property in *The Dunciad* to Lawton Gilliver, the publisher. The document was executed 16 Oct. 1729. On 21 Nov. Gilliver entered *The Dunciad Variorum* at Stationers' Hall (presumably in octavo: he had entered the quarto on 12 Apr.), and on 26 Nov. he issued the 'second edition' of the work in octavo.

[2] Mr. Thomas Harrison, register of the Exchequer Office, had died on 15 Sept. 1728. Possibly his chambers are in question.

[3] For *The Dunciad Variorum*, chief cause of the current war against Pope, Cleland had written 'A Letter to the Publishers'. Some Dunces attacked Cleland for this; others, preferring to believe no one but Pope would defend Pope, alleged that he himself had written the 'Letter'. In Apr. 1729 Savage had published in Pope's behalf, 'An Author to be Let'.

[4] This prophetic announcement is significant.

found out Mr. Holditch and returned him his Milton. To save you three pence I have scrawled this in a hurry for my lady's servant to carry with him to town, and he stays for it. I am ever your faithful humble servant.

POPE *to* CARYLL   8 *July* [1729]
Add. 28618

Twickenham July 8th.

If I have not so soon replied to your very friendly letter, as it well deserved, I must tell you it was not for neglecting, but thinking of you. For I have been these 3 weeks in full employment and amusement in reviewing the whole correspondence I have had with 2 or 3 of my most select friends, whose letters I have read quite thro', and thereby past over all my life in idea, and tasted over again all the pleasing intimacies and agreeable obligations I owed them. Some of my own letters have been returned to me,[1] which I have put into order with theirs; and it makes all together an un-important, indeed, but yet an innocent, history of myself. You make, I assure you, no small figure in these annals, from 1710 to 1720-odd. Upon my word, sir, I am glad to see how long and how often and how much I have been obliged to you, as well as how long, how often, and how much I've been sensible of and expressed it. I thank God (above all) for finding so few parts of life that I need be ashamed of, no correspondences or intimacies with any but good, deserving people, and no opinions that I need to blush for, or actions (as I hope) that need to make my friends blush for me.

This I say to encourage you still, to think well of me (that is as you used to do) and to continue that friendship which I shall always value, and wish to deserve, at your hands.

It looks, I confess, a little reserved, and as if I locked up something in my bosom from a friend, when I own I care not to tell you what you ask of the Lady *Sola*. The truth is, I know too much to imagine my discovery wou'd do any good, or operate upon her shame. If it would, I would tell; first tell her, then you. But 'tis too late: the *scandal* may be saved by silence, tho' the *vice* cannot. If her own conduct brings it to light, she will be past the help of any creature, even the most charitable upon earth. I will say no more to you, than that I wish the poor woman the mother were in a r[eligious] house.

If ever (as I sincerely wish) I see you here 2 or 3 such agreeable days as you lately gave me, I could be inclined to open this affair to you; and if it be so long first, as I fear it will, I also fear I may speak of it as no secret. I wish to God your G. D.[2] were anywhere else;

---

[1] Some of his letters Pope was evidently preparing for deposit in the Harleian Library. See Pope to Oxford, 15 Sept. 1729.

[2] Your god-daughter, Martha Blount. The Lady Sola is Teresa, of course.

tho' she her self will really never be to blame, she may happen to seem so.

My head aches. I have very ill health, and 'tis one of the causes that makes me so bad a correspondent. But I must not end without my hearty assurance to your whole family of my best wishes and prayers. I am ever (with that old-fashioned thing, truth) | Dear sir | Yours | A: P:

POPE *to* MRS. RACKETT   9 *July* 1729

Ushaw College

July 9. 1729.

Dear Sister,—I am glad to hear so good an account of the mony from Barckam & Mrs Walpole, &c. You have nothing more to do but to see the Bond Smith talks of. If it be Mr Rackets hand, it must be pay'd, I do not see Couwys[1] has any thing more to do, if Mrs. Walpole owns it, but to get Abbot's answer which you yourself may also write for, if it comes not soon.

As to taking the Principal mony from Lady Carington,[2] I directly advis'd you against it: and you say it is a loss of 15 a year, to change it into East India. I writ a week ago to dissuade you from any such thought, and do absolutely dis-approve of it. You may send an attorney forthwith to Mr Mackenzie & Enter on the Estate: This is the best advice I can give you: and I will write so to my Cosen Michael.[3] The Rent of Hallgrove will soon be due & doubtless they will pay Barkham's mony. I am your affect. Brother | A. Pope

POPE *to* MRS. CÆSAR[4]   10 *July* [1729?]

Rousham

Madam,—If this paper could blush, it ought, for its master's seeming Indolence. But the truth is, my Mothers continu'd Incertainty of health for 6 months past, kept me almost in daily attendance, & obligd me (whenever I went to town) to dispatch my business in a few hours & return. Your Behavior toward me is charming, & equal to any Virtue in the most heroic Romance. Your forgiveness extends to every point but one; you still remember the Drawing on the back of a Certain Letter; which after all was but joyning together the two things my heart was most full of, my Friend & my Garden.

---

[1] For *Cruwys*; see earlier letters of this year to Fortescue concerning Mrs. Rackett's troubles.
[2] On Lady Carrington and Mr. Mackenzie see Pope to Caryll, 8 Apr. 1729, and note.
[3] Michael Rackett, the eldest son of Pope's sister.
[4] The year is uncertain but probable.

I expect you all with joy next week, on Wednesday or Thursday, which you shall agree to. On Tuesday I'll send the Waterman. My faithful Services attend Mr Cæsar, & the young Gentleman & Lady.[1] I am, with ancient zeal (tho with modern practise) | Madam | Your most obligd | & obedient Servant, | A. Pope.

July 10th

Address: To | Mrs Cæsar, in | Poland street, | near | Golden Square | London.
Postmark[2]: 8/IY.

POPE *to* CARYLL[3]   20 *July* 1729
Add. 28618

                Twittenham July 20. 1729.
Your speedy letter on the occasion I hinted only at, proves how soon a good man takes fire on any occasion of doing good or preventing evil. I have not forgot (or if I had, an excellent letter of yours, which I lately read, would not have let me) what a generous part you took formerly in Mrs Weston's affairs, and have long known the warmth and vertue of your mind.

But in the present case there seems to be but little hope from any human wisdom, but from accident. You make me infinitely too great a compliment, as well as place too great a trust in a judgment which is, God knows, at best but too fallible, when you say that by my thoughts upon the whole you'll regulate your actions. I am, however, therefore obliged to give 'em you sincerely as I will in this letter since by opening 'em to you, I shall place a trust in my turn in your prudence, which will not, I'm sure, suffer you to reveal such faults, as can only be made worse by discovery, unless there were some plain and probable means of remedying them at the same time.

In a word the faults are two. That lady has an intrigue of half a year's standing (as the servants of the family, who were turn'd away once a month last winter, loudly declared, and as both the town and country begin to talk very largely of) with a married man. The circumstances of this I care not to tell, but (if those nearest her say true) [they] are very flagrant.

 [1] The son and daughter of the Caesars. In Oct. 1729 the son eloped with a fortune of £30,000. See Lord Oxford to Pope, 9 Oct. 1729.
 [2] The postmark is perplexing. Either it or Pope's dating must be wrong.
 [3] Elwin regarded this letter as an attempt to blacken Teresa's character in revenge for gossip she *may have* spread earlier about Pope and Martha. Doubtless Pope by this time had a prejudice against Teresa, the grounds for which must now be hypothetical. It must be remembered that Caryll's intimate acquaintance with the Blounts was of longer standing than Pope's. He does not dismiss Pope's gossip brusquely, as does Elwin. Evidently the family life of the mother and two daughters was at times painful to all of them. Lacking dowries, attractive ladies like Teresa and Martha were by the mores of the day condemned either to frustration or indiscretion. Both avenues were frequented—at least by others.

The other fault is outrage to the mother beyond all imagination,—striking, pinching, pulling about the house, and abusing to the utmost shamefulness. This also is so public that the streets in London and villages in the country have frequently rung of it.—those of the family declaring it everywhere, and some of them parting immediately upon these violences, which are frequent on all trifles, and repeated.

But these faults your ———¹ has laboured every way to conceal, nor did I come to the knowledge how true each was but by other and numerous hands. With great difficulty at last she owned her knowledge of 'em: but of the former I could not get her to confess she was certain of any direct guilt, but the circumstances she could not deny, nor the asseverations of every servant.

You see, sir, there can be no hopes on the mother's side: she who endures at this rate, can never command her daughter from two such things as the town and a gallant, I wished her in a monastery, not only to be out of the way of what might happen, but to be removed from a tyranny, which she cannot ('tis plain) resist. 'Twas but a wish and you see in its own nature, impossible; for she will never dare to do it: the attempt would only cause her to be worse used.

As to the other lady, 'tis as impossible to hope to reclaim her, after so many years continuance of one hellish practice without any good principles, and indeed no shame of owning all that are bad. As to the other matter one would not help to divulge it; for if it should come out, it should not be by us. The danger indeed is great, but the mother can not dare to control her, much less draw her away, and she has been told and warned of it by those people in the most respectful way.

———,² indeed, may share the shame of being thought conscious of her ———s³ proceedings, if not a party in them, and I know several proofs that the mother would accuse her as such rather than have her own beatings laid on her favorite. I therefore think the same if the other affair comes to an *éclat*.

All that can be done in my sentiment is to try to separate the innocent any gentle way from them. She thinks such reasons as these for it would hurt them, and that keeps her in a daily course of such usage as must ruin her health, her humour, and the whole enjoyment of life. It is not to be conceived how brutally she has been treated these many years. I do not, therefore, see any thing to be done in the compass of your power, but (without any notice of this reason) inviting as strongly as possible ———⁴ by her self. You may then tell her what you have heard, and what conduct your opinion is she should follow as to her self and them. Or if you care to write to the mother of the reports of her eldest daughter's intimacy with a ———⁵ or only try what she will

¹ Instead of the dash Elwin prints '[god-daughter]'. ² [Your god-daughter]—Elwin.
³ [sister]s—Elwin. ⁴ [your god-daughter]—Elwin. ⁵ [married man]—Elwin.

say of her own ill usage, blows, &c., so notorious in town and country
with your advice to her, you may; but I believe 'twill be to no purpose.
Perhaps if the son knew the fact of his mother's oppression and were
seriously inclined to remedy it by separating her from the tyrant and
taking her to his own house, some good might be done—but I doubt in
every way. All I'm sure of is that your desires and mine are just to
help the injured, to reclaim the bad, and to separate the innocent from
the guilty. Indeed, the second article is seldom practicable: bad people
constantly procure contempt. That they effectually have from all
that know 'em, and therefore daily step lower and lower into worse
acquaintance. But 'tis possible they may escape infamy; there may
be guardian devils as well as guardian angels; otherwise it must be
their lot at last. But this no good man would precipitate.

   To conclude, I wish the Scripture may not be verified on the only
good branch of the family: that *those who dwell with the wicked, shall
perish with 'em.* You will be as tender as you can with this subject
which I could not conceal from your request. I am ever with the best
wishes for your own happiness, and (in that, for your whole family's)
with true esteem and affection. | Dear Sir | Your most sincere, obliged |
friend and humble servant | A. P.

†SWIFT *to* POPE   11 *August* 1729
1740

                                                   Aug. 11, 1729.
I am very sensible that in a former letter I talked very weakly of my
own affairs, and of my imperfect wishes and desires, which however I
find with some comfort do now daily decline, very suitable to my state
of health for some months past. For my head is never perfectly free
from giddiness, and especially towards night. Yet my disorder is very
moderate, and I have been without a fit of deafness this half year; so
I am like a horse which though off his mettle, can trot on tolerably;
and this comparison puts me in mind to add that I am returned to be a
rider, wherein I wish you would imitate me. As to this country, there
have been three terrible years dearth of corn, and every place strowed
with beggars, but dearths are common in better climates, and our evils
here lie much deeper. Imagine a nation the two-thirds of whose
revenues are spent out of it, and who are not permitted to trade with
the other third, and where the pride of the women will not suffer them
to wear their own manufactures even where they excel what come
from abroad: This is the true state of Ireland in a very few words.
These evils operate more every day, and the kingdom is absolutely
undone, as I have been telling it[1] often in print these ten years past.

           [1] telling it often] telling often *1741 Labc.*

What I have said requires forgiveness, but I had a mind for once to let you know the state of our affairs, and my reason for being more moved than perhaps becomes a Clergyman, and a piece of a Philosopher: and perhaps the increase of years and disorders may hope for some allowance to complaints, especially when I may call my self a stranger in a strange land. As to poor Mrs. Pope (if she be still alive) I heartily pity you and pity her: her great piety and virtue will infallibly make her happy in a better life, and her great age hath made her fully ripe for heaven and the grave, and her best friends will most wish her eased of her labours, when she hath so many good works to follow them. The loss you will feel by the want of her care and kindness, I know very well, but she has amply done her part, as you have yours. One reason why I would have you in Ireland when you shall be at your own disposal, is that you may be master of two or three years revenues, *provisae frugis in annos copia*,[1] so as not to be pinch'd in the least when years increase, and perhaps your health impairs: And when this kingdom is utterly at an end, you may support me for the few years I shall happen to live; and who knows but you may pay me exhorbitant interest for the spoonful of wine, and scraps of a chicken it will cost me to feed you? I am confident you have too much reason to complain of ingratitude; for I never yet knew any person, one tenth part so heartily disposed as you are, to do good offices to others without the least private view.

Was it a Gasconade to please me, that you said your fortune was increased 100 *l.* a year since I left you? you should have told me how. Those *subsidia senectuti*[2] are extreamly desirable, if they could be got with justice, and without avarice; of which vice tho' I cannot charge myself yet nor feel any approaches towards it, yet no usurer more wishes to be richer (or rather to be surer of his rents) but I am not half so moderate as you, for I declare I cannot live easily under double to what you are satisfied with.

I hope Mr. Gay will keep his 3000 *l.* and live on the interest without decreasing the principal one penny; but I do not like your seldom seeing him. I hope he is grown more disengaged from his intentness on his own affairs, which I ever disliked, and is quite the reverse to you, unless you are a very dextrous disguiser. I desire my humble service to Lord Oxford, Bathurst, ⌐Lord B——st,⌐[3] and particularly to Mrs. B——, but to no Lady at court.[4] God bless you for being a greater Dupe than I: I love that character too myself, but I want your charity. Adieu.

---

[1] A Stock of Wine laid up for many Years.—Footnote in 1741 Dab. Curll (1741 Lc) made another translation.

[2] Supports of old Age.—Footnote in 1741 Dab. Curll reads differently in 1741 Lc.

[3] Omitted in all texts except [1740], 1741 Dab, and 1742 La.

[4] i.e. NOT to Mrs. Howard!

FENTON *to* BROOME   11 *August* [1729]

Elwin–Courthope, viii. 155

Easthampstead Park, August 11, [1729].

Dear Broome,—Upon the receipt of your last, I writ immediately
to Tonson to send Waller as you directed, and I believe it is long
before this arrived safe at Pulham, where I hope to find myself about
the middle of September, and I desire to be received, not as a formal
visitor, but a friend to board. In your next, which favour me with,
as soon as possibly you can, let me know if the old road by Colchester
and Ipswich will not be the best. My trunks I know how to send from
the Saracen's Head.

A gentleman of our county, some time since, sent to know whether
I would take his son till I went into Lord Gower's family. If I hear
anything more of his proposal,—which I am not very fond of, though
he will be heir to four or five thousand pounds per annum,—would
Mrs. Broome and you care to receive him?

My thoughts at present are rather turned to finish a tragedy, and
then *cæstus artemque repono*;[1] and as I would bring as little luggage as
possible, let me know exactly what dramatic writers you have got.
My humble service to Mrs. Broome and Mr. Burlington concludes in
haste—but you shall hear again before I set out—from your ever
affectionate humble servant.

P.S.—You are apt to forget to answer to particulars, but prithee
be punctual in your next.

POPE *to* CARYLL   12 *August* 1729

Add. 28618

12 Aug. 1729.

Your sense of the matter about which you write is truly generous and
honorable. As I before told you when you pressed me concerning the
daughter's wicked usage of the mother, so I tell you concerning the other
article, that what I said was extorted merely for force of what I knew
was due to so long a friendship as yours (when you so strongly desired it),
and little from any hope I could entertain of amendment on their parts.
Therefore it is my sentiment rather to conceal what one cannot remedy,
if you [find] upon tryal made by Mrs C—'s[2] letter to the poor mother
(which I perfectly approve) she should not open herself fairly or dare to
show [that] she feels and would redress her grievance. It is much my

---

[1] *Aeneid*, v. 484.
[2] Mrs. Caryll's letter has invited Mrs. Blount (the mother) to visit Ladyholt or East
Grinstead, without the daughters.

opinion that she will not, from several instances I've heard and some I've seen. Nay, I've known her, when she could not exclude one daughter from the censure, speak of both as unkind to her, &c., tho' the fact was wholly transacted when the younger was absent.

I think it not impossible if the mother should consent to visit you (with whatever intent) that the elder uninvited would go with her. It is exactly what I've known her do to many people. At least if both the mother and younger daughter comply with your invitation (which I dare say the first will not without leave from or concert with the elder) I durst lay a wager she would not stay behind, so that I really think there's little hope on that side.

On the other I find your ———¹ takes your letter as only a kind civility, which you have been some years hindered from offering because *the whole family might* (indeed very well) *be too much for any civil society*; and that since her sister had behaved so admirably to you, it gave you a handle to ask them separately, which she concludes you would always willingly have done to herself. If, therefore, you took occasion just to tell her you had a particular reason for inviting her, from some reports (in general) that touched the credit of her family, and someway endangered her own by being linked with them and censured with them, it might have more effect. Otherwise she knows what a weary life she must lead, if she does it by herself, when she returns to them. And as I told you, she has so much weak tenderness for them, in thinking her residence with them conceals and softens many things, that she is in danger of sacrificing every regard of her self,—health, character, interest, &c., to that alone.

The trial is all you can make: there is no serving any people without their co-operation. Your part is good and generous; but in truth that's all. I expect little success, but from some accident which by ruining one may save the other. I am with great sincerity (as the manner of my dealing with you on this whole affair undisguisedly may be one proof) | Dear sir | Your very Affect. friend and obliged | faithfull Servant | A. P.

POPE *to* THE EARL OF OXFORD²   14 *August* [1729]

Longleat Portland Papers, xii

Twitenham. Aug. 14th [1729]

My Lord,—Your Enquiry after me is particularly kind, if I can call particular any Kindness you show me; which indeed you honour me with so constantly on all occasions. The reason that hinderd my giving your Lordship under my hand an account of my easy & safe arrival

---

¹ your god-daughter.—Elwin.
² The year is added in Lord Oxford's hand, and the letter (in Pope's hand) is unsigned.

was an Illness that succeeded it next day before Night, which made me glad that I had parted even from my best friends. Such a violent Fit of the Headache & Cholick as held me three days & nights. I am now taking physick, which I hope will carry off the Remains of it. I beg my Lady's acceptance of my real Service & Respect I ought to have payd my thanks to my Lord & Lady Morpeth[1] for the honour which thro your means I receivd from them. I inteat your Lordship to do it for me. I am with all Truth | My Lord: Your Ever obligd faithful Servant.

Address: To | The Right Honble the Earl | of Oxford, in Dover street, | Piccadilly, | London.
Endorsement: Mr Pope | Twitenham Augt. 14 | 1729
Postmark: 15/AV

POPE *to* CARYLL   30 *August* 1729
Add. 28618

Twickenham. 30 Aug. 1729.

The satisfaction I naturally should take in writing to a friend is greatly increased, when I find occasion in every letter to esteem him for his goodness and honour. Yours about this unhappy family, without flattery, greatly augments my value for you. Would to God they prevailed as much and operated the right way, with those to whom they are directed. But it is certainly (as I at first told you) in vain upon two of them: what may be the effect upon the third, I know not. She is at present confined to her bed and chamber with a violent rash and some fever that attends it, but I hope in a way of recovery. She is very sensible of the kindness of your second letter, and I'm in hopes some good may be done upon her,—at least she may be retrieved from some evil. If you pursue the stroke in the manner I would here suggest, it might alarm her so far as to oblige her to open herself, and discover a part (I don't think she [will][2] the whole) of this dangerous truth, to you.

What if yourself or Mrs C[aryll] writ her word that you had heard from incontestable hands how the family suffered in a general disreputation from the extravagant behaviour of her sister from the highest to the lowest, and the barbarous treatment of her mother (public to such numbers in town and country); and also hinted at a suspicion of her s——r's conduct with regard to a married man (as no secret in either places); that you certainly as a relation have a right to

---

[1] On the Morpeths see Pope to Oxford, 15 Aug. 1727. Pope has presumably been visiting Lord Oxford either in town or in the country.
[2] Here Elwin reads *knows*. Elsewhere in the letter matter in brackets comes from Elwin's text.

enquire in of her, and to demand the truth from her, as a thing that must affect if not endanger her own character to act in privity to or live in conjunction with—there being as many ways of losing one's own character as of being accessory to sin in another: and perhaps this will draw out the truth from her; and I think when once it is out, she cannot but act in the rest as you shall direct, and as I wish really for justice and honour's sake. For the consequences and habits contracted from suffering ill things to be done, and seeing 'em daily about us, are in time too powerful, even in minds naturally good, and often betray our steps into measures that grow irrecoverable.

I must inform you that the moment the m[other] read your l[ady]s letter, she carried it to the eldest daughter, whom I saw in the afternoon looking very much out of humour. From this circumstance you'll see, how unable the poor woman is to act in her own relief. I made no doubt she would consult with her daughter, what answer to send you: tho one particular I cannot but take notice of,—her representing herself, as obliged to her in part of her housekeeping (which I've heard alleged and possibly may to you), whereas her own jointure is more than double the daughter's income, and she on the contrary lives much more upon her, if she live in common. But enough of this. I have had a very bad share of health of late, and my mother weakens and decays daily: my office is a melancholy one; 'tis like watching over a dying taper. God mend us, the best way, not in this life, but in the other, where happiness will either increase, or be at a stay; not as here always diminish and pass away from us!

I wish you, dear sir, all true happiness: what that is, He only knows who knows what are our true merits of it, and never fails to reward 'em. My faithful service attends Mrs C— and your son. I am sincerely yours. | A. P.

‖BOLINGBROKE *to* SWIFT[1]   30 *August* N S –5 *October* O S. 1729

Add. 4805

⌐Aix la Chapelle Aug: the 30th N:S: | 1729⌐

⌐I took a letter of yours from Pope, and brought it with me to this place, that I might answer att least a part of it. I begin today, when I shall finish I know not, perhaps when I get back to my farm. the waters I have been perswaded to drink, and those which my friends drink, keep me fuddled or employed all the morning. the afternoons are spent in airings or visits, and we go to bed with the chicken.⌐

---

[1] The text here printed is that of the original letter. The text that Pope printed in 1741 was based on the somewhat shortened version made for Lord Oxford, now in the Longleat Portland Papers, xiii, which, in printing, Pope further slightly abbreviated. His omissions are here placed in half brackets. Notably these include the first paragraph, Oxford's name in the second and some trivial matters about Bolingbroke's journey.

Brussels Sep: the 27th N:S: | 1729

I have brought your french acquaintance[1] thus far on her way into her own country, and considerably better in ⌈her⌉[2] health than she was when she went to Aix. I begin to entertain hopes that she will recover such a degree of health as may render old age Supportable. Both of us have closed the 10th Luster, and it is high time to determine how we shall play the last act of the Farce. might not my life be entituled much more properly a *What d'ye call it* than a Farce? Some Comedy, a great deal of Tragedy, and the whole interspersed with Scenes of Harlequin, Scaramouch, and Doctor Baloardo, the prototype of your Hero Oxf—d.[3] I used to think sometimes formerly of old Age and of Death, enough to prepare my mind, not enough to anticipate Sorrow, to dash the joys of youth, and to be all my life a dying. I find the benefit of this practice now, & ⌈shall⌉[4] find it more as I proceed on my journey. little Regret when I look backwards, little apprehension when I look forwards. you complain greivously of your situation in Ireland. I could[5] complain of mine too in England, but I[6] will not, nay I ought not, for I find by long experience that I can be unfortunate without being unhappy. I do not approve your joyning together the *figure of living* and *the pleasure of giving*, tho' your old prating friend Montagne does something like it in one of his Rhapsodys[7]. to tell you my Reasons would be to write an Essay, & I shall hardly have time to write a letter. but if you will come over, & live with Pope & me Ile shew you in an instant why those two things should not aller de pair,[8] and that forced Retrenchments on both may be made without making us even uneasy. you know that I am too expensive, & all mankind knows that I have been cruelly plundered, and yet I feel in my mind the power of descending without anxiety two or three Stages more. in short Mr Dean if you will come to a certain farm in Middlesex,[9] you shall find that I can live frugally without growling att the world, or being peevish with those whom fortune has appointed to eat my bread, instead of appointing me to eat theirs, and yet I have naturally as little disposition to frugality as any man alive. you say you are no Philosopher, and I think you are in the right to dislike a word which is so often abused, but I am sure you like to follow Reason, not custom, which is sometimes the Reason & oftner the Caprice of others, of the Mob of the world. now to be sure of doing this, you must wear your philosophical Spectacles as constantly as the Spaniards used to wear theirs. you must make them part of your dress, and sooner part with your broad brimmed Beaver,

---

[1] Lady Bolingbroke.—Footnotes in 1741 Dab.
[2] Omitted in all Pope's texts, 1741–2. [3] Hero Oxf—d] Hero —— *1740–42.*
[4] Omitted in the Longleat text and in the printed texts of 1740–2.
[5] could] would *1740–42.* [6] but I will] but will *Longleat.*
[7] Possibly in his chapter on friendship (Bk. I. xxvii or xxviii).
[8] Go together.—Footnote in 1741 Dab. [9] Dawley.—Footnote, 1741 Dab.

your Gown, your Scarf, or even that emblematical vestment your Surplice. thro' this medium you will see few things to be vexed att, few persons to be angry att. ⌐ostend Oct: the 5th⌐[1]

and yet there will frequently be things which we ought to wish altered, and persons whom we ought to wish hanged. ⌐Since I am likely to wait here for a wind, I shall have leisure to talk with you more than you will like perhaps. if that should be so, you will never tell it me grossly, and my vanity will secure me against taking a hint.⌐ In your letter to Pope you agree that a Regard for fame becomes a man more towards his Exit than att his entrance into life, and yet you confess that the longer you live the more you grow indifferent about it. your Sentiment is true & natural, your Reasoning I am afraid is not so upon this occasion. Prudence will make us desire fame, because it gives us many real & great advantages in all the affairs of life. fame is the wise man's means, his ends are his own good & the good of Society. you Poets and orators have inverted this order, you propose fame as the End, and good, or att least great, actions as the means. you go further. you teach our Self Love to anticipate the applause which we Suppose will be pay'd by posterity to our names, and with idle notions of immortality you turn other heads besides your own. I am afraid this may have[2] done some harm in the world.

⌐Calais oct. the 9th. I go on from this place, whither I am come in hopes of getting to sea, which I could not do from the port of Ostend.⌐ Fame is an object which men pursue successfully by various & even contrary courses. your Doctrine leads them to look on this End as essential, & on the means as indifferent, so that Fabricius & Crassus, Cato & Cæsar pressed forward to the same goal. after all perhaps it may appear from a consideration of the Depravity of Mankind that you could do no better, nor keep up virtue in the world, without calling this passion, or this direction of Self Love in to your aid. Tacitus has crowded this excuse for you, according to his manner, into a Maxim. contemptu famæ contemni virtutes.[3] But now whether we consider fame as an useful Instrument in all the occurrences of private & publick Life, or whether we consider it as the cause of that pleasure which our Self Love is so fond of, methinks our entrance into Life, or to Speak more properly, our youth, not our old age, is the Season when we ought to desire it most, & therefore when it is most becoming to desire it with ardor. if it is useful, it is to be desired most when we have, or may hope to have a long Scene of action open before us. towards our Exit, this Scene of action is, or should be closed, and then methinks it is unbecoming to grow fonder of a thing which we have no longer occasion for. If it is pleasant the sooner we are in possession

---

[1] Here Pope's printed texts omit the date and join the sentence on the same line.
[2] may have] has *Longleat*.   [3] Tacitus, *Annals*, Bk. IV, ch. 38, at the end.

of Fame the longer we shall enjoy this pleasure. when it is acquired early in life it may tickle us on till old age; but when it is acquired late the sensation of pleasure will be more faint, and mingled with the Regret of our not having tasted it sooner.

From my farm Oct the 5th ⌐O: S:⌐ I am here, I have seen Pope, & one of my first enquirys was after you. He tells me a thing I am sorry to hear. you are building it seems on a piece of Land you have acquired for that purpose in some County of Ireland.[1] tho' I have built in a part of the world which I prefer very little to that where you have been thrown & confined by our ill fortune and yours, yet I am sorry you do the same thing. I have repented a thousand times of my Resolution, and I hope you will repent of yours before it is executed. ⌐Pope tells me he has a letter of yours which I have not seen yet. I shall have that Satisfaction shortly, and shall be tempted to Scribble to you again, which is another good Reason for making this Epistle no longer than it is already.⌐ Adieu ⌐therefore⌐ my old & worthy Friend, may the physical evils of life fall as easily upon you as ever they did on any man who lived to be old; and may the moral evils which surround us, make as little impression on you, as they ought to make on one who has such superior sense to estimate things by, and so much virtue to wrap himself up in.

my Wife desires not to be forgot[2] by you. She is[3] faithfully your Servant, & Zealously your admirer. She will be concerned & disappointed not to find you in this Iland att her Return, which hope both She & I had been made to entertain before I went abroad.

Swift's endorsement: Lord Boling Aug. 30. 1729.

JERVAS *to* MRS. CÆSAR   2 *September* 1729

Rousham

Madam,—My wife laid her commands upon me to make all possible haste out of Ireland, & like a most dutiful husband I travell'd day & night, little less than seven hundred miles in five weeks, & anybody may see by my face that I defy'd wind & Sun. The first words I spoke when I arrived were to know how all our friends did, Mr Pope was soon named, & from Twickenham my wife's maid had a Message to deliver to her Mistress who was to convey it to me   That if I return'd in Ven'son time I should have a piece from Mrs Cæsar: my wife, you may be sure Madam was Critic enough to observe that if I did

---

[1] The best commentary on this project (which Swift abandoned) is found in his verses called 'The Dean's Reasons for not Building at Drapier's Hill'. The footnote at this point in 1741 Dab reads: 'In the County of *Armagh* called *Drapier's Hill*.'

[2] forgot] forgotten *Longleat and 1740–2*.

[3] She is]; she's *Longleat and 1740–2, except 1741 Lc (Curll)*.

not come home she should have no Ven'son, tho' she should have
wanted more than she is like to do now—All Europe is to be at Peace,
Greater difficultyes are adjusted—A smal Bribe may do wonders, &
Mrs C . . . r has not been so long a States woman but she knows how
to bestow her favours & upon whom—How Penelope[1] can be of any
use I cannot discern but your Ladyship may—She dictates no more
& of my own I can only say that I am | Madam | Your Ladyship's |
most obliged & most obedient Servant. | Charles Jarvis.

Cleaveland Court | Sepr 2. 1729,
    My wife gives her Service to Mr Cæsar—& so must I—

Address: To | Mistress Cæsar.

*POPE *to* LORD DIGBY[2]   8 *September* [1729]

Add. 6911 (transcript)

My Lord,—I beg you to use an unlimited Power over those Verses,
which have nothing in them that is not defective or alterable, except
the Affection that prompted them. The second line may be as it was at
first, or if you better like it

> knowledge
> Of modest wisdom & of candid truth.

I do not see any material Objection to the word associate, tho' some
Time did really pass between the Death of each—will *attendant* do?
or these

> And thou too close attendant on his Doom
> Blest Maid! hast followed to the silent Tomb
> .Trod the same Path—

> Or

> And yon blest Maid, sad follower of his doom
> Succeeded pensive to—
> Took—

I hope one of these will remove that Ambiguity. I have of late been
conversant with nothing but melancholy Subjects, my own Mother's
Decays giving me a daily Dejection of Mind, which has very much
affected my own state of Body. I should long ago have written to Mr

---

[1] In Jan. 1726/7 Jervas had married Penelope Hume, a lady of some fortune.
[2] The year is determined by the fact that Mary Digby died 31 Mar. 1729 and the epitaph
was printed in May of 1730. Its readings here suggested were later improved. In printing,
Pope with typical carelessness about dates gave in his heading for the epitaph the year 1727
which is obviously an error. Pope's friend Robert Digby had died in 1726.

Digby,[1] but for my own Indisposition, yet I assure him, to hear he is happy is one of the best amends I receive for the melancholy about me. Your Lordship is too good, in saying a word more on the few lines I writ on this mournful occasion.

It is you My Lord, that perpetuate your Family the best way, by transmitting thro' yourself all the Virtues of it into your Posterity. Your whole family is an example of what is almost now lost in this Nation, the Integrity of ancient Nobility. That you may long live to see them imitate, & that after your Death the World may long see them continue you in all those Virtues is the sincere wish of My Lord | Your true Honourer & most | obliged humble Servant | A. Pope.

Twickenham. | Sepr 8th

POPE *to* FORTESCUE   13 *September* [1729?]

1817 (Warner)

September 13.

I take your letter the more kindly, as I had not written to you myself; at least it must have been so, for all you could know; for though indeed I did write once, yet I know it never reached you. I am sorry for poor White,[2] who died just then. I could wish, if you are not fixed on a successor, you had a relation of mine in your eye; but this, I fear, is a hundred to one against my hopes. I am truly glad you have safely performed your revolution,[3] and are now turning round your own axle in Devonshire; from whence may we soon behold you roll towards our world again! I can give you no account of Gay, since he was raffled for, and won back by his Dutchess,[4] but that he has been in her vortex ever since, immoveable to appearance, yet I believe with his head turning round upon some work or other. But I think I should not in friendship conceal from you a fear, or a kind-hearted jealousy, he seems to have entertained, from your never having called upon him in town, or corresponded with him since. This he communicated to me

---

[1] Edward, one of three sons who predeceased his father. Edward's son succeeded as 6th Baron.

[2] Possibly this is the John White who died 26 Aug. 1729. He had been Secondary of the Poultry-Compter (i.e. deputy keeper of that prison), a place to which, clearly, Pope's young nephew Henry Rackett, who at this time was hoping to begin the practice of law without taking the oaths, could hardly aspire.

[3] i.e. his duties on the circuit.

[4] The 'raffle' was the subscription to *Polly*. The junior Duchess of Marlborough, whom (with Congreve) Gay had in 1728 accompanied to Bath, had subscribed £100; but the Duchess of Queensberry had 'won' Gay by her activity in the subscription, which caused her to be forbidden attendance at Court. Gay spent the summer of 1729—and most of his remaining days—with the Queensberrys. His attack on the Court in *Polly* must have embarrassed Fortescue (who was receiving promotions from Walpole) and Pope (whose *Dunciad* was well received at Court), and perhaps most of all Mrs. Howard, who was genuinely Gay's friend—though Swift believed otherwise.

in a late letter, not without the appearance of extreme concern on his part, and all the tenderness imaginable on yours. This whole summer I have passed at home; my mother eternally relapsing, yet not quite down; her memory so greatly decayed, that I am forced to attend to every thing, even the least cares of the family, which, you'll guess, to me is an inexpressible trouble, added to the melancholy of observing her condition.

I have seen Sir R. W.[1] but once since you left. I made him then my confidant in a complaint against a lady, of his, and once[2] of my, acquaintance, who is libelling me, as she certainly one day will him, if she has not already. You'll easily guess I am speaking of Lady Mary.[3] I should be sorry if she had any credit or influence with him, for she would infallibly use it to bely me; though my only fault towards her was, leaving off her conversation when I found it dangerous. I think you vastly too ceremonious to Mrs. Patty, but I shewed her what you wrote. I beg your family's acceptance of my heartiest services, and their belief that no man wishes them and you more warmly all prosperity, than, dear Sir, | Your ever affectionate friend and servant, | A. Pope.

I've only seen Mrs. Howard twice since I saw you, but hear she is very well, since she took to water drinking. If you have any correspondence at Lincoln or Peterborough, a friend of mine desires to procure a copy of Mr. —'s last will.[4]

Address: To William Fortescue, Esq; at Fallapit in Devonshire.

POPE *to* THE EARL OF OXFORD[5]   [*c.* 15 *September* 1729]

Longleat Portland Papers, xii

My Lord,—I have been for some days hindered by an Indisposition, from troubling you with a line or two, upon your setling in full family att Wimpole: where I heartily hope, you all enjoy perfect Health, Peace, & fair Weather, (The Three Wishes of Sir William Temple.)[6] My Mother is not better, you will too naturally conceive, but she has sufficient memory to think often & acknowledge your Lordships & Lady Oxfords favours. I wish her Situation were such, as would allow me to take so great a pleasure at any distance from her, as it would be to me to be with You a few weeks at Wimpole, & while you used

---

[1] Walpole.   [2] *Once* is Elwin's emendation for Warner's improbable *one*.
[3] Lady Mary was angry with Pope because of 'The Capon's Tale', published in the *Miscellanies* (Mar. 1728, dated 1727), and doubtless she had other reasons for rage. She was thought to have a hand in *A Pop upon Pope* (June 1728), and very likely had made more recent attacks.   [4] Not identified.
[5] The date is inferred from Oxford's endorsement giving the date of receipt.
[6] In his essay 'Of Health and Long Life'. *Works*, iii (1754), 268.

Manlyer Exercises to nod over a Book in your Library. The mention of your Library (which I should Envy any man, but One who both makes a good use of it himself, & suffers others to do so) brings back into my mind a Request I have had at heart, for half a year & more; That you would suffer some Original papers & Letters, both of my own and some of my Friends, to lye in your Library at London. There seems already to be an occasion of it, from a publication of certain Posthumous pieces of Mr Wycherley; very unfair & derogatory to His memory,[1] as well as injurious to me; who had the sole supervisal of 'em committed to me, at his Earnest desire in his Life time: And Something will be necessary to be done, to Clear both his & my reputation, which the Letters under hand will abundantly do: for which particular reason I would desire to have them lodgd in your Lordships hands. As the rest of the Work I told you of, (that of Collecting the papers & Letters of many other Correspondents) advances now to some bulk; I think more & more of it; as finding what a number of Facts they will settle the truth of, both relating to History, & Criticisme, & parts of private Life & Character of the eminent men of my time: And really My Lord, I am in hopes I shall, in this, make you no disagreeable, & no unvaluable Present to your Manuscript-Library.

I beg to have the pleasure of a Line sometimes from your Lordship, as at all times the Notice of your Welfare & Felicity will add to mine. I am, with my sincere compliments to Lady Oxford & Lady Margaret, with the truest Esteem & affectionate respect, | My Lord | Your most obliged & | ever faithful Servant | A. Pope.

Address: To the Rt. Hon. the Earl of | Oxford & Mortimer, at | Wimpole, | Cambrigeshire.

Endorsement (in Oxford's hand): R. Wenesday Sepr 17. 1729.

Second Endorsement (in a clerk's hand): Mr Pope.

FENTON *to* BROOME   28 *September* [1729]

Elwin–Courthope, viii. 156

Easthampstead Park, Sept. 28, [1729].

I was in hopes, my dear Doctor, that I should have eaten a Michaelmas goose with you at Pulham, but my friends here have prevailed with me to continue with them till they remove to London, which I believe they will not do before the latter end of November. As to the young gentleman whom I mentioned was offered to my care, I am come to no resolution about him, and I have not heard from his father since I wrote last. In my next you may probably hear more of that affair.

---

[1] See the Introduction to this edition, pp. ix–x.

Poor Mr. Blount[1] is the most miserable young man now living. I question not but you have heard what a fury he is yoked with. Sir Clement told me that she insists on separation, to which, were I in her spouse's place, I should most willingly agree, and view nothing in common with her, as Anthony says, but the sun and skies.[2]

I hope you have received Waller, which I desired Tonson to send you unbound, because some of the plates were wrought off so late that they would have been spoiled in the beating. Pope is very profuse of his praises of the performance, *sed non ego credulus illis.*[3] My humble service to Mrs. Broome, Mr. Burlington, etc., concludes me ever your most affectionate humble servant.

POPE *to* THE EARL OF OXFORD   6 *October* 1729

Longleat Portland Papers xii

Oct. 6. 1729.[4]

My Lord,—I long since writ you a Letter, principally to enquire of your Lordships & Familys health: secondly to tell you of what I know you have the goodness to interest yourself in, my own; & thirdly to ask your leave to deposite certain Memorandums of me, & the best part of me, (my Friendships & Correspondence with my Betters) in your Library. I foresaw some dirty Trick in relation to my Friend Wycherley's papers which they were publishing; & nothing can at once do justice so well to Him & to Me, who was by him employd in them, as the divulging some parts of his & my Letters (with proper Guard & Caution to reserve what should not be publishd of private Letters pour raisons (as the French express it) d' Honneteté.) It will be evident by these at one glance that neither He nor I thought those pieces by any means worthy the publick; but on the contrary that he fully determin to turn them entirely into another form[5] which would have been consistent with His Reputation. All the favor I would beg of your Lordship herein, is to give leave that it may be said the Originals are in your Library, which they shall be as soon as you will give orders to any one to receive them into it, which I earnestly request.

I would not appear myself as publisher of 'em, but any man else may, or even the Bookseller be suppos'd to have procurd Copies of 'em

---

[1] The marriage of Henry Pope Blount to Mrs. Cornwallis had taken place almost within the year. See Fenton to Broome, 15 Sept. 1728. The couple presently separated but were later reconciled.

[2] See Dryden's *All for Love*, the end of Act iv.   [3] Virgil, *Eclogue*, ix. 34.

[4] In the superscription the date is in Oxford's hand; in the endorsement we have that of an amanuensis.

[5] Prose maxims or apothegms. See Pope's Preface to his vol. ii of Wycherley's *Posthumous Works* here, vol. i, pp. xxxii–xxxiii.

formerly, or now, it is equal. But certain it is, that no other way can Justice be renderd to the Memory of a Man, to whom I had the first obligations of Friendship, almost in my childhood.[1]

My Lord, I can only repeat, & repeat again, my constant & unalterable wishes for your felicity, in which a great part of my own is really included, and my professions which will never vary of being sincerely | Your most obligd, obedient & faithful | Servant | A. Pope.

I've often enquird of your Health in Doverstreet & of Lord Duplin, who has lately much obliged me in a piece of Service to a nephew of mine.[2] My poor Mother holds up pretty well & is most sensibly Yours, & my Lady Oxfords obligd Servant.

Endorsement: Mr Pope | Octr. 6. 1729.

THE EARL OF OXFORD *to* POPE   9 *October* 1729

Longleat Portland Papers, xii

Oct: 9: 1729.

Sir,—I received the favor of your letters both and designed troubling you before the last came, you may be assured I shall think my library very much Honoured by the deposite you propose, and if you please to have those papers put in a box and left with my porter he has orders to put the Box into the library, and what ever mention you make of that Library I shall be pleased with.[3]

I know you will be rejoyced at any good fortune that happens to your Friends   young mr caesar is married to a very great Fortune & much to the satisfaction of his Father & mother,[4] I write this because I belive you will take notice of it to them.

my Wife & I desire you will make our Sincere compliments to good mrs pope.   my Wife desires your acceptance of her humble Service. I am your most affectionate | and most humble Servant | Oxford.

---

[1] This attitude of Pope's is fully treated in his Preface to Wycherley's *Posthumous Works*, vol. ii. See here vol. i, pp. xxxii–xxxiii.

[2] Presumably Henry Rackett, now trying to establish himself as an attorney.

[3] After this generous approval of 'whatever mention you make of the library' Pope did not hesitate to make his lordship publicly responsible for the edition. See his prefatory 'To the Reader', *Posthumous Works of Wycherley*, ii.

[4] On the 3rd of October young Cæsar had eloped with Miss Long under circumstances that evoked comment in prose and verse. See *Modern Philology*, xxxvii (1939), 197 for an account (published by Professor Helen S. Hughes) given in a letter from Miss Grace Cole to the Countess of Hertford. About this time Pope dined with the Cæsars and Miss Cole in town, and was witty and charming (ibid., p. 198). Elwin cites a ballad on the match called 'The Royston Bargain, or the Alehouse Wedding'. If Pope dined with the Cæsars, on the 14th as seems likely, he was also busy getting the three noble lords to convey their (or his?) rights in *The Dunciad* to Lawton Gilliver.

peggy desires I will tell you that she is yours & mrs popes humble Servt. | I write this in some haste.

Address: For | Alexander Pope Esqr at | Twickenham in | Middlesex | By way of London.

Frank: Oxford.

Postmark: 10/OC

†POPE *to* SWIFT   9 *October* 1729

1740

Oct. 9, 1729.

It pleases me that you received my books at last;[1] but you have never once told me if you approve the whole, or disapprove not of some parts, of the Commentary, &c. It was my principal aim in the entire work to perpetuate the friendship between us, and to shew that the friends or the enemies of one were the friends or enemies of the other: If in any particular, any thing be stated or mention'd in a different manner from what you like, pray tell me freely, that the new Editions now coming out here, may have it rectify'd. You'll find the octavo rather more correct than the quarto, with some additions to the notes and Epigrams cast in,[2] which I wish had been encreas'd by your acquaintance in Ireland. I rejoyce in hearing that Drapiers-Hill is to emulate Parnassus; I fear the country about it is as much impoverish'd. I truly share in all that troubles you, and wish you remov'd from a scene of distress, which I know works your compassionate temper too strongly. But if we are not to see you here, I believe I shall once in my life see you there. You think more for me, and about me, than any friend I have, and you think better for me. Perhaps you'll not be contented, tho' I am, that the additional 100*l.* a year is only for my life? my mother is yet living, and I thank God for it: she will never be troublesome to me, if it but please God[3] she be not so to herself: but a melancholy object it is to observe the gradual decays both of body and mind, in a person to whom one is tyed by the links of both. I can't tell whether her death itself would be so afflicting.

You are too careful of my worldly affairs; I am rich enough, and I can afford to give away 100*l.* a year. Don't be angry; I will not live to be very old. I have Revelations to the contrary. I would not crawl upon the earth without doing a little good when I have a mind to do it: I will enjoy the pleasure of what I give, by giving it, alive, and seeing another enjoy it. When I die, I should be asham'd to leave

---

[1] His copies of *The Dunciad Variorum*.
[2] Not yet sent to Swift as it was not yet off the press. See Pope to Swift, 28 Nov. 1729. Also Griffith, book 224.   [3] if . . . she] if *1741 Labc*; *1742 Lbc.*

enough to build me a monument, if there were a wanting friend above ground.[1]

Mr. Gay assures me his 3000 *l.* is kept entire and sacred; he seems to languish after a line from you, and complains tenderly. Lord Bolingbroke has told me ten times over he was going to write to you. Has he, or not? The Dr.[2] is unalterable, both in friendship and Quadrille: his wife has been very near death last week:[3] his two brothers buried their wives within these six weeks. Gay is sixty miles off, and has been so all this summer, with the Duke and Duchess of Queensberry. He is the same man: So is every one here that you know: mankind is unamendable. *Optimus ille Qui minimis urgetur*[4]—Poor *[5] is like the rest, she cries at the thorn in her foot, but will suffer no-body to pull it out. The Court-lady[6] I have a good opinion of, yet I have treated her more negligently than you wou'd do, because you like to see the inside of a court, which I do not. I've seen her but twice. You have a desperate hand at dashing out a character by great strokes, and at the same time a delicate one at fine touches. God forbid you shou'd draw mine, if I were conscious of any guilt: But if I were conscious only of folly, God send it! for as no body can detect a great fault so well as you, no body would so well hide a small one. But after all, that Lady means to do good, and does no harm, which is a vast deal for a Courtier. I can assure you that Lord Peterborow always speaks kindly of you, and certainly has as great a mind to be your friend as any one. I must throw away my pen; it cannot, it will never tell you, what I inwardly am to you. *Quod nequeo monstrare, & sentio tantum.*

POPE *to* THE EARL OF OXFORD   16 *October* [1729]

Longleat Portland Papers, xii

Oct. 16. | 1729[7]

My Lord,—I am extreamly obliged to you for your kind permission to Quote your Library, and to mention it in what manner I pleas'd: I consulted Mr Lewis upon the Turn of the Preface to those papers relating to Mr Wycherley and have exceeded perhaps my Commission in one point, (tho we both judged it the Right way) for I have made the Publishers say, that Your *Lordship permitted them a Copy* of some of the papers from the Library,[8] where the Originals remain as Testimonies of the Truth. It is indeed no more than a justice due to the

---

[1] Pope had so arranged the family monument in Twickenham Church that upon his death the only change necessary was the addition of the two words: *et sibi.*

[2] Arbuthnot, much in demand among quadrille players.

[3] She died 3 May 1730.   [4] Horace, *Sermones*, i. iii. 68–69.

[5] Poor *] Poor Mrs. * *1741 Dab.* (Martha Blount is doubtless intended.)

[6] Mrs. Howard.   [7] The year was added by Lord Oxford.

[8] See 'To the Reader', here vol. i, pp. xxxii–xxxiii.

Dead, and to the Living author; one of which (I have the happiness to know) You are Concernd for; and the other had too much Merit to have his Laurels blasted fourteen years after his death by an un-licencd & presumptuous Mercenary. The other Manuscripts I intend to trouble or burthen your Library with, I am causing to be fairly written & hope at Your Lordships return to be the Presenter of them to you in person.

Our affair with Gilliver is at last [like to be]¹ finishd² by Mr Taylor, who directed me to trouble you with your signing it speedily; by post, or by any safer way we beg your Lordships quick Return of the paper. Lord Burlington will be in Town in a few days, & till this is over, Our New Edition cannot come out. It will be in vain & Endless for me to pretend to say how many, daily & repeated favors of yours continue to bind me ever with all truth & Esteem | My Lord | Your most obedient | most affectionate faithfull | Servant | A. Pope.

My faithfull services to my | Lady & Lady Margaret | & Lord Duplin, if with you.

Address: To the Rt. Hon. the | Earl of Oxford.

Endorsement: Mr Pope | Octr. 16. 1729.

LADY MARY WORTLEY MONTAGU *to* DR. ARBUTHNOT³

17 *October* [1729]

The Royal College of Surgeons of England

Oct. 17

Sir,—I have this minute receiv'd your Letter, & can not remembr I ever was so much surpriz'd in my Life. The whole contents of it being matter of astonishment. I give you sincere & hearty thanks for your Intelligence & the Obliging manner of it. I have ever valu'd you, as

---

¹ The ink is blurred at this point.

² The indenture conveying copyright of *The Dunciad* to Lawton Gilliver was drawn on this date, 16 Oct. The dates of signing are not given on the document, now preserved in the British Museum as Egerton 1951, f. 7. Taylor's name does not appear on the indenture. He may, however, have been the attorney who drew it up.

³ The two letters from Lady Mary to her doctor here printed have hitherto been placed in 1730. That year was chosen because of the fact that the letters seem to refer to the *One Epistle to Mr. A. Pope*, published late in Apr. 1730. But since Dr. Arbuthnot flogged the supposed author of this libel (upon Swift and himself as well as upon Pope) in June 1730, it is unlikely that he would be telling Lady Mary of her own suspected authorship of it in October. The authorship was variously assigned: James Moor-Smythe was the man flogged in June (see Pope to Bethel, 9 June 1730). The poem was long in preparation; for it was announced as early as 1 Feb. 1728/9 in *The Universal Spectator* 'as the due Chastisement of Mr. Pope for his *Dunciad*, by James Moore Smythe, Esq; and Mr. Welsted'. One suspects that it circulated not too privately as early as October. Lady Mary's noble willingness to *prevent* the villainy may be interpreted as being earlier than publication of the *One Epistle*; her eagerness in protesting her own innocence is extreme. There is no real evidence of her connexion with this attack on Pope.

a Gentleman both of sense & merit, & will joyn with you in any method you can contrive to prevent or punish the authors of so horrid a villainy. I am with much Esteem | Your Humble Servant | M Wortley M

Oct 17

LADY MARY WORTLEY MONTAGU *to* DR. ARBUTHNOT[1]

[*October* 1729]

The Royal College of Surgeons of England

Sir,—Since I saw you, I have made some enquirys, & heard more of the story you was so kind to mention to me. I am told Pope has had the surprizing Impudence to assert, he can bring the Lampoon when he pleases to produce it under my own hand, I desire he may be made to keep this offer, if he is so skillfull in Counterfeiting Hands, I suppose he will not confine that great Talent, to the gratifying his Malice, but take some Occasion to encrease his fortune by the same Method, & I may hope (by such practices) to see him exalted according to his Merit which no body will rejoyce at more than my selfe. I beg of you Sir (as an Act of Justice) to endeavor to set the Truth in an Open Light, & then I leave to your Judgment the Character of those who have attempted to hurt mine in so barbarous a manner,[2] I can assure you (in particular) you nam'd a Lady to me, (as abus'd in this Libel) whose name I never heard before,[3] & as I never had any Acquaintance with Dr Swift am an utter Stranger to all his Affairs, & even his person, which I never saw to my knowledge. & am now convinc'd the whole is a contrivance of Pope's to blast the Reputation of one who never injur'd him, I am not more sensible of his injustice, than I am Sir of the Candor, Generosity, & good sense, I have found in you, which has oblig'd me to be with a very uncommon Warmth your real Friend & I heartily wish for an Opertunity of shewing I am so more effectually than by subscribing my selfe your very | humble Servant | M Wortley Montagu

POPE *to* CARYLL

19 *October* 1729

Add. 28618

Twickenham 19 Oct. 1729.

My mother and I have both been ill and your god-daughter, I think, is never well two days together. There is no wonder in all three: old

---

[1] This letter seems almost certainly a sequel to the one just preceding it.

[2] She is injured obviously by assertions of her authorship of the libel.

[3] This sentence associates the letter with *One Epistle to Mr. Pope*, the last eight lines of which slander Swift and 'Vanessa'. Evidently Lady Mary has not seen (or pretends not to have seen) the text; for it is Arbuthnot who told her the name of Esther Vanhomrigh (Vanessa), which she had never heard before.

age in the first, a crazy constitution in the second, and uneasiness and ill usage in the third, may equally induce and continue diseases. Indeed, it is some comfort to me (in the daily mortifying sight of the decay and gradual loss of a person so dear to me as a parent, to whose care I've been obliged thro' a whole life) to know I can in some measure now pay that debt, by softening her last hours; especially when I reflect how much more unhappy some poor old mothers are, than ever mine shall.

That miserable scene will never alter, and indeed I fear 'twill draw along with it the ruin (or at least the certain unhappiness) of an innocent woman. 'Tis a strange fate for one very ill creature to be concealed, and indeed by the concealment, encouraged, by the very two people that suffer from her. All others would detest her, and therefore could not suffer. I shall say no more on this subject but if she could be drawn from them, it would be one of the most virtuous deeds, and to the most deserving person, you ever could do. I can scarce commend any thing to you as worth reading that has been produced in this Age of the *Dunciad*. They write nothing but politics and those as bad as their poetry, or impieties worse than even their politics, but as soon as any thing starts that will entertain you, I'll send it you. Believe me | Dear sir | Your ever faithful and obedient servant. | A.P.

I should be vastly pleased if you would pass a few days here, as kindly as you did the last.

*POPE to THE EARL OF BURLINGTON 29 October [1729]

Chatsworth

My Lord,—I hope your self & my Lady are return'd in perfect health thro' all the perils of Yorkshire Roads, which were so Terrible to me ten years agoe.[1] I have twice or thrice enquird of both, at Burlington house; having receivd an alarm which I am heartily glad was a false one, that you were ill of a Fever. I would not write to you, because I car'd not to tell you so: 'twas a kind of Ill Omen, now that distemper is so Epidemical; And because your Ldship lately chanc'd to tell me you kept some of my silly Letters.

I'm in pressing need of you, to set flying the new Edition of the Dunciad: which the Bookseller retards, till the writing gives him a Title from the Lords who were pleas'd to be slanderd so far as to owne themselves Publishers of that poem. My Lds Bathurst & Oxford having signd it, there only waits the honour of your Ldship's name to compleat the favor you begun me.[2] I would wait on you with it, did

---

[1] More than ten years. See Pope to Lady Mary, 10 Nov. [1716].

[2] Burlington seems to have signed on 2 Nov. See the letters of that date.

I know when, or how, being confin'd (as I have been now seven days) by a violent Cold, which betrayd me into a sort of Fever. Yet if your Ldship would rather see me than not, in this pickle, I'll come whenever you'l send hither: If not, shall I trouble you with the Paper?

No one can be, with more Esteem & Truth, a Wellwisher at this Day's Solemnity;[1] than I am yours. Adding to it, what all those must want, an *affection* which it would be an affront to offer to Kings, & belongs only to Friends. I am ever therefore | My Lord | Your most obliged | most faithfull humble Servant | A. Pope.

Twitn'am: | Oct. 29.

POPE *to* THE EARL OF OXFORD   29 *October* [1729]

Longleat Portland Papers, xii

Twitenham Oct. 29. 1729.[2]

My Lord,—The quick dispatch your Lordship was pleasd to give to the Assignment[3] was very obliging: Mr Taylor had it some days before I dreamt of it. I have added another Odd sort of Errata to this Edition which you'l see I believe next week: I've orderd one to be sent to Doverstreet directed to Wimpole, & also one of Mr W'.s Remains,[4] which are strangely jumbled things as they have printed them, of no congruity, nor colour, nor Equality of any sort. I hope you will not take amiss, since you allowd me to mention the Library in what way I would, that we mentiond the Master of it, not in the Way I would could I have appeard in this; & particularly not as I would, because I would appear publickly in any thing said of You. Tis but like the sorry compliment of a Bookseller, to preserve Propriety.

I hope that Good health, Good Company, and Good Weather[5] all conspire to make Wimpole agreeable. Yet I shall wish they may not do so too long, lest we should be deprivd of you for half the Winter

I have reservd to the last a piece of news your good nature will not like: namely that last week, all on a sudden, from being in as much health as ever falls to My Lot, I was seiz'd with a Fever, knockd down to my Bed some days in London, & carryd very closely boxed & glass'd up to this place three days since, from which time I have never quitted my Room. But no part of the fever is on me; and probably I may live to be troublesome, grateful, & importunate to you, My Lord, some time longer. Be assurd with fidelity I shall, as long as I last, continue ever | Your most obligd faithful humble Servant | A. Pope.

1 The celebration that came the evening of King George II's birthday (30 Oct.).
2 The year is in Lord Oxford's hand.
3 Of *The Dunciad*. On Taylor see Pope to Lord Oxford, 16 Oct.
4 Wycherley's *Posthumous Works*.
5 For Sir William Temple's similar three goods see Pope to Lord Oxford, 15 Sept.

My Mother is as well as can be expected & always with respect Your Lordships & Lady Oxfords Servant. I hope Her Ladyship & Lady Margaret will accept of my best wishes.

Endorsement: Mr Pope | Twitenham Octr 29 | 1729

||SWIFT *to* BOLINGBROKE   31 *October* 1729
Longleat Portland Papers, xiii
                                                              Dublin Octr 31th 1729.

I received your Lordships travelling letter of several dates, at several States, and from different Nations, Languages and Religions. Neither could any thing be more obliging than your kind remembrance of me in so many places. As to your Ten Lustres, I remember when I complain'd in a letter to Prior, that I was fifty Years old, he was half angrey in jest, & answered me out of Terence, ista commemoratio est quasi exprobratio.[1] How then ought I to rattle you when I have a dozen Years more to answer for, all Monastically passed in this Country of Liberty and delight and Money and good company. I go on answering your Letter; it is you were my Hero, but the other ne'er was,[2] yet if he were, it was your own fault, who taught me to love him, and often vindicated him in the beginning of your Ministry, from my Accusations. But I granted he had the greatest inequalitys of any Man alive, and his whole Scene was fifty times more a what d'ye call it, than Yours, for I declare yours was *Unie*[3] and I wish you would so order it, that the wild World be as wise as I upon that Article. And Mr Pope wishes it too, and I believe there is not a more honest Man in England, even without Wit. But you regard us not. I was 47 Years old[4] when I began to think of death; and the reflections upon it now begin when I wake in the Morning, and end when I am going to Sleep. My Lord I writ to Mr Pope, and not to you. My Birth although from a Family not undistinguished in its time is many degrees inferior to Yours, all my pretensions from Persons[5] and parts infinitely so; I a Younger Son of younger Sons,[6] You born to a great Fortune. Yet I see you with all your advantages Sunk to a degree that could never have been so without them. But yet I see you as much esteemed, as much beloved, as much dreaded, & perhaps more (though it be almost impossible) than e'er you were in your highest exaltation, but I

---

[1] *Andria*, 1. i. 17. Footnote in 1741 Dab: *By putting me in Mind of your Favours, you in a Manner upbraid me with them.*

[2] Lord Oxford.—Warburton, 1751. This passage in depreciation of Oxford can hardly have pleased the 2nd Earl of Oxford. If Pope had had the transcripts now at Longleat prepared outside the Harleian library, one would have expected the expunging of the passage; but Pope seldom 'revised' the letters of others.   [3] Footnote in 1741 Dab: *Of a Piece.*

[4] Footnote in 1741 Labc; 1742 Lc: *The Year of Queen Anne's Death.*

[5] Persons] person *1741 Labc*; *1742 Lc*.

[6] Swift had no brothers: hence was not himself a younger son.

grieve (like an Alderman) not so rich. And yet, my Lord I pretend to value mony as little as You, and I will call 500 Witnesses, (if you will take Irish witnesses) to prove it. I renounce your whole Philosophy, because it is not your practice   by the figure of Living, (if I used that expression to Mr Pope) I do not mean the Parade, but a Suitableness to your mind; and as for the pleasure of giving I know your Soul suffers when you are debarred of it. Can you when your own generosity and contempt of outward things, (be not offended, it is no Ecclesiastical but an Epictetian Phrase) can you, could you, come over and live with Mr Pope and Me at the Deanery when you are undone. I could almost wish the Experiment were tryed.—No—God forbid, that ever such a Scoundrel as *want* should dare to approach you. But in the meantime do not brag; Retrenchments are not your Talent, but as old Weymouth[1] said to me ⌈in your Ministry⌉,[2] and in his Lordly Latin Philosophia verba, ignava opera.[3] I wish you could learn Arithmetick, that that 3 and 2 make 5, and will never make more. My Philosophical Spectacles which you advise me to, will tell me that I can live on 50ll a Year (Wine excepted which my bad health forces me to) but I cannot endure that your Otium should be sine dignitate. My Lord what I would have said of Fame is meant of Fame which a Man enjoys in his Life, because I cannot be a great Lord, I would acquire what is a kind of Subsidium, I would endeavour that my betters shall seek me by the merit of something distinguishable instead of my seeking them. But the desire of enjoying it in after times is owing to the Spirit and folly of Youth: but with age we learn to know the house is so full that there is no room for above one or two at most, in an age through the whole World. My Lord I hate and love to write to you, it gives me pleasure, and kills me with Melancholy. The D— take Stupidity that it will not come to supply the want of Philosophy.

†SWIFT *to* POPE   31 *October* 1729
1740
                                                    Oct. 31, 1729.

You were so careful of sending me the Dunciad, that I have received five of them, and have pleased four friends. I am one of every body who approve every part of it, Text and Comment; but am one abstracted from every body, in the happiness of being recorded your friend, while wit, and humour, and politeness shall have any memorial among us. As for your octavo edition, we know nothing of it, for we have an octavo of our own, which hath sold wonderfully considering our poverty, and dulness, the consequence of it.

---

[1] The first Viscount Weymouth (d. 1714).
[2] Omitted in all London texts of 1741–2, except 1742La (a reissue of 1740).
[3] Footnote in 1741 Dab: *Philosophical Writings are idle Treatises.*

I writ this post to Lord B. and tell[1] him in my letter, that with a great deal of loss for a frolick, I will fly as soon as build; I have neither years, nor spirits, nor money, nor patience for such amusements. The frolick is gone off, and I am only 100 *l.* the poorer. But this kingdom is grown so excessively poor, that we wise men must think of nothing but getting a little ready money. It is thought there are not two hundred thousand pounds of species in the whole island; for we return thrice as much to our Absentees, as we get by trade, and so are all inevitably undone; which I have been telling them in print these ten years, to as little purpose as if it came from the pulpit. And this is enough for Irish politicks, which I only mention, because it so nearly touches my self. I must repeat what I believe I have said before, that I pity you much more than Mrs. Pope. Such a parent and friend hourly declining before your eyes is an object very unfit for your health, and duty, and tender disposition, and I pray God it may not affect you too much. I am as much satisfied that your additional 100 *l. per Annum* is for your life as if it were for ever: you have enough to leave your friends, I would not have them glad to be rid of you, and I shall take care that none but my enemies will be glad to get rid of me. You have embroiled me with Lord B— about the figure of living, and the pleasure of giving. I am under the necessity of some little paltry figure in the station I am; but I make it as little as possible. As to the other part you are base, because I thought my self as great a giver as ever was of my ability,[2] and yet in proportion you exceed, and have kept it till now a secret even from me, when I wondred how you were able to live with your whole little revenue.[3]

⌈Lord — who does his duty of a good governor in enslaving this kingdom as much as he can, talks to me of you in the manner he ought.⌉[4]

POPE *to* MALLET[5]   1 *November* [1729]

Sir John Murray

Twitenham, Novr 1st.

Sir,—I think it a sillier sort of Vanity to undervalue one's Capacity,

---

[1] tell] told *1741 Dab.*

[2] Elwin remarks: 'Swift spoke the bare truth. "He laid himself out," says Dr. Delany, "to do more charities in a greater variety of ways, and with a better judging discernment, than perhaps any other man of his fortune in the world." '—Elwin, vii. 164 n.

[3] Bowles (ix [1806], 163) remarks, on unknown authority: 'Pope's revenue, it is said, was 800*l. per annum.*'

[4] Lord —] L— C— *1741 Dab. The sentence was omitted in 1741 Labc, and 1742 Lc.* (Lord Carteret is intended.)

[5] Elwin, perhaps rightly, placed this letter in 1730. It evidently concerns the making of interest to get Mallet's *Eurydice* accepted at Drury Lane. Since the play was acted there in February of 1730/1, Nov. 1730 seems late for the sort of appeal to Dr. Arbuthnot and others that Pope was undertaking. He was aware that 'Cibber and I are luckily no friends'. The address indicates that Mallet was still with the Montrose family, which he left in 1731.

when it can be of use to another, than to over-rate it, when it can be of none. Therfore I would not decline your favourable opinion of my Judgment in Poetry; since what I have, be it more or less, is at your Service: But it is no more than honesty to tell you at the same time, that in Dramatic Poetry I am less than in any other. To say truth, I think any common Reader judges there, of the most material part, as well as the most Learned, that is, of the Moving the Passions: and you'l agree with me, that if a Writer does not move them, there is no art to teach him. As to the Particular Conduct, the Incidents, the working up of those Incidents, & the Gradation of the Scenes to that end, as far as I can judge by the course of these first Acts, you proceed judiciously & regularly. The Single Sentiments & Expressions are surely generally correct, & where I can fancy otherwise, I will mark, & tell you my doubts.

But the Second difficulty I fear, will to you be greater than the first. you'l find it easier to write a good Play, than to produce it on the Stage without displeasing Circumstances. You judge very naturally, that I can have no great Influence over Cibber &c. If I had, he should never have hindred some plays from the publick, nor plagud you with his own. To answer you fairly in a word; if Any Person of Distinction that is in the compass of my acquaintance, or that I can come at by any other mans Influence, can be pitchd upon by you to do you that Serv[ice], I will do my best to have him ingaged in it: For it would really be a great pleasure to me, to contribute any way to increase your friendship for me.

You need no Apology for your letter; it gives me trouble on no other account, than that I am anxious with the fear of not succeeding so much as I would in your affair. You should rather make me an apology for hiding from me a Paper of Verses relating either to myself, or my Brother Dunces, (which Savage told me obscurely of.)[1] I believe any thing you do will please me, for a very good reason, because hitherto every thing you have done has pleasd me. I thank you for your Quotation from Salust.

I am with esteem | Sir | Your very faithful humble Servant, | A. Pope.

I have not yet given your papers to Dr Arbuthnot. If it be only to keep, I fear they will not be so safe in his custody as mine, the Doctor sometimes forgetting where he lays his papers: But if tis for him to read, he shall have them.

Address: To Mr Mallet, at his Grace | the Duke of Montrose's, at | Shawford near | Winchester | Hantshire.

Postmark: 1/NO

[1] Mallet's only known contribution to Pope's wars, 'Of Verbal Criticism', appeared in Apr. 1733, and was inspired in part by Bentley's Milton (published in Jan. 1731/2). Presumably some less ambitious effort is here in question.

*POPE *to* THE EARL OF BURLINGTON   2 *November* [1729]
Chatsworth

Twitenham Nov. 2d.

My Lord,—I trouble your Lordship with this Paper,[1] rather than be obliged to trouble you with myself, in so ticklish a state of health as mine is at present. The favour you permitted me, of making use of your name on this occasion, I take as a very distinguishing one, as it makes you in some degree Author & Proprietor of my Follies, or (which perhaps is worse) Partaker & Promoter of my Resentments: Both at least are great proofs of Friendship in you. It will be necessary to be witnessed, & by none so properly as two of your own Servants.

Notwithstanding what I take the liberty of doing by the Bearer, (to whom you'l please to give it seald up) I repent of losing the occasion this would have given me of waiting myself on your Lordship, & if I know when you shall next be at Chiswick, I would gladly repair it.

I beg my Lady Burlingtons acceptance of my most humble Services, & that you will ever know me for | My Lord, Your long-obliged & mindful Servant | A. Pope.

My Mother lives and is your Lordships faithful old Servant.

Address: To the Rt. Honble the | Earl of Burlington.

*THE EARL OF BURLINGTON *to* POPE[2]
Chatsworth

[2 *November* 1729]

enclosed I send you the paper which I signed with that pleasure, that I shall always take, in every thing where I can be of the least use to you. I am very sorry to find your cold continues, I hope you keep warm, which I take to be the only remedy at this dismal season. I intend to call upon you in a day or two, and will have more leasure, than I can have now, for both dinner and company wait for me. I am dear Sir your most affecte. | humble servant | Burlington

Kent is much your servant. pray my sincere compliments to Mrs Pope

POPE *to* JOHN KNIGHT   8 *November* 1729
Bowles (1806), x. 99–101

Nov. 8, 1729.

I have several times had cursory informations, at your door in Dover-street, of your health, and your several motions. I hoped you had

---

[1] The indenture assigning *The Dunciad* to Gilliver is sent for Burlington's signature; Pope requests its return by the messenger who brings it.
[2] See the preceding letter from Pope to Burlington.

intended to have moved this way before the year was so far advanced; but I find you are yet in Warwickshire. I am desirous (in the epidemical distemper that now afflicts us all, and, I am told, all over the nation) to know how Mrs. Knight and yourself have escaped it, or have you escaped it? I have lain-in these three weeks, and narrowly missed a fever. Mrs. Blount, hitherto, has been free from it, but is going next week to London, with open arms to receive that and all other town blessings. She very often commemorates Gosfield, and you and Mrs. Knight. Her love for the place she banished herself from in so few days, resembles Eve's passion for Paradise, in Milton, when she had got herself turned out of it. However, like Eve, who raves upon tying up the rose-trees, and cultivating the arbours in the midst of her grief, this Lady too talks much of seeing the lawn enlarged, and the flocks feeding in sight of the parterre, and of administering grass to the lambs, and crowning them with flowers, etc. In order whereto, she had got two beauties in their kind ready to send thither at your first order. The season, I have several times admonished her, would be too cold for such tender creatures to travel, unless she made her friend give them her forthwith. So, in short, whenever you will direct your servant in town, or her (who will be your servant in town in a few days), they shall be delivered, and sent in what manner you appoint.

My mother still remembers Mrs. Knight, though it is not to be told how much she is decayed since you saw her. I thank God she lives, and lives not in pain, though languid, and void of pleasure. I wish for you both, and all my friends, a life extended no longer than the enjoyment of it, and the possession of that understanding which will make us contented to part with the one, when we cannot preserve the other.

I am, with sincerity, and all good wishes to each of you, dear Sir and dear Madam, | Your, etc.

GAY *to* SWIFT   9 *November* 1729

Add. 4805

I have long known you to be my friend upon several occasions and particularly by your reproofs & admonitions. There is one thing which you have often put me in mind of, the overrunning you with an answer before you had spoken, you find I am not a bit the better for it, for I still write & write on without having a word of an answer. I have heard of you once by Mr Pope. Let Mr Pope hear of you the next time by me. By this way of treating me, I mean by your not letting me know that you remember me you are very partial to me, I should have said very just to me: you seem to think that I do not want to be put in mind of you, which is very true, for I think of you very often and as often wish to be with you. I have been in Oxfordshire with the Duke of Queensberry for these three months, & have had very little correspondence with any of our Friends. I have employ'd my time in new writing a damned play, which I writ Several Years ago call'd the Wife of Bath,[1] as 'tis approv'd or disapprov'd of by my friends when I come to town I shall either have it acted or let it alone if [we]ak Brethren do not take offence at it. The ridicule turns upon Supe[rsti]tion, & I have avoided the very words Bribery & corruption. Folly indeed is a word that I have ventured to make use of, but that is a term that never gave fools offence. 'Tis a common saying that he is wise that knows himself; what hath happened of late I think is a proof that it is not limited to the wise. My Lord Bathurst is still our Cashier, when I see him I intend to settle our accounts, & repay myself the five pounds out of the two hundred that I owe you. Next week I believe I shall be in town. Not at Whitehall for those lodgings were judg'd not convenient for me & disposed of. Direct to me at the Duke of Queensberrys in Burlington Gardens near Piccadilly. You have often twitted me in the teeth with hankering after the Court, in that you mistook me, for I know by experience that there is no dependance that can be sure but a dependance upon ones-self. I will take care of the little fortune I have got, I know you will take this resolution kindly; and you see my inclinations will make me write to you whether you will write to me or no. | I am | Dear Sir | Yours most sincerely & | most affectionately. J.G.

Middleton Stoney. Novemr. 9. 1729.

To the Lady I live with I owe my Life & fortune. Think of her with respect, & value & esteem her as I do, & never more despise a Fork with three prongs. I wish too you would not eat from the point of your knife.[2] She hath so much goodness, virtue & generosity that if you knew her you would have a pleasure in obeying her as I do. She often wishes she had known you.

Address: To | The Revd Dr Swift Dean | of St Patrick's in | Dublin | Ireland.
Endorsements (two by Swift): Mr Gay. Nov. 9th 1729

*POPE *to* BUCKLEY[3]   13 *Nov.* [1729]
Harvard University

Nov. 13th Thursday

Tho I am at all times willing to pass some time with you, My many

---

[1] Gay's play was, when acted in revised form in Jan. 1729/30, just as unsuccessful as it had been in 1713. See Irving, pp. 278–9.

[2] On Swift's habits with knives and forks see Gay to Swift, 15 Feb. 1727/8.

[3] The letter is bound into an extra-illustrated copy of Johnson's *Works* (1825), the leaves of which are inlaid in large folio sheets.

The year is probable. 13 Nov. was a Thursday only (during the years 1731–41) in 1729, 1735, and 1740. In 1729 Pope was in London on the 13th (see his letter to Caryll of that

infirmities make it difficult, if not a little dangerous, at this season: therfore if it were equal to you to do it at my house, it would be, properly, favouring my Weakness: If not, can we meet next Saturday for 2 or 3 hours, & dine with Dr Mead? We may be sure of some time in his Library before dinner, & I'll bring you the Preface I have made. I'll be there at 2 a clock or as much sooner as you will; or meet you any where else, if I have a Line from you pretty early on Saturday morning at Sir Tho. Lyttelton's at the admiralty.[1] Adieu, & all health attend you. | Yours A. Pope.

Address: To | Sam. Buckley, Esqr: at | his house in Little Britain | in | London
Postmark: PENY POST PAYD

POPE *to* CARYLL   13 *November* 1729
Add. 28618
London: 13. Novb. 1729.

Sir,—A friend of yours[2] (who does not think it prudent to sign his name in the same paper with this letter) advises you to give a caution for the future to your indiscreet correspondents lest you suffer for their sins. I take this opportunity to answer yours to me of a nature, I thank God, quite different from this. I assure you my merit (if it be any to be just) in the affair I recommended to you of the lady, ought not to be suspected of *tendresse* or any partiality. I know myself too well at this age to indulge any, and her too well, to expect as much folly in my favour as she shows for her relations. For truly that would be more than one poor woman could supply. I can add no more than my sincere services to yourself and family. | Yours ever | ——

‖BOLINGBROKE *to* SWIFT[3]   19 *November* 1729
Longleat Portland Papers, xiii
Novr 19th 1729.

I find you have laid aside your Project of building in Ireland, and that

---

date) and his health was bad. The 'Preface' presumably was one that he had tinkered with for Buckley, and it may have something to do with the great edition of Thuanus, though Pope did no Preface to that work. The indications for 1735 and 1740 are vague.

[1] Sir Thomas Lyttelton, father of Pope's friend, was one of the Lords of the Admiralty, 1727–41.

[2] The friend, so Elwin thought, is William Pulteney, who had earlier leased Ladyholt, and had a continuing friendship with Caryll. In 1724 letters passing between them (found in Add. MS. 28240) indicated political services rendered by Pulteney for Caryll. See Pope's letter of 20 Nov. 1729 to Caryll. After this first sentence, which concerns Jacobite activities, the rest of the letter concerns Martha Blount. The letter, except for the first sentence, is certainly by Pope. It is *possible* that Pope wrote it all to warn Caryll that his letters to Teresa's mother are indiscreet. See iii. 74.

[3] Published by Pope in his folio and quarto of 1741 as Letter XLIII. Pope's continuation of this letter, here mentioned by Bolingbroke near the end, is Letter XLIV (Pope to Swift, 28 Nov. 1729). The natural assumption is that Pope did not get around to finishing the letter until ten days after Bolingbroke wrote.

we shall see you in this Island Cum Zephyris,—et Hirundine prima.[1]
I know not whether the love of fame increases as we advance in age.
Sure I am that the force of Friendship does; I lov'd you almost twenty
Years ago, I thought as well as I do now, better was beyond the power
of conception, or to avoid an Equivoque, beyond the extent of my
Ideas. Whether you are more obliged to me for loving you as well
when I knew you less, or for loving you as well after loving you so
many Years, I shall not determine. What I would say is this, whilst
my mind grows daily more independant of the World, and feels less
need of leaning on external objects, the Ideas of friendship return
oftner, they busy me, they warm me more, is it that we grow more
tender as the moment of our great separation approaches? or is it that
They who are to live together in another State, (for vera amicitia non
nisi inter bonos)[2] begin to feel more strongly that Divine Sympathy
which is to be the great band of their future Society? there is no one
thought which sooths my mind like this. I encourage my imagination
to pursue it, and am heartily afflicted when another faculty of the
Intelect comes boisterously in and awakes me from so pleasing a dream,
if it be a Dream. I will dwell no more on Oeconomicks than I have
done in my former letter, thus much only I will say, that otium cum
Dignitate[3] is to be had with 500ll a Year as well as with 5000ll the
difference will be found in the value of the Man, not in that of the
Estate. I do assure you that I have never quitted the Design of Collecting, revising, improving, and extending several Materials which are
still in my power; and I hope that the time of setting my self about
this last Work of my life is not far off. Many papers of much curiosity
and importance are lost, and some of them in a manner which would
surprize and anger you. However I should[4] be able to convey several
great Truths to Posterity, so clearly and so Authentically, that the
Burnets and the Oldmixons of another Age, might rail, but should not
be able[5] to deceive. Adieu my friend, I have taken up more of this
paper than belongs to me, since Pope is to write to you; no matter, for
upon recolection the rules of proportion are not broken; He will say
as much to you in one Page, as I have said in three. Bid him talk to
you of the Work he is about.[6] I hope in good earnest; it is a fine one:
it will be in his hands an Original. His sole complaint is, that he finds
it too easy in the execution. This flatters his laziness, it flatters my
Judgment, who always thought that, (universal as his Talents are)

---

[1] Horace, *Epistles*, i. vii. 13. Footnote in 1741 Dab: 'With the soft Zephyrs, and the first
Swallow.'
[2] Footnote in 1741 Dab: 'True Friendship is found between good Men only.'
[3] Footnote in 1741 Dab: 'Retirement with Honour.'
[4] should] shall *1741 Labc; 1742 Lc.*
[5] might rail . . . be able] may rail, but not be able *1741 Labc; 1742 Lc.*
[6] Footnote in 1741 Dab: ' *Essays on Man.*' (An early, if not the first, mention of this work.)

this is eminently and peculiarly his, above all the Writers I know living or dead; I do not Except Horace. | Adieu.

Endorsement (by Oxford?): Dr. Swift to Ld Bolin | Ld Bolin to Dr Swift.—

SWIFT *to* GAY   20 *November* 1729

Longleat Portland Papers, xiii

Dublin Nov. 20. 1729.

In Answer to your kind Reproaches of the 9th Instant I declare myself to have not received above 2 letters from you at most since I left England. I have every Letter by me that you writ since I first knew you. Although neither those nor of some other Friends are in such Order as I have long intended them.[1] But one thing you are to consider, because it is an old compact, that when I write to you or Mr Pope I write to both, and if you are such a Vagabond and absent as not to see your Friends above on[ce] a Quarter, who is to blame? Who could write to you in Scotland? Yet I am glad you were in a Country nine times worse than this, wherein I speak very favourably of the Soil, the Climate, and the Language; but you were among a brave People, and Defenders of their Liberty, which outbalances all our advantages of Nature. Here I will define Ireland a Region of good eating and drinking, of tolerable Company, where a Man from England may sojourn some years with Pleasure, make a Fortune, and then return home, with the spoyls he has got by doing us all the Mischeif he can, and by that make a Merit at Court. Pray tell Mr Pope what a wise thing he has done. He gave my Lord Allen's Lady a Commission to buy him here a Bed of Irish Stuff. Like a right Englishman he did not imagine any Nation of human Creatures were deprived of sending their own Goods abroad. But we cannot send an Inch of wrought Woollen to any foreign Place without the Penalty of 500ll and forfeiture of the Stuff, and the English sea publicans[2] grumble if we carry our own Nightgowns, unless they be old. Lady Allen used all endeavours, but found it impossible and I told her she was a fool to attempt it. But if he will come over he shall lye in one of mine. I have heard of the Wife of Bath, I think in Shakespear,[3] if you wrote one it is out of my head. I had not the Cant word *Damned* in my head; but if it were acted and *Damned* & printed I should not be your Councellour to new lick it. I wonder you will doubt of your Genius.

The world is wider to a Poet than to any other Man, and new

---

[1] This remark, which Pope doubtless saw, may have served to heighten his anxiety to retrieve his own letters to Swift from their casual deposit. It was at this time that he was having the Harleian transcripts made.

[2] Common in Swift's time for tax-collector. See *OED*.

[3] Probably a thoughtless or jocose remark, designed to indicate a lack of interest in the Wife.

follyes and Vices will never be wanting any more than new fashions. Je donne au diable the wrong Notion that *Matter* is exhausted. For as Poets in their Greek Name are called Creators, so in one circumstance they resemble the great Creator by having an infinity of Space to work in. Mr Pope hath been teazed ten times to pay your 5 Guineas, and in his last letter he says it is done.[1] But you say otherwise. However I do not understand Lord Bathurst to be my Casheer, but my Cully and Creditor upon Interest; else you are a bad Manager, and our Money had better been in the Funds. I assure you I will give Lord Cartaret a note on him for nine guineas, which his Excellency hath squeez'd from many of us for a Jobb to Buckley the Gazetteer, who in conjunction with a Jacobite Parson is publishing a most monstrous unreasonable Edition of Thuanus.[2] I understand the Parson is only to be paid as a Corrector of the Press, but Buckley is to have all the Profit. The Parson's name is Cart. I wish you would occasionally inquire into this Matter, for the Subscribers on your side are many and glorious. I cannot be angry enough with My Lord Burlington. I sent him an Order of the Chapter of St Patrick's desiring the Dean would write to his Lordship about his Ancestor's Monument in my Cathedrall. The Gentlemen are all Persons of Dignity and Consequence, of Birth and Fortune, not like those of your hedge[3] Chapters in England; and it became him to send an answer to such a Body on an Occasion where onely the Honor of his Family is concerned. I desir'd in England that he would order the Monument to be repair'd, which may be done for 50ll and that he would bestow a bit of Land not exceeding 5ll a year to repair it for ever; which I would have ordered to be enter'd in our records in the most solemn manner. This he promised me.[4] I believe the Dean and Chapter are worth in Preferments and real Estates above ten thousand pounds a year, they being 25 and the Dean, and he cannot imagine they would cheat his Posterity to get about 3*s.* 6*d.* a man. Pray tell him this in the securest Manner, and charge it all upon me, and so let the Monument perish.

So, they have taken away your Lodgings.[5] This is a Sample of Walpole's Magnanimity. When Princes have a private quarrel with the Subjects, they have always the worst of the Lay.[6]—You have sent

---

1 This letter is not extant.

2 It appeared in seven large folio volumes in 1733. It was dedicated to Dr. Mead in an epistle signed by Thomas Carte. Buckley obviously was a chief promoter and editor of the edition. Its list of subscribers is of perhaps unparalleled distinction.

3 'Hedge,' says Dr. Johnson, 'prefixed to any word, notes something mean, vile, of the lowest class, perhaps from a hedge, or hedge-born man, a man without any known place of birth.'—Elwin.

4 Swift's letter to Burlington, 22 May 1729 (Ball, iv. 82), shows that Burlington had promised to repair, not to endow, the monument.

5 The result of his political indiscretion in printing *Polly.*

6 Elwin emends *Lay* to *fray.*

us over such a Cargo of violent Colds, that [the] well are not sufficient to tend the Sick, nor have we servants left to deliver our Orders. I apprehend myself to be this moment seized, for I have coughed more these three minutes past, than I have done in as many years.

I wish for her own sake that I had known the Dutchess of Q.[1] because I should be a more impartial Judge than you: But it was her own fault, because she never made me any advances. However as to you, I think the Obligation lyes on her Side, by giving her an Opportunity of acting so generous and honourable a Part, and so well becoming her Dignity & Spirit. Pray tell her Grace that the fault was in Mr Pope's Poetical forks, and not in my want of manners; and that I will rob Neptune of his Trident rather than commit such Solecism in good breeding again; and that when I return to England I will see her at the tenth Message, which is one fewer than what I had from another of her Sex.[2] With my humble respects to her Grace, I beg she will be your Guardian, take care to have your money well put out, and not suffer you to run in debt or encroach on the Principal. And so, God continue to you the felicity of thriving by the Displeasure of Courts and Ministreyes; and to your Goddess, many disgraces that may equally redound to her honour with the last. My most humble Service to my Lord Peterborow, Lord Oxford, Lord Boling—Lord Masham, Lord Bathurst, Mr Pulteney, the Doctor, Mr Pope and Mr Lewis. Alass poor Alderman Barber I doubt he hath left me Nothing.

POPE *to* CARYLL   20 *November* 1729
Add. 28618

Twit. 20 No: 1729.

Very soon after I wrote to you three words in Mr. P—'s[3] letter I returned from London and at home found your second most honorable and well-intended epistle. I must first premise a serious word or two in answer to a hint in your former, which I rallied rather than replied to in my short postscript. But it is truly a lamentable consideration[4] that we live in such [a] worthless world, that if any one acts but honestly, and does his duty to mother, friend, or any human creature, it is immediately questioned if we have not some interest, a passion, or selfish gratification in it. I've often heard that I expect much at my mother's death as a reason assigned for my behaving to her with no more than duty and humanity. And it pleases me not a little to know (tho' I seldom tell anybody as much) that I shall not get but lose by her death. In the same manner I receive a secret contentment in knowing

---

[1] Queensberry.   [2] Thought to mean Queen Caroline.
[3] Thought to mean Pulteney. See Pope's letter to Caryll on 13 Nov.
[4] The scribe first wrote *Condition* and then tried to change it into something that may be *Consideration.*

I have no tie to your God-daughter but a good opinion, which has grown into a friendship with experience that she deserved it. Upon my word, were it otherwise I would not conceal it from you, especially after the proofs you have given how generously you would act in her favour;[1] and I farther hope, if it were more than I tell you that actuated me in that regard, that it would be only a spur to you, to animate, not a let to retard your design. But truth is truth. you will never see me change my condition any more than my religion, because I think them both best for me.

This day I went to see her, and she shewed me your letter which came by the post from London. It gives me a full view of your worth and I will say no more on that side, which relates to you. On the other, which relates to her, I find her weakness (from the good principle that the junction of her fortune or income with theirs prevents the approach of the ruin of their affairs) operates too unreasonably in her own prejudice. I have often represented to her of late since this conduct of her sister's, that even in that View she had better lend them the equivalent and live out of the danger and discredit.

It is not possible to tell you too much of the sense she seems to have, and certainly has, of your kindness, and how right she takes it of you. But it is one thing to take it right *of you*, and an other, to take it right *to herself*. I fear she will not do the latter, unless you join with me in a strong representation of the matter. Above all, conceal that you had the hint from me; she'll think, very naturally, it [is] from a servant maid whom Lady B.[2] sent them, and who left 'em partly on account of this scandalous affair last winter. She will be willing I dare say to soften the thing to you, as she did to me till I had a too strong conviction of it from others, and even then I'm satisfied she concealed all she could from me; but you are sensible her tenderness here must ruin her own character, while she hopes to cover her sister's, which made me want a coadjutor in so important an advice. It is certain moreover she'll be the last woman, whom anybody will speak to, on what so nearly concerns her family, therefore liable most to suffer, and know of the scandal least, even when it becomes public. Of course she must be thought privy or consenting to it. It was chiefly this consideration moved me to own this to you, joined to your own earnest adjuration, and in friendship both to you and her I thought it a duty. God send your endeavours, in so worthy a cause and to so innocent, and endangered a woman, may succeed better than my own have been able to do. I am with sincere esteem | Your and all your family's faithful servant A. Pope.

[1] The remark seems to indicate that if Pope wished to marry Martha, Caryll might provide a dowry. The passage is Pope's most explicit statement on this matter.
[2] Thought to refer to the lady of Sir Cecil Bishop of Parham.

‖ATTERBURY *to* POPE¹   20 *November* 1729

Longleat Portland Papers, xiii (Harleian transcripts)

Nov. 20. 1729

⌐ Yes, dear Sir I have had all you design'd for me; and have read all (as I read whatsoever You write) with Esteem and Pleasure. But your last Letter, full of Friendship and Goodness, gave me such Impressions of Concern and Tenderness, as neither I can express, nor You, perhaps, with all the force of your Imagination fully conceive.⌐

I am not yet Master enough of my self, after the late Wound I have receiv'd, to open my very Heart to you; and am not content with less than that, whenever I converse with you. My Thoughts are at present, vainly, but pleasingly employ'd on what I have lost, and can never recover. I know well, I ought, for that reason, to call them off to other Subjects: but hitherto I have not been able to do it: by giving them the Rein a little, and suffering them to spend their force, I hope, in sometime, to check and subdue them—Multis fortunæ vulneribus perculsus, huic uni me imparem sensi, et penè succubui——This is Weakness, not Wisdom, I own; and, on that account, fitter to be trusted to the Bosom of a Friend, where I may safely lodge all my Infirmitys. As soon as my Mind is in some measure corrected and calm'd, I will endeavour to follow your advice, and turn it towards something of use & moment, if I have still life enough left, to do any thing that is worth reading and preserving. In the mean time I shall be pleased to hear, that you proceed in what you intend, without any such melancholy Interruptions, as I have met with. ⌐You outdo Others, on all occasions: my hope, and my opinion is, that on Moral Subjects, and in drawing Characters, you will outdo your self.⌐ Your mind is as yet unbroken by Age, and ill Accidents; your Knowledge and Judgment are at the height: use them in writing somewhat, that may teach the present and future times, and, if not gain equally the Applause of both, may yet raise the Envy of the one, and secure the

---

¹ This Harleian text agrees verbally with the transcript made by Birch and preserved as Add. 5144 as well as with the copy made by Atterbury's son-in-law William Morice for inclusion in his MS. 'Diary of a Journey and Voyage from London to Bordeaux. Anno 1729'. This 'Diary' is preserved with other Atterbury papers in the Library of Westminster Abbey. The present letter concerns the death of Atterbury's daughter Mrs. Morice.

Pope's text, first printed in the Cooper octavos of 1739, makes extensive excisions, possibly to conceal the fact that Atterbury had received letters from him since 1723—when it became technically a felony to correspond with the exile. With this letter was printed also that from Atterbury dated 23 Nov. 1731. Pope was still pretending that he had no part in the publication, and Cooper footnotes expressed doubts as to the authenticity of the letters. The note for the present letter in 1739a reads: 'This also seems genuine; tho' whether written to Mr. P or to some Learned friend in France, is uncertain: but we doubt not it will be acceptable to the Reader.' Nichols (i. 245–50) printed the letter faithfully from an unspecified source in 1783. The letter seems to be written at Montpellier.

Pope's omissions are placed in half-brackets.

Admiration of the other. ⌐Remember, Virgil dy'd at 52, and Horace at 58; and, as bad as both their Constitutions were, Yours is yet more delicate and tender.¬ Employ not your precious Moments, and great Talents, on little Men, and little things: but choose a Subject every way worthy of you; and handle it, as you can, in a manner which no body else can equal, or imitate. As for me, my Abilitys, if I ever had any, are not what they were; and yet I will endeavour to recollect and employ them—

gelidus tardante Senecta
Sanguis hebet, frigentque effæto in corpore Vires.¹

However, I should be ingrateful to this place, if I did not own, that I have gain'd upon the Gout, in the South of France, much more than I did, at Paris; tho' even there, I sensibly improv'd. ⌐What happen'd to me here last Summer was merely the Effect of my Folly, in trusting too much to a Physician, who kept me 6 weeks in a Milk-dyet, without purging me, contrary to all Rules of the Faculty. The Milk threw me at last into a Feaver; and that Feaver soon produced the Gout; which, finding my Stomach weak'ned by a long disuse of Meat attack'd it, and had like at once to have dispatch'd me. The excessive Heats of this place concurr'd to heighten the Symptomes; but in the midst of my distemper I took a sturdy Resolution of retiring 30 Miles into the Mountains of the Cevennoes; and there I soon found relief from the Coolness of the Air, and the Verdure of the Climate: tho' not to such a degree, as not still to feel some reliques of those Pains in my Stomach, which till lately I had never felt. Had I stay'd, as I intended, there, till the end of October,¬ I believe, my Cure had been perfected: but the earnest desire of meeting One I dearly lov'd, call'd me abruptly to Montpellier: where, after continuing two Months under the cruel torture of a sad and fruitless expectation. I was forc'd at last to take a long Journey to Toulouse; and even there I had miss'd the Person I sought, had She not with great Spirit & Courage, ventur'd all Night up the Garonne, to see me, which She above all things desir'd to do, before She dy'd. By that means, She was brought, where I was, between 7 & 8 in the morning, and liv'd 20 hours afterwards: which Time was not lost on either side, but pass'd in such a manner, as gave great Satisfaction to both, and such as, on her part, every way became her Circumstances and Character. For She had her Senses to the very last Gasp, and exerted them, to give me, in those few hours, greater Marks of Duty and Love than She had done in all her Life-time; tho' She had never been wanting in either. The last Words She said to me were the kindest of all; a Reflection on the Goodness of God, which had allowed us in this manner to meet once more, before we parted for

¹ *Aeneid*, v. 395–6. For *effæto* read *effetæ*.

ever. Not many Minutes after that, She lay'd her self on her Pillow, in a Sleeping Posture

placidàque ibi demum morte quievit.

Judge you, Sir what I felt, and still feel, on this occasion; and spare me the Trouble of describing it. At my Age, under my Infirmitys, among utter Strangers, how shall I find out proper Reliefs and Supports? I can have none, but those with which Reason and Religion furnish me; and those I lay hold, and make use of, as well as I can: and hope,[1] that He, who lay'd the Burthen upon me (for wise and good Purposes no doubt) will enable me to bear it, in like manner as I have born others, with some degree of fortitude and firmness.

You see how ready I am to relapse into an Argument, which I had quitted once before in this Letter. I shall probably again commit the same fault, if I continue to write, and therefore I stop short here, and with all Sincerity, Affection, & Esteem, bid you adieu, till we meet, either in this World, if God pleases, or else, in another.

⌐A Friend, I have with me, will convey this safely to your hands; tho' perhaps it may be some Time before it reaches you: Whenever it does, it will give you a true account of the Posture of mind I was in, when I writ it, and which I hope, may, by that time, be a little alter'd.⌐

POPE *to* THE EARL OXFORD   22 *November* 1729

Longleat Portland Papers, xii

Novr 22d | 1729.

My Lord,—I had sooner thankd you for Enabling us to begin Christmass so early by an excellent Collar of Brawn, which Dr Arbuthnot is of opinion is better than a Collar of SS.[2] But I was absent from thence for 4 or 5 days with Lord Bathurst. My Mother is heartily your humble Servant, for she eats heartily of it, & drinks yours & Lady Oxfords health after it: I thank God she is rather better than worse which at this Season, & in so sickly a time, is all that could be expected. It would be a Sincere Satisfaction to hear that all at Wimpole are as well as I wish them, and as free from the Infection of this ill Air, as from all other bad things of our Climate.

I have had two Letters from the Dean of St. Patricks, who has been free from his deafness these five entire months, & talks of seeing us once again next Summer. He has spent 100ll in beginning to build, & values himself upon desisting, and spending nothing to finish it.

I think you stay very long from us, tho I can say little to invite you to London: except you would come to *see* the Peace: or as people did

---

[1] lay hold . . . hope] lay hold on, and grasp as fast as I can. I hope *1739–42*.

[2] During the Christmas season for some years Lord Oxford sent the Popes a collar of brawn. An SS collar was worn by various civic officers.

some years ago, to *see* the Plague: Both of which we are in expectation of, with equal hope for the one & fear for the other: I hope whatever God sends us will be for our Good. I am, with the truest Esteem & sincerity, at all times, | My Lord | Your most Obligd & affectionate faithful Servant | A P.

Address: To | The Right Hon. the Earl | of Oxford.
Endorsement: Mr Pope | Novr 22d 1729

†POPE *to* SWIFT   28 *November* 1729
1740
                                                        Nov. 28, 1729.

This letter (like all mine) will be a Rhapsody; it is many years ago since I wrote as a Wit.[1] How many occurrencies or informations must one omit, if one determin'd to say nothing that one could not say prettily? I lately receiv'd from the widow of one dead correspondent, and the father of another,[2] several of my own letters of about fifteen or twenty years old; and it was not unentertaining to my self to observe, how and by what degrees I ceas'd to be a witty writer; as either my experience grew on the one hand, or my affection to my correspondents on the other. Now as I love you better than most I have ever met with in the world, and esteem you too the more the longer I have compar'd you with the rest of the world; so inevitably I write to you more negligently, that is more openly, and what all but such as love another will call writing worse. I smile to think how Curl would be bit, were our Epistles to fall into his hands, and how gloriously they would fall short of ev'ry ingenious reader's expectations?

You can't imagine what a vanity it is to me, to have something to rebuke you for in the way of Oeconomy? I love the man that builds a house *subito ingenio*,[3] and makes a wall for a horse; then cries, "We wise men must think of nothing but getting ready money." I am glad you approve my annuity; all we have in this world is no more than an annuity, as to our own enjoyment: But I will encrease your regard for my wisdom, and tell you, that this annuity includes also the life of another,[4] whose concern ought to be as near me as my own, and with whom my whole prospects ought to finish. I throw my javelin of Hope no farther, *Cur brevi fortes jaculamur ævo*—&c.[5]

The second (as it is called, but indeed the eighth) edition of the

---

[1] He used to value himself on this particular.—Warburton, 1751.
[2] Thought to be the letters to Edward Blount of Blagdon and those to Lord Digby's son Robert; but there must be some doubt: the letters Pope printed as to Blount may not have been in most cases sent to Blount.
[3] Footnote in 1741 Dab: 'With a Start of Genius.'   [4] His mother's.
[5] Horace, *Carmina*, ii. xvi. 17. Translated as footnote in 1741 Dab, as 'Why do we dart, with eager Strife, | At Things beyond the Mark of Life?'

Dunciad, with some additional notes and epigrams, shall be sent you
if I know any opportunity; If they reprint it with you, let them by all
means follow that octavo edition—The Drapier's letters are again
printed here, very laudably as to paper, print, &c. for you know I disapprove Irish politicks (as my Commentator tells you) being a strong
and jealous subject of England. The Lady you mention, you ought
not to complain of for not acknowledging your present;[1] she having
just now[2] receiv'd a much richer present from Mr. Knight of the
S. Sea; and you are sensible she cannot ever return it, to one in the
condition of an out-law: it's certain as he can never expect any favour,
his motive must be wholly dis-interested.[3] Will not this Reflexion
make you blush? Your continual deplorings of Ireland, make me wish,
you were here long enough to forget those scenes that so afflict you:
I am only in fear if you were, you would grow such a patriot here too,
as not to be quite at ease, for your love of old England. It is very possible, your journey, in the time I compute, might exactly tally with
my intended one to you; and if you must soon again go back, you
would not be un-attended. For the poor woman decays perceptibly
every week; and the winter may too probably put an end to a very
long, and a very irreproachable, life. My constant attendance on her
does indeed affect my mind very much, and lessen extremely my
desires of long life; since I see the best that can come of it is a miserable
benediction ⌜at most: so that⌝[4] I look upon myself to be many years
older in two years since you saw me: The natural imbecillity of my
body, join'd now to this acquir'd old age of the mind, makes me at
least as old as you, and we are the fitter to crawl down the hill together;
I only desire I may be able to keep pace with you. My first friendship
at sixteen, was contracted with a man of seventy, and I found him not
grave enough or consistent enough for me, tho' we lived well to his
death. I speak of old Mr. Wycherley; some letters of whom (by the
by) and of mine, the Booksellers have got and printed not without the
concurrence of a noble friend of mine and yours,[5] I don't much
approve of it; tho' there is nothing for me to be asham'd of, because
I will not be asham'd of any thing I do not do myself, or of any thing
that is not immoral but merely dull (as for instance, if they printed this
letter I am now writing, which they easily may, if the underlings at the
Post-office please to take a copy of it.) I admire on this consideration,

---

[1] Queen Caroline. Robert Knight (not Pope's good friend John) had been outlawed in
consequence of absconding in the South Sea scandal. His present, if made, would be in the
nature of a bribe. Warburton notes that Knight was pardoned in 1742.
[2] just now] lately *1741 Labc*; *1742 Lc*.   [3] Pope speaks with extreme irony.
[4] Omitted in all Pope's London texts, 1741–2, except 1742 La.
[5] In reissuing the sheets of the clandestine volume (1740) as vol. vii of his *Works* (1742 La)
Pope cancelled leaf [H6] (pp. 107–8) in part so as to insert the following footnotes: 'See
the occasion of this, in the preface before the first vol. of Letters.' In 1742 Lb and Lc this
reads: 'See the occasion, in the second and third Paragraphs of the Preface. . . .'

your sending your last to me quite open, without a seal, wafer, or any closure whatever, manifesting the utter openness of the writer. I would do the same by this, but fear it would look like affectation to send two letters so together.—I will fully represent to our friend (and I doubt not it will touch his heart) what you so feelingly set forth as to the badness of your Burgundy,[1] &c. He is an extreme honest man, and indeed ought to be so, considering how very indiscreet and unreserved he is: But I do not approve this part of his character, and will never join with him in any of his idlenesses in the way of wit. You know my maxim to keep clear[2] of all offence, as I am clear of all interest in either party. I was once displeas'd before at you, for complaining to Mr. Dodington[3] of my not having a pension, and am so again at your naming it to a certain Lord.[4] I have given some proofs[5] in the course of my whole life, (from the time when I was in the friendship of Lord Bolingbroke and Mr. Craggs even to this, when I am civilly treated by Sir R. Walpole) that I never thought myself so warm in any Party's cause as to deserve their money; and therefore would never have accepted it; but give me leave to tell you, that of all mankind the two persons I would least have accepted any favour from, are those very two, to whom you have unluckily spoken of it. I desire you to take off any impressions which that dialogue may have left on his Lordship's mind, as if I ever had any thought of being beholden to him, or any other, in that way. And yet you know I am no enemy to the present constitution; I believe, as sincere a well-wisher to it, nay even to the church establish'd, as any minister in, or out of employment, whatever; or any Bishop of England or Ireland. Yet am I of the Religion of Erasmus, a Catholick; so I live; so I shall die; and hope one day to meet you, Bishop Atterbury, poor Craggs,[6] Dr. Garth, Dean Berkley, and Mr. Hutchenson,[7] in that place, To which God of his infinite mercy bring us, and every body!

Lord B's answer[8] to your letter I have just receiv'd, and join it to this pacquet. The work he speaks of with such abundant partiality, is a system of Ethics in the Horatian way.[9]

---

[1] The wine had been sent by Robert Arbuthnot, the Doctor's banker brother, as later letters show.   [2] keep clear] keep as clear *1741 Labc; 1742 Lc.*

[3] Mr. Dodington] Mr.* The name occurs only in the clandestine volume. Both Dublin and London reprintings omit it, and apparently it first reappeared in Elwin's text. The reissue (1742 La) of the clandestine volume reprinted the leaf [H6] (pp. 107–8) in order to cancel this name as well as to insert the footnote on Wycherley's *Posthumous Works*. For the asterisk Curll (1741 Lc) absurdly inserted Gay's name.

[4] Lord Carteret, then Lord-Lieutenant of Ireland.

[5] proofs] proof *London texts of 1741–2.*

[6] poor Craggs] the younger Craggs *1741 Labc; 1742 Lc.*

[7] John Hutchinson, author of *Moses's Principia* (1724) and other works.

[8] i.e. that dated 19 Nov.

[9] In the 'Design' prefixed to the *Essay on Man* Pope speaks of the poem as 'a short yet not imperfect System of Ethics'.

POPE *to* MALLET　　　　　　　　　　　　12 *December* 1729
Sir John Murray

Decr. 12. 1729.

Sir,—A violent fit of the Headake (which perhaps you'l see from the
very blind hand I write in) makes me unable to say more to you than
the short Fact. & I thought it necessary to defer no longer telling you
That. I have but just yesterday been able to have the Lord Chamberlain spoken to by Lord Burlington: your Play is delivered into my
Lady Burlington's hands to give to the Duke.¹ I lik't that way best:
& will wait on him, or not, afterwards as shall be necessary: I know
this was the more Efficacious Way of addressing him. I've done as you
suggested, & not sent the Duke of Montrose's Letter till now. I beg
you to desire my Lord Duke of Montrose to remember I had once the
honor of being casually known to him at Mrs Murray's,² & that I
have not forgot the respect I owe him. I am (with the Sincerest Intent
& wishes to do you this triffling office, or, if I could a much better)
Dear Sir, your most humble | Servant | A. Pope.

THE EARL OF BURLINGTON *to* POPE³　　　[*December* 1729]
Sir John Murray

not knowing that you were in towne, I intended to have called upon
you at your villa, to acquaint you, that our party⁴ is put off, by an
affaire that I cou'd no ways prevent, I have spoke to the Duke, who
desired me to tell you, that he wou'd obey your commands, and shou'd
be glad of all occasions, wherein he cou'd shew you any mark of his
esteem. he begs the favour of your Company at dinner, on Monday
next. | I am dear Sir ever Yours | Burlington

I shall be glad to see you in the evening

POPE *to* MALLET⁵　　　　　　　　　　21 *December* [1729]
Sir John Murray

Sir,—A vehement Headache forces me to be so short in this Letter,
but the Companion of it will show you I have discharged my promise.

---

¹ The Duke of Grafton (Lord Chamberlain) was a close friend of both Lord and Lady
Burlington.
² Later Lady Murray, wife of Sir Alexander Murray of Stanhope. Before this time she
had quarrelled with Lady Mary Wortley Montagu.
³ On receiving this response concerning attempts to interest the Duke of Grafton (Lord
Chamberlain) in Mallet's tragedy Pope immediately wrote on the same sheet his letter to
Mallet dated 21 Dec. [1729], sending this letter along as proof of his efforts.
⁴ For *party* Elwin mistakenly reads *journey*.
⁵ A vehement headache may excuse misdating. The postmark (though blurred) indicates
that Pope was writing on the 20th or earlier.

I can only wish it may proceed successfully, for that part which is not my own. Could I have brought it myself on the Stage & done the whole, it would have pleasd me; but all I can do, you must take in good part. I believe the sooner you sent the last act now, the better. I am | Your affect: humble | Servant | A Pope.

Decr. 21.

Address: To Mr Mallet, at his Grace | the Duke of Montrose's at | Shawford | near | Winchester
Frank: Free Bathurst
Postmark: 20 / DE

POPE *to* THE EARL OF OXFORD   24 *December* [1729]
Longleat Portland Papers, xii
Twick'nham, Decr 24th | 1729.[1]

My Lord,—I think it but reasonable to be Forward in wishing you the Compliments of this Season, as you were so very early in putting me in mind of christmass by a Collar of Brawn after All hallows tide; Part of which Memorial is now on the Table before me, & with which I Shall, laudably & reputably, bring the Season to an end.

I have (as often as I've seen London) enquird of your faithful Porter after the health of all at Wimpole. I long since was told, you had paid off the Universal Fine, a Cold, & were perfectly well again. But it is as long since, your Lordship has done me the favor of a Line; which would have not only told me more pleasingly that You were better, but have made me so. Indeed I have been twice Revisited with this distemper, & am yet afraid of a third compliment before it takes leave of me: My Mother (I thank God) continues yet.

I am concern'd to find your Lordship grow so wise in Retirement, as to like it better & better the longer you stay in it: Many Good Men have done so before you, who could find nothing to be out of humour with in themselves; and it was much the worse for the world, & for those that wishd for, & wanted, them in it. I am of that number, & shall have nothing for it but to grow Spleenatick, & if I can't see you, see no body else, & stay at Twitnam, as I almost constantly do.

I have a Story to tell you; My Lord, that you will tell my Lady— But it shall be kept till I see you; And will astonish you less than it does me. Pray have you any Quarrel to me? Have I done any mischief to my Lady O. or to Lady Margaret? Have I ravishd Miss Walton?[2] For I lay in your house all last winter, and I am lately informd there is not in this Earth so Terrible a Monster of Iniquity as your Servant

[1] The year is added by Lord Oxford.
[2] Elwin suggests that Miss Walton may have been Lady Margaret's governess.

That I have had criminal Correspondence with my old Nurse of 70, I have seen in Print: What may not be dreaded from such a Youth? I assure you, one you *well know*, has taken the alarm upon it.—But of these, when Fate permits, & when I have the pleasure to tell you that I am | My Lord, | Your sincere, obligd (every way) | & faithful Servant, | A. Pope.

To give my heartiest wishes for Lady Oxford's & Lady Margarets happy New years, is Tautology, at the same time that I so much wish yours.

Endorsement: Mr Pope | Twick'nham 24 Decr 1729.

In this year Pope's letters go chiefly to Swift, Gay, Lord Oxford, Caryll, and Fortescue, and they throw as much light on the careers of others as on Pope's own employment—which was to arrange numerous fragments of verse into parts of the *Essay on Man* or other poems. His character is shown in his kindly interest in the affairs of others and in his friendly (or at least diplomatic) visits to Sir Robert and Lady Walpole, in his mysterious rejection of £100 from the Duchess of Buckingham, and in his reconciliation with Broome after Fenton's death in the summer. Throughout the year he seems on more friendly terms with the Court than in other years, and he is thus naturally much annoyed by Swift's tactless talk of Pope's contempt of Courts in the 'Libel on Dr. Delany'. In the autumn a lady (Martha Blount?) advised him to spend more time in 'study'. This, one judges from a letter to Lord Bathurst, seems to be his intention. A painful occurrence in October was Mrs. Pope's fall into the fire, which might have proved fatal. One may note that during this year *The Grub-street Journal* began its career and that it receives only one mention and no covert allusion in the letters of the year.

---

*ATTERBURY *to* POPE¹   [1730?]

Add. 5143–4

I venture to thank you for your kind & friendly Letter, because I think myself very sure of a safe Conveyance, & I am uneasy till I have told you what Impressions it made upon me. I will do it, with the same Simplicity & Truth, with which I wrote to you from Montpelier,² upon a very melancholy occasion. The memory of which would have been in the most touching manner awakened by what you writ, had it been entirely laid asleep, as it never will, or can be. Time, & a Succession of other objects, added to Reason & Religion (for even these great Principles, that should command our Nature, want now & then some Assistances from it) may divert the attention of my mind from what it loves too much to think of, tho' it finds no pleasure in such Thoughts: they may deaden the quick Sense of Grief, and prevent the frequent Returns of it: but where it is well fix'd, they cannot extinguish it.

¹ This fragment is here printed from an early transcript found in the British Museum. Nichols (i [1783], 259–60) printed it in a text verbally identical with this. It is not in Elwin. Nichols misdated the letter 'Nov. 20, 1729'—the date of the Montpellier letter on the occasion of the death of Atterbury's daughter. This letter is clearly of a later date.
² On 20 Nov. 1729.

*MALLET *to* POPE¹ [*January* 1729/30]

Chatsworth

After I parted from you, I called upon Mr. Upton,² who is the Centre of all trifling Intelligence: but he had heard nothing of what you mentioned to me, which makes me believe that Sophonisba is still to be played this Season.

He has heard, it seems, that Mr. D.³ publickly lays claim to a share in the Writing of that Tragedy, at which he is most divertingly angry. I pity my poor Friend betwixt them. And the kindest Wish I can form for him is, that his Performance may defend it self against the vain Applauses of the One, and the officious Impertinence of the other.

As for my little Affair, I only wish that my Lord Chamberlain would recommend it to the Players Wilks and Cibber⁴ to appoint me a Meeting, where my play may be read over, and at once either rejected or received. For I am indiferent what its Fate may prove, since it has given me an Opportunity to know, that what I have written is not indiferent to you. I am, with perfect Truth & Gratitude, | Sir, your most obliged | humble Servt. | D. Mallet.

*POPE *to* THE EARL OF BURLINGTON

16 *January* 1729/30

Chatsworth

Twitenham: | Jan. 16. 1729.

My Lord,—I have been often unhappy in my attempts to wait on you: I've been 4 times at your Gate in London & twice at Chiswick. and if I knew when or where, would be then and there again, with much satisfaction. My chief Impatience was my owne, but there is now joind to it that of a Poet (generally an Impatient race of men) who has been this week in town & whom I keep in suspence as to his Play. I doubt not your Lordship long since gave the Last Act to my Lord Chamberlain,⁵ but whether His Grace has yet spoken of it to Wilks, I wish I knew by a line from your Lordship. For the rest, I renew my

---

¹ Evidently Pope sent this letter to Lord Burlington together with his own letter of 16 Jan.—in which he speaks of Mallet's being in town for a week. The letter postdates Pope's to Mallet of 21 Dec. 1729 and antedates the first performance of Thomson's *Sophonisba* (28 Feb. 1729/30). The letter lacks its cover, but Lord Burlington has inscribed it: 'written to Mr. Pope'.

² Perhaps John Upton, Esq., who subscribed to *The Seasons* (1730). See Professor A. D. McKillop, *The Background of The Seasons*, p. 177, for a gay apparition of the gentleman.

³ At the foot of the page Burlington has here written in the name *Dodington*. Thomson had dedicated *Summer* to Dodington in 1727. Upton may be the divertingly angry person, whose applauses were as vain as Dodington's officiousness.

⁴ *Eurydice* has not yet got to the players.

⁵ See the letters of Dec. 1729 to Lord Burlington and Mallet about the latter's tragedy *Eurydice*.

own, old, constant Inclination of seeing you, when you have no better
Companion, or when you are deprivd of Mons. Battalia, by his Fitts
of the Headache or of Kinde Retirement with Betty Mews. I am at
present in His Condition, and have a Fellow-feeling with him in all
but the wench: It is He therfore that ought to Pity Me, & not I Him.
I am, with the sincerest esteem, | My Lord | Your most obligd & |
most affectionate faith- | ful Servant | A. Pope.

I have been often told, that my Lady Burlington is pretty well:[1] I
hope it is true, & am her most humble Servant.

POPE *to* MALLET[2]   [20 *or* 27 *January* 1729/30?]

Sir John Murray
                                                            Munday.

I have fixed next Saturday for my Friend to dine with you at chiswick,
who is extremely desirous to know you. Therfore pray fail us not,
Your best way of coming will be by the Hampton Coach, which innes
at the chequer at Charing cross & takes in passengers at the Inn over
against Dover street End in Piccadilly. about 9 aclock in the morning.
But I should like it much better if you could come the Day before to
me, who am with the sincerest affection | Dear Sir | Your faithfull |
humble Servant | A. Pope.

POPE *to* THE EARL OF OXFORD[3]   [29 *January* 1729/30]

Longleat Portland Papers, xii
                                    Thursday. | Jan: 29: 1729/30.

My Lord,—This day I intended you a Long Letter, but Sickness
interposd, and I could only send my Waterman to enquire of Yourself
& my Lady Oxford? On Munday I will be with you certainly, if I
live, move, and have my Being. For I know no Better use of it, than
to pass the few days we are allotted here, in the Company of such as
your Lordship: don't force me to join you with the other branch of
the Company, who has done ignominiously tother day in Your House.

---

¹ Pope's inquiry may in part be due to the fact that Lady Burlington gave birth to a son
on 25 Dec. 1729—according to the Chronological Diary of the *Historical Register*, xv. 4.
The child 'dy'd soon after he was born'.
    ² Dating this letter must be mere guess-work. Mallet seems to be acquainted with Lord
Burlington, at whose table Pope hopes to introduce him to an influential 'friend'. Since
Mallet seems to have been at Shawford in 1729 when his play was first being considered,
and since here he seems to be in London, the letter is placed in 1730, when in January he
visited London briefly. See the letter immediately preceding.
    ³ The date, except 'Thursday', is superscribed in Lord Oxford's hand. The endorsement is
that of a scribe.

I am with sincere esteem (a word not to be prophaned) | Your Lord-
ships most obedient | most faithful Servant | A. Pope.

> & Lady Oxford's
> Pray impose silence on Mrs Caesar.

Address: To the Earl of Oxford. | Present.
Endorsement: Mr. Pope | Thursday Jan: 29. 1729/30

POPE *to* CARYLL   *February* 1729/30

Add. 28618

Twittenham. Febr. 1729:30

I wish I could have prevailed with you to return home with me the
day I met you on the road: the rather because I fear the paternal
spirit will operate so far in you upon sight of the lady who is to be your
daughter,[1] that twill be hard to separate you a day or two from her
after you have seen her. I once saw your son at Mr. Pigot's this
Christmas for a moment (not knowing till I was going out that he was
in the house) and I begged him to see him at mine, but had not that
satisfaction. The latter part of the holidays I was upon the ramble,
and now am here with a friend whom I've great reason to believe
you would be pleased to be acquainted with, from a resemblance in a
very strong point, your friendships and opinions. I mean Mr. Robert
Arbuthnot,[2] to whose character I think you are not a stranger. If you
can spare a day or two, here you will find us till Monday or Tuesday,
I beleeve, and you need not be assured by many words or speeches that
it will be a true pleasure to | Dear sir. | Your most affectionate faith-
ful | and humble servant | A. Pope

Your god-daughter was the last person I saw in town. I agree
entirely with you as to her situation, but fear little good will come of
our joint opinions or persuasions. She makes the least that can be made
now of the matter, & seems resolved to think the best for them,
and do the worst for herself. You will give my hearty services to Mr
Pigot when you know I rank him as one of my best friends, for he
once in a manner saved my life, and has always taken care to keep me
out of law.[3]

---

[1] The marriage of Edward Caryll, third and only surviving son of Pope's friend, to Miss
Pigott, daughter of Pope's friend and neighbour at Whitton, was about to be celebrated.
[2] The banker brother of the Doctor, whose business was in France.
[3] Pigott had helped Pope when Lady Kneller wished to have the Pope monument in
Twickenham Church removed (1725), and to Pigott's house he had been carried when
nearly drowned in 1726. Thereafter Pope presented Pigott with a copy of his *Odyssey* in
which he inscribed a grateful quatrain, for which see *Harvard Library Bulletin*, ii (1948),
122, and Pope's *Minor Poems* (ed. Ault and Butt), p. 255.

POPE *to* CARYLL   *February* 1729/30

Add. 28618

Twittenham Febr. 1729:30

The fear I'm in of missing any way the satisfaction of seeing you (tho' considering the material Business[1] that engages you, it must needs be very uncertain what time you can spare me) makes me, after my letter yesterday, trouble you again with this, to acquaint you that the Gent[leman] I mentioned whose company I expected till Monday or Tuesday, has disappointed me, which determines me to try to find you in town first (supposing it to be ten to one that you could not come so speedily). I will therefore be with you, God willing, on the first day of the week, and if you'll leave a note at Mrs Blount's, on Monday morning, I will call there the moment I can get to London and meet you any where, or hour. I can add no more but in haste, and not in health | Ever yours | A. P.

SWIFT *to* POPE   6 *February* 1729/30

Longleat Portland Papers, xiii

Dublin Feb. 6th 1729

There are three Citizens wives in this town;[2] one of them whose name is Grierson, a Scotch Booksellers wife, She is a very good Latin and Greek Scholar, and hath lately published a fine Edition of Tacitus, with a Latin Dedication to the Lord Lieutenant and she writes *carmina Anglicana non contemnenda*. The second is one Mrs Barber, wife to a Wollen Draper, who is our chief Poetess, and upon the whole hath no ill Genius. I fancy I have mentioned her to you formerly. The last is the bearer hereof, and the wife of a Surly rich husband who checks her vein; whereas Mrs Grierson, is only well to pass, and Mrs Barber as it becomes the chief Poetess is but poor. The bearer's name is *Sikins*. She has a very good tast of Poetry, hath read much, and as I hear hath writ one or two things with applause, which I never saw, except about six lines she sent me unknown, with a piece of Sturgeon, some Years ago on my birth day. Can you shew such a Triumfeminate in London? They are all three great Friends and Favourites of Dr Delany, and at his desire, as well as from my own inclination, I give her this Passport to have the honor and happyness of seeing you, because She hath already seen the Estrich, which is the only rarity at present in this Town, and her ambition is to boast of having been well

---

[1] The marriage of his son Edward to Miss Pigott.

[2] Of this trio Mrs. Constantia Grierson (1706?–33), whose Tacitus is dated 1730, and Mrs. Mary Barber (1690?–1757) will be found enshrined in *DNB*. The third, Mrs. Sykins (or *Sican*, as Ball prints it), is more obscure. See Ball, iv. 121 n.

received by you, upon her return; and I do not see how you can well refuse to gratify her, for if a Christian will be an Estrich, and the only Estrich in a Kingdom he must suffer himself to be seen, and what is worse, without money.

I writ this day to Mr Lewis to settle that Scrub affair with M——.[1] It is now at an end, and I have all the money or receipts for it, except 20l. which is in Mr Lewis's hands; so that I have come off better than you.

I am enquiring an opportunity to send your four Bottles of Usquebagh. Pray God bless Mrs Pope. I despair of seeing her in this World, and I believe the most pious person alive would be glad to share with her in the next.

You will see 18 lines relating to your self,[2] in the most whimsical paper that ever was writ, and which was never intended for the publick.

I do not call this a letter, for I know I long owe you one, for I protest you must allow for the Clymate, and for my disposition from the sad prospect of affairs here, and the prostitute Slavery of the Representers of this wretched Country

I have not been deaf these 10 Months but my head is an ill Second to my feet in the night

To Alexander Pope Esq

POPE *to* CARYLL   12 *February* 1729/30

Add. 28618

12 Febr. 1729:30

My ill fortune extremely followed me when we so often missed of each other: the least intimation beforehand would have fixed me either in town or country. I went to Convent Garden the day after you left it. I can now only this way congratulate you on the Marriage of Mr Caryll, and with great sincerity wish the gentleman and lady all felicity. The last time you found me gone from home 'twas to Mr Morice, who returned some weeks ago a melancholy Widower of one of the best of women that ever lived.[3] He charged me with his service. to you when I should see you.

---

[1] Motte has now paid Swift, but Pope had not come off so well with regard to payments for the *Miscellanies*.

[2] In Swift's 'Libel on the Reverend Dr. Delany'. The lines represent Pope as detesting statesmen and 'contemning courts', and they may have been slightly embarrassing at a time when through the influence of the Burlingtons Pope was probably on better terms with the Court than at any time in his career. He was perhaps hoping to reinstate Gay in courtly favour.

[3] See Atterbury to Pope, 20 Nov. 1729, and for Pope's epitaph see E–C, iv. 390.

I was very sorry you had no time to see and talk with your god-daughter. I find, to my concern, the same story has spread into Northumberland,[1] relating to the sister's affair. I could not see Mr Pigot as yet, but this day I have received from him, by the Post, the letter you mentioned as having been given to you to deliver into my own hands. The contents of that letter are so extraordinary that I must desire you fairly to tell me who gave it you? and if instead of your giving it to Mr Pigot, he did not give it you? However, I've returned what it contained to the person, whom only I can conceive it came originally from, as having myself not the least right to it.[2]

I am at present very sick, and had chosen a time to write, when I might have said much more to you, but that I thought it not proper to delay acquainting you with this. The rest is but over and over to repeat my being to you and all yours | Dear sir | a most faithful affectionate | Servant | A. P.

---

*POPE to FORTESCUE   20 *February* [1729/30]

The Pierpont Morgan Library
                                        Twitenham Feb. 20.

I think it very long since we mett. I calld once in the view of dining, & once in the view of Supping with you, both times unfortunately. I have been twice in town, or thrice, since I saw you, but for the most part sick, and now returnd with a violent Cold &c. I've had another Vexation, from the sight of a paper of verses said to be Dr Swift's,[3] which has done more by praising me than all the Libels could by abusing me, Seriously troubled me: As indeed one indiscreet Friend can at any time hurt a man more than a hundred silly Enemies. I can hardly bring myself to think it His, or that it is possible his Head should be so giddy.—Another thing concerns me very much, the strange Delays in my Sisters affairs; Surely there must be some Neglect on Mr Cruwys's Side. I beg you would look into it, or hers (& consequently My, affairs) will be greatly incommoded. Mrs Blount makes you many acknoledgments in your absence for your repeated favors to her. When can you find a day or two? to see | Your ever faithful Friend & Servant | A. Pope.

---

[1] Teresa's aunt, Lady Swinburne (daughter of Anthony Englefield), lived in Northumberland, and it is presumably to her or her family that rumours had come.

[2] On this matter see later letters to Caryll—10 May, 16 June, and 29 July of this year. The strange proceeding supposedly is an attempt of Katherine, Duchess of Buckingham, to repay Pope for services for which she knew he would not readily accept money. *The Athenaeum*, 4 Aug. 1860, deals with the affair—which remains very mysterious. Pope and the duchess were not friendly for some years after 1729.

[3] See Swift to Pope, 6 Feb. 1729/30. Swift's verses had been published in London as early as 9 Feb. It is natural that Pope should complain to Fortescue, his chief tie with Walpole.

SWIFT *to* POPE   *26 February* 1729/30

Longleat Portland Papers, xiii (Harleian transcript)

Dublin Feb. 26. 1729.

My memory is so bad, that I cannot tell whether I answered a Letter from you, and another from Lord Bolin—that I received in Jan. last.[1] I have read them so often, that I should think I answered them, and yet I cannot recall one particular of what I said to either of you. I find you have been a writer of Letters almost from your infancy, and by your own confession had Schemes even then of Epistolary fame. Montaigne says that if he could have excelled in any kind of writing, it would have been in Letters; but I doubt they would not have been naturally, for it is plain that all Pliny's Letters were written with a view of publishing, and I accuse Voiture himself of the same crime, although he be an Author I am fond of. They cease to be Letters when they become a jeu d'esprit.

I am innocent of half your reproaches on the Subject of O'economy. It is true I did some years ago at a great expence build a Wall to enclose a Field for horses,[2] being tired with the knavery of Grooms who foundered all my horses, and hindred me from the only remedy against encreasing ill health: But the house is no more than a Plan, and shall never be more, for Sublata causa tollitur effectus. I wish these were the worst parts of my management; for I am in danger of losing every groat I have in the World by having put my whole fortune no less than 1600l. into ill hands upon the advice of a Lawyer and a friend. I have absolutely got clear of M—[3] and have all the money in my hands, or paid to Mr L—.[4] I believe he is poor, or too great an undertaker, and rich only in the worst kind of Stock.—I have not seen the new 8º. Dunciad nor do I believe they will reprint it here: The Kingdom cannot afford it. I think you have had some correspondence with my Lady Allin. Her Lord hath shewn an odd instance of his Madness. He hath for some years professed a particular Friendship for me; but a peny paper having been lately printed called a Libel on D.D. and a certain great Lord, meaning as it suppos'd Dr Delany and the Lord Lieutenant This same Allin about a fortnight ago, at the Privy Council, the Lord Mayor being sent for, accused me for the Author, and reproached the City for their resolution of giving me my freedom in a Goldbox, calling me a Jacobite Libeller &c.[5] and hath now brought the same affair into the H. of Lords, that the Printer &c

---

[1] This letter seems to answer those of 19 Nov. (from Bolingbroke) and 28 Nov. (from Pope). No letter is known that he might have received in January from Bolingbroke.

[2] The garden or field that he called Naboth's Vineyard.

[3] Motte.   [4] Lewis.

[5] For the 'Advertisement by Dr. Swift, in his Defence against Joshua, Lord Allen', see *Works* (ed. T. Scott), vii. 175. See also Swift's *Poems* (ed. Williams), pp. 794–5.

may be prosecuted. And there is a circumstance in this Affair, that when it is over, may be worth your hearing. There is not much in the paper, and they say it was printed in London before we had it. I have done with Court Ladyes and their Mistress: yet I think to write a moral letter to our half discarded friend.[1] I suppose it was purposely intended as a Slur, what was in some of the prints, that she was to be preferr'd to the place of Maid of Honour. I allow the great dis-interestedness of the other, which is fully acknowledged by the most Loyal Whigs among us—I have some Usquebagh, ready to be sent to you on the first opportunity. These happen so seldom that I am out of patience, there are but four quart bottles, for the lightness of carriage from Chester: but since they were pack'd up I am advised to send them by long sea, and directed to Lord Bathurst, because a Lords name will give them a Sanction. But this I have mentioned to his Lordship, and may you, that he may not be at a loss. My coming to England depends on two things the settlement of my health, and of my little affairs. The times are so miserable I can get in no Money, and among us Clergy here, all go to wreck in absence: for although Tythes be of Divine institution they are of diabolical execution: and God knows how long my Law Suit may last for my 1600ll. As much as I love you, to establish your health I would load you (not from myself) with half a Score Years. Yet on condition not to abate one grain of your Genius. For, (a mischief on it) I find neither prose nor Rime will come to me as it used, but that is not the worst, for I am daily harder to please, and less care taken whether I am pleas'd or not I dine alone, or only with my House keeper. I go to my Closet immediately after dinner there sit till eleven and then to bed. The best company here grows hardly tolerable, and those who were formerly tolerable, are now insupportable. This is my life five nights in Seven. Yet my Eyes are hurt with reading by candle-light, so that I am forced to write and burn whatever comes into my head. If I sent my last letter without a Seal it was an honest pure blunder, of which I make fifty every day, and what encreases them, is my fear of encreasing them. I'll hold a crown that in revising this letter I shall be forced to make thirty verbal corrections. Yet I hope to mend a little, being cured of Irish Politicks by despair: and I have ordered in my will that my body shall be buried at Holy-head with an Epitaph whereof this is a part[2]

As to my Hermitage misfortune,[3] it is a very afflicting trifle, whereof your abstemiousship is no judge: but I am very serious in telling you, that I expect the Doctor will this very Summer make his Brother give me ample satisfaction. I suppose he is rich else it would not be

---

[1] Mrs. Howard.   [2] The Harleian scribe here omitted the epitaph?
[3] Pope thought it was burgundy; see 28 Nov. 1729.

contemptible if he got the Custom of several Persons here who liked my first Hermitage so well (which was sent by Robin Arbuthnot) that they resolved to send for Cargoes if I succeeded in my Second, and I tell you, that good wine is 90 per Cent in living in Ireland, but in you, I sing to the deaf: I will refer it to our friend Gay, who hath writ to me lately, and you must promise my answer. I have not writ to Lord Burlington, but will soon with a vengeance, unless you prevent it— Sure, I answered your last before, about what you say of Doddington &c.[1] I would not be so nice about poking in a sore eye as in doing any thing wrong in so tender a point neither am I guilty in the least: but the Lieutenant knows himself and hath often known from me your Spirit in this matter. I hope your Ethick System is towards the umbilicum[2] I will write to Lord Bol— My most humble service to him and Lord Masham Lord Oxford, Mr Pulteney, and Dr Mr Lewis.[3] I will write to Lord Bath—t from whom I received a very kind letter.

GAY *to* SWIFT   3 *March* 1729/30

Add. 4805

I find you are determin'd not to write to me according to our old stipulation. Had I not been every post for some time in expectation to have heard from you I should have wrote to you before to have let you know the present state of your affairs, for I would not have you think me capable of neglecting yours whatever you think of me as to my own. I have receivd 21l–13–4 interest from Lord Bathurst, for your 200l from October 1727 to Xmas 1729 being two years and two months at 5l p Cent. Lord Bathurst gave me a note for your 200l again, & to allow interest for the same dated January 15 1729/30. If you would have me dispose of your money any other way, I shall obey your orders; Let me know what I shall do with this interest money I have receiv'd. What I have done for you I did for myself, which will be always the way of my transacting any thing for you. My old vamp'd Play got me no money, for it had no success. I am going very soon into Wiltshire with the D of Queensberry with intention to stay there all the winter; since I had that severe fit of sickness I find my health requires it, for I cannot bear the town as I could formerly. I hope another Summer's Air & exercise will reinstate me. I continue to drink nothing but water, so that you cannot require any Poetry from me; I have been very seldom abroad since I came to town, & not once at Court; this is no restraint upon me, for I am grown old enough to wish for retirement. I saw Mr Pope a day or two ago in

---

[1] See Pope to Swift, 28 Nov. 1729.   [2] i.e. towards a conclusion.
[3] Swift more than once in sending service thus combines Dr. Arbuthnot and Erasmus Lewis.

good Spirits, & with good wishes for you, for we always talk of you; the Doctor does the same. I have left off all great folks but our own family; perhaps you will think all great folks little enough to leave off us in our present situation. I dont hate the world but I laugh at it; for none but fools can be in earnest about a trifle. | I am Dear Sir | Yours most affectionately.

London. March 3. 1729/30.

    direct to me at the D. of Q. in Burlington Gardens.

Address: To | The Revd Dr Swift Dean | of St Patricks in | Dublin | Ireland.

Endorsements (by Swift): March 3d 1729–30 | Mr Gay | About money in | Lord Bathursts hands.
    Mr. Gay. Mar 3d 1729 | Answerd. Mar. 19
    ¹Lord Bathurst | Feb 12 1729–30

†POPE *to* SWIFT²   [4 *March* 1729/30]
1740
                                           April 14, 1730.
This is a letter extraordinary, to do and say nothing, but to recommend to you, (as a Clergy-man, and a charitable one,) a pious and a good work, and for a good and an honest man: Moreover he is above seventy, and poor, which you might think included in the word honest. I shall think it a kindness done myself if you can propagate Mr. Westley's subscription for his Commentary on Job,³ among your Divines (Bishops excepted, of whom there is no hope) and among such as are believers, or readers, of scripture. Even the curious may find something to please them, if they scorn to be edified. It has been the labour of eight years of this learned man's life; I call him what he is, a learned man, and I engage you will approve his prose more than you formerly could his poetry. Lord Bolingbroke is a favourer of it, and allows you to do your best to serve an old Tory, and a sufferer for the Church of England, tho' you are a Whig, as I am.

We have here some verses in your name, which I am angry at. Sure you wou'd not use me so ill as to flatter me? I therefore think it is some other weak Irishman.

---

¹ This last endorsement, at first sight strange, is simply Swift's record of Bathurst's letter (Ball, iv. 123–5) of the given date, which like Gay's dealt with Swift's finances.
² One may assume that the original letter was undated, and that when Pope edited it for printing he guessed its date as 14 Apr. It is obviously a sort of covering letter sent with that of the Earl of Oxford, whose letter is dated 4 Mar. In printing Pope joined his letter, which is unusually brief, to that of Bolingbroke to Swift, 9 Apr. 1730, giving the two letters the date of 14 Apr. Harleian transcripts of the letters of Oxford and Bolingbroke exist at Longleat. The Oxford letter is printed in Ball, iv. 131–2.
³ *Dissertationes in librum Jobi*, by Samuel Wesley (1662–1735), father of the founders of Methodism, was printed in 1735, after the author's death.

||SWIFT *to* GAY[1]   19 *March* 1729/30

Longleat Portland Papers, xiii (Harleian transcripts)

Dublin Mar. 19. 1729.

I deny it:[2] I do write to you according to the old Stipulation, for when
you kept your old Company, when I writ to one I writ to all. But I
am ready to enter into a new Bargain, since you are got into a new
world, and will answer all your Letters. You are first to present my
most humble respects to the Dutchess of Queensberry, and let her
know that I never dine without thinking of her, although it be with
some difficulty that I can obey her, when I happen to dine with Forks
that have but two prongs, and the Sawce is not very consistent; and I
desire she will order Lady Charlotte Hyde[3] to read before me when I
go next to my Lord Clarendon's; for when I saw her last she behaved
herself like a young Sempstress, or a Country Parson's Daughter.
You must likewise tell her Grace that she is a general Toast among all
honest Folks here, and particularly at the Deanery even in the face of
my Whig subjects. I will leave my money in Lord Bathurst's Hands,
and the Management of it (for want of better) in Yours. But I hope
you have paid yourself the five Guinneas; and pray keep the Interest
Money in a bag, wrapt up and sealed by itself, for fear of your own
fingers under your Carelessness and necessityes. I pay an Annuity of
15ll per Ann: in Surrey,[4] and shall soon send you a direction for part
of it, And besides My Lord Lieutenant hath forced me against my
will to pay nine Guinneas for the New Edition of Thuanus which I
know to be a jobb for Buckley, and I shall put the Payment on you or
Mr Lewis, who likewise hath some money of mine in his Hand. And
now I have learnt a way of making my Friends write, it is but letting
them keep my money, for till then I never had a line from Mr Lewis,
nor hardly from you. Mr Pope talks of you as a perfect Stranger. But
the different pursuits and manners and Interests of Life as fortune
hath pleased to dispose them, will never suffer those to live together,
who by their Inclinations ought never part. I hope when you are rich
enough, you will have some little oeconomy of your own, either in
Town or Country, and be able to give your friend a pint of Port and

---

[1] This is the first of a group of 12 letters from Swift to Gay printed by Pope as Letters
XLVIII–LIX in his editions of 1741–2. To the heading preceding this letter was appended
a footnote: 'Found among Mr. *Gay*'s papers, and return'd to Dr. *Swift* by the *Duke* of *Queensbury* and Mr. *Pope.*' The note did not appear in the clandestine volume or in the Dublin
editions (1741 Dab). It did appear in the London texts. Evidently before the letters were
returned to Swift they were copied by Pope's or Oxford's amanuensis, and printed from
these transcripts. The footnote was intended to deceive readers into thinking that the
Swift–Pope letters were published by Swift.

[2] i.e. that I do not write to you. See Gay to Swift, 3 Mar.

[3] Younger sister of the Duchess. Both were daughters of Henry, Earl of Clarendon.

[4] To his sister.—Ball.

a bit of mutton; for the domestick Season of Life will come on. We are taught to hope here, that Events may happen in no long time, which may give the Court another face with reguard to you as well as all wellwishers to their Country. But I hope you will be wise enough after you have got your bit to go decently off. I had never much hopes of your Vampt Play, although Mr Pope seem'd to have, and although it were ever so good: But you should have done like the Parsons,[1] and changed your Text, I mean the title and the Names of the Persons. After all it was an Effect of Idleness, for you are[2] in the Prime of Life when Invention and Judgement go together. I wish you had 100ll a year more, for Horses. I ride and walk whenever good Weather invites, and am reputed the best Walker in this Town and five Miles round. I writ lately to Mr Pope, I wish you had a little Villakin in his Neighborwood; but you are yet too Volatile, and a Lady and[3] Coach and Six Horses would carry you to Japan.[4] ⌈I complain to you as I did to Mr Pope of the Doctor's Roan[5] Brother, who sent me 150 Bottles of Hermitage, that by the time they got into my Cellar cost me 27ll and in less than a year all turned sowr; tho' what I had formerly from his Brother Robin was not fit to drink till two years, and grew better at seven, as a few left, yet shew. For this I expect satisfaction. The Dissappointment is five times more than the loss. But what care you for this, who have left off drinking Wine; and would not now think it hard if Mr Pope should tell us towards the bottom of a pint: Gentlemen I will leave you to your wine. And by the way, this is an ill encouragement for me to come among you, if my Health and buissiness would permit. Mr Pope's Usquebagh is, I hope, at sea, and directed to my Lord Bathurst. Tell his Lordship I will write to him soon with one enclosed to my Lord Bolingbroke, whose address I do not well know and wish you would tell me. My humble service to the Doctor; what other Acquaintance of mine you see I know not, except Mr Pulteney, whose humble servant I shall ever be, in all Fortunes, and he is another of our Stock-Healths. I Know not your Duke but love him for his Spirit. In my Conscience I forget whether your Dutchess be daughter of my Mistress Rochester,[6] or no. Pray venture on Horseback when you are in Wiltshire, there is very cold riding if you are near Salisbury. Adieu, and God preserve you.⌉

---

[1] like the Parsons] like Parsons *1741 Lab.* (N.B. This small variant indicates that the later octavos were not based on the quarto or folio texts of 1741.)

[2] are] were *1741 Dab.*

[3] and] in *1740; 1741 Dab.*] with *1741 Labc; 1742 Labc.*

[4] As printed by Pope the letter stopped at this point.

[5] For *Rouen*, where Robert Arbuthnot had offices as well as in Paris.

[6] She was. Her mother, Jane Leveson-Gower, married the 3rd Earl of Clarendon and Rochester in 1692. She had died in 1725.

†SWIFT *to* BOLINGBROKE[1]   21 *March* 1729/30

1740

Dublin, March 21, 1729.

You tell me you have not quitted the design of collecting, writing, &c. This is the answer of every sinner who defers his repentance. I wish Mr. Pope were as great an urger as I, who long for nothing more than to see truth under your hands, laying all detraction in the dust—I find my self disposed every year, or rather every month, to be more angry and revengeful; and my rage is so ignoble, that it descends even to resent the folly and baseness of the enslav'd people among whom I live. I knew an old Lord in Leicestershire who amused himself with mending pitchforks and spades for his Tenants *gratis*. Yet I have higher ideas left, if I were nearer to objects on which I might employ them; and contemning my private fortune, would gladly cross the channel and stand by, while my betters were driving the Boar out of the garden,[2] if there be any probable expectation of such an endeavour. When I was of your age I often thought of death, but now after a dozen years more, it is never out of my mind, and terrifies me less. I conclude that providence hath order'd our fears to decrease with our spirits; and yet I love *la bagatelle*[3] better than ever: for finding it troublesome to read at night, and the company here growing tasteless, I am always writing bad prose, or worse verses,[4] either of rage or raillery, whereof some few escape to give offence, or mirth, and the rest are burnt.

They print some Irish trash in London, and charge it on me, which you will clear me of to my friends, for all are spurious except one paper,[5] for which Mr. Pope very lately chid me. I remember your Lordship us'd to say, that a few good speakers would in time carry any point that was right; and that the common method of a majority, by calling, To the question, would never hold long when reason was on the other side. Whether politicks do not change like gaming by the invention of new tricks, I am ignorant? but I believe in your time you would never, as a Minister, have suffer'd an Act to pass thro' the H. of C—'s,[6] only because you were sure of a majority in

---

[1] Pope placed this letter as if it were written in 1729. It must be 1730 because of the allusion to the 'Libel on Dr. Delany' though the mention of 'this sixteen years' of peace favours the earlier date.

[2] The figure of the boar for statesman is apparently common. Pope used it to Sarah, Duchess of Marlborough, in late Aug. 1742, and it was commonly used of Junius later in the century. Its remote derivation may owe something to Psalm lxxx. 5–13 or to Ovid's boar-hunt in the eighth *Metamorphosis*, but it probably owes more to some unidentified political pamphlet. All London texts of 1741-2 read *boars*, which made the remark less pointed at Walpole.

[3] Footnote in 1741 Dab: 'Trifling.'   [4] verses] verse *1741 Dab*.

[5] Footnote in all texts, 1740-2: 'Entituled, A Libel on Dr. Delany, and a certain great Lord.'

[6] H. of C—'s] House of Commons *1741 Dab*.

the H. of L——s¹ to throw it out; because it would be unpopular, and consequently a loss of reputation. Yet this we are told hath been the case in the qualification-bill relating to Pensioners. It should seem to me, that Corruption, like avarice, hath no bounds. I had opportunities to know the proceedings of your ministry better than any other man of my rank; and having not much to do, I have often compar'd it with this sixteen years² of a profound peace all over Europe, and we running seven millions in debt. I am forc'd to play at small game, to set the beasts here a madding, meerly for want of better game, *Tentanda via est qua me quoque possim &c.*³—The D— take those politicks, where a Dunce might govern for a dozen years together. I will come⁴ in person to England, if I am provok'd, and send for the Dictator from the plough. I disdain to say, *O mihi praeteritos*⁵—but *cruda deo viridisque Senectus.*⁶ Pray my Lord how are the gardens? have you taken down the mount, and remov'd the yew hedges? Have you not bad weather for the spring-corn? Has Mr. Pope gone farther in his Ethic Poems? and is the head-land sown with wheat? and what says Polybius? and how does my Lord St. John?⁷ which last question is very material to me, because I love Burgundy, and riding between Twickenham and Dawley.—I built a wall five years ago, and when the masons play'd the knaves, nothing delighted me so much as to stand by while my servants threw down what was amiss:⁸ I have like-wise seen a Monkey overthrow all the dishes and plates in a kitchen, merely for the pleasure of seeing them tumble and hearing the clatter they made in their fall. I wish you would invite me to such another entertainment;⁹ but you think as I ought to think, that it is time for me to have done with the world, and so I would if I could get into a better before I was called into the best, and not die here in a rage, like a poison'd rat in a hole. I wonder you are not ashamed to let me pine away in this kingdom while you are out of power.

I come from looking over the *Melange* above-written, and declare it to be a true copy of my present disposition, which must needs please you, since nothing was ever more displeasing to myself. I desire you to present my most humble respects to my Lady.

---

¹ H. of L——s] House of Lords *1741 Dab.*
² with this sixteen] with these last sixteen *all printed texts except 1740 and 1742 La.*
³ Virgil, *Georgics*, iii. 8. Footnote in 1741 Dab gives the translation from Dryden's version.
⁴ come] go *1741 Dab.* (Bolingbroke posed as a willing Cincinnatus.)
⁵ *Aeneid*, viii. 560. Similarly footnoted in 1741 Dab with Dryden's translation.
⁶ *Aeneid*, vi. 304. Likewise translated by Dryden in the footnote of 1741 Dab.
⁷ Footnote in 1741 Dab: 'Lord St. John of Battersea, Father to Lord Bolingbroke.'
⁸ Mrs. Letitia Pilkington, *Memoirs* (1928), pp. 62–63, also gives an account of this episode in the walling of Naboth's Vineyard.
⁹ That is, one of inculcating political honesty.

FENTON *to* BROOME   22 *March* [1729/30]
Elwin–Courthope, viii. 157

Easthampstead Park, March 22, [1730].

Six or eight months have passed in expecting a letter from the Rector
of Pulham.¹ *Ut valet? ut meminit nostri?*² I should be glad to have an
answer to the former question; the other I can pretty well resolve
myself. You see by the date that I am still in the same place, and I
think on the same chair from which I wrote to you last, and it is the
easier under me, because I am somewhat useful in the family: for
upon making up accounts with the trustee, we find no less than nine
thousand pounds deficiency in one article, besides a long arrear of
interest for the principal. The squire,³ who presents his service to you,
bears it like a man; and is not only preferring a suit in chancery, but
another in the court of love.

About a month since I was in town about this unfortunate affair,
where a friend of ours told me of your epistolary *eclaircissement* with
Pope,⁴ who had showed him your letters and his answers. I was not
surprised to hear that it ended with declaring off from any further
commerce with him; but I should be glad to know whether or no your
resentment extends to E. Fenton.

POPE TO THE EARL OF OXFORD⁵   [2 *April* 1730]
Longleat Portland Papers, xiii.

Tis granted Sir; the Busto's a damn'd head
    Pope is a little Elf.
All he can say for't, is, He neither made
    The Busto, nor himself.

Address: To | The Right Honble | The Earl of Oxford | in Doverstreet |
London

Postmark: 2/AP

¹ Broome became rector of Pulham in 1728.   ² Horace, *Epistles*, i. iii. 12.
³ The squire, William Trumbull (b. 1708), had now reached his majority, and the condition of his estate was being examined.
⁴ This part of the correspondence is not among Broome's papers.—Elwin.
⁵ The day and month are from the postmark. The year is very likely wrong. It assumes
that the bust of Pope made by Rysbrack about 1725 was made for Lord Oxford, and is now
being 'placed' in the new library at Wimpole. See the later letters to Oxford here dated [June
1730] and 1 Oct. 1730. This quatrain was published in *The Nut-Cracker* (1751) and perhaps
elsewhere. It is printed under the title 'On some Reflections on Pope's Busto', and has an
additional quatrain:

Rysbrake, to make a *Pope* of Stone
    Must labour hard and sore;
But it would cost him Labour none
    To make a Stone of *Moor*.

The second quatrain hardly reads as if from Pope's own pen.

||POPE *and* BOLINGBROKE *to* SWIFT[1] [9 *April* 1730]

Longleat Portland Papers, xiii (Harleian transcripts)

⌐I have received two or three Letters of one kind or other from you, and answer'd them either jointly or seperately as I could. I also saw a Letter of one Mrs Sykins, but mist the sight of the Lady by an accident. She came from London one night, sent yours to my house about 7. it raining very hard, I sent word I would be at home all the next day at her Service. The next morning it raining still, I sent my Servant by nine, to ask at what hour I should send a Chariot for her, and she was gone 2 hours before, back to London: So she has seen no greater monster, yet, than the Estrich. I don't wonder, if people from all parts should flock to see me, after the Picture lately drawn of me by a very peculiar Painter in Ireland,[2] who has made the finest Show-Board of me, in the World: I forgive that Painter, tho' there may be others who do not, and tho he flatters my Virtue, which is a Greater Sin sure than to flatter one's Vanity.—I am pleased to see however your partiality, and 'tis for that reason I've kept some of your Letters and some of those of my other friends. These if I put together in a Volume, (for my own secret satisfaction, in reviewing a Life, past in Innocent amusements & Studies, not without the good will of worthy and ingenious Men) do not therefore say, I aim at Epistolary Fame:[3] I never had any Fame less in my head; but the Fame I most covet indeed, is that, which must be deriv'd to me from my Friendships.

I am truly and heartily concern'd at the Prospect of so great a Loss as you mention, in your fortune, which I wish you had not told me, since I can't contribute to help it by any remedy. For God's sake acquaint me if you come off well. I shall be thoroughly uneasy till I know the Event. If there be any Virtue in England I would try to stir it up in your behalf, but it dwells not with Power: it is got into so narrow a Circle that 'tis hard, very hard, to know where to look for it. Among your Friends I have been seeking it, and have hopes, there, some Occasion may arise, which will not be neglected, to invite you to us once again. I don't dislike your writing a Moral Letter to a Courtier, provided you inclose it to me, but the Slur you mention in the News was not level'd at her,[4] but at a poor Maid of Honour. As to

---

¹ This letter is in general a reply to that of Swift dated 26 Feb. The date is pencilled in the Harleian transcript by a later hand. It is not far wrong certainly. Pope's part of this letter was first printed by Elwin. Bolingbroke's part Pope printed (1741) as a PS. to his own brief letter to Swift here dated [4 Mar. 1729/30].

² This alludes to the eulogy of Pope in the 'Libel on Dr. Delany'.

³ On Pope's alleged appetite for epistolary fame see Swift to Pope 26 Feb. 1729/30. After what Pope writes here Swift could never fail to realize Pope's ambition to publish their letters. He will publish, not for Fame, but as a monument to their friendship.

⁴ Not levelled, that is, against Mrs. Howard. Pope's attempt to keep Swift from being offensive to Mrs. Howard and Lord Burlington is interesting.

your writing to Lord Burl. I would by no means have you, 'twill tend to no good, and only anger, not amend. You are both of you Positive men.—I shew'd Arbuthnot the passage in two of your letters about the bad wines: his answer I doubt not will be fully Satisfactory to you. He own'd the Wines were execrable, for (sayd he) so were all the wines my Brother had at that time. And to make you amends he thinks highly reasonable, which (sayd he) My Brother will surely do as soon as he returns from China, whither he set out some three Weeks since. In the meantime if the Dean will step and see my Brother at his house in China I'm sure he will make him welcome to the best wine the Country affords—

—what can a Man desire more?

You make me smile at appealing to Gay, rather than to me, for pitying any Distress in a friend, but particularly this of your bad wine: Do not you know he has wholly abstain'd from wine almost these two years? and I drink nothing else. I am really heartily vext at this piece of ill luck, and wish you would come and revenge it upon our good wines here, rather than follow the Doctor's direction to China. If your Lawsuit (Quod Deus bene vertat) can be finish'd, why not? You'l see here more of what you like, or less of what you hate, at least. I am in hope your health is tolerable, and cannot be worse in a better Clime (for so I believe ours is, in respect to Deafness, as the Air is rather clearer.)

Dr Whalley[1] has given me his Cases again, upon a Rehearing and you may be confident I will do him whatever Service I can. I lately saw your Cosen Lancelot,[2] who is a man extreamly affectionated to you, and to me. Every man here asks of you, Lord Oxford lately wrote to you in behalf of a very valuable Clergyman's Father's Book.[3] I wish you could promote it, but expect little from poor Ireland, by your accounts of it. The best thing it affords is what you have sent me, its Usquebagh, but we hear nothing, yet, of it: nor by what Ship it comes.⌐

⌐[4]I did not take the pen out of Pope's hands I protest to you, but since He will not fill the Remainder of the Page, I think I may without offence. I seek no Epistolary fame, but am a good deal pleased to think that it will be known hereafter that you and I lived in the most friendly intimacy togather.—Pliny writ his letters for the Publick, so did Seneca, so did Balzac, Voiture &c. Tully did not, and therefore these give us more pleasure than any which have come down to us from Antiquity.   when we read them, we pry into a Secret which was

<hr />

[1] See Ball, iv. 132 (Lord Oxford to Swift, 4 Mar. 1730).
[2] Swift's cousin Patty's second husband was William Lancelot.
[3] Samuel Wesley's work on Job. See Ball, iv. 131–2.
[4] At this point Bolingbroke begins, and at this point Pope began to print.

intended to be kept from us, that is a pleasure. We see Cato, and Brutus, and Pompey and others, such as they really were, and not such as the gaping Multitude of their own Age took them to be, or as Historians and Poets have represented them to ours, that is another pleasure. I remember to have seen a Procession at Aix la Chappelle, wherein an Image of Charlemagne is carried on the Shoulders of a Man, who is hid by the long Robe of the Imperial Saint; follow him into the Vestry, you see the Bearer Slip from under the Robe, and the Gigantick figure dwindles into an image of the ordinary Size, and is set among[1] other lumber.—I agree much with Pope, that our Climate is rather better than that you are in, and perhaps your publick Spirit would be less grieved, or oftener comforted, here than there. Come to us therefore on a Visit at least, it will not be the fault of several persons here if you do not come to live with us. But great good will and little power produce such slow and feeble effects as can be acceptable to Heaven alone and heavenly Men.—

I know you will be angry with me, if I say nothing to you of a poor Woman,[2] who is still on the other side of the Water in a most languishing State of health, if She regains Strength enough to come over, and She is better within a few Weeks, I shall nurse her in this Farm[3] with all the care and tenderness possible, if she does not, I must pay her the last dutys of friendship wherever she is, tho' I break thro' the whole plan of life which I have formed in my mind. Adieu.

I am most faithfully and affectionately yours.[4]

POPE *to* THE EARL OF OXFORD[5]   [16 *April* 1730]

Longleat Portland Papers, xii

April. 16: 1730.

My Lord,—The inclosed will shew you how desirous I am, because my Friend is, that your Lordship would attend Lady Howards Cause.[6] I cannot leave this place this week, but hope by the beginning of the next to see you with that pleasure I always wait on You. I beg my Lady Oxfords acceptance of my Services, and can only add with what

---

[1] set among] set by among *1740–2 all texts.*

[2] Lady Bolingbroke.—Footnote in 1741 Da.

[3] Lord Bolingbroke's Seat at Dawley in Middlesex.—Footnote in 1741 Da.

[4] The first Dublin text (1741 Da) follows this conclusion with the initial *B* as signature. The footnotes in this edition, not reprinted in the London editions, together with the *B* seem to the present editor evidence that Swift himself edited the letter for Faulkner's texts. Curll (1741 Lc) reprinting from the London texts found no sufficient indication as to the authorship of this part of the letter and so added the note: 'This Postscript was wrote by Lord Bolingbroke.'

[5] The date superscribed is in Lord Oxford's hand; that of the endorsement is by a clerk.

[6] The cause of Lady Howard has not been identified. Somewhat informally several ladies might be called Lady Howard, including Mary Blount, daughter of Pope's deceased friend Edward, and now married to Lord Edward Howard, later the 9th Duke of Norfolk.

Truth I ever am | My Lord Your most obligd & most | affectionate faithful Servant | A. Pope.

Address: To the Right Honble the | Earl of Oxford.

Endorsement: Mr Pope | April 16. 1730

POPE *to* THE EARL OF OXFORD[1]   [24 *April* 1730]

Longleat Portland Papers, xii

April. 24: 1730.

My Lord,—Your letter is perfectly kind; & implies your knowledge, how much in my heart is what the Dean our friend desires. I am heartily glad of two things, that a worthy Clergyman (a very scarce thing) is Easy;[2] & that a Prig & Flatterer Clergyman (no Scarce thing) is disappointed. I hope to wait on your Lordship in a few days. Till then, may what you merit, befall you, that is, may Health, happiness, & all prosperity be yours.

I am Ever sincerely | with Respect & with Love, | Your Lordships faithfull | Servant | A. Pope.

Address: To the Right Hon. the Earl | of Oxford. | Dover street.

Endorsement: Mr Pope | April 24. 1730.

POPE to SAMUEL WESLEY THE YOUNGER[3]

Welbeck   24 *April* 1730

April 24: 1730

Sir,—I have received from mr morice a Poem which I must be insensible not to thank you for, your elegy on the Death of Mrs Morice. It is what I cannot help an impulse upon me, to tell you under my own hand, the satisfaction I feel, the approbation I give, the envy I bear you for this good deed & good work as a poet, and as a man, I thank, I esteem you. I hope you will pass a day with me when you can: Ld Oxford says he will come soon perhaps you may with him.

When you see mr Lewis, pray answer his letter for me. the epitaph[4]

---

[1] The date is superscribed in Oxford's hand: the endorsed date is that of a clerk.

[2] Dr. Whaley's merits had been urged on Lord Oxford by Swift as early as 21 Sept. 1728, when an appeal to the House of Lords was pending. See Ball, iv. 46n.

[3] Here printed from a transcript made by Norman Ault and proofread by Francis Needham, Esq. The MS. is a transcript in the hand of the 2nd Earl of Oxford. Wesley, with whom Pope had been in communication concerning Thomas Cooke and *The Dunciad*, was at this time head usher in Westminster School. He was devoted to Atterbury and was a friend of Lord Oxford.

[4] Pope's epitaph is that for the Digby monument. It is printed in David Lewis's miscellany of poems published early in May (Griffith, Book 232). Pages 123–4 were cancelled so as to omit lines 3 and 4 of the Epitaph as later printed. The reason for the omission is not clear.

he writes about may (I think) pass if he cancel only the 2 lines (he will understand this) without altering the next page, I will be at that charge. if he & you have two or three days leasure why not take them here. no man is more than I Sir your real servant, | A. P.

Endorsement (in the second Lord Oxford's hand): A copy of mr Popes letter to mr Wesley upon the elogy of Mrs Morris.

POPE *to* THE EARL OF OXFORD¹   [*May* 1730]
Longleat Portland Papers, xii
May. 1730.

My Lord,—Being seiz'd by two Ladies before nine, I was transported to Parsons green,² & thence home; so that I could not carry even my Lamprey along with me. I send the Waterman for it, but much more to desire your Lordship to make your next Riding to Twit'nam. I am (with unfeigned respect, & sincere obligation) Ever, | My Lord, | Your most faithfull | Servant, | A. Pope.

Address: To the Right Hon. the | Earl of Oxford.
Endorsement: Mr Pope May 1730

POPE *to* BROOME   2 *May* 1730
Elwin–Courthope, viii, 157
May 2, 1730.

Yours lay a fortnight at my house, before I received it at my return from a little journey. I am really glad I was mistaken in what I fancied of your new acquaintance,³ and I take it kindly that you set me right; for an old friend will always, I believe, be worth ten new ones, even though they may chance to differ sometimes, and nothing is truer than that verse, I forget by whom,

> 'Tis sure the tend'rest part of love
> Each other to forgive.⁴

I heartily wish you the continuance of that enjoyment which you so often and so feelingly express in your present situation, and indeed am, as I ever was, your sincere servant. I was moved at nothing the scribblers said of you further than to a just desire of having it known that I had not engaged your pains for nothing, than which you are

---

¹ The superscribed date is in Lord Oxford's hand; the endorsement is that of a scribe.

² Parson's Green was where Lord Peterborow lived. *The Whitehall Evening Post*, 25 Apr. 1730, reports his lordship as 'dangerously indisposed at his house at Parson's Green'. To identify the ladies is probably impossible. Mrs. Anastasia Robinson might well be one.

³ The 'new acquaintance' were suspected to be Pope's dunces. It is more than possible that Broome considered joining them.

⁴ From 'The Reconcilement', a song by Sheffield, Duke of Buckingham, whose *Works* as edited by Pope had been reissued in 1729.

sensible there could not be any part more disreputable to me. And since
you yourself had not found any means publicly to disprove that wicked
and false slander, it was necessary another should.[1] As to all the rest,
I told you the whole truth in my first letter, though these scoundrels
made, and still make, no scruple to affirm strongly the flattest lies, as
I see by a thing just now published, called an Epistle to me, by James
Moore and others,[2] where they tell a formal story how the Dunciad
was composed out of a larger poem, and how the Profound was, in a
manner, wholly mine, &c., and where they again trump up the same
old lies about Wycherley and yourself.[3] It becomes any honest man to
speak of himself as such, and in this one point of honesty no man can
use a style too high of himself. I know full well what my behaviour
and principles have been, are, and will be; and that my heart is better
than my head. I know that in your particular regard, I meant to serve
you, and did it to my utmost, both as to fame and profit, in that
undertaking. And really if these rascals shall continue to publish such
a lie, it would be but honourable in any fair man concerned to contradict the fact in my justification, since for my own part I think it
beneath me to answer them, nor do I judge it right to appear my
own single defendant in truths which are as well known to others as
to myself.

I never looked in the least awry on your translating that book of
Homer in blank verse, I assure you, but think it was very reasonable,
after what you had suffered to be printed of that kind in your youth.
What you mention of that passage of the Zodiac is very just. It has
been said by several, and to your catalogue I can add Cowley, at the
end of one of his Pindarics:

The lion and the bear,
Bull, centaur, scorpion, all the radiant monsters there.

[1] So *The Dunciad Variorum* had annotated the line 'And Pope's translating three whole
years with Broome' (Bk. III, l. 328) as follows: 'Whoever imagines this a sarcasm on the
other ingenious person [Broome] is greatly mistaken. The opinion our author had of him was
sufficiently shown, by his joining him in the undertaking of the *Odyssey*: in which Mr.
Broome having ingaged without any previous agreement, discharged his part so much to
Mr. Pope's satisfaction, that he gratified him with the full sum of *Five hundred pounds*, and
a present of all those books for which his own interest could procure him Subscribers, to the
value of *One hundred more*. The author only seems to lament, that he was imploy'd in Translation at all.' The sum of £600 should have impressed all hackney writers, but it did not
impress Mr. Elwin, who was convinced that Broome was underpaid.

[2] *One Epistle to Mr. Alexander Pope* appeared 28 Apr. 1730. An item in *The Daily Journal*,
25 Apr. 1730, says, 'We hear that the Satire upon P–pe, which the Town has been so long
in Expectation of, will be published next Week, under the Title of an Epistle to him'. Moore-
Smythe and Welsted were most commonly said to be the authors. Pope suspected Lady
Mary Wortley Montagu of a hand in it. Dr. Arbuthnot, because of abuse of himself in the
poem, is said to have flogged Moore-Smythe. Pope especially wished Broome and others to
believe that the 'Bathos' and the notes to *The Dunciad* were in part by others. Such aid was
probably not extensive.

[3] The old lies were that Broome was 'half-paid' and that Pope wrote Wycherley's lines
'To Mr. Pope'.

Indeed, when I saw that passage in the book,[1] I never suspected it to be yours, but imagined I had remembered it in Cowley, mistaking the one for the other.

I have filled my paper and conclude with an assurance of being to you what I ever was. Honest Fenton I saw yesterday. He is in bed with the gout, and he spoke cordially of you. By the way I just now found, in the libel called an Epistle, that he and I were no friends. See what gentlemen these are! and join with me to despise them. I am ever yours.

SWIFT *to* POPE   2 *May* 1730

Longleat Portland Papers, xiii (Harleian transcripts)

Dublin May 2d. 1730.

I have yours mentioning one Mrs Sykins, whom at her earnest request I ventured to recommend that she might come back full of vanity with the honor of seeing you. It is to be understood that the only women of tast here are three Shopkeepers wives? of The other two, one is both a Scholar and Poet,[2] the other a Poet only, and Mrs Sykins but a good reader and a judge. Mrs Barber who is a Poet only, but not a Scholar, is going to England but I shall give her no letter of recommendation, and you will pardon me for what I did to Mrs Sykings. I must tell you that the Mortal Sin of your painter was praising a *Papist*, for we have no other zeal or merit than what arises from the utter detestation of your Religion.[3] *Ludlow* in his Memoirs mentions one Lord Fitzwilliam with this Character, that he was a civil Person, *though a Papist.*—[4]

The Lawyers say I have absolutely recovered my fortune, for my Creditor has done what you understand not; he hath levyed a fine[5] and suffered a recovery, to sell his Estate, and my money with costs and Interest will be payd me at Michaelmas, and I hope I shall never complain again upon my own affairs (like friend Gay) except I am compelled by Sickness; but the noise will not be loud enough for you to hear it.—As to Virtue, you have more charity than I, who never attempt to seek it, and if I had lost all my money I would disdain to seek relief from Power. The loss would have been more to some wanting friends and to the Publick than my self. Besides, I find that the

---

[1] The 'Bathos' was originally a project of the Scriblerus Club, and the 'high flights' satirically quoted had been collected, not all collected by Pope, over a period of something like fifteen years. Pope had revised and 'in a manner written it all', and he may be sincere here, but is probably disingenuous.

[2] Mrs. Grierson. See Swift to Pope, 6 Feb. 1729/30.

[3] Swift implies that Irish protestants objected to his commendation of Pope in the 'Libel on Dr. Delany.'

[4] Edmund Ludlow, *Memoirs* (ed. Firth), i. 426–7.

[5] See *NED* under *fine*, II b.

longer I live I shall be less expensive. It is growing with me as with Sir John Mennis,[1] who when he grew old, boasted of his happiness to a friend, that a groat would make him as drunk, as half a Crown did formerly, and so with me, half a pint of wine will go as far as a pint did some Years ago, and probably I shall soon make up an abstemious Triumvirate with you and Mr Gay. Your Usquebagh is set out by long Sea a fortnight ago.[2] I wish I may be once lucky in my commissions from hence. Some Rascal in London hath *packeted* me as far as two shillings with a Paper writ in favor of Wood the Copperman on a project of his to make Iron with pit-coal.[3] I shall not upon third thoughts trouble your female Courtier with a letter, any more than Lord Burlington.[4] As to the Wine I give it up; for positively I will not go to China till I receive my law money. Nothing could keep me from seeing you but the dread of my deafness returning, although I must tell you that almost three years in my share of life to come make a difference as much as an inch in a man's nose, yet I hitherto walk as much, and ride oftner than formerly. I intend to make no distant journey this Summer even here, nor be above two nights out of the power of returning to my home. I certainly expect that neither Tyths, nor Lands let to the full value will in a Year or two yield any money at all. All my comfort is, that I have 250l. a year which I receive from lands of above three times the value, and that will support me in some sort while there is any remnant of trade or money left among us. And so much for my scurvy Domestick. It is current here that the D. of Dorset[5] will be Lieutenant I have known him from his Youth. But, see the misfortune. There is one Lady Allen whom you employ'd in a commission. Her Lord and she have been some years caressing me in the most friendly manner when the Lord on a sudden without the least provocation rayl'd at me in the Privy Council and the H. of Lords as a Jacobite, and Libeller of the Government &c. He hath been worryed by some well-wisher of mine[6] in a Paper called a Vindication of Lord Carteret &c. and all this is lay'd on me. The libel is that paper of verses where you are mentioned, the other thing is Prose. Now this Lady hath been an old Favorite of the D. of D. and consequently will use all means to put me on a worse foot than my Station requires me to be with a Chief Governor, and who can help it,

---

[1] Sir John Mennes (1599–1671) was an admiral, much valued by Samuel Pepys, and a witty poet, author of verses in *Musarum Deliciae* (1655), &c.

[2] Consigned (as was this letter) to Lord Bathurst, who on 30 June acknowledged its arrival.—Ball, iv. 157.

[3] *An Account of Mr. Wood's Iron made with pulverized Ore and Pit-coal* may be the pamphlet sent to Swift. An inconvenience of the post in such matters was that the recipient, not the sender, paid.

[4] In his letter to Swift, 9 Apr., Pope had discouraged such writing.

[5] The appointment was almost immediately official.

[6] The *Vindication* was by the best of his well-wishers, himself.

for I shall not so much as desire Lady Betty Germain to mend the matter,[1] but rather, when the Parliament sits here a year and a half hence I will if my health permits pass that winter between you and London.

I writ to my Lord Oxford t'other day, and told him Sincerely that I had no credit to get one Subscriber for Mr Wesley, except myself.

I am not acquainted with one Lord either Temporal or Spiritual, nor with three Squires, half a dozen middling Clergymen are all the Croneys I have, who never will be worth a Guinea before hand.—I will say nothing to my Lord Boling— here, but write to him inclosed as this is to my debtor.[2] It is the safest way to his Lordship and you, though it may reach you later. There is a knot of little fellows here either in the University or among the Younger Clergy, who deal in verse and sometimes shrewdly enough. These have been pestering Dr Delany for several Months past, but how they have been provoked I know not, unless by envy at seeing him so very domestick with the Lord Lieut. The Doctor as a man of much strickness in his Life was terribly mortifyed with two or three of the first Squibbs, but now his Gall is broke. He hath a Country House very agreeable within a Mile of this Town, fit to lodge you, in a fine college[3] much more retired than Twickenham. But the Deanary is your habitation. He is a Man of the easyest and best conversation I ever met with in this Island, a very good listner, a right reasoner, neither too silent nor talkative, and never positive; but hath too many acquaintance.—I am now told I may drill on five years more without my money. My most humble service to Lord Burlington, Lord Bathurst Lord Masham, Mr Poulteney, the D.[4] Mr Lewis, and friend Gay. None to Lord Boling— for I will write to him and my particular services to Mrs Pope; and love to Patty Blount and to Mrs Howard if you please, when you see her, and Mrs Howard if she has a mind may present my Duty to the Qu— and by the way is Her M— angry at the Line where your Painter hath named her with relation to you,[5] or hath she by chance heard of it. Pray God bless you and restore and preserve your health.

To Mr. Pope.

POPE *to* CARYLL   10 *May* 1730

Add. 28618

Twitenham. 10 May 1730.

Many accidents, besides a short journey have thus long retarded my acknowledging your last. A very odd adventure has lately befallen me

---

1 See Lady Betty's letter (19 Sept. 1730), Ball. iv .164.   2 Lord Bathurst.
3 This clearly written word was changed by Elwin to *country*; *cottage* occurs to one as a possible reading.   4 The D[octor Arbuthnot].
5 A doubtless offensive line in Swift's 'character' of Pope in the 'Libel on Dr. Delany' was that in which he alleged that Pope 'Refused the visits of a queen'.

in consequence of the letter you sent me enclosed to Mr Pigot which contained a note for 100l. And it gives me a great curiosity to know what person put it into your hands. I soon found out the original plotter, but am at a loss for the instruments made use of, which this may give me some light into. I told your god-daughter what you said in your last, who takes it as she ought, with all possible kindness. But I expect little good to her, thro' her own indolence and goodness (not to say weakness) of nature. I hope for every happiness that you merit and wish in regard to your own family, the elder, and younger, and so *in sæcula sæculorum*. Pray my sincere services to Mrs Caryll, &c., and to my quondam neighbour of Whitton,¹ who I doubt not likes Ladyholt better than any place she liked before. I have often wished to see the pleasures of that place which are external, and yet more the pleasures of it, that are internal in the good will and unity of its cheerful inhabitants. But my mother continues not sick, but decaying, and in a condition that will not admit me to leave her, tho' I cannot help her. Whenever I am my own master (which yet God knows I cannot wish to be) I should prove myself more your servant by being longer, and more, a partaker of your life and enjoyer of your friendship. | Dear sir | Yours ever faithfully | A. P.

POPE *to* THE EARL OF OXFORD   [17 *May* 1730]
Longleat Portland Papers, xii

Sunday. May: 17: 1730.

My Lord,—I shall with great pleasure see your Lordship to morrow, the sooner the better, & we'll dine at two. And pray bring every one with you that you like. I am sure to like 'em too.

I am Ever sincerely & | with all true respect | Your Lordships faithful | Servant | A. Pope.

I've just now seen the Grubstreet Journal, & disapprove it.²
My faithful services to my Lady.

Address: To the Rt Honble the | Earl of Oxford.
Endorsement: Mr Pope May 17. 1730.

¹ Miss Pigott, now Mrs. Edward Caryll.   ² The remark is puzzling. One assumes that Pope has just seen the last number of the *Journal* (14 May). He may disapprove of the attention given briefly to *One Epistle to Mr. A. Pope*, but that hardly calls for much disapprobation. The leader of the number is concerned with the scandal over the case of the late Lady Abergavenny, who has died just as her husband was suing Richard Lyddel, Esq., for damages in *crim. con.* The leader discusses *An Epistle from Calista to Altamont*, concerning the authors of which and others of its sort 'a great Author writing to one of our Members well observes, they richly deserve not only to be *satyrized*, but *to be whipp'd and pillory'd'*. Also discussed, and not approved, is the 'Character of the late Lady A—y', which with modifications by Maevius was printed in the *Journal* for 16 Apr. 1731. The peculiar interest of Pope or Oxford in this scandal is unknown. The GEC Peerage ascribed the 'Character of the late Lady A—y' to the Duke of Dorset—meaning probably the 2nd Duke, who was Pope's friend and Spence's. Abergavenny was Oxford's neighbour in Dover Street.

*POPE *to* THE EARL OF BURLINGTON   22 *May* 1730
Chatsworth

May the 22d 1730.

My Lord,— I have try'd to wait upon you, unsuccessfully; It was to Condole with you for being made Knight of the Garter,[1] having known you to be so many Better Things before. Some of them, I think, will be rememberd, longer than that you had this Honour; if either marble or Virtue can long remain—However, Princes are honourd for having plac'd Honors justly, & it will be said that King George the Second made the Earl of Burlington Knight of the Garter, &c. I need not say I am too good a subject to Envy Him this; or too sincerely Your Lordships Friend & Honourer not to be Pleasd he has done it: being so truly | My Lord, | Your most Obedient faithful Servant | A. Pope.

Pray, if you dare, tell my Lady B. I know you are Embrac'd by something better than a Garter.

POPE *to* THE EARL OF OXFORD   2 *June* 1730
Longleat Portland Papers, xii

June 2d 1730.

My Lord,— I hear with pleasure that yourself, Lady Oxford & Lady Margaret, are arrived well at Oxford:[2] It pleasd me to see two such fine & temperate Days as you made your Journey in: It will please me greatly to hear your Health & pleasure continue; which is all I can say at present, being myself very sick: & If you write no more to me than these few lines, 'twill yet be a great Satisfaction, to one so sincerely Yours as | My dear Lord | Your most Obliged, | obedient & Real Servant | A. Pope

I hope Dr Middleton will not forget me, especially when he sees Herne:[3] I rememberd Him to day, over one whom I took to be Dr Bentley.

Address: To | the Earl of Oxford & | E. Mortimer.

Endorsement: Mr Pope | June 2d. 1730.

[1] At a Chapter of the Garter held at St. James's Palace on 18 May Burlington, Chesterfield, and Prince William were elected to the order. The installation came on 18 June.

[2] Thomas Hearne in his *Collections*, x. 287–90, details the movements of Lord Oxford at this time. He and his family arrived in Oxford on 28 May; his lordship was created D.C.L. on 4 June, and left for Wimpole on 6 June.

[3] Dr. Conyers Middleton, 'Protobibliothecarius' of Cambridge, was incorporated at Oxford, also on 4 June. Upon the death of Wanley Lord Oxford had wished to have as his librarian the great antiquarian scholar Thomas Hearne. Since in *The Dunciad* Pope had commented on Hearne as 'Wormius' (*Dunciad* [1728, 1729], iii. 181–6) he suggests that as he had remembered Middleton upon seeing (or reading) Middleton's violent enemy Bentley, Middleton may remember the author of *The Dunciad* when he sees Hearne.

POPE to FORTESCUE   7 *June* 1730
Harvard University

June 7th 1730

I am so taken up with Hospitality, (now the Season is arrived when all a mans Fairweather-Friends come about him in the Country,) that I cannot find a day to see you in London. I wishd to do it that morning I was there, at Sir Robert's:[1] but thought men of business should be left to each other, especially just when you were Return'd after a fortnights absence. I wish you could pass a night here at your best leisure. Next Sunday I am incouragd to call at Sir R.'s[1] where I therefore desire you would dine. In the mean time, I find by my sister, that Essington will not pay the Debt, but by driblets, and she can get but one hundred more of him at present. I beg you would write to him in such a manner as you judge proper, that his account may be ended fairly at once, for indeed His Delays are suspicious, and I find Her sollicitations are to little purpose. I have also another Lady's Comission to you, which your Politesse will, I'm sure, attend to. Mrs Patty Bl. desires you to renew the Insurance for the next year and to get her the money as soon as you conveniently can, having been very extravagant of late in purchases of Chince Beds & Furniture. If she adorns her Rooms, so as to invite you to pass sometimes an hour in them, her end will be answer'd. And so I bid you heartily farewell

Dear Sir, Yours & your fair family's | Very faithfull Friend & | Servant, | A. Pope.

Address: To | Wm Fortescue; Esqr.
Endorsement: 1730

THE EARL OF OXFORD *to* POPE   8 *June* 1730
Longleat Portland Papers, xii

June 8. 1730.

Sir,—I am obliged to you for your kind letter but am sorry you have been so much out of order, I cannot give you at present a particular account of our progress, only this that We have seen Rowsam[2] where mr Dormer received us very kindly, this I place to your account, I think the place extreamly pritty, We have been at Stow. The Ladies

---

[1] At Sir Robert Walpole's, where in view of Swift's picture of Pope as 'Detesting all the statesman kind' in the 'Libel on Dr. Delany', the poet might need Fortescue as a shield.
[2] On their way to Wimpole his lordship and family, including Dr. Middleton, have called at Rousham, home of James and Robert Dormer, friends of both Gay and Pope. They have also seen Stowe, seat of Viscount Cobham, celebrated by Pope in his *Epistle to the Earl of Burlington*.

are much pleased with both these places which I think is doing themselves & their Sex much honor.

my Wife, peggy and the Dr are much your Servants and send their compliments to you.

I am with great truth Sir your most | affectionate humble | Servant. | Oxford.

my Wives and my humble Service to mrs pope.

Address: For | Alexander Pope Esq; | at Twickenham | Middlesex
Frank: Oxford
Postmark: 8/IV

*POPE to HUGH BETHEL   9 June 1730

Egerton 1948

I was in hope of hearing a word or two, just to tell me you was safe at the end of your Journey, which in truth had not been ill bestowd upon me, for no man living can, with greater sincerity, wish you well, & think more frequently of, and about you. Now I am forced to write, to ask this; which had you written first, I had been happier, in knowing your welfare all this time that I am uncertain of it. It pleases God that my Mother is much the better for the advance of the Summer Season, and I think I am so too, (tho often put in mind of my ill Constitution by Headakes on the least Turn of weather) I lately commemorated you with Mr Day,[1] who for three hours could talk of nobody but Sir Robert Walpole & yourself. So equally are his affections & Respect divided. For my own part, I cannot but make some difference; on which side it lies, I will not say, to You.

Mrs Blounts came to the Country not till this week.[2] It pleases Heaven that it is not yet the Country, nor properly deserves that odious name, for the Court is yet at Richmond. It removes next week to Windsor. Our Friend is as usual in her health, and as usual in her endeavors to amend it. But this day she had a Conversation with Dr Arbuthnot, & he has Prescribed her a Bitter & Spaw waters, which she will, or will not, take. Lady Denbigh[3] is also arrived here, with a Sett of horses that might create Envy even in Breeders of Yorkshire. Mr Cleland remembers you over his Volumes; & over his Cups, and sends you hearty & honest Services: I have had a New Lampoon (I

---

[1] Possibly Thomas Day, Collector of Customs for the Port of London, and father of the author of *Sandford and Merton*.

[2] To Petersham, where the Blount ladies usually spent their summers.

[3] The Countess of Denbigh was the daughter of Peter de Jonge, burgomaster of Utrecht. She seems to be one of many ladies interested in what Mr. Pope was doing. See Pope's letter to her ladyship here placed in late May 1742 (iv. 397).

think it was since you went) in which He is spared, & Dr Arb. horribly abused.[1] which I'm the less sorry for, because he went to Expostulate with the Scrub Writers of it. It is below all notice, & contains as many Lyes as Lines; being purely Personal. James Moore own'd it but twas made by three others, and he will disown it whenever any man taxes him for it. I write you a Short letter, that you may not be discouraged from corresponding. And I would not have you hold yourself obliged any way to come to the Third Side of the paper, tho' I take that Space to turn, before I call myself what with great Truth I am, | Dear Sir | Your ever affectionate | faithfull Friend & Servant | A. Pope

Twitnam | June 9th 1730.

Tell Dr Key, my Bees do not | Swarm yet, & take that occasion | of giving him my Services. | My Mother is heartily yours.

Address: To | Hugh Bethel, Esqr | to be left at Mr Tho. Coolings | in the Shambles, in | City of Yorke.

Postmark: 9/IV

POPE *to* THE EARL OF OXFORD[2]   [*June* 1730?]
Longleat Portland Papers, xii

My Lord,—I attended you from Stage to Stage by the accounts I had from your faithfull Porter. I thought you would stay longer at that most agreeable Place, Down-Hall, than you first proposed; and as soon as I imagine you at your Journy's end, Wimpole, I send to welcome you. I put my self in the place of one of your wood-men or Stewards, (or rather of the Whole Country & University) to Hail your Arrival. I will fancy I am standing on the Stone-Steps at the Great door to receive you, & that I have just been Setting the Bells a-ringing in your parish church. I am impatient to follow you to the New-roof'd Library, & see what fine new lodgings the Ancients are to have? I salute the Little Gods & antiquities in my way in the Anti-room, wishing them joy of the New Temples they are to be Inshrined in, and I admonish that Prior's Lamp be set in a private corner. I advise;

---

[1] Major Cleland, who had been attacked as Pope's aid on *The Dunciad* in *Pope Alexander's Supremacy*, was spared in *One Epistle to Mr. Pope*. Dr. Arbuthnot's 'expostulation' is recorded in *The Grub-street Journal* for 11 June: 'Last Friday, at the Prince William Tavern, a very modest young gentleman, alias Moore, alias Smith, who had been concerned in a libel against an eminent physician, had the correction of the cane bestowed upon him by a relation of that physician.'

[2] The year of this letter seems fixed by the mention of the new library at Wimpole. How long after his lordship's letter to Pope of 8 June this should be placed is doubtful. Apparently Oxford was back in London by 2 July, when Pope again wrote to him. In this interpretation the stages of Oxford's journey would be from Oxford to Rousham, to Stowe, to Down Hall, to Wimpole.

that two Poets Heads, which I see in another room, be always kept together, as being both Odd-headed fellows (Cleveland & Another[1]) & kept at a convenient distance from the Library, not to be of ill Example to those who shall come to study there. I wish a small Cellar of strong beer, were somewhere under the Library, as a proper (brown) Study for the Country-Gentlemen; while the Cantabrigians are imploy'd above; unless any of the latter (for change and amusement) shall chuse to Descend to the former, & De-*sipp*-ere in loco, as Bentley's Horace has it.[2] I hope my Lord you use Exercise & *Bowl* daily, that Homer's saying[3] may be fulfilled,

Διος δ' ετελειτο Βουλη

& that Lady Margaret rides, because Martial[4] says

Ride si sapis, O puella, ride.

This advice is the best I can give, being perfectly Classical & Cantabrigian. I must be forced to tell Lady Oxford in plain English that I wish her all Health & pleasure, and that I am while I live | My Lord | Your Lordships | Most obliged faith|ful Servant | A. Pun.[5]

Mrs Gibs & Wootton[6] have been with me (as you see)

Endorsement: Mr Pope.

POPE *to* CARYLL · 16 *June* 1730

Add. 28618

Twitenham. 16 June 1730.

I had the pleasure of yours by the care of Mr Caryll,[7] whom I have since seen with his lady. I intend tomorrow to return them their kind visit but I must tell you satisfactions of this sort which result from one's love to the parents (like satisfactions of old folks and men of the last age like yourself and me) are imperfect, unless we see them also, and

---

[1] The 'another' is obviously Pope, who jokingly associates himself with a poet then out of fashion.
[2] Bentley here (*Carmina*, iv. xii. 28) does not differ from his predecessors textually. Horace, Pope seems to say, is now 'Bentley's'.
[3] *Iliad*, i. 5. (Here given as Pope wrote it.)   [4] Martial, ii. xli.
[5] With habitual austerity Elwin (viii. 272–3) comments: 'Pope had formed a very humble conception of what constituted a pun.'
[6] Elwin would like to identify these people as the wife of the architect Gibbs and the painter John Wootton. These two artists have connexions with Lord Oxford as employer or patron; but Gibbs was a bachelor, and the two persons may be mentioned as notable punsters, who have encouraged Pope in humble imitations.
[7] Mr. and Mrs. Edward Caryll had brought the letter when on a visit to her parents at Whitton.

I am rather uneasy at wanting you than pleased at seeing them. May this compliment soon vanish, by your company amongst us.

Our neighbour at Petersham is pretty well: I say our neighbour in the singular, for in good faith I am ashamed to say neighbours, that history being by no means unfinished; but in the general eye, almost as public as any history whatsoever. The mother will certainly never come to you; she is become as necessary to the daughter as any other utensil of the house.

I can't help telling you, so well as I love you, that I'm ready to take ill of you, and the more ill the more I love you, your silence and evasion of my question, Who it was that put into your hands that letter which contained a bankbill of 100l. I found out, as I told you, the original plotter, and returned the bribe back, as an honest man ought, with the contempt it deserved, by the hands of Lord Bathurst, to the lady. Therefore, sir, the plot failed, and 'twas not a farthing to my advantage. Must I be forced to assure you I can refuse anything I don't deserve, or don't seek, be it a hundred, or a thousand. And I thank God for having bestowed upon me a mind and nature more beneficent than craving.

Adieu. Think of me as I merit, for I really am no worldly man, tho' but a poor one, but a friendly one where obliged, and therefore very mindfully to yourself and all yours | Dear sir | A faithful and affectionate | humble servant | A. P.

My mother is better, and I the better for it.

POPE *to* BROOME   16 June [1730]

Elwin–Courthope, viii. 161

June 16, [1730].

I take yours very kindly, and would make use of it against so lying a slander, did not my contempt of the liars prevail infinitely above any regard of what such fellows can say. It is unfeignedly a great pleasure to me that you writ some time since to me with freedom upon these subjects. You and I shall never quarrel, nor do I think I ever shall with any honest man alive. But *scoundrels* I hate, though *fools* I pardon. So much for them!

But I must do justice in a point in which I perceive you mistaken. Dr. Arbuthnot knew no more than I of the verses cited from your book.[1] I think I told you before, that some others contributed to the collections of examples, and the person that sent those was an utter stranger to you, but moved, as he afterwards owned, by the opinion you had spread the reports to my prejudice, &c. I am sure it will be a

---

[1] Pope is still struggling to explain the quotations from Broome in the 'Bathos'.

satisfaction to you to know so ingenious and honest a man as the doctor was no way your enemy.

I have been almost daily employed in attending the last sparks of a dying taper,—the last days of my good old mother. This next week[1] she is ninety years complete; her memory decayed, but not lost; her eye-sight good; her temper easy and beneficent. She remembers you well, and sends you her service.

I hope you enjoy all the comforts of domestic life, and that you will long enjoy them. I would have written more, had I not written so soon and been at this time very much taken up. But I would not let you remain in an opinion so much undeserved by Dr. Arbuthnot. I am, with all hearty goodwill and affection, dear sir, yours.

†POPE *to* SWIFT[2]   [*c.* 19 *June* 1730]

1740

My Lord has spoken justly of his Lady; why not I of my Mother? Yesterday was her birth-day, now entering on the ninety-first year of her age; her memory much diminsh'd, but her senses very little hurt; her sight and hearing, good; she sleeps not ill, eats moderately, drinks water, says her prayers; this is all she does. I have reason to thank God for continuing so long to me a very good and tender parent, and for allowing me to exercise for some years, those cares which are now as necessary to her, as hers have been to me. An object of this sort daily before one's eyes very much softens the mind, but perhaps may hinder it from the willingness of contracting other tyes of the like domestic nature, when one finds how painful it is even to enjoy the tender pleasures. I have formerly made some strong efforts to get and to deserve a friend: perhaps it were wiser never to attempt it, but live Extempore, and look upon the world only as a place to pass thro', just pay your hosts their due, disperse a little charity, and hurry on. Yet am I just now writing, (or rather planning) a book, to make mankind look upon this life with comfort and pleasure, and put morality in good humour.—And just now too, I am going to see one I love very tenderly; and to-morrow to entertain several civil people,

---

[1] Mrs. Pope was baptized in Worsborough (York), 18 June 1642. Pope thought she was born in 1640: on the family tomb that is the date given. Writing on Tuesday the 16th it is more than strange that he should say 'this next week' she is ninety. One would like to see the original letter!

[2] This evident fragment seems originally to have been a postscript to a letter from Boling-broke to Swift (now lost) of June 1730. In 1741 Pope transferred it to the end of another Bolingbroke letter to Swift dated by Pope as 29 Mar. (see 20 March 1730/1). The Harleian transcript of Bolingbroke's letter bears in Lord Oxford's hand the date 20 Mar. The date here assigned to the Pope fragment is based on the poet's mistaken idea of his mother's age. See note 1.

whom if we call friends, it is by the Courtesy of England.[1]—*Sic, sic juvat ire sub umbras.*[2] While we do live, we must make the best of life,

> *O Vita! Stulto brevis, sapienti longa!*
> *Cantantes licet usque (minus via laedat) eamus,*[3]

as the shepherd says[4] in Virgil, when the road was long and heavy. I am yours.

---

*POPE *to* MRS. CÆSAR[5]   30 *June* [1730?]

Rousham

Twit'nam. June 30.

Madam,—It is with great & unaffected Concern that I heard (but 2 days since) that you have been long very ill. My Life has past in so absolute a Retirement for many months, that I never knew of it: and my Lord & Lady Oxford, (of whom I never failed to speak and ask of you) having been out of Town, has occasiond my Ignorance of that, which I faithfully assure you will always be my Concern. I beg the Bearer may learn the State of your health & inform me, who am with true regard & obligation, Madam | Your most obedient and mind-|ful humble Servant | A. Pope.

Mr Cæsar will know me for his humble Servant.

Address: To Mrs Cæsar: in | Poland street.

POPE *to* THE EARL OF OXFORD   2 *July* 1730

Longleat Portland Papers, xii

July 2d 1730.

My Lord,—I am much rejoicd at the news of your Arrival in Town, in perfect safety, Post varios *casus* (I do not mean after many *Falls,* but variable accidents.) I must come & trouble you with my joys in a few days, when I can suppose you are setled. I hope my Lord the pleasing Memory of so many agreeable Places & Partyes will not render you utterly disdainful of the Thames & Twitenham. I heard with real concern, since you were gone, of our friend Mrs Cæsars

---

[1] Pope's attitude towards his prospective guests is probably inhospitable. 'Courtesy of England' is a phrase he uses loosely (e.g. his Epistle to Augustus, l. 62), here meaning that he may enjoy these 'civil people' without their being claimed by others who might be expected to claim them. The escapist words of the dying Dido might support this interpretation.

[2] *Aeneid*, iv. 660.

[3] *Eclogues*, ix. 64. Only this second line seems to be Virgilian. The first line appears only in 1740, and 1741 Dab. The Dublin texts translate both lines in a footnote.

[4] says] said *1741 Labc*; *1742 Lbc, Da.*

[5] The year is uncertain, but Lord Oxford has been out of town for about a month, and in welcoming him back (letter of 2 July) Pope speaks of Mrs. Caesar's illness.

illness. I should be very sorry to lose so good a Mediatrix, and hope my Lady Oxford will recollect she owes the Water nymphs some Honours, yet unpayd this season. My Mother is your faithful Servant, and drank all your healths (as I hope You will all do each other's) on her Birthday in the Ninetieth year of her Age.

I am truly, & with | constant Esteem, | My Lord, | Your most Obligd & | most faithful Servant, | A. Pope.

Endorsement: Mr Pope | July 2d 1730.

GAY *to* SWIFT[1]   4 *July* 1730

Add. 4805

You tell me that I have put myself out of the way of all my old acquaintance, so that unless I hear from you I can know nothing of you; is it not barbarous then to leave me so long without writing one word to me? If you wont write to me for my sake methinks you might write for your own. How do you know what is become of your money? If you had drawn upon me when I expected it you might have had your money, for I was then in town; but I am now at Amesbury near Salisbury in Wiltshire at the Duke of Queensberry's; the Dutchess sends you her services; I wish you were here, I fancy you would like her, and the Place; you might fancy yourself at home, for we have a Cathedral near us, where you might find a Bishop of the same name.[2] You might ride upon the Downs & write conjectures upon Stonehenge. We are but five & twenty miles from the Bath, and I was told this very Evening by General Dormer who is here that he heard somewhere or other that you had some intentions of coming there the latter Season; I wish any thing would bring us together but your want of health. I have left off wine & writing, for I really think that man must be a bold writer who trusts to Wit without it.

I took your Advice, & some time ago took to Love, & made some advances to the Lady you sent me to in Soho, but I met no return, so I have given up all thoughts of it, & now have no pursuit or Amusement. A State of indolence is what I dont like; tis what I would not chuse; I am not thinking of a Court or preferment; for I think the Lady I live with is my friend, so that I am at the height of my ambition. You have often told me, there is a time of life that every one wishes for some settlement of his own; I have frequently that feeling about me; but I fancy it will hardly ever be my Lot; so that I will endeavour to pass away Life as agreeably as I can in the way I am. I

---

[1] Pope did not publish this letter, but he did publish Swift's reply to it, dated 10 Nov. It was first published by Hawkesworth.

[2] Dr. Benjamin Hoadly, bishop of Salisbury, whose brother Dr. John Hoadly succeeded archbishop King in the see of Dublin, Jan. 19, 1729-30.—Hawkesworth.

often wish to be with you or you with me, & I believe you think I say true. I am determin'd to write to you, though those dirty fellows of the Post office do read my Letters, for since I saw you I am grown of that consequence to be Obnoxious to the man I despise; so that it is very probable in their hearts they think me an honest man. I have heard from Mr Pope but once since I left London. I was sorry I saw him so seldom but I had business that kept me from him. I often wish we were together again. If you will not write, come. I am, Dear Sir, | Yours most sincerely & | affectionately.

Amesbury, near Salisbury in Wiltshire. July 4. 1730.

Endorsement: Mr Gay. | Jul. 3d. 1730

POPE *to* THE EARL OF OXFORD¹   [18 *July* 1730]

Longleat Portland Papers, xii

Saturday, July. 18. 1730.

My Lord,—I hold it most unfortunat that your Lordship could not give me a days foreknowledge when you could come hither; Since I am promised to Lord Bathurst, whose Chaise I ev'ry minute expect to go to Riskins. This fretts me to the heart, & I can think of no Remedy but your appointing forthwith another day: I shall return to morrow Evening—I've thought of another thing: If you can be here before one, I'll stay & disappoint Lord B. till Night, & keep his Horses till then in expectation.

     I am, with the greatest Esteem | & Sincerity, | My Lord, | Your faithful humble | Servant | A: Pope.

Address: To the Earl of Oxford. | at 11 a Clock.
Endorsement: Mr Pope July 18. 1730.

POPE *to* THE EARL OF OXFORD²   [20 *July* 1730]

Longleat Portland Papers, xii

My Lord,—I thank you for yours & My Lady's obliging Message: by which, since I see you remember me, I hope you also do your Promise to pass a day here: On Wednesday I am obligd to be abroad, & on Thursday morning in London. I hope to see your Lordship that Night, and to attend you back hither the first day you can after. Or if to morrow would do, you would vastly oblige me, who shall not stirr out the whole day. I beg my Mothers & my faithful Services may be acceptable to your self, my Lady Oxford, & Lady Margaret. I need

¹ The entire date is in Lord Oxford's hand. The endorsement is that of a scribe.
² The date is subscribed in Lord Oxford's hand.

not repeat how unlucky I thought my self the other day, when I dined alone, after one, it being too late as I thought for Lord Bathursts dinner, & Lost You into the bargain, tho He stay'd for us: I got thither at 4, & he sends you his Service. I am just come home, & in all places, ever | My Lord | Your most obliged | & real humble | Servant | A Pope.

Munday | morn. July. 20: 1730.

Address: To | the Earl of Oxford.

Endorsement: Mr Pope July 20, 1730

†POPE *to* GAY¹   21 *July* [1730]

¹⁷³⁵
                                                Twick'nam, July 21

Dear Gay,—You have the same share in my memory that good things generally have; I always know (whenever I reflect) that you should be in my mind; only I reflect too seldom. However, you ought to allow me the Indulgence I allow all my Friends, (and if I did not, They would take it) in consideration that they have other avocations; which may prevent the *Proofs* of their remembring me, tho' they preserve for me all the friendship, and good will, which I deserve from them. In like manner I expect from you, that my past life of twenty years may be set against the omission of (perhaps) one month: And if you complain of this to any other, 'tis you are in the spleen, and not I in the wrong. If you think this letter splenatick, consider I have just receiv'd the News of the death of a Friend, whom I esteem'd almost as many years as you; poor *Fenton*: He died at *Easthamstead*, of Indolency and Inactivity;² let it not be your fate, but use Exercise. I hope the Duchess will take care of you in this respect, and either make you gallop after her, or teize you enough at home to serve instead of Excercise abroad. Mrs. *Howard* is so concern'd about you, and so angry at me for not writing to you, and at Mrs. *Blount* for not doing the same, that I am piqu'd with Jealousy and Envy at you, and hate you as much as if you had a great Place at Court; which you will confess a proper Cause of Envy and Hatred, in any Poet-militant, or unpension'd. But to set matters even, I own I love you; and own, I am as I ever was, and just as I ever shall be, | *Yours*, &c.

¹ All superscription is omitted in 1737b (quartos and folios).
² He died 13 July. 'At Easthamstead' was omitted in the quartos and folios of 1737 (1737b).

POPE *to* CARYLL   29 *July* 1730

Add. 28618

29. July. 1730.

I know 'tis longer than it ought to have been since I wrote to you, and many accidents have prevented it. My life is so taken up with duties and complacencies to one or other that little of it is my own, and so much ill health as renders that little almost nothing. I take very kindly the warmth and concern you shew in apprehending I fancied your opinion of me to be less favorable than it is. Indeed, I did not; but was merely desirous to tell you I am the man I am, in respect to temptations of interest. Nor was the pretence taken to send me that 100l. any proposal to me to do what was dishonourable, but only a notion that I would receive reward for what I had formerly done out of pure friendliness. A lady who imagined herself obliged to me on that score, imagined she could acquit herself of an obligation by money, which she cared not to owe on a more generous account, and Mr Pigot[1] can tell you the whole story, and so will I when we meet—which I'm extremely pleased to hear may be soon. Mr Caryll told me so yesterday when he did me the favour to dine with me, as I hope the same company will again, when you come this way. I beg I may know by a line a day or two beforehand, I am so often abroad, tho' I generally come home at night, or seldom stay longer from my mother than two nights at most, who by the way is a good deal better this summer.

I think [it] as you do, a singular piece of good luck for a certain lady, that her conduct reaches not so far as to scandalize Sussex: I the rather believe so, since I hear she is going (*sola*) to the Lady Bishop,[2] either there or in Bucks. That will not be till her ill-chosen friend (who is one of the oddest gallants alive) removes from hence into Yorkshire; he has been pretty constant to her this summer to the knowledge of all this neighbourhood. I think there's truth in what I formerly said to you that some folks have guardian devils, to defend 'em & continue 'em in their iniquities. I have only to add my sincere wishes for yours and your whole family's welfare and prosperity, the long and constant prayer of | Yours affectionately | A. P.

POPE *to* JOHN KNIGHT   30 *July* 1730

Stowe 755

Sir,—I have long intended to tell you & Mrs Knight, that I live, & live very faithfully a Servant to you both. Accidents prevented my

---

[1] Pigott had been counsel for the Duchess of Buckingham in 1727 in her prosecution of John Ward; hence he might know of her recent attempt to reward or 'bribe' Pope.

[2] See Pope to Caryll, 18 Aug. Teresa was going to visit the widow of Sir Cecil Bishop (of Parham, Sussex) in Buckinghamshire.

seeing you before you left London, and I had (after many Enquiries which would have seemed impertinent had I not thought Mrs Knight in extreme danger) the Satisfaction of hearing she was recoverd enough to go a journey, almost the same day that she went: For the very next I got to Town, & found you had left it. Since that, your Servant there told me she continud well; I hope it, but should be better satisfyed to be ascertaind by yourself. I hope you both enjoy whatever is to be enjoyd in the Country, & where Two, well-gathered together, make a thousand. (For Mrs K's sake indeed, I wish a little Quadrille in the midst of you.) I am stuck at Twit'nam, as fast as my own Plants, scarce removeable at this season. So is Mrs Patty Blount, but not stuck with me, but removeable to all other Gardens hereabouts. Women seldom are planted in the Soil that would best agree with them, you see Carnations fading & dirty in Cheapside, which would blush and shine in the Country. Mrs Cornish is (just now) going to some such soft Retreat, at Hampsted, or Richmond, or Islington, having read the following Epigram,

> When other Fair ones to the Shades go down,
> Still Cloë, Flavia, Delia, stay in Town.
> Those Ghosts of Beauty wandring here reside
> And haunt the places where their Honor dy'd.[1]

Mrs Bl. bids me assure you she is faithfully your Servant & I have only to add, that my Mother is much better this Summer, than she ought to be not having seen Mrs Knight: and that I am Sick every other day, as usual, & this day for one: but truly & always, | Dear Sir, | Your most affectio-|nate & most humble | Servant. | A. Pope.

July 30. | 1730.

Address: To | John Knight Esq; in | Dover street | Piccadilly, | London.
Postmark: 30/IY
Endorsement: Mr Pope | July the 30th 1730

POPE *to* THE EARL OF OXFORD[2]   [3 *August* 1730]

Longleat Portland Papers, xii

My Lord,—This is only to thank your Lordship for yours, & to tell you I shall impatiently expect the honour you promise me to morrow.

---

[1] This epigram, sometimes called 'On Certain Ladies', had been published in D. Lewis's *Miscellaneous Poems* early in May 1730. The last two lines were remade to become lines 241–2 of Pope's second Moral Essay.
[2] In dating Pope gave only the day of the week : the remaining date is subscribed by Lord Oxford himself.

If this finds you at home, I beg one line that I may know your receipt of it, it not coming by my own Waterman.

I am ever | My Lord | Your most Obedient | faithful Servant | A. Pope

Munday. | Aug. 3. 1730

Address: To the Rt Hon. the | Earl of Oxford, in | Dover street.
Endorsement: Mr Pope | Augt 3. 1730.

POPE *to* BRIAN FAIRFAX   14 *August* 1730

[At Sotheby's sale of 12–15 May 1851 was sold as lot 643 this letter said in the Catalogue to be 'a letter of recommendation'. On Fairfax see *DNB*, vi. 994. The letter was dated from Twickenham. For its text see vol. v. 8.]

BROOME *to* POPE   17 *August* 1730

Elwin–Courthope, viii. 163

Pulham, Aug. 17, 1730.

Dear Mr. Pope,—By the public news I find we have lost Mr. Fenton,[1] the sincerest of men and friends. Of what a treasure has one moment robbed me! The world is really become of less value to me since he is out of it. Of all men living I knew him best, and therefore no man loved him more. How many happy hours have we passed in retirement! How many more did I expect, if Providence had lengthened his days! He intended to have withdrawn to me, and to lay his bones by mine, that, as we had been inviolably united in our lives, death itself might not make an entire separation. But he is gone before me. I shall go to him, but he shall not return to me. He has left me to lament him, which I will do most affectionately.

It is said by Pausanias[2]—if it be not too light to mention fables upon this melancholy occasion—that the nightingales near the tomb of Orpheus had sweeter notes than others of the same kind. I will endeavour to catch harmony from my friend's sepulchre; I will labour to write something equal to my affection for him. It is a tribute due to our uninterrupted friendship. Yet why should I lament him? Why should I grieve because he is so soon become an angel? The inoffensive, unambitious, undesigning, and peaceful Fenton is gone to his peace, and despises this world, which indeed is no wonder, for he always despised it.

---

[1] Fenton had died in the country on 13 July. *The Grub-street Journal* of 23 July announced the fact, which would get to Pulham from London perhaps slowly.

[2] Pausanias, ix. xxx. 6.

I dare say you will not be silent upon this occasion. You will build a monument over his ashes, by some elegy or epitaph more durable, as it will be more honourable, than the proudest marble. But after all, if reason, not affection were to speak, might we not rather with Camden, author of Sir P. Sidney's character, say, Providence has recalled him, as more worthy of heaven than earth.[1] Let us not celebrate his memory with tears, but admiration, and, to crown all, his virtues with imitation. Dear sir, adieu. Be pleased to give an account of him in his last hours. Yours affectionately.

†POPE *to* GAY[2]   18 *August* [1730]

1735

Aug. 18.

Dear Gay,— If my friendship were as effectual as it is sincere, you would be one of those people who would be vastly advantag'd and enrich'd by it. I ever honour'd those Popes who were most famous for Nepotism, 'tis a sign that the old fellows *loved Somebody,* which is not usual in such advanced years. And now I honour Sir *Robert Walpole,* for his extensive Bounty and Goodness to his private Friends and Relations.[3] But it vexes me to the heart when I reflect, that my friendship is so much less effectual than theirs; nay so utterly useless that it cannot give you any thing, not even a Dinner, at this distance, nor help the General whom I greatly love to catch one fish. My only consolation is to think you happier than myself, and to begin to envy you, which is next to hating[4] (an excellent remedy for Love). How comes it that Providence has been so unkind to me, (who am a greater object of compassion than any fat man alive) that I am forc'd to drink wine, while you riot in water, prepar'd with oranges by the hand of the Duchess of *Queensberry?* that I am condemn'd to live on a High-way side, like an old Patriarch, receiving all Guests, where my Portico (as *Virgil* has it)

Mane salutantum totis vomit ædibus undam,[5]

while you are wrapt into the *Idalian* Groves, sprinkled with Rose-water, and live in Burrage, Balm and Burnet up to the chin, with the Duchess of *Queensberry?* that I am doom'd to the drudgery of dining at Court with the Ladies in waiting at *Windsor.* while you are happily

---

[1] Camden in his *History of . . . Elizabeth* (1675), p. 329, praises Sidney highly, but does not use this somewhat trite observation.

[2] The year was added to the superscription in editions of 1737–42.

[3] By 1735 Pope was evidently willing to take sly, if public, shots like this at Walpole: he would not have published such a statement in 1730.

[4] hating [an] hating you (an *1737–42.*   [5] *Georgics,* ii. 462.

banish'd with the Duchess of *Queensberry*? So partial is Fortune in her dispensations! for I deserv'd ten times more to be banish'd than you, and I know some Ladies who merit it better than even her Grace. After this I must not name any, who dare do so much for you as to send you their Services: But one there is, who exhorts me often to write to you, I suppose to prevent or excuse her not doing it herself; she seems (for that is all I'll say for a Courtier) to wish you mighty well. Another who is no Courtier frequently mentions you, and does certainly wish you well—I fancy, after all, they both do so.

¹I writ to Mr. *Fortescue* and told him the pains you took to see him. ⌐Dr. *A.* for all that I know may yet remember you and me, but I never hear of it⌐. The Dean is well; I have had many accounts of him from *Irish* Evidence, but only two Letters these four months, in both which you are mentioned kindly: He is in the North of *Ireland*, doing I know not what, with I know not whom. Cleland always speaks of you: he is at *Tunbridge*, wondring at the superior Carnivoracity of the Dr.² He plays now with the old Duchess of *M*—,³ nay dines with her, after she has won all his money. Other News know I not, but that Counsellor *Bickford* has hurt himself, and has the strangest⁴ walking-staff I ever saw. He intends speedily to make you a visit at *Amesbury*. I am my Lord Duke's, my Lady Duchess's, Mr. *Dormer's*, General *Dormer's*, and | *Your*, &c.

POPE *to* CARYLL   18 *August* 1730

Add. 28618

Aug: 18: 1730. Twittenham.

I am heartily to thank you for a side and a haunch of venison and so is your god-daughter; but sure she had the worst luck in the world, and the worst usage (from me) that ever she had. I was absent at Windsor⁵ when it came, and my sister chancing to be here (very innocent of frustrating the intentions of the donor) sent the haunch to a friend, and potted the side for me. When I came home three days too late, I found the wrong done, which [I] could no ways repair, and for which I was sufficiently rebuked by Mrs P[atty] who values Ladyholt venison above any other out of a laudable partiality to the owner, so that I can make her no amends with any other. She is now alone with her mother, her sister being at Lady B[ishop]'s in Bucking-

---

¹ This whole paragraph, full of personalities, was omitted in the quartos and folios of 1737, but not in the octavo editions. The sentence about Dr. A (here in half-brackets) was omitted in all editions of 1737–42.   ² of the Dr.] of our friend *1737–42*.
³ Duchess of *M*—, nay] Duchess, nay *1737–42*.
⁴ strangest] strongest *1737–42*.
⁵ See on this visit to Court, Bathurst to Pope, 19 Sept. 1730, and note.

hamshire. If the poor old gentlewoman could see with her eyes, or judge by her feeling, I should think she could perceive the difference of the two daughters, or at least find the difference of being beaten or not beaten. God knows witchcraft here seems allied in a new sense to rebellion; for the mother is enchanted as well as ill used. However, I hear she speaks very well of this daughter's kind conduct to her, and her constant staying at home to dine with her, now she is alone. *Quod Deus bene vertat!*

I am going this evening to try to find Mr Pigot and your son, having scarce been at home, since I had the pleasure of seeing them here at dinner. I am extremely glad to hear how much the young lady pleases your family, as I unfeignedly do and ever shall rejoice at the felicities of it. 'Tis a concern to me to hear no more yet of your intent to travel this way. I hope the gout is not the impediment, tho' I was told you lately had it. My mother is remarkably better, and I am not worse: both which I tell you as one of the few that are sincere in friendship, and a partaker of your friend's happiness or ease. I hope soon to have a line from you. You now have in my neighbourhood that which is worth coming to see. May you long enjoy all you wish here, and at length exchange all happiness here for much greater hereafter. I am Mrs Caryll's and | Dear sir | Your most affectionate and | Faithful servant | A. P.

POPE *to* FORTESCUE   24 *August* 1730

1797 (Polwhele, i. 323)

August 24th, 1730

I had no sooner received your kind letter, with the ill news of your being seized with the gout, at Buckland, but your clerk acquainted me that you were extremely ill, which gives me unexpressible concern. My fears of your being distant from your family, and what help by physicians may be to be procured in a lone country, do sincerely much trouble me. I beg to know by the first opportunity, by a line either from yourself, or any other hand, how you are; and that you are not in so much danger as I apprehended. I will add no more words, since none can tell you how much I am in pain about you, and since they can only be troublesome to yourself if you are very ill. But God and my own heart know with what warm affection, and wishes for your recovery, and for your every happiness and comfort, I am ever, dear Sir, yours, | A. Pope.

Address: To Wm. Fortescue, esq. to be left at his house in Bell-yard, near Lincoln's Inn, London. Speed.

POPE *to* BROOME[1]   29 *August* 1730

I intended to write to you on this melancholy subject, the Death of Mr Fenton, before yours came; but stayd to have informd myself & you of the Circumstances of it. All I hear, is, that he felt a Gradual Decay, tho' so early in Life;[2] & was declining for 5 or 6 months. It was not, as I apprehended, the Gout in his Stomach, but I believe rather a Complication first of Gross Humors, as he was naturally Corpulent, not discharging themselves, as he used No sort of Exercise. No Man better bore the approaches of his Dissolution (as I am told) or with less ostentation yielded up his Being. The great Modesty which you know was natural to him, & the great Contempt he had for all Sorts of Vanity & Parade, never appeared more than in his last moments: He had a conscious Satisfaction (no doubt) in acting right, in feeling himself honest, true, & un-pretending to more than was his own. So he dyed, as he lived, with That Secret, yet Sufficient, Contentment.

As to any Papers left behind him, I dare say they can be but few; for this reason, He never wrote out of Vanity, or thought much of the Applause of Men. I know an Instance where he did his utmost to Conceal his own Merit that way; And if we join to this his natural Love of Ease, I fancy we must expect little of this sort: at least I hear of none except some few further Remarks on Waller (which his cautious integrity made him leave an order to be given to Mr Tonson) and perhaps, tho' tis many years since I saw it, a Translation of the First Book of Oppian. He had begun [a] Tragedy of Dion, but made small progress in it.

As to his other affairs, he dyed poor but honest, leaving no debts, or Legacies; except of a few pds to Mr Trumbull & my Lady,[3] in token of respect, gratefulness, & mutual Esteem.

I shall with pleasure take upon me to draw this Amiable, quiet, deserving, unpretending, Christian & Philosophical character, in His Epitaph. There, Truth may be spoken in a few words: as for Flourish, & Oratory, & Poetry, I leave them to Younger & more lively Writers, such as love Writing for writing-sake, & would rather show their own

---

[1] The letter was printed in Dr. Johnson's Life of Fenton. It had been transcribed on 7 Nov. 1780 ('Snowy day and not well') by William Cole whose copy, now Add. 5860, ff. 30–31, is prefaced by a note extolling the letter as an example of Pope's goodness of heart. The editor has another transcript made by John Hoole, the translator of Tasso, 'from a printed Copy (a few being struck off) sent to Rev. Mr. Tho. Warton of Trinity Coll. Ox. from Mr. Nichols, Printer of London   Sept. 27. 1782'.

[2] Fenton died aged 47. He was almost exactly five years older than Pope.

[3] Lady Judith Trumbull, widow of Pope's early friend, Sir William. It is an easy assumption that Pope was serviceable through Sir Clement Cottrell in getting Fenton his post in this family.

Fine Parts, than Report the Valuable ones of any other man. So the Elegy I renounce.

I condole with you from my heart on the Loss of so worthy a Man, & a Friend to us both. Now he is gone, I must tell you, he has done You many a good office, & Set your character in the fairest light, to some who either mistook you, or knew you not. I doubt not he has done the same for Me.

Adieu. Let us love his Memory, & profit by his Example. I am very sincerely | Dear Sir | Your affectionate | & real Servant | A. Pope.

Aug. 29th 1730.

Address: To | The Revd Mr Broome | at Pulham, near | Harlestone | By Beccles Bag. Suffolke

Postmark: 29/AV

POPE *to* FORTESCUE   6 *September* [1730?]

1797 (Polwhele, i. 322)

Twitnam, Sept. 6th.

I cannot express the joy your letter gives me. I was in great fears after I had written,[1] learning no further of your state, when I sent three days to Mr. Thory. Your giving me these lines under your hand, is a kindness I shall long remember. I hope in God your recovery increases as fast as I really wish it; one of my great apprehensions was, you might not have a skilful physician in a distant country place, of which you have eased me; I hope you keep him near, or with you. I desire earnestly to hear of you soon again, tho' I hope the danger of a relapse is over, but surely you must not hazard cold, by too quick a removal. Without pretences I am, and have been so long and so sincerely your friend, that this alarm was a lively and deep felt one to me; God forbid it should ever be renewed: I may now have spirits enough to quote Homer to you, who says, "a friend is better than a kinsman." Your sister, I hope, is well, and as she ought to receive no harm from so virtuous an enterprize, so, I trust, she will have her reward compleat in seeing you perfectly restored. I am ever, dear Sir, your truly affectionate and faithful friend, | A. Pope.

Is there any thing at this distance that I can procure for you, or any corroborative advice that I can get for you from any of our physicians, or any business I could ease you the care of, or any thing you would have said or done?

Address: To Wm. Fortescue, esq. at Buckland Filleigh.

[1] See Pope to Fortescue, 24 Aug. 1730.

POPE *to* LORD BATHURST[1]   11 *September* 1730

Cirencester

                                                    Sept. 11. 1730

My Lord,—If you have read in any Newspaper that I am dead, there
are many Reports spread that way which are false, & I could have
wishd you had *Enquird* whether this were so or not? If you have only
Forgot I was alive, I can the better account for your Forgetfulness
about a Month before you left this Neighbourhood; when I was daily
in hopes to have waited on you at the summons you promisd me. It is
observd of Very Aged people, & such whose memories Long Life &
much Business have worn away, that they better recollect Things
long since past than those which are nearer. I therfore hope, My Lord
you may have yet some glympse of remembrance, that there was at
the latter End of Queen Anne's reign, a Poet of the name of Pope,
to whom you sometimes afforded an hour of Conversation as well as
reading (tho' indeed the former was the lesser Task of the two, for
his Works were much longer than his Visits) you sometimes also, in
those days, & evn to the middle or later end of the Reign of George 1st
honor'd him with your Letters. I know the succeeding Reign, as it was
a Time of greater Actions & Designs, and a Busier Scene, both at
home & abroad, did much engross your Lordships Thoughts & hours,
& hurryd you (like all other true Patriots) to the public paths of Glory
from the private ones of Friendship, Amusement, & Social Life. I also
am sensible, that many Great & Noble Works, worthy a large Mind
& Fortune, have employd your cares & time; such as Enclosing a
Province with Walls of Stone, planting a whole Country with Clumps
of Firs, digging Wells (which were extremely wanted in those parts
for the very necessities of Life) as deep as to the Center, erecting
Palaces, raising Mounts, undermining High ways, & making Com-
munications by Bridges. Not to enumerate those many & Various
Studies which possess your Lordships mind; in which it may suffice
to say Every thing has place except Polemic Divinity, but chiefly &
principally Natural Philosophy, & the Art of Medicine: Witness those
Instructions, which Physicians, instead of giving, Receive from You,
even while you are their Patient: They come, to feel your pulse, &
prescribe you physick! presumptuous Men! they return with their
own pulses examind, & their own Bodies purgd, vomited, or blooded.

Among all these Employments how can I expect to be rememberd?
I am more reasonable My Lord; I only expect to be thought of when
you see my hand or person. I ask & hope no more than to be thought
what I merit to be thought, & to be rememberd for what I merit to

---

[1] It is interesting to compare this complaint for lack of letters with the similar complaint
made by Lord Bathurst to Swift two days earlier. See Ball, iv. 162–4.

be rememberd, Your true Wellwisher, client, Lover, Friend; and (to the last of my life) | My Lord, Your Faithful Servant, | A. Pope.

Sanders[1] somtimes tells me, how yourself my Lady, & your family do, He knows I once livd much with you, & has not forgot me, tho' he is a Lords Porter, & (I think) Elder than his Lord. Old David too, (who is old enough to be your Grandfather) has some notion of me.

†POPE *to* GAY   11 *September* 1730

1735

Sept. 11, 1730.

I may with great Truth return your Speech, that I think of you daily; oftner indeed than is consistent with the character of a reasonable man; who is rather to make himself easy with the things and men that are about him, than uneasy with those which are not. And you, whose Absence is in a manner perpetual to me, ought rather to be remembered as a good man gone, than breathed after as one living. You are taken from us here, to be laid up in a more blessed state with Spirits of a higher kind: such I reckon his Grace and her Grace, since their Banishment from an earthly Court to an heavenly one, in each other and their friends; for I conclude none but true Friends will consort or associate with them afterwards. I can't but look upon myself (so unworthy as a man of *Twitnam* seems, to be rank'd with such rectify'd and sublimated Beings as you) as a separated Spirit too from Courts and Courtly Fopperies. But I own, not altogether so divested of terrene Matter, nor altogether so spiritualized, as to be worthy admission to your Depths of Retirement and Contentment. I am tugg'd back to the world and its regards too often; and no wonder, when my retreat is but ten miles from the Capital. I am within Ear-shot of Reports, within the Vortex of Lyes and Censures. I hear sometimes of the Lampooners of Beauty, the Calumniators of Virtue, the Jokers at Reason and Religion. I presume these are creatures and things as unknown to you, as we of this dirty Orb are to the inhabitants of the Planet *Jupiter*: Except a few fervent prayers reach you on the wings of the post, from two or three of your zealous Votaries at this distance; as one Mrs. *Howard*,[2] who lifts up her heart now and then to you, from the midst of the *Colluvies* and Sink of Human Greatness at *W—r*: One Mrs. *B.* that fancies you may remember her while you liv'd in your mortal and too transitory State at *Petersham*: One Lord

---

¹ Sanders and old David are presumably servants at Bathurst's house in St. James's Square.

² Howard] H. *1737–42.*

B.[1] who admir'd the Duchess before she grew quite[2] a Goddess; and a few others.

To descend now to tell you what are our Wants, our Complaints, and our Miseries here; I must seriously say, the Loss of any one Good woman is too great to be born easily: and poor Mrs. *Rollinson,*[3] tho' a private woman, was such. Her Husband is gone into *Oxfordshire* very melancholy, and thence to the *Bath,* to *live on,* for such is our Fate, and Duty. Adieu. Write to me as often as you will, and (to encourage you) I will write as seldom as if you did not. Believe me | Your, &c.

*JOSEPH SPENCE *to* POPE*[4]   11 *September* 1730

Professor R. H. Griffith

Winton   Sept. 11, 1730

We have a particular Accident here I cannot forbear communicating to you. All our conversation turns on it; & every body is surpriz'd that hears it. Tis a Man without anything of what is cald Education, grown up into an Excellent Poet all at once.[5] The Man is yet a comon Thresher: plain & modest in his behaviour; but when you come to talk to him, of particular good sense; & of more knowledge than could possibly be expected. Tis not yet a year ago that he was first employd to write on a Subject; & he lately producd a little Poem that is good every way: even in its Design, as well as in the Language, & the Numbers. Tis the Story of the Shunamite from the book of Kings. Any one who has not talkd with the man, would think it impossible for such an one to have written it: & any body that has, will soon be sure that tis his Own. Lord Macclesfield & the Dean of Peterborough[6] sent for him some days ago: & the Dean, (whom I happend to see since) assured me that he went through the strictest examination imaginable. The

---

[1] Windsor, Mrs. Blount (Martha), and Lord Bathurst are concealed (?) in the abbreviations.

[2] grew quite a goddess] grew a goddess *1737–42.*

[3] Thought to be Sarah, wife of William Rollinson, Esq., friend of Swift, Gay, and others of the circle. Rollinson, when in financial straits, had become a wine merchant. His wife had been the widow of Charles, 4th Earl of Winchilsea.

[4] This letter in draft form is among the collections of Professor Griffith. The text here is taken from that printed by Dr. Margaret Lee Wiley in *English Studies in Honor of James Southall Wilson* (University of Virginia Studies, iv [1951], 261–2).

[5] Spence thus introduces to Pope 'the thresher poet' Stephen Duck.

[6] The Earl of Macclesfield and Dr. Francis Lockier, Dean of Peterborough, were early sponsors of Duck. Lockier was a friend of Pope's, and contributed anecdotes to Spence's collection. If such men approved of Duck, Pope might. That Duck's sponsors were very nervous about a possible inclination on Pope's part to place Stephen among the Dunces may be seen in the letters of Dr. Alured Clarke to Mrs. Clayton, printed in *Memoirs of Viscountess Sundon* (ed. 'Mrs. Thomson', 1847), i. 183–206. Dr. Clarke (i. 187) thought Duck 'a superior genius to Mr. Pope', and he also remarked: 'I am not fond of paying compliments to Mr. Pope; I think he deserves them not from anybody that has a true love for the Royal Family' (i. 197). Pope's bias as to the royal family was far less marked in 1730 than it was later.

Man is now in Winton; & I had him all the last Evening & this
Morning to myself: I cant say that I ever spent many hours more
agreably. One sees the Strugles of a great Soul in him; much light he
has, & much he wants: but there's so much more knowledge in
the man than could be expected & so much goodness in this man,
that even his Ignorance as he manages it has something even agreeable
in it. If you have not yet heard of him, this account I hope wont be
impertinent: & if you have not seen his Poem above mentiond, I shall
take a great deal of pleasure in writing it out & sending it to you. I
had almost forgot one particular. The Man is so out of the world, that
he never saw your Essay on Criticism till his coming to Winton this
week: & reads it with so much taste, that I was surprizd to find he
could repeat the best part of it by heart this morning. You see that I
am just full of the Man, & I could not help giving you an account of
him. I hope Mrs. Pope & you enjoy all the health which is ever very
sincerely wisht to you by Sir | Your most obligd | Humble Servant.

Endorsement (at top): *Draft* | Spence to Pope | on Stephen Duck.

LORD BATHURST *to* POPE   19 *September* 1730
Longleat Portland Papers, xii

Cirencester Sepr 19th 1730

It was no small satisfaction to me to find you are alive for I had great
reason to beleive you were either Dead or transported. I cou'd not
conceive that for so long a time I shou'd not have had one line from
you. you knew where I was to be found but you are perpetually roving
& one must shoot flying (to speak in the language of the Country)
to hit you. besides there's another reason why I shou'd expect that
you shou'd write first. You know I never have any pen Ink or Paper
in the way, and you have them always by you at home, & are allways
calling for them abroad, witness that you put me to the Charge of
buying a tin Standish for you at Richkings. I may truly say with one
of the Ancients—toto non quater anno membranam posco,[1] why then
shou'd you expect to hear from me? but by some flying reports which
have peirc'd even thro' Oakly-wood, I have reason to beleive you have
some great projects on foot, & can't have leasure to turn your thoughts
to the mean consideration of preserving an old useless friendship, or of
enquiring after a Man who is out of the Grande monde. one who is
sent for to Court in a hurry & kept there all night[2] despises a poor
Country Gentleman, & looks upon him as a Creature of a different

[1] Horace, *Satires*, ii. iii. 1–2 (adapted).
[2] Mrs. Howard wrote to Gay, 22 Aug.: 'Mr. Pope has been to see me, Lord Burlington
brought him; he dined and supped with my lady [Burlington] all the time he staid; he was
heartily tired, and I not much pleased, though I thought myself exceedingly obliged to him
for the visit.'—*Suffolk Correspondence*, i (1824), 384–5. Mrs. Howard may also have written
to Lord Bathurst about the visit.

Species. Know then that I am still a Man according to the true defini-
tion, Animal implume bipes. as to the Heterodox notion of Animal
rationale I disclaim it, for it wou'd certainly have excluded the whole
race of Verse-men from the beginning of the world to this day. being
then your fellow creature & not one of the fowls of the Air why wou'd
you mortifie me so much as to make me think you had totally forgot
me. I have often seen you write in your Sleep, nay & to my knowledge
you translated half Homer when you were scarce awake; how easy
then wou'd it have been for you to have writt me half a dozen times
in all this time. Now you see I don't thank you for writing to me now
but am angry you did not write sooner. Patty Blount has been ill I
hear, which I'm very sorry for, why did not you send me word of that?
the newspapers say Lady Mary is very ill[1] pray inquire after her in
your own name & mine; we have both been her humble Admirers at
different times. I am not so changeable as you, I think of her now as
I allways did.

I design to stay here all the next month at least, if you have a mind
to make up the quarrell I have with you, you must come down to me;
your curricle can bring you with a Pair of Horses as far as Abingdon
My Chaise shall meet you there & bring you to dinner the next day;
I will meet you there my self & drive you hither for the security of
your Person; if you stay but one day with me, you can't be much tir'd
with the Place or the Company. I'll cutt you off some little corner of
my Park (500 or 1000 acres) which you shall do what you will with,
& I'll immediately assign over to you 3 or 4 millions of plants out of
my Nursery to amuse your self with. if you refuse coming I'll immediately send one of my wood-Carts & bring away your whole house &
Gardens, & stick it in the midst of Oakly-wood where it will never be
heard off any more, unless some of the Children find it out in Nutting-
season & take possession of it thinking I have made it for them. I beg
of you, if it be possible lett me see you here. You know that I love
& Esteem you most heartily & Sincerely.

My service to Mrs Pope Patty Blount Mrs Howard, & Capt Gray.[2]
These you see often.

†POPE *to* GAY   1 *October* 1730

1735
                                                                Oct. 1, 1730

I am something like the Sun at this Season, withdrawing from the
World, but meaning it mighty well, and resolving to shine whenever

---

[1] *The Grub-street Journal*, 17 Sept., reports Lady Mary as ill at her house in Covent
Garden. The *Journal* ordinarily gleaned its news from earlier items in other papers. Pope's
relations with Lady Mary were by now past even such politeness as Bathurst suggests.

[2] Captain John Gray was a resident of Twickenham, from whom Mrs. Howard had leased
or purchased grounds. He died in 1736.

I can again. But I fear the Clouds of a long Winter will overcome me to such a degree, that any body will take a farthing candle for a better Guide, and more serviceable companion. My Friends may remember my brighter days, but will think (like the *Irishman*) that the *Moon* is a better thing when once I am gone. I don't say this with any allusion to my Poetical capacity as a Son of *Apollo*, but in my Companionable one, (if you'll suffer me to use a phrase of the Earl of *Clarendon*'s) For I shall see or be seen of few of you, this Winter. I am grown too faint to do any good, or to give any pleasure. I not only, as *Dryden* fairly says, *Feel my notes decay* as a Poet, but feel my Spirits flag as a Companion, and shall return again to where I first began, my Books. I have been putting my Library in order, and enlarging the Chimney in it, with equal intention to warm my Mind and Body (if I can) to some Life. A Friend, (a Woman-friend, God help me!) with whom I have spent three or four hours a day these fifteen years,[1] advised me to pass more time in my studies: I reflected, she must have found some Reason for this admonition, and concluded she wou'd compleat all her kindnesses to me by returning me to the Employment I am fittest for; Conversation with the dead, the old, and the worm-eaten.

Judge therefore if I might not treat you as a Beatify'd Spirit, comparing your life with my stupid state. For as to my living at *Windsor* with Ladies, &c. it is all a dream; I was there but two nights, and all the day out of that company. I shall certainly make as little Court to others, as they do to me; and that will be none at all. My Fair-Weather-Friends of the Summer are going away for *London*, and I shall see Them and the Butterflies together, if I live till next year; which I would not desire to do, if it were only for their sakes. But we that are Writers, ought to love Posterity, that Posterity may love us; and I would willingly live to see the Children of the present Race, meerly in hope they may be a little wiser than their Parents. | I am, &c.

POPE *to* THE EARL OF OXFORD   1 *October* 1730

Longleat Portland Papers, xii

Oct. 1st 1730.

My Lord,—I heartily thank you for yours, as I always shall, let them be ever so short, provided they tell me what That Letter did, that you are all in perfect health. My old Woman is wonderfully well; if the Decline of the Year does not make itself too soon felt. I shall hope she may last one year more amongst us. My own health is bad enough

---

[1] If Martha Blount is intended (and who else could be?) the statement is an obvious exaggeration. The whole letter seems designed to excuse his going to Court, an act that might seem disloyal to his friend Gay. Apparently while at Windsor in August he visited the Burlingtons and practically no one else. Mrs. Howard felt neglected!

to make me wish for no more years than I shall be able to bear, which sure cannot be many. I never have layn in Town but one night since you went, nor have I seen it one day; for I got thither but at 10 in the Evening, & went away by 8 next morning, to take leave of Mr Morice.[1] I have a long letter from the Dean,[2] who says he has sent another to your Lordship: he has promisd me some Verses, not to be printed, which however may increase the Collection in the Harley Library, where I look upon all good papers to have a sure retreat, safe from all Present & Future Curlls. I rejoice at the finishing your New Room, the Palace of Learning. I wish my Head had as good right to be with the Authors there, as my Heart has to be with the Master; to whom, by Right Hereditary, Acquir'd, & Elected, I entirely belong, and am ever to be (in the fullest & truest sense of the words) his | Most faithfull, obligd, and | obedient Servant. | A. Pope.

I am always Lady Oxfords humble Servant, & Lady Margarets humble chamber fellow, (I think at Cambrige you call it *Chum*)

Endorsement: Mr Pope Octr 1st 1730.

POPE *to* LORD BATHURST   1 *October* [1730]
Cirencester

My Lord,—I am sorry to find one I took for a Just Patriot, so tyrannical & oppressive in his disposition, as to think of taking from another his house & Lands, only because they are less than his own. At this rate your Lordships poor Neighbours will fare ill, & all be swallowd in Oakley Wood. I hoped at least my Distance from you might have securd me from those terrible Designs of the Greater upon the Less. But if your Cart does come, & carry away my Buildings & Gardens it shall carry me too a-top of 'em; that I may be sure of a tight & safe Roof at least to lye under, better than that to which you were once pleasd to commit the best Brains of the Nation, (I mean Swift's.)[3] In good earnest, my Lord, I wish I were your Tenant in the Wood on any terms, if I were not certain you would run away from me as soon as I was setled. My Lord B. & I hope, since you say you shall not stir this month or two, that you are already on the road hither: And I doubt not if I meet you, at Abingdon,[4] it will be to return to

---

[1] Morice had government permission to visit his exiled father-in-law (Atterbury) in this year, and was probably visited by Pope before departing for the Continent.

[2] An unknown letter.

[3] Swift long remembered the inconveniences of Lord Bathurst's 'guest house'. See Ball v. 34 (Mrs. Pendarves to Swift, 24 Oct. 1733) and 252 (Swift to Lord Bathurst, 21 Oct. 1735).

[4] Pope jokes over Bathurst's supposed unpredictable journeyings by suggesting that if he met Bathurst at Abingdon his lordship would be *en route* to London and not ready to take Pope back to Cirencester. See Bathurst's letter, 19 Sept.

London. I could tell you something from Court that would bring you up, You have had at least three good words spoken of you by a great person:[1] Only I make a scruple of telling them to you, for fear you should depend upon 'em. You stand fair, by what I also hear from Dr Burton,[2] to be made an Honorary Physician to her Majesty: and as I take it your ambition would be gratifyd by that, more than any other way. I have compliments to you from a Lady there, & from a Lady here, not Lady Mary (who wishd you & all of us at the devil last week, because she thought of going to him herself, but is now recover'd & cares not a pin for you, or any Man of honour in Christendom). Mrs Patty has always a Partiality for you, notwithstanding your eternal neglect, of which she thinks there cannot be a greater proof than your never proposing to put her among the other things in the Cart. She can't be so humble as not to imagine, Her Person might be as much an Ornament to your Wood, as a Leaden Statue. She says she could look after the children that you resolve to give My House to; and for my part I assure your Lordship, I should think myself not so much disgracd by the Company you assign me, but be proud to pass my time with the only honest & unprejudic't Part of the Nation; Those children, my Lord who may come to assert, what their Fathers have given up.

I know you think this does not concern you; no more it does; but however I have a wish left to be revengd on you by. May your own children come to assert what you have asserted, but with so much better success, as to Eclypse their Fathers Fame, & leave Posterity nothing to say for him, but that He wishd & labourd to do the same thing which They accomplishd.

I hear Mr Bathurst is coming over?[3] Is it true? Are you in perfect health? is my Lady so? and all yours? Capt. Grays Boat is in my Custody ready equippd with Sails, flags, Pennons, &c. What shall be done with it? tho' I can keep it in my Boathouse all the Winter if you please. Lady Bolingbroke I hear is expected this week. Will you not come, to dispute with her for her health? On any terms I wish to see you, or to hear from you. Other people of my rank may respect you, & so do I, but I love you so much more, that I forget many Degrees of that respect. Indeed my Lord, I am to all intents entirely | Your Lordships ever | obligd, affectionate | Servant, | A. Pope.

Oct. 1st

[1] Perhaps by the Queen?

[2] Simon Burton, M.D. (1690?–1744), was a fashionable doctor consulted by both Bathurst and Pope. He attended Pope in the poet's last illness, and survived him less than a fortnight.

[3] If the reference is to Bathurst's son, the inquiry is probably concerning a return from abroad. At this time there is no evidence that his lordship was eager to see his nineteen-year-old son in politics, but he was anxious to see one of his brothers (Peter or Benjamin) elected to Parliament. See *Suffolk Correspondence*, i. 276.

The Dean, Lewis, Gay, Cleland, at all times ask of you. I remember something you spoke of about buying English Elms at a Nursery in Isleworth, which Gray told you of: can I do any thing in it?

†POPE *to* GAY¹   *October* 1730

1737

It is true that I write to you very seldom, and have no pretence of writing which satisfies me, because I have nothing to say that can give you much pleasure: only merely² that I am in being, which in truth is of little consequence to one from whose conversation I am cut off, by such accidents or engagements as separate us. I continue, and ever shall, to wish you all good happiness: I wish that some lucky event might set you in a state of ease and independency all at once! and that I might live to see you as happy, as this silly world and fortune can make any one. Are we never to live together more, as once we did? I find my life ebbing apace, and my affections strengthening as my age encreases: not that I am worse, but better, in my health than last winter: but my mind finds no amendment nor improvement, nor support to lean upon, from those about me: and so I feel my self leaving the world, as fast as it leaves me. Companions I have enough, friends few, and³ those too warm in the concerns of the world for me to bear⁴ pace with; or else so divided from me, that they are but like the dead whose remembrance I hold in honour. Nature, temper, and habit, from my youth made me have but one strong desire; all other ambitions, my person, education, constitution, religion, &c. conspir'd to remove far from me. That desire was to fix and preserve a few lasting, dependable friendships: and the accidents which have disappointed me in it, have put a period to all my aims. So I am sunk into an idleness, which makes me neither care nor labour to be notic'd by the rest of mankind; I propose no rewards to myself, and why should I take any sort of pains? here I sit and sleep, and probably here I shall sleep till I sleep for ever, like the old man of Verona.⁵ I hear of what passes in the busy world with so little attention, that I forget it the next day: and as to the learned world, there is nothing passes in it. I have no more to add, but that I am with the same truth as ever, | Yours, &c.

---

¹ Pope in all his editions places this letter between those to Gay dated 1 Oct. and 23 Oct. Only in the quartos and folios of 1737 did he give the letter a date and then it was dated 'October 1730'. In the summer of 1730, however, he has not been remiss in writing, and the friends are not separated by 'accidents and engagements' but by the fact that Gay is in Amesbury. Yet the position of the letter is not impossible—simply somewhat improbable.
² only merely that] only that *1737b*
³ and] but *1737b*.   ⁴ bear] keep *1737b*.
⁵ Is the allusion to Claudian's 'old man of Verona' (*De Sene Veronensi*)? He stayed at home but did not concentrate on sleep. Claudian's poem had perhaps a connexion with Pope's 'Ode on Solitude'.

BOLINGBROKE *to* LORD BATHURST[1]   8 *October* 1730

Elwin–Courthope, viii, 340–1

EXCERPT

I expect to see Pope to-morrow, for my servant says he is at home, in which case I shall dine with him. You will not be forgot by us, for though we are at present deep in metaphysics, there will be some gay scenes interspersed, which will of course lead us to your lordship, and give Pope occasion to ask your information and corrections.

*POPE *to* FORTESCUE[2]   [*October* 1730]

Harvard University

It is but justice you do me in thinking so great a truth, as that to hear you are got abroad will be a sensible pleasure to me. I have frequently enquir'd of the Progress of your amendment, of Mr Thory, and was again in some fear last week till I receivd this kind letter. I could wish to see you well arrived in Town for the Winter, but surely it must be with great caution that you must venture to travel, especially if the Season grow cold. Methinks a Coach would be the proper Vehicle, & it might bring Mrs Fortescue with you, whose assistance would be very necessary in case you should not be perfectly well either on the road or after your journey. My mother, tho' she now forgets almost every one, remembers you & heartily joins with me in wishes for your recovery: so does Mrs Blount, who has often askd me of you: (By the way you forgot to leave orders with your clerk for her 25ll.) We hear not a word of Mr Roberts, to whom a Letter was sent by Mr Bethel, & promisd by one of his Lawyers (whom Mr Thory found out) to be forwarded to him, long agoe. I can tell you no news but that Mrs Howard is well & exprest much concern at your Illness. I've seen her but twice this whole Summer at Windsor, and I was at the same time to wait on Sir Robert, but he was ingaged. I have liv'd constantly at home, & had my health but ill.

As to the Letter you sent me inclosed, I see the Gentleman has applyd himself to the matter he mentions with industry.[3] You must

[1] Elwin prints the whole of this letter, which he found among the Bathurst Papers. The parts here omitted tell us that Bolingbroke is back from a (political?) visit to Sir William Wyndham, and hopes for the return of Bathurst to London and of Lady Bolingbroke from France. The accident to Mrs. Pope is not mentioned, and may not yet have occurred.

[2] Early in September (letter to Fortescue, 6 Sept.) Fortescue was recovering from his long summer affliction of gout, and now he is planning to return to London. His clerk has no orders to pay Martha Blount her quarterly allowance from her brother. Cf. Pope to Fortescue, 2 Aug. 1735. The letter postdates that of 6 Sept. and antedates the date (1731) when Mrs. Howard became a countess. It also antedates, presumably, the accident to Mrs. Pope (falling into the fire) in October of this year—at least that accident is unmentioned.

[3] The unidentified author of a projected work on rhythm in verse and oratory would doubtless have liked to quote Pope. It is uncertain whether Pope did not wish to be quoted or did not wish to be quoted by this author.

excuse my not answering it, to him, any way your Friendship can invent, for I've found many Inconveniencies from writing too liberally on Subjects where my name has come to be used as an Autority, where I only meant a modest opinion or Civility. But what I think of it shall be put into the next leaf which may be shown him separately.

I think the Gentleman's Observations upon the Rythmus every way right, & incontestable; and if he extends them in Particulars, it cannot but be an useful Discourse; to lay down Methods to give the Last Grace & finishing (for so the Rythmus in the sense he uses it may be calld) to a Poem or Oration. But he must give me leave to say, this can be done only by Examples from Homer, Virgil, Demosthenes, Tully, & a very few more. I have no thoughts of writing upon it, but would Practise it where ever I could; which if perform'd so as to be seen & felt by the judicious reader, is the same thing; and it ought to be done so distinctly & constantly (had a man time to write correctly) as not to need being Pointed out. The Author he mentions, Dionysius of Halicarnassus, is much the nicest critick on that Subject, I fear rather too minute: I know of none besides those whom he names, except in one chapter of Quintilian & in the Book of Rhet: Ad Herennium, a few Observations. Our English Language is certainly more capable of this Beauty, than the French & Italian; their Pauses in the Verse are too Equal, & too near a Monotony, ours more Various; & I think the better for the Consonants, if discreetly manag'd. Those Languages *Flow smoothly*, but ours *Rowls fully* & freely. I need say no more to the Gentleman, who (I can see) knows his subject too well for me to pretend to give him Hints. Pray thank him for having so much a higher notion of me, & my Poetry & Prose both, than I deserve.

You will return my very sincere Services to your Sister & Daughter. I am ever | Dear Sir | Yours most Faithfully, | A. Pope.

POPE *to* FORTESCUE[1]   [? *October* 1730]

1797 (Polwhele, i. 322)

Dear Sir, I quite forgot, in the place of business, where I last saw you, to mention a commission of lady Walpole's,[2] that you will not forget her laver. I shall readily speak to Chiselden what you desire, and to St. Andre if you will; the others I have not the least knowledge of: I will put Mrs. Howard also in mind of it, that lady is now better;

---

[1] This letter concerns the choice of some protégé (Mr. Wise?) of Fortescue for one of the recently established scholarships in surgery. It is further tied to Oct. 1730 by the next letter which adds the fall of Mrs. Pope into the fire. Cheselden and St. Andre were leading surgeons of the day. Boucher may also have been connected with one of the London hospitals. Cheselden was at St. Thomas's, where he had for years lectured on anatomy.

[2] The laver suggests further intimacy of Pope and Fortescue with Sir Robert and his lady.

she has been in some danger of a fever, and in extreme pain since you saw her on Sunday, she has hitherto kept her bed since that day. I will see her as soon as I can. If Dr. Arbuthnot knows Mr. Boucher, I will speak to him on his return to town; or in any thing, any way in my power, do my utmost that you can suggest, being, with lasting truth, and all good wishes for you and yours, ever your affectionate friend, | A. Pope.

Pray leave me a memorandum where Mr. C—s[1] is to be found, and give him all directions needful. I heartily wish you health and a good journey. Sit tibi cura mei. Sit tibi cura tui.

Address: To Wm. Fortescue, esq.

POPE *to* FORTESCUE[2]   [? *October* 1730]

Professor C. B. Tinker

Tis in the utmost hurry I send this, not to omit a Post; my Mother had had a most unfortunate accident of a Fall, which has much bruisd her, & almost had burned her but for a great Escape. Mr Cheselden had no sooner writ me the inclosed (for I sent a letter to his house but just before as soon as I received yours) but he came hither to assist her. What he further tells me, is, that he has the power of putting in four in a year: for the next two he stands indispensably ingagd, but will make Mr Wise the third: which will be in about half a year. He will then certainly serve him The terms it seems are 29ll. for the Course of the Hospitals & the Anatomy. He assures me he will forward and assist him all he can. Pardon my haste, I am really in great trouble & she in great pain. God knows the Event of such a Shock at her Years. God prosper you all. pray write how you continue recovering. Adieu. Yours A. Pope.

Address: To | Wm Fortescue Esqr.

POPE *to* CARYLL   22 *October* 1730

Add. 28618

Twittenham. 22. Oct. 1730.

I see you either forget me, or spare me, in regard to the many things which yet take up my life. I would have it the latter for two reasons; one, that I cannot reconcile my mind to the thoughts of your being less kind to me than you have been so many years; the other, that I would rather be beholden to your forgiveness and considerateness

---

[1] Cruwys?

[2] This letter evidently follows closely that to Fortescue immediately preceding, and names Fortescue's protégé as Mr. Wise. It seems also to follow closely Mrs. Pope's accident, which is first reported, in a dated letter, to Caryll on 22 Oct. It seems to have happened early in the month.

than fancy I incur your neglect. Indeed I have not written to you since your last, but that last was not six lines and only about venison. I hope the lady paid you her own thanks, as I punctually discharged your commission. She has been but ill in health this whole summer: but what will please you better than ill news in relation to her is, that the sister is happily forsaken by the person for whom she unaccountably exposed herself so much. He has proved to be very near a mad man; which you'll say he more than half proved before, by being attached to her: *Deus dedit his quoque finem.*[1]

I was and still am much concerned for Mrs Pigot. My own poor mother is yet a partaker of her reason, which renders all other decays less grievous; but her memory is very near gone. She had within this month a very extraordinary escape from a terrible accident: She fell into the fire without touching her body, tho' it consum'd the clothes she had on, at least a yard about. Her back lay on the grate, but her head (tho' dressed in Musselin) reclining sideways was not burnt. The shock of the fall and blow has much hurt her, but after a week or two she recovered of all but her feebleness. I am willing to think it a preservation of God, whose providence is surely sometimes particular, as 'tis always general. I shall ever rejoice to hear of the welfare and prosperity of all your family. Pray assure your son and daughter (I should first have your Lady) of my sincere services, and believe me ever | Dear sir | Your most faithful and affect. servant | A. Pope.

†POPE *to* GAY   23 *October* 1730

1737

Oct. 23, 1730.

Your letter is a very kind one, but I cant say so pleasing to me as many of yours have been, thro' the account you give of the dejection of your spirits. I wish the too constant use of water does not contribute to it; I find Dr. Arbuthnot and another very knowing physician of that opinion. I also wish you were not so totally immers'd in the country; I hope your return to Town will be a prevalent remedy against the evil of too much recollection. I wish it partly for my own sake: We have liv'd little together of late, and we want to be physicians for one another. It is a remedy that agreed very well with us both, for many years, and I fancy our constitutions would mend upon the old medicine of *Studiorum similitudo*, &c. I believe we both of us want whetting; there are several here who will do you that good office, merely for the love of wit, which seems to be bidding the town a long and last adieu. I can tell you of no one thing worth reading, or seeing; the whole age seems resolv'd to justify the Dunciad, and it may stand for a

---

[1] Adapted from *Aeneid*, i. 199.

publick Epitaph or monumental Inscription, like that at Thermopylae, on a *whole people perish'd*! There may indeed be a Wooden image or two of Poetry set up, to preserve the memory that there once were bards in Britain; and (like the *Giants* at *Guildhall*) show the bulk and bad taste for our ancestors: At present the poet Laureat[1] and Stephen Duck serve for this purpose; a drunken sot of a *Parson*[2] holds forth the emblem of *inspiration*, and an honest industrious *Thresher* not unaptly represents *Pains* and *Labour*.[3] I hope this Phænomenon of Wiltshire has appear'd at Amesbury, or the Duchess will be thought insensible to all bright qualities and exalted genius's, in Court and country alike. But he is a harmless man, and therefore I am glad.

This is all the news talk'd of at court, but it will please you better to hear that Mrs. Howard talks of you, tho' not in the same breath with the Thresher, as they do of me. By the way, have you seen or convers'd with Mr. Chubb, who is a wonderful Phænomenon of Wiltshire? I have read thro' his whole volume[4] with admiration of the writer: tho' not always with approbation of the doctrine. I have past just three days in London in four months, two at Windsor, half an one at Richmond, and have not taken one excursion into any other country. Judge now whether I can live in my library? adieu. Live mindful of one of your first friends, who will be so to the last. Mrs. Blount deserves your remembrance, for she never forgets you, and wants nothing of being a friend.

I beg the Duke's and her Graces acceptance of my services: the contentment you express in their company pleases me, tho' it be the barr to my own, in dividing you from us. I am ever very truly Your, &c.

POPE *to* MALLET[5]   29 *October* [1730]

Sir John Murray

Oct. 29th

Sir,—I thank you for writing to me, & I find I am to thank you for

---

[1] poet Laureat] poor Laureat *1737e–1742*

[2] Pope evidently did not know that the Rev. Lawrence Eusden, called here 'a drunken sot', had died on 27 Sept. There may have been rumours to that effect, but the earliest direct statement of his death in Lincolnshire noted is in *The Universal Spectator*, 31 Oct. 1730. *The Grub-street Journal*, 15 Oct., retailing a rumour from *The Daily Journal* that Stephen Duck will succeed as laureate, comments, 'I wonder at this article, since the bodily life of . . . Eusden is at present in no danger.'

[3] Pope's possible reactions to the genius of this untaught thresher from Wiltshire caused considerable trepidation at Court. It can be seen in letters printed in *Memoirs of* [Charlotte Clayton] *Viscountess Sundon*, edited by K. Thomson in 1850. Pope behaved rationally and very charitably—at least in public.

[4] Thomas Chubb's *Collection of Tracts, on Various Subjects* (1730) was a heavy quarto in 474 pages. At work on his *Essay on Man*, Pope had unusual interest in such tracts.

[5] The year is doubtful; but in 1729 Mallet was at Shawford, and now he is in town. In 1731 (1 Sept.) he was with the Duke of Montrose in Norfolk, and before 1732 he had left the Montrose family.

not writing to me, since your motive was a kind & considerate one. Indeed when I do not correspond, or converse as I wish to do, with those I esteem; it is not my heart, but my Constitution is to blame. I shall, with great truth, be glad to see you any day you appoint, the end of this, or in the next week; being sincerely | Sir | Your most affectionate | humble Servant, | A. Pope

Address: To | Mr Mallet, at the Duke | of Montrose's in Hanover Square | London.

Postmark: 30/OC

POPE *to* THE EARL OF OXFORD   3 *November* 1730

Longleat Portland Papers, xii

My Lord,—A very unhappy accident which befell my Mother, of a Fall into the Fire (from which however it pleasd God she has escapd without more hurt than her back bruis'd, & now well, and her Clothes burnt off) has kept me many days from writing to your Lordship & acknowledging your kind Memory of me, which I will not say is shown by the kind Present of Brawn, it is shown so many hundred ways. I am sensible of the Particular Providence of God, as well as of His General, on this occasion: and I flatter myself, that after my long Care & attendance (which is no more than Duty however, & gratitude) upon Her Infirm Condition, He would not suffer her to End tragically.

I wish sincerely all felicity to your Lordship & Family, & have nothing to say, but that I beg you, & my Lady Oxford to know me for what I am. That indeed, as the world goes, and as its Censure & Rash Judgment goes, is almost an unreasonable request: But I take you to be of the charitable & Just part of that world, & so I expect & hope it.

I have a Petition to your Lordship, which you would extremely oblige me in. My Friend Cleland has a Son,[1] Student in Christchurch, Oxon: whose welldoing is of great importance to his Father: He apprehends he may fall into mean company, unless some experienced worthy Man would countenance, & have an eye over him, or recommend him to proper Companions. If your Lordship would favor Cleland, (that is *Me*) with your recommendatory Letter to Any Such worthy men of his College (with whom it is my own fancy You have Interest) it would be a means of doing my Friend a great Service in so tender a part as his Favorite Son, & I need not tell so good a Parent as Yourself, What that is?

[1] Henry Cleland, son of Major William Cleland of Kingston, Surrey, had matriculated at Christ Church (Lord Oxford's college) in 1728. His older brother John, later a novelist of notoriety, was a rolling stone, and evidently the father (who helped Pope on *The Dunciad Variorum* and in other ways) was worrying about the younger son. Major Cleland was also a friend of the Earl of Marchmont and the Earl of Chesterfield.

I was not a little concernd to hear your Coach was this day to go empty back to Wimpole. Had not this unhappy accident befallen my Mother, I had infallibly put myself into it. My Lord, I am with Truth | Your most affectionate, & | Most obliged | humble Servant | A. Pope.

My Mother is yet | your Servant

Twitnam, | Nov. 3d 1730

Endorsement: Mr Pope | Twitnam Novr 3. 173[0]

GAY *and* THE DUCHESS OF QUEENSBERRY *to* SWIFT[1]

8 *November* 1730

Add. 4806

So you are determin'd never to write me again, but for all that you shall not make me hold my tongue, you shall hear from me (the Post office willing) whether you will or no. I see none of the Folks you corespond with, so that I am forc'd to pick up intelligence concerning you as I can, which hath been so very little that I am resolv'd to make my complaints to you as a friend who I know love to relieve the distress'd; and in the circumstances I am in, where should I apply but to my best friend? Mr Pope indeed, upon my frequent enquirys hath told me that the Letters that are directed to him concern me as much as himself, but what you say of yourself, or of me, or to me I know nothing at all. Lord Carteret was here yesterday in his return from the Isle of Wight where he had been a shooting; & left 7 pheasants with us. He went this morning to the Bath to Lady Carteret who is perfectly recover'd. He talk'd of you for three hours last night, & told me that you talk of me; I mean that you are prodigiously in his favour, as he says, & I believe that I am in yours; for I know you to be a just & equitable person, and tis but my due. He seem'd to take to me; which I take to proceed from your recommendation; though there is another reason for it, for he is now out of Employment, and my friends have generally been of that sort; for I take them as being naturally inclin'd to those who can do no mischief. Pray, do you come to England this year, he thinks you do, I wish you would, & so does the Dutchess of Queensberry. What would you have more to induce you? Your Money crys come spend me; and your friends cry come see me. I have been treated barbarously by you; if you knew how often I talk of you, how often I think of you, you would now & then direct a Letter to me, & I would allow Mr Pope to have his share in it, in short I dont care to keep any Man's money that serves me so; Love or money I

---

[1] This, the first of a series of joint letters from Gay and his beautiful Duchess, was published by Hawkesworth. Pope had earlier printed Swift's reply (19 Nov.).

must have, & if you will not let me have the comfort of the one, I think I must endeavour to get a little comfort by spending some of the other. I must beg that you would call at Amesbury in your way to London, for I have many things to say to you, & I can assure you, you will be welcome to a three prong'd fork. I remember your prescription, & I do ride upon the Downs, and at present I have no Asthma; I have kill'd five brace of Partridges, & four Brace & a half of Quails, & I do not Envy either Sir Robert, or Stephen Duck, who is the favorite Poet of the Court. I hear sometimes from Mr Pope, & from scarce any body else; Were I to live here never so long I believe I should never think of London, but I cannot help thinking of you. Were you here, I could talk to you, but I would not, for you shall have all your share of talk which was never allow'd you at Twickenham. You know this was a grievance you often complain'd of, & so in revenge you make me write all, & answer nothing. I beg you my compliments to Dr Delany. I am Dear Sir, | Yours most Affectionately. | JG.

Amesbury near Salisbury in Wiltshire.

Novr. 8. 1730

I ended the Letter as above to go to the Dutchess, & she told me I might go down & come a quarter of an hour hence; I had a design to have asked her to have sign'd the invitation that I have made you as I dont know how much she may have to say to you, I think it will be prudent to leave off that she may not be stinted for want of room. So much I will say, that whether she signs it or no, both the Duke & Dutchess would be very glad you would come to Amesbury; & you must be persuaded that I say this without the least private view; for what is it to me whether you come or no? for I can write to you, you know.

I would fain have you come, I cannot say you'll be welcome—for I don't know you, & perhaps I shall not like you, but if I do not (unless you are a very vain person) you shall know my thoughts as soon as I do my self.— | C Q

Endorsement: Mr Gay, and the Dutchess | of Queensberry | Novr 8th 1730

THE EARL OF OXFORD *to* POPE   10 *November* 1730

Longleat Portland Papers, xii

Wimpole. Nov: 10: 1730

I dare say, Dear Sir, you will belive me when I tell you that I was very sensibly toucht when I read the account of the accident that befell your mother, it is a great happiness it was not worse, I will take the liberty to say I feel for you and am very much affected when ever I think what you must feel, and when ever it pleases God to remove her from you by taking her more to himself, your comfort and consolation must arise from your having payed a constant Duty and from your own Virtue;

you may be assured I should have been very glad to have seen you. my Wife desires in particular to be remembered to you and to mrs pope peggy does the same. I am mrs popes humble servant.

I am very busie about my new Room,[1] there I hope to spend some days with you, and there I hope to be free from the impertinence (to give it no other name) of this world. I am about some plantations, Dr middleton is here with me and desires you will accept of his most humble Service.

I am with true respect and esteem | Sir your most | obliged & most | Faithfull humble Servt. | Oxford.

I will write to you about the | major son[2] in a little time.

||SWIFT *to* GAY[3]   10 *November* 1730

Longleat Portland Papers, xiii (Harleian transcript)

Dublin Nov. 10. 1730.

When my Lord Peterborow in the Queen's time went abroad upon his Ambassyes, the Ministry told me, that he was such a vagrant, they were forced to write *at* him by guess, because they knew not where to write *to* him. This is my case with you, sometimes, in Scotland, sometimes at Ham walks, sometimes God knows where. You are a man of business, and not at leisure for insignificant correspondence. It was I got you the Employment of being my Lord Duke's premier Ministre; for his Grace[4] having heard how good a manager you were of my ⌈Bathurst⌉ revenue, thought you fit to be intrusted with ten talents. I have had twenty times a strong inclination to spend a Summer near Salisbury downs, having rode over them more than once, & with a young parson of Salisbury reckoned twice the stones at Stonehenge, which are either 92 or 93: ⌈I thank you for offering me the neighborhood of another Hoadly; I have enough of one; he lives within 20 yards of me, our gardens joyn, but I never see him except

---

[1] His new library.

[2] The son of Major Cleland; see Pope to Lord Oxford, 3 Nov. 1730.

[3] This letter, published by Pope in 1741 and here printed from the Harleian transcript, illustrates well Pope's methods of editing and also the interrelationships of the editions of 1740 (the clandestine volume), 1741, and 1742. Half-brackets are here used to indicate omissions from all the printed texts of 1740–2.

[4] his Grace . . . thought] his Grace heard how a good manager you were of my revenue, and thought *1740*. (*This reading, not reprinted in either the Dublin or London texts of 1741–2, seems to indicate that, independently, Swift and Pope hit upon identical reforms of this sentence.*)

upon business.⌐ I desire to present my most humble acknowledgements
to my Lady Dutchess in return of her civility. I hear an ill thing, that
she is matre pulchra filia pulchrior.¹ I never saw her since she was a
girl, and would be angry she should² excell her Mother, who was long
my principal Goddess. I desire you will tell her Grace, that the ill
management of forks is not to be helpt when they are only bidential,
which happens in all poor houses, especially those of Poets, upon
which account, a knife was absolutly necessary at Mr Pope's, where it
was morally impossible with a bidential fork to convey a morsel of
beef with the incumberance of mustard & turnips into your mouth
at once. And her Grace hath cost me 30 pounds to provide tridents for
fear of offending her, which Sum I desire she will please to return me.
—I am sick enough to go to the Bath, but have not heard, it will be
good for my disorder ⌐You remember me giddy sometimes, & very
violently; I am now constantly so, but not to so high a degree. I
ride often every week, & walk much; but am not better. I thank God
the pain is not great, nor does it spoyl my sleep. But I grow listless, &
good for nothing.⌐ I have a strong mind to spend my 200ll next
Summer in France. I am glad I have it, for there is hardly twice that
Summ left in this Kingdom. ⌐I have left of writing, but not wine though
I have lost six hogsheads that grew muddy in the bottles, and I have
not one family upon whom I can spunge.—⌐ You want no settlement,
I call the family where you live, & the foot you are upon, a Settlement,
till you increase your fortune to what will support you with ease &
plenty, a good horse³ & a garden; The want of this I much dread in⁴
you. For I have often known a she cousen of a good family & small
fortune passing months among all her relations, living in plenty, &
taking her circles, till she grew an old maid, & every body weary of her.
Mr Pope complains of seldom seeing you, but the evil is unavoidable,
for different circumstances of life have always separated those whom
friendship would joyn, God hath taken care . . . of that⁵ to prevent any
progress towards real happyness here, which would make life more
desirable & death too dreadfull. I hope you have now one advantage,
that you allways wanted before, and the want of which made your
friend⁶ as uneasy as it did yourself. I mean⁷ that sollicitude about your
own affairs which perpetually filled your thoughts & disturbed your
conversation; For if it be true what Mr Pope seriously tells me, ⌐that
you are principal manager of the Duke's affairs,⌐ you will have oppertunity of saving every groat of the interest you receive, and so, by the
time he and you grow weary of each other, you will be able to pass

---

¹ Horace, *Carmina*, I. xvi. I.
² she should] should she *1740*. (*Again in this letter the clandestine volume is followed by no
text of 1741–2*.)   ³ horse] house *1740–2*.   ⁴ in] for *1741 Dab; 1742 La*.
⁵ care . . . of that] care of this, *1740–2*.   ⁶ friend] friends *1740–2*.
⁷ I mean that] I mean the removal of that *1741 Labc; 1742 Lbc*.

the rest of your wine-less life in ease & plenty, ⌜with as good a house & gardens as Mr Pope, and⌝ with the additional triumphial comfort of never having received a penny from a tasteless ungratefull court,[1] from which you deserved so much, and which deserves no better Genius's than those by whom it is celebrated,—so let the Post rascal open this letter, and let Walpole read it.—Mr Ford is with us upon the death of his Mother, who has left him money enough to supply the nole wancyes[2] of rents for 2 years in London. He tells me, that he heard I was out of favour with the — The loss is not great. I made a present, or rather it was begged from me, of about 35ll. The trifle promised me, worth about 15ll was never remembered,[3] & after I had made my present shame would not suffer me to mind them of theirs. If you see Mr Cesar present my humble service to him, & let him know that the Scrubb libel printed against me here, & reprinted in London, for which he shew'd a kind concern to a friend of us both, was written by my self,[4] and sent to a whig printer. It was in the style & Genius of such scoundrels, when the humor of libelling ran in this town,[5] against a friend of mine whom you know.—But my paper is ended. ⌜My most humble service to Lord Peterborow, Bolin.— Masham, Bathurst, Lord Oxford, Mr Poulteney, the Doctor Mr Lewis, Mr Pope, &c.—Ever Yours.⌝

⌜Lord Burlington never remembers the request made him in a Solemn manner about his ancester's tomb: however he owed in civility an answer to a letter from so considerable a body. he that would not sacrifice twenty acres out of two hundred thousand to the honor of his family may live to see them not return him two hundred thousand pence, towards which I believe he feels enough already.⌝

POPE *to* THE EARL OF OXFORD   16 *November* 1730

Longleat Portland Papers, xii

                                        Nov. 16. 1730.

My Lord,—I am growing, your Lordship will find, a troublesome Correspondent, & Sollicitor; who have no sooner askd you a favor for one Young man, but must ask something for another. It happens,

---

[1] from a tasteless . . . from which] from those tasteless ungrateful people, from whom *1740–2*. (The Court, that is, is not mentioned in the texts printed by Pope and Swift.)

[2] The legal phrase is badly inserted in Lord Oxford's hand. (The scribe evidently could not decipher it.) Elwin and Ball print in its place *not receiving*, but that is not what is written in the transcript.

[3] In 1726 Swift had sent Irish silk plaids to Mrs. Howard, which had greatly pleased her mistress, then Princess of Wales. The Princess asked Mrs. Howard to get Swift to send similar plaids for herself and her (four or five) daughters, which Swift did—at a cost, he here says, of 35*l*. The Princess expected to pay for the plaids, but Swift (see Ball, iii. 366) professed himself 'highly affronted with such a base proposal'. His complaints here are obviously due to his general and implacable animosity to political Power.

[4] This seems possibly a reference to *A Libel against Dr. Delany*.

[5] town] strain *1740–2*.

that a Nephew of mine,[1] who for his Parents Sins & not his own, was Born a Papist, is just coming (after nine or ten years Study & hard Service under an Attorney) to practise in the Law. Upon this depends his whole wellbeing & Fortune in the world, & the Hopes of his Parents in his Education: all which must inevitably be frustrated, by the Severity of a late opinion of the Judges, who, for the major part, have agreed to admit no Attorney to be sworn the usual oath which qualifies them to practise, unless they also give them the Oaths of allegiance & Supremacy. This has been occasiond solely by the Care they take to inforce an Act of Parliament in the last Session but one, against *fraudulent Practises of attornies*, & to prevent *Men not duly qualifyd for attornies from practising as such*. It is very Evident, that the *Intent* of the act is no way leveld at Papists, nor anyway demands their being Excluded from practising, *more than they were formerly*. Therfore I hope the Favor of a Judge may be procurd, so far as to admit him to take the usual attorneys Oath, without requiring the Religious one. I am told (having fully informd myself of this) that if possibly one of the Judges will be good naturd enough to do this, it would be Judge Price;[2] with whom I think your Lordship has good Interest: and I have try'd in vain every other means. In one word, the poor Lad will be utterly undone in this case, if this Connivance cannot be obtain'd in his behalf. I know your Charity and Humane Consideration will endeavor it, and I have no other possibility of bringing such a thing about for him. Which is all I need say to So good a Man, and so good a Friend.

What further troubles me is, that I am told it will be too late unless this admission be procurd this present month, & I was ignorant of the whole till now.

Surely your Lordship will believe me, I am more heartily vext to be obligd to trouble you thus, than You can be to be so troubled: But to be Obligd to you, would be as great a pleasure to me, as it would even to you, to do me the good. I can say no more; & if your Lordship finds the thing impracticable, my best consolation will be, that You endeavord at least to assist me.

I have but just room for my sincerest Respects to Lady Oxford & Lady Margaret. My truest & best wishes, my Memory & my Gratitude, attend you always.

I am My Lord | Your most obligd & most | affectionate humble Servant | A. Pope

My Mother is a little better, & faithfully your Servant

Endorsement: Mr Pope Novr 16. 1730.

---

[1] Henry Rackett was the lawyer in the Rackett family. Elwin mistakenly thought it was Robert (EC viii. 277). See also Pope to Lord Oxford, 2 Dec. 1730.

[2] Robert Price (1655–1733) had been a distinguished judge since about 1700.—*DNB*.

‖SWIFT *to* GAY *and* THE DUCHESS OF QUEENSBERRY[1]
19 *November* 1730

Longleat Portland Papers, xiii (Harleian transcript)

Dublin novr 19th 1730.

I writ to you a long Letter about a fortnight past concluding you were in London, from whence I understood one of your former was dated; nor did I imagine you were gone back to Aimsbury so late in the year, at which Season I take the Country to be onely a Scene for those who have been ill used by a Court on account of their Virtues; which is a State of Happyness the more valuable, because it is not accompanyed by Envy; although nothing deserves it more. I would gladly sell a Dukedom to lose favour in the Manner their Graces have done. I believe, my Lord Carteret, since he is no longer Lieutenant, may not wish me ill, and I have told him often, that I hated him onely as Lieutenant.[2] I confess he had a genteeler manner of binding the Chains of this Kingdom, than most of his Predecessors; and I confess at the same time that he had six times a regard to my recommendation, by preferring so many of my Friends in the Church,[3] and the two last Acts of his Power[4] was[5] to add to the Dignityes of Dr Delany and Mr Stopfort, the last of whom was by you and Mr Pope put into Mr Pulteney's hands. I told you in my last that a continuance of giddyness, tho' not in a violent degree prevented my thoughts of England at Present. For in my Case a domestick Life is necessary, where I can with the Centurion say to my Servant go and he goeth, and do this and he doth it. I now hate all people whom I cannot command,[6] and consequently a Dutchess is at this time the hatefullest Lady in the World to me, one onely excepted, and I beg her Grace's Pardon for that exception, for in the Way I mean her Grace is ten thousand times more hatefull. I confess I begin to apprehend you will squander my money, because I hope you never less wanted it, and if you go on with Success for two years longer, I fear I shall not have a farthing of it left. The Doctor hath ill informed me, who says that Mr Pope is at present the cheif poeticall favorite;[7] yet Mr Pope himself talks like a Philosopher and one wholly retired. But the vogue of our few honest folks here is that Duck is absolutely to Succeed Eusden in the Lawrell, the contention being between Concannan or Theobald, or some other Hero of the Dunciad. I never charged you for not talking, but the Dubious State of your Affairs in those Days was too much the

---

[1] Printed with practically identical texts in Pope's editions of 1740-2.
[2] as Lieutenant] as a Lieutenant *1740*; *1742La.*
[3] Church, and the two] Church; the two *1741 Labc*; *1742 Lbc, Da.*
[4] Power] favour *1740-2.*
[5] was] were *1741 Labc*; *1742 Lbc, Da.* [6] The transcriber wrote *commend.*
[7] In a letter of November Arbuthnot had written to Swift, 'Pope is now the great reigning poetical favourite.'—Ball. iv. 171.

Subject; and I wish the Dutchess had been the Voucher of your Amendment.

Nothing so much contributed to my ease as the turn of Affairs after the Queen's Death, by which all my hopes being cut off, I could have no Ambition left, unless I would have been a greater Rascal than happened to Suit with my Temper. I therefore sat down quietly at my morsel, adding onely thereto a principle of hatred to all Succeeding Measures and Ministryes, by way of Sauce to relish my meat; and I confess one point of Conduct in My Lady Dutchess's Life hath added much poignance to it. There is a good Irish practical Bull towards the End of your Letter, where you Spend a dozen lines in telling me you must leave off, that you may give my Lady Dutchess room to write, and so you proceed to within[1] three Lines of the bottom, tho' I would have remitted you my 200ll to have left place for as many more.

To the Dutchess

Madam,—My beginning thus low[2] is meant as a Mark of respect, like receiving your Grace at the bottom of the Stairs. I am glad you know your Duty; for it hath been a known and established rule above twenty years in England that the first advances have been constantly made me by all Ladyes who aspired to My Acquaintance, and the greater their Quality the greater were their advances. Yet, I know not by what Weakness, I have condescended gratiously to dispense with you upon this important Article. Tho' Mr Gay will tell you, that a Nameless person[3] sent me eleven Messages before I would yield to a Visit. I mean a Person to whom he is infinitely obliged for being the Occasion of the happyness he now enjoys under the Protection and favor of my Lord Duke and your Grace. At the same time I cannot forbear telling you, Madam, that you are a little imperio[us] in your Manner of making your advances. You say; perhaps, you shall not like me: I affirm you are mistaken, which I can plainly demonstrate; for I have certain Intelligence, that another Person dislikes me of late, with whose likings yours have not for some time past gone together. However, if I shall once have the Honor to attend your Grace, I will out of fear and Prudence appear as vain as I can that I may not know your thoughts of me. This is your own direction; but it was needless, for Diogenes himself would be vain to have received

---

[1] to within three] to within two or three *1740–2*.

[2] In imitation doubtless of the original letter the transcript here printed leaves a wide vacant space between the end of Gay's letter and the bottom of the page where, four lines from the bottom, begins the portion addressed 'To the Dutchess'. Deference to rank is thus indicated.

[3] Swift doubtless means the Queen. His footnote in the first Dublin edition (1741 Da) is: 'The Princess of Wales, afterwards Queen Caroline.' Pope, naturally, did not reprint such notes!

the Honor of being one Moment of his Life in the thoughts of your Grace.

⌈I am with the greatest │ Respect Your Grace's &c.⌉[1]

POPE *to* THE EARL OF OXFORD   [*c. 2 December* 1730]

Longleat Portland Papers, xii

My Lord,—I have great reason to thank you for the ready Favour you did me, in recommending my Nephew to Mr Baron C.[2] He shewed him what possible regard he could, and lamented his Inability to admit any in that Circumstance, as it really is a Case of Compassion. I fear there is no remedy for it, without some particular Sanction of Parliament: But my Sense of your Lordships Intention is the same as if it could have succeeded. It is a Whole Education Lost,[3] and one of those Miseries, which Individuals are subject to, from the Two General Distribution of Laws.

> Delirant Optimates, plectuntur Populi[4]

I know it will please you My Lord, to hear that the Painful Part of my Mother's Accident is over, & that she lives at least out of torment: Her Condition is now half Sleep, half Quiet awake; & the Decays are gradual: I hope, when the time comes, her Dissolution will be, in the Scripture Phrase, a *Sleep in the Lord.*

> And fall, like Autumn fruit that mellowd long,
> Ev'n wondred at, because it dropt no sooner.

You are busie about your New Room to lodge Books in, and I am as busy about a Book[5] to lodge in it: Very Unworthy indeed of Such Company, but not wholly unworthy it will be, because it will consist of nothing but such Doctrines as are inoffensive, & consistent with the Truest Divinity and Morality: what it will want in Spirit, it will make up in Truth. It is with both that I affirm my self, (from Love, & long Experience) │ My dear Lord, │ Your ever obliged & │ affectionate Servant, │ A. Pope

Pray forget not Cleland's Son: It is certainly an honest desire, in a

---

[1] The conclusion is omitted in the editions of 1740–2.

[2] Either Baron Carter (Lawrence Carter, 1672–1745) or Baron Comyns (Sir John Comyns, *d.* 1740), probably the latter.

[3] For some years young Rackett had been preparing for the practice of law, and at the end of his training or thereabouts was passed (May 1729) 'An Act for the better regulation of attorneys and solicitors' that presented an insuperable barrier. Rackett apparently became an estate manager or steward.

[4] An ironic adaptation of Horace, *Epistles,* i. ii. 14: *delirant reges plectuntur Achivi.*

[5] *An Essay on Man.*

Parent, to save a Youth of his own bringing into the World, from the Perils of it.

Lady Oxford & Lady Margaret will know me for their real Servant: My Mother's Prayers will do you, & them, no harm.

Will you never come to London?

Endorsements [In Oxford's hand]: R. Dec. 2: 1730 | at Wimpole.
[In clerk's hand]: Mr Pope.

POPE *to* CARYLL   6 *December* 1730

Add. 28618

Twittenham, 6. Dec. 1730.

I received your very kind letter with real satisfaction, having long wished to hear of you, and being a little sunk in my spirits by two or three such accidents as only affect me, of all with which this world abounds. I mean the misfortunes of some of my friends, and the loss of others. One I have buried, and my mother I had like to have buried: but she is yet (I thank God) lent me a little longer, and lives out of pain.

One of my troubles is about a nephew of mine, a very honest, reasonable, and religious young man, who having nothing, (or very little more than nothing) to depend on but his practice as an attorney, and just come to be qualified in it by fourteen[1] years' application, is deprived all at once of the means of his subsistance by the late act of Parliament disqualifying any from practicing as such, without taking the oaths. After having tried all methods to find favour by personal interest made to the judges, I am convincd no way is left him to live, unless I can procure some nobleman to employ him as a steward, or keeper of his courts on some part of their estates. My own acquaintance (as you know) has happened not to run much in a Catholic channel; and of all the rest I despair. I know, if 'tis possible for you to help me you will. Mr Fortescue (now a great man and the Prince's attorney general) assured me there can nothing else be done, and suggested to me the thought if he could be employed in this capacity by the Lord Petre, offering me to speak to Sir Robert Abdey[2] for him, with whom he has a particular intimacy. I naturally thought of applying to you on my part, and could such a thing be brought about, I should be very happy. The young man's character is every way unexceptionable as well as his capacity, or (I believe you know) I would not propose the

---

[1] Pope had told Lord Oxford (letter of 16 Nov. 1730) of 'nine or ten' years of study. In any case it was a long period.

[2] Sir Robert Abdy was one of the trustees under the settlement of the previous Lord Petre, and Caryll was one of the guardians to his children, under his will.—Elwin.

nearest relation I had, to this, or any other worthy family, or thro' your mediation.

As to your question, if I am writing, I really very rarely dip my pen. The vanity is over: and unless I could hope to do it with some good end, or to a better pitch than I've hitherto done, I would never return to the lists. But the truth is, it is now in my hopes (God knows whether it may prove in my power) to contribute to some honest and moral purposes in writing on human life and manners, not exclusive of religious regards, and I have many fragments which I am beginning to put together, but nothing perfect, nor finished: nor in any condition to be shown, except to a friend at a fire side[1]; I wish you would have so much curiosity to come and pass a few days to see them here. I beg to hear from you sometimes. No man more sincerely wishes the prosperity of your self and family, or better remembers the long friendship with which you have favoured me. My mother is your servant. I am Mrs Caryll's, your son's and both your daughters'. They have an hereditary right to | Dear sir | Your ever affectionate, and | obliged servant | A. Pope.

POPE *to* BROOME

Elwin–Courthope, viii, 165

14 *December* [1730]

Dec. 14, [1730].

I was glad to see your letter this last time, more particularly as I had heard a report from some newspaper of the death of one of your name.[2] I presume it might be the neighbouring clergyman you mention, to whom some of your correspondents' letters have been delivered by mistake, and which makes the distinction needful of doctor to yourself. I will take care of it for the future, whether the gentleman be dead or not. I am sorry to answer yours one way—that is, in recounting the misfortunes of my little family, out of which I have lost one,[3] and been in very great fear of the loss of the best of it, my mother. She had a fall into the fire, but escaped almost miraculously, without being touched, though the gown was consumed on her back, and her head, dressed in muslin, lay upon the coals heaped over the fire. I think there are many reasons to believe as well a particular as a general providence,[4] and the effect of such a belief is of singular use in our

---

[1] Pope in May 1730 had thus shown fragments of the *Essay on Man* and other projects to Joseph Spence. See *Essays on the Eighteenth Century, presented to David Nichol Smith* (1945), pp. 50–51.

[2] *Read's Weekly Journal* (and also *Fog's*) for 21 Nov. had announced: 'The Rev. Mr. Brome, Vicar of Debenham, died some Days ago.'

[3] The identity of the deceased is not clear; such a loss is mentioned also to Caryll, 6 Dec. 1730.

[4] In his *Essay on Man*, now in process of composition, Pope states the case for general Providence and seems to deny particular Providences. Here he says there are many reasons for belief; he probably also assumes that there are reasons *not* to believe in particular interventions of Providence.

life and conduct. I hope you think yourself you have experienced a
part of it, and that your own family is perfectly restored to health.
Sir Clement Cottrell and I remember you sometimes, and never fail
to name poor Fenton and you together. The epitaph on him I thought
you must have seen, as they had got it into the public prints. However,
such as it is, here take it. It is not good in any sense but as it is true, and
really therefore exemplary to others:

> This modest stone, what few vain marbles can,
> May truly say, Here lies an honest man;
> A poet blessed above the poet's fate,
> Whom Heav'n kept sacred from the proud and great;
> Foe to loud praise, and friend to learned ease,
> Content with science in the vale of peace,
> Calmly he looked on either life, and here
> Saw nothing to regret, nor there to fear;
> From nature's temp'rate feast rose satisfied,
> Thanked Heav'n that he had lived, and that he died.

Believe me, with sincerity, and the truest wishes for your felicity,
dear sir, your affectionate friend and servant.

Mr. Fenton's brothers have claimed his effects, papers, &c., and
Mr. Trumbull has delivered them. I hear of nothing but the Book of
Oppian.

POPE *to* LORD BATHURST[1]   18 *December* [1730?]

Elwin–Courthope, viii. 359

Dec. 18.

My Lord,—I am no stranger to the manner in which your life is
passed, the state of your health and the amusements and operations in
your retirement, all which I have heard, as I never fail to inquire, of
your friends or correspondents. In sincere truth I often think myself
(it is all I can do) with your lordship: and let me tell you my life in
thought and imagination is as much superior to my life in action and
reality as the best soul can be to the vilest body. I find the latter grows
yearly so much worse and more declining that I believe I shall soon
scruple to carry it about to others; it will become almost a carcase,
and as unpleasing as those which they say the spirits now and then
use for vehicles to frighten folks. My health is so temporary that if I
pass two days abroad it is odds but one of them I must be a trouble to

---

[1] Elwin printed from the original letter, then in the possession of Lord Houghton, and
the letter has not been seen by the present editor. Its year is uncertain, but it pretty clearly
falls in the period during which Pope was considering the composition of a poetical epistle to
Lord Bathurst.

any goodnatured friend and to his family; and the other, remain dispirited enough to make them no sort of amends by my languid conversation. I begin to resolve upon the whole rather to turn myself back again into myself, and apply to study as the only way I have left to entertain others, though at some expense both of my own health, and time. I really owe you and some few others some little entertainment, if I could give it them; for having received so much from them, in conscience and gratitude I ought not to go to my grave without trying at least to give them an hour or two's pleasure, which may be as much as half the pains of my remaining life can accomplish. And without flattery, my lord, I hope to show you, some day, that I made it one of my first vanities, to be thought your friend, not only while I lived, but when I am gone.[1]

The last time you were in London and Riskins, had I but received the favour of the least knowledge while you was in town, I had gone to see you; and the only day I heard (accidentally) you should be in the country I was in town upon business. Dr. Burton, I hope, told you our joint endeavour to get to you the next day, and then he concluded you gone to Cirencester; but it seems the day after that, and after I had left the town, your lordship sent for him. It was really vexatious to me to be disappointed of that pleasure. I hope your speedy return will make me amends. I am sick at this present writing, but the more I feel the want of health, or of anything else myself, the more I wish them to you and yours. I desire Lady Bathurst, Mr. Bathurst, and the young ladies to accept my services, and yourself, my lord, to believe there is no man living more inclined, more desirous, more impatient, to render you any, were my capacity equal to the sincerity with which I am everlastingly your faithfully obliged servant.

*POPE to [MALLET][2]   29 *December* 1730

The New York Public Library (Berg)
                                                        Decr 29. 1730.

You may judge of the Dissipation of my Life, when I tell you I have lost your Letter, and must answer it at randome and by memory. I have been from home six days, in several places, and only remember that there were in yours many obliging things which ought to be acknowledged. one particular I recollect, about my neighbour Johnson's criticismes, which (I verily believe) are as wild in Poetry as in

---

[1] It is such remarks that lead one to believe Pope wishes to talk with Bathurst about a projected epistle to be addressed to his lordship.
[2] Mallet's *Eurydice* has been accepted and is preparing for presentation. It was acted at Drury Lane 22 Feb. 1730/1. It has recently been presented to the Queen by Pope's neighbour, Secretary James Johnstone, said to have been a great favourite with the Queen but never such with Pope, who would not have chosen him as a messenger.

Politicks! But I must tell you something about him, relating to your Play & to myself, very odd. He carried yours to her Majesty, telling her, it was I that sent, & recommended it to her perusal. The person who heard him say this,[1] reported it to me innocently, as supposing it a matter of fact; I desird her to tell the Queen, that indeed I had read and much liked the Play, that the author was my friend, & that I would say, not only to her Majesty but to Men and Angels, that I both esteemd the author and his Work: But that I did not take upon me to Send it her, and if I had done so, it had been by a Better Messenger.

I hope you will soon be here to look after your child. I wish it good fortune, which is almost all I can do, and I fear it, considering what sort of animals it is to be born among; Things that come into the world with Hair, Teeth, and Tails; rough mischievous, obscene Births. God send you well out of this World! I think it a better wish than well in it; for to be well in it, you must be a Cibber.

I was sorry, not surprisd, in relation to Savage.[2] I have seen him once since I saw you. I have not heard from Mr. Thomson.[3] I wish every ingenious (& still more every honest man) all happiness. Therefore I will not, I need not, tell you how sincerely I am Dear Sir | Yours. | A. Pope.

[1] Lady Burlington?
[2] In November certain newspapers reported that Richard Savage was to succeed Eusden as poet laureate. About the 1st of December Cibber's appointment was announced. Pope is 'sorry, not surprised'.
[3] James Thomson, the author of 'The Seasons'.

The year 1731 was quietly spent by Pope working on the poems that were to appear in 1733–4. In April he sent a form of his Epistle on Taste to Lord Burlington, to whom in print it was to be addressed. For others—Bolingbroke and Pulteney, for example—the year was politically exciting, but the letters reflect little of this, and they reflect no close connexion on Pope's part with the controversial *Grub-street Journal*. In the spring Pope saw much of Bolingbroke, since he went to Dawley when on his diet of asses' milk. To Fortescue the letters, perhaps significantly, say less about Walpole, and confine themselves to business affairs concerning Miss Blount and Mrs. Rackett. The tone of Pope's established friendships does not much change: Gay, Swift, and the Queensberrys loom large in the correspondence, chiefly for what they wrote and Pope edited rather than for what Pope wrote to them. More recent friendships were adjusting themselves—that with Aaron Hill painfully, with David Mallet more smoothly. The background of these and other less evident friendships—with Savage, for example—was Pope's ability to be of service, especially (and curiously) with relation to the production of plays at Drury Lane, where Pope and the players were 'luckily no friends'. In the middle of December appeared his Epistle to Lord Burlington, the first poem by Pope to be printed since *The Dunciad*. Its reception indicated what for the future Pope might expect from his Dunces.

POPE *to* THE EARL OF OXFORD[1]   [1731?]

Longleat Portland Papers, xii

My Lord,—I have much ado to write a word: I have indeed sufferd much pain, & don't know when I shall be able to stir. I dreamt I was with you. I wish I were. But when God knows. Believe me truly sensible of your friendship, and if ever you can My Lord, let me see you with any one you like to bring, The Weather mends I hope, & I'm not quite so bad to day   our faithfullest Services to you all. My Lord affectionatly | & with all respect | Yours

Address: Lord Oxford
Endorsement: Mr Pope

[1] This letter might be written at any time when Pope was suffering from either rheumatism or headaches. Early 1731 was a time when he suffered from both: hence it is at best a possible moment for the letter. Obviously no moment could be sufely determined for it.

POPE *to* JONATHAN RICHARDSON[1]   13 *January* [1730/1]
1739 (and Elwin, ix. 496)

Twitenham, Wednesday the 13th.

I have at last got my Mother so well, as to allow myself to be absent from her for three days. As sunday is one of them, I do not know whether I may propose it to you to imploy in the manner you mention'd to me once. Sir Godfrey call'd imploying the pencil, the prayer of a painter, and affirm'd it to be his proper way of serving God, by the talent he gave him. I am sure, in this instance, it is serving your friend; and you know we are allowed to do that, (nay even to help a neighbour's oxe or ass) on the sabbath: which tho' it may seem a general precept, yet in one sense particularly applies to you, who have help'd many a human oxe, and many a human ass, to the likeness of man, not to say of God.

[If you will let me dine with you I'll get to you by one or very soon after: otherwise if that hour be inconvenient let it be another day.]

[Be pleased to give me a line to Lord Peterboro's in Bolton Street, where I shall either be or at least from whence it will be conveyed to me in time.]

Believe me, dear Sir, with all good wishes for yourself and your family (the happiness of which tyes I know by experience, and have learn'd to value from the late danger of losing the best of mine) |
[your affectionate friend and servant]

SWIFT *to* POPE   15 *January* 1730/1

Longleat Portland Papers, xiii (Harleian transcripts)

Dublin Jan. 15. 1730-1

I have just finished a letter to my Lord Bolin- It is one of my many evenings when I have nothing to do, and can do nothing. read at night I dare not for my eyes, and to write any thing but letters, or those to any but a few friends I find all inclination is gone. I awake so indifferent to every thing which may pass either in the world or my own little domestick, that I hardly think it worth my time to rise, and would certainly ly all day a bed if decency and dread of Sickness did not drive me thence. This I ow not so much to years (at least I would hope so) as to the Scene I am in. . . .

---

[1] This letter was published in the octavo *Works* of Pope, issued by Cooper in 1739. See vi. 225–6 (*1739a*). Elwin printed from an unidentified source called by him 'the Richardson transcript'. The parts here placed in brackets come from Elwin. Pope printed the letter under date of 'Jan. 13, 1732'; but this seems to be an error. Elwin's source gives merely the day of the week, the month, but not the year. In 1731 the 13th of January was a Wednesday, and the remark about 'the late danger of losing' his mother makes 1731 a more plausible year. Lord Peterborow, as other letters show, was at this time available as a host.

I dine tête à tête five times a week with my old Presbyterian House-keeper, whom I call Sir Robert, and so do all my friends & Neighbours. I am in my Chamber at five, there sit alone till eleven, and then to bed. I write Pamphlets and follys meerly for amusement, and when they are finished, as¹ I grow weary in the middle, I cast them into the fire, partly out of dislike, and chiefly because I know they will signify nothing. I walk much every day and ride once or twice a week and so you have the whole State of my life. What you dislike in the letter you saw to a Lady,² I ought also to dislike, and shall do so, although my conscience be clear. For I meant only a reproach in a matter long since at an end, for I did ill explain my self, if it was not understood that I talked of Schemes long since at an end; for sure, if I had any the least hopes left, I would not have writ in a manner to render them desperate, as I think I did, and as I am sure, I intended, both in what I related to her & her Mistress; and therefore I intreat when you see her next, to let her know, that from the moment I saw her last, to the moment I writ to her last, and from that moment to this moment, I never had one single imagination, that the least regard would ever be shown for me.

You reproach me very unjustly for my apology in giving you an account of my self and my little affairs; and yet in your letter there is not a Syllable that concerns your health, which I know is always so precarious, and so seldom as it should be. I can walk 8 or ten Miles a day, & ride 30 Irish ones. You cannot ride a mile nor walk two— Will you dare to think that this doth not hang on my Spirits. I am unhappy in Sickly friends. There are my Lord and Lady Bolin—the Doctor You, and Mr Gay, are not able to contribute amongst you to make up one Sturdy healthy person. If I were to begin the World, I would never make an acquaintance with a poor or Sickly Man, with whom there might be any danger of contracting a friendship. For I do not yet find that years have begun to harden me. Therefore I argue that avarice and hardness of heart are the two happiest qualitys a man can acquire who is late in his life, because by living long we must lessen our friends, and may increase our fortunes.

I have inquired for Mr Brandreth,³ but cannot hear he is yet landed. I shall be very glad of such an acquaintance if he be but one half of what he is described to you; but I shall probably have more need of his countenance than he of mine. Yet with all his Merits, the D. of D. if I had been his Councellor would have waited till himself came over, at least, it would have been more popular to have bestowed those

---

¹ The Harleian scribe wrote *as*; Swift probably wrote *or*.
² For Swift's reproachful letter to Mrs. Howard (21 Nov. 1730) see Ball, iv. 181–4. Pope's natural protest against it was conveyed in a letter not preserved.
³ The Rev. John Brandreth, former tutor to the son of the Duke of Dorset, was now being given valuable preferments in Ireland by his patron the new Lord Lieutenant.

midling preferments at first, to Persons of this Kingdom, as well as
the first great one;[1] and yet he hath already acted otherwise in both,
though he has time enough before him. Lord T[2] in what you write
of him acts directly suitable to his Character, he hath treated twenty
persons in the like manner. Pray tell me whether your Col. Cleland
be a tall Scots Gentleman, walking perpetually in the Mall, and fast-
ning upon every body he meets, as he hath often done upon me? As
to his letter before the Dunciad, I know not the Secret, but should
not suspect him for it.[3] I must tell you how affairs pass between Lord
Chesterfield and me. By your encouragement I writ to him, but named
you not. He sent me a long and gracious answer.[4] As to the point, it
was that he had five dependars, and as many prior Engagements; after
which he would provide for Mr Launcelet. This I took as a jest, but
my answer was thankful and serious: that I hoped his Lordship would
not continue in any post where he could be only an Ornament to the
Court so long till a dozen vacancys should fall and God forbid there
should be ever such a Mortality in any one branch of the Kings family,
that a Dozen people in low offices should dye in less than a dozen
years. So I suppose he finds that we understand each other, and there
is an end of the matter. I have writ to Mr Poulteney to congratulate
with him on his Son.[5] I wait but an opportunity to supply Sir C.
Cotterell's refusal, and when you receive them it will be left entirely
to you, provided you will be as severe a judge as becomes so good and
dear a Friend.[6] My humble service (I must still name them) to my
Lord Bathurst, Oxford, Peterborow (how is his health?) Mr Poulteney,
the Doctor Mr Lewis and Mr Gay; and particularly Mrs Pope.

And pray tell Patty Blount, that I am her constant lover and
admirer.

I had a letter lately from Mr Budgel,[7] the direction a feign'd hand

---

[1] The Duke had made a nephew of Archbishop Tenison (a royal chaplain) Bishop of
Ossory.

[2] Townshend is thought to be meant. Since he ceased to be a member of the Cabinet in
June 1730, the occasion for reference is not clear. Could the reference possibly be to Lord
Tyrconnel, who had hoped to get the laureateship for Savage?

[3] Everyone thought—and perhaps rightly—that Cleland merely signed the 'Letter to
the Publisher' in *The Dunciad Variorum* after Pope had written it. Doubtless Cleland *could*
have written it. It is not clear that Pope's Cleland was ever more than a major. See *DNB*, under
'William Cleland'.

[4] On this unsuccessful attempt to get Chesterfield's patronage for Swift's cousin Launce-
lot see Ball, iv. 177–8 (Swift to Chesterfield, 10 Nov. 1730), 184–5 (Chesterfield's reply,
15 Dec.), and 191–2 (Swift's 'gracious answer', 5 Jan. 1730/1).

[5] Pulteney's only son, recently born, died a year before his father.

[6] One assumes this is a reference to contributions to the final volume of the *Miscellanies*.
Sir Clement is disinclined to let Pope have any of Fenton's poems, and so Swift is supplying
the deficiency and begging Pope to be the severe judge that a dear friend should be. Later he
was dissatisfied with Pope's judgement in the matter.

[7] Budgell's eccentricities were increasing upon him, and after his curious failure in Ireland
he was not likely to win support from Swift. Budgell was already regarded by many as a
madman.

and inclosed to Mr Tickel. He desires I would write to some of my
great friends in England to get him into the H. of Commons there,
where he will do wonders what shall I do? I dare not answer him, and
fear he will be angry. Can nobody tell him that I have no great
friends in England, and dare not write to him.

To Alexander Pope Esq at | Twitenham in Middlesex | By way of London.

BOLINGBROKE *to* SWIFT[1]   *January* 1730/1

1740

                                                        Jan. 1730–1.

I begin my letter by telling you that my wife has been returned from
abroad about a month, and that her health, tho' feeble and precarious,
is better than it has been these two years. She is much your servant,
and as she has been her own physician with some success, imagines
she could be yours with the same. Would to God you was within her
reach. She would I believe prescribe a great deal of the *medicina animi*,
without having recourse to the Books of Trismegistus. Pope and I
should be her principal apothecaries in the course of the cure; and
tho' our best Botanists complain, that few of the herbs and simples
which go to the composition of these remedies, are to be found at
present in our soil, yet there are more of them here than in Ireland;
besides, by the help of a little chymistry the most noxious juices may
become salubrious, and rank poison a specifick[2]—Pope is now in my
library with me, and writes to the world, to the present and to future
ages, whilst I begin this letter which he is to finish to you.[3] What good
he will do to mankind I know not, this comfort he may be sure of,
he cannot do less than you have done before him. I have sometimes
thought that if preachers, hangmen, and moral-writers keep vice at a
stand, or so much as retard the progress of it, they do as much as human
nature admits: A real reformation is not to be brought about by
ordinary means, it requires these extraordinary means which become
punishments as well as lessons: National corruption must be purged by
national calamities. Let us hear from you. We deserve this attention,
because we desire it, and because we believe that you desire to hear
from us.

---

[1] Warton and Bowles dated this letter 17 Jan. Elwin puts the 17 in brackets. Pope gives
no day of the month in his editions, but in the view that Warton may have had a reason for
adding it, the letter is left in its place as if dated the 17th. That day was Sunday—the Sunday
that Pope in the preceding letter planned to spend in town with Richardson.

[2] Thus Pope, 'writing to the world', says that the bee—
     From pois'nous herbs extracts the healing dew.
                                        —*Essay on Man*, i. 220.

[3] The two are in consultation, evidently, over the *Essay on Man*. Pope's part of this letter
was not printed.

HILL *to* POPE   18 *January* 1730/1.
1753 (Hill)

Petty France, Westminster.
January 18, 1731.

Sir,—I wish the *plain dealers*[1] may be worth a place in your library, since, being most of them mine, they are too much your due, to deserve your thanks, and too insignificant to reward your notice.

I send you, with them, a little present, still more due to you; because it was derived from your inspiration three or four years since, in a small branch of my family, not then eleven years old. She came to me one day in my study, to return me your poems, and supply herself with some new book, as usual; being willing to try her taste, I gave her Blackmore's *Prince Arthur*, and told her very gravely, that it was so extraordinary a poem, that the author had been *knighted* for writing it. She took it, with great expectation, and shut herself up in her closet the whole remainder of that day. But, next morning I was surprized to see the book upon a table, placed purposely in my way, with the paper, I enclose you, sticking out between the leaves of it.

You have more right, than I, to the verses, because they are the effect of your own genius, outworking nature, and creating judgment, in an infant, who could see you, but as she saw the *sun*, by a light of your own lending.

You have them, as they came out of her hand, without the least retouching or alteration. I will remark but two things; first, that the eight concluding lines (at an age too weak for *art*, and speaking the language of pure truth and nature) contain a forceful example of the influence of *good* poetry, and of *bad*, which might have given *rest* to the *muse of Sir Richard Blackmore*, had he lived to see and consider it. And the *second* remark (which I make with most pleasure) is, how natural it is in my family to love and admire you.

If, after this, I should inform you, that I have a gentle complaint to make to, and against you, concerning a paragraph in the notes of a late edition of the *Dunciad*,[2] I fear, you would think your crime too

---

[1] A reprint of *The Plain Dealer*, Nos. 1–117, 23 Mar. 1724–7 May 1725, appeared in two volumes dated 1730. It is this reprint that Hill sends with the critique of *Prince Arthur*, which was not printed.

[2] Friendship with Hill was a continual invitation to what Fenton well called *éclaircissement*. This ominous ending of the letter shows concern over the note to *Dunciad* ii. 285 in 1729. The note concerned an unnamed champion in the diving contest who does not sink in mud, but 'mounts far off, among the swans of Thames'. In the 1728 texts the champion had been 'H—'; in 1729 two asterisks suggested 'Aaron'. In no text was he 'Hill'. But the note applied to Hill, and, though in part complimentary, might well serve to remind the swan of 1729 that in chapter vi of 'The Art of Sinking' he had been 'A.H.' among the 'flying fishes'. The footnote in *The Dunciad* kept alive memories of Hill's other errors—graciously forgiven him!

little to deserve the punishment of so long a letter, as you are doomed to, on that subject, from, | Sir. | Your most humble, and | Most obedient Servant, | A. Hill.

POPE *to* HILL   26 *January* 1730/1

1751 (Hill)

Jan. 26. 1730–31.

Sir,—I am oblig'd to you for your Compliment,[1] and can truly say, I never gave you just Cause of Complaint. You once mistook on a Bookseller's idle Report,[2] and publickly express'd your Mistake; yet you mistook a second time, that two initial Letters, only, were meant of you, tho' every Letter in the Alphabet was put in the same manner: And, in Truth (except some few), those Letters were set at Random to occasion what they did occasion, the Suspicion of bad and jealous Writers, of which Number I could never reckon Mr. *Hill.* and most of whose Names I did not know.

Upon this Mistake you were too ready to attack me, in a Paper of very pretty Verses, in some publick Journal.[3]—I should imagine the *Dunciad* meant you a real Compliment, and so it has been thought by many, who have ask'd, to whom that Passage made that oblique *Panegyrick?* As to the Notes, I am weary of telling a great Truth,[4] which is, that I am not Author of 'em; tho' I love Truth so well, as fairly to tell you, Sir, I think even that Note a Commendation, and should think myself not ill us'd *to have the same Words said of me*: Therefore, believe me, I never was other than friendly to you, in my own Mind.

Have I not much more Reason to complain of *The Caveat?* Where give me Leave, Sir, to tell you, with the same Love of Truth, and with the Frankness it inspir'd (which, I hope, you will see, thro' this whole Letter), I am falsly abus'd, in being represented '*sneakingly to approve, and want the Worth to cherish, or befriend Men of Merit.*' It is, indeed, Sir, a very great Error: I am sorry the Author of that Reflection knew me no better, and happen'd to be unknown to those who could have better inform'd him: For I have the Charity to think, he was misled only by his Ignorance of me, and the Benevolence to

---

[1] The compliment was allegedly that of the ten-year-old Urania Hill. See 18 Jan. 1730/1.
[2] See the Preface 'To Mr. Pope' in Hill's *Northern Star* (1718), which attacks, and *The Creation* (1720), which apologizes; more recently *Plain Dealer*, No. 116, had found fault with Pope's Shakespeare, and in 1730 appeared (in reply to either *The Dunciad* or 'The Art of Sinking') Hill's *Progress of Wit: a Caveat. For the Use of an Eminent Writer.* This purported to be by Gamaliel Gunson, but was immediately known to be Hill's.
[3] These are unidentified, but see iii. 170 and n. 1.
[4] In spite of the reiterations of this 'great truth' it has been regarded as a great lie. Pope must have written many of the notes, but he may have had more help than we know of. We know he asked Swift for help, but he probably got none there.

forgive the worst Thing that ever (in my Opinion) was said of me, on that Supposition.

I do faithfully assure you, I never was angry at any Criticism, made on my Poetry, by whomsoever: If I could do Mr. *Dennis* any humane Office, I would, tho' I were sure he would abuse me personally To-morrow; therefore it is no great Merit in me, to find, at my Heart, I am your Servant. I am very sorry you ever was of another Opinion. —I see, by many Marks, you distinguish'd me from my cotemporary Writers: Had we known one another, you had distinguish'd me from others, as a *Man*, and no ill, or ill-natur'd one. I only wish you knew, as well as I do, how much I prefer Qualities of the Heart to those of the Head: I vow to God, I never thought any great Matters of my poetical Capacity; I only thought it a little better, comparatively, than that of some very mean Writers, who are too proud.—But, I do know *certainly*, my moral Life is *superior* to that of most of the *Wits* of these Days. This is a silly Letter, but it will shew you my Mind honestly, and, I hope, convince you, I can be, and am, | Sir, | Your very affec-tionate | and humble Servant, | A. Pope.

HILL *to* POPE　　　　　　　　　　　　28 *January* 1730/1

1751 (Hill)

　　　　　　　　　　　　　　　　　　Jan. 28. 1730–1.

Sir,—Your Answer, regarding no Part of mine, but the Conclusion, you must pardon my Compliment to the Close of yours, in return; if I agree with you, that your Letter is *weaker*, than one would have expected.

You assure me, that I did not know you so well, as I might, had I happened to be known to others, who could have instructed my Ignorance; and I begin to find, indeed, that I was less acquainted with you, than I imagined: But your last Letter has enlighten'd me, and I can never be in Danger of mistaking you, for the future.

Your Enemies have often told me, that your *Spleen* was, at least, as distinguishable, as your *Genius*: And it will be kinder, I think, to believe them, than impute to Rudeness, or ill Manners, the Return you were pleased to make, for the Civility, with which I addressed you.[1]

I will, therefore, suppose you to have been *peevish*, or in *Pain*, while you were writing me this Letter: And, upon that Supposition,

---

[1] This letter has been praised as a manly reply to Pope's letter of two days earlier. Pope understood better than some critics have done the true situation between himself and Hill. Hill, who had recently published, under a pseudonym, an attack on Pope (*The Progress of Wit*), sends Pope a complimentary letter with a copy of *The Plain Dealer* in two volumes. But Pope knew of Hill's attack, and replied to the attacker's 'civility' in a way that annoyed. Now Hill retorts, and his remarks on Pope's 'sneaking' procedures must have hurt.

shall endeavour to undeceive you.—If I did not love you, as a good
Man, while I esteem you, as a good *Writer*, I should read you without Reflection: And it were doing too much Honour to *your* Friends,
and too little to my *own Discernment*, to go to *them* for a Character of
your Mind, which I was able enough to extract from your Writings.

But, to imitate your Love of Truth, with the Frankness you have
taught me, I wish the *Great* Qualities of your Heart were as strong
in you as the *Good* ones: You would then have been above that Emotion and Bitterness, wherewith you remember Things which want
Weight to deserve your Anguish.

Since you were not the Writer of the Notes to the *Dunciad*, it
would be impertinent to trouble you with the Complaint I intended:
—I will only observe, that the Author was in the *Right*, to believe
me capable of a second *Repentance*; but, I hope, I was incapable of
that second *Sin*, which should have been previous to his Supposition.
—If the initial Letters *A.H.* were not *meant* to stand for my Name,[1]
yet, they were, everywhere, read so, as you might have seen in *Mist's
Journal*, and other publick Papers; and I had shewn Mr. *Pope* an
example, how reasonable I thought it to clear a Mistake, publickly,
which had been publickly propagated.—One Note, among so many,
would have done me this Justice: And the Generosity of such a Proceeding could have left no Room, for that offensive *Sneakingly*, which,
though, perhaps, too harsh a Word, was the properest a Man could
chuse, who was satirizing an Approbation, that he had never observed
warm enough to declare itself to the World, but in Defence of the
Great, or the *Popular*.

Again, if the Author of the Notes knew, that *A.H.* related not to
me, what Reason had he to allude to that Character, as mine, by
observing, that I had published Pieces bordering upon *Bombast*—A
Circumstance so independent on any other Purpose of the Note, that
I should forget to *whom* I am writing, if I thought it wanted Explana-
tion.

As to your oblique Panegyrick, I am not under so blind an Attachment to the *Goddess* I was devoted to in the *Dunciad*, but that I knew
it was a *Commendation*; tho' a dirtier one than I wished for; who am,
neither fond of some of the Company, in which I was listed—the
noble Reward, for which I was to become a Diver;—the allegoric
Muddiness, in which I was to try my Skill;—nor the Institutor of the
Games, you were so kind to allow me a Share in.

Since, however, you could see, so clearly, that I ought to be satisfied with the Praise, and forgive the Dirt it was mixed with, I am

---

[1] Possibly, but not probably, 'A. H.' might have been intended to refer to Anthony
Hammond or Anthony Henley. Pope's enemies would gain by asserting Hill was meant;
for Hill would be vocal in reply. Hill probably was meant.

sorry, it seemed not as reasonable, that you should pardon me for
returning your Compliment, with more, and opener, Praise, mixed
with less of that Dirtiness, which we have, both, the good Taste to
complain of.

The *Caveat*, Sir, was mine.—It would have been ridiculous to
suppose you ignorant of it: I cannot think, you need be told, that it
meant you no Harm;—¹ and it had scorn'd to appear under the
borrow'd Name, it carries, but that the whimsical Turn of the Preface, would have made my own a Contradiction.—I promise you,
however, that, for the future, I will publish nothing, without my
Name, that concerns you, or your Writings. I have, now, almost
finished, *An Essay on Propriety, and Impropriety, in Design, Thought,
and Expression, illustrated, by Examples, in both Kinds, from the
Writings of Mr. Pope*; and, to convince you how much more Pleasure
it gives me, to distinguish your *Lights*, than your *Shades*;—and that
I am as willing as I ought to be, to see, and acknowledge my Faults;
I am ready, with all my Heart, to let it run thus, if it would, otherwise,
create the least Pain in you:—*An Essay on Propriety, and Impropriety,
&c. illustrated by Examples, of the first, from the Writings of Mr.* Pope,
and of the last, from those of the Author.

I am sorry to hear you say, you never thought any great Matters of
your *Poetry*.—It is, in my Opinion, the Characteristic you are to
hope your *Distinction* from: To be *Honest* is the Duty of every *plain
Man*! Nor, since the *Soul* of Poetry is Sentiment, can a *Great Poet*
want *Morality*. But your *Honesty* you possess in common with a
Million, who will never be *remembered*; whereas your *Poetry* is a
Peculiar, that will make it impossible, you should be forgotten.²

If you had not been in the *Spleen*, when you wrote me this Letter, I
persuade myself, you would not, immediately after censuring the *Pride*
of Writers, have asserted, that you, *certainly, know* your moral Life,
above that of most of the Wits of these Days: At any other Time, you
would have remembered, that *Humility* is a moral Virtue. It was a
bold Declaration; and the *Certainty* with which you know it, stands
in need of a better *Acquaintance* than you seem to have had with the
Tribe; since you tell me, in the same Letter, that many of their
Names were *unknown* to you.

Neither would it appear, to your own Reason, at a cooler Juncture,
over-consistent with the Morality you are so sure of, to scatter the
Letters of the whole Alphabet, annexed, at Random, to Characters of

---

¹ This is one of the many astonishing statements of the letter. Hill affects the position
that he only wished to cure Pope's spleen—to do him good! And he follows the statement
with threats of further medicine. *An Essay on Propriety* will reappear later in the letters, but
it was never published.

² This paragraph and the next two strike home at the sort of pride in honesty and moral
virtue that was notably excessive in Pope. They had no apparent curative effect.

a light and ridiculous Cast, confusedly, with Intent to provoke jealous Writers, into Resentment, that you might take Occasion, from that Resentment, to expose and depreciate their Characters.

The Services, you tell me, you would do Mr. *Dennis*, even tho' he should abuse you, in Return, will, I hope, give him some Title to expect an Exertion of your recommendatory Influence in his Behalf: A Man, so *popular*, as you, might secure him a great Subscription: This would merit to be called a *Service*; and, the more the World should find you abused in the Works you had recommended, so much the more glorious Proof would they see, that your Morals were, in Truth, as superior, as you represent them, to those of your Cotemporaries. Tho' you will pardon me the *Pride* of wondering, a little, how this Declaration came to be made to *me*, whose Condition not standing in need of such Services, it was not, I think, so necessary you should have taken the Trouble to talk of them.

Upon the Whole, Sir, I find, I am so sincerely your *Friend*, that it is not, in your own Power, to make me your Enemy: Else, that unnecessary Air, of Neglect, and Superiority, which is so remarkable in the Turn of your Letter, would have nettled me to the Quick; and I must triumph, in my Turn, at the Strength of my own Heart, who can, after it, still find, and profess myself, most affectionately and sincerely,[1] | Your humble Servant, | A. Hill.

POPE *to* HILL[2]   *5 February* 1730/1

1751 (Hill)

Parsons Green, Feb. 5. 1730-1.

Sir,—Since I am fully satisfy'd we are each of us sincerely and affectionately Servants to the other, I desire we may be no further misled by the Warmth of writing on this Subject. If you think I have shewn too much *Weakness*, or if I think you have shewn too much *Warmth*, let us forgive one another's Temper. I told you I thought my Letter a silly one; but the more I thought so, the more in sending it I shew'd my Trust in your good Disposition toward me. I am sorry you took it to have an Air of *Neglect*, or *Superiority*: Because I know in my Heart, I had not the least Thought of being any way superior to Mr. *Hill*; and, far from the least Design to shew Neglect to a Gentleman who was shewing me Civility, I meant in Return to shew

---

[1] This affectionate, if hypocritical, conclusion reminds one of l. 112 of the *Epistle to Dr. Arbuthnot*: One 'more abusive calls himself my friend'. But Hill was not there intended, probably.

[2] Pope is writing from Lord Peterborow's house, where he is on a visit. See the end of the letter. No one can imagine that Pope makes a strong reply in this letter, but no one can doubt that he is capable of strong replies! He wishes to be conciliatory. Possibly one would have preferred a stronger tone.

him a better Thing, Sincerity; which I'm sorry should be so ill express'd as to seem Rudeness. I meant but to complain as frankly as you, that all Complaints on both Sides might be out, and at a Period for ever: I meant by this to have laid a surer Foundation for your Opinion of me for the future, that it might no more be shaken by Mistakes or Whispers.

I am sure, Sir, you have a higher Opinion of my Poetry than I myself. But I am so desirous you should have a just one of me every way, that I wish you understood both my Temper in general, and my Justice to you in particular, better than I find my Letter represented them. I wish it the more, since you tell me how ill a Picture my Enemies take upon 'em to give, of the Mind of a Man they are utter Strangers to. However, you will observe, that much *Spleen* and *Emotion* are a little inconsistent with *Neglect*, and an Opinion of *Superiority*. Towards Them, God knows, I never felt any Emotions, but what bad Writers raise in all Men, those gentle ones of Laughter or Pity: That I was so open, concern'd, and serious, with respect to you only, is sure a Proof of Regard, not Neglect. For in Truth, nothing ever vex'd me, till I saw your Epigram against Dr. *S.* and me come out in their Papers:[1] And this, indeed, did vex me, to see *One Swan amongst the Geese.*

That the Letters *A. H.* were apply'd to you in the Papers, I did not know (for I seldom read them); I heard it only from Mr. *Savage*, as from yourself, and sent my Assurances to the contrary. But I don't see how the Annotator on the *D.*[2] could have rectify'd that Mistake, *publickly*, without particularizing *your Name*, in a Book where I thought it too good to be inserted. No doubt he has apply'd that Passage in the *D.* to you, by the Story he tells; but his Mention of *Bombast, only* in some of your *Juvenile Pieces*, I think, was meant to shew, that Passage hinted only at that *allegorical Muddiness*, and not at any *worse sort of Dirt*, with which some other Writers were charged. I hate to say what will not be believ'd: Yet when I told you, "Many ask'd me to *whom* that Oblique Praise was meant?" I did not tell you I answer'd, it was *you.* Has it escap'd your Observation, that the Name is a Syllable too long? Or (if you will have it a Christian Name) is there any other in the whole Book? Is there no Author of two Syllables whom it will better fit, not only as getting out of the allegorical Muddiness, but as having been *dipt in the Dirt of Party-writing*, and recovering from it betimes? I know such a Man, who would take it for a Compliment, and so would his Patrons too—But I ask you not to believe this, except you are vastly inclin'd to it. I will come

---

[1] This epigram, with verses hostile to Pope, appeared in *The Daily Journal*, 16 Apr. 1728, according to Dorothy Brewster in *Aaron Hill* (1913), p. 208.

[2] *D.* is for *Dunciad.*

closer to the Point: Would you have the Note *left out*? It shall. Would you have it expressly said, *you were not meant*? It shall, if I have any Influence on the Editors.

I believe the Note was meant only as a gentle Rebuke, and friend-lily: I understood very well the *Caveat* on your Part to be the same; and complain'd (you see) of nothing but two or three Lines reflecting on my *Behaviour* and *Temper to other Writers*; because I knew they were not true, and you could not know they were.

You cannot in your cool Judgment think it fair to fix a Man's Character on a Point, of which you do not give one Instance? Name but the Man, or Men, to whom I have unjustly omitted Approbation or Encouragement, and I'll be ready to do them Justice. I think I have *publickly* prais'd all the best Writers of my Time, except yourself, and such as I have had no fair Opportunity to praise. As to the *Great* and *Popular*, I've prais'd but few, and those at the Times when they were *least popular*. Many of those Writers have done nothing else but flatter'd the Great and Popular, or been worse employ'd by 'em in Party-stuff. I do indeed think it *no great Pride* in me, to speak about *them* with some Air of Superiority; and this, Sir, must be the Cause (and no other) that made me address *that Declaration* of my Temper towards *them*, to *you*, who had accus'd me of the contrary; not, I assure you, from the least Imagination of any Resemblance between you and them, either in Merit or Circumstances.

I nam'd Mr. *Dennis*, because you distinguish him from the rest: So do I. But, moreover, he was uppermost in my Thoughts from having endeavour'd (*before* your Admonition) to promote his Affair, with Lord *Wilmington*, Lord *Lansdown*, Lord *Blandford*, and Mr. *Pulteney*, &c. who promis'd me to favour it. But it would be unjust to measure my Good-will by the Effects of it on the Great, many of whom are the last Men in the World who will pay Tributes of this sort, from their own un-giving Nature; and many of whom laugh at me when I seriously petition for Mr. *Dennis*.[1] After this, I must not name the many whom I have fruitlessly sollicited: I hope yet to be more success-ful. But, Sir, you seem too iniquitous in your Conceptions of me, when you fancy I call'd such Things *Services*. I call'd 'em but *humane Offices*: Services I said I *would* render him, *if I could*. I *would* ask a Place for Life for him; and I *have*; but that is not in my Power: If it was, it would be a *Service*, and I wish it.

I mention'd the *Possibility* of Mr. *D.*'s abusing me for forgiving him, because he actually did, in Print, lately represent my poor, unde-

---

[1] The implication is that Pope petitioned for subscribers to the projected edition of Dennis's *Works*. The subscription failed. In 1733 Pope aided in organizing a benefit for Dennis, at which *The Provoked Husband* was acted. The benefit came on 18 Dec., and Dennis died on 6 Jan. 1733/4. The Prologue for the benefit was written by Pope. It contained some phrases honest but unkind.

signing, Subscriptions to him, to be the Effect of Fear and Desire, to stop his Critiques upon me. I wish Mr. *Hill* would (for once) think so candidly of me, as to believe me sincere in one Declaration, that "I desire no Man to belye his own Judgment in my Favour." Therefore, tho' I acknowledge your generous Offer to give *Examples* of *Imperfections* rather out of your own Works than mine, in your intended Book; I consent, with all my Heart, to your confining them to *mine*; for two Reasons: The one, that I fear your Sensibility that way is greater than my own (by observing you seem too concern'd at that Hint given by the Notes on the *D.* of a little Fault in the Works of your *Youth* only): The other is a better, namely, that I intend to amend by your Remarks, and correct the Faults you find, if they are such as I expect from Mr. *Hill's* cool Judgment.

I am very sensible, that my *Poetical* Talent is all that may make me *remember'd*: But it is my *Morality* only that must make me *Beloved*, or *Happy*: And if it be any Deviation from *Greatness of Mind*, to prefer Friendships to Fame, or the honest Enjoyments of Life to noisy Praises; I fairly confess that Meanness. Therefore it is, Sir, that I much more resent any Attempt against my moral Character (which I know to be unjust) than any to lessen my poetical one (which, for all I know, may be very just).

Pray then, Sir, excuse my weak Letter, as I do your warm one. I end as I begun. You guess'd right, that I was sick when I wrote it: Yours are very well written, but I have neither Health nor Time to make mine so. I have writ a whole Book of Retractions of my Writings (which would greatly improve your Criticisms on my Errors), but of my Life and Manners I do not yet repent one Jott, especially when I find in my Heart I continue to be, without the least Acrimony (even as little as I desire you should bear to myself), sincerely, Sir, | Yours Affectionately, | A. Pope.

If I did not acknowledge as I ought, both the Father's agreeable Present, and the Daughter's pretty one, which you sent me, I very ill express'd myself. If Miss *Urania Hill* has not my 4*to* Edition of the *Odyssey*, I beg your leave to send it her. You had sooner heard from me, but I saw yours, here, but three Days ago. I return Home To-morrow.

POPE *to* CARYLL   6 *February* 1730/1

Add. 28618

Twittenham 6 Feb. 1730/1

I thank you for your kind promise in relation to my nephew in case of any future opportunity in Lord Petre's family, and I doubted not your long experienced friendship would have assisted me, in him, had the occasion presented. Mr Pigot you know, has lost his son,[1] which I am concerned for. But he told me there was no way for our poor conscientious papists to take but to pass for clerks to some protestants, and get into business thereby, laying hold of their cloaks, as they used to try to get to heaven by laying hold of a Franciscan's habit.

Your recommendation of Pascal's *Pensées* is a good one, (tho' I've been beforehand with you in it) but he will be of little use to my design, which is rather to ridicule ill men than preach to 'em. I fear our age is past all other correction.

I'll now answer all your queries as they lie. *Mount Caburn* I never read, but some little things[2] of that gentleman's Lord Wilmington shewed me, and I liked. *The Art of Politicks* is pretty.[3] I saw it before 'twas printed. There is just now come out another imitation of the same original, *Harlequin Horace*:[4] which has a good deal of humour. There is also a poem upon satire writ by Mr Harte[5] of Oxford, a very valuable young man, but it compliments me too much: both printed for L. Gilliver in Fleet street. I would have sent you some ballads, &c., but your god-daughter was too quick for me, and I suppose you've had a cargo from her. My sister Rackett[6] was my own father's daughter by a former wife. Lady Sola is not so *sola* as I described to you in my last; for her innamorato is returned. I'll say no more of 'em, since I can say nothing good: the thing is too much talked of here. I've seen nothing of Swift's of late, but *Pandora*,[7] which I take to be his, in the *Grub Street Journal*. That paper would often divert you, tho' 'tis very unequal. I'm taken up very unpleasantly in a law suit of my sister's,[8] which carries me too often to London, which neither agrees with my health nor my humour. Adieu | Dear sir | Yours | A. Pope.

HILL *to* POPE   10 *February* 1730/1

1751 (Hill)

[9]Feb. 10. 1731–32.

Sir,—I am oblig'd to you for your Letter from *Parsons Green*, and come heartily into the Proposal, it begins with: A mutual Resolution

---

[1] Counsellor Pigot's son died at his house in Great Ormond Street on 29 Dec. *The Political State* reports him 'a Gentleman of an universal good character'.

[2] By William Hay, who lived near Lord Wilmington in Sussex. Pope had known the Earl of Wilmington (as Spencer Compton) when they both lived in Chiswick.

[3] By James Bramston, vicar of South Harting, near Caryll's place.

[4] By James Miller. It like Bramston's poem praised Pope.

[5] By Walter Harte of St. Mary Hall, Oxon.

[6] On Mrs. Rackett see *The Athenaeum*, 30 May 1857.

[7] 'Pandora' appeared in *The Grub-street Journal*, 28 Jan. 1730/1.

[8] This suit dragged on for years.

[9] The text of Hill's *Works* (1753) adds *Westminster* to the superscription. The *Collection* of 1751 is obviously wrong in its date of 1731–2.

to forget in each other, the Appearance of every Thing, that has been distasteful to either, agrees, I am sure, with the Affection, I feel for you, at my Heart, where it is founded on a natural Strength, both of *Reason*, and *Inclination*.

The *Caveat* began, originally, with the Vision: I added not, till after it was finish'd, those Lines, among which are the unlucky Ones, that displeas'd you. I was fearful, lest, without something of that kind, by way of Introduction, the Reader might think himself push'd, too abruptly, into the Allegory: But, I confess, it was unreasonable in me to cover your *Praise*, which I delighted in, under the Veil of an Allegory; and explain my *Censure*, too openly, in which I could take no Pleasure.

The Truth is, I lov'd you so well, and thought of you so often, that it was not easy for me, in any Humour, to write Verse, and not dwell upon you.—Have you never been *jealous* of a favourite *Mistress?*—Have you never, under a *Pique*, at her suppos'd *Neglect*, said, what she could no more deserve, than you could think she did, upon cooler Reflection?—And have you not found, after all, that you was never the less her *Lover?*

Your Offer is very kind, to prevail on the Editor of the *Dunciad*, to leave out the Note, or declare, that I was not meant in it; But I am satisfied:—It is over;—and deserves no more of your Application.

I agree with you, It is *Morality* makes us belov'd: I know it, from the Effect of your Writings; where I *but admire* the Harmony, and the Elegance, while I *love* the Generosity, and the Candor of the Sentiments. I prefer too, as you do, *Friendships*, and the honest Enjoyments of Life, to *Fame*, and noisy *Praises*; but I am glad you are happier, than you wish to be, who enjoy both Benefits, together.

Yet, if there was nothing desirable in *Fame*, there could be nothing detestable in *Slander*; and your honest Uneasiness, at being *thought* worse than you *are*, would, in that Case, be in Danger of passing for a *Weakness*.

I know, however, that you consider *Praise* in a nobler Light than *Vanity*.—There is, in Fame, the Promulgation[1] of a good Man's Example, which his natural Life being too short to extend so far as he wishes, *That* Defect is supplied by the second Life, he receives, from his *Memory*.

I have seen, and been asham'd of that low Turn, which Mr. *Dennis* gave, to your Good-nature.—Where a Man's *Passions* are too strong for his *Virtues*, his *Suspicion* will be too hard for his *Prudence*: He has often been weak enough to treat you in a Manner that moves too much Indignation against Himself, not to leave it unnecessary for you, also, to punish him.—Neither of us would chuse him for a

---

[1] Promulgation] prolongation *1753*.

Friend; but none of the *Frailties* of his *Temper*, any more than the heavy *Formalities* of his *Style*, can prevent your acknowledging, there is often *Weight*, in his *Arguments*; and *Matter*, that deserves Encouragement, to be met with, in his *Writings*.

I will soon, Sir, convince you, that my Sensibility is not so tender, as you suppose it to be: I am so far from an Inclination to defend some *Pieces*, which I was too much a Boy, when I publish'd, that I embrace all Occasions of exposing 'em, myself, to the Contempt they have merited.¹

I am already too much oblig'd, not to blush at your Mention of the *Odyssey*, with a View of sending it to my Daughter; and *She* is too inquisitive a Lover of what gives her *Instruction* with *Delight*, to have been satisfied without finding, in her Closet, whatever she had heard *you* had publish'd.

As a Proof, how determin'd I am, to throw nothing upon the World, that may give you Cause of Complaint, I will send you, in Manuscript, the *Essay on Propriety*, as soon as it is finish'd: I do the same, now, by a smaller Piece, I am about to publish, because you will find yourself concern'd in some Part of it.²—I am, Sir, with great Truth, | Your most humble, | and most obedient Servant, | A. Hill.

POPE *to* THE EARL OF OXFORD   [11 *February* 1730/1]

Longleat Portland Papers, xii

Thursday Evening. ³[Feb: 11: 1730/1]

My Lord,—Till this day, the violent pain of the Rheumatism in my left arm was such, that I could not bring it near enough to a Table, to write with my other hand. I am like to be confined many days, & am more dissapointed in not being able to wait on your Lordship, than in any other circumstance of my Confinement. Lord Bathurst was here yesterday & found me not fit to be seen: But he promisd me to believe, that notwithstanding the Wry faces I made, I should possess myself Stoically enough in 2 or 3 days, to deserve another Visit, &

---

¹ The text of 1751, edited perhaps by Hill himself, here omits the following sentence printed in his *Works* (1753): 'Let me appeal, for one instance, to the *Plain Dealer*, Numb. 10, wherein you may see I am so unnatural a parent, as to have lost all my primitive fondness, of an offspring, you may imagine to be still my favourite.'

² The text of 1751 here omits a significant sentence that was printed in Hill's *Works* (1753), as follows: 'I do the same now by a smaller piece, I am about to publish, because you will find yourself concerned in some part of it; and I will alter and give a general turn to any particular that relates to *you*, if you but mark the place with a ⛯, when you send back the paper to | Sir, | Your most humble. . . .'

If the 'smaller piece' was Hill's *Advice to the Poets*, its publication came in Mar. 1731. The *Advice* compliments Pope but urges that he should not,

> Stung, by *wit's wasps*, all rights of rank forego,
> And turn, and snarl, and bite, at every foe.

³ The date is in Lord Oxford's hand.

that he would ask you, my Lord, to accompany him & dine here. If you Can pass a day out of town, when nothing invites you but charity, for Gods sake do, on Sunday, or Munday, or Tuesday next. To entertain you, I will show you (as I promisd Him) a Phænomenon worth seeing & hearing, Old Jacob Tonson,[1] who is the perfect Image & Likeness of Bayle's Dictionary; so full of Matter, Secret History, & Wit & Spirit; att almost fourscore.

I've felt so much that Pain is an Evil, that I hope there neither is, nor will be, any in your family. My sincerest wishes are ever for their health & I have a Heart every day telling me what I beg leave to tell your Lordship, that I am wholly | My Lord | Your most obligd, affectionate, | faithfull Servant | A. Pope

If your Lordship can comply with this Extravagant Desire, pray let me know time enough to send for Jacob: there is no depending on Lord B's being punctual in a Message.

Endorsement: Mr Pope Feb. 11. 1730

POPE *to* THE EARL OF OXFORD   [15 *February* 1730/1]

Longleat Portland Papers, xii

One a clock [2][Feb: 15. 1730/1]

My Lord,—I will not say that Our Letters cross each other; but (what is a more pleasing Turn of Thinking,) I will rather say we think of each other mutually at the *Same times*: I am much obligd for your Lordships kind Enquiries: My arm is out of pain, but not yet usefull to me. I am much concernd you could not find a day to pass here: the weather is so inviting, & I so desirous, & which is most rare, Lord Bathurst as setled as the weather itself. My Lord: I am, to you all, a most | Faithfull & obedient humble | Servant | A. Pope

My Mothers Prayers never fail you & Lady Oxford & Lady M.

Address: To the Rt Hon. the | Earl of Oxford. | present
Endorsement: Mr Pope. Feb. 15. 1731/0

POPE *to* HILL   15 *February* 1730/1

1751 (Hill)

Feb. 15. 1731.

Sir,—Ever since I return'd Home, I have been in almost roaring Pain, with a violent Rheumatism in my Shoulder, so that all I am

---

[1] There is a delightful description of Tonson in his old age given in a letter from Samuel Croxall to Jacob Tonson, Jr., 10 Mar. 1732/3, in Add. MS. 28275, ff. 491–2. It has been printed by Professor S. L. C. Clapp in *Jacob Tonson in Ten Letters by and about him* (University of Texas Press, 1948), pp. 19–21.   [2] The date is Lord Oxford's.

able to do is to return you Thanks for yours. The Satisfaction it gave me is proportion'd to the Regard I have for you. I will not praise your Poem further than to say, the Generosity of its Sentiments must charm every Man: Its other Merit you know well. You'll pardon the few Doubts I start in the Interlinings; they are such as you can efface as easily as they may deserve. I wish to tell my Lord *Peterborough* (who has so long honour'd me with so particular and familiar an Acquaintance) the Honour done him.[1]

I am very desirous to leave out that *Note*, if you like so. The two Lords, and one Gentleman, who really took and printed that Edition, I can (I doubt not) bring easily to it.[2]

The chief Objection I have to what you say of myself in this Poem, is, that the Praise is too strong. I may well compound for the rest.

Suffer me to send the young Lady the *Odyssey*, full of Faults as I know it to be, before she grows old enough to know how mean a Present it is. I am, with great Truth, | Sir, | Your most humble | obedient Servant, | A. Pope.

POPE *to* MALLET[3]   [18 *February* 1730/1 ?]
Sir John Murray

Lord Bolingbroke desires you to pass a few hours with him to morrow Evening. I will be there about 6 to meet you, (being in the meantime to go to Parsons green.) I am now getting out of a violent fit of the Headake, which incapacitated my writing in answer to yours, but at all times, sick or well dives, inops, &c Yours faithfully. | A. Pope.

Thursday, twelve a clock

I will try to determine to morrow in what manner to go to the Play, if my health permits it, I fain would.

POPE *to* THE EARL OF OXFORD[4]   [2 *March* 1730/1]
Longleat Portland Papers, xii

My Lord,—Mr Gay tells me of a very kind Design of your Lordships,

---

[1] In his *Advice to the Poets* (1731) Hill urged bards to honour properly captains 'form'd for War's Controll', and in so doing ''spite of *Marlbro's*, do a *Mordaunt* Right'. In the *Works* (1753) the two heroes are reduced to initial M—'s and dashes. Mordaunt, of course, is Peterborow's family name.
[2] The note concerning Hill (*Dunciad* [1728], ii. 283) was omitted. The publication of *The Dunciad* in Mar. 1729 was managed by Lords Bathurst and Oxford and by the Hon. Edward Digby. See Pope to Lord Oxford, 27 Mar. 1729.
[3] On the possibly wild assumption that the postscript of this letter concerns Pope's hope to be present at the first performance of Mallet's tragedy *Eurydice* (22 Feb.), this letter is dated as written on the preceding Thursday. The fact that Pope complains of headache rather than of rheumatism is perhaps against this dating.
[4] Pope subscribed the date 'Tuesday morn.' The more specific dating is in Lord Oxford's hand.

to dine here on Friday, & to bring him & some others with you. Pray do so, it will be the greatest Joy I can receive. I am much more at ease, tho not able, I fear, a long time to go from home, partly for fear of cold, partly from Inability of my arme. Your answer by the bearer will extremely oblige | My dear Lord | Your Ever-sincerely | obligd, faithful Servant | A. Pope.

Tuesday | morn. march. 2. | 1730/1

Lady Oxf. will accept my faithfullest respects.

Address: To the Rt Honble the Earl | of Oxford, | These.

Endorsement: Mr Pope March 2 | 1730/1

POPE *to* THE EARL OF OXFORD   [3 *March* 1730/1]
Longleat Portland Papers, xii

[March 3, 1730/1]

My Lord,—I will with great Joy Expect you. Pray come early | Your Ever-faithful | A. Pope

Address: To Lord Oxford
Endorsement (by a clerk): Mr Pope | March 3. 1730/1
Endorsement (by Lord Oxford): March 3. 1730/1

POPE *to* THE EARL OF OXFORD[1]   [5 *March* 1730/1]
Longleat Portland Papers, xii

[March: 5: 1730/1]
[R. march: 6:]

My dear Lord,—After asking & hoping, that you got well home, tho sorry you made so short a Day of it, (for 'twas almost the Only Day I could count, of so many that I have livd, either in Pain, or without Pleasure.) I recollect, that you was inquisitive to procure this Pamphlet.[2] Pray save yourself the trouble, & accept of This.

I think you will not be displeasd at My Phænomenon:[3] & when I am able, we will go together to see it again I doubt not, my Room[4] will be well aired when I tell your Lordship I hope to inhabit it in five days, if I grow no worse again: (For this very Evening I am in some Pain)

I am, My Lord, with sincere Esteem and gratefulness, | Your most affectionate | faithfull Servant | A. Pope.

Endorsement: Mr Pope March 5. 1730/1

---

[1] The superscribed datings ('R' for 'Received') are both in Lord Oxford's hand.
[2] Unidentified.
[3] Jacob Tonson, with whom Pope, Oxford, and others dined on 19 Mar. See Gay to Swift, 20 Mar. 1731. Pope's remark indicates that Tonson had not been able to come to the dinner at Pope's villa on this day.   [4] At Lord Oxford's house in Dover Street.

POPE *to* THE EARL OF OXFORD[1]   [13 *March* 1730/1]

Longleat Portland Papers, xii

My Lord,—I hoped to have seen you this day, but could find no convenient Vehicle to carry me, without apprehension of cold or accidents. I know the Unmerited Care your Lordship has of me, & beg your pardon for the trouble which I believe airing my apartment &c has given the Good Family. I will some way or other have the pleasure of being yours & my Lady's Domestick in 2 days: I am in the meantime with the sincerest Esteem, her Ladyships, and | My Lord | Your most oblig'd | faithful Servant | A. Pope.

Saturday. | march: 13: 1730/1

Address: To the Rt Hon: the Earl | of Oxford & Mortimer.

Endorsement: Mr Pope | March 13. 1730/1

‖SWIFT *to* GAY *and* THE DUCHESS OF QUEENSBERRY[2]
                                        13 *March* 1730/1

Longleat Portland Papers, xiii (Harleian transcripts)

                                        Dublin, March 13th 1730–1.

⌐Before I go to answer your Letter, I must tell you, that I am perpetually battling against my disorders by riding and walking whether the weather favors or no. I have not for almost two years been rid of a kind of giddyness, which tho' not violent as formerly, keeps me low in Spirits and humor, and makes me a bad Walker whenever it grows towards night: This and some smal returns of deafness have hindred me from Acknowledging yours of above two months old, but that I matter not. What is worse, I have wanted Courage to return my humblest thanks to her Grace the Dutchess of Qu— which I shall leave till I come to her Grace's Part. Mr Pope in all his letters complains he has no Acquaintance with you, and is utterly ignorant of your Affairs.⌐ Your Scituation is an odd one. The Dutchess is your Treasurer, and Mr Pope tells me you are the Duke's. And I had gone ⌐on⌐ a good way in some verses on that Occasion, prescribing Lessons to direct your Conduct, in a negative way, not to do so and so &c like other Treasurers; how to deal with Servants, Tenants and[3] Neighboring Squires, Which I take to be Courtiers, Parliament[4] and Princes in Alliance, and so the Parallell goes on; but grew[5] too long to please me.

---

[1] The date is subscribed by Lord Oxford.
[2] The considerable omissions made by Pope in printing this letter are here placed in half-brackets.
[3] and Neighbouring] or neighbouring *1740–2*.
[4] Parliament] Parliaments *1740–2*.   [5] grew] grows *1740–2*.

⌐I will copy some Lines.¹

> Let some reward to merit be allow'd;
> Nor with your Kindred half the Palace crowd:
> Nor think yourself secure in doing wrong,
> By telling Noses with a Party strong;
> Be rich; but of your Wealth make no parade
> At least before your Master's debts are paid.
> Nor in a Palace built with Charge immense
> Presume to treat him at his own Expence &c²

Then⌐ I prove that Poets are the fittest Persons to be Treasurers and Managers to great Persons, from their Virtue and contempt of money &c—Pray why did not you get a new heel to your Shoe;³ unless you would make your Court at St James's, by affecting to imitate the Prince of Lilliput—But the rest of your letter being wholly taken up in [a] very bad Character of the Dutchess, I shall say no more to you, but apply myself to her Grace.

Madam,—Since Mr Gay affirms that you love to have your own way, and that⁴ I have the same Perfection; I will settle that matter immediately to prevent those ill consequences he apprehends. Your Grace shall have your own way in all Places, except your own house, and the demains about it. There and there onely I expect to have mine. So that you have all the world to reign in, bating onely two or three hundred Acres, and two or three houses in Town and Country. I will likewise out of my *Special grace, certain Knowledge, and meer Motion,* allow you to be in the right against all human kind, except myself, and to be never in the wrong but when you differ from me. You shall have a greater Priviledge in the third Article, of speaking your Mind, which I shall graciously allow you now and then to do even to myself, and onely rebuke you when it does not please me—

Madam—I am now got as far as your Grace's Letter, which having not read this fortnight (having been out of Town, and not daring to trust myself with the Carriage)⁵ the presumptuous manner in which you begin had slipt out of my memory. But I forgive you to the seventeenth line; where you begin to banish me for ever, by demanding me to answer all the Kind⁶ Character⁷ some partial Friends have

---

¹ These five words are in Lord Oxford's hand.
² These lines were included in 'An Epistle to Mr. Gay', where Swift, instructing Gay in duties as agent for the Duke of Queensberry, satirizes the 'stewardship' of Walpole.
³ On shoes and heels see Gay's letter to Swift, 6 Dec. 1730 (Ball. iv. 186). The heir to the throne of Lilliput had one heel higher than the other (a compromise between the factions of high heels and low heels), a fact which caused him to hobble in his gait.
⁴ that] since *1740–2*.   ⁵ Carriage) the] Carriage of it) the *1740–2*
⁶ Kind] good *1741 Labc; 1742 Lbc, Da*.
⁷ Character] Characters *1741 Dab*

given me—Madam, I have lived sixteen years in Ireland, with onely
an Intermission of two Summers in England; and consequently am
fifty years older than I was at the Queen's Death, and fifty thousand
times duller, and fifty million times more peevish perverse and morose;
so that under these disadvantages I can onely pretend to excell all
your other Acquaintance about some twenty barrs length. Pray,
Madam, have you a clear Voice, and will you let me sit at your left
hand, at least within three of you; for of two bad ears, my right is
the best. My Groom tells me that he likes your Park, but your House
is too little. Can the Parson of the Parish play at Backgammon and
hold his tongue? Is any one of your Women a good nurse, if I should
fancy myself sick for four and twenty hours? How many dayes will
you maintain me and my Equipage? When these preliminaries are
settled, I must be very poor, very sick, or dead, or to the last degree
unfortunate, if I do not attend you at Aimesbury. For I profess you
are the first Lady that ever I desired to see since the first of August
1714.[1] And I have forgot the date when that desire grew Strong upon
me, but I know I was not then in England, else I would have gone
on foot for that happyness as far as to your house in Scotland. But I
can Soon recollect the time, by asking Some Ladyes here the Month
the day and the hour when I began to endure their company, which
however I think was a Sign of my ill judgment; for I do not perceive
they mend in anything but envying or admiring your Grace, I dislike nothing in your letter but an affected apology for bad writing
bad Spelling and a bad pen; which you pretend Mr Gay found fault
with wherein you afrount Mr Gay, you affrount me, and you affrount
your self: False Spelling is onely excusable in a chamber-maid for
I would not pardon it in any of your waiting women—Pray God
preserve your Grace and family and give me leave to expect that you
will be So just to number[2] me among those who have the greatest
regard for Virtue, goodness, prudence, Courage and generosity; after
which you must conclude that I am with the greatest respect and
gratitude Madam, your Graces most obedient and most humble
Servant &c

— to Mr Gay.

I have just got yours of Feb. 25[3] with a Postscript by Mr Pope. I
am in great concern for him, ⌈for I did not know that the Rhumatism
was in the number of his disorders. I ow him for a Letter some time
ago that I had from Mr Brandrath, who is gone to his preferments that
are about 300ll. per ann: if any money is to be got by Lands or Tythes
in this most miserable country. God knows I have inducements

---

[1] The day on which Queen Anne died.   [2] number] remember *1740–2.*
[3] Feb. 25] February 24 *1740–2.*

enough to be with you, besides the uneasiness of beggary and desolation in every Scene and person round me. But that law suit of mine, wherein almost my whole fortune depends, is still on foot, for land is to be Sold to pay me, and that is Still delay'd, but I am told will be done in may, I hope from drinking wine by advice, you will arrive to drink it by inclination, else I Shall be a bad companion; for I do it indeed onely by advice, for i love ale better⌐—I find Mr Pope dictated to you the first part ⌐of what he would Say⌐, and with great difficulty some days after added the rest.[1] I See his weakness by his hand-writing, How much does his Philosophy exceed mine, I could not bear to See him, I will write to him Soone.

⌐I received lately a very friendly letter from Mr Pulteney.[2] Adieu, pray God preserve you both. Dr Delany keeps much at his villa about 2 miles from this town, he will be very happy with Mr Pope's kind remembrance of him, I am not perfectly master how to direct to the Duke's house pray tell me.⌐

POPE *to* HILL   14 *March* 1730/1

1751 (Hill)

                                         Twickenham, March 14. 1731.

I am not more happy, nor feel a greater Ease in comparison of my former Pain, in the Recovery from my Rheumatism, than in that from your Displeasure. Be assur'd, no little Offenders ever shall be distinguish'd more by me.[3] Your Dedication pleases me almost equally with the Poem; our Hearts beat just together, in regard to Men of Power and Quality: But a Series of Infirmities (for my whole Life has been but one long Disease) has hinder'd me from following your Advices. I this Day have writ to Lord *Peterborough* a Letter with your Poem. The Familiarity in which we have liv'd some Years, makes it not unusal, in either him or me, to tell each other any thing that pleases us: Otherwise you might think it arrogant in me, to pretend to put so good a Thing into his Hands, in which I have no Merit. Your Mention of our Friend Mr. *Mallet* I thank you for, and should be glad he would give me an Opportunity of thanking you in Person, who am, with Sincerity, | Sir, | Your obliged, and | faithful Servant, | A. Pope

---

[1] Gay wrote to Swift, 20 Mar. 1730/1, 'About a fortnight since I wrote to you from Twickenham, for Mr. Pope and myself. He was then disabled from writing by a severe rheumatic pain in his arm.' The letter of 'a fortnight since' is lost.

[2] Dated 9 Feb. 1730/1. See Ball, iv. 198.

[3] Pope had abandoned 'little Offenders' for the Great in his Epistle on Taste, which he must have been polishing at this time. He sent it to Lord Burlington 4 Apr. (q.v.).

*POPE to THE EARL OF BURLINGTON[1]   [1731?]

Chatsworth

Tuesday.

My Lord,—I am to acquaint your Lordship, that agreably to your Proposal, my Lord Bolingbroke will dine at Chiswick in his way to Twitnam, on Thursday next, where I hope to have the pleasure again of meeting you & him; tho I th[   ][2] you may account me a Domestic[2] already, it being so lately that I left you. I am with constant Truth & Esteem | Your Lordships most obliged & most faithful Servant, | A. Pope.

Address: To the Rt. Hon. the Earl of Burlington.

‖BOLINGBROKE *and* POPE *to* SWIFT[3]   [20 *March* 1730/1]

Longleat Portland Papers, xiii (Harleian transcripts)

[march: 20. 1730|1]

[Bolingbroke writes:]

I have delayed several posts answering your letter of January last,[4] in hopes of being able to speak to you about a Project which concerns us both, but me the most, since the success of it would bring us together,[5] it has been a good while in my head, and at my heart. if it can be set a going you shall hear more of it. I was ill in the beginning of the Winter for near a Week, but in no danger either from the nature of my distemper or from the attendance of three Physicians. Since that bileous intermitting Fever, I have had, as I had before,— better health than the regard I have payed to health deserves. We are both in the decline of life, my Dear Dean, and have been some years going down the hill, let us make the passage as smooth as we can, let us fence against Physical Evil by care, and the use of those means which Experience must have pointed out to us. Let us fence against moral Evil by Philosophy. I renounce the Alternative you propose. But we may, nay if we follow[6] nature, and do not work up imagination against her plainest Dictates; we shall of course grow every year more indifferent to life, and to the affairs and interests of a System out of which we are soon to go, this is much better than Stupidity. the decay of passion strengthens Philosophy, for passion may decay, and stupidity not Succeed, Passions, says our divine Pope,[7] as you will see one time

---

[1] This letter is obviously undatable. Pope in a letter to Lord Oxford, 13 Mar. 1731, uses a phrase similar to 'count me a domestic'; but he might echo himself at a long interval as well as a short.   [2] The edge of the sheet is here torn away.
[3] The date is in the hand of Lord Oxford. In all Pope's texts (1740–2) it is printed March 29.   [4] Unknown.
[5] For settling Swift in England.—Elwin.   [6] follow] will follow *1740–2*.
[7] our divine Pope] Pope, our Divine *1741 Labc*; *1742 Lbc, Da*.

or other, are the Gales of life, let us not complain that they do not blow a Storm. What hurt does Age do us in Subduing what we toil to Subdue all our lives? It is now, six in the morning. I recal the time, and am glad it is over, when about this hour I used to be going to bed, Surfeited with pleasure, or jaded with business, my head often full of Schemes, and my heart as often full of anxiety. Is it a misfortune, think you, that I rise at this hour; refreshed, Serene, and calm? that the past, & even the present affairs of life stand like objects at a distance from me, where I can keep [off]¹ the disagreeable so as² not to be strongly affected by them and from whence I can draw the others nearer to me? Passions in their force would bring all these, nay even future contingencys, about my ears at once, and Reason would but ill defend me in the Scuffle. I leave Pope to speak for himself, but I must tell you how much my Wife is obliged to you. She says she would find strength enough to nurse you, if you was here, and yet God knows She is extreamly weak. The slow Fever works under, and mines the constitution. We keep it off sometimes, but still it returns, and makes new breaches before nature can repair the old ones. I am not ashamed to say to you that I admire her more every hour of my life. Death is not to her the King of Terrors, She beholds him without the least. When She suffers much, she wishes for him as a Deliverer from pain; when life is tollerable, she looks on him with dislike, because He is to separate her from those friends to whom She is more attached than to life it self. You shall not stay for my next, as long as you have for this letter; and in every one Pope shall write something much better than the Scraps of old Philosophers, which were the presents, munuscula, that Stoical Fop Seneca used to send in every Epistle to his Friend Lucilius.

[Pope writes:]³

⌜My Lord promises too much for me. I can write nothing, not even so much as good Scraps, for I'm become but a Scrap of my self, and quite exhausted by a long Pain and Confinement[.] The Doctor puts me into Asses Milk, and I must neither use Study nor Exercise, I'm too weak. I am to do nothing but Sleep and Eat (if I can) were my Life my own, even without Health, I would come and show you the last of me in Ireland. My Spirits continue good, and Fear is a Stranger to me. Mrs. Barber desires I would correct her Verses, truly I should do it very ill, for I can give no Attention to any thing. Whatever Service I can render her, by speaking well &c. I will. Whatever Friends I can get to Subscribe to her, I will. But you know my Circle

---

¹ keep the] keep off the *1740–2*.   ² so as] so far as *1741 Dab.*
³ Pope's portion of this letter was not printed by him. In its place he substituted the postscript properly dated in June 1730 (q.v.). The omission was probably made because this present letter contains trivial personalities.

is vastly Contracted, as I seldom have been out of the Country[1] these two Years. All your Friends She will have without me; and all their Friends. But I'll do all I can. I must in return press you to speak well (as You justly may) of an Abridgment of the Roman History,[2] a Subscription for which is going in Ireland and the Profit of which the Gentleman (who is a very valuable Man and my particular friend) gives to the repairing of St Mary Hall in Oxford. Pray also desire Mr Brandreth from me to promote it what he can.

⌈My hearty Services to Dr Delany. I writ to you the first time I was able, with Mr Gay, about two weeks since. My Mother is yours, and at this present, better than I. I hope your Lawsuit is well ended: how is your health? | Adieu.⌉

Endorsement (Lord Oxford's): Ld. B. & Mr Pope to | the Dean of St. Patricks.

GAY *to* SWIFT[3]   20 *March* 1730/1

Add. 4806

I think 'tis above 3 months ago that I wrote to you in partnership with the Dutchess. About a fortnight since I wrote to you from Twickenham for Mr Pope and myself, he was then disabled from writing by a severe rheumatic pain in his arm but is now pretty well again and at present in town. Lord Oxford, Lord Bathurst, He and I din'd yesterday at Barnes with old Jacob Tonson where we drank your Health. I am again by the advice of Physicians grown a moderate Wine drinker after an abstinence of above two years, and I now look upon myself qualified for society as before.

I formerly sent you a state of the Account between us. Lord B[4] this day hath payd me your principal & interest; the interest amounted to twelve pounds; and I want your directions How to dispose of the principal which must lye dead 'till I receive your orders. I had a Scheme of buying two Lottery Tickets[5] for you & keeping your principal entire; and as all my good fortune is to come, to show you that I consult your advantage, I will buy two more for myself, and you and I will go halves in the ten thousand pounds. That there will be a Lottery is certain, the Scheme is not yet declar'd, but I hear it will

---

[1] Meaning Twickenham. 'Country' is frequently used as 'region' or 'county'.

[2] Elwin thought this a project of Pope's young friend Walter Harte, who had been a student in St. Mary Hall. But it seems more likely to concern the work of Nathaniel Hooke, who was a friend (as Swift was) of Dr. William King, Principal of St. Mary Hall, in which his eldest son was later a student. The son (Thomas Hooke) was not a Catholic, as the father was.

[3] Though not printed by Pope, this letter is inserted because of references to it in other letters of this year.   [4] Bathurst.

[5] Gay was apparently still a commissioner of the State lottery, but ceased to be so in this year.

not be the most advantageous one for we are to have but 3 per Cent. I sollicit for no Court favours so that I propose to buy the tickets at the market price when they come out; which will not be these two or three months. If you do not like to have your money thus dispos'd of, or if you like to trust to your own fortune rather than to share in mine Let me have your orders, and at the same time tell me what I shall do with the principal Summ.

I came to town the 7th of January last with the Duke & Dutchess about business for a fortnight, as it depended upon others we could not get it done 'till now. Next week we return to Amesbury in Wiltshire for the rest of the year; But the best way is always to direct to me at the Duke's in Burlington Gardens near Piccadilly. I am order'd by the Dutchess to grow rich in the manner of Sir John Cutler;[1] I have nothing at this present writing but my Frock that was made at Salisbury and a Bob periwig. I persuade myself that it is shilling weather as seldom as possible and have found out that there are few Court visits that are worth a shilling, in short I am very happy in my present independency, I envy no man, but have the due contempt for the voluntary slaves of Birth and fortune. I have such a Spite against you that I wish you may long for my company as I do for yours; though you never write to me you cannot make me forget you, so that if it is out of friendship you write so seldom to me it doth not answer the purpose. Those, who you would like should remember you, do so, whenever I see 'em. I believe they do it upon their own account, for I know few people who are solicitous to please or flatter me. The Dutchess sends you her compliments & so would many more if they knew of my writing to you.

March 20. 1730/1

Address: To | The Revd Dr Swift | Dean of St Patrick's in | Dublin | Ireland
Postmark: 20/MR

Endorsement: (by Swift) Mr Gay. | Mar. 20th 1730-1 | Answered Apr. 13th | 1731

POPE *to* THE EARL OF OXFORD[2] [3 *April* 1731]

Longleat Portland Papers, xii

[April 3. 1731]

My Lord,—I arrived better than I expected; and am much less in pain, by day, but in the nights, a little Fever, & great Headake returns. I am taking Sweats, which I fear weaken too much, but there's no

---

[1] On Sir John see Pope's third Moral Essay (to Bathurst), ll. 315-34.
[2] The date is in Lord Oxford's hand.

help for't. I will keep within doors and wish to see you. It vexes me to have Better Days without You; reflecting how uneasy I made Your Lordship, as well as felt myself—Instead of writing yesterday a Letter, I resolved to equip my Manuscript[1] to set forward this day But I depend on your Lordships not showing it to any one: You'l lock it up, & when you are weary of Herne & the author of Virgilius the Magicians Life, then cast an eye over it. In the blank leaves after Mr Morice's Letters, I wish the Discourse about Iapis[2] were transcribed, at leisure. You'l see a Memoir in a strange hand at the Beginning of your Manuscript, which mentions some original Letters not yet in your Lordships Library, but they are ready.

I humbly desire Lady Oxford & Lady Margaret to accept my Thanks, the one for her humanity & assistance during my illness, the other for her obliging, sweet, & Thisbæan Conversation thro the Wainscote Wall.

I hope my Lord you'l bring Mr Thomas[3] when you can come this way. Tis better travelling hither even now, than when he set out for Wales last Winter.

My Mother is pretty well, & to all your worthy Family, as I am, an Ever faithfull humble | Servant | A. Pope

Address: To | The Right Hon: the Earl of | Oxford. | with a Book
Endorsement (by a clerk): Mr Pope April 3d 1731.

*POPE to THE EARL OF BURLINGTON   4 April [1731]

Chatsworth
                                                Twitenham Ap. 4th.

My Lord,—I send you the Inclosed[4] with great pleasure to myself. It has been above ten years on my conscience to leave some Testimony of my Esteem for your Lordship among my Writings. I wish it were worthier of you. As to the Thought which was just suggested when last I saw you, of its attending the Book,[5] I would have your Lordship think further of it; & upon a considerate perusal, If you still think so, the few Words I've added in this paper may perhaps serve two ends at once, & ease you too in another respect. In short tis all submitted to your own best Judgment: Do with it, & me, as you will. Only I beg

---

[1] Pope sends with this letter, apparently, some of the transcripts of his correspondence with Atterbury, made very likely during a recent visit to Dover Street and Lord Oxford.

[2] The Discourse about Iapis (by Atterbury) deals with an episode in *Aeneid* xii.

[3] The Rev. Timothy Thomas, Lord Oxford's chaplain, seems to have had much to do with making the transcripts of Pope's correspondence. See Thomas Hearne's *Collections*, ix. 16.

[4] Enclosed is Pope's Epistle to Lord Burlington, 'Of Taste', which was published in December of this year. Lord Burlington evidently had a transcript made (still preserved at Chatsworth) and returned Pope's MS.

[5] i.e. of being prefixed to Burlington's folio vol. of Palladio's designs.

your Lordship will not show the thing in manuscript, till the proper time: It may yet receive Improvement, & will, to the last day it's in my power. Some lines are added toward the End on the Common Enemy, the Bad Imitators & Pretenders, which perhaps are properer there, than in your own mouth. I am with all truth, my Lord | Your most obedient & affectionate | Servant | A. Pope

I hope Lady B. thinks me as I am, her most faithful servant.

POPE *to* HILL   4 *April* 1731
1751 (Hill)

Twickenham, April 4. 1731.

It is a serious Pleasure to me to find you concern'd, that I should do your good Sense and Discernment the Justice it deserves. It is impossible for me not to think just what you would have me on this Head; the whole *Spirit* and *Meaning* of your Poem[1] shews all little Thoughts to be Strangers to your Soul. I happen to know many Particulars relating to the Earl of *Peterborough's* Conduct, and just Glory, in that Scene you draw so well: But no Man ought (I think) to attempt what you hint at, or can pretend to do him more Honour than what you yourself here have done, except himself: I have long press'd him to put together many Papers lying by him, to that End. On this late Occasion he told me you had formerly endeavour'd the same, and it comes into my Mind, that, on many of those Papers, I've seen an Endorsement *A. H.* which I fansy might be those you overlook'd.[2] My Lord spoke of you with great Regard, and told me how narrowly you both miss'd of going together on an adventurous Expedition.[3] The real Reason I carry'd him your Poem was, that I imagin'd you would never send it him, of all Mankind; and that I was truly pleas'd with it.

I am troubled to reflect, how unequal a Correspondent I am to you, partly thro' want of Health (for I have since had a Fever), partly thro' want of Spirits, and want of Solitude; for the last Thing we Poets care to own, is the other Want; that of Abilities.

But I am sensibly pleas'd with your Letter, not only with that which seem'd to prompt it, but with the Things said in it: And I thank you for both—Believe me desirous to see you: When, and where, you shall determine; tho' I wish it were here: You'll see a Place seeming more fit for me than it is; looking Poetical, yet too much in the World; Romantic, and not Retir'd: However, I can lock up all Avenues to it sometimes, and I know no better Reason for doing so, or for shutting out the World, than to enjoy such an one as yourself.

I am, Sir, with Esteem and Sincerity, | Your most obedient | faithful Servant, | A. Pope.

[1] *Advice to the Poets.*   [2] i.e. looked over.
[3] On an Expedition to the West Indies.—Hill, 1751.

POPE *to* MALLET   [*Spring of* 1731]

Sir John Murray

Dawley, Friday.

I am truly sorry to hear of your Illness, in which I ought had I known it to have payd you the Visit of a Friend, in return to your very kind one to me, in Mine. I've been almost constantly here, ever since I began my Regimen of Asses milk.[1] I will not fail to be at home next Thursday or Friday, which of them Yourself can best appoint, for the pleasure of seeing Mr Hill, whose Time I believe may be less at his own disposal than yours, therfore pray try to accomodate it. If I cannot have both pleasures, let me have one: but pray assure him I much desire it: Bowry shall wait on you on Munday or Tuesday next, to know your Day: pray leave a line for him in case you go out, & it shall guide my Motions. My real Service to Mr Savage, & know me for | Yours, | A. Pope

POPE *to* MALLET[2]   [*Spring of* 1731?]

Sir John Murray

Dawley, Saturday.

I hope Dear Sir, you had my Letter on Friday last, in which I sent my Compliments to Mr Hill, (or rather my Desires to see him with you) Pray let a line be left on Munday for my Waterman, to tell me whether you come on Thursday or Friday? for I must go home purposely to meet You, & would chuse not to lye from hence, if possible, in order to continue some Medicines which I take every morning. Contrive to come as early as possible, & stay as late! and if it be by Coach or Water, inform me on Munday; that if I can, I may make it more convenient to you.

adieu. I am sincerely | Dear Sir Your affectionate Servant | A. Pope.

Address: To Mr Mallet, at the | Duke of Montrose's in | Hanover Square. | with speed.

POPE *to* CARYLL   15 *April* 1731

Add. 28618

Apr. 15. 1731.

'Tis indeed true that I had not been hinderd from writing to you, but by such a continued succession of accidents as made [me] incapable

---

[1] The letter is doubtfully dated by the fact that on 20 Mar. Pope and Bolingbroke were together writing to Swift, and in the letter Pope speaks of his diet of asses' milk. He also mentions this to Lord Oxford, 22 Apr. 1731.

[2] One guesses from the compliments sent to Mr. Hill that this letter follows the preceding letter to Mallet by eight days.

of it. First, a violent rheumatic pain settled in the shoulder joint, which was a distemper quite new to me: that kept me sleepless so long till a fever succeeded. A constant course of evacuations and plasters and phlebotomy and blisters, &c., &c., &c. Lastly, another fever from a cold taken after I went out. In the whole, nine weeks pain, confinement, and sickness; from all which I am just now free, whilst God pleases. I know to tell you This, is the chief thing you would hear from me, and next that I am not utterly unresigned to bear them again, if it must be so.

I am going into a course of asses' milk to repair the weakness left behind by those disorders. This very drying cold easterly wind retards my recovery, by preventing the use of exercise and air. I will soon give you a farther account of myself: in the meantime pray think I am always desirous to hear the best I can off from your own hand.[1] It has been particularly happy, that during my disorders, my mother has continued tolerably well, better than for this half year last past. My services wait upon your good family. Believe [me] with sincerity, while I live | Sir | Your affect obliged humble servant | A. Pope.

SWIFT *to* POPE   20 *April* 1731

Longleat Portland Papers, xiii (Harleian transcripts)

Dublin April 20. 1731.

From your own letters as well as one I just had from Mr Gay, I have by no means a good account of your health. The common saying of life being a Farce is true in every sense but the most important one, for it is a ridiculous tragedy, which is the worst kind of composition: I know but one temporal felicity that hath fallen to your share, which is, that you never were a strugler for bread. As to the rest, I mean the esteem of friends, and enemys of your own and other Countrys, your Patience and fortitude, and a long et cetera,[2] they are all Spiritual blessings. The misfortune I most lament is your not being able by exercise to battle with your disorders, as I do by riding and walking, at which however I repine, and would not do it meerly to lengthen life, because it would be ill husbandry, for I should save time by Sitting still, though I should dye seven Years sooner; but the dread of pain and torture makes me toyl to preserve health from hand to mouth as much as a laborer to support life. I am glad you are got into Asses milk. It is a remedy I have a great opinion of, and wish you had taken it sooner. And I wish too you were rich enough to keep a Coach and use it every day you are able; and this you might do if your private Charitys were less extensive, or at least suspended till you were able *nare sine cortice*:[3] I believe you have as good reason as any Christian

---

[1] can . . . hand] can of you from your own hand *Elwin*.
[2] Swift refrains from naming the long care of Mrs. Pope.
[3] Based on Horace, *Satires*, i. iv. 120.

man to be a Stranger to fear, But I cannot endure the thought that you should live in pain, and I believe when Horace said *Quisquis erit vitæ scribam color*;[1] he understood, that Pain was to be excepted. Mrs Barber acted weakly in desiring you to correct her Verses, I desired her friends here to warn her against every thing of that kind. I do believe there was a great Combat between her modesty and her Ambition. I can learn nothing of this Roman history, you did not tell me the Gentleman's name and I know not where to enquire. Mr Brandreth is gone to his livings and will stay there till the D. of D.'s[2] arrival hither, or at least till towards the end of Summer. Perhaps you may hear that I and my Chapter are erecting a Stone over the body of the old Duke of Schomberg, killed at the Boyn, We had applyed often to the Countess of Holderness, now Lady Fitzwalter, for a monument over her Grandfather, and could receive no answer. The Latin inscription hath been printed by the News-writers here, and hath I suppose reached England, and I hear the relations are angry: Let them take it for their pains. I have ordered the Stone to be fixed up. I long to know the Success of your Ass's milk, if it hinders you from Study the world will be the chief Sufferer. Descend in the name of God, to some other amusements as common Mortals do. Learn to play at Cards,[3] or Tables, or Bowls, get talking females, who will go on, or stop at your commands, contrive new tramgams in your Garden or in Mrs Howards, or my Lord Bolingbroke's; or when you are able, go down to Aymsbury, and forget your self for a fortnight with our friend Gay and the Dutchess. Sweeten your milk with mirth and motion. For my own part, I think when a Man is Sick, or Sickly, great Lords and Ladies let them be ever so civil, so familiar and so friendly, are not half so commodious as middling folks, whom one may govern as one pleases, and who will think it an honor and happiness to attend us, to talk or be silent, to laugh or look grave just as they are directed. The old Lord Sunderland was never without one or more of these, Lord Sommers had a humdrum Parson with whom he was used to forget himself for three pence at Backgammon, and our friend Addison had a Young fellow (now of figure in your Court)[4] whom he made to dangle after him, to go where, and to do whatever he was bid. I often thought you wanted two or three of either Sex in such an employment, when you were weary, or Sick, or Solitary, and you have my probatum est; if that be of any value. My old Presbyterian Housekeeper tells me, that if you could bring your Stomach to woman's Milk, it would be

---

[1] *Satires*, ii. i. 60.
[2] Duke of Dorset, the Lord Lieutenant, whose chaplain Brandreth was.
[3] This seems to imply Pope was not a card-player. The celebrated game of ombre in *The Rape of the Lock* would indicate otherwise, and there is at Chatsworth a small drawing that has been thought possibly of Pope with cards in his hand as if playing. But see Kneller's remark, ii. 9.   [4] Carey or Tickell might be intended.

far better then Asses. I would have you contrive to get as much of Summer Air as it is possible, of which we have yet had nothing here but a long run of Northeast winds that have almost ruined my fruit, for I suffer peach and Nectarin and pear-weeds to grow in my famous Garden of Naboth's Vineyard, that you have heard me boast of. I protest to you, that nothing so much discourages me from an English journey as the prospect of Domestick easments when I am from home, and at a distance of such a kind that I cannot come back but by the pleasure of Waves and Winds. However if my health and Law will permit me I shall venture once more to see you.[1] For as to my Law, the land of my Creditor is not sold, but after a dozen hopes I have the thirteenth that it will be done in a Month. Yet then I know not what to do with the money; for Mr Gay tells me I can hardly expect even 4 per Cent. besides the trouble of returning it and safely putting it out: and here I hope to have Six on good Security of Land; if land continues to yield any thing at all, for without a Miracle we are just at our last gasp, beyond the imagination of any one who does not live in this Kingdom. And most of my sorry revenues being of the Tyth-kind; I am forced to watch my Agents and farmers constantly; to get nothing. This, and Years, and uncertain health have sunk my Spirits, and I often wish my self a Vicar in Wales. I ride constantly here but cannot afford to support a couple of horses in England.—

Pardon this particular impertinence of relating my difficulties so contrary to my desires. I was just reading one of your letters three Months old, wherein you are hard on me for saying you were a Poet in favour at Court:[2] I profess it was writ to me either by Lord Bol. or the Doctor. You know favor is got by two very contrary qualitys, one is by fear, the other by ill taste; as to Cibber if I had any inclination to excuse the Court I would alledge that the Laureats place is entirely in the Lord Chamberlain's gift; but who makes Lord Chamberlains is another question. I believe if the Court had interceded with D. of Grafton for a fitter Man, it might have prevailed. I am at the end of my Paper, you are in my constant prayers to your health. I hope you will present my humble service to my List Lord Per[3] Lord Oxford Lord Bol. & Lady Lord Bathurst Lord Masham, Mr Poulteney the Dr Mr Lewis Mrs Pope and Patty very heartily. Nothing to Mrs Howard, you drew me in to write to her, and see how she hath served me,[4] for which She is a—

Endorsement (Lord Oxford's): April. 20: 1731. | Dean Swift to Mr Pope.

---

1 This is not the only remark that contradicts any assumption that after 1727 Swift had no expectation of ever seeing England again.

2 Possibly that of 9 Apr. 1730. There is no such letter of three months back.

3 For *Peterborow*. The scribe more than once in this letter could not read Swift's hand and Lord Oxford wrote in the word for him. Here no addition was made.

4 By not answering. Words fail Swift, and he ends with a dash.

POPE *to* THE EARL OF OXFORD[1]   22 *April* [1731]

Longleat Portland Papers, xii

Apr. 22d | [1731]

My Lord,—I shall be very much obliged to your Lordship in letting this Poem be fairly transcribed in a Folio paper, about   lines[2] in a page. I am daily drinking Asses Milk, which will confine me from rambling farther than betwixt this place & my Dam's Pasture, which is 4 miles off.[3] I lye there & come hither daily, then go to Suck at night again. I hope your Lordship & the Ladyes are in perfect health: one of the best uses I can make of mine, when I have confirm'd it a little more, will be to wait on you again. I am with truth & respect | My Lord, | Your most faithfull | & obligd Servant. | A. Pope.

Endorsement: Mr Pope | April 22. 1731.

POPE *to* THE EARL OF OXFORD[4]   [27 *April* 1731]

Longleat Portland Papers, xii

[April. 27. 1731]

I wish my Lord Oxford would dine at Twitnam next Sunday, or fix any day after it. Witness my hand, | A. P.

If you bring none but Mr Thomas, I dare show you many of my Papers: and I will take This as a Visit only to my said Papers, & Expect another to myself, with what Company your Lordship pleases.

Endorsement (Lord Oxford's hand): mr Pope. | April. 27. 1731

POPE *to* FORTESCUE[5]   [*April* 1731?]

1797 (Polwhele, i. 323)

Thursday morn.

You may reasonably wonder to have not heard of me so long; but for four or five days I intended to see you in town, and have been prevented by a terrible cold, which yet confines me to my chamber. The first day I can get to you I will; in the mean time I write to tell you I cannot forget you and yours. I hope you and they are well. I just now hear Mr. Gay is come to town. I hope to meet all together about Sunday at farthest, for I have three or four days' business, which is very inconveniently put off by my present indisposition. Mrs. Blount

---

[1] The year is superscribed in Lord Oxford's hand; the subscribed endorsement is that of his amanuensis.
[2] The space is left blank in the original.   [3] At Dawley.
[4] The date in both cases is in Lord Oxford's hand.
[5] Gay made visits to London from Amesbury at this time, and the Fortescues were all there by May at least. The letter is undatable.

sends you her services, and will be in town on Saturday. Believe no man more affectionately yours. I am your faithful friend and servant, |
A. Pope.

Address: To Wm. Fortescue, esq. in Bell-yard, near Lincoln's Inn.

GAY *to* SWIFT   27 *April* 1731

Add. 4806

Amesbury, April 27. 1731

Yours without a date I receiv'd two days after my return to this place from London where I stayd only four days, I saw Mr Pope who was much better. I din'd with him at Lord Oxford's who never fails drinking your health & is always very inquisitive after every thing that concerns you. Mr Pulteney had receiv'd your Letter & seem'd very much pleas'd with it, & I thought you very much too in the good graces of the Lady. Sir W Wyndham, who you will by this time have heard hath buried Lady Catherine, was at Dawley in great Affliction.[1] Dr Arbuthnot I found in good health & spirits; His neighbour Mr Lewis was gone to the Bath. Mrs Patty Blount I saw two or three times who will be very much pleas'd when she knows you so kindly remember her; I am afraid Mrs Howard will not be so well satisfied with the compliments you send her. I breakfasted with her twice at Mrs Blounts, & she told me that her indisposition had prevented her answering your Letter, this she desir'd me to tell you & that she would write to you soon and she desires you will accept of her compliments in the mean time by me. You should consider circumstances before you censure;[2] twill be too long for a Letter to make her Apology, but when I see you, I believe I shall convince you that you mistake her. The day before I left London I gave orders for buying two South sea or India Bonds for you which carry four per cent & are as easily turn'd into ready money as Bank Bills; which by this time I suppose is done. I shall go to London again for a few days in about a fortnight or three weeks, and then I will take care of the twelve pound affair with Mrs Lancelot as you direct; or if I hear of Mr Pope's being in town, I will do it sooner by a Letter to him. When I was in town (after a bashfull fit for having writ something like a Love Letter, and in two years not making one visit) I writ to Mrs Drelincourt to Apologize for my behaviour, & receiv'd a civil Answer but had not time to see her; they are naturally very civil so that I am not so sanguine to interpret this as any encouragement. I find by Mrs Barber

---

[1] Lady Catherine (Sir William's first wife) was the daughter of the 6th Duke of Somerset.

[2] Most creditably Gay, Pope, and others defend Mrs. Howard against Swift, who by this time was the only one of the group who still had expectations of her using influence in his favour.

that she very much interests herself in her Affair, and indeed from every body who knows her she answers the character you first gave me. Whenever you come to England if you will put that confidence in me to give me notice I will meet you at your Landing place & conduct you hither, you have experience of me as a traveller, & I promise you I will not drop you upon the road for any visit whatever. You tell me of thanks that I have not given; I dont know what to say to people who will be perpetually laying one under obligations; my behaviour to you shall convince you that I am very sensible of 'em though I never once mention 'em. I look upon you as my best friend & counsellor I long for the time when we shall meet & converse together; I will draw you into no great company besides those I live with, in short, if you insist upon it I will give up all great company for yours. These are conditions that I can hardly think you will insist upon after your declarations to the Dutchess who is more & more impatient to see you, & all my fear is that you will give up me for her which after my ungallant declaration would be very ungenerous. But we will settle this matter together when you come to Amesbury. After all I find I have been saying nothing, for sp[ea]king of her, I am talking as if I were in my own power. You us'd to blame me for oversolicitude about myself, I am now grown so rich that I don't think myself worth thinking on, so that I will promise you never to mention myself or my own Affairs; but you ow'd it all to the inquisitiveness of your friendship; and ten to one but every now and then you will draw me to talk of myself again. I sent you a gross state of my Fortune already, I have not room to draw it out in particulars. When you come over the Dutchess will state it to you. I have left no room for her to write, so that I will say nothing till my Letter is gone, but she would not forgive me if I did not send her compliments.

Address: To | The Revd Dr Swift | Dean of St Patrick's | in Dublin | Ireland | by way of London

Postmark: 28/AP

Endorsement (by Swift): May. 4th 1731 | Mr Gay | Answered Jun. 29th | 1731

*POPE to HUGH BETHEL[1]   [*April* 1731 ?]

Egerton 1948

I can't let the Servant go, without sending you my most hearty Wishes

---

[1] Pope wrote two similar farewell notes to Bethel here placed in Apr. 1731 and May 1732. The two notes might have been written in almost any year after 1721 (when Bethel's brother-in-law, William Codrington, became Sir William) and before 1738, when in December Sir William died. Bethel spent almost every summer in Beverley (Yorkshire), and the farewell notes are placed in these years simply because in them we can definitely date his departures.

for your Health, Prosperity, Pleasure, and Success, in your Journey.
May every thing that can give You, (what you do more than any man
I know to give Others) Ease and Satisfaction, conspire & agree. And
may you as soon, & as well, return to us, as is consistent with your
own Desire. I assure you faithfully, no man's is greater to enjoy your
Conversation & Friendship than that of | Dear Sir | Your ever
Sincere, & obligd | Servant | A. Pope.

I shall come soon & ask Sir Wm how you did when you set out?

Address: To | Mr. Bethel

*POPE to FORTESCUE   1 May [1731]

The Pierpont Morgan Library

I hope this finds you in perfect health & happy, with all your family
in London. & that when next I goe thither I may See You Entire.
I have ever since your absence been creeping up-hill, but slowly, &
now am drinking asses Milk which makes it not proper for me to
interrupt my Course of medicines by going to Town. I writ to you
long since, which I hope you receivd. I had a particular Request that
you will be my Sisters Trustee instead of Essington, who is intractably
troublesome about paying the Money as Mr Cruwys can inform you.
I understand it will be small trouble to you & a matter of meer form.
You will oblige me in it; as I hope twill be putting the last hand to my
Sisters long Vexations, to the freeing her from which You have been
the Sole Instrument all along. I beg one word in answer, when you
have spoken to Mr Cruwys.

I thank God my Mother holds up pretty well, & is your he[ar]ty
Servant. In a little time I hope the Season will invite you, as well as
I do, to look on this place, where you will always find the same sincere
welcome & the same unfeigned Friend in Dear Sir | Yours Ever, |
A. Pope.

May 1st

Address: To | William Fortescue Esq; | in Bell Yard, by | Lincolns Inne. |
London
Endorsement (by Fortescue): Mr Pope | May. 1731.

*POPE to HUGH BETHEL   1 May [1731]

Egerton 1948

I hope you are now happily arrived at the end of your journey, & that
you receivd the advantage of the fine weather & good roads that
ensu'd your departure from London, that you had no reliques of your

Indisposition, and that your affairs will prosper, on which depends that which is the Health of the Mind, Ease. I would fain be told, after you have taken a View about your Tenants &c, that you are loosen'd from the Earth and have shov'd off the dirty acres upon other shoulders than your own: that we may form prospects of living more uninter-ruptedly together; I speak for many besides myself, who I am sure, value you for the same reasons that I do.

Lord Bathurst desires you will take the Lodgings for his Son[1] at the same time that you secure your own, at Scarborough. And Dr Burton will be obliged to you if you can procure him an Exact account from the Physicians at York, what several minerals the Waters are impregnated with? I sent your Letter to Mr Roberts, but from the Supiness or Dishonorable temper of the man, I fear there may be more trouble occasiond than perhaps will be convenient; and in case our friend thinks best to part with it, do you think Coronell could put it off? I think you mentiond something to that Effect, pray did he offer to sell it for you? that in case that part be chosen, we may have a line from you to commission him.

My health is much the same, but I am made to hope better, & an increase of strength (which I find I much want) from the Asses Milk; which I now regularly drink at Dawley, & temper all my other diet accordingly. I desire Mr Moyzer's acceptance of my Services, and am only sorry my Services are worth nothing to my Friends, whom I wish I could some way Serve, and you Dear Sir in particular: I am sincerely tho un-usefully, | Yours affectionately & | faithfully. | A. Pope.

May 1st

Address: To | Hugh Bethel Esqr to be left | at Mrs. Pecket's, in the Shambles in | Yorke

Postmark: 4/MA

POPE *to* THE EARL OF OXFORD   2 *May* [1731]

Longleat Portland Papers, xii

My Lord,—An Accident falls out that will engage me on Wednesday, so I hope it was not the day you thought of passing here, and pray fix any other, why not Thursday? I am with Truth, and (My Lord) as you see, without ceremony, | Your faithfull, affec-|tionate, & obligd Servant | A. Pope.

May 2d | [1731][2]

Address: To the R. Hon. | The Earl of Oxford.

Endorsement (by a clerk): Mr Pope May 2d 1731.

---

1 Probably Benjamin, eldest son of Lord Bathurst.
2 The year comes from the hand of Lord Oxford and of his clerk.

*POPE *to* FORTESCUE¹   [*Spring of* 1731]

Harvard University

I found myself under a mistake as to our Invitation to Mrs Henley: it
being her Sister Mrs. Cornish in Conduit-street. I hope we shall find
Mrs. Fortescue & yourself there about 3, or sooner. Mrs Blount gives
you both her most faithful Services. I have been layd up with my cold,
& ill ever since. I am sincerely ever | Dear Sir | Your affectionate |
Friend & Servant | A. Pope.

    I lye at Lord Bathursts.

Address: To | Wm Fortescue Esqr | in Bell-yard | near | Lincolns Inn

*POPE *to* FORTESCUE²   [*Spring of*] 1731

Harvard University

I was to have waited on you last night (had not a violent fit of the
Headake &c prevented) with a message from Mrs Patty Blount. It
seems Mrs Cornish & she were to have come to you this morning, but
the latter sent word to the contrary, so that she hopes twill be no
disappointment. I fear You have forgot to send to Mr Roberts attorney
(whom Mr Thory knows) to represent to him the necessity either of
paying his annuity or of his Certificate. It would be a favor to Her, if
you would yourself talk to him, for as the matter now stands, tis quite
dead. If I can prevail with a friend who brought me to town, not to
go out of it this day, I'll try to see you in the Evening. I wish you
could pass Sunday or to morrow with us at Twit'nam. Dear Sir,
adieu, I am | Sincerely ever yours, | A. Pope.

Friday 9 oclock

Address: To Wm Fortescue Esq. his | Royal Highness's Attorney | General
in | Bell Yard
Endorsement: 1731.

POPE *to* BROOME   19 *May* [1731]

Elwin–Courthope, viii. 167

                    Twitenham, May 19 [1731].
It was particularly unlucky that I received your letter in an hour
after I had come from London on Thursday evening here. I

---

¹ The letter has to be placed at a time when the ladies concerned and Pope and Fortescue
were in London. As a pure guess it is placed in the spring of 1731.
² This letter bears in two places the date 1731, not in Pope's hand, however. For the
rest, the placing is guess-work.

could otherwise have certainly seen you yesterday or the day before. I had used the precaution to write to Lintot, in case you came to town this month, which in your last you gave me some hope of, to let me know a day or two beforehand, that I might not miss of you. I have been drinking asses' milk these three weeks at a friend's country house some miles from hence,[1] and never lay at home one night, making only a few day visits to my mother. I am pretty well recovered from a very low state, and shall always continue to be affectionately, dear sir, your true friend and hearty servant.

POPE *to* THE EARL OF OXFORD   21 *May* [1731]

Longleat Portland Papers, xii

My Lord,—I was not unmindful of the Command you layd upon me, in relation to further particulars of the Story I told you from Lord B.[2] concerning your Lordships Father & himself. The Persons present at that Meeting, where they consulted about Violence to their Persons, were most of those at that time called the Juncto; the Duke of Marlborough, Lord Sunderland, Lord Wharton, E. of Orford, &c. Prince Eugene in particular was the person, who advised it should be done as either the Treasurer or Secretary went home in an Evening, so as to have the Air of a *Quarrel* or *Rencounter*: (which they thought more practicable in the latter than the former, who kept more regular hours abroad.) Monsieur Buisse the Envoy of Holland in my Lord Bolingbrokes hearing, receivd the whole story from your Father, with the utmost silence & confusion; & afterwards confest it to Lord B. in France. I am uncertain when I shall have the pleasure of seeing you in town, which made me write you this: but whenever Lady Oxford & your self can afford me a Day at Twitnam, I'll pay the Duty of a Night to you on the Water, after this present Week. I am with truth her Ladyship's and | My Lord, | Your most obliged, affectionate Servant, | A. Pope.

Dawley: | May 21st

Address: To the Right Hon: the | Earl of Oxford. | Dover Street | London.
Postmark: 25/MA
Endorsement (by a clerk): Mr Pope | Dawley May 21st 1731

---

¹ At Dawley. In the joint letter to Swift of 20 Mar. Pope had mentioned the asses' milk as in prospect. Apparently the diet was in operation by 15 Apr. Pope's statements as to lapse of time are habitually vague.

² Lord Bolingbroke repeats a story of conspiracy against the 1st Earl of Oxford and himself. The plot arose during the political and military hysteria of 1712, when Prince Eugene was in England. How authentic Bolingbroke's story was is doubtful.

*THE EARL OF BURLINGTON *to* POPE¹   1 *June* [1731]
Chatsworth

an unavoidable accident hinders me from sending my coach this day
to Dawly but if to morrow will be as convenient to you it shall attend
you where you please I hope I need not tell you what concern the
least delay of enjoying your company gives me nor that I am with
the greatest truth dear Sir | your most affectionate faithfull servant |
Burlington

I beg my compliments to | my Lord Bolingbroke

Chiswick June 1

*POPE *to* THE EARL OF BURLINGTON   1 *June* [1731]
Chatsworth

June 1st [1731]
My Lord,—I am always ready & desirous to enjoy the favour &
honour of your Company, & therfore concernd at any disappointment
of it. I find myself under a necessity to be in London all to morrow &
next day: but if Friday will be a Day of Leisure to your Lordship, I
will with great pleasure, wait on you there from Town. My Lord
Bolingbroke bids me to assure you, no man is more your humble
Servant than himself. I am with the greatest Esteem, My Lord, at
all times, | Yours most faithfully, | affectionately, | & mindfully, | A.
Pope.

POPE *to* HILL²   5 *June* 1731
1751 (Hill)

Jan. 5, 1730–1.
Sir,—I was unwilling to answer your too obliging Letter (which puts
much too great a Stress upon my Opinion) till I had read your Play
with the Attention it deserves; I mean, not once, but several times
over. In a Word, to comply with my Judgment will cost you no
Trouble, except to your Modesty; which is, *to act it as soon as possible.*
Nothing but Trifles have I to object, and which were such as did not
once stop me at the first Reading; the Spirit, Design, and Characters,
carrying me on, without Stop, Check, or even Intermission. You certainly are Master of the Art of the Stage, in the manner of forming

---

¹ Pope's reply to this letter, written the same day, is written on a Tuesday, and in 1731
1 June was a Tuesday—and at this time Pope was much at Dawley.
² The first (1751) editor of this letter evidently misread the date as *Jan.* instead of *June.*
In January Pope and Hill were furious with each other; presently friendly, they begin the
comment on Hill's tragedy *Athelwold* in this letter, Elwin first corrected the date.

and conducting the Design, which I think impossible to be mended; of that Great Part, and of the other, the raising the Passions, I will say nothing to you, who know them so much better than myself. I would only point out a few Particularities in Thought or Expression, as material as excepting to a Button on your Coat, or a loose Hair. Two or three Lines I have with great Timorousness written on one of your blank Leaves, in Black Lead, half afraid to be legible, and not without some Hope that *before* you see them, they may be vanished: So may perhaps my Objections, every one of them. Shall I see you soon, to tell you these Nothings? Whenever I shall see you, I hope to find, we can employ the Time better, than I, in telling, or you, in hearing them. Or must I return you the Play now? Your Orders will be obey'd as soon as you give them.—I really rejoice at your Lady's Recovery: I would have her and you think, the Air of *Richmond* is particularly good to re-establish her. Pray let Miss *Hill* know, I am ready to believe all the good Things her own Father can see in her: I can safely trust both his *Judgments*, and his *Affections*. I am, truly, | Sir, | Your obliged and sincerely | affectionate Servant, | A. Pope.

*POPE *to* THE COUNTESS OF BURLINGTON[1]

8 *June* [1731]

Chatsworth

June 8th.

Madam,—As a Proof of my real Gratitude, & in full Recompence for all the Pamphlets you have preserved for my perusal, I beg leave to send you this one; which I am sure will be no small Iniquitous Delight to you, tho not the production of | Madam, | Your most obedient & faithfull | Servant | A. Pope.

I hope, at the end of the week, to come & receive your thanks in person.

POPE *to* THE EARL OF OXFORD[2]   15 *June* [1731?]

Longleat Portland Papers, xii

My Lord,—I am truly obliged for your Lordships very kind Enquiryes after me: I've been once more at Dawley, where my Lameness left me in 2 days, & am now returnd home, which I like as well as any

---

[1] The year date can only be guessed at. The postscript suggests that the letter was written early in the week: 8 June was Tuesday in 1731, and in other years when Pope was in known correspondence with the Countess, the 8th comes late in the week. *The Craftsman* of 22 May had inspired a spate of pamphleteering. Pope's disclaiming authorship of his enclosure may be true or false; he is not known to have written anything in prose at this time.

[2] The year is guess-work. On the original the year 1728 has been pencilled in; but 1731 seems more fitting.

place, since I have a Hope to see you & Lady Oxford here. You'l
be so good to bring whom you like with you, I suppose you'l not forget
Lady Margaret. I am both Theirs, & My Lord, with the sincerest
respect, | Your Ever faithfull | obliged humble Servant | A. Pope.

Twickenham, | June 15.

I believe Sunday is the only day I am ingagd from hence.

Address: To the Rt. Hon. the | Earl of Oxford:
Endorsement: Mr Pope Twickenham | June 15.

POPE *to* KNIGHT[1]   20 *June* [1731?]

Elwin–Courthope, ix. 447

Twitenham, June 20.

It was my intention and my hope to have been able to see Mrs. Knight
and yourself before you left London, which now I fear will not be in
my power, if my sober waterman's account be true. I received to-day
the enclosed, which gives you a farther picture of my friend's desire
to serve you: I am satisfied it is all he can do towards it. And really I
wish it could answer your purposes, because there lives not a more
moral, laborious, nor (I believe) one more proper to educate youth
this way, considering the difficulty of finding people willing, able, and
inoffensively tractable in such a situation. I hope you both enjoy good
health, as (at this very present point of time) I do. That you may long
and together enjoy that and all other earthly felicities is truly the wish
of, dear sir, &c.

‖SWIFT *to* GAY   29 *June* 1731

Longleat Portland Papers, xiii (Harleian transcripts)

Dublin Jun. 29th 1731

Dear Friend,—Ever Since I received your letter, I have been upon a
balance about going to England, and landing at Bristol, to pass a
Month at Aimsbury, as the Dutchess hath given me leave. But my[2]
difficultyes have interfered; first, I thought I had done with my law-
suit, and so did all my Lawyers; but my adversary after being in
appearance a Protestant these 20 years, hath declared he was always a
Papist, and consequently by the law here cannot buy nor (I think) Sell,
So that I am at Sea again for almost all I am worth, But I have Still
a worse evil; for the giddyness I was Subject to, instead of coming

---

[1] Since in this year David Mallet left the family of the Duke of Montrose and became
tutor to Knight's step-son, young Newsham, one infers that this is a letter recommending
Mallet for the place.
[2] my] many *1740–2*.

Seldom, and violent,¹ now constantly attends me, more or less, tho
in a more peaceable Manner, yet Such as will not qualify me to live
among the young and healthy, and the Dutchess in all her youth
Spirit and grandure will make a very ill nurse, and her women not
much better. Valitudinarians must live where they can command, and
Scold; I must have horses to ride, I must go to bed, and rise when I
please, and live where all mortals are Subservient to me. I must talk
nonsense when I please; and all who are present must commend it. I
must ride thrice a week, and walk three or 4 miles besides every day.
I always told you Mrs² Howard was good for nothing but to be a rank
Courtier, I care not whether She³ ever writes to me or no, She³ ⌐has
Cheated us all, and may go hang her Self, and so may her —⌐and you
may tell this to the Dutchess, and I hate to See you so Charitable, and
Such a Cully, and yet I love you for it, because I am one my Self. ⌐A
P— on her for hendring me from going to France where I might
have recovered my health,⁴ and She did it in a most treacherous manner,
when I layd it upon her honor,⌐ you are the Sillyest lover in Christendom, If you like Mrs⁵ why do you not command her to take you, if
She does not, She is not worth pursuing, you do her too much honor,
She hath neither Sense nor taste if She dares to refuse you, though She
had ten thous'd pounds. I do not remember to have told you of thanks
that you have not given, nor do I understand your meaning, and I
am Sure I had never the least thoughts of⁶ my Self. If I am your friend
it is for my own reputation, and from a principle of Self-love, and I do
Sometimes reproach you for not honoring me by letting the world
know we are friends:⁷ I See very well how Matters go with the
Dutchess in regard to me. I heard her Say, ⌐prethee⌐ Mr Gay fill your
letter to the Dean that there may be no room for me, The frolick is
gone far enough, I have writ thrice I will do no more, if the man hath
a mind to come let him come; what a clutter is here? ⁸*poliliveles* I
will not write a Syllable more, ⌐The jest is grown Stale.⌐ She is an
ungratefull Dutchess considering how many adorers I have procured
her here over and above the thousands She had before, I cannot allow
you rich enough till you are worth 7000ll, which will bring you 300ll
per ann. and this will maintain you with the perquisite of Spunging

---

¹ violent] violently *1741Dab.*   ² Mrs. Howard] Mr.—*1740–2.*
³ She] he *1740–2.* Passages in half-brackets are omitted, *1740–2.*
⁴ In his letter to Mrs. Howard, 27 July 1731 (Ball, iv. 247), Swift urged this reproach,
and she, replying 25 Sept. 1731 (Ball, iv. 263–5), makes a sensible and dignified defence.
⁵ Mrs. Drelincourt is the mistress here alluded to.
⁶ of my] of any my *1741 Labc.* (This strange passage refers to Gay's letter to Swift, 27
Apr. 1731.)
⁷ This was a persistent vanity with Swift. As far back as 1709 (Ball, i. 169) he urged
Ambrose Philips to mention him in a poem, and he repeatedly begged Pope, '*Orna me!*' He
was not content with the mention of him in *Dunciad* I, but valued highly that in Pope's
Imitation of the First Epistle of the Second Book of Horace, ll. 221–4.
⁸ As gloss on this word in the margin of the sheet is written, *positively.*

while you are young, and when you are old will afford you a pint of Port at night, two Servants and an old Maid, a little garden, and pen and ink provided you live in the Country,⌐—you never mentioned whether you were Seriously a manager for my Lord Duke in his estate, which the Doctor and Mr Pope absolutely affirm. And pray what will you do with my 200ll? will it yield nothing in the funds?[1] and what are you doing towards encreasing your fame and your fortune,⌐ have you no Scheam either in verse or prose? The Dutchess Should keep you at hard meat, and by that means force you to write; and So I have done with you.

Madam,—Since I began to grow old I have found all Ladyes become inconstant without any reproach from their consciences.[2] If I wait on you, I declare that one of your women, which ever it is that had designs upon a Chaplain, must be my nurse, if I happen to be Sick or pevish at your house: and in that case you must Suspend your domineering Claim till I recover. your omitting the usuall appendix to Mr Gay's Letters, hath done me infinite mischief here; for while you continued them, you would wonder how civil the Ladyes here were to me, and how much they have altered Since. I dare not confess that I have descended So low as to write to your Grace after the abominable neglect you have been guilty of; for if they but Suspected it, I Should lose them all, one of them who had an inclin of the matter (your Grace will hardly believe it) refused to beg my pardon upon her knees, for once neglecting to make my rice milk—Pray consider this, and do your Duty, or dread the consequences.[3] I promise you Shall have your will Six minutes ⌐in⌐ every hour at Aimsbury, and Seven in London, while I am in health. But if I happen to be sick, I must govern to a Second. Yet properly speaking there is no man alive with so much truth and respect Your Grace's most obedient and devoted Servant the Dean.

Pray tell Her Grace, that Mr Ford (whose affairs keep him here against his heart) toasts her every day, which is a great matter, for he hath thrown off all except Her Grace and Harrietta Pitt.[4]

THE DUCHESS OF QUEENSBERRY *and* GAY *to* SWIFT[5]
18 *July* 1731

Add. 4806

July thee Eighteenth | 1731

[DUCHESS:] You are my Dear freind, I am sure, for you are hard to

---

[1] In his letter of 27 Apr. Gay had told Swift the bonds were at four per cent.
[2] consciences] conscience *1740-2*.   [3] consequences] consequence *1740-2*.
[4] This lady was either the mother or the sister of William Pitt, Earl of Chatham.—Elwin.
[5] This letter is written solidly, without paragraphing or indication as to which of the two writers was holding the pen. Their handwriting was somewhat similar, and the whole

be found; that you are so is certainly owing to some Evil genius, for if you say true this is the very properest place you can repair to, there is not a Head here upon any of our Shoulders that is not at some times worse than yours can possibly be att your worst & not one to compare with yours when at best (except your friends are your sworn Lyars) so in one respect at least you'll find things just as they could be wishd tis farther necessary to assure you that the Dutchess is neither young or healthy. She lives in all the Spirits that she can and with as little grandeur as she can possibly, she too as well as you, can scold & command, but she can be silent, & obey, if she pleases—& then for a good Nurse tis out of dispute that she must prove an excelent one, who has been so experienc'd in the infirmitys of others & of her own. as for talking nonsense provided you do it on purpose she has no objection. there's some sense in nonsense when it does not come by Chance. in short I am very sure that she has set her Heart upon seeing you att this place. here are women enough to attend you, if you should happen not to approve of her. she has not one fine Lady belonging to her, or her house. She is impatient to be govern'd, & is chearfully determin'd that you shall quietly enjoy your own will & pleasure as long as ever you please. [GAY:] You shall ride; you shall walk, & She will be glad to follow your example, and this will be doing good at the same time to her & your self.

I had not heard from you so long that I was in fears about you & in the utmost impatience for a Letter. I had flatter'd myself your Lawsuit was at an end & that your own money was in your own pocket, & about a month ago I was every day expecting a summons to Bristol.[1] Your Money is either getting or losing something for I have plac'd it in the funds, for I am grown so much a man of business, that is to say so covetous, that I cannot bear to let a summ of money lye idle. Your friend Mrs H. is now Countess of Suffolk,[2] I am still so much a dupe that I think you mistake her. Come to Amesbury & you & I will dispute this matter & the Dutchess shall be judge. But I fancy you will object against her, for I will be so fair to you as to own that I think she is of my side. But in short you shall chuse any impartial referee you please. I have heard from her, Mr Pope hath seen her, I [be]g that you would suspend your judgment 'till we talk over this affair together, for I fancy by your Letter you have neither heard from her or seen her, so that you cannot at present be as good a judge as we are. I'll be a Dupe for you any time, therefore I beg it of you that you would let me be a Dupe in quiet.

constitutes a sort of game or trick played upon Swift, who has to distinguish authors as best he can. The implied friendly informality existing between her Grace and Gay is pleasing. This sort of joking is continued in later letters to or from Swift and his epistolary pair at Amesbury. [1] To meet Swift, who might land there.
[2] Her husband succeeded his brother in the title in June of this year.

As you have had several attacks of the giddiness you at present complain of, & that it hath formerly left you, I will hope that at this instant you are perfectly well; though my fears were so very great before I receiv'd your Letter that I may probably flatter myself & think you better than you are.

As to my being a Manager for the Duke you have been mis-inform'd. Upon the discharge of an unjust Steward, he took the Administration into his own hands. I own I was call'd in to his assistance when the state of affairs was in the greatest confusion; like an Ancient Roman I came, put my helping hand to set Affairs right, and as soon as it was done, I am retir'd again as a private man. [DUCHESS:] What you imagin'd you heard her say was a good deal in her Stile, t'was a thousand to one she had said so, but I must do her the justice to say that she did not either in thought or word; I am sure she wants to be better acquainted with you, for which she has found out ten thousand reasons that we'll tell you if you'll come. [GAY:] By your Letter I cannot guess whether we are like to see you or no. Why might not the Amesbury Downs make you better? [DUCHESS:] Dear Sir Mr Gay tells me I must write on upon his line for fear of taking [up] too much room. T'was his fault that I omitted my Duty in his last letter, for he never told me one word of writing to you till he had sent away his letter, however as a mark of my great humility, I shall be ready & glad to aske your pardon upon my knees as soon as ever you come, tho not in fault. I own this is a little mean Spirited, which I hope will not make a bad impression, considering you are the occa-tion. I submit to all your conditions, so pray come, for I have not only promis'd myself, but Mr Gay also the Satisfaction to hear you talk as much nonsense as you can possibly utter. [GAY:] You will read in the Gazette of a friend of yours who hath lately had the dignity of being disgrac'd;[1] for he & every body (except five or six) look upon it in the same Light. I know were you here, you would congratulate him upon it. I payd the twelve pounds to Mrs Lancelot for the uses you directed. I have no Scheme at present either to raise my fame or fortune; I daily reproach myself for my idleness; you know one cannot write when one will; I think and I reject; one day or other perhaps I may think on something that may engage me to write. You and I are alike in one particular, (I wish to be so in many) I mean that we hate to write upon other folk's Hints. I love to have my own Scheme and to treat it in my own way; this perhaps may be taking too much upon myself, & I may make a bad choice, but I find I can always enter into a

---

[1] William Pulteney had in Jan. fought his bloodless duel with Lord Hervey, and had joined in violent attacks on Walpole centring on *The Craftsman* for 22 May 1731. Early in July his name was ordered to be struck off the list of privy councillors and from commissions of the peace. Thus he joined the Queensberrys in the joys of 'disgrace'.

Scheme of my own with more ease & pleasure than into that of any
other Body. I long to see you, I long to hear from you; I wish you
health, I wish you happiness; & I [shou]ld be very happy myself to be
witness that you [enjoy my wishes].

Address: To | The Reverend Dr Swift | Dean of St Patrick's | In Dublin |
Ireland | by way of London.

Postmark: 19/IY

Endorsement (by Swift): Rx Jul 25th 1731 | Mr Gay and | Du—s of Qu—

SWIFT *to* POPE[1]   20 *July* 1731

Victoria & Albert Museum (Forster)

Jul. 20th, 1731.

I writ you a long letter not many days ago which therefore did not
arrive till after your last that I receivd yesterday with the inclosd from
me to the Qu—. You hinted something of this in a former letter. I
will tell you sincerely how the affair stands. I never was at Mrs Bar—s
house in my life, except once that I chancd to pass by her shop, was
desird to walk in and went no farther, nor stayd three minutes. Dr
Delany hath been long her Protector, and he being many years my
acquaintance desired my good offices for her, & brought her several
times to the Deanery. I knew she was poetically given, & for a woman,
had a sort of genius that way. She appeard very modest & pious, and I
believe was sincere, and wholly turnd to Poetry. I did conceive her
Journey to England was on the score of her trade, being a woollen-
draper, till Dr Del— said she had a design of printing her poems by
subscription, and desired I would befriend her; which I did chiefly by
your means. The Dr still urging me on, upon whose request I writ to
her 2 or 3 times, because she thought that my countenancing of her
might be of use. Lord Carteret very much befriended her, and she
seems to have made her way not ill. As for those 3 letters you mention
supposed all to be writ by me to the Qu on Mrs B's account, especially
the letter which bears my name, I can only say, that the apprehensions
one may be apt to have of a friend doing a foolish thing is an effect of
Kindness, and God knows who is free from playing the fool some time

---

1 The torn and fragmentary original of this letter is preserved in the Forster Collection
of the South Kensington Museum. With it is preserved the 'counterfeit' letter of 22 June
sent from Dublin to the Queen, and signed with Swift's name. The letter is not in his hand,
and he had some reason to be angry with Mrs. Barber, whom the letter recommended to
Her Majesty. Any anger speedily vanished, but in 1733 when Mrs. Barber was concerned
in the publication of Swift's *Of Poetry: A Rhapsody* she fell into legal difficulties, and the
possibility that she had written forged letters to the Queen may have served her ill as background to this later difficulty. She was innocent in the matter of this and two other letters
to the Queen, and remained high in Swift's favour.

or other: but, in such a degree as to write to the Qu— who hath used me ill without any cause, and to write in such a manner as the letter you sent me, and in such a Style, and to have so much zeal for one almost a stranger, and to make such a description of a woman as to prefer her before all mankind, and to instance it as one of the greatest grievances of Ireland, that Her M— hath not encouragd Mrs B—, a woollen-drapers wife, declind in the world, because she hath a knack at versifying, was to suppose or fear a folly so transcendent that no man could be guilty of who was not fit for Bedlam. You know the letter you sent inclosed is not my hand; and why I should disguise and yet sign my name, should seem unaccountable; especially when I am taught and have reason to believe that I am under the Qu—'s displeasure on many accounts, and one very late, for having fixed up a Stone over the burying place of the D. of Schomberg in my Cathedrale, which however I was assured by a worthy person, who sollicited that affair last summer with some relations of the Duke, Her M, on hearing the matter, said they ought to erect a monument. Yet I am told assuredly, that the K— not long ago on the representation and complaint of the Prussian Envoy (with a hard name) who hath marryd a granddaughter of the Duke, said publickly in the drawing room, that I had put up that stone out of malice to raise a quarrell between His M. and the K. of Prussia. This perhaps may be false, because it is absurd, for I thought it was a Whiggish action to honor D. Schomberg, who was so instrumental in the Revolution and was Stadtholder of Prussia, and otherwise in the service of that Electorate which is now a Kingdom. You will observe the letter you sent me, concluded Your Majesty's loyall Subject, which is absolutely absurd; for we are only Subjects to the K; and so is Her M— herself. I have had the happyness to be known to You above 20 Years; and I appeal whether you have known me to exceed the common indiscretions of mankind, or that when I conceived my self to have been so very ill usd by her Majesty, whom I never attended but on her own commands, I should turn sollicitor to her for Mrs B. If the Qu had not an inclination to think ill of me, she knows me too well to believe in her own heart, that I should be such a coxcomb. I am pushed on by this unjust suspicion to give up so much of my discretion, as to write next post to my Lady Suffolk on this occasion, and to desire she will shew what I write to the Qu— though I have as much reason to complain of her as of Her M— upon the score of her pride and negligence, which make her fitter to be an Irish Lady than an English one. You told me she complaind that I did not write to her; when I did upon your advise, and a letter that required an answer, she wanted the civility to acquit her self. I shall not be less in the favor of God or the esteem of my friends, for either of their Majesty's hard thoughts, which they only take up from misrepresentations. The first time I saw the Qu, I took occasion upon the subject of Mr Gay to complain of that very treatment which innocent persons often receive from Princes and great Ministers, that they too easily receive bad impressions; and although they are demonstrably convincd that those impressions had no grounds, yet they will never shake them off. This I said upon Sir R. W's treatment of Mr Gay, about a libel, and the Qu fell intirely in with me; yet now falls into the same error. As to the Lett¹ *************************** of accidents, & out of perfect commiseration, &c.

Endorsement (by Swift): Letter to Mr. Pope | about my pretended | Letter to the Qu— &c.

*POPE *to* HUGH BETHEL   28 *July* 1731

Egerton 1948

July 28. 1731.

According to my Promise of writing to you, conditionally, that you will not put your eyes to the trouble of answering me, except when something happens to you, good or ill, which a Friend has a right, (from his Desire) to know: I now assure you of the Continuance & un-interrupted Series of my best Wishes & Concerns for you. My own health is not worse than usual, my Mothers is better, and Mrs Bs much as it is accustom'd to be; & She herself much as she is accustom'd to be: not so careful of it as we wish. These are the persons, about whom your friendship will be most interested in this Neighbourhood; tho to tell you Lady Suffolk is happy, will give you (I doubt not) that Pleasure, which I fancy the happiness of all Man- & Woman-kind would give you. I have just finished an Epistle in Verse, upon the Nature & Extent of Good nature & Social affection; & am going upon another whose subject is, The True Happiness of Man, in which I shall prove the Best Men the happiest, & consequently you should pull off your hat to me, for painting You² as the happiest man in the Universe. I do not think it will at all diminish that felicity, if I should acquaint you that the King does not go his Progress this Summer, and that even your (too-much-beloved) Yorkshire, will be deprivd of the Joy his Aspect would have given it. Do you think the County would

---

¹ Here the paper is accidentally torn. There seem to be wanting eight small quarto lines, and the letter concludes with those few words on the back of the page which follow the asterisks.—Deane Swift.

² The Epistle finished is the third of the *Essay on Man*; that now in process is the fourth. Epistle IV, ll. 123–30, has especial reference to Bethel. Bethel's love of simple living and diet led Pope to use him as substitute for Horace's Ofellus in the Imitation of the Second Satire of the Second Book, which Pope published in 1734, about six months after the fourth Epistle of the *Essay on Man* was in print.

This sentence about happiness was printed by Ruffhead (1769), p. 256 n.

be the less Northern, if his Majestys gracious Countenance had shined upon it? tho Horace said of his Augustus,[1]

> Instar veris enim, Vultus ubi tuus
> Affulsit, populo gratior it Dies,
> Et Soles melius nitent.

I fear the People of your Climate must expect their health & Spirits this year rather from the Scarborow waters. I fancy you are there, & I wish I were with you. Mr Bathurst, you perceive by the Newspapers,[2] is preparing to dip & taste of another sort of Spring, which has not often the same Effect of invigorating the nerves, and easing pains & Tumours in the Head, but the contrary. Mr Cleland has been here 2 days: & every day I've seen him, here or elsewhere, drinks your health. Mr Fortescue was to write to you for some Receits for Roberts &c. and a letter for him (which is but too necessary) therfore I say no more of it here; and Mrs B.[3] is just as sollicitous and careful, of her Pecuniary Life, as of her Bodily one: But she forgets not You so much as she does herself, & always is enquiring of you. My Mother is your mindful Servant, and I with all sincere Esteem | Dear Sir, | Your faithful Friend | & affectionate Servant | A. Pope.

Address: To Hugh Bethel Esqr to | be left at Mrs Pecket's in | Yorke
Postmark: 29/IY

BOLINGBROKE *to* SWIFT[4]   2 *August* 1731

Add. 4806

I am indebted to you, my Reverend Dean, for a letter of a very old date. the Expectation of Seeing you from week to week which our friend Gay made me entertain hindered me from writing to you a good while, & I have since deferred it by waiting an opportunity of sending my letter by a safe hand. that opportunity presents itself att last, and Mr Echlin[5] will put this letter into your hands. You will hear from Him and from others of the general State of things in this Country, into which I returned, and where I am confined, for my Sins. if I entertained the notion, which by the way I believe to be much older than Popery, or even than Christianity, of making up an account

---

[1] *Carmina*, IV. v. 6–8.
[2] The newspapers evidently printed reports as to projected matches for Lord Bathurst's son Benjamin. On the day of this letter his lordship was writing to Lord Strafford concerning newspaper reports on negotiations. The son was finally married late in 1732.
[3] Martha Blount.
[4] The letter is printed only in part by Elwin. Hawkesworth printed it entire in 1766, and it is so printed here from the original.
[5] Presumably the Rev. John Echlin, a friend and adviser of Swift.

with Heaven, and demanding the Ballance in Bliss, or paying it by good works & sufferings of my own & by the merits & sufferings of others, I should imagine that I had expiated all the faults of my life, one way or other, since my return into England. one of the circumstances of my Situation which has afflicted me most, and which afflicts me still so, is the absolute inutillity I am of to those whom I should be the best pleased to serve. Success in serving my friends would make me amends for the want of it in disserving my Enemys. it is intollerable to want it in both & yet both go togather generally. I have had two or three projects on foot for making such an Establishment here as might tempt you to quit Ireland. one of them would have succeeded, & would have been agreable in every respect, if Engagements to my Lady's Kinsman, who did not I suppose deserve to be your Clarke, had not prevented it. another of them cannot take place without the consent of those who would rather have you a Dean in Ireland than a Parish Priest in England, & who are glad to keep you where your sincere friend[1] my late Lord Oxford sent you. a third was wholy in our power. But when I enquired exactly into the value, I found it less than I had beleived, the Distance from these Parts was great, & besides all this, an unexpected, & groundless Dispute about the right of presentation, but still such a Dispute as the Law must determine, had arisen. you will please to beleive that I mention these things for no other Reason than to show you, how much those friends deserve you should make them a visit att least, who are so desirous to settle you amongst them. I hope their endeavours will not be always unsuccessful.

[2]I received some time ago a letter from Dr Delany, & very lately Mr Pope sent me some sheets which seem to contain the substance of two sermons of that gentlemans. the Philosophia prima is above my reach, and especially when it attempts to prove that God has done or does so and so, by attempting to prove that so and so is essential to his attributes or necessary to his design, and that the not doing so and so would be inconsistent with the former, or repugnant to the latter. I content my self to contemplate what I am sure He has done, & to adore Him for it in humble Silence. I can demonstrate that every cavil which has been brought against the great system of the world, physical and moral, from the Days of Democritus and Epicurus to this day, is absurd. But I dare not pronounce why things are made as they are, state the ends of infinite wisdom, & shew the proportion of the means.

Dr Delany in his letter to me mentioned some errors in the critical part of learning which he hoped he had corrected, by shewing the

---

[1] The description is intended as irony.
[2] Elwin omitted this and the following two paragraphs.

mistakes, particularly of Sir J: Marsham, on whose authority these
errors were built. Whether I can be of use to him even in this part I
know not, for having fixed my opinions long ago concerning all
ancient History & chronology, by a careful examination into the first
principles of them, I have ever since layed that study totally aside. I
confest in the letter I writ lately to the Doctor, notwithstanding my
great Respect for Sir John Marsham, that his authority is often precarious, because He leans often on other authoritys which are so. But
to you I will confess a little more. I think, nay I know, that there is
no possibility of making any system of that kind without doing the
same thing, & that the defect is in the Subject not in the writer. I have
read the writings of some who differ from him, & of others who undertook particularly to refute him. it seemed plain to me that this was the
case. all the materials of this sort of Learning are disjoynted & broken.
Time has contributed to render them so, & the unfaithfulness of those
who have transmitted them down to us, particularly of that vile fellow
Eusebius, has done even more than Time itself by throwing these
fragments into a different order, by arbitrary interpretations, & it is
often impossible to make any others, in short by a few plausible guesses
for the connexion & application of them, a man may with tollerable
ingenuity prove almost any thing by them. I tryed formerly to prove
in a learned dissertation, by the same set of authoritys, that there had
been four Assyrian monarchys, that there had been but three, that
there had been but two, that there had been but one, & that there
never had been any.

I puzzled myself, & a much abler man than myself, the friend to
whom I lent the manuscript, & who has I beleive kept it. in short I
am afraid that I shall not be very useful to Dr Delany in making
Remarks on the work he is about. His communication of this work
maybe useful, & I am sure it will be agreeable to me. if you and He
are still in Ireland, pray give my best services to Him, but say no more
than may be proper of all I have writ to you.

I know very well the project you mean, & about which you say
that Pope & you have often teazed me.[1] I could convince you, as He is
convinced, that a publication of any things of that kind would have
been wrong on many accounts, & would be so even now. Besides, call
it Pride if you will, I shall never make either to the present Age, or to
Posterity, any Apology for the part I acted in the late Queen's Reign.
But I will apply myself very seriously to the composition of just and
true Relations of the Events of those times, in which both I and my
friends & my Enemys, must take the merit or the Blame which an
authentick & impartial Deduction of fact will assign to us: I will
endeavour to write so, as no man could write, who had not been a

---

[1] They urged that he write the history of his own times.

Party in those transactions, & as few men would write who had been concerned in them. I beleive I shall go back in considering the political Interests of the principal Powers of Europe as far as the Pyrenæan treaty. But I shall not begin a thread of History till the Death of Charles the 2d of Spain, & the accession of Q: Anne to the Throne of England. nay even from that time downwards, I shall render my Relation more full, or piu magra, the word is Father Pauls,[1] just as I have or have not a stock of authentick Materials. these shall regulate my work, & I will neither indulge my own vanity, nor other men's curiosity in going one step further than they carry me. You see my Dear Swift that I open a large feild to my self. with what success I shall expatiate in it, I know as little as I know whether I shall live to go thro' so great a work. But I will begin imediately, & will make it one principal Business of the rest of my life. this advantage att least I shall reap from it, and a great advantage it will be. my attention will be diverted from the present scene. I shall greive less att those things which I cannot mend. I shall dignify my Retreat, and shall wind up the labours of my life in serving the cause of truth. you say that you could easily shew by comparing my Letters for twenty years past how the whole system of Philosophy changes by the several gradations of Life. I doubt it. as far as I am able to recollect, my way of thinking has been uniform enough for more than twenty years. true it is, to my shame, that my way of acting has not been always conformable to my way of thinking. my own passions, & the passions & Interests of other men still more, have led me aside. I launched into the Deep before I had loaded Ballast enough. if the ship did not sink, the Cargo was thrown overboard. the storm it self threw me into Port.[2] my own opinion my own Desires would have kept me there. the opinion the desires of others sent me to sea again. I did, and blamed myself for doing, what others, & you among the Rest, would have blamed me if I had not done. I have payed more than I owed to Party, and as much att least as was due to friendship. if I go off the stage of publick life without paying all I owe to my Enemys, & to the Enemys of my Country, I do assure you the Bankrupcy is not fraudulent: I conceal none of my effects.

does Pope talk to you of the noble work which, att my instigation, he has begun, in such a manner that He must be convinced by this time I judged better of his tallents than He did?[3] the first Epistle which considers man, and the Habitation, of man, relatively to the whole system of universal Being, the second which considers Him in his

---

[1] Paolo Sarpi, the historian.

[2] Bolingbroke had taken refuge in the port of philosophy in 1708, when he retired from politics, and more notably when in exile after the death of Queen Anne. The remark about too little ballast may indicate that the earlier retirement is here in mind.

[3] This passage concerns Pope's progress on the *Essay on Man*. See also iii. 209.

own Habitation, in Himself, & relatively to his particular system, & the third which shews how an universal cause

works to one end, but works by various laws,

how Man, & Beast, & vegetable are linked in a mutual Dependancy, parts necessary to each other & necessary to the whole, how human societys were formed, from what spring true Religion and true Policy are derived, how God has made our greatest interest & our plainest Duty indivisibly the same, these three Epistles I say are finished. the fourth he is now intent upon. 'tis a noble subject. He pleads the cause of God, I use Seneca's Expression, against that famous charge which atheists in all ages have brought, the supposed unequal Dispensations of Providence, a charge which I cannot heartily forgive you Divines for admitting. you admit it indeed for an extream good purpose, and you build on this admission the necessity of a future state of Rewards & punishments. But what if you should find that this future state will not account for Gods justice, in the present state, which you give up, in opposition to the atheist? would it not have been better to defend God's justice in this world against these daring men by irrefragable Reasons, and to have rested the proof of the other point on Revelation? I do not like concessions made against Demonstration, repair or supply them how you will. the Epistles I have mentioned will compose a first Book. the plan of the Second is settled.[1] you will not understand by what I have said that Pope will go so deep into the argument, or carry it so far, as I have hinted.[2] You enquire so kindly after my wife that I must tell you something of her. she has fallen upon a Remedy invented by a surgeon abroad, & which has had great success in cases similar to hers. this Remedy has visibly attacked the original cause of all her complaints, and has abated in some degree by one gentle & uniform effect all the greivous & various symptoms. I hope, & surely with Reason, that she will receive still greater benefit from this method of cure which she will resume as soon as the great heat is over. if she recovers, I shall not for her sake abstract myself from the world more than I do att present in this place. But if she should be taken from me, I should most certainly yeild to that strong desire, which I have long had, of secluding my self totally from the Company & affairs of mankind, of leaving the management even of my private affairs to others, and of securing by these means for the rest of my life an uninterrupted tenor of philosophical Quiet. I suppose you have seen some of those volumes of scurrility which have been thrown into the world against

---

[1] Of the plan of his 'ethic epistles' Pope gave various accounts. See Spence, pp. 16, 48, 315.

[2] Pope has practically nothing on 'a future state' in the *Essay on Man*. The absence of mention need not imply absence of belief since the *Essay* pretended to have a rationalistic or empirical basis.

Mr P: and myself,[1] and the Craftsman which gave occasion to them. I think, and it is the sence of all my Friends, that the Person who published the final answer took a right turn in a very nice & very provoking circumstance. to answer all the falsitys, misrepresentations, & Blunders which a club of such scoundrels as Arnold, Concanen, and other Pensioners of the Minister, crowd togather, would have been equally tedious & ridiculous, and must have forced several things to be said neither prudent, nor decent, nor perhaps strictly honourable to be said. to have explained some points, & to have stopped att others, would have given strength to that impertinent suggestion Guilt alone is silent in the Day of Enquiry. it was therefore Right to open no part of the scene of the late Queen's Reign, nor submit the passages of her admini-stration, & the conduct of any of her Ministers, to the examination of so vile a Tribunal. this was still the more Right because upon such points as relate to subsequent transactions and as affect me singly, what the Craftsman had said was justifyed unanswerably, and what the Remarker had advanced was proved to be infamously false. the effect of this paper has answered the Design of it, and, which is not common, all sides agree that the things said ought to have been said, & that more ought not to have been said. the publick writers seem to be getting back from these personal altercations to national affairs, much against the grain of the Minister's faction. what the effects of all this writing will be I know not, But this I know that when all the information which can be given is given, when all the spirit which can be raised is raised, and all to no purpose, it is to no purpose to write any more. even you men of this world have nothing else to do, but to let the ship drive till she is cast away, or till the storm is over. for my own part I am neither an owner, an officer, nor a foremast man. I am but a Passenger, said my Lord Carbury.

it is well for you that I am got to the end of my paper, for you might else have a letter as long again from me. if you answer me by the post, remember whilst you are writing that you write by the post. Adieu my Reverend Friend—

Aug: the 2d | 1731.

Endorsement (In Swift's hand): Lord Bolingbroke. | Dated Aug. 2d. 1731 | Rx Octr 10th. 1731 | Answerd Octr 30: 1731

---

[1] Bolingbroke's letter in *The Craftsman*, 22 May 1731, had provoked many attacks, both on himself and on Pulteney. One was *Remarks on The Craftsman's Vindication*. Pulteney's reply to this caused his dismissal from the Council. Bolingbroke himself was the author of the *Final Answer*.

THE EARL OF OXFORD *to* POPE   : 10 *August* 1731

Longleat Portland Papers, xii

Aug: 10: 1731.
Down Hall

Sir,—It is a very long time Since I have heard from you,   I trouble
you to ask how you do, & how good mrs pope does,   I have staid
here much longer then I designed but found the air so agreable and the
quiet of the place that I have in some degree laid aside all thoughts of
London but that I hear there is nobody in town, & as I have some
hopes of seeing you there that I shall I belive be tempted to see it
soon but not Sooner then a letter from you will reach this place. my
compliments to your good mother   my Wife & peggy desire the Same
to her & to you.—

Lord Dupplin & Dr middleton desire you will accept of their
humble Services. I am with true respect & esteem | Sir your most
faithfull humble | Servant | Oxford

Address: For | Alexander Pope Esq; | at Twickenham | Middlesex
Frank: Oxford
Postmark: 11/AV

POPE *to* THE EARL OF OXFORD[1]   15 *August* [1731]

Longleat Portland Papers, xii

Aug. 15.

My Lord,—Your Lordships Letter gave me great pleasure, & the
greater, as it was a mere Deed of Goodness without my Merit, so a
proof of your Partiality to me, as well as Favour. The true reason of
my silence was Expectation every day of your return, which at length
was driven so far off, that in despair of you, I ran away to Lord Cobham's at a single days warning. I was transported hither by the
Impetuous Spirit of the Brigadier Dormer,[2] & am to be hurryd back
by a Reflux of the same violent Tyde in two days. I hope to find your
Lordship in Town on Thursday: if I do, all the Happiness which
that place can give me, will be mine. & if I do not see You, I will not
see It, this whole season.

I desire Lady Oxford to know I am much her Servant, & as a
proof, I have the happiness to give her the good News of Faustina's
Health, & safe Delivery. which my Lady Cobham just now receivd
under her own hand, but not in her own name,[3] but that of Madam

---

[1] The letter is written from Stowe, where Pope is the guest of Lord Cobham.
[2] James Dormer, brother of Col. Robert Dormer of Rousham.
[3] Faustina Bordoni, operatic soprano, who in 1726 won great popular success in rivalry
to Cuzzoni, in 1730 married the composer J. A. Hasse.

Hessé, the person she has married. I presume it will not be long before Lady Oxford has it notifyed to her in like manner. For we here are of opinion, that these two Ladies will be pitched upon (to the Envy of all the other Ladies of Great Britain Italy & Germany) to stand God Mothers.

More-over the said Faustina, alias Mrs Hesse, hath sent to Lady Cobham divers Notes of Musick & New Airs, which those that can play & sing shall communicate to the less deserving who are meer Auditors & Auditoresses.

Pray let Lord Duplin remember me as his most humble Servant; and believe me (My Lord) my head must have lost its Sense, & my hand its cunning, if I am not always glad to feel myself & proud to call and write myself | Your most obliged & most | faithfull Servant | A. Pope.

Lord Cobham desires your acceptance of his real Service. Lady Cobham has charged me with hers to my Lady. I shall never meet Dr Middleton[1] any other way than with my services.

Address: To | the Right Hon. the | Earl of Oxford, in | Doverstreet | Piccadilly | London |
Postmark: 16/AV
Endorsement: Mr Pope Augt 15. 1731.

POPE *to* JOHN KNIGHT[2]   23 *August* [1731]

Stowe 755

Stowe, Augst the 23d [1731]

Sir,—The Place from which I write to you will be a proof, alone, how incapable I am of forgetting you & your Gosfield; for if any thing under Paradise could set me beyond all Earthly Cogitations; Stowe might do it. It is much more beautiful this year than when I saw it before, & much enlarged, & with variety. Yet I shall not stay in it by a fortnight so long, as I did (with pleasure) with you. You must tell Mrs Knight She has been spoken of, & her health toasted, here; & that Ld Cobham sends his Services, with a Memorandum to perform her promise of seeing this place. If she keeps it, I do not despair to live, (partly by my own exemplary Temperance, & partly by the assistance of Mother Vincent,) to meet you both here another Season. I [shall] yet think it a diminution to my happiness, to miss of half our

---

[1] Presently Lord Oxford was less intimate with the Cambridge librarian, and in the *Epilogue to the Satires* (Dialogues I, l. 75) Pope bravely ventured to disparage the Latinity of Middleton.

[2] The year is in an early hand, but not Pope's. It is probably correct, but in that case Pope did not return to London 'in two days' as he had planned to do. See Pope to Oxford, 15 Aug.

Companions & Compotators of Syllabub, not to have Mr Newsham, and his Dogs, & his Præceptors, and his dearly beloved Cosen, and his Mathematics, & his Greek, & his Horses. Without a Complement to all, or any of them, I never passed an easier & more agreeable Month, in spite of some Ill health, & some Melancholy, than that of July last. I hope you will long enjoy that Tranquillity & that Satisfaction, which you spread over all that is about you. I often wish Mr Mallet joy[1] in my own heart of his having exchangd such a whining, valetudinary, cloudy, journalier Companion as my Self, for the Goodhumour, Serenity, & Indulgence of your Family. I am pretty sure he will deserve it all. Mrs Patty languishes in Town, & diets there on Fools, in defect of Friends. I am sorry to forsake her at such a time, & she is more sorry you live at such a distance: her Sister affirms, nobody of Sence can live 6 miles out of London, and indeed I know nothing that can set her right, but the free Use of the Cane you bestowd upon me, & which I could wish to bestow upon her. I can't say my Rambles contribute much to my health, yet I take no corporeal medicaments, but wholly apply to remedies of the mind: if human Philosophy will not do, I must desire Mrs Elliot to pray for me. My next Journey is to Southampton to my Lord Peterborow, where also I have a Catholick Friend[2] who will take care of my soul & shall dine with a Jesuit, thrice a week, worth all the Priests in Essex, if you except Mr Tripsack.

I desire you all to accept of my faithfull Services, and to know no man is more mindful of you, than | Dear Sir | Your most obliged | & affectionate | Servant, | A. Pope.

Address: To John Knight Esqr; at | Gosfield, near | Braintree | Essex.

Postmark: 25/AV

||SWIFT *to* GAY[3]   28 *August* 1731

Longleat Portland Papers, xiii (Harleian transcripts)

                                     ⌜The Country.⌝ Aug. 28. 1731

You and the Dutchess use me very ill, for I profess I cannot

---

[1] We do not know at what precise date Mallet became tutor to Mr. Newsham. The decision to leave the Montrose family was contemplated in June (see Pope to Knight, 20 June), and the decision has now been made. But since the address of Pope's letter to Mallet, 1 Sept. 1731, indicates that Mallet is still with the Montroses, one must here assume that Pope is happy over Mallet's prospects rather than over a status actually achieved. Mention of *preceptors* in the plural suggests a transitional stage in young Newsham's education. The letter can hardly date 1732, since Pope was not at that time at Stowe. In Aug. 1731 he was there. Evidently in 'July last' Pope was at Gosfield.

[2] Mrs. Robinson, secretly married to Lord Peterborow, was a Catholic. The *also* refers to the fact that Mrs. Elliot, Mrs. Knight's sister, was a convert to Catholicism.

[3] Pope's texts of this letter (1740–2) make several omissions, here placed in half-brackets. Swift's comments on the handwriting of Gay and his duchess refer to their letter to Swift, 18 July 1731.

distinguish the Style or the handwriting of either. I think Her Grace writes more like you than her self, and that you write more like her Grace than yourself. I would swear the begining of your letter ⌜was⌝ writ by the Dutchess, though it is to pass for yours; because there is a cursed lye in it, that she is neither young or healthy, & besides it perfectly resembles the part she owns. I will likewise swear, that what I must suppose is written[1] is your hand, & thus I am puzzled & perplexed between you, but I will go on in the innocency of my own heart. I am got eight miles from our famous Metropolis to a Country Parsons, to whom I lately gave a City living, such as an English chaplain would leap at.[2] I retired hither for the publick good having two great works in hand, one to reduce the whole politeness wit, humor & style of England into a short System for the use of all persons of quality, and particularly the Maids of Honor:[3] The other is of almost equal importance; I may call it the whole duty of servants, in about twenty several Stations from the Steward & waiting woman down to the Scullion & Pantry boy.[4]—I believe no mortal had ever such fair invitations as ⌜I⌝ to be happy in the best company of England. I wish I had liberty to print your letter with my own comments upon it. There was a fellow in Ireland called Conolly,[5] who from a shoe-boy grew[6] to be several times one of the chief Governors, wholly illiterate, & with hardly common sence.[7] a Lord Lieutenant told the first K.[8] George, that Conolly[9] was the greatest subject he had in both Kingdoms, and truly this Character was gotten & preserved by Conolly's[10] never appearing in England, which was the only wise thing he ever did except purchasing sixteen thousand pounds a year. Why you need not stare: it is easily applyed. I must be absent in order to preserve my credit with her Grace. ⌜One thing I like well enough, that you & the Dutchess absolutely govern the family, for I have not heard one syllable of my Lord Duke, who I take for granted, submits to all your decrees. I writ some time ago to your new lady Suffolk,

---

¹ is written is] is written by the Duchess is *1740–2*.

² Swift is visiting the Rev. John Towers at Powerscourt, to whom he has given the living of St. Luke's, Dublin.—Ball, iv. 258 n.

³ The reference is to his *Complete Collection of Genteel and Ingenious Conversation* (1738).

⁴ This was to be *Directions to Servants in General* (1745).

⁵ fellow ... who ... grew] fellow in Ireland called C——, who from a shoe-boy grew *1740* person in Ireland called ****, who from a very low birth grew *1741 Dab.* fellow in Ireland who from a shoe-boy grew *1741 Labc; 1742 Labc, Da.*

⁶ The shoe-boy was the exceedingly influential William Conolly (d. 1729), Speaker and Lord Justice in Ireland. In the first of his *Drapier's Letters* Swift had advertised Conolly's wealth by saying: 'Squire C——y has Sixteen Thousand Pounds a Year, now if he sends for his Rent to Town, as it is likely he does, he must have Two Hundred and Forty Horses to bring up his Half Years Rent [in Wood's halfpence], and Two or Three great Cellars in his House for Stowage.'

⁷ wholly illiterate ... sence] very illiterate and with no great share of sense *1741 Dab.*

⁸ K. George] King George *1741 Labc; 1742 Lbc, Da.*

³ Conolly] he *1740–2*.   ¹⁰ Conolly's] his *1740–2*.

and old friend; but have received no answer. she will probably be
more civil when she comes to be a Dutchess, but I do not think her
sincerity worth disputing; nor will disturb you in your Dupery because it is of no consequence, besides my quarrell with her is partly
good manners, and she is a good servant who does the office of a
¹skreen⁷.—Lo here comes in the Dutchess again (I know her by her
dd's;² but am a fool for discovering my Art) to defend her self against
my conjectures³ of what she said. Madam, I will imitate your Grace
and write to you upon the same line. I own it is a base un-Romantick
Spirit in me, to suspend the honor of waiting at your Graces feet, till
I can finish a paultry Law-suit. It concerns indeed almost my whole
fortune; it is equal to half Mr Pope's, & two thirds of Mr Gay's, and
about six weeks rent of your Grace's. This cursed accident hath
drill'd away the whole summer. But Madam, understand one thing,
that I take all your Ironicall Civilities in a literal sense, and when ever
I have the honor to attend you, shall expect them to be literally performed, though perhaps I shall find it hard to prove your hand writing
in a Court of Justice; but that will not be much for your credit. How
miserably hath your grace been mistaken in thinking to avoyd envy
by running into exil, where it haunts you more than ever it did even
at Court: Non te civitas, non Regia domus in exilium miserunt, sed
tu utrasque,⁴ so says Cicero (as your Grace knows) or so he might
have said.

⌜Sir I profess it was in my thoughts to have writ that congratulatory
letter⁵ you mention; I never saw the Paper which occasioned the disgrace, It was not suffered to be visible here; But I am told there was
something wrong in it, that looked like betraying private coversation.
Two Ministers may talk with freedom of their master's wrong notions,
&c. and it would hardly agree with honor to communicate what was
spoken, to any third person, much less to the publick; this I say at a
venture; for all things are here misrepresented, and I wish my self
better informed.⌝ I am told that the Craftsman in one of his papers is
offended with the publishers of (I suppose) the last edition of the
Dunciad, & I was asked whether you & Mr Pope were as good
friends to the new disgraced person⁶ as formerly. This I know⁷
nothing of, but suppose it⁸ the consequence of some Irish mistake.⁹ As
to writing; I look on you just in the prime of life for it, the very
season when Judgement & invention draw together. But Scheams are

---

¹ skreen] shrew *Elwin and Ball* (wrongly!).
² The Duchess retaliated for this remark about her dd's in two 'Coptic' lines appended to
Gay's and her letter of 1 Nov. 1731. ³ conjectures] conjecture *1740–2*.
⁴ You have not been sent into Exile by the City or by the Royal Family; but both City and
Royal Family have been banished by you.—1741 Dab (footnote).
⁵ To William Pulteney. ⁶ Pulteney. ⁷ know] knew *1740–2*.
⁸ it the consequence] it was the consequence *1740–2*.
⁹ some Irish mistake] some mistake *1741 Labc*; *1742 Lbc, Da*.

perfectly accidental; some will appear barren of hints & matter, but prove to be fruitfull; and others the contrary. And what you say is past doubt, that every one can best find hints for himself; though it is possible, that sometimes a friend may give you a lucky one just suited to your own imagination. But all this is almost past with me, my invention & judgement are perpetually at fisty cuffs, till they have quite disabled each other; And the meerest trifles I ever wrote are serious Philosophical lucubrations in comparison to what I now busy my self about; as (to speak in the Authors phrase) the world may one day see.[1]⌐—I must desire you (raillerie a part) to let my Lady Dutchess know, that no man is or can be more sensible than my self of her Grace's undeserved civility favour and condescention, with my thanks, for all which I could fill this paper & twenty more to the bottom. but an oppertunity just happening to send this letter to town (for I am out of post rodes) I must here conclude.⌐

POPE *to* THE EARL OF OXFORD[2]   [30 *August* 1731]
Longleat Portland Papers, xii

Munday. [Aug. 30. 1731.]

My Lord,—I have Re-examin'd the Waterman about the book, who is positive he had it not, & indeed I never saw it after it lay on the Table in your Lordships room. I have been careful to return This, which I took to read but could not, it is so silly, and I send Persius with it. You'l please to give him the *Folio*.

I once more Wish you (my Lord) & my Lady Lady Margaret a good Journey, & a pleasant Evening of this Season. I was so sick when I left you that I was ashamd to be seen, or I had payd my respects to Lady Oxford. May every Good & Pleasure attend you all! and pray remember sometimes a man, of little other merit, than that of being with constant Sincerity & Respect | My Lord | Your most faithful & | ever obligd Servant | A. Pope

Address: To the Rt Hon. the | Earl of Oxford.
Endorsement: Mr Pope | Augt 30. 1731.

POPE *to* MALLET   1 *September* 1731
Sir John Murray

Sept. 1st 1731.

I am, I assure you, at all times pleasd to hear from *You*, nor should you think *Me* so ignorant of your good & indulgent nature, as not to take it for granted, you would allow for my Infirmities of body & Avocations of Life, even if I did not answer every Proof of your Regard, by

---

[1] The reference is to the two works mentioned early in the letter.
[2] Pope gave, as date, only the day of the week. The rest is added by Lord Oxford.

punctual Replies in Writing. Therfore pray let not That which is my Unhappiness in itself, be the occasion of another misfortune to me additional to it, that of your Silence. Whenever the Spirit prompts, let it work; & pour forth your kind Breathings upon me.

When yours arrived here, I was absent for a week with Ld Cobham. Your Epitaph on that worthy modest Man, poor Aikman, pleases me greatly.[1] It is honest, it is just, it is tender: I return it to you, & can make no other alteration in it. These sort of writings are so prostituted, it's become hard to say truth, it goes for nothing: The best way I know is to be very modest & reservd in the Commendation that it may be believd not to be *Hired*, or not to be *Partial*. You have hitt this, & there is too much Nature in what you say, to be attributed to Art of any sort. In a word, I think it perfectly right. Tell me if this was a mere Impulse of your Friendship, to write on a Man, because he deservd it, or is there any body so generous (or rather—so just) to intend him a Monument? Your answer to this question will please me, because (if it does no other good) it will bring me another of your Letters. I am truly your Wellwisher, your Friend & your Servant. To add the Esteem I justly bear you as a Poet, is not so great a matter in yours and my opinion as what I bear you as a Good & humane Man, Let John Dennis & the Wits take it as they will— | I am | Dear Sir | Ever yours. | A. Pope.

Address: To | Mr Mallet, at his Grace | the Duke of Montrose's, | at Clye, near | Swafham | Norfolke.

Frank: Free | Bathurst

Postmark: 2/SE

POPE *to* HILL   1 *September* 1731

1751 (Hill)

Sept. 1. 1731.

I could not persuadĕ myself to write to you since your great Loss,[2] till I hop'd you had receiv'd some Alleviation to it, from the only Hand which can give any, that of Time. Not to have mention'd it, however fashionable it may be, I think unnatural, and in some Sense inhuman; and I fear the contrary Custom is too much an Excuse, in reality, for that Indifference we too usually have for the Concern

---

[1] The epitaph is printed in Mallet's *Works* (1759), i. 13.I concerns both William Aikman the painter, who died 7 June 1731, and his son, who had died shortly before, aged 17. Father and son were buried in the same grave, and it is curious that Pope makes no comment on the son. Mallet sent the epitaph to Hill in a letter of 29 Sept. 1731 (now in the Theatre Collection of Harvard University), and Hill replied with commendation on 2 Oct. (*Works*, 1753, i. 83–86).

[2] Miranda, 'consort of Aaron Hill,' as she liked to sign herself, had died on 25 June 1731.—D. Brewster, *Aaron Hill*, p. 221.

of another: In truth, that was not my Case: I know the Reason of one Man is of little Effect toward the Resignation of another; and when I compar'd the Forces of yours and mine, I doubted not which had the Advantage, even tho' in your own Concern. 'Tis hard, that in these tender Afflictions the Greatness of the Mind and the Goodness are opposite to each other; and that while Reason, and the Consideration upon what Conditions we receive all the Goods of this Life, operate towards our Quiet; even the best of our Passions (which are the same Things with the softest of our Virtues) refuse us that Comfort. But I'll say no more on this melancholy Subject. The whole Intent of this Letter is to tell you how much I wish you capable of Consolation, and how much I wish to know when you find yourself so. I would hope you begin to seek it, to amuse your Mind with those Studies of which *Tully* says, *Adversis perfugium & solatium præbent*,[1] and to transcribe (if I may so express it) your own Softnesses and generous Passions into the Hearts of others who more want them. I do not flatter you in saying, I think your Tragedy will do this effectually (to which I had Occasion, the other Day, to do justice to Mr. Wilks),[2] or whatever else you chuse to divert your own Passion with, and to raise that of your Readers.—I wish the Change of Place, or the Views of Nature in the Country, made a Part of your Scheme.— You once thought of *Richmond*—I wish you were there, or nearer. I have thrice miss'd of you in Town, the only Times I have been there: My last Month[3] was pass'd at my Lord *Cobham's*, and in a Journey thro' *Oxfordshire*: I wish you as susceptible, at this time, of these Pleasures as I am. I have been truly concern'd for you, and for your Daughter, who I believe is a *true Part* of you. I will trouble you no farther, but with the Assurance that I am not unmindfully, | Sir, | Your most sincere | humble Servant, | A. Pope.

---

*POPE to THE DUKE OF —[4]   2 *September* 1731

J. M. Osborn

Twitenham Sept. 2d

My Lord,—It was with great Satisfaction I heard some time ago that

---

[1] *Pro Archia poeta*, vii.

[2] Robert Wilks, the actor-manager at Drury Lane, approved Hill's *Athelwold* but declined to create the title-role. See his letters to Hill in Hill's *Collection* (1751), pp. 85–87. His reason was very likely ill-health. The tragedy was first acted 10 Dec. 1731, and Wilks died 27 Feb. 1732.

[3] For varying estimates of the time Pope spent at Stowe see his letters of 15 Aug. (to Lord Oxford), 23 Aug. (to Knight), and 1 Sept. (to Mallet). He first intended to be absent two days, and probably spent a week at Stowe and then went on with Brigadier Dormer to Rousham. He was back in London before the end of August.

[4] Lacking the estate papers of Hallgrove, one finds it impossible to identify the duke who is perhaps 'agreeing' for that house. The lands are being let to a farmer. Apparently when Mr. Rackett died in 1728, his widow went to live with her son Henry (destined for the law)

your Grace had agreed for Hallgrove, knowing in how good hands by that means the affairs of my Nephew & Sister in law would fall. I am most disagreably surpriz'd to find the mistake her Ignorance has put her under, in the Imagination that her *Son's Letter of Attorney* impow'red her to let the Lease. In fact, she continued the Lease to Mr Butler before, upon the same supposal. I dare take upon me to assure your Grace of the Integrity of Her Intentions, as well as of my Nephew (who is a very honest & tractable man) making good the Lease to your Grace, in any the Securest manner you can desire: either by cutting off the Intail (if it be intaild on the younger Brothers) or by the joint Consent of the Brothers, & Concurrence in your Lease. I dare further assure your Grace of your being indemnifyd as to Expences &c: in case this be not made good. What I humbly beg of your Grace is, that you will enter upon it at present, conditionally, the Title to be secured, which may doubtless be done in a few months, (my Nephew being abroad.) I hope that to do so will be no less to your Grace's Conveniency than to my Kinswoman's, to whom it will otherwise be of infinite Prejudice, & hinder as well her agreement with the Farmer for the Land: as Country people will be afraid of the least difficulty, tho none can be more easily removd (as I conceive) than this, by my Nephew's giving the Lease himself: I wonder indeed this thing should have been put in so wrong a Train at first, for I ever knew the Estate to be vested in the Son, tho it's true his Mother has transacted all his affairs many years with his full Consent, & indeed the Debt he is in to her for her jointure & a farther Sum of money, (due from her having sacrific'd very much, her own Interests to her Family's) has made him act in all things with the utmost complyance & tenderness to her; As I am sure he will immediately, in the present Instance.

Your Grace will be weary of so long a Letter, but the Thing not only vex'd, but Piqu'd me, as I had been concernd in recommending it to your Grace. If you please to honour me with any of your Commands in this, or to order me to wait on you thither, I shall be (as with great respect I am, in every regard besides) | My Lord Duke | Your most obedient & | most humble Servant | A. Pope.

Endorsement: Mr Pope received | Sepr the 4th | 1731

POPE to FORTESCUE[1]   [2 *September* 1731]

Harvard University

I had written to you the first post, but that I was not at home when

in Bloomsbury, and leased Hallgrove presumably to 'Mr. Butler'. The house is now being considered by the unidentified duke, but the letter of attorney from her eldest son, Michael, does not give her sufficient power to execute a lease. Michael seems to have lived on the Continent, perhaps to avoid difficulties arising from his own or his father's debts.

[1] The year date is difficult; the day and month are from the postmark. The year should

yours arrived. I partake in the contentment you now taste in your domestick Employments. As to your Building, I heartily wish you had sent me a plan of it, in which I might possibly be of more Service to you than by barely sending you the Proportions you desire. It is not easy to answer your question of the Doors & Windows, the Dimension of them being to b[e] suited to the Size & Height of the Room, which you do not tell me. But in general both Doors & Windows should be a double Square, & the Solid of the Walls between Window & Window rather more than the Opening: no harm in exceeding in the Solids to near twice the dimension of the windows. If the Windows be large (above 3 foot broad) the Doors need be no larger; but if the Windows be less, make the doors rather above 3 feet wide: the height just double to whatever be the width.¹

I must add one caution about your Gardening. If you happen to cutt away old trees or copsewood for Hedges, do not cut them upright in a perpendicular, much less (as the common gardeners use) over hanging, for all Hedges so cutt will dye at the bottom in a year or two & appear very thin & ugly. But cutt the hedge side in this first form

cut thus /   not thus | much less thus \

This will constantly preserve all parts of the Hedge: tho this may seem a triffle, 'tis a great secret & practisd hardly any where & has another excellent effect in widening the Walk & giving air in the closest woodworks.

Mrs Blount sends you her best Services & wishes for all your prosperity. You will take some care for Hers, & I fear there is all possible need of it. I beg no delay may be admitted, provided you proceed safely, for nothing (I am informd many ways) is to be expected from the man² otherways. Dear Sir adieu We are all pretty well—Write to me as often as you can, & know me for one entirely & affectionately Yours. | A. Pope.

Address: To | Wm Fortescue Esqr at Buck-|land-Filleigh, near | Great Torrington, | Devonsh:
Postmark: 2/SE

postdate 1728 when Fortescue began to concern himself for Martha Blount's finances, and should antedate 1733 when Pope's mother had died. 'We' in the last sentence should include Mrs. Pope, though her health was bad at the time. Years other than 1731 seem improbable for various reasons.

¹ Notable perhaps is the fact that panelling for a new room installed at Castle Hill about 1740 is now to be seen as a Georgian drawing-room in the art gallery of the Huntington Library.   ² On the man Roberts see iii. 233.

POPE *to* HILL[1]   *3 September* 1731

1751 (Hill)

Sept. 3. 1731.

I have been, and yet am, totally confin'd by my Mother's Relapse, if that can be call'd so, which is rather a constant and regular Decay. She is now on her last Bed, in all Probability, from whence she has not risen in some Weeks, yet in no direct Pain, but a perpetual Languor. I suffer for her, for myself, and for you, in the Reflection of what you have felt at the Side of a sick Bed which I now feel, and of what I probably soon shall suffer which you now suffer, in the Loss of one's best Friend. I have wish'd (ever since I saw your Letter) to ask you, since you find your own House a Scene of Sorrows, to pass some Days in mine; which I begin to think I shall soon have the same melancholy Reason to shun. In the mean time, I make a sort of Amusement of this melancholy Situation itself, and try to derive a Comfort in imagining I give some to her. I am seldom prompted to Poetry in these Circumstances; yet I'll send you a few Lines I sent t'other Day from her Bed-side to a particular Friend.[2] Indeed I want Spirits and Matter, to send you any thing else, or on any other Subject. These too are spirit-less, and incorrect.

> While ev'ry Joy, successful Youth! is thine,
> Be no unpleasing Melancholy mine.
> Me long, ah long! may these soft Cares engage;
> To rock the Cradle of reposing Age,
> With lenient Arts prolong a Parent's Breath,
> Make Languor smile, and smooth the Bed of Death.
> Me, when the Cares my better Years have shown
> Another's Age, shall hasten on my own;
> Shall some kind Hand, like B***'s[3] or thine,
> Lead gently down, and favour the Decline?
> In Wants, in Sickness, shall a *Friend* be nigh,
> Explore my *Thought*, and watch my asking *Eye*?
> Whether that Blessing be deny'd, or giv'n,
> Thus far, is right; the rest belongs to *Heav'n*.

[1] It has been thought strange that Pope should write to Hill on both the 1st and 3rd of this month. Viewed in its chronological sequence after the letter to Fortescue (2 Sept.), in which Pope's mother and he are 'pretty well', and before the letter to Bethel (8 Sept.) where his mother is 'better than when you saw her'—viewed thus, the letter at first sight becomes very questionable in date. The truth probably is that Hill has shown some sign (which he did not print) of wishing to visit Pope, and Pope is using his mother's health as excuse for not inviting him. Later in the month, however, Hill is invited.

[2] The particular friend ('successful Youth') is not identifiable. Dr. Johnson in his *Life of James Thomson* tells of an Epistle addressed to Thomson while on the Continent (as he was at this time). The youth may be Thomson, or Lyttelton. It can hardly be Murray, who had not yet been called to the bar. The lines will be easily recognized as a part of the ending of the Epistle to Dr. Arbuthnot.   [3] Bolingbroke's.

Excuse this, in a Man who is weak and wounded, but not by his Enemies, but for his Friends. I wish you the Continuance of all that is yet dear to you in Life, and am truly | Yours, | A. Pope.

*POPE *to* HUGH BETHEL   8 *September* 1731

Egerton 1948

Sept. 8th | 1731.

I would have written to you sooner, if you had not, (contrary to my good & reasonable Expectations of you) been at the trouble of a long letter yourself, which but too manifestly shews the ill state of your Eyes. Pray do so no more; only write three lines if you are well &c. or if you would entertain me farther, let another write for you. Your Question of the date of Roberts receit I answer first, it should be for half a year due last Midsummer. No more has yet been heard of him, but Mr Fortescue proposes to inquire of his Effects & the Estate lyable to Distraining, after Michaelmas; if he gives no good account in the mean time. I now come to Friendship: Mrs Patty often thinks & speaks of you. So does Cleland; & Mr Gay is here, who inquir'd of you. I hope the Scarborow waters have done you service; my own health is as usual, but better in the Summer than Winter; So I will not complain till the Evil day comes.

I have been busy in the Moral Book I told you of: many exemplary Facts & Characters fall into it daily, but which render it less fit for the Present Age. The Fate of the Marlborough family is a Great one, which the death of the Marquess of Blandford[1] has renewd my Reflections on. *Solus sapiens dives*[2] is very true. I have been so pleasd, when I meet with a Good Example or character (as it is a Curiosity now) that I have sent Express Enquiries after the Particulars to be Exact in the celebration of it and with great contentment find, that what I writ of the Good Works of the Man of Ross, is to a Tittle true.[3] I think you saw those Verses—

I begin to hope for your return, tho there are here few people to entertain you, but it is natural to think more how ones self shall be pleas'd, than how another shall: therfore I wish you here. Mrs Blount has so mean an opinion of herself, that she never will think it can be

---

[1] The Marquess (son of Henrietta, Duchess of Marlborough) died 24 Aug. 1731, leaving no heir. Pope's 'reflections' on this event may well have been the passage designed to be inserted in the *Essay on Man* but cancelled. The passage is available in the facsimile used as frontispiece to vol. iii of the Elwin–Courthope *Works.*

[2] The sixth Stoic Paradox; see Cicero, *Paradoxa,* and possibly Horace, *Satires,* i. iii. 124–5.

[3] The sentence was quoted in Ruffhead (1769), p. 297. Bethel has supposedly seen the manuscript of the character of this Man, which was published (*Moral Essay III,* ll. 249–84) in Jan. 1734. See Pope to Tonson, 14 Nov. 1731 and 7 June 1732. In November Pope seems eager for more facts about the Man.

any motive to you, to come where she is; I wish she thought so rever-
endly of herself, as to be abstracted from all worse Company than
you or me: for I fear she has none so truly her friends as ourselves.
My Mother (God knows) is now no companion, [tho] her Health
rather is better than wh[hen you] saw her, her memory much at on[ ]
I've lately had a Service to you from Dean Swift, who says he will
write Histories, or rather small Penny-Story-books, of the Good Men
of this age.[1]—Adieu. pray remember me to Mr Moyzer, & believe me
ever with sincere affection Dear Sir your truely faithful Servant. |
A. Pope.

Address: To Hugh Bethel Esqr to | be left at Mrs Pecket's in the | Shambles |
Yorke.

Postmark: 9/[S]E

HILL *to* POPE[2]   *17 September* 1731

1753 (Hill)
                                                        Sept. 17, 1731.

It will never be in my power to forget, how compassionate you have
been, in *calling* and *sending* so often.—It is plain, you have none of
the *fashionable want of feeling, for the calamities of others*; and, when I
reflect, that you are kind enough to *concern* yourself for *mine*, it brings
me nearer to *comfort*, than either resignation, or philosophy.

The part you are pleased to take, in my *loss of a wife*, who had the
misfortune of being a *stranger* to you, would have been as *just*, as it is
generous, had you been qualifyed to measure it, by an acquaintance
with her *virtues*. It was *one* of those virtues—that she admired Mr.
Pope, and knew, *why* she admired him. She wish'd for nothing, with
more liveliness, than the pleasure of seeing you, and (such is the
illusion of our prospects!) the very *day*, on which she promised herself
the enjoyment of that wish, she became insensible to *all wishes*, on
this side eternity!

I chose a place for her, in the *Abbey-Cloister*; the Wall of the
church, above, being so loaded with marble, as to leave me no room,
to distinguish her monument.

---

¹ Part of the letter from Swift dated 20 July is missing. It or some totally lost letter must
have contained the materials here mentioned.

² The date Hill (or his daughter) assigned to this letter is impossible. The first sentence
of the last paragraph indicates that it was written during the first half of a month. In the
next to the last paragraph Hill has heard from Wilks that Pope thinks highly of *Athelwold*.
Since Hill first confessed to Wilks the authorship of the tragedy in a letter of 22 Sept. (*Works*
[1753], i. 71), the letter can hardly date in the first half of September, where Elwin placed it.
Writing again to Wilks on 25 Sept. Hill talks (as here) of a monument for his wife, and
encloses a six-line epitaph of his own composition. Since inconsistencies in details cannot be
reconciled under any date resembling that originally printed, the impossible date is allowed to
stand. Possibly it was written about 1 Oct. 1731.

Give me leave to hope the benefit of your advice, on this mournful occasion. I cannot suffer her to lie unnoticed, because a monument, in so frequented a place as *Westminster-Abbey*, restoring her, to a kind of second life, among the living, it will be in some measure, not to have *lost* her. But there is a low and unmeaning lumpishness, in the vulgar style of monuments, which disgusts me, as often, as I look upon them; and, because I would avoid the censure I am giving, let me beg you to say, whether there is *significance*, in the draught, of which I enclose you an aukward *scratch*, not a *copy*: the flat table, behind, is *black*, the figures are *white* marble.

The *whole* of what you see, here, is but *part* of the monument; and will be surrounded by *pilasters*, arising from a pediment of *white marble*, having its foundation on a *black marble mountain*, and supporting a *coronice* and *dome*, that will ascend to the point of the cloister arch. About half way up a craggy path, on the *black mountain*, below will be the figure of *time*, in *white marble*, on an attitude of *climbing*, obstructed by little *Cupids*, of the same colour; some rolling rocks, into his path, from *above*; some throwing *nets*, at his *feet* and *arms*, from *below*: others in *ambuscade*, shooting *arrows* at him, from *both sides*; while the *Death*, you see in the *draught*, will seem, from an opening between *hills*, in *relievo*, to have found admission by a shorter way, and prevented *time*, at a distance.

I cannot forbear to inclose you an anonymous favour, which I received, in a penny-post letter, from some kind hand disguised, that I should not guess at the obliger. I find, in it, a strong and touching *simplicity*; nature, nervous, and undressed; striking, from and to the heart, without pomp or affection! you will be pleased with these four verses, if my melancholy has not helped their impression on me. It is true, they seem rather the moving words of a *wife*, while dying, than the inscription of her monument, *after death*; but I have never been able to read them, without emotion; and being charmed with them myself, I wished you a part of the pleasure.

I had heard of the obliging opinion you expressed of my *Tragedy*, when you had, lately, an occasion of speaking to Mr. *Wilks*, concerning the affairs of the *stage*. I assure you, without complement, I had rather it should please you, singly, than a dozen crowded audiences. And one thing I can be sure of, in its favour,—It will be the *better* for some marks of your *pencil*. If you would have the goodness, to allow me to put a copy of it into your hands, and speak of it occasionally, with the same kind partiality, to some of those, who can give success to Tragedies; *That* alone, might determine me, to venture it on the *stage*, next winter.

I have thoughts, about the middle of this month, of taking your advice, and *Tully's*; I will try what *change of place*, and the pleasure

of being nearer *you*, can do, toward dispelling a *grief*, that time seems
to threaten increase of: I will fly from it, if I can, but the *atra cura
post equitem*, will sit too close to be parted with. I am, truly, and
unalterably, | Dear Sir, | Your most affectionate, | And most obedient
Servant, | A. Hill.

POPE *to* HILL   25 *September* 1731
1751 (Hill)
                                        Twickenham, Sept. 25. 1731.
Sir,—The Hurry I was in to send to you, made it a Message instead of
a Letter, which I ask your Excuse for by this. If now you have
Thoughts of the Country, pray think no further than my own House:
I am wholly at your Service. The Weather is yet inviting: I could
wish (if Miss *Hill*, under a Father's Authority, might venture), she
saw me before I am quite decay'd (I mean all of me that is yet half
flourishing, my Garden). You'll very much oblige me, and give
Countenance to my Judgment, in letting your Tragedy pass thro' my
Hands to any Persons to whom you care I should shew it. Believe me
with great Truth (and a real Concern for what must so much afflict
a good Mind), | Sir, | Your affectionate | obedient Servant, | A. Pope.

HILL *to* POPE   30 *September* 1731
1753 (Hill)
                                              Sept. 30, 1731.
You are very good, and obliging:— your last letter[1] came not to my
hands 'till yesterday; I will thank you for it, in person, one day, next
week, if possible, and give you notice, a day before.

My daughter, under encouragement of your invitation, promises
herself the pleasure of admiring your gardens; and wishes the weather
may continue, as it is, till I can give her the opportunity of an afternoon's walk in them.

My Brother is writing over another copy of the Tragedy, which I
will take the liberty to put, a second time, into your hands, as soon as
it is ready: I propose no benefit, to myself, from it, leaving its profits
to the players: but, as I know it necessary, to prepare the expectation
of persons of the first rank, if one would wish a play that kind of fame
which noise can give it, (and without which indeed it were to no purpose, to have it brought on the stage), I am therefore, greatly oblig'd,
by the hope, you permit me to nourish, that you will suffer it to pass
thro' your hand, to the notice of some of those, who speaking of it,

---

[1] In Hill's *Collection of Letters* (1751) was printed a letter from Pope under date of 29
Sept. 1731 which is here placed in 1738 (q.v.). Bowles, Elwin, and others placed it also in
1731; but Pope's last letter, which Hill is answering, was that of the 25th.

with favour, will be a direction to others, how far they may *dare* to be pleas'd with it. I am, | Dear Sir, | Your most oblig'd | And affectionate Servant, | A. Hill.

POPE *to* HILL   1 *October* 1731

1751 (Hill)

Oct. 1. 1731.

It was my Hope you had Thoughts of passing a few Days hereabouts, that made me impertinent enough to wish, you would make use of this Place, which is as much at your Service as its Master. It is otherwise too great a Trouble to you, no less than too great a Distinction shewn to me, to have you come purposely; much less to give the young Lady the Fatigue of an Afternoon's Visit to what so little merits it. My Wish was, that you could have taken a Bed here, as long as you could allow yourself to be in the Country; and have done me the Pleasure to see the Person you, now, love best in the World, with you; either as giving you to me, or receiving you from me, on the Day that you came, or that you went. Be assur'd I always am with Truth, | Dear Sir, | Your most oblig'd, | affectionate, faithful Servant, | A. Pope.

If Miss *Hill* does not dine with us, I shall think all the Rites of Hospitality violated.

POPE *to* JONATHAN RICHARDSON[1]   3 *October* [1731]

Elwin–Courthope, ix. 495

Twickenham, Oct. 3. [1731].

If I was not much mistaken you told me you wanted this edition of Milton. I made it my endeavour, at least, upon that supposition to procure and send it you. If I erred, you have only to return it by the bearer. I am ready when you will to look over your notes, as I truly am (at any time) to please you, and to please myself, both which I think I shall on reading them. I am with my service to your son, dear sir, your affectionate friend.

POPE *to* HILL[2]   [4] *October* 1731

1751 (Hill)

Monday Night, Oct. 9. 1731.

I see the Season will not allow me the Pleasure of seeing you, nor of

---

[1] Elwin prints from 'Richardson's Transcript'. The 'notes' are doubtless the *Explanatory Notes and Remarks on Paradise Lost*, which Richardson and his son published in 1734.

[2] The full date is given in the *Collection*, but unfortunately the 9th was Saturday—a day not normally confused with Monday. Since a 4 as made by Pope could be misread as a 9 (though that would not normally be probable), and since the 4th was Monday, the revised date is suggested. The year is determined by the circulation of *Athelwold*.

shewing my faded Garden this Year to Miss *Urania*. I assure you I would willingly make a Trip to *London* on purpose to see you and her, but my Constitution, of late, has been faster in Decline than the Year. I have been as ill, as when I writ you that peevish Image of my Soul, a Letter, some Time since, which had the good Effect of making us know one another.¹

This is the first Day I have been able to see Lady *S*.² who shew'd me a very polite Letter of yours that put her out of Countenance. The Truth is, she makes no Pretension to judge of Poetry. But the Tragedy will be shewn, as I told you, to One, or rather (I think) to Both will be better. I wish you was not so soon to bring it on, by what Mr. *Savage* tells me of Mr. *Booth* and Mrs. *Porter*.³ I think it will be a Loss both to the Play, and to them, if they do not make one another shine: I hope, in a Week, to wait on you in *London*, and tell you with what plain Truth I am, dear Sir, | Yours, | A. Pope.

My Book⁴ I have no manner of Thought of publishing: It is of so various a Nature, that I know not under what Denomination, yet, to rank the many Parts of it; and shall write, just as I live, without knowing the *End* of my Works, or Days: The Whole will proceed, as my Life proceeds; and probably die, as I die.

*MARTHA BLOUNT and POPE to HUGH BETHEL*⁵

[*8 October* 1731]

Egerton 1948

Sir,—My Long Silence has not been owing to any want of Leisure here, (where there has been no court, and which is worse no company at all) but to a fear of doing too often that which I can not help doing some times, inquiring of your health. I hope it is improved by Scarborough; of which the Duke of Argyle tells wonders, tho he was there but a short time, and is much the better. I am now of another party, and on the Side of the Hott waters, which I'm taking by Dr Burtons advice, together with other Medicines. I would not have you Judge from hence that I am ill, but (what is a wonder) I take 'em only in hopes of being better. Miss Betty Poulteney has been in this Neighbourhood

---

¹ The letter of 26 Jan. 1730/1.   ² Lady Suffolk (Mrs. Howard).

³ Barton Booth died in 1733; consequently the tragedy in question must be *Athelwold* and not the unacted *Roman Revenge*, in which Pope had a tepid interest in the period after 1737. Mrs. Porter's crippling accident in 1731 kept her from the stage for the most part after that time. In *Athelwold* Mrs. Booth created the role of Elfrid. See Hill's *Collection of Letters* (1751), p. 78.

⁴ The *Essay on Man* is here represented as more inchoate than it appeared in Bolingbroke's letter of 2 Aug. It was doubtless still in composition, but here Pope is already concealing intentions as to publication.

⁵ The day and month are implied in the postmark; the year is inferred from the fact that this letter continues topics treated in Pope to Bethel, 8 Sept. 1731.

some time, and I've withstood all her temptations, as to bad hours, &c but as the season draws near for that universall Temptation of all Women, the Town, I shall want you to preach to me for my own good, and keep me (if you can) in that health I'm now endevoring to lay up. I begin to think of you and your Sisters, a warm fire-side, two or three friends in a room, a party at quadrille, and no door open at one's neck. I hope Colonell Moyser[1] will not hinder you long from seeing these things, and me, who sincerely want to see you, and so does Mr Pope. but he is Just come in and says he will fill the rest of this letter himself. | Adieu. MB

[POPE]

I have just receivd from Mr Cleland a Letter relating to Mr Roberts' affairs (but first I must give you his hearty Services in a Parenthesis, which is his own manner of telling things, and he is here for some days at Twitenham) In it we have an account that his Father is dead,[2] & that he seems in quiet possession of the Estate, but that there is a report an Extent has been granted on some part of it. But upon the whole they think him now responsable. We have never heard more of him nor of his Rent. He is told by his Lawyers (as Mrs. Drelincourt[3] acquaints us who lives in that Country & is one of his Creditors) that his Wife & he by passing Fines & recoverys may sell, & satisfy the debts. Whatever Estate in Denbighshire he was possest of before his fathers death, is made liable to Mrs B's Rent, as I find by the writing to you.

It is very true that I always wish to see you, & that you are never out of my thoughts a day. I could be glad you could find some remedy for your Eyes, which I think & hope is now your greatest Complaint. By Lord Burlingtons former accounts of you you want not bodily strength, for he said you were foremost in the field a Hunting. May it continue, if you have it! [Ma]y it encrease, if you want it! Let Mr Moyser know [I a]m his Servant, & envy him your constant neighborhood: I never see you but in the worst season, winter, & when I am worst to be seen; for if I have any Life, it is with the Butterfly. Adieu. My Mother is as well as she has been of late years. We often remember you in our Cups. We want Rain extremely, tho I hear you in Yorkshire [d]o not. I'm going in haste to plant Jamaica

---

[1] Col. James Moyser lived in Beverley, not far from Beswick, where Bethel lived.

[2] *The Universal Spectator*, 11 Sept. 1731, reports the death at Place-Newidd in Denbighshire of John Roberts, Esq., 'possess'd of upwards of 2000*l.* per Annum, which descends to his only son Major Roberts'. The major is probably the elusive Roberts who from 1729 on for some years is to be dilatory in payments to Miss Blount.

[3] Probably the Mrs. Drelincourt, widow (after 1722) of the Dean of Armagh, to whom John Gay paid intermittent and diffident court. She was wealthy, and like Roberts had property in Denbighshire. See *Notes & Queries*, 10 S. xi (1909), 275.

Strawberries, [wh]ich are to be almost as good as Pineapples, they say they resemble them in flavor. Once more adieu. I am truly | Yours.

Address: To Hugh Bethel Esqr | at Mrs Pecket in the Shambles | Yorke
Postmark: 9/OC

HILL *to* POPE[1]   29 *October* 1731
1753 (Hill)
                                                        Oct. 29, 1731.

Beginning to fear, I shall not have the pleasure of returning to *Richmond*, this season, I take the freedom of replacing *Athelwold* in your hands, with the scenes I have added, lately.

But, observing some new marks of your pencil, in places, which you had formerly distinguished, in the same manner, I am obliged, (for fear, you should think me fonder of my follies than I really am) to confess, that when I altered all the rest of the places, I left these few, as they were, because my judgment could not, so clearly as it wished, fall in with your objections.

In the first, for instance, instead of—shorten your *meant* absence—you would read it—to make your absence *shorter*.—Methinks, your correction intends but one signification, that is—to make his absence *shorter* than he *meant to make it*. And, in that sense, it is exactly the same, as my own. But, to make his absence *shorter*, is equivocal, and, therefore, not elegant. His absence could not be *shorter*, than it *was*.—It might be *shorter*, than he *intended it*.

If I am doubtful, too, in your second exception, against *wishes*, in the plural, I shall have your second thoughts on my side; for *Athelwold* had wanted delicacy, had he said, that *Ethelinda* blessed his *wish*; as if he had felt but *one*, only which the *ladies* would have called a *gross* one, unaccompanied with those politer, of partiality, tenderness, and confidence, from a mistress, who could *bless* him, in one general possession, with all those different accomplishments, he had *wished for*, among women.

But, it would look, like growing serious, upon a trifle, should I go on, in this manner, and expect you to read all the reasons, I could give, in defence of the other places. And you will conclude, I have such as, I think, you would approve of; since I send you the Play, again with all those places, unaltered.

It is time to forbear persecuting you, about this Tragedy:—It is to come on before *Christmas*: But, tho' you have given me leave, to tax your condescention with some concern for its success, it will, I

---

[1] This letter seems to have been written before receipt of Pope's letter of the same day—though Pope's letter is improperly dated.

fear, be too much to wish, you would recommend it to an assembly, or two, of the leaders, in parties of this nature, as a Play, to be acted for the benefit of the house, not the author; who has no other interest, in their encouraging its reception, but the distinction of having *power* to *please*, at a time, when Tragedy seems to have lost all its influence.

Perhaps, this is too much for the Play;—I am sure, it is too much for the author: And therefore, if you have any reason, (which you *may* have, and I not apprehend it) why this would, in the least, be an improper step for you to take, I shall, sincerely be pleased, that you decline it.—For I have better reasons, than any, which concern myself, to be, | Dear Sir, | Your most affectionate, | And obedient Servant, | A. Hill.

P.S. I long to hear when your Ethic piece is to be published.

POPE *to* HILL[1]   29 *October* 1731

1751 (Hill)
                                              Thursday, Oct. 29. 1731.

There is an ill Fate hangs upon me in relation to the Pleasure I've often (from the very first Time I saw you at Dr. *Young*'s) propos'd in our Acquaintance. I really stay'd that Night in Town, upon *Bowry*'s Notice, which he left in Writing, that you should *be at Home all* Wednesday, and had dedicated three Hours to you, or, more properly, to myself with you. I ask'd, particularly, for Miss *Urania*; but thought myself, tho' old enough, not familiar enough to ask to see her. I desire your first Notice, if you come this Way; or, rather, I wish you would take up your Lodging with me. In the mean time, pray send the Tragedy of *Athelwold* (for so I would call it), under Cover, to the Countess of *Suffolk*, before *Monday*, at her Lodgings in *St. James*'s. I promis'd it her again; and if you think of any Consequence that the K.[2] should see it in Manuscript, I think nothing more easy. In Truth, all this is doing it no Credit; 'tis only doing some to those who may commend it. I could not imagine in what Parts it needed Addition; sure every Incident is well prepar'd: But no Man can see so far into his own Work as the Author, if a good one; so little, if a bad or indifferent one.—I am with Truth, | Sir, | Your very obliged | and faithful Servant, | A. Pope

---

¹ Although the full date is impossible (since the 29th was a Friday), it is allowed to stand. Possibly a change to the 28th is preferable, but one may mistake the day of the week as easily as that of the month. It is of course possible that Pope wrote only 'Thursday', and that the editor copied the day and month from the postmark. Hill's letter also dated the 29th seems to have been written before he received this from Pope.

² The King.

HILL *to* THE COUNTESS OF SUFFOLK   30 *October* 1731
1753 (Hill)

Oct. 30, 1731.

Madam,—Mr. Pope has desired me to send this Tragedy, in his name, to the Lady in the world, I should most *wish* to have it with, could any thing be found, in it, deserving the distinction.

It cannot be without delight, that I put *Athelwold* into a hand, for which he would have been proud to give up *Elfrid's*; if, in *life*, I could have given him my sentiments, with the authority which his *death* has lent me.

I have no pretence to tax your condescention, with any concern for the *success* of this Play, or I should most earnestly, wish your vote in its favour; tho' I have no meaner interest, in its good, or ill fortune, than the *ambition* of some *power* to *please*.

But, whatever reception it may meet with, from the public, it can never have been written in vain, since Mr. *Pope* has partiality enough to believe, it will be agreeable to such a taste, as the *Countess of Suffolk's*, whose servant I have the honour to be, | With the utmost Obedience, | And Devotion, | A. Hill.

POPE *to* THE EARL OF OXFORD[1]   [31 *October* 1731]
Longleat Portland Papers, xii

Munday night [Oct. 31. 1731]

My Lord,—The Desire which is Constant in me to wait upon your Lordship, made me readily agree to dine with you on Wensday, as I wish'd it the first day I could, without reflecting, that I have been præ-engaged that day to Mr Fazakerly, Mr Murray & Mr Noel, in Lincoln's Inne.[2] I beg you to excuse me, as knowing these are Men not to be disappointed, & who Command the Time of much greater Folks than myself. Any day after, I shall with the sincerest pleasure obey your Summons, & hope in the meantime to come & ask you. No man alive is with more Truth, & Obligation, | Your Lordships ever faithful Servant | A. Pope.

Address: To the Rt Honble the | Earl of Oxford.

---

[1] In dating Pope wrote only 'Munday night'. The bracketed date, added in the hand of Lord Oxford, may be wrong. The 31st was a Sunday. Oxford is ordinarily far more reliable in his datings than Pope, but one or the other is here wrong.

[2] Fazakerley, Noel, and Bootle were the principal attorneys for the defence in the famous trial in which Richard Francklin was found guilty of publishing a libel in *The Craftsman* of 2 Jan. 1730/1. The libel was by Lord Bolingbroke, and it is conceivable that the conference concerned the approaching trial. If Murray is Pope's young friend (later the 1st Earl of Mansfield), this is early to find him concerned in an important case. He was, however, a member of Lincoln's Inn, and Fazakerley and Noel were Templars. In delivering judgment in 1784 as Lord Chief Justice Mansfield (Murray) cited the Francklin case with familiarity. See John, Baron Campbell, *Lives of the Chief Justices of England* (1849), ii. 541.

POPE *to* CARYLL   1 *November* 1731

Add. 28618   Twittenham. Nov. 1. 1731.

I know it to be long since I wrote to you; and I feel it to be long since you wrote to me. In truth, I am always rejoiced to be remembered by you, but I think I writ last; however, that had not hindered my writing again, and I had begun one to you when I received yours. Mr Pigot knows we never meet without talking of you. Mrs Patty knows I never see her without enquiring when she heard from Mrs C. But the matter is I grow dull and seldom correspond at all. I find myself fitter for conversation than writing, except some serious subject calls upon my whole attention, and flatters me I may do some good by writing. How rarely that happens you may guess—Would to God I might hope to enjoy your conversation: we have been separated very long, and my letters are cold things; but I would hope my friendship is not cold, as I'm sure yours is valuable.

Lord Bathurst was, and yet is, full of raptures about your park. I sincerely long to see it, but much more to be there with you. It is my mother only that robs me of half the pleasure of my life, and that gives me the greatest at the same time. If a week could carry me to you and home again next season I would readily come, but the fact is I have never been absent from her longer; for there being none but servants about her, if she should die, it would rest upon my mind that it might have happened for want of my personal care.

I am truly pleased to see you already living in your grand-son, and anticipating the honour of your posterity. I congratulate sincerely on the fair expectations you conceive of him, and may God fulfill and complete them.

Your *singular* friend P[atty] is so so: she would be better if more *singular*. She has too much affection for people she cannot help, nor mend. And God forbid her excess of good nature should involve her in the curse pronounced in Scripture, *Those that love the Wicked shall perish with 'em*, since her affection, tho' weak, is yet virtuous.

I have seen Mr Pigot three hours since, who after a troublesome fit of the gravel is much recovered. News here's none to send you,— only that the D. of Lorraine was converted from popish fasting to protestant fleshpots on Saturday sevenight,[1] when dining with the King: they forgot to get him fish. Adieu, dear sir, let your lady, son, and daughters know me for theirs and | Your ever faithful, obliged, affectionate servant, | A. Pope

[1] Possibly Pope refers to a dinner at Hampton Court on 23 Oct., but probably he has in mind a more elaborate festivity on the 16th, which was reported in the newspapers (*London Evening Post*, 19 Oct.) somewhat later. On the 16th the Duke dined 'at an oval Table in the Beauty Gallery' at Hampton Court, with the King, the Prince of Wales, two members of the Duke's train, four English dukes, and other noblemen. The Duke was in England from 13 Oct. until 9 Dec. 1731.

POPE *to* HILL · 1 *November* 1731
1751 (Hill)
Chiswick, Nov. 1. 1731.

Sir,—I troubled you with a hasty Scrawl at Lord *Tyrconnel*'s,[1] in which I mention'd *Gilliver*'s[2] Desire to be the publisher of your Tragedy: Since, he requests my Letter to recommend him. I find Mr. *Savage* has rais'd his Hope, by saying you had kept *yourself unengag'd*, *in Expectation that I would* plead for him, and that *you wonder'd I did not sooner.* If this be not one of those Things in which Mr. *S.* speaks upon Imagination, I am more oblig'd to you than ever I intended. For I assure you, I had no Thought of *imposing*, nay, not even of *proposing* a Bookseller, for fear your great Complacency toward me, should lead you, more, than your own Inclination, to another Bookseller. But if you have no such Byass, this Man I really think honest, and capable in his Business. I hope in a few Days to meet you in Town, and am sincerely yours, and the young Lady's, | A. Pope.

I just now receive your very kind Letter, but can answer it no otherwise than by going about what you propose. I'll write first, and then see every body I can in Town on *Tuesday*, &c.

[3]GAY *and* THE DUKE OF QUEENSBERRY *to* SWIFT
Add. 4806
[1 *November* 1731]

For about this month or six weeks past I have been rambling from home or have been at what I may not improperly call other homes, at Dawley & at Twickenham; & I really think at every one of my homes you have as good a pretension as myself, for I find 'em all exceedingly disappointed by the Lawsuit that hath kept you this summer from us. Mr Pope told me that Affair was now over, that you have the Estate that was your security. I wish you had your own money, for I wish you free from every Engagement that keeps us one from another. I think you decypher'd the last Letter we sent you very judiciously. You may make your own conditions at Amesbury where I am at present; you may do the same at Dawley, and Twickenham you know is your own; But if you rather chuse to live with me, (that is to say, if you will give up your right & title) I will purchase the house you & I us'd to dispute about over-against Ham walks on purpose to entertain you. name your day & it shall be done. I have liv'd with you,

---

[1] Lord Tyrconnel, together with Pope and other friends, was at this time aiding Richard Savage financially. His Lordship was the nephew of the unfortunate woman (now Mrs. Brett, formerly Countess of Macclesfield) whom Savage claimed as mother. Pope's hasty scrawl and Hill's letter mentioned here in the postscript have disappeared.

[2] Lawton Gilliver had recently become Pope's bookseller, and Hill allowed him to bring out *Athelwold*.

[3] First published by Hawkesworth. The date is inferred from the postmark. Pope published the answer, dated 1 Dec.

& I wish to do so again in any place & upon any terms. The Dutchess does not know of my writing, but I promis'd to acquaint the Duke the next time I writ to you, & for aught I know he may tell the Dutchess, & she may tell Sir W. Wyndham, who is now here, & for fear they should all have something to say to you I leave the rest of the paper 'till I see the Duke.

[1]Mr Gay tells me you seem to doubt what authority my Wife & he have to invite a person hither who by agreement is to have the government of the place during his stay, when at the same time it does not appear that the present master of these Demesnes hath been consulted in it. The truth of the matter is this; I did not know whether you might not have suspected me for a sort of a pert coxcomb had I put in my word in the late correspondence between you & my Wife. Ladies (by the Courtesie of the World) enjoy priviledges not allow'd to men & in many cases the same thing is call'd a favour from a Lady which might perhaps be look'd upon as impertinence from a man. Upon this reflection I have hitherto refrain'd from writing to you having never had the pleasure of conversing with you otherways & as that is a thing I most sincerely wish I would not venture to meddle in a negotiation that seem'd to be in so fair a way of producing that desirable end; but our friend John has not done me justice if he has never mention'd to you how much I wish for the pleasure of seeing you here & tho I have not till now avowedly taken any steps towards bringing it about, what has pass'd conducive to it has been all along with my privity & consent & I do now formally ratify all the preliminary articles & conditions agreed to on the part of my Wife & will undertake for the due observance of them. I depend upon my friend John to answer for my sincerity. I was not long at Court & have been a Country gentleman for some time.

Poll manu sub linus darque dds[2]
Sive Nig fig gnipite gnaros

Address: To the Revd Doctor Swift | Dean of St Patricks | in Dublin | Ireland
Postmark: 1/NO
Endorsement (In Swift's hand): Mr Gay and the | Duke of Queensberry | No date | Rx Novr 8th 1731

[1] The rest of the letter is by the Duke, except the two lines of gibberish(?) appended at the very end by the Duchess.

[2] These two lines evidently—as Swift divines in his answer to the letter—are added by the Duchess, and refer somehow to Swift's reflection on her dd's in his letter of 28 Aug. 1731. The second of the two lines comes from a piece of gibberish known to the editor only as existing in a letter from Lord Percival to his son written in Bath, 12 May 1730, and preserved as Add. MS. 47032, pp. 329–30. The item copied into Percival's letter is alleged to be taken from an inscription 'found upon Malcoms Cross', but it is obviously jocose gibberish of a sort Swift might enjoy. The 'inscription' is in rough hexameters, and the second line reads: 'Spalando Spados sive nig fig Knippite gnaros.' Where the inscription was printed or how the Duchess got hold of it is unknown. See *Notes & Queries*, 198 (1953), 160–1.

POPE *to* JONATHAN RICHARDSON[1]   2 *November* [1731]

Elwin–Courthope, ix. 495

Twitnam, Nov. 2, [1731]

It is true that some accident, as well as some bad health, have conspired to hinder me from seeing London and you. But I am now in a tollerable way, and taken up also with some friends here. I shall be one day in town this week, but fear it will not be in my power to see you. If it is, I shall not fail. You will give the bearer those notes on Milton which I want to read, and also the second edition, which I committed a piece of violence (not to call it injustice) to procure for you, in the mistake I was under about it. My services attend your son, and my most hearty wishes are yours. Believe me, dear sir, yours.

POPE *to* THE EARL OF OXFORD[2]   7 *November* [1731]

Longleat Portland Papers, xii

Novr 7th | [1731]

My Lord,—Whether your Lordship or I, desire most, & are most impatient, to know of the others Welfare, may be determin'd by the Need one has of the other, & the Good one does to the other: Wherfore (I presume in common Interest) you must allow Me to be the person most concern'd to hear it. I beg to be acquainted in your own hand, more particularly than your Porter can satisfy my longing, What you do, how you do, where you are, & where you will be? How stands the Library, which since the Loss of the Cottonian[3] is the greatest Care of the Republick of Learning? Has not B—y done Great things for Literature, in publishing his own papers, & burning those? That public Calamity has happend under this Tyrant, while he was *fidling* upon Milton & Manilius.[4]

---

[1] Elwin prints from 'Richardson's transcript'.

[2] The year is probably Lord Oxford's addition.

[3] *The London Evening Post*, 21–23 Oct. 1731, reports: 'This Morning early a Fire broke out in the late Earl of Ashburnham's House, near Westminster-Abbey, where the famous Cotton Library is kept; it did great Damage to the House, and destroy'd several of the valuable MSS., belonging to that noble Collection, and damag'd others, which Loss is irreparable.' The Library had been presented to the nation in 1700. Since 1694 Pope's critic, Richard Bentley, had been Keeper of the King's Libraries in England, and though Bentley was probably at this time resident in Cambridge, Pope affects to blame him for the fire. Only MSS. were damaged in this famous fire, not printed books.

[4] Bentley's edition of *Paradise Lost* was published early in 1732. Manilius was a longtime favourite of Bentley's, and the edition (published in 1739) was a lifework. Bentley's enemies loved to fling at him his remark that 'Ovid and Manilius were the only poets that had *wit* among the ancients'. See J. H. Monk, *Life of Bentley*, p. 26 n. Pope was condemning Bentley's Milton partly on hearsay and partly on specimens given pre-publication by his enemies in Cambridge; notably by (one supposes) John Martyn (presently to become professor of botany at Cambridge, where he was already studying while helping to edit *The Grubstreet Journal*).

I can give your Lordship so bad an account of my own studies, that I ought not to condemn another man's; tho, bad as my Verses are, I dare say such Verbal Criticks as may follow B—y's track, can make them worse, if they attempt to correct them. However, I have made some little leisurely progress, & taken the Liberty to call at Your Door, in my way to Moral Virtue;[1] as you will see when we meet. That it may be soon, is what I heartily wish; & that it may be in the utmost Good health, of yourself, Lady Oxford, & Lady Margaret: I am sure it will be in the utmost Good humour.—My sincere Services & respects are theirs, and ever, Spiritus dum hos reget artus, | My Lord, | Yours, | A. Pope.

My Mother & I drink your healths often: She is pretty well still.

Address: To the Earl of Oxford, in | Dover street, Piccadilly. | London.
Postmark: 10/NO

THE DUKE OF DORSET *to* LADY SUFFOLK[2]

9 November 1731

1824 (*Suffolk Correspondence*, ii. 33)

Excerpt

I will not add to my impertinence by making you the messenger of my compliments to Mr. Pope: when I see him I will make them myself, in the best manner I am able, and at the same time I hope he will grant me a *free conference* upon the subject matter of the epitaph. . .

POPE *to* TONSON, JUN.

November [1731]

The Gentleman's Magazine, clix (1836), 27.

Twitenham, Nov. [1731]

Sir,—I learn from an Article published in a late daily journal,[3] that Tibbald is to have the *text* of Shakespear, *together* with his remarks,

---

[1] Pope had inserted a compliment in his third Moral Essay (to Bathurst), ll. 243–8.

[2] This letter (found in Add. 22626, f. 20) was written from Dublin Castle: his grace was Lord Lieutenant. The fragment here printed concerns an epitaph for the Duke's father, the 6th Earl of Dorset (d. 1706), which Pope printed in his *Works* (1735). In 1731 the Duke's son, Charles, Earl of Middlesex, was travelling on the Continent with Joseph Spence as companion—through Pope's intervention. In Jan. 1732 Savage (or Pope?) dedicated to the Earl of Middlesex the *Collection of Several Pieces . . . publish'd on Occasion of the Dunciad*, and Pope's further interest in the Sackville family is seen in his encouraging Spence to edit *Gorboduc* in 1736. In the 'last' volume of the *Miscellanies* (1728) Pope had printed his 'Artemisia' as imitation of the famous Restoration wit, the 6th Earl of Dorset.

[3] On 11 Nov. *The Grub-street Journal* reprinted from *The Daily Journal* the item: 'We hear that Mr. Theobald, being now intirely ready to give the publick an edition of Shakspear's Plays, with his remarks and emendations, has articled with Mr. Tonson for publishing the same in 6 Volumes in 8vo, with all possible dispatch.' Pope must have known that such an edition had for some time been preparing, but he effectively pretends surprise.

printed by *you*. As I have heard nothing of this from you, I presume
it is not so; at least that you, with whom I have liv'd ever upon amic-
able terms, will not be the publisher of any impertinencies relating
any way to my character, of which you cannot but know, that man's
specimens and letters concerning them have been full. In a word, I
doubt not but you wou'd some way have acquainted me with any
design of yours concerning Shakespear. I desire you'l tell me the truth
of this matter, tho' I believe 'tis no more than some idle report crept
into the News, or perhaps put into it by himself. | I am, Dear Sir,
your affectionate humble servant, | A Pope.

When did you hear of your Uncle?

TONSON, JUN. *to* POPE   13 *November* 1731

The Gentleman's Magazine, clix (1836), 27.

13 Nov. 1731.

Sir,—I have rec'd yours, *wherein you desire me to tell you the truth
whether I have agreed with Theobald to print the Text of Shakespear
together with his Remarks*. The truth is this, other persons being concerned in the Text of Shakespear with myself, Mr Theobald treated
with them to print it, and as I found the work wou'd go on by the
other parties concern'd (tho I had not come into the agreement), so I
could not avoid being concern'd in the edition: this is the truth.[1] I
am sensible of the many instances of your friendship, and shall never
do any act to forfeit your opinion of me; and since Theobald's Shakespear must come out, I cannot think you will like it the worse that a
friend of yours is one of the printers. As for the advertisement, or
piece of news in the daily Journal, I knew nothing of it till I read it
in the Paper, nor ever thought it worth my time to enquire how it
came there. I had a letter from my uncle last post, who is well, and
will be very glad to hear that you are so.

I am Sir, your most obliged and most obedient servant, | J. T.

POPE *to* TONSON, JUN.   14 *November* 1731

The Gentleman's Magazine, clix (1836), 28.

Nov. 14, 1731.

You may guess how far I am from being unwilling that Tibbald's
Notes should come out, when I long since desir'd and commission'd

---

[1] Tonson and Theobald signed articles on 28 Oct. 1731, according to a letter printed
in R. F. Jones, *Lewis Theobald*, p. 277. The letter indicates that other booksellers had
approached Theobald, but that Tonson had bought him off by offering double their terms.
Tonson wished to preserve his pretended perpetual copyright in Shakespeare's plays.

you to try to procure them against our second edition. The worst I wish is, that Shakespear and you may be serv'd by 'em. But all I shou'd be sorry for would be, if *you* were made the *publisher* of any falsity relating to my *personal character*, who not only am a man that wish you well, but have suffer'd a little on your account, by one lye of this man's venting. Having a mind to write to your uncle, I've taken this for part of a subject of a letter, where you will see what further I have to say of it.[1] I am fully satisfied by what you tell me, and always ready to be truly, Sir, your affectionate humble servant |
A. Pope.

POPE *to* TONSON, SR.   14 *November* 1731

Egerton 2869
                                                      Nov. 14th 1731.

Sir,—I had a Letter from your Nephew, who tells me what I am pleasd always to hear, that you are well, but not a word when you return to Barnes. Your stay has been much longer than I hopd, & you proposed. I was almost ready to be angry with your Nephew on hearing He was to be the Publisher of Tibbald's Shakespear; who, according to the laudable Custom of Commentators, first servd himself of my Pains, & then abused me for 'em. But I am satisfy'd, since he tells me other Proprietors in the Copy of Shakespear would have printed it without him; And I am the better pleasd he has a Share in it, because if any Slander on my Personal character should be inserted in the Book, He doubtless would be enabled to testify in the same book, any such Truth in my justification as I could call upon him to witness. I never understood, when I was concernd in this Edition, that any other Proprietors could be ballancd with himself in it: This you must know too.[2] But if an Edition of the Text can be printed without his Consent, & if the Propriety to this Author be so wandring, I'm very sure that however my Edition, or Tibbald's, may sell, I know a way to put any Friend upon publishing a new one that will vastly outsell them both (of which I will talk with you when we meet.) And not of this author only but of all the other best English Poets, a Project which I am sure the Publick would thank me for, & which none of the Dutch-headed Scholiasts are capable of executing.

I think I should congratulate your Cosen[3] on the new Trade he is commencing, of publishing English classicks with huge Commentaries.

---

[1] Evidently the letter to the uncle (then living in Ledbury) was enclosed with this to the bookselling nephew. See the following letter.

[2] When Theobald's edition appeared in 1733 Tonson's name on the title-page came third in a list of six booksellers; but one doubts if he recognized the other five as actual sharers in the copyright.

[3] *Cousin* to Pope frequently means *relative*; here, *nephew*.

Tibbalds will be the Follower of Bentley, & Bentley of Scriblerus. What a Glory will it be to the Dunciad, that it was the First Modern Work publish'd in this manner? In truth I think myself happier in my Commentator than either Milton or Shakespear; & shall be very well content if the same hands proceed to any other mans works, but my owne, and in this I depend upon your Friendship, & your Interest with your Cosen, that you will not let the Tibbalds ever publish notes upon such things of mine, as are your Property yet, or shall be here-after—*Oh shade those Laurels which descend to you!*[1]

I writ you a long letter about 2 months since, since when I have not heard from you. If you are now upon returning, you'l probably find Lord Bathurst at Cirencester, who I know would rejoice to show you all his works there. I past a week lately with Lord Cobham & Mr Stanyan. I think all your friends are well. Lord Wilmington I dined with the day he left Chiswick for the Season. My Mother is pretty well & remembers [you]. I know nothing more to tell you but that I am, with sincere good will, ever | Dear Sir | Your affectionate Friend & Servant | A. Pope.

I have a very pretty Poem to show you of a near Relation of Lord Cobhams, which he has inscribed to me & some others.[2]

You live not far from *Ross*. I desire you to get me an Exact information of the *Man of Ross*, what was his Xtian & Surname? what year he dyed, & about what age? and to transcribe his Epitaph, if he has one. And any Particulars you can procure about him. I intend to make him an Example in a Poem of mine.[3]

Address: To | Mr Tonson, Senr at | Ledbury, | Herefordshire.
Postmark torn away.

TONSON, JUN., *to* POPE   18 *November* 1731

The Gentleman's Magazine, clix (1836), 28

                                                    18 Nov. 1731.

Sir,—I have fully answer'd your first about Shakespear. As to any other matters, I shall be so far from doing, or suffering any thing to be done, to make you uneasy, that on the contrary, I shall be glad of any opportunity of obliging, and, if possible, serving you; and in the plainest words I tell you, that whoever I employ in publishing any of

---

[1] From Dryden's 'Epistle to Congreve'.

[2] Both George Lyttelton and Gilbert West were nephews of Lord Cobham, and both were friends of Pope throughout the rest of his career. Pope seems to have in hand West's poem on *Stowe: The Gardens of the . . . Viscount Cobham* (1732). *Stowe* was 'Address'd to Mr. Pope'.

[3] Pope still wishes further checks on his information concerning the Man of Ross. See his letter to Bethel, 8 Sept. 1731.

the copy's I am entitled unto (more especially any pieces of yours), I will conclude on nothing till I have your opinion. I am much obliged to you for the compliment of sending your letter to my uncle open to me; but as (in my humble opinion) it will look much better for that letter (or any other of yours) to come immediately from yourself than under my cover, so I return it as I rec'd it, and am, Sir, your most humble servant | J. T.

POPE *to* THE EARL OF OXFORD   [20 *November* 1731]

Longleat Portland Papers, xii

Nov. 20. 1731

My Lord,—I came yesterday to Towne, & enquird at your house of the welfare of your family. I was most extremely surprized to hear that Lady Margaret has been dangerously ill,[1] & still tho in a fair way of Recovery, confined to her chamber. My drunken Sot of a Waterman has thrice told me all your Lordships Family were well; and the Concern this has given me is what I really feel more than can be exprest. I partly feel what you yourself must have felt, & what Lady O. must have felt on this occasion. Such an Experience of the Errors of Servants, and the Dissatisfaction of such accounts, to a Man Who is truly concernd for you, makes me urgently beg a Line from your own hands, of the State of Lady Margarets health. I am more than I can tell you, | My Lord | Your sincere obliged, af-|fectionate Servant | A. Pope

I've just receivd a Collar of Brawn, for which my Mother & I heartily thank you.

Address: To | the Earl of Oxford.
Endorsement: Mr Pope Novr 20. 1731.

ATTERBURY *to* POPE[2]   23 *November* 1731

1735 (*A General Dictionary*, ii. 447)

Paris Nov. 23d, 1731[3]

You will wonder to see me in print; but how could I avoid it? The

---

[1] *The London Evening Post*, 13 Nov. 1731, contains verses dated Wimpole, 1 Nov. 1731, 'To Dr. Mead, on the Recovery of the Lady Margaret Harley'. These may have first informed Pope concerning an illness in the country.

[2] This letter, dated three months before Atterbury's death, was included in the last edition of Pope's letters published in the poet's lifetime (1742Ld2). Its earlier printings have a complicated history. Atterbury's *Vindication . . . relating to the Publication of Lord Clarendon's History* was a reply to Oldmixon's charges that Atterbury had helped falsify the
[*Note 2 continued on next page.*

[3] 1731] 1732 1735*kim* (An impossible date, months after Atterbury's death!)

dead and the living, my friends and my foes, at home and abroad, call upon me to say something; and the reputation of an History, which I and all the world value, must have suffered, had I continued silent. I have printed here, in hopes that somebody afterward may venture to reprint in England, notwithstanding the two frightening words at the close of it.[1] Whether that happens or not, it is fit you should have a sight of it, who I know will read it with some degree of satisfaction, as it is mine, tho' it should have (as it really has) nothing else to recommend it. Such as it is,

Extremum hoc munus morientis habeto

For that may well be the case, considering that within a few months I am entering into my seventieth year; after which even the healthy and the happy cannot much depend upon life, and will not, if they are wise, much desire it. Whenever I go, you will lose a friend, who loves and values you extremely, if in my circumstances I can be said to be lost to any one, when dead, more than I am already whilst living. I expected to have heard from you by Mr. M—,[2] and wondered a little, that I did not; but he owns himself in a fault for not giving you due notice of his motions. It was not amiss that you forbore writing ⌐to me⌐ on a head, wherein I promised more than I was able to perform. Disgraced men fancy sometimes, that they preserve an influence, where, when they endeavour to exert it, they soon see their mistake. I did so, my good friend, and acknowledge it under my hand. You sounded the coast, and found out my error, it seems, before I was aware of it. But enough of this subject. What are you

text of Clarendon's *History*. The *Vindication*, dated 26 Oct. 1731, had been published in French in the *Bibliothèque raisonnée* for October–December of 1731 (pp. 457–72). An English edition (advertised in *LEP* for 2 Dec.) was simultaneously published, but the date of this letter to Pope perhaps implies that copies of the French text were sent to him with this covering letter. Probably without permission the letter was first printed in *A General Dictionary, Historical and Critical*, ii. 447. The *General Dictionary* originally appeared in monthly fascicules, and that containing the life of Atterbury (and this letter to Pope) was published either in Sept. or Oct. 1734, as advertisements in *The Universal Spectator* indicate. Pope learned of the publication while at Bath (see *Modern Philology*, xxxvi [1938], 25–46), and, still timid about avowing correspondence with the attainted exile, immediately persuaded Birch and Lockman (editors of the *Dictionary*) to cancel the leaf containing the letter. It appears, however, in some copies of the *Dictionary*. It was reprinted by [William] Dawson in his volume of *Miscellaneous Poems* (*LEP*, 5 Dec.) and in *The London Evening Post* itself, 12 Dec. Curll included it in 1735k and it appears in two possibly piratical 'Booksellers' editions, 1735im. In 1742Ld2 occurs the following footnote: 'We have ventured to insert this Letter, which was plainly intended for Mr. Pope, tho' we are inform'd that on second thoughts it was not judg'd proper to send it him. A Copy was preserved, and published soon after in the English additions to Bayle's Dictionary, under the Article of Atterbury.' Whether this represents a coy authorization of the letter by Pope will perhaps be a matter of opinion. The different early texts of the letter vary frequently, but vary only slightly. Here only more significant variations from the text of 1742 are given. Other texts have slight or no connection with Pope as editor. Half-brackets indicate omissions in 1742.

[1] His Name.—*1735k; 1742 Ld2*.   [2] M—] Morice *1742Ld2*.

doing in England to the honour of Letters? And particularly what are
you doing?

Ipse quid audes?
Quae circumvolitas agilis Thyma?[1]

Do you pursue the moral plan[2] you marked out, and seemed sixteen
months ago so intent upon? Am I to see it perfected e'er I die? And
are you to enjoy the reputation of it whilst you live? Or do you rather
choose to leave the marks of your friendship, like the legacies of a will,
to be read and enjoyed only by those who survive you? Were I as near
you as I have been, I should hope to peep into the manuscript even
before it was finished. But alas! there is and ever will probably be a
great deal of land and sea between us. How many Books have come
out of late in your parts, which you think I should be glad to peruse?
Name them; the Catalogue, I believe, will not cost you much trouble.
They must be good ones indeed to challenge any part of my time, now
I have so little of it left. I, who squandered away whole days hereto-
fore, now husband hours, when the glass begins to run low, and care
not to mispend them on trifles. At the end of the lottery of life our
last minutes, like ⌜benefit-⌝ tickets in the wheel, rise in their valua-
tion. They are not perhaps of so much worth in themselves, as those,
which preceded, but we are apt to prize them more, and with reason.
I do so, my dear friend, and yet think the most precious minutes of my
life are well employed in reading what you write. But this is a satisfaction I cannot much hope for; and therefore must betake myself to
others, ⌜which are⌝ less entertaining. Adieu, dear Sir, and forgive me
engaging with one, whom you, I think, have reckoned among the Heroes
of the Dunciad.[3] It was necessary for me either to accept of his dirty
challenge, or to have suffered in the esteem of the world by declining
it. My respects to your mother; I send a paper[4] for Dean Swift, if
you have an opportunity, and think it worth your while to convey it.
My country at this distance seems to me a strange sight. I know not
how it appears to you, who are in the midst of the Sun, and your self
a part of it. I wish you would tell me. You may write safely to Mr.
M—[5] by the honest hand, that conveys this, and will return to these
parts before Christmas. Sketch out a rough draught of it, that I may
be able to judge whether a return to it be really eligible, or whether
I should not like the Chymist in the bottle upon hearing Don
Quevedo's account of Spain,[6] desire to be cork'd up again. After all
I do and must love my country with all its faults and blemishes; even
that part of the constitution, which wounded me unjustly (and itself

---

[1] Horace, *Epistle*, i. iii. 20–21.   [2] The *Essay on Man.*—*1735k; LEP 1734.*
[3] In *The Dunciad* of 1729 Oldmixon is mentioned several times.
[4] Another copy of the *Vindication*.   [5] M—] Morice *1735k; 1742Ld2.*
[6] In the second of the *Visions* of Don Quevedo Villegas, very popular in the translation
of Sir Roger L'Estrange.

thro' my side) will ever be dear to me. My last wish shall[1] be like that of Father Paul, *Esto perpetua*; and when I die at a distance from it, it will be in the same manner as Virgil describes the expiring Peloponnesian,

Sternitur, & dulces moriens reminiscitur Argos.[2]

Do I live[3] in the memory of my friends, as they certainly do in mine? I have read a good many of your paper-squabbles about me, and am glad to see such free concessions on that head, tho' made with no view of doing me a pleasure, but of loading another. Fr. Roffen.

†GAY *and* POPE *to* SWIFT　　　　　　　I *December* 1731
1740

December 1, 1731.

You us'd to complain that Mr. Pope and I would not let you speak: you may now be even with me, and take it out in writing. If you don't send to me now and then, the post-office will think me of no consequence, for I have no correspondent but you. You may keep as far from us as you please, you cannot be forgotten by those who ever knew you, and therefore please me by sometimes shewing that I am not forgot by you. I have nothing to take me off from my friendship to you; I seek no new acquaintance, and court no favour; I spend no shillings in coaches or chairs to levees or great visits, and as I don't want the assistance of some that I formerly convers'd with, I will not so much as seem to seek to be a dependant. As to my studies, I have not been entirely idle, though I cannot say that I have yet perfected any thing. What I have done is something in the way of those fables I have already publish'd.[4] All the mony I get is by saving, so that by habit there may be some hopes (if I grow richer) of my becoming a miser. All misers have their excuses; The motive to my parsimony is independance. If I were to be represented by the Duchess (she is such a downright niggard for me) this character might not be allow'd me; but I really think I am covetous enough for any who lives at the court-end of the town, and who is as poor as myself: for I don't pretend that I am equally saving with S—k.[5] Mr. Lewis desir'd you might be told that he hath five pounds of yours in his hands which he fancys you may have forgot, for he will hardly allow that a Verse-man can have a just knowledge of his own affairs. When you got rid of your law-suit, I was in hopes you had got your own, and was free from every vexation of the law; but Mr. Pope tells me you are not entirely out of

---

[1] The word is inserted from the text of 1742.　　　　　　　[2] *Aeneid*, x. 781–2.
[3] Do I live] Do I still live *1735kim, 1742Ld2, LEP.*
[4] Gay's second series of *Fables* was on the point of completion.
[5] Charles, 2nd Earl of Selkirk, a generally disliked courtier, who had the fortune to be satirized by both Pope and Lord Hervey—among others.

your perplexity, though you have the security now in your own possession; but still your case is not so bad as Captain Gulliver's, who was
ruin'd by having a decree for him with costs. I have had an injunction
for me against pyrating-booksellers, which I am sure to get nothing by,
and will, I fear, in the end drain me of some mony. When I begun this
prosecution I fancy'd there would be some end of it, but the law still
goes on, and 'tis probable I shall some time or other see an Attorney's
bill as long as the Book. Poor Duke Disney is dead, and hath left
what he had among his friends, among whom are Lord Bolingbroke
500 *l*[1] Sir William Wyndham's youngest son, 500 *l*. Gen Hill, 500 *l*.
Lord Massam's son 500 *l*.

You have the good wishes of those I converse with, they know they
gratify me when they remember you; but I really think they do it
purely for your own sake. I am satisfied with the love and friendship
of good men, and envy not the demerits of those who are more[2]
conspicuously distinguish'd. Therefore as I set a just value upon your
friendship, you cannot please me more than letting me now and then
know that you remember me (the only satisfaction of distant friends!)

P.S. Mr. Gay's is a good letter, mine will be a very dull one; and
yet what you will think the worst of it is what should be its excuse,
that I write in a head-ach that has lasted three days. I am never ill
but I think of your ailments, and repine that they mutually hinder our
being together: tho' in one point I am apt to differ from you, for you
shun your friends when you are in those circumstances, and I desire
them; your way is the more generous, mine the more tender. Lady —[3]
took your letter very kindly, for I had prepared her to expect no
answer under a twelve-month; but kindness perhaps is a word not
applicable to courtiers. However she is an extraordinary woman there,
who will do you common justice. For God's sake why all this scruple
about Lord B—'s[4] keeping your horses who has a park, or about my
keeping you on a pint of wine a day? We are infinitely richer than you
imagine; John Gay shall help me to entertain you, tho' you come like
King Lear with fifty knights—Tho' such prospects as I wish, cannot
now be formed for fixing you with us, time may provide better before
you part again: the old Lord[5] may die, the benefice may drop,[6] or at
worst, you may carry me into Ireland. You will see a word of Lord
B—'s and one of mine;[7] which, with a just neglect of the present age,
consult only posterity; and with a noble scorn of politicks, aspire to
philosophy. I am glad you resolve to meddle no more with the low

[1] The London texts (1741–2) insert after Bolingbroke's 500 *l*., 'Mr. Pelham, 500 *l*.'
[2] more] most *1741Labc*; *1742Lbc, Da*.   [3] *Suffolk* presumably.
[4] Bolingbroke's.   [5] Lord St. John, Bolingbroke's aged father.
[6] The benefice (unidentified) that Bolingbroke intended for Swift—to bring Swift back
to England.
[7] The 'words' were Pope's *Essay on Man* and Bolingbroke's parallel prose writing.

concerns and interests[1] of parties, even of countries, (for countries are but larger parties) *Quid verum atque decens, curare, & rogare, nostrum sit.*[2] I am much pleased with your design upon Rochefoucault's maxim, pray finish it. I am happy whenever you join our names together: so would Dr. Arbuthnot be, but at this time can be pleas'd with nothing; for his darling son is dying in all probability, by the melancholy account I received this morning.[3]

The paper you ask me about is of little value.[4] It might have been a seasonable satire upon the scandalous language and passion with which men of condition have stoop'd to treat one another: surely they sacrifice too much to the people, when they sacrifice their own characters, families, &c. to the diversion of that rabble of readers. I agree with you in my contempt of most popularity, fame, &c. even as a writer I am cool in it, and whenever you see what I am now writing, you'll be convinced I would please but a few, and (if I could) make mankind less Admirers, and greater Reasoners.[5] I study much more to render my own portion of being easy, and to keep this peevish frame of the human body in good humour. Infirmities have not quite un-mann'd me, and it will delight you to hear they are not increas'd, tho' not diminish'd. I thank God I do not very much want people to attend me, tho' my Mother now cannot. When I am sick I lie down, when I am better I rise up: I am used to the head-ach, &c. If greater pains arrive (such as my late rheumatism) the servants bath and plaster me, or the surgeon scarifies me, and I bear it, because I must. This is the evil of Nature, not of Fortune. I am just now as well as when you was here: I pray God you were no worse. I sincerely wish my life were past near you, and such as it is I would not repine at it.—All you mention remember you, and wish you here.

‖SWIFT *to* GAY *and* THE QUEENSBERRYS

[1 *December* 1731]

Longleat Portland Papers, xiii (Harleian transcripts)

[Dec. 1. 1731][6]

If your ramble was on horseback I am glad of it, on account of your

---

[1] interests] interest *1741 Dab.*

[2] We spend our Time in the Search and Enquiry after Truth and Decency.—Footnote in 1741 Dab.

[3] Rev. Charles Arbuthnot (1704–31), second son of the Doctor, died 2 Dec.

[4] Probably Arbuthnot's *Brief Account of Mr. John Ginglicutt's Treatise concerning the Altercation or Scolding of the Ancients*, published in Feb. 1730/1. It is probably being considered for the *Miscellanies* of 1732.

[5] The poem he means is the *Essay on Man*. But he could never compass his Purpose: His readers would in spite of him *admire* his poetry, and would not understand his *reasoning*—Warburton, 1751.

[6] The subscribed date on the transcript is added by Lord Oxford. Swift usually dated his letters, and since this is an answer to Gay's letter 'received' 8 November, Lord Oxford's date

health, but I know your arts of patching up a journy between Stage coaches and friends coaches, for you are as arrant a cockney as any hosier in Cheap-Side, and one clean Shirt with two Cravats and as many Handkerchefs make up your equipage, and as for a night gown, it is clear from Homer, that Agamemnon rose without one I have often had it in my head to put it into yours, that you ought to have Some great work in Schemes, which may take up Seven years to finish; besides two or three under-one's, that may add another thousand pounds to your Stock; and then I shall be in less pain about you, I know you can find dinners, but you love twelve penny coaches too well, without considering that the interest of a whole thousand pounds brings you but half a crown a day. I find a greater longing than ever to come amongst you, and reason good; when I am teised with Dukes and Dutchesses for a visit; all my demands complyed with and all excuses cut off; you remember; O happy Don Quixet, Queens held his horse, and Dutchesses pulled off his armor, Or Something to that purpose. He was a mean Spirited fellow, I can say ten times more O happy &c *Such* a Dutchess was designed to attend him, and *Such* a Duke invited him to command his Palace Nam istos reges ceteros memorare nolo, hominum mendicabula:[1] go read your Plautus, and observe Strobilius vaporing after he had found the pot of gold: I will have nothing to do with ⌜the house over against Ham-walks, or with⌝ the owner of it,[2] I have long hated her on your account, and the more because you are So forgiving as not to hate her. ⌜I writt her a long letter lately, in answer to her last and let her know I would write to her no more, all⌝ though She has Good qualityes enough to make her esteemed; but not one grain of truth or honour.[3] I onely wish She were ⌜as great⌝ a fool ⌜as She is a knave⌝. I have been severall months writing near five hundred lines on a pleasant Subject, onely to tell what my friends and enemyes will say on[4] me after I am dead.[5] I Shall finish it soon, for I add two lines every week, and blott out four, and alter eight, I have brought in you and my other friends, as well as enemyes and Detractors.

It is a great comfort to See how corruption and ill conduct are instrumental in uniting Virtuous Persons and lovers of their country of all denominations ⌜Lord B— with W. P. Sir W W with the Aimsbury;⌝[6] Whig and Tory high and low Church as Soon as they

---

is very likely what Swift wrote. Pope in 1741 curiously dated the letter 10 Sept. 1731—which seems impossible.

[1] Plautus, *Aulularia*, IV. viii. 2–3. Translated in a note in 1741Dab as 'I pass by those other Princes, poor mendicants of Mankind.'

[2] All printed texts 1740–2 read, 'I will have nothing to do with that Lady.'

[3] truth or honor] feeling *1740–2*.   [4] on] of *1741Dab*.

[5] *Verses on the Death of Dr. Swift* (1739).

[6] That is, Lord Bolingbroke is united with William Pulteney, and Sir William Wyndham with the Duke and Duchess at Amesbury.

are left to think freely, all joyning in opinion. If this be disaffection, pray God Send me allways among the disaffected; And I heartily wish you joy of your Scurvy treatment at Court, which hath given you leisure to cultivate both publick and private Virtue, neither of them likely to be Soon met within[1] the Walls of St James's or Westminster,—But I must here dismiss you that I may pay my Acknowledgments to the Duke for the great honor he hath done me

My Lord,—I could have Sworn, that my pride would be always able to preserve me from vanity, of which I have been in great danger to be guilty for some months past, first by the conduct of My Lady Dutchess and now by that of your Grace, which had like to finish the work; And I should have certainly gone about Shewing my letters under the charge of Secrecy to every blab of my acquaintance, if I could have the least hope of prevayling on any of them to believe that a man in So obscure a corner quite thrown out of the present world, and within a few Steps of the next, Should receive Such condecending invitations, from two Such persons to whome he is an utter Stranger, and who know no more of him than what they have heard by the partial representations of a friend; But in the mean time, I must desire your Grace, not to flatter your Self, that I waited for your consent, to Accept the invitation. I must be ignorant indeed not to know, that the Dutchess ever Since you met, hath been most politically employd in increasing those forces., and Sharpening those arms with which She Subdued you at first., and to which, the braver and wiser you grow, you will more and more Submit. Thus I know my Self on the Secure Side, and it was a meer piece of ⌜my⌝ good manners to insert that clause, of which you have taken that advantage; But, as I cannot forbear informing Your Grace, that the Dutchess's great Secret in her art of government, hath been to reduce both your wills into one; So I am content in due observance to the forms of the world to return my most humble thanks to your Grace for so great a favor as you are pleased to offer me and which nothing but impossibilityes Shall prevent me from receiving. Since I am with the greatest reason, truth and Respect My Lord Your Graces most obedient &c.

Madam,—I have consulted all the learned in occult Sciences, of my acquaintance, and have Sate up eleven nights to discover the meaning of those two hieroglyphicall lines in your Graces hand at the bottom of the last Aimsbury letter; but all in vain Onely tis agreed, that the language is Coptick, and a very profound Behmist Assures me the Style is poetick containing an Invitation from a very great person of the Femal Sex to a Strange kind of man whom She never Saw, and

---

[1] met within] met with within *1740–2*.

this [is] all I can find, which after So many former Invitations will ever confirm me in that respect wherewith I am, Madam | Your Grace's most obedient &c.

Decr 1st 1731

POPE *to* HILL[1]   [9 *December* 1731]

1751 (Hill)

Nov. 12. 1731.

I shall have the Pleasure (sick or well) to be at the first Representation of your Play To-morrow, with Lord *Burlington* and Lord *Bathurst*, and one or two more. Another noble Lord, who understands you best,[2] must be contented to read the two last Acts in his Study: But Sir *Will. Wyndham*, with Mr. *Gay*, and some others, will be there also, in another Place, in his stead.—I write this that I may not take up a Minute of your Time in calling on me Tomorrow; but if you will send to the Office To-night for Places for four People, we will order a Man or two to go to keep 'em for us: Lord *Burlington* comes on purpose to Town. I am, with great Truth, | Yours, | A. Pope.

I've yet heard no Account from Court.[3]

POPE *to* HILL[4]   [11 *December* 1731]

1751 (Hill)

Sat. Morn. Nov. 14. 1731.

I cannot leave *London* without thanking you for the Pleasure you gave me last Night, by which I see you can as well make Actors, as Plays: Yet I own I receive more Pleasure from reading, than seeing your *Athelwold*. I thought the best Part of the Audience very attentive, and was told, several Ladies were mov'd to Tears. It is a Pity Mrs. *Cibber's* Voice and Person were not a little higher;[5] she speaks extremely justly, and seems to be Mistress of her Part. I could not come soon enough for the Prologue, but the Epilogue is a very humorous one. I am asham'd to trouble you; but being gone out of Town, and fearing the Mistakes of Servants, I beg a Box may be

---

[1] The November date for this letter appears in 1751 and in all editions including Elwin's. But the play in question seems to be *Athelwold*, and since it was first acted on 10 Dec. 1731, the date is here changed. The play had only three performances.

[2] Very likely Bolingbroke, who might be in ill health.

[3] That is, there is no report from Lady Suffolk on His Majesty George II's opinion of the play.

[4] The letter is obviously misdated in the *Collection* of 1751. Pope evidently wrote as date 'Sat. morn', and an editor added 'Nov. 14. 1731'. That day was on Saturday, and obviously the letter is written the day after *Athelwold* was first performed, which was Friday, 10 Dec.

[5] Mrs. Cibber (wife of Theophilus) acted Ethelinda.

had for *Monday*, the third Night (if there be any empty), for Mrs.
Blount, a particular Friend of mine. I yesterday saw Lady *Suffolk*, and
found, tho' their Majesties had not had Time to read, yet they were
possess'd with a good Opinion of the Play; and she would not part
with the Copy, expecting it would be call'd for every Day. I must
once more acknowledge the very obliging Manner in which you
favour'd the Bookseller, as well as the particular Generosity to him.
I can add no more, but an Assurance of the Sincerity with which I
am, | Dear Sir, | Your most oblig'd | and affectionate Servant, | A.
Pope.

I am hasten'd away, on hearing my Mother is not well: As soon
as I return, I hope we may pass some Time together.

[WILLIAM CLELAND] *to* GAY¹   [16 *December* 1731]

The Daily Post-Boy, 22 December 1731

Sir,—I am *astonished* at the Complaints occasion'd by a late *Epistle*
to the *Earl* of *Burlington*; and I should be afflicted were there the
least just Ground for them. Had the Writer attacked Vice, at a Time
when it is not only tolerated but triumphant; and so far from being
concealed as a Defect, that it is proclaimed with Ostentation as a
Merit; I should, ⌈while I admired his Courage,⌉ have been appre-
hensive of the Consequence: Had he satirized Gamesters of one
hundred thousand Pounds Fortune, acquired by such Methods as are
in daily Practice, and almost universally encouraged; had he over-
warmly defended the *Religion of his Country*, against such Books as
come from every Press, are publickly vended in every shop, and
greedily bought by almost every Rank of Men; or had he called our
excellent *Weekly Writers* by the same Names which they greatly²
bestow on the greatest Men *in* the Ministry and *out* of the Ministry,
for which they are all unpunished, and most rewarded: In any of

¹ This letter with omissions and slight revisions appeared in all Pope's editions except
1735ab and 1737b. The date appears in those texts, and must be approximately correct.
The letter first appeared as here given in *The Daily Post-Boy*, and it was reprinted on 23
Dec. in *The Daily Journal*, where the postscript (not found in any of Pope's editions) was
printed as a separate letter immediately following the other. The second letter had a date
of 19 Dec. In Pope's texts of 1735 the heading was 'To J. Gay, Esq;' and in those editions,
as in the newspapers, there was no mention of Cleland. In the octavos of 1737–43 the heading was 'Mr. Cleland to Mr. Gay'. The belated occurrence of this ascription to Cleland,
together with the nature of the *apologia*, has led to the belief that Warburton was right
when in 1751 (footnote) he remarked: 'This was written by the same hand that wrote the
Letter to the Publisher, prefixed to the Dunciad.' Warburton means that while both effusions
are ascribed to Cleland officially, Pope wrote both.
   The notable variants in text are omissions (here in half-brackets); there are some verbal
changes, as here noted.
² greatly] openly *1735–43*.

these Cases, indeed, I might have judged him too presumptuous, and perhaps have trembled for his Rashness.

I could not but hope better for this small and modest Epistle, which attacks *no one Vice* whatsoever; which deals only in *Folly* and not Folly in general, but a single Species of it; that only Branch, for the opposite Excellency to which, the Noble Lord to whom he writes must necessarily be celebrated, I fancied it might escape Censure, especially seeing how tenderly he treated these Follies, and seemed less to accuse them, than to make their Apology.[1]

> Yet hence the Poor are cloath'd, the Hungry fed,
> Health to himself, and to his Infants Bread,
> The Lab'rer bears.

Is this such a *Crime*, that to impute it to a Man must be a grievous Offence? 'Tis an *Innocent Folly* and much more *Beneficent* than the Want of it; for *Ill Taste* employs more Hands, and diffuses Expence more than a *Good* one. Is it a *Moral* Defect? No, it is but a *Natural* one; a *Want of a Taste*. It is what the best good Man living may be liable to: The worthiest Peer may live exemplarily in an ill favoured House, and the best reputed Citizen be pleased with a vile Garden. I thought (I say) the Author had the common Liberty to observe a Defect, and to compliment a Friend for a Quality that distinguishes him? Which I know not how any Quality should do, if we were not to remark that it was wanting in others?

But they say the Satire is *Personal*. I thought it could not be so, because all its Reflexions are on *Things*⌐; unless the Pictures, Statues, trimmed Trees, and Violins, are *Persons*¬. His Reflections are not on the *Man*, but his House, Garden, &c. Nay, he respects[2] (as one may say) the *Persons* of the Gladiator, Amphitrite,[3] the Nile, and the Triton: He is only sorry to see them (as he might be to see his best Friends) ridiculous, by being in the wrong Place, and in bad Company. Some fancy, that to say a Thing is *Personal*, is the same as to say it is *Injust*, not considering, that nothing can be *Just* that is not *Personal*: I am afraid that all such Writings and Discourses as touch no Man, will mend no Man. The *Good Natured* indeed are apt to be alarmed at any thing like Satire; and the *Guilty* readily concur with the *Weak* for a plain Reason, because the Vicious look upon Folly as their Frontier. *Iam proximus ardet Ucalegon.*[4] No wonder those who know Ridicule belongs to them, find an inward Consolation in removing it from themselves as far as they can; and it is never so far, as when they

---

[1] tenderly . . . Apology] tenderly these follies are treated, and really less accused than Apologized for. *1735–43*.

[2] respects] expects *Daily Post-Boy* (here emended).

[3] Amphitrite] Amphitheatre *1735* (omitted *1737–42*). (*The Daily Journal* has *Amphitheatre*.)

[4] *Aeneid*, ii. 311–12.

can get it fixt on the *best Characters*.[1] No Wonder, those who are Food for Satirists shou'd rail at them as Creatures of Prey; every Beast born for our Use, would be ready to call a Man so.

I know no Remedy, unless People in our Age would as little frequent the Theatres, as they begin to do the Churches; unless Comedy were forsaken, Satire silent, and every Man left to do what seems good in his own Eyes, as if there were no King, no Priest, no Poet, in Israel.

But I find myself obliged to touch a Point, on which I must be more serious; it well deserves I should: I mean[2] the malicious Application of the Character of *Timon*, which I will boldly say, they would impute to the Person the most different in the World from a *Manhater*, and the Person whose *Taste* and *Encouragement* of *Wits* have ever[3] been shewn in the *highest*[4] *Place*. The Author of this Epistle must certainly think so, if he has the same Opinion of his own Merit as Authors generally have; for he has been ⌐always distinguished and¬ favoured[5] by this very Person. Why, in God's Name, must a *Portrait* apparently collected from twenty different Men, be applied to one only? Has it his *Eye*? No, it is very unlike. Has it his *Nose* or *Mouth*? No, they are totally differing. What then, I beseech you? Why it has the *Mole on his Chin*. Very well: but must the Picture therefore be his, and has no other Man that Blemish? ⌐Would to God I had it together with his Magnificence, Beneficence, Generosity and Goodness! Then I would add one Vanity more to the Catalogue, and firmly believe myself the best Man of my Age and Country, because I have *honoured my God* with most Dignity, and done most *Good* to my *Neighbour*.¬

Could there be a more melancholy Instance how much the Taste of the Publick is vitiated, and turns the most salutary and seasonable Physick into Poyson than if amidst the Blaze of a thousand bright Qualities in a Great Man, they should only remark there is a *Shadow* about him, as what Eminence is without ⌐one¬? I am confident the Author is[6] incapable of imputing any such to a Person, whose whole Life (to use his own Expression in Print[7] of him) *is a continued Series of good and generous Actions*. ⌐I say I am confident, for I have known this Author long and well; and¬ I know no ⌐good¬ Man who would

[1] *The Daily Journal* accidentally omitted this sentence.

[2] *Wear* in *The Daily Post-Boy* is *mean* in all Pope's texts; so here emended. *The Daily Journal* also made this correction.

[3] ever] often *1735–43*.

[4] highest] rightest *1735–43*. (*The Daily Journal* has *rightest*.)

[5] favoured] distinguished *1737–43*.   [6] is] was *1735–43*.

[7] *The Daily Post-Boy* had printed here *private*, which did not make good defensive sense. The misprint was doubtless one reason for reprinting the letter on the 23rd in *The Daily Journal*. Pope had printed his opinion of Chandos in 1715 (when his grace was Earl of Carnarvon) in the Preface to the *Iliad*: 'I could say a great deal of the pleasure of being distinguish'd by the Earl of *Carnarvon*, but it is almost absurd to particularize any one generous action in a person whose whole life is a continu'd series of them.'

be more concerned, if he gave the least Pain or Offence to another;[1] and none who would be less concerned, if the Satire were challenged by any one at whom he would really aim it. If ever that happens, I dare engage he will own it, with all the Freedom of a Man whose Censures are just, and who sets his Name to them. ⌜I am, | Sir, | Your humble Servant.⌝

[2]⌜I really cannot help smiling at the Stupidity, while I lament the Slanderous Temper of the Town. I thought no Mortal singly could claim that Character of *Timon*, any more than any Man pretend to be Sir *John Falstaff*.

⌜But the Application of it to the D. of Ch. is monstrous; to a Person who in *every particular* differs from it. 'Is his Garden crowded with *Walls*? Are his Trees cut into *Figures of Men*? Do his Basons want *Water*? Are there *ten steep Slopes* of his Terrass? Is he piqued about *Editions* of *Books*? Does he exclude all *Moderns* from his *Library*? Is the *Musick* of his Chappel bad, or *whimsical*, or *jiggish*? On the contrary, was it not the best composed in the Nation, and most suited to grave Subjects; witness *Nicol. Haym's*, and Mr. *Hendel's* noble *Oratories*? Has it the Pictures of naked Women in it? And did ever Dean Ch—w—d[3] preach his Courtly Sermons there? I am sick of such Fool-Applications.'⌝

HILL *to* POPE   17 *December* 1731
1753 (Hill)

Dec. 17, 1731.

I ought, sooner, to have thanked you, for the pleasure you have given me, by that excellent letter to Lord *Burlington*,—If the title had been *Of False Taste*, would it not have been properer?[4]

We have *Poets*, whom heaven *visits* with a *taste*,[5] as well as planters and builders.—What other inducement could provoke some of them, to mistake your epistolary relaxation of numbers, for an involuntary defect in your versification?

We have printers, too, of better *taste* than *morals*, who *like* you so well, that they cannot endure, you should be made a monopoly.—

---

[1] to another] to any innocent person *1735-42*.
[2] The headnote in *The Daily Journal* implies that the erection of this postscript into a second letter (which has hitherto not been reprinted) was a principal object. It reads: 'The following Letters having been incorrectly printed in a Daily Paper Yesterday, and the one being subjoined to the other as a Postscript from the same Hand, it was thought necessary to reprint them in this Paper correctly and separately, as they should be.' It may be remarked that both the newspapers printing the material gave it the place of a leader.
[3] Possibly Dr. Knightly Chetwood, Dean of Gloucester (d. 1720). See Pope's own note to l. 150 of his Epistle to Burlington, in which no name is mentioned.
[4] Pope agreed and his next edition was called 'Of False Taste' (Griffith 267).
[5] Line 17 of the Epistle to Burlington.

The *hawker's* wind is upon you, already; and your last incense, to the muses, is blown about the streets, in thinner, and less fragrant expansions.—The pictures of your *mind*, like those of other great men's *persons*, are to be multiplied and extended, that we may have you at whole length, and in miniature.[1]

I send you a piece, that is safe enough, from this danger:—*Athelwold* will have nothing to *fear*, from the *pirates*: I believe, I need not inform you, how it dragg'd itself along, for two lean nights, after the first; as lame, and as wounded as the snake, in your poem[2]—but, not half so delightfully.

It would be affectation, not modesty, to deny, that I am nettled at the monstrous reception which the *town* has given this Tragedy.[3]—But, I find, there is a two-fold obligation, upon a tragic writer, if he would engage attention at our theatres.—He must make *Audiences*, as well as *Plays*.—He must become the solicitor of his own commendation.— That is, in the other words, if he *desires* to be *known*, he must *deserve* to be *forgotten*.

Bating the reverence, due to fashion,—this is putting the *Poet* upon the foot of the *Prize-fighter*.—He must not only submit himself to be *wounded*, for the *public Diversion*, but must also march about, with his *drum*, from one end of the town to the other, to stir up *fools curiosity*, and draw together the company.

I should feel the liveliest indignation, upon such an occasion, as this, in the cause of *another*: But, as the case is *my own*, I think,—and *smile*,—and am *satisfied*.—I had rather be *neglected*, to my *mortification*, than become *popular*, to my *infamy*.

It is possible, after all, that some persons of *rank*, and distinction to *bespeak* Plays, and compel audiences, may be kind enough to *Athelwold*, to introduce him, now and then, into civiler company, for the sake of the *Players*.—It were a downright shame, if these good People, who gave the Tragedy all its merit, of fine dressing and *sceneing*, should be suffered to lose their money, while the good for nothing author, who was guilty of the *dull* part of the entertainment, has lost nothing, but his labour.—But enough of this subject.

I hope the good lady, whose illness hastened you home, found a recovery, in your return.—*Who* can blame her for missing you, in a world so few are like you—Believe me, with much acknowledgment and esteem, Dear Sir, | Your faithful and obedient Servant, | A. Hill.

[1] Evidently the Epistle was promptly pirated *in miniature*. There was an octavo printing (Griffith 264).

[2] *Essay on Criticism*, l. 357.   [3] It ran only three nights.

*POPE *to* THE EARL OF BURLINGTON   21 *December* 1731
Chatsworth

Twitenham Decr 21. [1731]

My Lord,—Having been confined at home for ten days by my Mothers being in extreme danger, I never heard till two days since of a most Extravagant Censure, which they say the whole Town passes upon the Epistle I honourd myself in addressing to your Lordship, as if it were intended to expose the D. of Chandos.[1] Either the whole Town then, or I, have lost our Senses; for nothing is so evident, to any one who can read the Language, either of English or Poetry, as that Character of Timon is collected from twenty different absurditys & Improprieties: & was never the Picture of any one Human Creature. The Argument is short. Either the Duke these folks would abuse, *did* all those things, or he *did not*. If he did, he would deserve to be laughd at with a Vengeance; and if he did *not*, then it's plain it cannot be the Duke: and the latter is really the case.

I beg to know what are your Lordships Sentiments, that I should do in this unaccountable affair? I hope You are not abused too, because I meant just the Contrary; I can't tell, but I fancy your Lordship is not so easy to be persuaded contrary to your Senses, even tho the whole Town & Court too should require it. I doubt not the Justice, the more than justice, you will do me, on this or any other Injury: but I really want to know your Thoughts of it, being (as I perceive) a Man out of the World, & delirious: but still my dear Lord with understanding enough to Love and Adhere to you.

Yours ever faithfully, | A Pope

POPE *to* HILL   22 *December* 1731
1751 (Hill)

Twickenham, Dec. 22. 1731.

I thank you for your Tragedy, which I have now read over a sixth Time, and of which I not only preserve, but increase, my Esteem. You have been kind to this Age, in not telling the next, in your Preface, the ill Taste of the Town, of which the Reception you describe

---

[1] Lacking this letter and other evidence now available commentators on the Epistle to the Earl of Burlington formerly accepted the assertions of Pope's enemies that 'Timon' of the poem was the Duke of Chandos. The view is no longer tenable. For a marshalling of the evidence see *The Huntington Library Bulletin*, No. 8 (1935), 131–52, and Pope's *Poems* (Twickenham ed.), iii, pt. 2 (ed. Bateson), pp. 164–82.

The outcry against the Epistle was instant. Hill had heard it by 17 Dec., and Dr. Delany, in London at the time, wrote Sir Thomas Hanmer (23 Dec.) an interesting reaction. See *Correspondence* of Sir Thomas Hanmer (1838), pp. 216–17. In part he says: 'There is a general outcry against that part of the poem which is thought an abuse on the D. Chandois —other parts are quarreld with as obscure & unharmonious. . . . I am surprized Mr. Pope is not weary of making enemies. . . .'

it to have given of your Play (worse, indeed, than I had heard, or could have imagin'd), is a more flagrant Instance than any of those Trifles mention'd in my Epistles; which yet, I hear, the sore Vanity of our Pretenders to Taste flinches at extremely—The Title you mention had been a properer to that Epistle—I have heard no Criticisms about it,[1] nor do I listen after 'em; *Nos hæc novimus esse nihil* (I mean, I think the Verses to be so): But as you are a Man of tender Sentiments of Honour, I know it will grieve you to hear another undeservedly charg'd with a Crime his Heart is free from: For, if there be Truth in the World, I declare to you, I never imagin'd the least Application of what I said of *Timon* could be made to the D. of *Ch—s*, than whom there is scarce a more blameless, worthy and generous, beneficent Character, among all our Nobility: And if I have not lost my Senses, the Town has lost 'em, by what I heard so late, as but two Days ago, of the Uproar on this Head. I am certain, if you calmly read every Particular of that Description, you'll find almost all of 'em point-blank the Reverse of that Person's *Villa*. It's an aukward Thing for a Man to print, in Defence of his own Work, against a Chimæra: You know not who, or what, you fight against: The Objections start up in a new Shape, like the Armies and Phantoms of Magicians, and no Weapon can cut a Mist, or a Shadow. Yet it would have been a Pleasure to me, to have found some Friend saying a Word in my Justification,[2] against a most malicious Falshood. I speak of such, as have known by their own Experience, these twenty Years, that I always took up their Defence, when any Stream of Calumny ran upon 'em. If it gives the Duke one Moment's Uneasiness, I should think myself ill paid, if the whole Earth admir'd the Poetry; and believe me, would rather never have written a Verse in my Life, than that any one of 'em should trouble a truly good Man. It was once my Case before, but happily reconcil'd; and among generous Minds nothing so endears Friends, as the having offended one another.

I lament the Malice of the Age, that studies to see its own Likeness in every thing; I lament the Dulness of it, that cannot see an Excellence: The first is my Unhappiness, the second yours. I look upon the Fate of your Piece, like that of a great Treasure, which is bury'd as soon as brought to Light; but it is sure to be dug up the next Age, and enrich Posterity.

I have been very sensible, on these two Occasions, to feel them (as I have done) at a Time, when I daily fear'd the Loss of (what is, and

---

[1] The criticisms—astonishingly prompt—were not of the poem but of the poet and his alleged ingratitude to the Duke of Chandos.

[2] The failure of friends to come to his defence is one of Pope's recurring griefs. The letter of Cleland to Gay came out in the evening of the day Pope writes to Hill—who also, it is implied, might print something in Pope's favour!

ought to be dearer to me than any Reputation, *but that of a Friend*, or than any thing of my own, *except my Morals*) the Loss of a most tender Parent—She is alive, and that is all! I have perceiv'd my Heart in this, and you may believe me sincerely, | Dear Sir, | Your faithful and | really affectionate Servant, | A. Pope.

HILL *to* POPE[1]   [24] *December* 1731

1753 (Hill)

Dec. 23, 1731.

Your letter, dear Sir, which I have this moment receiv'd, occasions me a double pain. The *fear*, which yours *ends* with, ought to give a *beginning* to mine; because I am, too sincerely, your *friend*, not to feel *myself*, first mov'd, by what concerns *you*, most nearly. I hope, however, your *joy*, for that good lady's recovery, will be the next of your *Passions*, that will be touched, upon this occasion.

Concerning your *Epistle*, it is no wonder, that the malice of a little herd of censurers, whom your wit has made your *enemies*, would awaken a resentment, of more consequence, than their own. *They* are glad to *mistake*, if they can make *others*, mistake *you*: or, perhaps, they do not misunderstand you, *themselves*, but are conscious, they must seem to *believe*, what they would fix on the *belief* of others.

I am doubtful, which of these is the case, because, I confess, at the first, and second reading, I was, myself, mistaken in your purpose; and fell into the general construction, that has been put upon the character of *Timon*: but upon a more deliberate examination of the particulars, discern'd those disagreeing circumstances, which have been remark'd, for your justification, with very good success, in yesterday's *Daily Journal*, and the *Daily Post-boy* of *Wednesday*, by a hand, most able to do *you* justice.

That unguarded absence of caution, which is a mark, by which one may be sure, a purpose was either angry or *generous*, has prevented you from examining your piece, before it was publish'd, with the sharpness of an *eye*, that is watchful of occasion to *slander*; or, you would have foreseen, that the unlucky name of *Timon*, would be applied, as it has since been, from a present reverse, (as is reported) to the splendor of that great man's fortune. This circumstance has not only help'd on the mistake, but given it malignance, from a kind of pity, which some, who hated his good fortune, from the good uses he made of it, affect now, to feel for his disappointments.

Two or three other *likenesses* concurr'd in the character; such as

---

[1] Hill dated his letter the 23rd, but he speaks of 'yesterday's *Daily Journal*', and must mean the *Journal* of the 23rd; hence the suggestion of the 24th as a better date. *The Daily Post-Boy* of the 22nd would be Wednesday's issue.

the *hundred foot-steps*; the exact number of his domesticks, for some years, at *Canons*. And the pomp of the chapel, and its musick; for, whether *jiggish*, or *solemn*, never struck the inquiry of a thousand, who remembered the Duke's magnificence, chiefly by that circumstance. And as to the many un-resembling particulars; they are drown'd, like the mistaken predictions, of eleven months, in an Almanack, where the events of the twelfth, come by chance, to be accomplish'd.

I am of opinion, that the Duke himself can never be among the mistakers. It is with *taste*, as it is with *genius*; a man, who *feels* he has *either*, will never too lightly *believe* it is *questioned*, by another, whom he knows to possess it.

But, that it is a *rule* with me, to consider the letters, I receive from my *friends*, as their own property, *still*, tho' trusted to my *possession*, I could more effectually, convince him, how *he* ought to *think*, by letting him see, how *you* think, on this subject, in an easy, undesigning, natural indignation, express'd in a private letter, than by all the most labour'd endeavours, of yourself, or your friends in *publick*.

It cannot be difficult, to dispossess the town of a notion, whose credit will gradually die away, in proportion to the daily discovery, that is made of the malicious industry, with which it was propagated: And I dare assert, that your friends are too many, and too sanguine, to let a slander be *long-liv'd*, that is levell'd against your *gratitude*; I use this word by an authority, which I borrow from your own generosity, in the preface to your translation of the *Iliad*. I am so pleas'd, to converse with you, any way, that I forgot, I have scarce room to declare myself, | Dear Sir, | Your most faithfully | Affectionate Servant, | A. Hill.

*THE DUKE OF CHANDOS *to* POPE[1]   27 *December* 1731

The Huntington Library

Cannons 27th Decr 1731

Sir—I am much troubled to find by your favour of the 22d you are under any uneasiness, at the application the Town has made of Timon's Character, in your Epistle to the Earl of Burlington. For my own part I have received so many instances of the will they bear me, that I am as little surprized as I am affected with this further proof of it; It would indeed be a real concern to me did I beleive One of your Judgment had designedly given grounds for their imbibing an Opinion, so disadvantageous of me. But as your obliging Letter, is sufficient to free me from this apprehension, I can with great indifference bear the insults they bestow, and not find myself hurt by 'em:

---

[1] This reply to Pope's 'favour of the 22d' (unfortunately not preserved) comes from the Chandos letterbooks, xxxix. 32. It is dignified and neither hostile nor cordial.

nor have I Reason to be much disturb'd, when I consider how many better persons are the daily objects of their unjust censures.

I heartily lament the Melancholly condition you are in on account of the approaching loss, of so near and tender a Relation; Such strokes of Providence are great tryals of humane Nature, and exercise its utmost Fortitude, but they proceed from the hand of One, whose power wee cannot resist, and whose will, it is our Duty to submit to. I need not I am confident enlarge on this subject to One, whose words have instructed many, and who hath so often upholden him that was falling, Religion and his own good Sense, will enable him to avoid the reproach that follows; but now it is come upon thee and thou faintest, is this thy confidence and thy Hope?—

I earnestly wish you may soon be restored to that quiet of mind you have hitherto possesst, and without which no happiness can be enjoy'd. I am | Sir Your &c

Much confined at home in this year by the condition of his mother, Pope was quietly busy at literary work. He had to defend his Epistle to Lord Burlington, and he had labour and worries over the final volume of the Swift–Pope *Miscellanies*, involving difficulties with booksellers and with Swift himself. Throughout the year studied improvements in the manuscript of the *Essay on Man* were made. Apparently Fortescue furnished a man to transcribe the poem once; possibly the younger Richardson made a later transcript for the printer. Fortescue and the Richardsons were among the friends who in advance knew of Pope's authorship of the poem. The Epistle to Lord Bathurst is a frequent topic in letters, and its delayed appearance (from November 1732 to January 1733) was irritating. At the first of the year Lady Burlington was mysteriously acting as Pope's amanuensis, and late in the year Pope reciprocated by arranging and transcribing some of the Savile Papers of Lady Burlington's family. Pope was also interested in the work of the Richardsons on their volume of *Explanatory Notes on Paradise Lost*, stimulated in part by Bentley's pedantic edition, which appeared this year. Pope's co-operation with Samuel Buckley in his edition of Thuanus is also notable. The deaths of Atterbury and Gay deprived Pope of close friends: no important new correspondents emerge, but the year is notable for the Swift–Gay correspondence as well as for Pope's letters to his noble lords—Bathurst, Burlington, Peterborow, and Oxford. It is a year of literary labour rather than of social amusement.

POPE *to* FORTESCUE[1] [1731/2?]

1797 (Polwhele, i. 322)

Sunday, six o'clock.

I have often wished, but twice only been, to see you. After an engagement of four or five days to a particular friend, (for whom I was confined entirely) I now beg the first days I have had to myself, that you will pass what time you can with us at Twitnam. I received a promise from Gay to be with us. I go home to-morrow evening, to stay all the week. Gay and I have been all about the Temple after you in vain. I wish you would sacrifice a few days to me, who am as sincerely (I faithfully assure you) as any man living, dear Sir, yours most affectionately, | A. Pope.

Address: To Wm. Fortescue, esq.

[1] An undatable letter. This placing seems possible,

POPE *to* FORTESCUE¹   [1731/2?]

1797 (Polwhele, i. 321)

Friday morning.

I was t'other day in town, but could not find you at any hour of it, except at night, when I could not be disengaged. I have got Gay with me here, to pass two or three days; we are quite alone and uninterrupted; if you can come to us on Saturday, and stay Sunday, it will be highly delightful to us both, and Gay will return with you. I am so much better in health here than in town, that² I think to pass my time almost entirely at home, for the remainder of the winter. I shall be much pleased if I find myself so much remembered by two or three (which is the most I either hope or wish) of my friends, as to be visited by them now and then; and as I have experimentally known you to be one of those, I beg you to continue thus mindful of him, who will always be so of you. Your true friend and affectionate servant, | A. Pope.

I recd your inclosed some days since. If his information be right, I think him in his profession, industrious, and able, besides which he will work cheap.

Address: To Wm. Fortescue, esq. at his house, at the upper end of Bell-yard, near Lincoln's Inn, London.

POPE *to* THE EARL OF BURLINGTON³   [*January* 1731/2]

1732 ("Of False Taste")

My Lord,⁴—The Clamour rais'd about this Epistle could not give me so much pain, as I receiv'd pleasure in seeing the general Zeal of the World in the cause of a Great Man⁵ who is Beneficent, and the particular Warmth of your Lordship in that of a private Man who is innocent.

It was not the *Poem* that deserv'd this from you; for as I had the Honour to be your Friend, I cou'd not treat you quite like a Poet: but sure the *Writer* deserved more Candor even from those who knew him not, than to promote a Report which in regard to that Noble

---

¹ The beginning of 1732 seems a plausible time for this undatable letter.

² Polwhele reads *yet*, an evident mistranscription of *yᵗ*.

³ The text comes from the third edition of Pope's Epistle to Lord Burlington, which was published 20 Jan. 1731/2. The letter was included, with no important alterations except the addition of the (wrong) date 'March 7', in all Pope's editions of his letters. He added two footnotes given below.

⁴ This salutation was omitted in 1737b.

⁵ The Duke of Chandos. See Pope to Burlington, 21 Dec. 1731. See also Professor John Butt, 'A Master Key to Popery', in *Pope and His Contemporaries* (1949), edited by J. L. Clifford and L. A. Landa, pp. 41–57.

Person, was *Impertinent*; in regard to me, *Villainous*. Yet I had no great Cause to wonder, that a Character belonging to *twenty* shou'd be applied to one; since by that means, *nineteen* would escape the Ridicule.

I was too well content with my Knowledge of that noble Person's Opinion in this Affair, to trouble the publick about it. But since Malice and Mistake are so long a dying, I take the opportunity of this third Edition to declare *His Belief*, not only of *My Innocence*, but of *Their Malignity*,[1] of the former of which my own Heart is as conscious, as I fear some of theirs must be of the latter. His Humanity feels a Concern for the Injury done to *Me*, while His Greatness of Mind can bear with Indifference the Insults offered to *Himself*.

However, *my Lord*, I own, that Critics of *this Sort* can intimidate me, nay half incline me to write no more: It would be making the Town a Compliment which I think it deserves, and which some, I am sure, would take very kindly. This way of Satire is dangerous, as long as Slander rais'd by Fools of the lowest Rank, can find any countenance from those of a Higher. Even from the Conduct shewn on this occasion, I have learnt there are some who wou'd rather be *wicked* than *ridiculous*; and therefore it may be safer to attack *Vices* than *Follies*. I will leave my Betters in the quiet Possession of their *Idols*, their *Groves*, and their *High-Places*; and change my Subject from their *Pride* to their *Meanness*, from their *Vanities* to their *Miseries*: And as the only certain way to avoid Misconstruction, to lessen Offence, and not to multiply ill-natured Applications, I may probably in my next make use of *Real* Names and not of Fictitious Ones.[2] I am, | My Lord, | Your Faithful, | Affectionate Servant, | A. Pope.

POPE *to* THE EARL OF OXFORD   22 *January* [1731/2]

Longleat Portland Papers, xii

Twickenham. Jan. 22d | [3][1731/2]

My Lord,—I have heard a sort of Rumor (tho I found your Servants in Town did not know of any such thing) as if Lady Margaret were again indisposed. I hope in God 'tis only the Rebound of the news of her former illness: but what gives me the more apprehension is, that you stay so long in the Country, which my fears interpret to be on her

---

[1] See the Duke's letter to Pope, 27 Dec. 1731. Pope (1735-42) added a footnote: 'Alludes to the Letter the Duke of *Ch*— wrote to Mr. *Pope* on this occasion, a Copy of which, together with Mr. *Pope*'s to his Grace, we hope to procure for the next Volume.' After 1735 the note was concluded with the word *occasion*. His grace of Chandos evidently cared not at all for further publicity in the matter.

[2] This he did in his next Piece, which was the Epistle to the Lord *Bathurst* of the use of Riches.—Pope, 1735 (not later!).

[3] The year is added in Lord Oxford's hand; the endorsement at the end is in the hand of a clerk.

account if her health be not perfectly established. I beg the favor of one line from your Lordship on this. For the rest, I have little to say, but that, which I hope to You & to Lady Oxford is needless Tautology, that I am most respectfully & (what is more) most cordially hers & your Lordship's Servant. I can't help this Style to my Betters, when they are such, as will make me Love as well as honour them: tho I have been much blamed by the Formalists of the Town for subscribing my Letter in print to Lord Burlington, with, *your Faithfull, affectionate Servant.*

The Noise which Malice has raisd about That Epistle has caused me to suppress a much better, concerning the *Use of Riches,*[1] in which I had payd some Respect, & done some Justice to the Duke of Chandos. I thought it a great proof of *both,* when the Celebration of him was joind with one of You, & of my Lord Bathurst. But to print it, now, would be interpreted by Malice (& I find it is Malice I am to expect from the World, not Thanks, for my writings) as if I had done it in attonement, or thro' some apprehension, or sensibility of having meant that Duke an abuse: which I'm sure was far from my Thought. The Comfort is, that his Grace from the first, assured me of his opinion of my Innocence, & confirmed it in the strongest, as well as most Humane Terms, by Letter to me.—I had almost forgot to thank you for 2 Collars of Brawn, which have prolonged my Christmas till now. As also to wish Your Lordship, Dr Middleton, & Dr Colbatch,[2] Joy of Bentley's Milton. I am, with all truth & all esteem, | My Lord | Your most obliged & faithfull Servant | A. Pope.

My Mother has been very ill.
If Lord Duplin be with you[3] I hope he will accept my Services.

Endorsement: Mr Pope Twickenham | Jan: 22. 1731/2

POPE *to* HILL   5 *February* [1731/2]
1751 (Hill)

Feb. 5. 1730-1.[4]

I made a strong Essay to have told you in Person how very kindly I took your two last Letters. The only Hours I had in my Power from a necessary Care that brought me back immediately, I would have imposed on you. It will please you to know the poor Woman is rather

---

[1] Finally published a year after this in Jan. 1733.

[2] Middleton and Colbatch were Cambridge dons, hostile to Bentley. See *DNB* for all three.

[3] Viscount Dupplin was Oxford's nephew; noted for his small talk he became in Jan. 1735 the 'prating Balbus' of the *Epistle to Dr. Arbuthnot* (l. 276).

[4] This year assigned to the letter in the edition of 1751 is obviously impossible. The letter concerns Pope's poem on taste, which in January had appeared under the title suggested by Hill, 'Of False Taste'.

better, tho' it may be but like the Improvement of a Light on the End of a dying Taper, which brightens a little before it expires.—Your Hint about my Title *Of false Taste*, you'll see, is made use of in the Second Edition. Your Opinion also of my giving some publick Dissent or Protest against the silly malicious Misconstruction of the Town, I agree to; but I think no one Step should be taken in it, but *in Concert* with the Duke whom they injure. It will be a Pleasure felt by you, to tell you, his Grace has written to me the strongest Assurance imaginable of the Rectitude of his Opinion, and of his Resentment of that Report, which to *Him* is an Impertinence, to *me* a *Villainy*.

I am afraid of tiring you, and (what is your best Security) I have not Time to do it. I'll only just tell you, that many Circumstances you have heard, as Resemblances to the Picture of *Timon*, are utterly Inventions of Lyars; the Number of Servants never was an Hundred, the Paintings not of *Venio*[1] or *La Guerre*, but *Belluci* and *Zaman*; no such Buffet, Manner of Reception at the Study, Terras, &c. all which, and many more, they have not scrupled to forge, to gain some Credit to the Application: And (which is worse) belyed Testimonies of Noblemen, and of my particular Friends, to condemn me. In a word, the Malice is as great as the Dulness, of my Calumniators: The one I forgive, the other I pity, and I despise both. Adieu; the first Day I am near you I will find you out, and shew you something you will like. My best good Wishes are yours, and Miss *Urania's*.

Your affectionate Servant, | A. Pope.

POPE to DR. WILLIAM COWPER[2]　　　　　*5 February* 1731/2

Harvard University

Sir,—Some accident[s, and above all,] the Sickness of a very deserving Parent, h[ave prevented,] till now my acknowledgment of the receit [of your obliging] Letter & Verses. Pray think I am one, wh[o would nei]ther be insensible to a Civil, or neglectful [to an ingeni]ous Man. I shall use you with the Justi[ce and the free]dom, which is due to both: and at the sa[me time that] I congratulate you upon the Revival of your Taste for the Ancient Authors, Exhort you not to cultivate

---

[1] A misprint in 1751 for *Verrio. Zaman* is probably *Zeeman* for Enoch Seemann.

[2] Dr. Cowper, physician, antiquary, and minor poet, is noticed in *DNB*. The original letter is imperfect, and the brackets indicate additions from a transcript now Add. 44919A in the British Museum. In its *Fifth Report* the Hist. MSS. Comm. (pp. 358–9) prints the letter with the following preamble: 'Pope's Elegy to an unfortunate lady was translated into Latin hexameters by Mr. Cowper. He sent a copy to Pope, who acknowledged it by the following letter.' At the end of the letter the *Report* adds: 'A copy of the Latin translation of the Elegy is with this letter.' The translation is not to be found now. Pope's letter certainly sounds as if one of the Pastorals had been translated by Cowper. If he is calling *Eloisa* more descriptive, more enthusiastic, and hence more 'classical' than the *Unfortunate Lady*, it is an interesting judgment. The late endorsement, assigning the *Messiah* as the poem translated, is a complication also.

them negligently, but by frequent Imitations of them. No Pleasures So well suit with Exercise as those of the Imagination, which can be pursued even in the Field, and when your Dogs are at a fault, can fill up the Intervall; None better suit with a Country Life, than those of Poetry. Your Choice indeed of my writings is what I cannot approve as the best, but if mine lead you [to better], they will have some merit, & I shall thank [you for think]ing so. When you write better (as you cer[tainly will if] you proceed) you will find Authors among the [Moderns more] worthy of your pains: but in the mean-[time (to giv]e you, Sir, a proof that what you have done [pleases me)] I should not be sorry if you tryed your hand upon Eloisa to Abelard, since it has more of that Descriptive, &, (if I may so say) Enthusiastic Spirit, which is the Character of the Ancient Poets, & will give you more occasions of Imitating them. I am sensible (Sir) of your Partiality to me, & desire you to think me | Your most obedient humble Servant, | A. Pope.

Twitenham in Middlesex | Febr. 5. 1731/2

Endorsement (later hand): from Alexander Pope Twitenham Feb. 5th 1732 to Dr Cowper respecting his Translation of the Messiah.

JACOB TONSON *to* HIS NEPHEW   [*February* 1731/2]

The Pierpont Morgan Library
                    EXCERPT

. . . pray give my most humble service to Mr Pope & shew him this & the manuscript of the first book. It woud rejoyce my heart to heare that he was likely to take the Dr to task, for medling with Subjects nature has not [intended?] him for . . . An edition from Mr Pope woud be most Joyfully receivd by the mankind.[1] . . . Once more my most hearty Service to Mr Pope, I hope it wil not be said:—*Pope are you asleep?*

POPE *to* JONATHAN RICHARDSON[2]

                              February [*or March*] 1731/2

Elwin–Courthope, ix. 496

Many and necessary attendances have long made my intention and

---

[1] The complete text of this letter is printed from the original by Miss Helen Darbishire in *The Manuscript of Milton's Paradise Lost Book I* (1931), pp. xi–xv. The excerpt here printed is from Miss Darbishire. The aged Tonson was most violent in his reprobation of Bentley's text and notes. For Pope's reaction see his letter to Tonson 7 June 1732. He was obviously too much beset to take on further combats.

The letter is vaguely placed in February since it seems a prompt response to Bentley's edition, which was advertised as published as early as 14 Jan.

[2] Elwin says the letter comes textually from 'Richardson's transcripts'. He adds, 'The date is inserted in the margin by Richardson.'

desires to see you impracticable. The only time I hoped it I was unlucky, and to have given you notice before, was not in my power, my
call to London was so sudden. I have arrived here this very hour, and
send you the edition of Milton you desire.¹ As to your question what
I am doing? I answer, just what I have been doing some years: first,
my duty; secondly, relieving myself with necessary amusements or
exercises which shall serve me instead of physic as long as they can;
thirdly, reading till I am tired; and lastly, writing when I have no
other thing in the world to do, or no friend to entertain in company.

My mother is, I thank God, the easier if not the better for my cares,
and I am happy² in that regard, as well as in the consciousness of doing
my best. My next felicity is in retaining the good opinion of honest men,
who know me not quite undeserving of it, and in finding no injuries
from others hurt me as long as I know myself. I will add the sincerity
with which I act towards good and ingenious³ men, and which makes
me always (even by a natural bond) their friend. Therefore believe me
very affectionately, dear sir, yours.

*POPE *to* FORTESCUE⁴ [*February* 1731/2?]

Arthur A. Houghton, Jr.

Thursday night

I left London the day after you carry'd me thither, & did not attempt
to see you, on account of the Sittings, which I guess kept you imployed.
As you go soon upon the Circuit, & as I always sincerely wish to be
with you, I would take any day most Convenient to your self, to come
to Town for that End, about the middle or End of next week, whenever you'l acquaint me—If the bearer finds you at home, pray give him

¹ Richardson notes in the margin: 'This was Tonson's 4to, two vol.'—Elwin. (See Pope
to Richardson, 2 Nov. [1731], where Pope is sending an unwanted edition.)
After the first two sentences the rest of the letter was printed by Pope in 1737 a (Roberts
octavo) as to Fenton, under date of 5 May (no year). In 1737 b (quarto and folio) Pope added
the impossible year, 1717; but his octavo editions later omitted that year date. In printing
the letter to Fenton Elwin dated it 1720, where it will be found in this edition. Elwin was
naturally perplexed over a verbatim identity in passages ostensibly written twelve years
apart. One hypothesis may be that, when in 1732 writing this letter to Richardson, Pope
was preparing his letters for publication and wished to indicate something as to the origin
of the partnership in the *Odyssey*. He saw that what he was writing to Richardson could be
used as if written earlier to Fenton—and so he fabricated the letter to Fenton. It is of course
possible (if not altogether probable) that after Fenton's death in 1730 Pope's letters to him
(presumably not numerous) had been returned to Pope, and that the Richardson letter is in
part transcribed from an actual letter to Fenton. One needs to see the original letters.
² happy] the happier *all texts of the Fenton letter*.
³ ingenious men] ingenious and undesigning men *all texts of the Fenton letter*.
⁴ Fortescue has visited Twickenham, taken Pope back with him to town, and taken also
one of the epistles (pretty certainly I or II of the *Essay on Man*) to be transcribed. Cf. the
next following letter to Fortescue. The date is thus 1732, and the time towards the end of
the sittings in the King's Bench and Court of Common Pleas, which fell in February. The
county assizes (the 'circuit') began the 1st of March.

the Epistle you took to have transcribed. I told Mr Bethel about Mr Roberts: He desires your Clerk will learn where he is to be found, in your absence, that he may either receive the Mony of him, or (if he does not pay it in) the Interest, with a further Insurance: I fancy it is impossible he sh'd have an Act of Parliament this sessions; & therefore one sh'd press the Rent to be paid up.—Mrs Blount gives you many Services & Thanks for the trouble she gives you. My Mother continues just as you saw, but sends you her Service. Mr Jervas is come hither for his health, to Hampton, & is to reside here some time every week. My sincerest wishes attend your family: and no man is, has been, and will be, more truly & affectionately Yours, | than | Dear Sir, | A. Pope.

Pray direct Bowry how to get the Cyder, & pay for it yourself, as I will, You, with thanks.

Address: To | Wm Fortescue, Esqr.
Endorsement: Mr. Pope. | 1731/2.

POPE *to* FORTESCUE¹   *[Early March* 1731/2?]

1797 (Polwhele, i. 321)

Mr. Gay and I am here, reading (but not writing) all day long. He is the reverse of you, and hates exercise,—nay, I can't so much as get him into the garden. I employ myself yet a little there, and a little in casting my eye upon the great heap of fragments and hints before me, for my large and almost boundless work, to remove as much of which as is in any method, out of the rest, is so much clearing the way: therefore it is that I trouble you with so much transcribing. I send the third of the first part, relating to society and government, which I believe Mr. Doves² may pick out. And if he has transcribed what last I left with you, pray send it by the bearer. I have no thought of going to town these five days. All health attend you and yours. Ever your affectionate friend and servant, | A. Pope.

Pray send some of your styptic.

Address: To Mr. Fortescue.

*POPE *to* THE COUNTESS OF BURLINGTON³   [1732?]

Professor C. B. Tinker

Madam,—I can't enough thank you. this is shorter & better than any

---

¹ The letter is placed chronologically by Gay's visit and by the fact that Fortescue's amanuensis is asked to transcribe the third epistle of the *Essay on Man*.

² Possibly Charles Deaves, later secretary to Fortescue, when Fortescue was Master of the Rolls.

³ An impossible letter to date; but since her ladyship's activities as copyist can be placed

Compliment I could make you. I hurry over my thanks as you do your obligations, you are so quick, that you are ready to confer another before one can take notice of the former. You shall soon have more work, but no more transcribing of this, for (whatever you think) when you do things as carelessly as you can, they will still be better than most other people's Finishd Works. I am (with great Respect tho without gilt paper) sincerely | Madam | Your most obliged & obedient | humble Servant | A. Pope.

Be pleased to tell my Lord Sir Clem. Cottrel is in London.

Address: To the Rt Hon. the | Countess of Burlington.
Endorsement: Mr Pope

POPE to THE EARL OF BURLINGTON[1]   [1732?]

Chatsworth

Munday. morn.

My Lord,—I know it will be a pleasure to you, to hear that I am well, by a Nights Rest. It would be a greater trouble to me to Dye while I feel such Friendships as yours, & such concerns as you show for me, For as for such Enemies as I have hitherto had, they serve only to raise my spirits.

I have a favor to beg of my Lady B. (after having given me a copy of Maister Johnson,[2]) to give me the Copy of my Pamphlet which she writ out, & to keep my original among her papers of greater value: the bearer will bring it me, & also the Laurels, which you (of all Mankind at this time) bestow upon me so liberally. If your Lordship happens not to return to London till this evening, My inclinations to see you are revived & to go thither with you: but it happens that till after dinner I must wait here for a Relation of mine[3] who comes upon business to dine here. I am with the greatest Truth | My Lord | Your most obliged most faithfull Servant | A. Pope.

Address: To the Earl of Burlington. | at Chiswick.

near this time, one may leave the letter here. Doubtless it could be placed elsewhere with almost equal plausibility.

  [1] To place this letter chronologically with accuracy is impossible. The mysterious Laurels, surprising 'at this time', suggest a period shortly after the publication of the Epistle to Burlington, now under attack. Lady Burlington's transcribing may be that of the 'Master Key to Popery', which we know she at this time copied for Pope, or it may be that of some other unidentified piece.

  [2] Probably (Secretary) James Johnstone (1655–1737), one of Pope's neighbours whom the poet did not affect. Lady Burlington was both a wit and an artist: it is possible that the 'copy' of Johnstone was a caricature drawing.

  [3] One of the Rackett nephews?

*THE EARL OF BURLINGTON *to* POPE[1]   [1732?]

Chatsworth

I shou'd not have failed enquiring after your health on Saturday morning, nor of sending my coach yesterday, but from a want of Cavalry both days. Ldy B came to towne in the morning thinking she was to have been in waiting. I hope I need not have been so particular in my justification since I flatter my self, that you know me too well to suspect, that any thing but an impossibillity, can at any time hinder me from the sincere pleasure of your company. since I came to towne, I told Ly B of your commands in relation to her copy. she says hers is locked up at Chiswick but when she goes back, shall be very desirous of the exchange. in the mean time not knowing what occasion you may have for the original, I now send it. on Thursday I intend to go for two days into Berkshire and at my return, will take the first opportunity of seing you. company is now in the room, and I have but time to assure you, that I am my dear friend most faithfully yrs | Burlington

*POPE *to* THE COUNTESS OF BURLINGTON[2]
[1732 or 1733?]

Chatsworth

Saturday.

Madam,—I promised your Ladyship some account of my great affair. It has taken an entire new Turn since I came to town, the particulars of which I must reserve for Conversation. I do not send your Paper till I can do it effectually, a most Compleat Copy; (which (it is ten to one) will be in Print.) But should the spirit of Contempt or Forgiveness operate too strongly upon me, Your Ladiship shall have an unalterable Copy, to remain with you as an Instance of my Great Goodness & Lenity to his Lordship. I sincerely wish your Ladyship better health, & am with real Esteem & Obligation | Madam | Your most Obedient & most humble Servant | A. Pope.

POPE *to* CARYLL   6 *March* 1731/2

Add. 28618

6 March 1731–2

Some months past I sent you a letter which I have since reason to think came not to your hands, not only because you have not written

---

[1] Remarks on Lady Burlington's work as amanuensis indicate that this letter follows that immediately preceding.

[2] The reason for placing the letter here is that the 'great affair' seems in some way connected with Lord Burlington. Otherwise the 'great affair' might refer to Pope's 'Letter to a Noble Lord' (1733?) or to the publication of his 'Narrative' concerning the publication of his letters in 1735. There are even further possibilities, such as 'The Master Key to Popery'.

to me, but as it was franked by a nobleman, whose servant took charge of it, and it seems was very drunk. I could say much to you on the death of our poor friend abroad,[1] which has suggested to me many reflections on human views and infelicities. I can't communicate most of them here but have a great deal to tell you when we meet in May. I was truly sorry for Mrs Caryll's miscarriage,[2] of which Mr Pigot informed [me] but last week.

I think one lives in this world but only to experience how much more melancholy and disappointing one year is than another. I have spent this whole winter at home by my mother's bed-side in that most dismal situation of wishing for what cannot be, her recovery. I've scarce any news but that of Mrs E—'s marriage.[3] She is a lucky woman to marry at these years and get an honest man; for such certainly Mr Webb is, and what is yet luckier for her, a good-natured one. I knew him at school, and he was the best-conditioned boy in the school, tho' the biggest, which shows his power and superiority will not be ill used; for I've heard of few instances where the virtues of youth did not precede those of age. I see your god-daughter as constantly as I go to London, and I think nobody should be changed towards her, as she is always the same.[4]

Time and experience lessen all my sollicitudes and concern every year except to the very few I find really honest and (therefore only) really valuable; for I assure you parts and wit are no more allurements to my acquaintance or conversation with anybody: much less those idle things, power and quality. I've nothing to add but my true wishes for yours and your family's prosperity and welfare, who am as I've been of so long standing | Sir | Your faithful friend and obliged | humble servant. | A. Pope.

†BOLINGBROKE *and* POPE *to* SWIFT[5]   [*March* 1731/2]

1740

You may assure yourself, that if you come over this spring, you will find me not only got back into the habits of study, but devoted to that

[1] Bishop Atterbury died in Paris, 22 Feb. (O.S.) or 4 Mar (N.S.). The date 15 Feb. is given in *The Gentleman's Magazine*.   [2] Mrs. Edward Caryll, Pigott's daughter.
[3] The widow of Henry Englefield.—Elwin.
[4] This is the theme—*semper eadem*—developed in compliment to Miss Blount in Pope's *Epistle on the Characters of Women* (published in Feb. 1735), where the rest of the sex is *varium et mutabile*.
[5] Elwin first assigned to this letter the bracketed date of Apr. 1732—which is definitely too late. By 13 Mar. (q.v.) Gay feared that Swift's lameness might keep him from visiting England: before April that news should have reached Pope. The first volume of Delany's *Revelation examined with Candour* was, according to *The London Evening Post*, published 4–6 May, and April is unduly late for submitting the MS. to Bolingbroke. Archbishop Boulter of Armagh had recommended the (completed?) work to the Bishop of London as early as Aug. 1731 (Boulter's *Letters* [Oxford, 1769–70], ii. 67).

historical task, which you have set me these many years.[1] I am in hopes of some materials which will enable me to work in the whole extent of the plan I propose to myself. If they are not to be had, I must accommodate my plan to this deficiency. In the mean time Pope has given me more trouble than he or I thought of; and you will be surprized to find that I have been partly drawn by him and partly by myself, to write a pretty large volume upon a very grave and very important subject;[2] that I have ventur'd to pay no regard whatever to any authority except sacred authority, and that I have ventured to start a thought, which must, if it is push'd as successfully as I think it is, render all your Metaphysical Theology both ridiculous and abominable. There is an expression in one of your letters to me, which makes me believe you will come into my way of thinking on this subject; and yet I am perswaded that Divines and Free-thinkers would both be clamorous against it, if it was to be submitted to their censure, as I do not intend that it shall[3]—the passage I mean, is that where you say that you told Dr.*[4] the Grand points of Christianity ought to be taken as infallible Revelations, &c.

It has happened that whilst I was writing this to you, the Dr. came to make me a visit from London, where I heard he was arrived some time ago: He was in haste to return, and is I perceive in great haste to print. He left with me eight Dissertations,[5] a small part, as I understand, of his work, and desired me to peruse, consider, and observe upon them against monday next when he will come down again. By what I have read of the two first, I find my self unable to serve him. The principles he reasons upon are begged in a disputation of this sort, and the manner of reasoning is by no means close and conclusive. The sole advice I could give him in conscience would be that which he would take ill and not follow. I will get rid of this task as well as I can, for I esteem the man and should be sorry to disoblige him where I cannot serve him.

As to retirement, and exercise, your notions are true: The first should not be indulged so much as to render us savage, nor the last neglected so as to impair health. But I know men, who for fear of being savage, live with all who will live with them; and who to preserve their health, saunter away half their time. Adieu: Pope calls for the paper.

[1] Bolingbroke's projected history of his own times. See Bolingbroke to Swift, 2 Aug. 1731.

[2] Bolingbroke was perhaps engaged at this time on his 'Letter to Mr. Pope' or perhaps on his 'Fragments'. These works were published in 1753 or 1754.

[3] Already Bolingbroke intended only posthumous publication.

[4] Dr. Patrick Delany. Swift's remark, whenever made, would have been in accord with his normal contempt of argument, especially on the subject of religion.

[5] *Revelation examined with Candour.* Eight Dissertations would be something like half the number published in 1732. Vol. i appeared on 6 May and vol. ii on 27 June.

¹P.S. I hope what goes before will be a strong motive to your coming. God knows if ever I shall see Ireland; I shall never desire it, if you can be got hither, or kept here. Yet I think I shall be, too soon, a Freeman—Your recommendations I constantly give to those you mention; tho' some of 'em I see but seldom, and am every day more retired. I am less fond of the world, and less curious about it; yet no way out of humour, disappointed, or angry; tho' in my way I receive as many injuries as my betters, but I don't feel them, therefore I ought not to vex other people, nor even to return injuries. I pass almost all my time at Dawley and at home; my Lord (of which I partly take the merit to my self) is as much estrang'd from politicks as I am. Let Philosophy be ever so vain, it is less vain now than Politicks, and not quite so vain at present as Divinity: I know nothing that moves strongly but Satire, and those who are asham'd of nothing else, are so of being ridiculous. ⌈I fancy if we three were together but for three years, some good might be done even upon this Age; or at least some punishment made effectual, toward the Example of posterity, between History, Philosophy, and Poetry, or the Devil's in it. Nay, and I think 'tis all among ourselves; at least, I yet see none likely to dispute it with us. Those who get your mony, can't get your Fame from you: that is one thing at least not always to be sold.⌉²

I know you'll desire some account of my health: It is as usual, but my spirits rather worse. I write little or nothing. You know I never had either a taste or talent for Politicks, and the world minds nothing else. I have personal obligations which I will ever preserve, to men of different sides; and I wish nothing so much as publick quiet, except it be my own quiet. I think it a merit, if I can take off any man from grating or satyrical subjects, merely on the score of party: and it is the greatest vanity of my life that I've contributed to turn my Lord Bolingbroke to subjects moral, useful, and more worthy his pen. Dr. D—'s³ Book is what I can't commend so much as Dean Berkley's,⁴ tho' it has many things ingenious in it, and is not deficient in the writing part: but the whole book, tho' he meant it *ad Populum*, is I think purely *ad Clerum*. Adieu.

GAY *to* SWIFT   [13 *March* 1731/2]

Add. 4806

I hope this unlucky accident of hurting your Leg will not prevent your

¹ Pope begins here.

² The bracketed material was entirely omitted by Swift and Faulkner in the Dublin texts of 1741. The sentence beginning 'I fancy . . . this Age' was printed in the London texts of 1741–2, and in the Dublin (1742) reprint of those texts.

³ Dr. D—'s] Dr.—'s *1741–2*. [Delany's, of course.]

⁴ Bishop Berkeley's *Alciphron*, advertised as published 2–4 Mar. 1732 (*The London Evening Post*).

coming to us this Spring though you say nothing about it; All your friends expect it, & particularly my Landlord & Landlady, who are my friends as much as ever, & I should not think 'em so, if they were not as much yours. The Downs of Amesbury are so smooth that neither horse nor man can hardly make a wrong step, so that you may take your exercise with us with greater security. If you can prevail with the Dutchess to ride & walk with you, you will do her good, but that is a motive I could never prevail with her to comply with. I wish you would try whether your oratory could get over this difficulty. General Dormer, Sir Clement Cotterel & I set out to morrow morning for Rousham in Oxfordshire to stay ten days or a fortnight. The Dutchess will undertake to recommend the Lords of her acquaintance to attend Mr Reeves his Cause[1] if it should come on before our return; the Duke will do the same. Her Grace too hath undertaken to answer your Letter. I have not dispos'd of your S. Sea Bonds; There is a years interest due at Lady day. But if I were to dispose of 'em at present I should lose a great deal of the premium I pay'd for 'em; perhaps they may fall lower, but I cannot prevail with myself to sell 'em. The Roguerys that have been discover'd in some other companys I believe makes 'em all have less credit. I find myself disquieted for want of having some pursuit; indolence & idleness are the most tiresome things in the world, & I begin to find a dislike to society. I think I ought to try to break myself of it, but I cannot resolve to set about it. I have left almost all my great acquaintance; which saves me something in Chair-hire, though in that article the Town is still very expensive.

Those who were your old acquaintance are almost the only people I now visit, and indeed upon trying all I like 'em best. Lord Cornbury refus'd the Pension that was offer'd him.[2] He is chosen to represent the University of Oxford, (in the room of Mr Bromley) without opposition. I know him and I think he deserves it. He is a Young Nobleman of Learning & Morals which is so particular that I know you will respect & value him, & to my great comfort he lives with us in our family. Mr Pope is in town & in good health I lately past a week with him at Twickenham.[3] I must leave the rest to the Dutchess for I must pack up my shirts to set out to morrow being the 14th of March the day after I receiv'd your Letter. If you would advise the Dutchess to

---

[1] On the suit of William Ryves (a friend of Swift's) against David Bindon, which had led to an appeal to the British House of Lords, see Ball, iv. 285, n. 2.

[2] Spence (p. 292) has preserved the often quoted anecdote concerning Lord Cornbury, the handsome and charming brother of Gay's duchess, concerning this pension. Upon his return to England Cornbury was told by his brother-in-law, the Earl of Essex, 'that he had got a pension for him. It was a very handsome one, and quite equal to his rank.—All Lord Hyde's [i.e. Cornbury's] answer was: "How could you tell, my lord, that I was to be sold? or at least, how could you know my price so exactly?"' Pope immortalized the moment in l. 61 of his Imitation of the Sixth Epistle of the First Book of Horace (To Mr. Murray).

[3] This remark helps to date earlier letters of this year that mention the visit.

confine me four hours a day to my own room while I am in the country I will write; for I cannot confine myself as I ought.

Address: To | The Revd Dr Swift | Dean of St Patricks | Dublin.
Frank: Cornbury | ffree
Postmark: 8/AP
Endorsement (In Swift's hand): Mr Gay Rx Apr. 19 | 1732 | Answd May 5th 1732.

POPE *to* THE EARL OF OXFORD[1]   16 [*March* 1731/2]

Longleat Portland Papers, xii

march. 16. 1731/2.
R. at Wimpole. 17.

My Lord,—It was a great Joy to me to see a few lines in your hand, which I had long wished, in regard to the State of Lady Margarets health, of which I heard different accounts, & could not collect much from what your own Servants told me from week to week. Dr Mead I went to enquire of, who but three weeks ago told me She was not perfectly recover'd, but had again been lately ill. I hope all your fears are over on that account, for indeed My Lord, Your own Fears & Concerns are shared by me with the sincerest tenderness. My affections & concerns at home I can hardly expect any one should partake with me, it is Scarce Reasonable to wish myself (much less to think another should) the longer Life of a person past Ninety. The Trouble which I've receivd from abroad, on the news of the death of that much-injured man,[2] could only be mitigated by the Reflection your Lordship suggests to me, His own Happiness, & Return into his Best Country, where only Honesty & Virtue are sure of their reward. I long to see you; Why must I not know when? I'll end like the Schoolboys, Nil mihi rescribas, attamen Ipse veni.

My dear Lord. | Your Ever obligd, ever affectionate, faithful | Servant.

Thursday the 16: I write in such haste not to omit this Post, that you'l forgive the want of Forms, & Services, from Your A. Pope

I forgot to tell you I have had a Fever in the Country, but recovered in four days at your House, tho I wanted the best Physitians, your Lordship & my Lady.

Address: To | The Rt Hon. the Earl of Oxford | & Mortimer at Wimpole | Cambridgeshire.
Postmark: 16/MR
Endorsement (in clerk's hand): Mr Pope March 16. 1731/2.

---

1 The superscribed dates are in the hand of Lord Oxford.   2 Bishop Atterbury.

POPE *to* CARYLL   29 *March* [1732]
Add. 28618

March 29.

The speed with which I answer yours (which I take the more kindly
for two things, first for your jealousy which is a sign of affection and
secondly for sincerely owning it)—let, I say, this speed atone in some
degree for my tardiness before. And pray do not make the punctuality
of my correspondence the measure of the temper of my heart. For
there are a hundred accidental causes for my omissions in a state of life
so dissipated when abroad, and so busied when at home as mine, I
think, is forever doomed to be. *Perditur hæc inter misero lux.*[1] Nay, it
often happens that I omit writing to my best friends, for this very
reason that I've too much to say to 'em, and would not do it unsatisfactorily. Some times an event has happened of which they must
naturally expect either an account, or a solution from me; and which
I can do at large and would not do by halves. Nay, the imperfect
manner in which I should be obliged sometimes by prudence and sometimes by friendship to mention these things would appear to them as
reserve or indifference. Therefore I often totally omit to write.

There was such an incident lately relating to an imaginary reflection on a worthy peer, in a poem of mine.[2] The report was almost universal, but so very groundless and silly, that I don't yet know the effect
it will have upon my conduct,—whether so great a stupidity in the
point of comprehending a poet's manner, (being the ignorance of
the very principle of that sort of writing) and so great malignity in the
point of applying it in the worst sense, should give me such a pique to
the world's malice, as never to publish anything, or such a contempt
of its judgment as to publish everything, which I think right myself,
without the least concern about what they think or say. I avoided
naming this to anybody whilst the report lasted, expecting my friends
should name it to me, and justify me to others. Certainly they have
known me long enough to know I am no immoral man.—I only
desired your friend Patty to send you the prose letter prefixed to the
last edition, which told you how the duke understood it, and how I
meant it—which was sufficient, it being no man's concern besides, unless my friends had made it theirs.

What you say of the condition of a certain family,[3] I'm heartily
sorry for; I hoped it would have been covered from most part of the
world. But I am more sorry that no remedy can be found to heal the
sore of one, and prevent the infection which may attend another.

[1] Horace, *Satires*, II. vi. 59.
[2] On the Duke of Chandos in the Epistle to Burlington.
[3] Obviously the Blount ladies. Evidently Pope was not alone in worrying about these
ladies.

Indeed nothing is more to be lamented than what the guilty and the bad bring upon themselves, except the fate of the good and the innocent, who are sometimes involved with them thro' their own goodness.—I must conclude.—I hope to see you as you promise. It was ill done in you to give so much way to your rash judgment as not to call last time. But pray to avoid *accidents*, for I'll never be guilty of *causes* that may offend, let me know 3 or 4 days beforehand, for I'm often abroad, and be assured no man will see you more joyfully than | Dear Sir | A. Pope.

POPE *to* THE EARL OF OXFORD   28 *April* 1732

Longleat Portland Papers, xii

April the 28th | 1732.

My Lord,—Absence makes some Minds forget, and quickens the memory of others, in regard of those we value. I assure you mine is of the latter kind, and I promise myself yours is so too. Your House, my Lord, which I inhabit when in town, is meerly like a Tomb; it serves now only to put me in mind of what I have Lost. The Ghosts of your Self, Lady Oxf. & Lady Margaret haunt me there, & will not let me rest, in the Quiet, & Pleasurable situation I once enjoyed in that place. Will you not only disappoint me from month to month, but not so much as give me a Hope, a Glympse, of a Joyful Resurrection, where we may all meet again? When will the Time come for the Kingdom of the Just upon Earth? This whole year has seem'd the Expiration of the Reign of the Wicked;[1] by its Enormities one would think their measure was full. I remember your Lordships Father loved a Town-Summer; I hope you will *Patrissare* in this sense too, and I may receive some Reward at last for taking care of your Leavings, that abandoned House, & Books, & Pictures in Dover street. For want of other Society, Lyon[2] & I are grown as intimate as Androcles (or Androgeus, I have forgot which) was with his Name-sake.

In casting my eye over what I've written, I find some Expressions which might, were I of the Clergy, render me suspected to my Brethren; & I might probably, (were This Letter, like Dr Middleton's,[3] directed to any Clergyman) be treated as Ill as he: For a Phrase, or a

---

[1] Elwin assumed that this millennial language referred to the 'reign' of Sir Robert Walpole. It seems far more likely that Pope is thinking of the gross corruption uncovered in the current investigation of the Charitable Corporation. (Cf. Peterborow's letters of this time.)

[2] Lion would seem to be the name given to the offspring of Pope's great dane, Bounce, presented by him to Lord Oxford. It is curious in view of the interest in the poor as cheated by the Charitable Corporation that Pope in 'Bounce to Fop' represents Lion as 'fawning' upon the poor at Oxford's house.

[3] In reply to Tindal Dr. Daniel Waterland, at this time vicar of Twickenham, had published *Scripture Vindicated* (1730–2), and was attacked by Middleton in an anonymous *Letter to Waterland*, which by its critical attitude towards the historicity of the Scriptures cost Middleton many friends—including Lord Oxford.

Mis-nommer, to that Genus irritabile is unpardonable. But You who are a Lay-Lord, will *Understand* my *meaning*; see, it has *no ill Tendency upon the whole*, and remain in charity with me, tho not in Communion. No Poet is *always*, & in *every word*, an Inspired person, 'Tis only when he Sings, & not when he Says, that this is his prerogative.

My Lord, I love you, I honor you, I have put you into my heart, I will put you into my Poems, Will either of them do you any good? I fear not.

Pray remember me, write to me & come to me. If I could, I would come to you: Indeed I would if there were no such thing as Duty to hinder me. I am sincerely & with respect, | My Lord | Your faithfull, | obliged, humble | Servant | A. Pope.

My Mother is every day weaker, but yet remembers you & Lady Oxford.

Address: To | The right Honble the | Earl of Oxford, at | Wimpole | Cambridgeshire.

Postmark: 27/AP

Endorsement (in Oxford's hand): Mr A: Pope | April 28th 1732.

†THE EARL OF PETERBOROW *to* POPE[1]   [*April* 1732]

1737

Whenever you apply as a good Papist to your female Mediatrix,[2] you are sure of success; but there is not a full assurance of your entire submission to Mother-church, and that abates a little of your authority. However if you will accept of country letters, she will correspond from the haycock and I will write to you upon the side of my wheelbarrow: surely such letters might escape examination!

Your Idea of the Golden Age is, that every shepherd might pipe where he pleased. As I have lived longer, I am more moderate in my wishes, and would be content with the liberty of not piping where I am not pleased.

Oh how I wish, to my self and my friends, a freedom which Fate seldom allows, and which we often refuse our selves! why is our Shepherdess in voluntary slavery?[3] why must our Dean submit to the Colour of his coat, and live absent from us? and why are you confined to what you cannot relieve?

---

[1] In Pope's editions 1737–42 this letter is placed, undated, as if it belonged in the spring of 1732. Since Peterborow was in London in May of this year, April seems a probable moment. In the Golden Age haycocks were timeless, and here they cannot be sure evidence against April.

[2] Anastasia Robinson (secretly married to his lordship) is here intended. She was a devout Catholic.

[3] Lady Suffolk was still Mistress of the Robes.

I seldom venture to give accounts of my journeys beforehand, because I take resolutions of going to London, and keep them no better than quarrelling lovers do theirs. But the devil will drive me thither about the middle of next month, and I will call upon You, to be sprinkled with holy water, before I enter the place of Corruption.[1] Your, &c.

†THE EARL OF PETERBOROW *to* POPE[2] [*Early May* 1732]
1737
                                                                           1732.

I am under the greatest impatience to see Dr. Swift at Bevis Mount, and must signify my mind to him by another hand, it not being permitted me to hold correspondence with the said Dean, for no letter of mine can come to his hands.

And whereas it is apparent, in this protestant land most especially under the care of divine providence, that nothing can succeed or come to a happy issue but by Bribery; therefore let me know what he expects to comply with my desires, and it shall be remitted unto him.

For tho' I would not corrupt any man for the whole world, yet a benevolence may be given without any offence to conscience; every one must confess that gratification and corruption are two distinct terms; nay at worst many good men hold, that for a good end some very naughty measures may be made use of.

But Sir, I must give you some good news in relation to my self, because I know you wish me well; I am cur'd of some diseases in my old age, which tormented me very much in my youth.

I was possest with violent and uneasy passions, such as a peevish concern for Truth, and a saucy love for my Country.

When a Christian Priest preached against the Spirit of the Gospel, when an English Judge determined against Magna Charta, when the Minister acted against common-Sense, I used to fret.

Now Sir, let what will happen, I keep my self in temper: As I have no flattering hopes, so I banish all useless fears: but as to the things of this world, I find my self in a condition beyond expectation; it being evident from a late Parliamentary inquiry, that I have as much ready money, as much in the funds, and as great a personal estate, as Sir Robert S—tt—n.[3]

---

[1] The Court? or the Town?

[2] Pope's editions (1737–42) give us the year of this letter and place it immediately after that which here precedes it. Elwin reversed this order without giving reason. There seems to be none for his change. See below, note 3, for comment on Sir Robert Sutton and the date. The theme of corruption that runs through the letters is connected with him.

[3] Cobbett tells us that the 'Further Report of the Committee relating to the Charitable Corporation' was brought in on 20 April. Because of his connexion with this disgraceful

If the Translator of Homer find fault with this unheroick disposition, (or what I more fear) if the Draper of Ireland accuse the Englishman of want of spirit; I silence you both with one line out of your own Horace, *Quid te exempta juvat spinis e pluribus una?*[1] For I take the whole to be so corrupted, that a cure in any part would be of little avail. | Yours, &c.

---

*POPE *to* FORTESCUE   [*May* 1732]

Harvard University

It was doubly a disappointment to me which I fancy my blundering Waterman occasiond: I was near 2 days in town & sent him on the first to know at whatever hour I might best find you at home? He never brought back the answer the first day; & the second said you was gone out. I was ingaged at Parsons green & at Chiswick on Saturday (& Sunday as I thought) but my Lord Peterborow gave me the Slip; & I was made to believe by Bowry you would be here on Sunday Evening which hastend me home, so that I mist too of dining with Lord Burlington, who dined late.—All this Evil you will repair by coming the first time you can; for believe it, there is no Lord in the Land I like better to see.

I had also some business with you which we must be pretty quick & very peremptory in, for our friend Mrs Blounts sake. You know the time he was indulged in is now elapsed,[2] for he gave Mr Bethel the st[ronges]t assurances of payment this *May*. We have so many fresh advices of the little Dependence there is on him, & the danger of delay, or complyance with so indolent a Creature, that I beg you to write him as by Mr Bethels order, a Positive Demand of prompt payment or to assure him you must Enter on the Lands. He owes 3 quarters of the year. Mr Thory can tell his Direction, if he be (as he said he should) at his house in the Country: or of Mr Eadnell where he is?

I have had 4 sick days in one week: I hope your health continues, or increases: & that all yours are well. My Mother is not worse . . . .[3]

Address: To | Wm Fortescue Esqr in | Bellyard, by | Lincolns-Inne | London
Endorsement (by Fortescue): Mr Pope | May. 1732.

---

affair (more than once mentioned by Pope in his satires) Sir Robert Sutton was on 4 May expelled from the House.— *Parl. Hist.* viii. 1077, 1161. This suggests the moment at which Peterborow was writing. Sir Robert was a patron of Warburton's. See Warburton to Pope, Jan. 1743/4 (iv. 492–4).

  [1] *Epistles*, ii. ii. 212.
  [2] This matter concerns, probably, the annuity purchased from the mysterious Roberts.
  [3] One line of text and the subscription have been torn away at this edge of the paper.

POPE *to* CARYLL   4 *May* 1732

Add. 28618

Your very welcome letter came hither when I was in town and where
I had been at Mr Pigot's enquiring when I might hope for you. That
very evening I found out your inn after you were gone out of Town,
and now answer you fairly and freely, that my mother's condition no
ways hinders me from seeing a friend here; but from seeing one abroad
for any time, her state of health absolutely denies me. Therefore, I've
a double reason to desire you to pass what days you can here, since God
knows when I shall be able to do it with you, how willing soever otherwise. Believe me, dear sir, sincerely to long for your appointment, and
I will not fail to be at home to enjoy it. Adieu | Dear sir | Your ever
faithful and obliged servant | A. Pope.

Twickenham | 4 May 1732.

POPE *to* CARYLL   20 *May* 1732

Add. 28618

Whitton 20 May 1732.

After an expectation (which I must call a pleasant one) of a week
which I stayed at home in hope of you, I am truly disappointed at the
receipt of yours, and worse than disappointed, grieved. The intention
you expressed in yours of getting home as fast as possible made me, till
now, imagine (and hope) that a letter would not find you any where
but at Ladyholt: but this day going the second time to see your son at
Whitton he tells me you are still detained at Ingatestone.[1] I would fain
hope you'll now stay there till a perfect recovery sufficient to bring you
hither. In good earnest I long extremely for a week of your company.
My necessary attendance on the last days of my mother (now wholly
confined to her bed) makes it impracticable to see you at your own
house, which, with all that is in it, I wish I could enjoy once more.
Mr Caryll (who is at my side) sends you his duty and writ to you last
post. As soon as you can, pray acquaint me of your better health,
which no friend you have more sincerely desires than | Yours ever | A.
Pope.

---

[1] The home of Lord Petre. Caryll was the guardian of the 8th Lord Petre, who at this
time (aged 18) had just married the daughter of the 3rd Earl of Derwentwater, 'a fortune
[so says *The Universal Spectator*, 29 Apr. 1732] of 30,000*l*.'

‖SWIFT *to* GAY[1]   4 *May* 1732

Longleat Portland Papers, xiii (Harleian transcripts)

Dublin May 4th 1732.

I am now as lame as when you writ your Letter, and almost as lame as
your letter it Self, for want of that limb from my Lady Dutchess,
which you promised, and without which I wonder how it could limp
hither. I am not in a condition to make a *true* Step even on Amesbury
Downs, and I declare that a corporeal false Step is worse than a
political one; nay worse than a thousand politicall ones, for which I
appeal to Courts and Ministers who hobble on and prosper without the
Sense of feeling, To talk of riding and walking is insulting me, for, I
can as soon fly as do ether⌐, I desire you will manage my South-Sea
estate, as you would do if it were your own, I mean in every circumstance except gaming with the public, that is buying or Selling lottery
tickets, as you once proposed to me from your own practice. I love Mr
Lewis's Device; Piano piano⌐. It is your pride or lazyness more than
Chair-hire, that make[2] the town expensive. No honor is lost by walking
in the dark, and in the day, you may becken a blackguard boy under a
gate, near your visiting place (experto crede)[3] Save eleven pence; and
get half a crowns worth of health, The worst of my present misfortune
is, that I eat and drink, and can digest neither for want of exercise; and
to encrease my misery the knaves are Sure to find me at home, and
make huge voyd Spaces in my Cellars, I congratulate with you for
losing your *great* acquaintance, in Such a case philosophy teaches that
we must Submit, and be content with *good* ones, I like Lord Cornbury's refusing his pension, but demur[4] at his being elected for Oxford,
which I conceive is wholly changed, and entirely, devoted to new
Principles,[5] ⌐directly contrary to those for which Lord Cornbury refused a pension, and⌐ appeared to me a most corrupt Seminary the two
last times I was there.

I find by the whole cast of your letter that you are as giddy and as
volatile as ever; just the reverse of Mr Pope, who hath always loved a
domestick life from his youth. I was going to wish you had Some little
place that you could call your own, but I profess I do not know you
well enough to contrive any one Systeem of life that would please you,

---

[1] Printed by Pope in 1740–2 with few revisions apart from omissions, here placed in
half-brackets. Oxford's scribe had more than usual trouble with Swift's antiquated *o*'s, which
are more than once mistaken for *e*'s or even *ee*'s. These errors are preserved as typical specimens.

[2] make] makes *1740–2*.

[3] Believe me who have experienced it.—Footnote in 1741 Dab.

Gay, as Elwin notes, was also experienced in getting a boy to clean his shoes before entering
a house as visitor. See *Trivia*, ii. 99–102—a passage which Swift may have had in mind.

[4] but demur] but I demur *1740–2*.

[5] Principles . . . appeared] Principles; so it appeared *1740–2*.

You pretend to preach up riding and walking to the Dutchess, yet from my knowledge of you after twenty years, you allways Joyned a violent desire of perpetually Shifting places and company, with a rooted Lazyness, and an utter impatience of fatigue. A coach and Six horses is the utmost exercise you can bear, and this onely when you can fill it with Such company as is best Suited to your tast, and how glad would you be if it could waft you in the air to avoyd jolting; while I who am So much later in life can or at least could ride 500 miles on a trotting horse, You mortaly hate writing onely because it is the thing you chiefly ought to do as well to keep up the vogue you have in the world, as to make you easy in your fortune; you are mercifull to every thing but money, your best friend, whom[1] you treat with inhumanity;—Be assured, I will hire people to watch all your motions, and to return me a faithfull account. Tell me, have you cured your absence of mind? Can you attend to trifles? Can you at Amesbury write domestick libels to divert the family and the Neighboring Squires for five[2] miles round; or venture So far on Horseback without apprehending a Stumble at every Step? Can you Set the footmen laughing[3] as they wait at dinner; and do the Dutchess's women admire your Wit.? In what esteem are you ⌐of⌐ with the Vicar of the Parish? can you play with him at Back-gammon? Have the Farmers found out that you cannot distinguish Rye from Barly, or an Oak from a crab-tree? You are Sensible that I know the full extent of your country Skill is in fishing for Roches, or Gudgeons at the highest.[4]

I love to do you good offices with your friends; and therefore desire you will Show this letter to the Dutchess, to improve Her Graces good opinion of your qualifications, and convince her how usefull you are like to be in the family. ⌐I Suppose you have Seen Dr Delany who hath been long amongst you, And we hear is printing many Sermons against free thinkers, besides one or more against eating blood. I advised him against preaching on those Subjects to plain believing Christians, but that he might print if he pleas'd, This I Suppose hindred him from taking me as his adviser, & he rather chose Lord Bolingbroke. We hear he has published a Poem inscribed to one of the Princesses.[5] Pray how does Dr Berkeleys book pass amongst you; It is too Speculative for me, I hope you Still See Ldy S— in her grandeur and think her as much your friend as ever; in which you do her justice. I desire to present my most humble respects to the Duke and Dutchess.⌐ Her Grace shall have the honor of my correspondance again, when She goes to Amesbury. Hear a piece of Irish news, I buried the famous General Mere-

---

[1] whom] which *1741 Dab.*   [2] five] four *1741 Db.*
[3] footmen laughing] footmen a laughing *1741 Labc; 1742 Lbc.*
[4] Gay and Swift both loved fishing.
[5] Delany's sermons and his pamphlets against eating blood are easily identified; but his poem to the Princess is not known to the editor.

dyth's father last night in my Cathedral, he was 96 years old:[1] So that
Mrs Pope may live Seven years longer.[2] You Saw Mr Pope in health,
pray is he generally more healthy than when I was amongst you, I
would know how your own health is, and how much wine you drink
in a day. My Stint in company is a pint at noon, and half as much at
night, but I often dine alone[3] like a Hermit, and then I drink little or
none at all, yet I differ from you for I would have Society if I could
get what I like, people of middle understanding middle rank, ⌜very
complying, and consequently Such as I can govern. Lord knows where
this letter will find you, but I think your will is that I Should always
[direct] to the Dukes in Burlington Gardens. There's a Lord[4] for you
wholly out of my favor whom I will use as I did Schomberg's Heiresses.
So⌝ adiu | ⌜ever your &c.⌝

*POPE to HUGH BETHEL[5]   [1732?]

Egerton 1948

Tho no Words can tell you how warmly I am yours, or how truly I
wish you all health & felicity, yet I can not help writing this one line
to bid you adieu (since it must be so.) Every Year that robs me of you,
makes me wish for the next to restore you. May it do so as whole &
as sound, & every way in body & mind as hearty & as tranquill, as I
think you have been this year. Be assured I shall long to hear of you, &
am ever with all True Esteem | Dear Sir | Yours | A. Pope.

Address: To | Mr. Bethel

*POPE to HUGH BETHEL[6]   5 *May* [1732]

Egerton 1948

May 5th

It is a real pleasure to me to hear that you are not only Safely, but
Well, arrived at York. It would be a grief to me to lose you, unless

---

[1] The General was, so Ball tells us (iv. 295 n.), a violent Whig; but Swift nevertheless
liked the family.

[2] As Swift was writing, Mrs. Pope was six weeks short of 90. One infers that Swift was
aware of the true age of Mrs. Pope, whereas her son always assumes wrongly that she was
born in 1640.

[3] alone] at home *1741 Dab.*

[4] i.e. Lord Burlington. Swift is still displeased at Burlington's lack of interest in the family
monument. On the Schomberg monument see Swift to Pope, 20 Apr. 1731.

[5] Since Bethel normally spent his winters in town and his summers in Yorkshire, this
note of formal farewell might have been written in many years. It is here tentatively tied to
the letter immediately following. One may compare this with the letter addressed to Bethel
in Apr. 1731.

[6] The year of this letter like that immediately preceding is most uncertain. The second
paragraph (which, beginning with 'I am tyed down' was quoted by Ruffhead, p. 473) indicates
that the letter antedates the death of Mrs. Pope in 1733.

your own Good, health, & happiness, made me amends. A Friend who takes care of himself, obliges every one that loves him truly: I am glad you will do what our friend Mrs Patty will not; and I hope to receive the fruit of your Journey at your return, in seeing you in such Spirits, as will enable you to enjoy yourself, & render us more capable of enjoying You.

I thank you for your Thoughts of me, & Wishes for me. but I am tyed down from any distant Flights; a Horse hereabouts must be like a Carriers horse, always in a Road, for my life (as you know) is perpetually carrying me between this place & London: To this narrow Horizon my Course is confined; & I fancy it will end here; & I shall soon take up my Inn, at Twitnam church or at Westminster, as it happens to be my last Stage.

I fear Mrs B. will fear the Scarborow waters; she has the Hydrophobia upon her; she is (with all her faults) your sincere Friend, & does you justice in every opinion & regard. We joyn in hearty Services to you. My poor old Woman is hardly able to be hearty, now, in anything. She is weak to such a degree as not to speak, even to me, thrice in 24 hours, & lyes almost wholly in bed, without any appetite. adieu, & be as well as I wish you. But do not write to me. Let your Parson but draw up a Certificate that you are in health, & just sign it yourself, that is enough. | I am ever, Dear Sir, | Your most faith|full affection|ate Servant. | A. Pope.

Address: To Hugh Bethel Esqr | to be left at Mrs. Peckets | in the Shambles, in | Yorke.

Postmark: 6/MA

GAY *to* SWIFT   16 *May* 1732

Add. 4806

London May 16. 1732

To morrow we set out for Amesbury where I propose to follow your advice of employing myself about some work against next winter. You seem'd not to approve of my writing more Fables; those I am now writing have a prefatory discourse before each of 'em by way of Epistle, & the Morals of most of 'em are of the political kind; which makes 'em run into a greater length than those I have already publish'd. I have already finish'd about fifteen or sixteen; four or five more would make a volume of the same size as the first. Though this is a kind of writing that appears very easy, I find it the most difficult of any that I ever undertook; after I have invented one Fable, and finish'd it, I despair of finding out another, But I have a moral or two more which I wish to write upon. I have also a sort of a Scheme to raise my finances by doing something for the Stage;[1] with this & some reading & a great deal of exercise I propose to pass my summer; I am sorry it must be without you. Why can't you come, & saunter about upon the Downs a Horseback in the Autumn to mark the partridges for me to shoot for your dinner? Yesterday I receiv'd your Letter, & notwithstanding your reproaches of Laziness I was four or five hours about business & did not spend a shilling in a Coach or a Chair. I receiv'd a years interest on your two Bonds which is Eight pounds. I have four of my own, I have deposited all of 'em in the hands of Mr Hoare to receive the half Year's interest at Michaelmas. The Premium of the Bonds is fallen a great deal since I bought yours; I gave very near six pounds on each bond, and they are now sold for about fifty shillings. Every thing is very precarious, & I have no opinion of any of these publick securitys, but I do not know what to do with our money. I believe the Parliament next Year intend to examine the Southsea Scheme. I do not know whether it will be prudent to trust our money there till that time. I did what I could to assist Mr Ryves, & I am very glad that he hath found Justice. Lord Bathurst spoke for him, & was very zealous in bringing on his Cause.[2] The Dutchess intended to write in my last Letter, but she set out all on a sudden to take care of Lord Drumlanrig,[3] who was taken ill of the Small pox at Winchester School. He is now perfectly well recover'd (for he had a favourable kind) to the great joy of our family. I think she ought, as she intends, to renew her correspondence with you at Amesbury. I was at Dawley on Sunday, Lady B— continues in a very bad state of health, but still retains her Spirits; You are always rememberd there with great respect & friendship. Mrs Pope is so worn out with Old Age, but without any distemper, that I look upon her Life as very uncertain. Mr Pope's state of health is much in the same way as when you left him. as for myself, I am often troubled with the Cholick, I have as much inattention, & have, I think, lower Spirits than Usual, which I impute to my having no one pursuit in life. I have many compliments to make you from the Duke & Dutchess, & Lord Bolingbroke, Bathurst, Sir W. Wyndham, Mr Pulteney, Dr Arbuthnot, Mr Lewis &c. Every one of 'em is disappointed in your not coming among us. I have not seen Dean Berkeley, but have read his Book, & like many parts of it, but in general think with you, that it is too Speculative, at least for me. Dr Delany I have very seldom seen; he did not do me the honour to advise with me about any thing he hath publish'd; I like your thoughts upon these sort of writings and I should have advis'd him as you did, though I had lost his good opinion. I write in very great haste; for I have many things to do before I go out of town. Pray make me as

---

[1] Possibly *Achilles*, staged in the following February, after Gay's death.
[2] See Gay to Swift, 13 Mar. 1731/2.   [3] Her eldest son.

happy as you can, & let me hear from you often; But I am still in hopes to see you; & will expect a summons one day or other to come to Bristol, in order to be your Guide to Amesbury.

Endorsement (in Swift's hand): Rx Jun. 10th 1732 | Mr Gay, by Mr Reeves | Answd Jul. 10th 1732

POPE *to* TONSON, SR.   7 *June* 1732

The Gentleman's Magazine, clix (1836), 29.

Twitenham, June 7th, 1732.

Before I received your last, I intended to write to you my thanks for the great diligence (or let me give it a higher title, zeal) you have shewn in giving me so many particulars of the Man of Ross. They are more than sufficient for my honest purpose of setting up his fame, as an example to greater and wealthyer men, how they ought to use their fortunes. You know, few of these particulars can be made to shine in verse, but I have selected the most affecting, and have added 2 or 3 which I learnd fro' other hands.[1] A small exaggeration you must allow me as a poet; yet I was determined the ground work at least should be *Truth*, which made me so scrupulous in my enquiries; and sure, considering that the world is bad enough to be always extenuating and lessening what virtue is among us, it is but reasonable to pay it sometimes a little over measure, to balance that injustice, especially when it is done for example and encouragement to others. If any man shall ever happen to endeavour to emulate the Man of Ross, 'twill be no manner of harm if I make him think he was something more charitable and more beneficent than really he was, for so much more good it would put the imitator upon doing. And farther I am satisfy'd in my conscience (from the strokes in 2 or 3 accounts I have of his character) that it was in his will, and in his heart, to have done every good a poet can imagine.

My motive for singling out this man, was twofold: first to distinguish real and solid worth from showish or plausible expence, and virtue fro' vanity: and secondly, to humble the pride of greater men, by an opposition of one so obscure and so distant from the sphere of publick glory, this proud town. To send you any of the particular verses will be much to the prejudice of the whole; which if it has any beauty, derives it from the manner in which it is *placed*, and the *contrast* (as the painters call it) in which it stands, with the pompous figures of famous, or rich, or high-born men.

I was not sorry he had no monument, and will put that circumstance

---

[1] The passage suggests that actually Pope had all the materials he wanted on the Man, but that he was eager for verification, and perhaps willing to create 'interest' in his portrait—which, however, he will not send to Tonson.

into a note, perhaps into the body of the poem itself (unless you entreat the contrary in your own favor, by your zeal to erect one). I would however, in this case, spare the censure upon his heir (so well as he deserves it), because I dare say, after seeing his picture, every body will turn that circumstance to his honour, and conclude the Man of Ross himself would not have any monument in memory of his own good deeds.

I have no thoughts of printing the poem (which is an epistle on the *Use of Riches*) this long time, perhaps not till it is accompanied with many others; and at a time, when telling truths, and drawing exemplary pictures of men and manners can be of no disservice to the author, and occasion no slanderer to mistake them, and apply them falsely, as I was lately serv'd in the character of Timon. But I wish for nothing more than to see you here, on these quiet banks of the Thames, where any of these things should be frankly shewn to you.

My portrait, by Dahl,[1] I have sent a week ago to your nephew. You oblige me in the copy of my old friend Dr. Garth; and you will always oblige me in continuing to write to me. As to Dr. Bentley and Milton, I think the one *above* and the other *below* all criticisme. Adieu, and health, and peace, and fair weather[2] attend you.

Yours, | A. Pope.

†SWIFT *to* POPE[3]   12 *June* 1732

1741 La

Dublin, June 12, 1732.

I doubt, habit hath little power to reconcile us to sickness attended by pain. With me, the lowness of spirits hath a most unhappy effect; I am grown less patient with solitude, and harder to be pleas'd with company; which I could formerly better digest, when I could be easier without it than at present. As to sending you any thing that I have written since I left you (either verse or prose) I can only say, that I have order'd by my Will, that all my Papers of any kind shall be deliver'd you to dispose of as you please. I have several things that I have had schemes to finish, or to attempt, but I very foolishly put off the trouble, as sinners do their repentance: for I grow every day more

---

[1] Dahl's portrait (now sent to be copied for Tonson) was painted in 1727 according to the Grolier Club *Catalogue* (1911).

[2] Sir William Temple's wish again.

[3] This letter was first inserted, out of chronological order, in the official London editions of the Swift letters (1741 Lab), from which it was thereafter added with six others to the Dublin edition (1741 Da) as a Supplement. Faulkner's headnote to the Supplement was: 'After we had reprinted the foregoing Sheets, we found the following Letters in the Folio Edition published by Mr. Pope in London; which we here insert to make our Collection as compleat as possible.' The letters in this group were not in the clandestine (1740) volume: speculation only can offer reasons for their omission. In all Pope's editions this letter unaccountably was placed after Swift to Gay, 3 Oct. 1732.

averse from writing, which is very natural, and when I take a pen say to my self a thousand times, *non est tanti.*[1] As to those papers of four or five years past, that you are pleas'd to require soon,[2] they consist of little accidental things writ in the country; family amusements, never intended further than to divert our selves and some neighbours, or some effects of anger on[3] Publick Grievances here, which would be insignificant out of this kingdom. Two or three of us had a fancy three years ago to write a Weekly paper, and call it an Intelligencer. But it continued not long; for the whole Volume (it was re-printed in London and I find you have seen it) was the work only of two, my self and Dr. Sheridan. If we could have got some ingenious young man to have been the manager, who should have published all that might be sent to him, it might have continued longer, for there were hints enough. But the Printer[4] here could not afford such a young man one farthing for his trouble, the Sale being so small, and the price one half-penny; and so it dropt. In the Volume you saw, (to answer your questions) the 1, 3, 5, 7, were mine. Of the 8th I writ only the Verses (very uncorrect, but against a fellow we all hated)[5] the 9th mine, the 10th only the Verses,[6] and of those not the four last slovenly lines; the 15th is a Pamphlet of mine printed before with Dr. Sh——'s[7] Preface, merely for laziness not to disappoint the town; and so was the 19th, which contains only a parcel of facts relating purely to[8] the miseries of Ireland, and wholly useless and unentertaining.[9] As to other things of mine since I left you; there are in prose a View of the State of Ireland; a Project for eating Children; and a Defence of Lord Carteret; in Verse a Libel on Dr. D—— and Lord Carteret; a Letter to Dr. D——[10] on the Libels writ against him: the Barack (a stol'n Copy) the Lady's Journal; the Lady's Dressing-room (a stol'n Copy) the Plea[11] of the Damn'd (a stol'n Copy); all these have been printed in London, (I forgot to tell you that the Tale of Sir Ralph was sent from England.[12]) Besides these, there are five or six (perhaps more) Papers of Verses

---

[1] It is not worth while.—Footnote in *1741 Dab.*
[2] For the 1732 volume of their *Miscellanies*.
[3] on] or *1741 Da*] at *1742 La.*   [4] John Harding.—*1741 Dab* (footnote).
[5] The verses attacked the Hon. Richard Tighe; see *Poems*, ed. Williams, pp. 772–82. The poem appeared in the *Miscellanies*.
     'but against a fellow we all hated'—omitted in *1741 Dab.*
[6] 'Tim and the Fables'; see Williams, pp. 782–3.
[7] Sheridan's.   [8] relating purely to] relating to *1742 La.*
[9] Swift's prose in *The Intelligencer* included: No. 1, Introduction; No. 3, On 'The Beggar's Opera'; Nos. 5 and 7, 'Essay on the Fates of Clergymen'; No. 9, 'Essay on Modern Education'; No. 15, 'A Short View of the State of Ireland'; and No. 19, 'On Coinage'. Pope reprinted in the *Miscellanies* iii, Nos. 5, 7, 9, and 16 (which Swift here does not acknowledge). He also reprinted 'A Modest Proposal' and the 'Vindication of Lord Carteret'.
[10] D——] Delany *1741 Dab.*
[11] Plea] Place *1741 Dab.* (Ball prints *Place* here, and *Plea* is certainly an error).
[12] 'Sir Ralph the Patriot' as 'The Progress of Patriotism' was reprinted in *Intelligencer* No. 12 from *The Craftsman* of 3 Aug. 1728. It has not been regarded as by Swift.

writ in the North, but perfect Family-things, two or three of which may be tolerable, the rest but indifferent, and the humour only local, and some that would give offence to the times.[1] Such as they are, I will bring them, tolerable or bad, if I recover this lameness, and live long enough to see you either here or there. I forget again to tell you that the Scheme of paying Debts by a Tax on Vices, is not one Syllable mine, ⌐but of a young Clergyman whom I countenance;[2] he told me it was built upon a passage in Gulliver, where a Projector hath something upon the same Thought. This young man is the most hopeful we have: a book of his Poems was printed in London; Dr. D— is one of his Patrons; he is marry'd and has children, and makes up about 100*l.* a year, on which he lives decently. The utmost stretch of his ambition is, to gather up as much superfluous money as will give him a sight of you, and half an hour of your presence; after which he will return home in full satisfaction, and in proper time die in peace.⌐[3]

My poetical fountain is drain'd, and I profess I grow gradually so dry, that a Rhime with me is almost as hard to find as a Guinea, and even Prose speculations tire me almost as much. Yet I have a thing in prose,[4] begun above twenty-eight years ago, and almost finish'd. It will make a four shilling Volume, and is such a perfection of folly, that you shall never hear of it till it is printed, and then you shall be left to guess. Nay I have another of the same age,[5] which will require a long time to perfect, and is worse than the former, in which I will serve you the same way. I heard lately from Mr.—[6] who promises to be less lazy in order to mend his fortune. But women who live by their beauty, and men by their wit, are seldom provident enough to consider that both Wit and Beauty will go off with years, and there is no living upon the credit of what is past.

I am in great concern to hear of my Lady Bolingbroke's ill health returned upon her, and I doubt my Lord will find Dawley too solitary without her. In that, neither he nor you are companions young enough for me; and I believe the best part of the reason why men are said to grow children when they are old, is because they cannot entertain themselves with thinking; which is the very case of little boys and girls, who love to be noisy among their play-fellows. I am told Mrs. Pope

---

[1] Of the poems named Pope chose for the *Miscellanies* iii the following: 'The Journal of a Modern Lady', 'Mad Mullinix and Timothy', the 'Barrack' ('A Soldier and a Scholar': see Williams, pp. 863–73), and 'Letter to Dr. Delany' (Williams, pp. 499–505). Of the prose he selected 'A Modest Proposal', 'A Vindication of Lord Carteret', 'An Essay on the Fates of Clergymen', 'An Essay on Modern Education', and two letters from *The Intelligencer*. These are the items mentioned here: other pieces by Swift appear in the volume.

[2] Matthew Pilkington, Chaplain to Alderman Barber, when Lord Mayor, by the Dean's Recommendation.—Curll, *1741 Lc.* The 'Scheme' was inserted in the *Miscellanies*.

[3] The passage in half-brackets was omitted in 1741 Dab for obvious reasons, among which was Pilkington's unsatisfactory behaviour after having the dean's 'countenance'.

[4] *Polite Conversation.*—Footnote in 1741 Dab.

[5] *Advice to Servants.*—Footnote in 1741 Dab.   [6] Mr. Gay?

is without pain, and I have not heard of a more gentle decay, without uneasiness to her self or friends; yet I cannot but pity you, who are ten times the greater sufferer, by having the person you most love so long before you, and dying daily; and I pray God it may not affect your mind or your health.

*POPE *to* BUCKLEY[1]   16 *June* [1732]

The Athenaeum, 17 May 1884, p. 631.

As One Instance (& I wish I could give you many) of my Desires to be serviceable to you, I have had the Articles examined betwixt Lintott & me, as to what I promisd of the use of the copper ornaments, Initials & Tailpieces, for your Work.[2] I am very certain they are wholly in my power. Therfore I have written to him an order to deliver them to you; upon your going or order[3] for them. But as he is a Grand Chicanneur, I would not have you tell him for what Book: and as he is a great Scoundrell to me, I would willingly have him receive the small punishment of imagining I am printing with you Something of my own, for which he has (upon Rumours, for I never converse with Him) lately been importuning me, and receivd no other answer than a very true one, that I would never imploy him more.

I am, with sincerity, Dear Sir, | Your obligd & affectionate Servant, | A. Pope.

Twit'nam, June 16.

Address: To Mr. Buckley at his house in Princes Court, near Storye's, Westminster.

POPE *to* CARYLL[4]   29 *June* 1732

Add. 28618

I assure you 'twas with true concern that I heard of the continuance of your illness, enough, God knows, to weary out any but Christian

---

[1] The year is determined by the fact that Buckley's Thuanus was in press in October of 1732. See Nichols, *Lit. Anec.,* iv. 401.

[2] Buckley used Pope's copper ornaments at the ends of some volumes of his great edition of Thuanus (1733). After the three Latin epistles prefixed to vol. i he makes acknowledgements, without compliment, to various gentlemen for medals, &c., used for engraving, and finally to Pope in the following glowing terms: 'Ornamentorum autem, quae ad calcem tomorum sunt adjecta, tabulas aeneas Alexander Pope armiger, Anglicorum poetarum hujus temporis facile princeps, ultro mihi perbenevole commodavit.' To modern tastes the ornaments (designed by William Kent) are imposing, heavy, and unattractive; but Buckley's edition in its day was all that magnificence could achieve.

[3] Should this read *giving an order*?

[4] Elwin prints 20 June as the date, but the transcript gives either 27 or 29—the second digit is not clear: it cannot be 20.

patience. I am certain you possess yourself as much as any man and can resign as well to the Disposer of all Men, but I wish and pray the trial may not be so hard, and that virtue may not be put to so severe an experiment. I will not say it doubles my concern to be deprived by this of your long-expected conversation; for indeed it makes but a very small part of it whatever is my loss alone. I am a thousand times more affected by the sense of your suffering, which, that it may please God to put a speedy end to in your perfect recovery, is the hearty desire of | Dear sir | Your ever faithful friend and servant | A. Pope

Twitnam. 27 June 1732.

POPE *to* LORD BATHURST   9 *July* [1732]

Cirencester

July 9th

My dear Lord,—I hope you now feel all the pleasure, which if I did not greatly love you I would envy, in the Sight of your own Improvements: those Certain Improvements, which Time bestows only on things Inanimate, & which will flourish, when we are gone. (does not that look like a Stroke of Envy?) No, it is a Reflexion arising from Tenderness, both to our Friends & ourselves, and draws with it a Sigh for both. I would not wish myself immortal, unless I could make my Friends so too; And then indeed, to out-live an Oak would be a thing desireable. Speaking of Oaks, poor Mr Lewis is not such Timber as I could wish, (tho' about the Girt he is according to the Statute) for he has been dangerously ill, and continues very much so. He is at a place called Pishobury, near Sawbridgworth in Hertfordshire, whither I wish you writ to him.—You can hardly think how pleasd you have made Cleland in expressing your memory of him in Venison, tho' to do him justice, tis the memory & not the Venison that delights him so much: but the Venison too was good, & I eat thereof. He intends to invite the Doctor[1] to the Hanch and next week he is to be here en famille, for 7 days, where he will find no venison. I intend to carry them one day to Riskins with a cold dinner, purely to propagate the Fame of your gardens here, while you desert them: and we are to see the Royal Workes at our leisure, afterwards. Lord Bolingbroke bids me to wish you all the Joys of Nebuchadonozor, all the pensile Gardens, the proud Pyramids, the Ninivehs and Babels, to aggrandise and ornament your Territories; & that at length, you may be turn'd into a Happy Beast, loose among a thousand Females, to grass.

There is One Woman at least that I think you will never run after, of whom the Town rings with a hundred Stories, *why* she run, &

---

[1] Dr. Arbuthnot.

whither she is run?[1] Her sober Friends are sorry for her, & truly so am I, whom she cutt off from the number of them three years agoe. She has dealt as mysteriously with you, as with me formerly; both which are proofs that We are both less mad, than is requisite, for her to think quite well of us. I am told in town, she is sending her Son to Oxford, and if you, (whose Gallantry is to make her amends for your defects in Politicks) intend to see him there.[2] I hope, my Lord, you'l bestow a few steps more of your galloping Horse, to make these parts a Visit: in which case I would lugg my crazy carcase ten miles, to meet you at Riskins, London, or wherever you will, hereabouts. It is a great truth that I often wish for Fortunatus's Hatt, to be with you; and yet I think that even that Hatt should have wings, like Mercury's, to make me sure of finding you any where. I hope I shall be happyer when I am a Seperated Spirit, & find at last a Vehicle active enough for such Souls as ours to keep pace with each other; I assure you my Lord I am taking pains to arrive at such a Vehicle, by such methods as will speedily destroy my present Crust in all probability. I have no news to tell, but desire to hear the best, I mean that of your Lordships, my Lady Bathurst's & all your Family's health & pleasure, which a few words from your hand will make me happy in. It is a sincere Truth I have few wishes equal, and no one wish superior, to those I shall always make for your happiness to which my own is attachd so many ways, as hardly leaves me any Merit in them. adieu my dear Lord, & think I want you never more, than when I have no worldly Interests for you to take care of; & particularly at this very time. My Mother is as usual, & my own health rather worse, but partly thro' my own fault.

‖SWIFT *to* GAY *and* THE DUCHESS OF QUEENSBERRY[3]

10 *July* 1732

Longleat Portland Papers, xiii (Harleian transcripts)

Dublin Jul. 10. 1732.

I had your Letter[4] by Mr Ryves a long time after the date for I suppose he stayd long in the way. I am glad you determine upon something ⌐that will bring you money. But you have misunderstood me, for⌐

---

[1] The Duchess of Buckingham had suddenly left for France. According to Elwin she wrote explanations to Sir Robert Walpole from Boulogne, 6 June 1732. Elwin must be wrong in thinking that the journey was due to a desire to get control of Atterbury's papers. According to *The Universal Spectator*, 6 May 1732, Atterbury's body and his effects were landed at Deal on 29 Apr. See also *Gent. Mag.* ii. 772. It is, then, barely conceivable that she feared incrimination by the bishop's papers, which were naturally seized for examination by the customs. She was notoriously a Jacobite of course.

[2] Bathurst was one of the young duke's trustees. His defects in politics would be defects in Jacobitism.

[3] This letter appears in all of Pope's texts (1740–2) with numerous excisions. These are here placed in half-brackets.   [4] Gay's letter of 16 May 1732.

there is no writing I esteem more than Fables, nor any thing so difficult to succeed in. which however you have done excellently well, and I have often admired your happyness in such a kind of performance, which I have frequently endeavoured at in vain. I remember, I acted as you seem to hint, I found a moral first, & then studyed for a Fable, but cou'd do nothing that pleased me, & so left off that scheme for ever. I remember one which was to represent what Scoundrels rise in Armys by a long War, wherein I supposed the Lyon was engaged, & having lost all his animals of worth, at last Serjeant Hog came to a Brigadeer,[1] & Corporall Ass a Colonell, &c. I agree with you likewise about geting something by the Stage, which when it succeeds, is the best crop for Poetry in England. But pray take some new scheme quite different from any thing you have already touched. The present humor of the Players, who hardly (as I was told in London) regard any new play, & your present Scituation at the Court, are the difficultyes to be overcome, but those circumstances may have altered (at least the former) since I left you. My scheme was to pass a month at Amesbury, & then go to Twitenham & live a winter between that & Dawly, & sometimes at Riskins, without going to London where I now can have no occasional lodgings.[2] But I am not yet in any condition for such removeals. ⌐I believe I told you that I have been about a month able to ride in Gambadoes which give my feet a support like a floor, but I can no more stand tiptoe on my left leg than I can dance the rope, nor know when I shall; for I mend slowly, & limp when I walk. For these reasons⌐ I would fain have you get enough against you grow old, to have two or three Servants about you & a convenient house. It is hard to want those subsidia Senectuti[3] when a man grows hard to please, & few people care whether he be pleased or no. I have a large house; yet I should hardly prevail to find one Visitor, if I were not able to hire him with a bottle of wine. So that when I am not abroad on horseback, I generally dine alone, & am thankfull if a friend will pass the evening with me ⌐over a bottle⌐. I am now with the remainder of my pint before me, ⌐that I drank with water at dinner, with no creature but two Servants attending while I eat about half a chicken; and⌐ so here's your health—And the second & chief is to my Tunbridge acquaintance,[4] My Lady Dutchess. And I tell you that I fear, my Lord Bolin. & Mr Pope, a couple of Philosophers would starve me; for even of Port wine I should require half a pint a day, & as much at night, and you were growing as bad unless your Duke & Dutchess have mended you. ⌐You have not forgot; Gentlemen I'll leave you to your wine,

---

[1] came to a Brigadeer] came to be a Brigadeer *1740; 1741 Dab; 1742La.*] to be Brigadeer *1741 Labc; 1742 Lbc.*

[2] Since Gay has been turned out of Whitehall where Swift had stayed with him.

[3] Supports to old Age.—Footnote in *1741 Dab.*

[4] i.e. an acquaintance to be owned at Tunbridge only, or in the country.

which was but the remainder of a pint when four glasses were drank. . .
I tell that story to every body, in commendation of Mr Pope's abstemiousness. If you please to manage my 200ll as your own, (though
I believe you are just such a manager as my self) I shall be obliged to
you. Yet if it ever comes to be at par, I will against my former maxims
return it hither, where I can get 10 per cent by the exchange, & 6 per
cent Interest, or 5 and a ½ with great safety but probably I shall have
occasion to spend it, for our tythes hardly yeild us any thing, & my
land rents are not half sufficient to maintain me. I congratulate with
my Lady Dutchess on her Son's passing so easily through the small pox.
I am heartily concerned for the Lady at Dawly. I fear she is in a bad
way. I owe her much gratitude for many civilities I recieved from her,
& have a great esteem for her good sence.⌉ Your Cholick is owing to
intemperance of the Philosophick kind. you eat without care, & if you
drink less than I, you drink too little. But your *inattention* I cannot
pardon, because I imagined the cause was removed, for I thought it
lay in your fourty Millions of Scheams by Court hopes & Court fears,
yet Mr Pope has the same defect, & it is of all others the most mortal
to conversation. Neither is my Lord Bolingbroke untinged with it. . . .
All for want of my rule Vive la bagatelle. But the Doctor is the King
of inattention. . . . What a vexatious life should I lead amongst you.
If the Dutchess be a *reveuse*, I will never come to Amesbury, or if I
do, I will run away from you both to one of her women, & the Steward
& Chaplain.

⌐Pray God bless you, & your Landlord & Landlady with the whole
family. I am ever sincerely yours, &c.⌉

Madam,—I mentioned something to Mr Gay of a Tunbridge acquaintance whom we forget of course when we return to Town, and
yet I am assured that if they meet again ⌐the⌉ next summer they have
a better title to resume their commerce. Thus I look upon my right
of coresponding with your Grace to be better established upon your
return to Amesbury, & I shall at this time descend to forget or at least
suspend my resentments of your neglect all the time you were in
London, ⌐tho'⌉ I still keep in my heart, that Mr Gay had no sooner
turned his back than you left the place in his letter voyd, which he had
commanded you to fill, though your guilt confounded you so far that
you wanted presence of mind to blot out the last line where that command stared you in the face. But ⌐I own⌉ it is my misfortune to quarell
with all my acquaintance & always come by the worst, and fortune is
ever against me, but never so much as by persuing me out of meer
partiality to your Grace, for which you are to answer. By your connivance she hath pleased by one stumble on the Stairs to give me a
lameness that six months have not been able perfectly to cure. And

thus I am prevented from revenging my self by continuing a month at Amesbury, and breeding confusion in your Grace's family. No disappointment through my whole life hath been so vexatious by many ⌜thousand⌝ degrees; and God knows whether I shall ever live to see the *invisible Lady* to whom I am[1] obliged for so many favours, & whom I never beheld since she was a brat in hanging sleeves. I am, shall[2] be ever with the greatest respect & gratitude Madam your Grace's most obedient | & most humble &c.

⌜I intreat your Grace to present my most humble respects to my Lord Duke & pray God of his mercy preserve you to see a Court worthy of your appearing in it.⌝

⌜Jul. 10. 1732.⌝

LORD BATHURST *to* POPE[3]   20 *July* [1732]
Elwin–Courthope, viii. 344

I return you a thousand thanks for your agreeable letter, and for the kind expressions in it, but what method you are in to hasten the demolition of that little tenement of yours, which was not designed by nature to bear any proportion of duration with the works of its partner, I am at a loss to guess. You say you are taking pains about it. Believe me there is no occasion to try any new method. You were sufficiently irregular before, and you need be under no apprehension of exceeding the age of your mother. But admitting that long life is not so desirable as the generality of mankind reckon, is health to be despised? and for God's sake what are you doing to make yours worse than it was? I am provoked at you to the last degree. I positively insist upon your coming down to me that I may put you into a new regimen. What the d— ails you? Is it not enough to have the headache four days in the week, and to be as sick as a breeding woman the other three? I shall come to Oxford very soon to meet the little duke,[4] and I beg it of you in the most earnest manner, that you will meet me there, and come back with me. I will give you due notice. If you can come half the way, which you may easily do with a pair of horses, and your curricle, you shall have my chaise to meet you. I long to see you excessively, for I have now almost finished my hermitage in the wood, and it is better than you can imagine, and many other things are done that you have no idea of. However there is enough remaining to employ you for a week

---

[1] am] was *1740–2*.   [2] am, shall] am, and shall *1740–2*.

[3] Elwin printed this from the original in 'the Oxford Papers'. The present editor has not discovered the original. It may have been offered for sale at Sotheby's on 16 Mar. 1852 as lot 106. The date Elwin took from the postmark, which should postdate the actual writing by a day perhaps. The letter is obviously an answer to Pope's of 9 July.

[4] Edmund, Duke of Buckingham.

at least, and occasion the consumption of a quire of paper in draughts.
I will venture to assert that all Europe cannot show such a pretty little
plain work in the Brobdingnag style as what I have executed here. If
you have any curiosity, come; if you have any regard for me, come; if
you have any value for your own health, come. In short I will never
forgive you if you do not come. I send half a buck for Mr. and Mrs.
Cleland by the coach this night, which will be left at the Red Lion at
Brentford to-morrow, and I hope it will be in your house[1] before this
comes to your hands. Adieu. Let me hear from you by the next post,
and frame no excuses about this journey, for I will not admit of any,
let them appear never so reasonable.

GAY *and* THE DUCHESS OF QUEENSBERRY *to* SWIFT
24 *July* 1732

Add. 4806

Ambresbury[2] July the 24th 1732

As the circumstances of our money affairs are alter'd I think myself
oblig'd to acquaint you with 'em as soon as I can which if I had not
receiv'd your Letter last post I should have done now. I left your two
S. Sea Bonds, and four of my own in Mr Hoare's[3] hands when I came
out of town. that he might receive the interest for us when due, or if
you should want your money that you might receive it upon your
order. Since I came out of town, the Southsea Company have come
to a resolution to pay off 50 per cent of their Bonds with the interest
of the 50 per cent to Michaelmas next, so that there is now half of our
fortunes in Mr Hoare's hands at present without any interest going on.
As you seem to be inclin'd to have your money remitted to Ireland I
will not lay out the summ that is paid into his hands in any other thing
till I have your orders. I cannot tell what to do with my own; I
believe I shall see Mr Hoare in this country very soon, for he hath a
house not above six miles from us,[4] & intend to advise with him,
though in the present situation of affairs I expect to be left to take my
own way. The remaining 50 per cent, were it to be sold at present
bears a premium, but the premium on the 50 that was paid in is sunk.
I do not know whether I write intelligibly to you upon this subject.
I cannot send you the particulars of your account, though I know I
am in debt to you for interest besides your principal, & you will understand so much of what I intend to inform you that half of your money
is now in Mr Hoare's hands without any interest; so since I cannot

---

[1] The venison had been sent, more or less at Pope's suggestion, to help him in entertaining
the Clelands.

[2] Professor Francis P. Magoun, Jr., tells the editor (referring him to *English Place-Name
Society*, xvi [1939], 358–9) that the spelling here used was in Gay's day known but archaic.

[3] Richard Hoare of the famous banking family.   [4] At Stourhead.—Ball.

send you the particulars of your account I will now say no more about it. I shall finish the work I intended this summer, but I look upon the success in every respect to be precarious. You judge very rightly of my present situation that I cannot propose to succeed by favour, & I don't think, if I could flatter myself that I had any degree of merit much could be expected from that unfashionable pretension. I have almost done every thing I propos'd in the way of Fables, but not set the last hand to them; though they will not amount to half the number, I believe they will make much such another volume as the last. I find it the most difficult task I ever undertook, but I have determin'd to go through with it, and after this, I believe I shall never have courage enough to think any more in this way. Last Post I had a Letter from Mr Pope who informs me he hath heard from you, and that he is preparing some scatter'd things of yours & his for the Press; I believe I shall not see him 'till the Winter, for by riding & walking I am endeavouring to lay in a stock of health to squander in town; You see in this respect my scheme is very like the Country Gentlemen in regard to their revenues. As to my eating & drinking I live as when you knew me, so that in that point we shall agree very well in living together; and the Dutchess will answer for me that I am cur'd of inattention, for I never forget any thing she says to me. for he never hears what I say, so cannot forget. if I served him the same way I should not care a farthing ever to be better acquainted with my Tunbridge acquaintance, which by my attention to him I have learnt to sett my heart upon   I began to give over all hopes & from thence began my neglect. I think this is a very good philosophical reason, tho' there might be another given; when fine Ladys are in London tis very genteel & allowable to forget their best friends, which if I thought modestly of my self, must needs be you, because you know little of me. till you do more pray dont perswaid Mr Gay that he is discreet enough to live alone; for I do assure you he is not, or I either   We are of great use to one another for we never flatter or contradict but when tis absolutely necessary & then we do to some purpose; particularly the first agrees mightily with our constitutions, if ever we quarrel twill be about a peice of Bread & butter for some body is never sick except he eats too much of it, he will not quarrel with y[ou] for a Glass or so for by that means he hopes to be able in time to Gulp down some of those forty millions of schemes that hindred him from being good company. I would fain see you here, there is so fair a chance that one of us must be pleasd, perhaps both, you with an old acquaintance & I with a new one, tis so well worth taking a journey for, that if the Mountain will not come to Mahomet Mahomet must come to the Mountain, but before either of our journeys are settled I desire you would resolve me one question—whether a man who thinks himself well where he is, should look out for his house & Servants before tis convenient, before he grows old, or before a person with whom he lives pulls him by the sleeve in private (according to oath) & tells him they have enough of his Company. he will not let me write one word more but that I have a very great regard for you &c &c The Duke is very much yours & will never leave you to your wine. many thanks for Drum.¹ I wish to receive your congratulations for the other Boy you may believe.

Address: For | the Revd Dr Swift Dean of St Patricks | in Dublin | Ireland | by way | of London
Postmark: 26/ [blur]
Endorsement (in Swift's hand): Mr Gay, & D—s | of Q— | Rx Aug. 1. 1732 [repeated on another part of the cover].

POPE *to* CARYLL   27 *July* 1732

Add. 28618

27 July 1732.

I am truly desirous to know in what state of health you continue since I saw you at Whitton. I've made the best inquiry I could, but shall not be satisfied till I have a line from your hand. You may with truth believe no man more heartily wishes your welfare than one who has so many years experienced your partiality to himself in all events. It was a great disappointment to me that you *did not*—I won't say *Would not*—pass some days at my house. I had so much to say to you that to attempt any part of it in writing would be beginning an immense work. I hate *words* without matter, and can here only repeat what I've so often said of my attachment to you, that I scarce care² to speak at all of a thing so known to all my friends. And all my long stories must be reserved only, as they are fit only, for conversation. Adieu, dear sir. May God preserve you as happy as I wish you. | Yours ever | A. Pope.

Pray let all your family know I am their faithful servant in being yours. My mother is tolerably well. Your god-daughter sends you her duty or (if you like another phrase better) her duteous love—

POPE to THE EARL OF BURLINGTON³   [?28 *July* 1732]

Chatsworth

Friday.

My Lord,—Being confined to pay Civilities to Mr C.⁴ & his Family

---

¹ Lord Drumlanrig was congratulated on his recovery from smallpox, which seems at the moment to afflict his brother.
² *Care* is Elwin's reading. What the scribe wrote looks more like *fanc*.
³ The Clelands seem to have been with Pope in the third week of July. The 28th was a Friday. A later Friday, in August, is perhaps possible.
⁴ Mr. Cleland.

who were here for a week, I had set apart to morrow to take my leave of your Lordship; when I find myself obliged to attend Lady Boling-broke at home. I wish another Lady knew, how it vexes me, not to have been on my knees to Her; to ask, for the last time, some of her Papers of Mr Savil's[1] ambassy to France, &c. (which I could read over during your stay in Yorkshire at full leisure.) If she will send them to me, I will keep the Deposite very faithfully. I fear it would be too near your Journey, to disturb you on Sunday, or would try to tell your Lordship & my Lady how truly I am always hers & | My Lord your most faithfull | & obligd Servant | A. Pope

‖SWIFT *to* GAY *and* THE DUCHESS OF QUEENSBERRY[2]

12 *August* 1732

Longleat Portland Papers, xiii (Harleian transcripts)

Dublin Aug. 12th 1732.

I know not what to say to the account of your stewardship and it is monstrous to me that the South-Sea should pay half their debts at one clap. But I will send for the money, when you put me into the way for I shall want it here, my Affairs being in a bad condition by the miseryes of the Kingdom, and my own private fortune being wholly embroyld, and worse than ever; so that I shall soon petition the Dutchess as an object of Charity to lend me 3 or 4 thousand pounds to keep up my dignity. That[3] 100ll will buy me six hogsheads of wine which will support me a year, provisæ frugis in annum copia;[4] Horace desired no more. for I will construe *frugis* to be wine. You are young enough to get some lucky hint, which must come by chance and it shall be a thing of importance, quod et hunc in annum vivet et plures[5] and you shall not finish it in hast, and it shall be diverting, and usefully satyri-call. and the Dutchess shall be your Critick, and betwixt you and me, I do not find she will grow weary of you till this time seven years. I had lately an Offer to change for an English living,[6] which is just too short by 300ll a year; and that must be made up out of the Dutchess's pin-money before I can consent. I want to be Minister of Amesbury,

---

[1] Henry Savile, great-uncle of Lady Burlington, was in an embassy to France in 1672. Her grandfather was the Marquess of Halifax, author of the 'Character of a Trimmer'.

[2] This letter, with slight modifications, appears in all the editions of 1740–2.

[3] That 100ll] My own hundred pound *1740; 1741 Dab; 1742 La.* My one hundred pound *1741 Labc; 1742 Lbc.*

[4] A Stock of Wine laid up for many Years.—Footnote in 1741 Dab. See Horace, *Epistles*, I. xviii. 109.

[5] Lord Oxford himself had to write in this tag from Horace, *Carmina*, I. xxxii. 3–4, and he mutilated it somewhat. Pope's texts read (1741 Labc; 1742 Lbc) *vivat et in plures*. The correct Dublin texts of 1741 have the footnote, 'Which may live this Year and many others.'

[6] The living was that of Burghfield (Berks.). Bolingbroke tried to arrange the gift of it. See Ball, iv. 320.

Dawly, Twitenham, Riskins and Prebendary of Westminster, else I will not stir a step, but content my self with making the Dutchess miserable 3 months next summer. But I keep ill Company, I mean the Dutchess and you; who are both out of favour and so I find am I, by a few verses[1] wherein Pope and you have your parts⌐; and tho the —,[2] told me 5 years ago they would make me easy amongst you, I find they take a pretence to be angry to such a degree, that they will not give me the medals they promesed me. Yet wheedled me out of a present that cost me 40ll. If my leg had been so well 2 months ago I should have been to see Amesbury this Summer, For with a little pain I can walk; and ride without Gambadoes⌐. You hear Dr D—y has got a wife with 1600ll a year,[3] I who am his Governor cannot take one under two thousd; I wish you would inquire of such a one in your Neighborhud, see what it is to write Godly books; I profess I envy you above all men in Engld, you want nothing but three thousand pounds more to keep you in plenty when your friends grow weary of you. To prevent which last evil at Amesbury you must learn to dominear and be peevish, to find fault with their vittals and drink; to chide and direct the servants with some other lessons which I shall teach you, and always practiced my self with success. I belive I formerly desired to know whether the Vicar of Amesbury can play at Backgammon. pray ask him the Question and give him my service.

To the Dutchess

Madam, I was the most unwary creature in the world, when against my old Maxims, I writ first to you upon your return to Tunbridge; ⌐for Mr Gay will depose, that all Ladyes of great quality ever made me the first Advances.⌐ I beg that this condescension of mine may go no farther, and that you will not pretend to make a president of it, I never knew any man cured of inattention[4] although the pretended causes were removed. when I was with Mr Gay last in London, talking with him on some poetical subjects, He would answer; Well; I am determined not to accept the Employment of Gentleman usher ⌐to the —⌐, and of the same disposition were all my poetical friends; and if you cannot cure him, I utterly despair. As to yourself I will say to you (though comparisons be odious) what I said to the — that your quality should be never any motive of Esteem to me. My compliment was then lost, but it will not be so to you, for ⌐you reason wrong;⌐ I know you more by any one of your Letters, then I could by six months

---

[1] These cannot be identified. They should be from verses hostile to all three men.

[2] Above the dash is entered by a modern hand the word *Court*.

[3] Dr. Delany, who had acquired some fame this year by his godly books, had in July married a rich widow, Mrs. Tennison.—Ball, iv. 336, n. 1. Swift as Dean was governor to Delany as Chancellor of St. Patrick's.

[4] of inattention] of any inattention *1741 Labc; 1742 Lbc.*

conversing, ⌜for⌝ your pen is always more naturall and sincere and unaffectd then your tongue. In writing you are too lazy to give yourself the trouble of Acting a part and have indeed acted so indiscreetly that I have you at mercy and although you should arrive at such a height of immorality as to deny your hand, yet whenever I produce it; the world will unite in Swearing this must come from the — of —.[1] I will answer your Question. Mr Gay is not discreet enough to live alone; but he is too discreet to live alone, and yet unless you mend him, he will live alone even in your Grace's company; your quarrelling with each other upon the subject of Bread and Butter, is the most usuall thing in the world, Parliaments, Courts, Cityes, and Kingdoms quarrell for no other causes, from hence and from hence onely arise all the quarrells between whig and Tory, between those who are in the Ministry, and those who are out; between all pretenders to Employments in the Church, the Law, and the Army, even the common Proverb teaches you this, when we say; It is none of my bread and butter; meaning, it is no business of mine. Therefore I despair of any reconcilement between you till the affair of Bread and butter be adjusted, wherein I would gladly be a Mediator. If Mahomet should come to the mountain, how happy would an excellent Lady be who lives a few miles from this Town; as I was talking[2] of Mr Gays way of Living at Amesbury, she offerd 50 Guineas you were[3] both at her house for one hour over a bottle of Burgundy which we were then drinking. To your question, I answer, that your Grace should pull me by the Sleeve[4] till you tore it off, and when you said you were weary of me, I would pretend to be deaf, and think, according to another proverb, that you tere my Cloaths to keep me from going. I never will believe one word you say of My Lord Duke, unless I see three or four lines in his own hand at the bottom of yours. I have a concern in the whole Family, and Mr Gay must give me a particular account of every branch, for I am not ashamed of you though you be Duke and Dutchess, though I have been of others who are &c. and I do not doubt but even your own servants love you; even down to your Postillons, and when I come to Amesbury before I see your Graces I will have an hours conversation with the Vicar, who will tel me how familiarly you talk to goody Dobson and all the Neighbors, as if you were their equalls,[5] and that you were Godmother to his[6] son Jacky.

I am and shall be ever with the greatest Respect ⌜and gratitud⌝ your Graces most obedient &c.

[1] the — of —] you only *1740–2*.   [2] talking] telling *1740–2*.
[3] you were] to have you *1740–2*.
[4] the Sleeve] Here Swift evidently used an abbreviation, which was transcribed by the scribe as *your*. Lord Oxford wrote in *the* (yᵉ) but failed to cancel *your*, which is here deleted.
[5] equalls] equal *1740*; *1741 Labc*; *1742 Lbc*.
[6] his son] her son *1740–2*.

POPE *to* MOTTE[1]   16 *August* [1732]

The Pierpont Morgan Library

Sir,—Had I had the least thought you would have now desired what
you before so deliberately refused, I would certainly have preferrd
you to any other Bookseller. All I could now do was to speak to Mr
Gilliver as you requested, to give you the share you would have in the
Property, & to set aside my obligation & Covenant with him so far, to
gratify the Dean & yourself. You cannot object I think with any
Reason to the Terms which he pays, & which at the first word he
agreed to.

I am | Sir | Your Friend & Servant | A. Pope

Aug. 16. 1732.

†POPE *to* THE EARL OF PETERBOROW[2]   24 *August* [1732]
1737

Aug. 24, 1728.

My Lord,—I presume you may before this time be returned from the
contemplation of many Beauties, animal and vegetable, in Gardens;
and possibly some rational, in Ladies; to the better enjoyment of your
own at Bevis-Mount. I hope, and believe, all you have seen will only
contribute to it. I am not so fond of making compliments to Ladies as
I was twenty years ago, or I wou'd say there are some very reasonable,
and one in particular there. I think you happy, my Lord, in being at
least half the year almost as much your own master as I am mine the
whole year: and with all the disadvantagious incumbrances of quality,
parts, and honour, as meer a gardiner, loyterer, and labourer, as he who

---

[1] At the end of the letter the year is added to the date in a different hand—presumably
Motte's. The letter concerns the tangled negotiations concerning the volume of *Miscellanies* presently (in October) to be published. Swift had in 1728 commissioned Pope to publish,
and he had more recently allowed the Rev. Matthew Pilkington to negotiate with Bowyer.
Swift himself was inclined to employ Motte, whom Pope disliked because of his poor hand-
ling of the *Miscellanies* of 1728. It is nonsense to assume, as Ball did (iv. 342 n.), that Pope
was being mercenary in his dealings with Swift. Swift had, through lack of interest, employed
Pope, Pilkington, and Motte; and the result was a tangle. The volume appeared in October
under the imprint of Motte and Gilliver. Ball assembles several relevant letters in Appendix
X of his Volume IV, but does not interpret them wisely.

[2] In all Pope's editions this letter appears (without notable changes in text) under the
year 1728. This seems a highly improbable year, supplied casually by Pope. The letter from
Peterborow almost immediately following seems to echo Pope's phrasing in this letter, to
which it is an answer: Peterborow's letter can hardly date 1728. The mention of the feasts
and 'laborious walks' of the Queen, &c., suggests a year when the King was in Hanover. In
1728 he was in England. In 1732 the newspapers carried in July and August frequent
notices of the amusements of the Queen and Royal Family during the absence of the King
in Hanover. There is of course always the possibility that Pope has amalgamated two or
more letters here. The year 1732 seems the best tentative placing in view of our present
information. By 4 Sept. 1728 both Pope and Peterborow were in Bath: here we have no
mention of such an intended excursion.

never had Titles, or from whom they are taken. I have an eye in the last of these glorious appellations to the style of a Lord degraded or attainted: methinks they give him a better title than they deprive him of, in calling him Labourer: *Agricultura*, says Tully, *proxima Sapientiæ*, which is more than can be said by most modern Nobility of Grace or Right Honourable, which are often *proxima Stultitiæ*. The great Turk, you know, is often a Gardiner, or of a meaner trade: and are there not (my Lord) some circumstances in which you would resemble the great Turk? The two Paradises are not ill connected, of Gardens and Gallantry; and some there are (not to name my Lord B.) who pretend they are both to be had, even in this life, without turning Musselmen.

We have as little politicks here within a few miles of the Court (nay perhaps at the Court) as you at Southampton; and our Ministers I dare say have less to do. Our weekly histories are only full of the feasts given to the Queen and Royal Family by their servants, and the long and laborious walks her majesty takes every morning. Yet if the graver Historians hereafter shall be silent of this year's events, the amorous and anecdotical may make posterity some amends, by being furnished with the gallantries of the Great at home; and 'tis some comfort, that if the Men of the next age do not read of us, the Women may.

From the time you have been absent, I've not been to wait on a certain great man, thro' modesty, thro' idleness, and thro' respect. But for my comfort I fancy, that any great man will as soon forget one that does him no harm, as he can one that has done him any good. Believe me my Lord yours.

GAY *and* THE DUCHESS OF QUEENSBERRY *to* SWIFT
28 *August* 1732

Add. 4806

Amesbury. Aug. 28. 1732.

Mr Hoare hath a hundred and odd pounds of yours in his hands, which you may have whenever you will please to draw upon me for it; I know I am more indebted to you (I mean besides the Southsea Bond of a hundred that still subsists) but I cannot tell you exactly how your account stands 'till I come to town. I have money of my own too in Mr Hoare's hands which I know not at present how to dispose of; I believe I shall leave it without interest till I come to town, & shall then be at the same loss how to dispose of it as now. I have an intention to get more money next Winter but am prepared for disappointments which I think it very likely I shall meet with. yet as you think it convenient & necessary that I shou'd have more than I have you see I resolve to do what I can to oblige you. If my designs should not take

effect I desire you will be as easy under it as I shall be; for I find you
so solicitous about me that you cannot bear my disappointments as
well as I can. If I don't write intelligibly to you ['tis] because I wou'd
not have the Clerkes of the Post Office know every thing I am doing.
If you would have come here this summer you might with me have
help'd to have drunk up the Duke's wine and sav'd your money. I am
grown so saving of late, that I very often reproach myself with being
covetous, and I am very often afraid that I shall have the trouble of
having money & never have the pleasure of making use of it. I wish
you could live among us, but not unless it could be to your ease &
satisfaction. You insist upon your being Minister of Amesbury,
Dawley, Twickenham, Riskings & prebendary of Westminster; for
your being Minister in those places I cannot promise you, but I know
you might have a good living in every one of them. Gambadoes I have
rid in, and I think 'em a very fine and usefull invention, but I have not
made use of 'em since I left Devonshire. I ride and walk every day to
such excess that I am afraid I shall take a surfeit of it; I am sure, if I
am not better in health after it, 'tis not worth the pains. I say this,
though I have this season shot 19 brace of Partridges. I have very little
acquaintance with our Vicar; he doth not live among us but resides
at another Parish and I have not play'd at Back-Gammon with any
body since I came to Amesbury but Lady Harold and Lady Bateman.[1]
As Dr Delany hath taken away a fortune from us I expect to be recommended in Ireland, if Godly Authors of Godly Books are intituled
to such fortunes, I desire you would recommend me as a Moral one,
I mean in Ireland, for that recommendation would not do in England.[2]
The Dutchess will not lend you two or three thousand pounds to keep
up your dignity for reasons best known to Strada dal Poe,[3] but she had
much rather give you that or ten thousand times more than to lay it
out in a fine peticoat to make her self respected. I believe for all you
give Mr Gay such good advice that you are a very indiscreet person
your self, or else you would come here to take care of your own affairs,
& not be so indiscreet to send for your monies over to a place where
there is none. Mr Gay is a very rich man for I realy think he does not
wish to be richer, but he will, for he is doing what you bid him, tho
if it may not be allow'd he will acquire greater honour & less trouble,
his Covetousness at present is for health which he takes so much pains
for that he does not allow himself time [to enjoy it], neither does he
allow himself time to be either absent or present, when he began to be

---

[1] Lady Harold was the Duke of Kent's daughter-in-law, and Lady Bateman, wife of an
Irish Viscount, was grand-daughter of the first Duke of Marlborough.—Ball.

[2] After this word, in the middle of Gay's line, the Duchess begins to write—without
warning. Her handwriting is very similar to Gay's, as Swift complained.

[3] Written in this form by the Duchess. A street in Turin is so named, but the Duchess
uses the name simply as a symbol for banking interests.

a sportsman he had like to have kill'd a dog & now every day I expect he will kill himself, & then the Bread & butter affair can never be brought before you, it is realy an affair of too great consequence to be trusted [to] a letter. Therefore pray come on purpose to decide it, if you do you will not hear how familiar I am with goody Dobson, for I have seen goody Dobson play at that with so ill a grace, that I was determind never to risque any thing so unbecoming I am not beloved neither Do I love any creature, except a very few, & those not for having any sort of merit but only because tis my humour, in that rank Mr Gay stands first & your self next if you like to be respected upon these conditions. now do you know me: he stands over me and scolds me for spelling ill & is very peevish (& sleepy) that I do not give him up the pen, for he has yawnd for it a thousand times, we both once heard a lady (who at that time we both thought well off)[1] wish that she had the best living in England to give you. it was not me, but I do wish it with all my heart, if Mr Gay does not hang out false lights[2] for his freind. [3]I had forgot to tell you that I very lately received a Letter from Twitenham in which was this paragraph: "Motte & another idle fellow I find have been writing to the Dean to get him to give them some Copyright which surely he will not be so indiscreet as to do when he knows my design (and has done these two months & more) Surely I should be a properer person to trust the distribution of his works with than to a common Bookseller. here will be nothing but the ludicrous & li[ttle thing]s, none of the political or any things of consequence, which are wholy at his own disposal; but at any rate it wou'd be silly in him to give a copy right to any which can only put the manner of publishing 'em hereafter out of his own & his friends power into that of Mercenarys."—I really think this a very useful precaution considering how you have been treated by these sort of fellows.[4]

The Duke is fast asleep or he wou'd add a line.

Address: To | the Revd | Dr Swift Dean | of St Patricks in | Dublin | Ireland| by way of London.

Postmark: 30/AV

Endorsement (In Swift's hand): Rx Sepr 5th 1732 | Mr Gay, and | D—s of Qu—ry | Ansd Octr 10 1732 [partly repeated elsewhere on the cover].

---

[1] Queen Caroline. [2] i.e. give Swift a false character.

[3] From here Gay (beginning in the middle of the line) resumes the pen.

[4] In their unjustly prejudicial notes to this letter Elwin and his follower, Ball, fail to recognize that Gay approves Pope's position. There is no evidence that Pope was being mercenary in the matter, as these editors assert. There is even some evidence (see Pope to Motte, 8 Mar. 1728/9) that Motte did pay Swift something for his part in the first three volumes of *Miscellanies*. The whole tangle is seen in Pope's letter to Pilkington, presumably written in October or November. (It is here placed just after 17 October.) Pope's reasons for not including *A Libel on Dr. Delany* in the *Miscellanies* of 1732 (an omission that annoyed Swift greatly) are apparent and rational. When he learns that Swift is annoyed, he excuses himself somewhat disingenuously in his letter to Swift of 16 Feb. 1732/3.

†THE EARL OF PETERBOROW *to* POPE[1]   [*August* 1732]

1737

I must confess that in going to Lord Cobham's, I was not led by curiosity. I went thither to see what I had seen, and what I was sure to like.

I had the idea of those gardens so fixt in my imagination by many descriptions, that nothing surprized me; Immensity, and Van Brugh appear in the whole, and in every part. Your joyning in your letter animal and vegetable beauty, makes me use this expression, I confess the stately Sacharissa at Stow, but am content with my little Amoret.[2]

I thought you indeed more knowing upon the subject, and wonder at your mistake: why will you imagine women insensible of Praise, much less to yours? I have seen them more than once turn from their Lover to their Flatterer. I am sure the Farmeress at Bevis in her highest mortifications, in the middle of her Lent, would feel emotions of vanity, if she knew you gave her the character of a reasonable woman.

You have been guilty again of another mistake which hinder'd me showing your letter to a friend: when you join two ladies in the same compliment, tho' you gave to both the beauty of Venus and the wit of Minerva, you would please neither.

If you had put me into the Dunciad, I could not have been more disposed to criticise your letter. What Sir, do you bring it in as a reproach, or as a thing uncommon to a Court, to be without Politicks? With politicks indeed the Richlieu's and such folks have brought about great things in former days: but what are they, Sir, who without policy in our times can make ten treaties in a year, and secure everlasting Peace?

I can no longer disagree with you, tho' in jest. Oh how heartily I join with you in your contempt for Excellency and Grace, and in your Esteem of that most noble title, Loiterer. If I were a man of many plums, and a good heathen, I would dedicate a Temple to Laziness: No man sure could blame my choice of such a Deity, who considers, that when I have been fool enough to take pains, I always met with some wise man able to undo my labours. | Yours, &c.

---

1 This seems clearly to be a reply to Pope's letter here dated 24 Aug. [1732]. Elwin dated this present letter [1731]. The many beauties 'animal and vegetable,' the compliment of reason offered to Mrs. Robinson (the 'farmeress'), the lack of politics at Court, and the noble title of 'Loiterer'—all mentioned by Pope are echoed in this letter. In his editions (1737–43) Pope gave the letter no date.

2 i.e. Bevis Mount (Southampton).

†POPE *to* THE EARL OF PETERBOROW[1] [*September* 1732]

1737

You were in a very Polemick humour when you did me the honour to answer my last. I always understood, like a true controvertist, that to answer is only to cavil and quarrel: however I forgive you; and you did it (as all Polemicks do) to shew your parts. Else was it not very vexatious, to deny me to commend two women at a time? It's true my Lord, you know women, as well as men: but since you certainly love them better, why are you so uncharitable in your opinion of them? surely one Lady may allow another to have the thing she herself least values, Reason, when Beauty is uncontested? Venus her self could allow Minerva to be Goddess of Wit, when Paris gave her the apple (as the fool her self thought) on a better account. I do say, that Lady P*[2] is a reasonable woman; and I think she will not take it amiss, if I should insist upon Esteeming her, instead of Toasting her like a silly thing I could name, who is the Venus of these days. I see you had forgot my letter, or would not let her know how much I thought of her in this reasonable way: but I have been kinder to you, and have shown your letter to one who will take it candidly.

But for God's sake, what have you said about Politicians? you made me a great compliment in the trust you reposed in my prudence, or what mischief might not I have done you with some that affect that denomination? Your Lordship might as safely have spoken of Heroes. What a bluster would the God of the winds have made, had one that we know puff'd against Æolus, or, (like Xerxes) whipp'd the seas? They had dialogued it in the language of the Rehearsal,

I'll give him flash for flash—
I'll give him dash for dash—

But all now is safe; the Poets are preparing songs of joy, and Halcyon-days are the word.

I hope my Lord, it will not be long before your dutiful affection brings you to town. I fear it will a little raise your envy to find all the Muses imployed in celebrating a Royal work,[3] which your own

---

[1] This letter, a reply to the preceding, is placed next to it as a reply undated—though pretty certainly it was written towards the end of September. The second paragraph in part is concerned with the dangerous seas when His Majesty King George II returned from the Continent. He landed on 26 Sept., and this letter seems written slightly before that joyous event.

[2] Pope evidently knows that Mrs. Robinson is secretly married, and hence calls her Lady P[eterborow].

[3] One Muse thus employed may be found in *The Gentleman's Magazine*, ii. 922 (Aug. 1732), where are verses 'On her Majesty's setting up the Bustoes of Mr Lock, Sir Isaac Newton, Mr. Woolaston, and Dr. Clark, in the Hermitage at Richmond'. The Hermitage (a grotto) was the 'Royal Work'. For other verses see Swift's *Poems* (ed. Williams), pp. 662–4.

partiality will think inferior to Bevis-Mount. But if you have any inclination to be even with them, you need but put three or four Wits into any hole in your Garden, and they will out-rhyme all Eaton and Westminster. I think Swift, Gay, and I, could undertake it, if you don't think our Heads too expensive: but the same hand that did the others, will do them as cheap. If all else shou'd fail, you are sure at least of the head, hand, and heart of your servant.

Why should you fear any disagreeable news to reach us at Mount Bevis? Do as I do, even within ten miles of London, let no news whatever come near you. As to publick affairs we never knew a deader season: 'tis all silent, deep tranquillity. Indeed they say 'tis sometimes so just before an Earthquake. But whatever happens, cannot we observe the wise neutrality of the Dutch, and let all about us fall by the ears? Or if you, my Lord, should be prick'd on by any old-fashion'd notions of Honour and Romance, and think it necessary for the General of the Marines[1] to be in action, when our Fleets are in motion; meet them at Spit-head, and take me along with you. I decline no danger where the glory of Great Britain is concern'd; and will contribute to empty the largest bowl of punch that shall be rigg'd out on such an occasion. Adieu, my Lord, and may as many Years attend you as may be happy and honourable!

LORD BATHURST *to* POPE[2]   9 *September* 1732

Elwin–Courthope, viii. 345

Cirencester, Sept. 9, 1732

I believe I am indebted to you for a letter, but really I am under such a scarcity of thought at present that I cannot find any matter to furnish out ten lines. I think of nothing out of my own circle, and though it is a large one, it only furnishes two ideas,—wood without timber, and land without water. But as my lot is cast here I must make the best of it, and I find employment from one day to another. My charitable vanity or folly supplies bread to many industrious labourers,[3] and therefore I would think no further. When your mind has shot through the flaming limits of the universe,[4] send me some account of the new discoveries. For my part I am grovelling upon this earth, and am contented with living in a state of indolence, doing a little good, and no mischief, to the best of my knowledge. When I come to town again, how I may be infected with bad company I know not, but I am sure

---

[1] This had been Peterborow's title for at least ten years.

[2] Elwin printed from the original in 'the Oxford papers'. The present editor has not seen the original.

[3] An allusion to Pope's Epistle on Taste (to Burlington), ll. 171–2.

[4] Alluding to Lucretius, i. 73, and the *Essay on Man*, now in composition.

at this time I am a most innocent creature. I may there think more wisely, and act more foolishly. Since you are resolved not to come to me I may freely own that I am in a perfect state to stupidity and should be the worst company in the world, but what alteration you might make in me I cannot tell. I have often thought myself the better for your company, though you have slept all the time you have been with me. The reflections I have made upon the soul at that time were of great use to me, to consider how your ideas were floating in it confused and loose, which at other times are so perfectly well ranged, and so ready to arise in their proper order. It was great consolation to me to think that there was no difference between you and I, but that I slept most, and for the most part one is happier asleep than awake. I am now taking a sound nap towards Christmas, and then the din and hurry of a parliament may make me give a loud yawn or two in your house, and I shall come back again here to rest. I remember Horace writes to somebody somewhere, something to this purpose:

> Quid aeternis minorem,
> Consiliis animum fatigas?[1]

I suppose it was to some metaphysical friend who he was afraid would wear out his body by letting his soul ride it too hard. I have some apprehensions this may be your case, but remember the Scripture says,[2] the good man is merciful to his beast, therefore do not whip and spur perpetually, but give it some rest. Adieu. Let me hear from you. Rouse me if you can; but however unbent and languid I am, I shall always be ready to exert myself when you have any occasion for a faithful friend or humble servant.

*POPE to THE EARL OF BURLINGTON 19 September 1732

Chatsworth

Sept. 19th 1732.

My Lord,—I need not to be put in mind of you by the Traces of your Art, your Buildings or your Gardens: but so it is, that a Good Writer is not more rememberd by his works, than you by yours. I hear with pleasure from Mr Bethel, that the finest thing he ever beheld, inspite of Italy, is your Egyptian Hall at York:[3] *And Bethel is an Honorable Man.* You have no Flatterer here in me, & I assure you Chiswick has been to me the finest thing this glorious Sun has shin'd upon. I have

---

[1] Horace, *Carmina*, II. xi. 11–12.   [2] Proverbs xii. 10?
[3] Within the month the new Assembly Room, built by Lord Burlington for the city of York, had been opened with concerts, balls, &c. It was commonly called at the time 'the most elegant room in Europe'. It is described in *Eboracum*, ii (1788), 338 ff. It also appears in Smollett's *Humphry Clinker*.

thrice made use of the obliging Privilege your Lordship allows me of bringing it admirers: & once I brought it a Censurer, whose name I will not tell you (for his sake) till we meet. My Lady Burlington has found me employment, but a very agreable one, in those Papers.[1] I am very certain it will be a deed reputable to her Ancestors memory, & very deserving to the world, to publish many of them. Almost all those loose maxims & Miscellaneous Thoughts, are perfectly worthy of Him; they need only be copied out, & divided under the two Heads of *Political & Moral* Maxims: These I would add to the *Heads for a Character* (for so I would call it, not to alter any part, but only by a very few connecting words) *of Charles the Second*; & 'twill make a Volume of equal bulk to that alredy printed. And the best of his Letters & Mr S.'s may make a third, very much to the credit of the Family.

I find few of Sir Lionel Jenkyns's & the others worth publishing, either as to matter or manner. Only every one of Algernon Sydney's, & (I think) some of his Sister my Lady Sunderland's,[2] are so. But these would be properer in a Volume apart.

I am of opinion, that the Book in which my Lord Halifax set down his private conferences with the King &c, will be very valuable, towards discovering the real Sources of the affairs at that time. I wish I had them, to compare with what I have, in that View; many things I meet with giving me that curiosity.

I beg my Lady's acceptance of my Services, & if in any instance relating to this, I can be of use, she may most freely command me; there is truly no man more respectfully her Servant. I hope she will forgive a Crime I've committed towards her, in putting into a Collection of Verses (which I will soon trouble you with at Lanesborough) that little paper-thing about her,[3] with the Addition only of one Stanza, to show I am as ready to commend as to blame her.

My Portico is in hand, & by an Expedient of Mr Kents which is here inclosed, the only difficulty we had is remov'd: but I will not proceed till I have your Lordship's Sanction of it. The Basement, if continued no farther on the Sides than the Pillars, would be too thin & want a flight of Steps to spread it: which would spoil a Design I have, to make that Basement include a Cold Bath & a fall of Water. Your opinion of this, as it stands, with relation to its connection to the rest of the Front, will greatly oblige me. Having told your Lordship all my

---

[1] The papers included writings of Lady Burlington's grandfather, the 1st Marquess of Halifax, of his brother Henry, and chiefly those of her father the 2nd Marquess. The papers were not published in Pope's lifetime.

[2] On Jenkins and Sidney see *DNB*. The Countess of Sunderland, Lady Burlington's great-grandmother, was Algernon Sidney's sister and was celebrated by Waller as Saccharissa.

[3] *Miscellanies* iii (October 1732), 74–75 (2nd series), prints Pope's lines 'On the Countess of B— Cutting Paper'.

business, I am asham'd to make this Letter speak what I never do myself, the language of Compliment; so have nothing left but to bid you believe me otherwise, if you can, than | My Lord, | Your long obliged & long affec-|tionate grateful Servant | A. Pope.

I hope Lady Dorothy[1] & Mr Battalia, & Mr Wood, are finished.

Endorsement (by Burlington): Mr Pope | Sepr 19 1732 | Concerning Lord Halifax's papers.

POPE *to* THE EARL OF OXFORD[2]   22 *September* 1732

Harl. 7525
                                                    Sept. 22d 1732.

My Lord,—It was a grief to me not to be able to snatch one day more, to be happy with you, before you left the town; & it added to the vexation, when I found myself within a week after obliged to do that for business which I could not for pleasure; for I was kept 4 days there, *multa gemens.* I am extremely sensible, my Lord, of the many & great distinctions you have shewn me, the Original of all which, I attributed to your Piety to your Father, for whom my respect was too Sincere to be exprest in poetry: And if, from the Continuance of your good Opinion, I may derive some Imagination, that you thought me not a worse Man than a Poet; it is a greater obligation to me personally, than even the other. I hope my having taken an opportunity, the only way my poor abilities can, of telling all men I no less esteem & love the Son, will not be ungrateful to you, or quite displeasing. If any Objection to the manner of it occurr to your Lordship, I depend on you, both as a Friend and a Judge, to tell me so.[3] Otherwise I will interpret your Silence as a Consent to let me acquaint every body that I am, (what I truly feel my self) | My Lord | Your ever affectionate | & ever obliged humble | Servant | A. Pope.

My Lady & Lady Margaret don't know how much I am theirs, unless your Lordship will tell them you believe it of me. And my poor old Woman heartily (tho feebly) expresses her Service to you all.

---

1 'Finished' is puzzling. Lady Dorothy was Burlington's daughter. Rev. Thomas Wood, rector in Chiswick, was a Yorkshireman, and may have been present at the opening of the Assembly Room. Battaglia was probably an artist or artisan employed by Burlington. See also Pope's remark to Swift (14 Dec. 1725): 'Jervas and his Don Quixote are both finished.'
2 This letter was printed in *Additions to the Works of Pope* (1776), ii. 23–24, and also printed in *St. James's Chronicle* for 27 July 1775.
3 Pope evidently is enclosing either the complete MS. of his Epistle to Lord Bathurst or (more probably) the passage that complimented Lord Oxford (ll. 243–8).

POPE *to* CARYLL   27 *September* 1732
Add. 28618
                                              Twittenham. 27. Sept 1732.
I own that I ought to have thanked you long since for a very kind
letter. I hoped to have done it by the hand of Mr Caryll when he left
Whitton, but by many accidents was prevented seeing him. I've been
much avocated from all that pleases me most, which is retirement and
study by troublesome business and by ill health, which I've increased
by following it.

I was so disappointed in not having a few entire days of your company that I can't find my heart to give you any account of my studies:[1]
It would be tedious to do it at length (for a few words will not suffice
to let you into the design of them), and to do it imperfectly and consequently unsatisfactorily would be worse than not doing it at all. Let
it suffice to tell you that they are directed to a good end, the advancement of moral and religious vertue, and the discouragement of vicious
and corrupt hearts. As to the former, I treat it with the uttmost
seriousness and respect; as to the latter, I think any means are fair and
any method equal, whether preaching or laughing, whatever will do
best. My work is systematical and proceeds in order; yet that does not
hinder me from finishing some of the particular parts, which may be
published at any time, when I judge particular vices demand them.
And I believe you'll see one or two of these next winter,[2] one especially
of the Use of Riches, which seems at present to be the favorite, nay,
the only, mistress of mankind, to which all their endeavours are
directed, thro' all the paths of corruption and luxury. My satire will
therefore be impartial on both extremes, avarice and profusion. I shall
make living examples, which inforce best, and consequently put you
once more upon the defence of your friend against the roar and
calumny, which I expect, and am ready to suffer in so good a cause.

I saw Mr Pigot the other day who is pretty well. I hope the same of
all your good family. Whenever you favour me with the knowledge
of it, you oblige me, who with old-fashioned sincerity, pray for you and
yours, and am ever | Dear sir | Your faithful friend and affectionate |
humble servant | A. Pope.

Your god-daughter always remembers you. She is by no means in
good health and by no means in the condition I wish her mentally, or
corporally, for the life at home continues a sad one, or rather worse.

---

[1] Pope's extensive plans for a series of epistles may be found in Spence, pp. 16, 48, 315.
The plans were not carried out as elaborately made.

[2] In Jan. 1733 he published his Epistle to Lord Bathurst, 'Of the Use of Riches', and in
February his imitation of *The First Satire of the Second Book of Horace*, as well as the first
epistle of the *Essay on Man*. This last appeared anonymously, whereas the other two had the
poet's name on the title-page.

†THE EARL OF PETERBOROW *to* POPE¹   [*October* 1732]

1737

You must receive my letters with a just impartiality, and give grains of allowance for a gloomy or rainy day: I sink grievously with the weather-glass, and am quite spiritless when opprest with the thoughts of a Birth-day or a Return.

Dutiful affection was bringing me to town, but undutiful laziness, and being much out of order, keep me in the country; however if alive, I must make my appearance at the Birth-day. Where you showed one letter you may shew the other; she that never was wanting in any good office in her power, will make a proper excuse, where a sin of Omission, I fear, is not reckoned as a venial sin.

I consent you shall call me Polemick, or associate me to any sect or Corporation, provided you do not join me to the Charitable Rogues,² or to the Pacifick Politicians of the present age. I have read over ³Barkley in vain, and find, after a stroak given on the left, I cannot offer the right cheek for another blow: all I can bring my self to, is to bear mortification from the Fair sex with patience.

You seem to think it vexatious that I should allow you but one woman at a time, either to praise, or love. If I dispute with you upon this point, I doubt every jury will give a verdict against me: So Sir, with a Mahometan indulgence, I allow you Pluralities, the favourite priviledge of our church.

I find you do not mend upon correction; again I tell you, you must not think of women in a reasonable way: You know we always make Goddesses of those we adore upon earth, and do not all the good men tell us, we must lay aside Reason in what relates to the Deity?

'Tis well the Poets are preparing songs of joy, 'tis well to lay in antidotes of soft rhyme, against the rough prose they may chance to meet with at Westminster. I should have been glad of any thing of Swift's, pray when you write to him next, tell him I expect him with impatience, in a place as odd, and as much out of the way, as himself. Yours.

¹ Printed in Pope's editions 1737–42, this letter seems certainly to be an answer to Pope's placed here early in September. The continued joke about Peterborow's 'polemic' tone, and the mention of 'the poets preparing songs of joy' connect the two. The mentions of the return from Hanover and the royal birthday (30 Oct.) date the letter vaguely.

² An allusion to the scandalous Charitable Corporation and, possibly, to the peace-at-any-price policies of the government.

³ Barkley's apology for the Quakers.—Footnote 1737–42. (i.e. the famous *Apology* of Robert Barclay, published in English in 1678 and often reprinted.)

†POPE *to* GAY   2 *October* 1732

1737   Oct. 2, 1732.

Sir Clem. Cottrel tells me you will shortly come to town. We begin to
want comfort, in a few friends about us, while the winds whistle, and
the waters roar. The sun gives us a parting look, but 'tis but a cold one;
we are ready to change those distant favours of a lofty beauty, for a
gross material fire that warms and comforts more. I wish you cou'd be
here till your family come to town: you'll live more innocently, and
kill fewer harmless creatures;[1] nay none, except by your proper deputy,
the butcher. It is fit for conscience sake, that you shou'd come to town,
and that the Duchess shou'd stay in the country, where no innocents
of another species may suffer by her. I hope she never goes to church:
the Duke shou'd lock you both up, and less harm would be done. I
advise you to make man your game, hunt and beat about here for cox-
combs, and truss up Rogues in Satire: I fancy they'll turn to a good
account, if you can produce them fresh, or make them keep: and their
relations will come, and buy their bodies of you.

The death of Wilks[2] leaves Cibber without a collegue, absolute and
perpetual dictator of the stage; tho' indeed while he lived, he was but
as Bibulus to Caesar. However Ambition finds something to be gratify'd with, in a mere name; or else, God have mercy on poor ambition!
Here is a dead vacation at present, no politicks at court, no trade in
town, nothing stirring but poetry. Every man, and every boy, is writing
verses on the Royal Hermitage: I hear the Queen is at a loss which to
prefer, but for my own part, I like none so well as Mr. Poyntz's[3] in
latin. You would oblige my Lady Suffolk if you tried your muse on
this occasion: I am sure I would do as much for the Duchess of
Queensberry, if she desir'd it. Several of your friends assure me it is
expected from you: one should not bear in mind all one's life, any little
indignity one receives[4] from a Court; and therefore I'm in hopes
neither her Grace will hinder you, nor you decline it.[5]

The volume of miscellanies is just publish'd,[6] which concludes all
our fooleries of that kind. All your friends remember you, and I assure
you no one more than, Yours, &c.

    [1] Gay wrote to Swift (28 August 1732) that he had during the hunting season shot
nineteen brace of partridges.
    [2] Booth had long ceased to act; Mrs. Oldfield died in 1730, and now the death of Robert
Wilks on 27 Sept. left Cibber as sole manager and as the only surviver of the long-established
group of players at Drury Lane.
    [3] Stephen Poyntz, governor to the Duke of Cumberland, presently married a niece of
Lord Peterborow's. She was the 'Fair Circassian' of Samuel Croxall's poem.
    [4] one receives] received *1737b*.
    [5] It is easy to reproach Pope for advising Gay to flatter the Queen; but Pope clearly
wished to win Gay back from his 'exile' with the Queensberrys. The advice is purely politic,
but it is disinterested.
    [6] The first advertisements noted of *Miscellanies the Third Volume* appeared on 4 Oct.,
but doubtless advance copies were already circulating.

‖SWIFT *to* GAY *and* THE DUCHESS OF QUEENSBERRY[1]

3 *October* 1732

Longleat Portland Papers, xiii (Harleian transcripts)

Dublin Oct. 3rd 1732.

I usually write to friends after a pause of a few weeks, that I may not interrupt them in better company, better thoughts, and better diversions. I believe I have told you of a great man who said to me that he never once in his life received a good letter from Ireland for which there are reasons enough without affronting our understandings: for there is not one person out of this country who regards any events that pass here unless he hath an Estate or employment, ⌐except the Court & the chief Governors who delight & endeavour to enslave & ruin us.—I am wondering at this proceeding in the Southsea people, to pay off half the company's debt at one clap. I will send for the mony when you are in town, for all my revenues that depend on tythes are sunk almost to nothing, & my whole personal fortune is in the utmost confusion. So that I believe in a short time I must be driven to live in Wales. God do so & more also to your special friends who have brought this upon us. I find, some other friends as well as you, are afraid of the Post rascals and would have me onely write by private hands, of which I cannot hope to get a conveniency twice a year.⌐ I cannot tell that you or I ever gave the least provocation to the present Ministry, and much less to the Court, & yet I am ten times more out of favor than you. For my own part I do not see the politicks of opening common letters, directed to persons generally known. For a man's understanding would be very weak to convey secrets by the Post, if he knew any, which I declare I do not: And besides I think the world is already so well inform'd by plain events, that I question whether the Ministers have any secrets at all. Neither would I be under any apprehension if a letter should be sent me full of treason; because I cannot hinder people from writing what they please, nor sending it to me; and although it should be discovered to have been opened before it came to my hand, I would only burn it, & think no further. I approve of the scheme you have to grow somewhat richer, though I agree you will meet[2] discouragments, & it is reasonable you should, considering what kind of pens are at this time onely employed & encouraged. For you must allow that the bad Painter was in the right, who having painted a Cock, drove away all the Cocks & hens, & even the chickens, for

---

[1] The Harleian transcript as well as the texts of 1740, 1741 Dab, and 1743 La have the year here given. In the London texts (1741 Labc; 1742 Lbc) the year is 1731. One assumes that this is merely a misprint, since the letter comes after letters dated in earlier months of 1732. Omissions in all the texts of 1740–2 are placed in half-brackets. In place of the first long omission Pope printed dashes, which indicate a willingness, unusual, to advertise an omission.

[2] meet discouragments] meet with discouragements *1740–2*.

fear those who pass'd by his shop might make a comparison with his work. And I will say one thing in spight of the Post officers, that since wit & learning began to be made use of in our Kingdoms, they were never professedly thrown aside, contemned & punished, till within your own memory, nor dullness & ignorance ever so openly encouraged & promoted. In answer to what you say of my living among you; if I could do it to my ease. Perhaps you have heard of a scheme for an exchange in Berkshire,[1] proposed by two of our friends: but besides the difficulty of adjusting certain circumstances, It would not answer. I am at a time of life that seeks ease & independence. You will hear my reasons when you see those friends; and, I concluded them with ⌐one⌐ saying: that I would rather be a freeman among slaves, than a slave among freemen. The dignity of my present Station damps the pertness of inferior puppyes & Squires, which without plenty & ease on your side the channel, would break my heart in a month. ⌐am ev—⌐

Madam,—See what it is to live where I do. I am utterly ignorant of that same Strado del Poe; and yet if that Author be against lending or giving money, I cannot but think him a good Courtier; which I am sure your Grace is not; no not so much as to be a maid of honor. For I am certainly informed that you are neither a free-thinker, nor can sell bargains, that you can neither spell, nor talk, nor write, nor think like a Courtier. That you pretend to be respected for qualityes which have been out of fashion ever since you were almost in your cradle; that your contempt for a fine petticoat is an infalible mark of disaffection, which is further confirmed by your ill tast for wit, in preferring two old fashoned Poets before Duck or Cibber; besides you spell in such a manner as no Court Lady can read, & write in such an old fashioned Style, as none of them can understand.—You need not be in pain about Mr Gay's stock of health, I promise you, he will spend it all upon lazyness, & run deep in debt by a winter[2] in town. Therefore I intreat your Grace will order him to move his chaps less & his legs more for the six cold months, else he will spend all his mony in Physick & coach-hire. I am in much perplexity about your Grace's declaration[3] of the manner in which you dispose what you call your love & respect, which you say, are not paid to merit but to your own humor. Now Madam my misfortune is, that I have nothing to plead but abundance of merit, & there goes an ugly observation, that the humor of Ladyes is apt to change. Now Madam if I should go to Amesbury with a great load of merit, & your Grace happen to be out

---

[1] On the offer to Swift of the living of Burghfield see Ball, iv. 320 (Bolingbroke to Swift, 18 July 1732), and here, Swift to Gay, 12 Aug. 1732.

[2] winter] winter's repose *1740–2*.

[3] declaration] decrarution *Longleat transcript*. All printed texts have *declaration*.

of humor, & will not purchase my merchandise at the price of your respect, the goods may be damaged, & no body else will take them off my hands. Besides you have declared Mr Gay to hold the first part, & I but the second, which is hard treatment, since I shall be the newest acquaintance by some years, & I will appeal to all the rest of your sex, whether such an innovation ought to be allowed. I should be ready to say in the common form that I was much obliged to the Lady who wished she could give me the best living—&c—if I did not vehemently suspect it was the very same[1] who spoke many things to me in the same style, & also with regard to the Gentleman at your elbow when you writ, ⌜&⌝ whose Dupe he was, as well as of her waiting woman, but they were both arrant knaves as I ⌜then⌝ told him & a third friend, though they will not believe it to this day. I desire to present my most humble respects to my Lord D—[2] & with my heartyest prayers for the prosperity of the whole family remain your Grace's most &c.

⌜Sir I must say something to your few lines at the bottom of your letter, which cites a Paragraph from our friend relating to me, to which I gave two or three full answers.⌝[3]

†GAY *to* POPE[4]   7 *October* 1732

1737

Oct. 7, 1732.

I am at last return'd from my Somersetshire expedition, but since my return I cannot so much boast of my health as before I went, for I am frequently out of order with my colical complaints, so as to make me uneasy and dispirited, though not to any violent degree. The reception we met with, and the little excursions we made were every way agreeable. I think the country abounds with beautiful prospects. Sir William Wyndham is at present amusing himself with some real improvements, and a great many visionary castles. We were often entertain'd with sea views and sea fish, and were at some places in the neighbourhood, among which I was mightily pleased with Dunster Castle near Mine-

---

[1] same who] same lady who *1740–2*.   [2] D—] Duke *1740–2*.

[3] This tantalizing sentence evidently began a reply to Gay's ending of his letter of 28 Aug. 1732, in which he supported Pope as the proper person to publish Swift's things in London. It is well to remember that when Gay died, the Duke of Queensberry turned over to Pope Gay's correspondence with Swift, to return to Swift. Pope had the letters copied before returning them to Swift, and here evidently suppressed all but the first sentence of the comment, which probably was not to his taste. In the Harleian transcript there is a vacant half-page below the sentence: the passage seems not to be missing by accident!

[4] This, the last letter that we have from Gay, appeared in all Pope's editions from 1737 to 1742. At the end of the first paragraph Pope in his octavo editions appended the following footnote: 'Mr. Gay dy'd the November following at the Duke of Queensberry's house in London, aged 46 years.' Actually Gay died on 4 Dec. That date is entered among the deaths recorded in Pope's Elzevir Virgil.

head. It stands upon a great eminence, and hath a prospect of that town, with an extensive view of the Bristol Channel; in which are seen two small Islands, call'd the steep Holms and flat Holms, and on t'other side we could plainly distinguish the divisions of fields on the Welsh coast. All this journey I perform'd on horseback, and I am very much disappointed that at present I feel my self so little the better for it. I have indeed follow'd riding and exercise for three months successively, and really think I was as well without it, so that I begin to fear the illness I have so long and so often complain'd of is inherent in my constitution, and that I have nothing for it but patience.

As to your advice about writing Panegyrick, 'tis what I have not frequently done.[1] I have indeed done it sometimes against my judgment and inclination, and I heartily repent of it. And at present as I have no desire of reward, and see no just reason of praise, I think I had better let it alone. There are flatterers good enough to be found, and I wou'd not interfere in any Gentleman's profession. I have seen no verses upon these sublime occasions, so that I have no emulation. Let the patrons enjoy the authors and the authors their patrons, for I know myself unworthy. | I am, &c.

*THE EARL OF BURLINGTON *to* POPE[2]   8 *October* 1732

Chatsworth

I flatter myself, you will believe it to be something more than ordinary that has made me so slow in thanking you for your last favour, but the truth is that I have been almost three weeks from home, constantly upon the road. and in all the time never a minute to myself, I am very glad that any of my performances please so good a Judge and so good a man as Bethel, and if they have the happiness of pleasing you, I despise the whole race of censurers with or without names. Lady B is very much obliged to you for the pains you have been pleased to take upon her account and begs that you wou'd put the papers[3] into what method you please, and get some trusty person to transcribe them, I have considered your front,[4] and am of opinion that my friend Kent

---

[1] Gay has been censured for superficiality and even cynicism, but underneath these seeming faults there was a sterling integrity that finds noble expression in this reply to Pope. One must envy him this final dignified bow as he leaves the stage.

[2] On the back of this letter Pope has written names as follows: '~~Ld Peterborow~~ | L. Cobham | L. Burlington, write (transcribing | Epist) | L. Argyle Islay, Hyde | Fortescue, Robts | Ld Bath. murry [*or* muny] | Ds Bs ann. deeds & Dr Burton | Sr Clem. Cottr. manusc? | Dr Arb. his nephew | Mr Gay, Lewis | Thursday 4 a clock, Ld Peterb | at Ld Bathursts.' To the right of these names is crowded in the following, still in Pope's hand: 'Campbell, | I hear the Storekeeper of|Woolidge is|dying|may he have|it? George.' Explanation of all this is perhaps futile. 'Campbell' might be General John Campbell, later 4th Duke of Argyll, and 'Woolidge' is doubtless Woolwich. The 'Ds Bs' is the Duchess of Bucks or Buckingham, from whom Pope had purchased an annuity.

[3] The Savile papers.   [4] The front of the villa with its newly designed portico.

has done all that can be, considering the place, I hope you will forgive the shortness of this epistle. which I write in the middle of company and cards, but let me be anywhere, I can never leave off without assuring you, that no mortal can be with more affection than I am | my dear friend | your most faithfull servant | Burlington

Londesburgh Oct 8 1732

*POPE *to* MATTHEW PILKINGTON[1]   17 *October* [1732]
1870 (Catalogue of John Weller)

Excerpt

Tuesday Oct. 17.

I am prepared, with great pleasure, to receive the friend of the Dean, and to find one in you. I am much concerned to be told you went yesterday to Twickenham, when I came hither. . . .

[Dated from] My Lord Oxford's in Dover Street, Piccadilly.

*POPE *to* MATTHEW PILKINGTON[2]   [1732]
The Huntington Library

Sir,—Since I mentiond to you the Pretension of Mr Bowyer the Printer, in order to be clear in my Intentions of doing Justice to him, as well as in those Intentions He appeal'd to, (namely the Dean's in that Paper he signed) I find by a long letter he sent to Gilliver, that he departs from that Foot he first put it upon, & does not seem to leave the matter to the Dean & me at all. His words to me in his Letter (which caused me to apply to the Dean) were, "that he would readily submit to have his claim bounded within such Limits as he & I should prescribe." In complyance to his pretension, I writ: the Dean answerd, *no man had any title from him more than Curll*; nevertheless I writ again, that Bowyer had something under his hand: He answerd, *his Intention was nothing of a perpetuity, but a Leave only to reprint to Mr Falkner & him, with promise not to molest 'em by any Interest of his as to such pieces as were imputed to him.* He declares he had no thought of giving them a perpetuity, but a Permission to the former end only, "however

---

[1] This scrap taken from Catalogue 83 issued by John Weller in 1870 (where it is lot 227) serves somewhat to date the arrival of Pilkington from Dublin, and seems to indicate a lack of previous acquaintance. It seems to antedate the letter immediately following.

[2] Ball in printing this letter (iv. 485–6) dates it [Nov. 1732]. It should postdate Pope's first interview with Pilkington after 17 Oct. One must infer that the letter does not concern what Pope *may* insert in *Miscellanies* iii, but rather what he *has inserted*. In other words, now that the arrangements between Pilkington and Bowyer have been frustrated by the appearance in early October of the *Miscellanies*, Bowyer is either threatening suit or demanding a share in the profits of the volume. Pope will let him settle the matter with Gilliver. Ball prints in his Appendix X of vol. iv relevant letters from Pilkington to Bowyer. See also here, iii. 309 and vol. v. 10, for Swift's 'assignment'.

Faukner & Boyer may have *contrived* to *turn* those *papers into a Property.*" These are his words.

I have done what Bowyer desired, & it's plain if he would be judgd by the *Dean's Intentions,* here they are. But I find he is a true Bookseller, & therfore shall leave it to himself & Gilliver; If there be a legal title I presume he will not wave it in any wise to oblige us; and if not, I will not presume to determine what I don't know, nor to meddle, if he rejects me as an Arbitrator. But I understand by you, that he has no Right to the Scheme for paying the Debts, nor to the Intelligencers, in the latter of which Dr Sheridan only has a right by a Prior Gift of the Dean's. Mr Bowyer also puts these into his Catalogue & two Pieces into the Bargain, which are *not* the Dean's. It is a very comprehensive assignment, this he speaks of, which claims not only what *is* own'd but what is *not* own'd, nay what is *not His.* He represented to me that it would be a hardship to print in our Collection what the Dean *might not care to owne,* and at the same time prints them *In his name.* Upon the whole, it is plain I was deceivd in thinking Mr Bowyer so civil & candid to the Dean & to me. When I suggested the best way he could take to please Him, (by seperating the Ludicrous things in the present Collection, & leaving to him to print the serious or political) his reply was, he thought I could not persuade him that *Half was more than the whole.* Yet this is a great Truth as Authors well know, tho' Booksellers do not. He also went so far as to ask *what authority* I had from the Dean, that was *prior* to his assignment when the authority was subsisting from the time he, & I published the 3 volumes of Our Miscellanies & in the Preface to them, he may see this other Volume then intended by the Dean as well as myself. Since he has no other Sense of my complying with his Plea, than to suppose he is arguing with me instead of Gilliver, pray assure him I will not take upon me to *limit* his Pretentions or to *enlarge* them, but leave the matter between the Booksellers as they can agree it, and that the only reason that made me offer *any* opinion about it, was his pretending to have his "*claim bounded by the Dean & me.*" If his assignment be plain & Legal, it is not I that will obstruct, or can obstruct, or intend to obstruct it. So there it rests: only let Mr Boyer know, he has, by the modest manner in which he first proposed it, given me more trouble than I find he thanks me for.

I am Sir | Your affectionate Servant | A. Pope.

THE EARL OF OXFORD *to* POPE   23 *October* 1732

Longleat Portland Papers, xii

Wimpole. Oct. 23. 1732.

Sir,—I return you many thanks for your obliging letter I am ashamed I have not made you the return I should, I have been much from home, We have had a ramble into Norfolk which was very pleasant we saw a great many fine places, I Wished for your company, I think you never was in that county it is much different from any that I ever saw & I am sure you would be pleased with some places. what you are so indulging to me to mention & in the manner you do, I must leave it entierly to yourself to do as you shall judge proper,[1] I am so conscious of my Self that I know I do not deserve it, and if any thing could raise my opinion of my self, it must be the notice you take of me, this I will say, that nothing can make me[2] more an affectionate humble Servant of yours, then I am at present and must allways continue so.

My Wife and peggy desire you will accept of their compliments and to present them to your good mother I desire mine.

I desire you will be so kind as to let me know, when mr Fenton died, where, & where buried, this is for an antiquary of my accquaintance.[3]

I am with true respect and esteem | Sir your most faithfull | & most humble Servant | Oxford.

Lord Dupplin is your most humble Servant.

Address: For | Alexander Pope Esqr | at his House | at Twickenham | Middlesex

Frank | Oxford.

Postmark: 25/OC

POPE *to* THE EARL OF OXFORD[4]   29 *October* [1732]

Longleat Portland Papers, xii

Oct. 29th | [1732.]

My Lord,—I am greatly obliged by your very kind letter, & in particular for the Privilege you allow me of mentioning the Son, in my mean way, as well as the Father. One Alteration in that place you must permit me to make; which is, not to joyn with your Name any other's for whom I have less affection & therfore you must stand Single, in that Verse which before mentiond the Duke of —'s.[5] As to your Lordships Query of Mr Fenton, he dyed at Easthampsted in Berkshire at a Seat of Sir William Trumbul's, to whose Son he was Tutor & is buried in the church of that Parish,[6] in   173   where the

---

[1] This is Lord Oxford's reply to Pope's request made in the letter of 22 Sept.

[2] Oxford miswrote *my* for *me.*

[3] The antiquary may be Thomas Hearne. His entries concerning Fenton, however, exceed the information sent by Pope to Oxford, 29 Oct. 1732. See Hearne's *Collections*, xi. 316 and 329. Hearne's entries were made in 1734.

[4] The year is added in Lord Oxford's hand.

[5] The Duke of Chandos had been mentioned with Oxford. Pope postponed the mention of His Grace, which appeared in the Moral Essay 'On the Characters of Men' (Jan. 1734), l. 54. See Pope to Lord Oxford, 22 January 1731/2.

[6] Pope had to leave these factual blanks. Fenton was buried in July 1730.

Inscription I wrote is set over him. Whoever mentions Mr Fenton, ought to do as much justice to his Integrity of Manners, Equality of Temper, & Moderation of Mind, as to his Learning & Genius.

I am particularly obliged to your Lordship & Lady Oxfords Regard for my poor Mother, who is your faithfull Servant, & in a supportable condition of life I thank God at present. I have seen your House twice, & lamented your absence. I hope at my next visit to find all in it that renders it delightful to him who is with true respect & warm affection,

My dear Lord, | Your ever faithfull | & most humble Servant | A. Pope

My Lord Duplin has my most humble Services, & my Envy for enjoying you so constantly.[1] I take it ill of Lady Margaret that she will not Love London as much as all other young women do.

Address: To the Earl of Oxford, at | Wimpole, in | Cambridgeshire.
Postmark: 31/OC
Endorsement: Mr A: Pope | Octr 29th 1732

POPE *to* JONATHAN RICHARDSON[2]   [*October* 1732?]

1739 (*Works*, vi. 227–8)

It is hardly possible to tell you the joy your pencil gave me, in giving me another friend, so much the same! and which (alas for mortality!) will out-last the other. Posterity will thro' your means, see the man whom it will for ages honour, vindicate, and applaud, when envy is no more, and when (as I have already said in the Essay to which you are so partial)

"The sons shall blush their fathers were his foes."

‖POPE *to* JONATHAN RICHARDSON[3]   2 *November* 1732

Roscoe (1824), i. 389–90

Sir,—The Essay ⌐on Man⌐ has many faults; but the poem you sent

---

[1] Oxford eventually found the family of his brother-in-law, the Earl of Kinnoul, a financial burden. Lord Dupplin lived much with his uncle.

[2] Since in 1739–42 Pope published this fragment as the first paragraph of a presumably conflated letter, the latter part of which Roscoe printed under date of 2 Nov. 1732, it seems wise here to place the fragment just before the rest of Pope's letter, which was printed by him without date. He placed it after a letter dated 10 June 1733, but one can believe both parts of the conflated letter antedate the publication of the *Essay on Man*, which the Richardsons saw in MS.

The fragment thanks Richardson for his drawing or engraving of Lord Bolingbroke, as the adaptation of the *Essay on Man*, iv. 388 shows.

[3] In Pope's octavos, 1739–42, this letter was united, as a second paragraph, with the paragraph printed here as a separate letter immediately preceding this. Roscoe evidently

me has but one, and that I can easily forgive. Yet I would not have it printed for the world; and yet I would not have it kept unprinted neither—but all in good time.¹ ⌜You will see another poem next week² to employ more of your speculations, which the author likewise does not own. I thank you for all. Your prudence I never doubt, nor your son's; to whom my services, and sincere ones.⌝ I am glad you publish your Milton.³ B—ly⁴ will be angry at you, and at me too shortly, for what I could not help; a satirical poem on verbal Criticism, by Mr. Mallet, which he has inscribed to me ⌜before I knew anything of it.⌝ But the thing itself is good (another cause of anger to any critic). As for myself, I resolve to go on in my quiet, calm, moral course, taking no sort of notice of men's, or women's ⌜anger, or⌝ scandal, with virtue in my eyes, and truth upon my tongue. Adieu, dear Sir. Yours | A. P.

Twitnam, Nov. 2, 1732.

---

*LORD LANSDOWNE to POPE   *3 November* 1732

New York Public Library (Myers)

Old-Windsor. Nov: 3d: 1732.

I hope my Booksellers have been punctual in sending you my volume of Comedies⁵ &c. according to my direction and a reply to some observations upon my vindications by one of your dunciad Heroes. You know very well that I am never satisfyed with my self till I have your particular opinion, independent of the Publick, and I hope you will not refuse it me without flattery or partiality. another of your Heroes Mr Thomas Burnet has been likewise at me with remarks

---

had an authentic source for his text unknown to other editors. Pope's text omits various phrases found in Roscoe and here placed in half-brackets. The date of 1732, furnished in Roscoe's source (?), hardly fits: in some ways 1733 is more probable. Roscoe thought the remark about another poem 'which likewise the author does not own' referred to the Epistle to Lord Bathurst (published in Jan. 1733); but that poem had Pope's name as author on the title-page. In 1733 'likewise' might refer to the three epistles of the *Essay on Man* already out and *The Impertinent*, published only as 'By an Eminent Hand' the week following 2 Nov. 1733.

¹ Richardson's lines 'To the Concealed Author of An Essay on Man' were printed in vol. ii of Pope's *Works* in 1739, with other commendatory verses. The Richardsons knew in advance of Pope's authorship of the *Essay*.

² Pope's 'next week' cannot be taken too seriously. His Epistle to Bathurst came out in January 1733: *The Impertinent* appeared 5 Nov. 1733.

³ The *Explanatory Notes and Remarks on 'Paradise Lost'* by the Richardsons was not published until 1734.

⁴ Bentley was attacked in Mallet's *Of Verbal Criticism*, which was delayed until 16 Apr. 1733, but its publication reinforces the date of the letter as 1732. Mallet's poem was advertised by Gilliver (*Lond. Eve. Post*, 14 Apr.) as 'An Epistle to Mr. Pope; occasion'd by Bentley's MILTON and Theobald's SHAKESPEAR'.

⁵ The second volume of Lansdowne's *Genuine Works in Verse and Prose*. It contains the comedy, *Once a Lover*, reworked from his earlier *She-Gallants*.

upon my Reply to Oldmixon:¹ I think it lawfull for a son, right or wrong, to say something for his Father & therefore shall return no animadversions upon it, nor indeed shall I trouble my self about any thing else that may hereafter come from such hands.

If you have had leisure or can have patience to read the Comedy of once a Lover &c alwayes a Lover, you will oblige me by a sincere Critick upon it. I hope you enjoy your health perfectly well and shall be glad to hear of it. I am alwayes with the most perfect affection & esteem Dear Sir | Your most faithfull | humble servant | Lansdowne

I expect no answer by the bearer, but at your leisure.

Address: To Mr Pope

POPE to THE EARL OF BURLINGTON² 6 November [1732]
Chatsworth

Novr 6th

My Lord,—The Hopes I had of your being a Better Courtier than to be absent on the Birthday, made me silent till now. Whatever Benedictions Cibber finds out so wisely, & sings so sweetly, accruing from his Majesty's birth, the greatest I expected from it, this Year, was to be blest with the Sight of you both. My Lady has found a way to give me a great deal of pleasure in her absence, in the fancying I obey her commands not unsuccessfully: For I think I clearly see all that can be done, or ought to be done, with the Papers she left me. I have got some transcribed as you directed, & might have done the same with more, but that I've found a shorter method, by figuring the Loose & Scatterd Thought first, to make one Transcription serve for all, which will at the same time reduce 'em under proper Heads. If she disapprove not of publishing Algn. Sydney's Letters, it must be Seperately: & in that case they need only be writ out just for the Press, which any Bookseller you'd employ may do himself, & save us the trouble. I think as to Lord Halifax's Works, they must be called, *Miscellanies, Political & Moral*. They will make a Volume about the size of that which was

---

¹ Earlier in 1732 Oldmixon had replied to Atterbury's defence of himself and Smallridge, and Lansdowne had entered the battle with *A Letter to the Author of Reflections Historical and Political, occasioned by a Treatise in Vindication of General Monck and Sir Richard Grenville.* Burnet had countered with *Remarks upon the Rt Hon Ld Lansdown's Letter . . . as far as relates to Bp. Burnet.*

² The year is inferred from the late absence of the Burlingtons in Yorkshire and Pope's work on the Savile papers. Doubtless he got pleasure out of the work, but nothing was apparently published in his lifetime except the correspondence of Algernon Sidney and Henry Savile (1742) which were advertised as 'Printed from the originals in Mr Sydney's own hand'. Pope later persuaded the Countess of Burlington to let Mallet have 'a considerable number of Letters of Col. Algernon Sidney written to the Marquis of Halifax'. This aid, called to the editor's attention by Professor J. L. Clifford, is noted in a letter of Thomas Birch to P. Yorke, 1 Oct. 1741, found in Add. MS. 35396.

formerly printed, with the character of K. Charles added; and without any of the Letters, which should (if publishd) be in another Volume apart, with his Brothers &c. Whatever orders my Lady gives I will punctually observe.

I am very impatient to be building my Portico, but Mr Kent admonishes me to defer the Brickwork & Plastering till Spring, which I grieve to comply with. Pray lay your Commands upon Kent, to send you the Short Dialogue[1] I writ in his behalf, between the General & myself, shewing the Cause why nobody takes notice of him when they speak of the Hermitage. He is modest, & afraid to give offence, so has kept it in his pocket, nor ever dared to show it the General, by which means my Wit is lost in obscurity.—Mr Dodington[2] is happily returnd from Italy, without any one Idea of Building more than he set out with, whereby Morris & He continue to admire each other. I am sorry Mr Wood is removed into the other world,[3] & cannot but pity Battalie & Chiswick: I assure you, never was Enoch, or Elijah so Transported as He. I suppose it is the wickedness of the men of his Parish that hath made him so willing to quit it. I hope his righteous Spirit will at last find Rest in Yorkshire; unless your Lordship's & my Lady's Advent every year, busy him as much as a Patriarch entertaining Angels, when they travel'd upon earth.

You'l be tired of this Stuff, and yet I wish I were with you to tire you more; tho I did (as I generally do) make myself sick when I make others so. My reall Services (I wish my Lord, they deserved that Epithet) attend yourself & Lady B. I hope she paints; I hope you build; I hope you are both well & happy whatever you do, or if you do nothing: which last is the situation (and one very much to be envyd) of | My Lord, | Your faithfull & ever | obliged Servant, | A. Pope.

POPE *to* MALLET[4]   *7 November* [1732]

Sir John Murray

Novr 7th.

I was in Town one day, & my Inability to see you was really vexatious to me. It will be more so, if I am not sometimes to have that pleasure

---

[1] Kent seems to have seen to it that this *Dialogue* was permanently 'lost in obscurity'. Kent had some part in designing Queen Caroline's Hermitage at Richmond (see B. S. Allen, *Tides of Taste*, ii (1937), 136).

[2] Doubtless Bubb Dodington, who at this time was agreeable to the Opposition party. Morris is possibly Robert Morris, the architect, who in 1728 was 'of Twickenham'. See *DNB*.

[3] Pope thinks Wood is being 'transported' from Chiswick to a parish in Yorkshire; actually he goes to Barrowby in Lincolnshire. There he will come to know Wm. Warburton of nearby Newark. The reference to Battaglia is obscure, but he was mentioned with Wood in Pope to Burlington, 19 Sept. 1732.

[4] This letter refers to Mallet's *Verbal Criticism*, addressed to Pope, and published in Apr. 1733. Elwin wrongly places the letter itself in 1733.

here, which you were used to give me. The great Hurry of your last
Visit perfectly disconcerted me. The Epistle I have read over & over,
with great & just Delight; I think it correct throughout, except one or
two small things that savor of Repetition toward the latter End. A
better Judge than any other I know is of the same opinion, who sees
enough in it to desire to be made of your Acquaintance;[1] and I know
no Man's that will please you so much. If you could let me know some
days beforehand when you can come this way, we will go together; or
he will meet you here. I am too much pleasd with the favor you have
done me in this Epistle, to be willing to part with it, till you absolutely
require it. Believe me with real Affection & Esteem |Dear Sir | Your
most faithfull & obliged | Servant | A. Pope.

POPE *to* JONATHAN RICHARDSON[2]   *November* [1732]

Elwin–Courthope, ix. 499

Nov.

I have with much ado contrived to get to this end of the town to see
you, but stopped, it being too late to dine with you, at Mr. Cheselden's
where I beg to see yourself and your son, as he likewise does. I must
be going before night, back again to St. James's, and to home to-
morrow, from whence I came but last night, being engaged in building
(a much better thing than poetry). Adieu, but come instantly.

POPE *to* JONATHAN RICHARDSON   *9 November* [1732]

Elwin–Courthope, ix. 499

9th November.

I send you back these verses, not knowing if you gave them me. Your
notes I have read over attentively, and like: in the view you intend
them, I think they are much to the purpose. Two or three trifles I have
marked, I could no more. Adieu, and send me the rest, and believe me
truly yours.

At my next journey to town I will come and tell you so.

RICHARDSON, JR., *to* POPE   [*November* 1732]

Elwin–Courthope, ix. 499

I was heartily vexed when I came home and found I had lost an
opportunity of your company, but have since seen your observations on

---

[1] Almost certainly Lord Bolingbroke; but in a letter of [18 Feb. 1730/31] there is indi-
cation that perhaps Mallet is already acquainted with his lordship. Possibly at that time
Mallet missed making the acquaintance, but early in 1733 Pope asks Mallet (letter of 18
Mar.) why he does not call upon Bolingbroke.

[2] Pope writes from Cheselden's, where he hopes to see the Richardsons before he returns
to Lord Bathurst's for the night. The year, of course, is most uncertain.

the notes with great pleasure, only we beg of you to let us know (if you recollect) some instances of an epithet that expresses any sort of smell for the gourd or cucumis among the ancients, which may very well be, but I can find none either in the gradus, or dictionaries, or indexes, and because that would be a main proof for the present reading,[1] though there are indeed some reasons for changing *smelling* to *swelling* (however scrupulous one should certainly be in such alterations), and however lawful and usual it is for a poet to derive epithets from any natural quality; in the first place the word was used but two lines before, and that in general, so that giving immediately after this particular instance, seems a little remiss. But then what is abundantly more considerable is that Milton has particularized all the productions that go in the same period with this by circumstances that offer themselves to the *sight*. He has given the pictures of them, but specified no one natural quality.[2] Forth flourished—clustering—crept—smelling —upstood—embattled, &c. *Humi repit—jacent crescunt* (Plin. xix. 45). My father gives his humble service to you, and I am your most obliged humble servant.

POPE *to* JONATHAN RICHARDSON   [*November* 1732]

Elwin–Courthope, ix. 500

Sir,—You will think it odd to see your letter returned instead of an answer. But the reasons you here give for the new reading are so strong (especially the last), that I would have you put these very words into the notes, in the room of what I writ there. You are of Bentley's mind, but for better reasons. My head aches, or I would say more.

*POPE *to* MRS. CÆSAR   15 *November* 1732

Rousham

Madam,—I assure you no Dean nor Lord can think of you more than I do. I have been but thrice in town this whole Summer, & as constantly enquired of you by Lord Oxford, & Dr Mead. The former I desired to make our usual Party with you & my Lady, the little time they were here, & was truly sorry they did not. My poor old Woman whom you so kindly ask after, is indeed the Cause I seem to forget many of my Friends; my Attendance being now become constantly

---

[1] The reading in question is that found in *Paradise Lost*, vii. 321. Bentley in his edition of 1732 wished to emend the *smelling* gourd to the *swelling* gourd. The Richardsons supported Bentley in their *Explanatory Notes on Paradise Lost* (1734), pp. 321–3.

[2] Richardson here and in his note shows an interesting consciousness of the neo-classical tendency to rely on 'natural qualities' of objects in describing rather than on the mere look of the object. It is what nowadays would be called an abstractionist tendency.

necessary to her. It is now near 2 years since I have been able to snatch a day even to dine with Dr Mead, whom I've sometimes met (as I was in a hurry always) & been ashamed so often to repeat both an Excuse & a Promise. Your Letter Madam is what I take as a particular mark of kindness considering how little I must appear to you to deserve it. And I beg you to tell me when you are in Town, & where? that I may show you (as I will the first day I can) you can never be forgotten, while there is any Grace or Goodness left in | Madam | Your most obliged and | most faithfull Servant, | A. Pope.

Novr 15th 1732.

Address: To | Mrs Cæsar. | To be left at Lord Oxford's & | sent on.

*POPE to THE EARL OF BURLINGTON[1]

24 *November* [1732]

Chatsworth

Twitenham, Novr 24. | [1732]

My Lord,—Tho' I am at all times ready to pour out my thoughts & wishes, to & for you, which would cause your Lordship more trouble from my affection, than is consistent with my Respect. Yet when I write meerly to ask you any thing, I make no Apology; because I am satisfied, then is the Time you like best to hear from me if it be in your power to oblige me. Your Lordship has more than once been so good as to think & to tell me you thought of helping my Friend Mr Walter Harte to a Living, & to promise me one for him either in Ireland, or (if you could) in England. I understand there is fallen the Parsonage of Barrowby in Lincolnshire (not far from Lord Tyrconnel's) If your Lordship is not better ingaged, (I mean more to your personal liking for another) I need not say to what a degree this would make Two men happy, Mr Harte & myself.[2] My Zeal for him was not only moved by his Ingenuity & Morals, but by his great Piety to his Parents both whom he has maintain'd in their old age upon the *whole* of his small Income by pupils in the university: & left himself nothing but his Clothes & Commons many years.

My Lord, I am in great want of you, & I hope you will follow your old rule, of coming on the sudden, tho' Kent knows nothing of it, and every body here gives you up till Christmas. My Lady Burlington's loss is very ill born at Court, I can tell her; and yet I believe there are

---

[1] The year is made sure from Burlington's fully dated reply of 30 Nov. 1732.

[2] Pope had known and valued Harte from the time when Harte was an undergraduate and published (1727) poems in praise of Pope. This application to Burlington was futile. By 1735 Harte was vicar at Gosfield, presumably through Pope's kind offices with the Knights. That living was not deemed sufficient, and Pope and Mrs. Knight (25 Nov. 1735) are trying to get him either a better or an added benefice.

those out of Court who know how to value her company as much, because I never was such a flatterer as to think or say all True Taste is confined to that Circle. I will add no more, than to beg her Ladyship's & Your Belief of the Sincerity & regard with which I shall ever be hers & | My Lord Your most obedient & | faithfull Servant, | A. Pope.

*THE EARL OF BURLINGTON *to* POPE   30 *November* 1732

Chatsworth

To pretend business in the life I lead here wou'd not bear water, and yet a constant hurry of doing nothing, is to be accounted for by those who experience it, but I am not to expect it shou'd be, by any that have not so great a stock of good nature as you are master of. this excuse I risk as it appears [it] is the only, and the true one, that I have to offer, for not having thanked you sooner for the favour (I was going to say pleasure) of your two last letters, but I can by no means give that phrase to that of the 24th as I am disabled from obeying your commands in it. the living you mention has been given to Mr Wood a considerable time in consequence of a long engagement and I can assure you that from the moment you mentioned Mr Harte he has been constantly in my thoughts, and shall be so whenever it is in my power, for promises apart, I shall always be proud to serve any man, that has merit enough to gain your esteem. The latter part of your letter makes some amends for the former, by your saying you want me, it has taken away all the chagrin, that the thoughts of a compulsive journey next week gave me. and I hope to see you early the week after. if part of this letter be as disagreable to you, as it is to me, I am sure it is high time to finish. and I will only beg you to believe me unalterably | dear Sir | your most obliged | affectionate servant | Burlington

Londesburgh Nov 30 1732

POPE *to* THE EARL OF OXFORD   1 *December* 1732

Longleat Portland Papers, xii

Decr 1st 1732

My Lord,—I ought sooner to have enquired of your health this way, if I was not so fortunate as by lodging in your house to hear of it daily. And as it is not with Ceremony but Sincerity that I am Yours, there would be a sort of Falseness in but seeming to be a common Well-wisher in the Forms. But I wish often that I had any thing to tell your Lordship which you might call either Good or Entertaining; if so,

my Letters would be a Weekly Paper, & keep pace with Fog,[1] & the
Journals. There are more Politicks in those than in all the Courts of
Europe, & more Verses in 'em too than half the Booksellers Shops.
Speaking of Verses, my Lord, those of mine which I lately showd you
will come out just at the same time with the Bell-man's,[2] & (I hope)
salute you, with them, in Town; where I earnestly long to see you,
& where nothing shall make me stay a whole Week, but your Coming.

I entreat my Lady Oxford, Lady Margaret, & Lord Duplin's
acceptance of my Services. I am, with all truth & Esteem, | My Lord |
Your ever faithfull | & obedient Servant | A. Pope

The Collar of Brawn is worth a Collar of SS. in the opinion of
Dr Arbuthnot & myself.

Endorsement (in a secretary's hand): Mr Alexander Pope | Decber 1st 1732.

POPE *to* ARBUTHNOT[3]   [*c. 5 December* 1732?]

Sotheby Catalogue

. . . if you would add anything I send it to you open. . . .

†POPE *and* ARBUTHNOT *to* SWIFT[4]   5 *December* 1732

1740

Dec. 5, 1732.

It is not a time to complain that you have not answered me two letters
(in the last of which I was impatient under some fears) It is not now
indeed a time to think of one's [5]self when one of the nearest and longest
tyes I have ever had, is broken all on a sudden, by the unexpected
death of poor Mr Gay. An inflammatory feaver hurried him out of
this life in three days. He died last night at nine a clock, not deprived

---

[1] When in 1728 the Jacobite proprietor of *Mist's Weekly Journal* (Nathaniel Mist) had
to run away for fear of charges of treasonable journalism, his journal was continued in his
absence as *Fog's Weekly Journal* (1728–37).

[2] The bell-man passed out (for a gratuity?) verses during the holiday season of Christmas
and New Years. Pope (letter to Richardson, 2 Nov.) expected to publish the Epistle to Lord
Bathurst even earlier than Christmas. It appeared about 15 Jan.

[3] The sentence here printed is from an untraced letter offered as item 22 in lot 355 in the
sale catalogue for 28 Nov. 1913. No date is given, but one guesses that this might be a
covering letter for the joint letter to Swift that follows immediately. That seems to be the
only joint letter preserved from the two friends to Swift.

[4] To the heading introducing this letter Pope appended (1741L) the following footnote:
'*On my dear friend Mr.* Gay's *death: Received* December 15, *but not read till the* 20th, *by an
Impulse foreboding some Misfortune.* [This note is indors'd on the original letter in Dr. Swift's
hand.] *Dublin Edit.*'
   The note appears in 1741 Dab; without, however, the words 'Dublin Edit', which Pope
added to stress the impression that the volume of letters emanated from Dublin.

[5] one's self] of my self *1741 L; 1742 L*.

of his senses entirely at last, and possessing them perfectly till within five hours. He asked of you a few hours before, when in acute torment by the inflammation in his bowels and breast. His effects are in the Duke of Queensbury's custody. His sisters, we suppose, will be his heirs, who are two widows; as yet it is not known whether or no he left a will[1]—Good God! how often are we to die before we go quite off this stage? in every friend we lose a part of ourselves, and the best part. God keep those we have left! few are worth praying for, and one's self the least of all.

I shall never see you now I believe; one of your principal Calls to England is at an end. Indeed he was the most amiable by far, his qualities were the gentlest, but I love you as well and as firmly. Would to God the man we have lost had not been so amiable, nor so good! but that's a wish for our own sakes, not for his. Sure if Innocence and Integrity can deserve Happiness, it must be his. Adieu. I can add nothing to what you will feel, and diminish nothing from it. Yet write to me, and soon. Believe no man now living loves you better, I believe no man ever did, than | A. Pope.

Dr. Arbuthnot, whose humanity you know, heartily commends himself to you. All possible diligence and affection has been shown, and continued attendance on this melancholy occasion. Once more adieu, and write to one who is truly disconsolate.[2]

Dear Sir,—I am sorry that the renewal of our correspondence should be upon such a melancholy occasion. Poor Mr. Gay dy'd of an inflammation, and I believe at last a mortification of the bowels; it was the most precipitate case I ever knew, having cut him off in three days. He was attended by two Physicians besides my self. I believed the distemper mortal from the beginning. I have not had the pleasure of a line from you these two years; I wrote one about your health, to which I had no answer. I wish you all health and happiness, being with great affection and respect, Sir, Your, &c.

†POPE *to* [MARTHA BLOUNT][3]   [*6 December?* 1732]

1737

Your letter dated at nine a clock on Tuesday (night as I suppose) has

---

[1] The amount of 6000*l.* was equally divided between his sisters, Katherine Baller and Joanna Fortescue.—Cunningham–Elwin. When very ill in 1729 Gay wrote Pope that he had made no will.

[2] Between Pope's part of the letter and what follows, the Dublin editions (1741 Dab) inserted the centred caption: 'P.S. By Dr. Arbuthnot.'

[3] Miss Blount first appears as the person to whom this letter is addressed in Warburton's edition of 1751. The letter seems written shortly after Gay's death, and answers one from Miss Blount (or another) informing Pope of the event. When first printing the letter in

sunk me quite. Yesterday I hoped; and yesterday I sent you a line or two for our poor friend Gay, inclos'd in a few words to you; about twelve or one a clock you should have had it. I am troubled about that, tho' the present cause of our trouble be so much greater. Indeed I want a friend, to help me to bear it better. We want each other. I bear a hearty share with Mrs. Howard,[1] who has lost a man of a most honest heart: so honest an one, that I wish her Master had none less honest about him. The world after all is a little pitiful thing; not performing any one promise it makes us, for the future, and every day taking away and annulling the joys of the past. Let us comfort one another, and if possible, study to add as much more friendship to each other, as death has depriv'd us of in him: I promise you more and more of mine, which will be the way to deserve more and more of yours.

I purposely avoid saying more. The subject is beyond writing upon, beyond cure or ease by reason or reflection, beyond all but one thought, that it is the will of God.

So will the death of my Mother be! which now I tremble at, now resign to, now bring close to me, now set farther off: Every day alters, turns me about, and confuses my whole frame of mind. Her dangerous distemper is again return'd, her fever coming onward again, tho' less in pain, for which last however I thank God.

I am unfeignedly tired of the world, and receive nothing to be call'd a Pleasure in it, equivalent to countervail either the death of one I have so long lived with, or of one I have so long lived for. I have nothing left but to turn my thoughts to one comfort; the last we usually think of, tho' the only one we should in wisdom depend upon, in such a disappointing place as this. I sit in her room, and she is always present before me, but when I sleep. I wonder I am so well: I have shed many Tears, but now I weep at nothing. I would above all things see you, and think it would comfort you to see me so equal-temper'd and so quiet. But pray dine here: you may, and she know nothing of it; for she dozes much, and we tell her of no earthly thing lest it run in her mind which often trifles have done. If Mr. Bethel had time, I wish he were your companion hither. Be as much as you can with each other: Be assur'd I love you both, and be farther assur'd, that friendship will encrease as I live on.

1737a (Roberts's octavo) Pope added a footnote: 'Mr. Gay's death, which happen'd in Nov. 1732, at the Duke of Queensberry's house in London, aged 46.' Actually Gay died on Monday the 4th of December, and Miss Blount presumably wrote to inform Pope of the fact on Tuesday at 9 a.m. (not *night*).

[1] Naturally, perhaps, in his emotional state Pope might speak of 'Mrs. Howard', but this is the only time after June 1731 (when her husband succeeded as Earl of Suffolk) that she is so spoken of by Pope.

POPE *to* CARYLL   14 *December* 1732

Add. 28618

Twittenham. 14 Decbr 1732.

I am indeed to blame, but the true reason of my not writing was, that I had a mind to give you some satisfaction in a point you have often asked after, viz., What I was doing? I [hoped] every week to have sent you a poem of mine,[1] which has been in the press a month, but most unexpected accidents have still retarded it. Perhaps they were merciful reprieves, from time to time; for I expect when ever it does come out, much noise and calumny will attend it, as those things generally attend all that is honest, or public spirited.—But I will not delay one post answering your last kind, tho' short, letter.

Take it then in three words. I am well. Poor Gay is gone before and has not left an honester man behind him; he had just put a play into the house,[2] which the D. of Queensbury will take care of, and turn to the benefit of his relations. I have read it, and think it of his very best manner, a true original. He has left some other pieces fit for the press.

Your god-daughter has been very ill. I no sooner saw the death of my old friend Mr Gay,[3] whom I attended in his last sickness (it was but three days), but she fell very ill, partly occasioned by the shock his death gave her. Dr Arbuthnot who attended the one was constantly with the other, and has had better success with her. During her whole illness, the worthy family set open all their windows and doors, and washed the house and stairs to her very door twice in the week in which her recovery depended upon being kept warm; and had a constant clatter of doors, and removal of chairs, and all the noise that could possibly be made, while she was ordered to be composed to rest by the Doctor. This I saw and heard, and so did Dr. Arbuthnot, who very humorously asked, as he went up and down their stairs, why they did not sell and make money of their shaftes,[4] and leave the windows quite open?

Pardon the bad hand I write. I am but just returned from those scenes of sickness and death[5] to Twittenham, and half starved with the

---

[1] His Epistle to Lord Bathurst, 'Of the Use of Riches'. It came out about a month after this letter was written.

[2] Gay's play was *Achilles*. It had a moderate success in 1733.

[3] Unless one suspects the preceding letter, here regarded as to Miss Blount, of being a fabrication, one must feel that Pope does not here intend to say he was at Gay's bedside when he died. Possibly Miss Blount was. The sentence would be more naturally coherent if Pope had written, '*She* no sooner saw the death . . . but she fell very ill.'

[4] For the scribe's clear *shaftes* Elwin substitutes *sashes*, which is very likely what Pope wrote. Bailey's *Dictionary* gives as one meaning of *shaft*, 'the tunnel of a chimney'—which like the windows might afford draughts.

[5] Pope may mean that he has visited Exeter Exchange where Gay's body lay in state. *The Weekly Miscellany*, 30 Dec., gives an account of the funeral, which took place on the 23rd: 'On Saturday Night last, about 11 o'clock, the Corpse of John Gay, Esq; Author of

journey; yet I will not delay longer, that I may send before the post goes. Adieu; no man is more sincerely than I | Dear sir | Your affect and obliged friend and servant, | A. Pope.

the Beggars Opera, and several other fine Poetical Pieces, was (after lying in State in Exeter Exchange) carry'd to Westminster-Abbey, and interred there with great Pomp and Solemnity. The Pall was supported by the Right Hon. the Earl of Chesterfield, the Lord Cornbury, the Hon. George Berkeley, the Hon. Levison Gower, Esq; General Dormer, and Alexander Pope, Esq; and the Funeral was attended by several Persons of Distinction.'

1733

This year is notable for the anonymous publication of three epistles of the *Essay on Man* and for other poems of which Pope avowed the authorship. The year—less obviously so far as the letters indicate—was one in which, partly as a result of Walpole's abortive project for an Excise, political allegiance was being shifted. Bathurst, Burlington, Cobham, Chesterfield, and others forsook Walpole and went into the Opposition. After the attention given the royal family in Pope's imitation of the *First Satire of the Second Book of Horace* the poet also was naturally less well regarded at Court. In this poem stray couplets, shot nauseously at Lady Mary Wortley Montagu and Lord Hervey (who at this time was forsaking Pulteney and the Prince of Wales for Walpole and Queen Caroline), provoked these 'top court wits' to extensive and equally nauseous replies. Such interchanges receive relatively little space in the correspondence of all three principals. The poet's private life was changed by the death of his mother on 7 June, which encouraged him to ramble away from Twickenham during the later summer. Visits to London, to Dawley, to Stowe, were followed by a fortnight in Essex, a possible (but doubtful) visit to Cirencester, three weeks at Ladyholt, and a like period at Bevis Mount. In October he returned briefly to London and thence to Twickenham. As 'P.T.' he was now endeavouring to entrap Curll into publishing his letters. An attempt to interest Curll earlier (in March) had failed, and letters of October and November aroused no immediate interest on Curll's part. The project seemed to Pope to eventuate in a proper and dignified reply to current attacks on his parentage and on his own personal character.

---

*POPE *to* HENRY RACKETT[1]   [1733?]

Ushaw College

Dear Cosen,—My sister spoke to me about my Cos. John's affair. I desird to have You draw up a State of the whole Case, that I might advise with Council upon it, which she promisd should be sent me next day to Dr Arbuthnot's in Cork street. But it has not come in two days. Pray draw it up carefully & let me have it to show. Let me also know what the Debt they challenge, is? and a Copy of the Action, or Writ, Particulars, &c.

As to getting a Protection, I told my Sister I did verily believe I

[1] Henry Rackett is the legally trained nephew, and John is the sailor. The time of this action against John for debt (incurred perhaps through some miscarriage of imported goods) is impossible to fix without further data. This letter was written before the death of Dr. Arbuthnot, and so at a guess is placed in or about 1733. It should date after Henry Rackett has some knowledge of the law; but since John had made four or five voyages by 1724, his trouble may date earlier than 1733. See Pope to Drummond, 1 Aug. 1724.

could not, having tryed formerly in vain. No Lord of my Acquaintance ever give[s] any, in case of Debt, and I have applyd to forein Ambassadors, but find that No ambassador can give a Protection against arrest for any matter of *Trade* or *Shipping*, but are expressly prohibited from any such by Act of Parliament. So that None from an ambassador can be of service to him. To have a just State of the Case is necessary, and is all it is possible for me to serve him in. I shall go to Twitnam on Munday: where the Paper will find me, & where I shall be till Thursday. No time should be lost. I go out of town by nine a clock Sunday. (to morrow) I am surprized to have heard nothing all this while.

I am your affectionate | Cosen & Servant | A. Pope

Saturday

Address: To | Mr Henry Rackett, at | the Green Canister in New | North-street | Bloomsbury.

POPE *to* CARYLL   *January* 1732/3

Add. 28618

Jan. 1732/3

The concern I've been in of late (as well as a great deal of ill health) made me forget when I wrote last to you, to tell you how very much I liked the verses you favoured me with of your grandson.[1] I like them so well, that I desire you to send me anything he does. If he is not assisted in them, they are extraordinary.—I would rather see him a good man than a good poet; and yet a good poet is no small thing, and (I believe) no small earnest of his being a good man.

This or the next post will bring you under two covers, my Epistle to Lord Bathurst, on the Use of Riches.[2] It is not the worst I have written, and abounds in moral example, for which reason it must be obnoxious in this age. God send it does any good! I really mean nothing else by writing at this time of my life.

I believe you will receive from the care of your poor god-daughter a prettier poem—I call her *poor*, for she deserves pity, both from the strange unnatural usage she meets with in her own family, and from her own weak but well-natur'd submission to endure it. Adieu, may this year, and every year add to your happiness, 'till you are weary of all this world can afford, and long for a better. I am always | Dear sir | Your most mindful, obliged, and | affectionate servant | A. Pope

---

[1] The grandson was John, the sixteen-year-old son of another John and his wife Lady Mary. The grandson was in the Scotch College (Jesuit) in Paris from Oct. 1726 to Apr. 1733. See Add. 28250, ff. 398, 400, and 403.

[2] It was published 15 Jan., after a long delay.

*POPE to THE COUNTESS OF BURLINGTON[1]

Chatsworth

Madam,—I fully purposed to have been myself the bearer of these Papers, and it is no small punishment to me that I am not. I believe it would be very proper, to have as many as are thus marked Θ of my Lady Sunderland's Letters, transcribed: and to joyn them with Algernon Sydney's (if not also some of Mr Savil's &c.)[2] which are dated in the years, 79, & 80: as they relate to the Same Facts & Occurrencies. If your Ladyship wants Employment, these will abundantly supply it, till I bring you all Lord Halifax's Maxims & single Thoughts, under their proper Heads, which I can in a few days; & if you would still inlarge the Collection, his loose papers will furnish wherewithall. But if this Task seems too great for your Self, I will employ an Amanuensis for the rest. Your Ladyships Commands will be a better thing than an Honour, they are really a Pleasure & Improvement to me.

The Picture is the best ornament to my New Room.[3] The merry old Gentleman has got a Name, which I will maintain to all Connoisseurs. That may make it more Valuable to Them, but to me, the Hand that painted it is Sufficient. I am with all respect & sincerity | Madam | Your Ladyship's most | obedient & oblig'd Servant | A. Pope.

Jan 13th | [1733].

*POPE to THE EARL OF BURLINGTON[4]   [1732/3]

Chatsworth

Tuesday morning.

My Lord,—The Inclosed is the Last Bill I shall draw upon your Lordship for stone, according to the Commands you layd upon me, that there should be nothing Durable in my building which I was not to owe to Chiswick. I am sure there will be nothing in it Beautiful besides, nor (I believe) in this nation, but what is owed to the Lord of

---

[1] The year is added by the 6th Duke of Devonshire.—Francis Thompson. It seems correct since the Burlingtons are now back from Yorkshire, and Pope is returning parts of the Savile papers for Lady Burlington to work on.

[2] These persons are Lady Burlington's great-grandmother, Countess of Sunderland (Waller's Sacharissa), her great-uncle Henry Savile, and Lady Sunderland's brother, Algernon Sidney.

[3] This seems to be the only mention at this time of a 'new room'. He enlarged his villa in 1736 somewhat. Lady Burlington dabbled in painting, and has evidently done a picture for Pope. Listed among the furnishings of his 'Little Parlor' after his death was a painting of an 'Oldman without a frame'. See *Notes & Queries*, 6 S. v (1882), 364.

[4] At several different times Pope was 'building' at Twickenham. The description of himself as a philosopher-poet leads one to assume that this letter concerns stone for his new portico. This hypothesis may be wrong, of course.

Chiswick.—We now stand still for Materials—I would not have faild dining with you on Saturday, had not my Engagement subsisted to carry a Friend home with me that morning. If your Lordship shall be in the Country this week or any part of it, I wish to meet you; & I am in a particular manner desirous to find my Lady Burlington there, since I think it would compleat her recovery—I am, in the sincerity of a Philosopher, & with the Flame & Warmth of a Poet, My Lord, your most faithfull, obedient humble Servant, | A. Pope.

Address: To the Rt. Hon. the Earl of Burlington.

HILL *to* POPE   16 *January* 1732/3
1751 (Hill)
                                                            Jan. 16, 1733.

Sir,—I thank you, with a double pleasure, for the present of your Epistle, *Of the use of riches*; because it brought me a proof, that you have good-nature enough, to remember one, who must have *seemed* not to have deserved the distinction. But my reason for not acknowledging, sooner,[1] the due sense I have of many other favours, you have been so obliging, as to intend me, is, from an occasion, I have in view, of doing it very shortly.

I am sorry, *The man of Ross*, who is, so beautifully, your *theme*, is not, like the *Thames* to Sir *John Denham*, your *example* also.—You will start, I make no doubt, at an accusation you are so unconscious of deserving.—Yet, we know ourselves too little! and I must, in spite of my friendship, join the world, in its censure of this manifest defect in your conduct, who can suppose it sufficient, to shake over us, now and then, a thin sprinkling, from stores so inexhaustibly rich and desirable![2]

I wish you an increase of happiness, and of health, in this, and every new year; and am, | Sir, | Your most faithful, | And obedient Servant, | A. Hill.

POPE *to* FORTESCUE[3]   [1732/3?]
Harvard University
                                                            Friday night.

You may think I have forgot you, and I may think you have forgot me; but I believe neither of us will think so wrong. The truth is, I

---

[1] Hill evidently received an advance copy.

[2] Even a compliment from Hill can contain an obvious barb!

[3] In 1733 Peterborow was ill at various times according to the newspapers and to letters, especially letters to and from Swift. The illness of January seems to have been the most serious. See *Lond. Eve. Post*, 25 Jan. and the letter of Lord Hervey to Henry Fox (23 Jan. 1732/3: ed. Ilchester), where Hervey remarks, 'They say Lord Peterborough cannot recover; so that of the veteran nobility there is now only his Grace (or rather Highness) of Somerset remaining.'

have been neither at home nor at London a day together: for my Lord
Peterborow came very ill from Hantshire to Kensington a fortnight
since, & has ever since kept his chamber, where I have been to help him
pass his time, almost daily. It was but yesterday that I left him well
enough to stay at Twitnam for a few days. If this reach you in time, &
at leisure, I hope it will bring you hither for a night. As soon as I
return to Town, you shall be troubled with me. Adieu, & may all
health attend you, as I wish! Yours always, | A. Pope.

Address: To Wm Fortescue Esqr

†SWIFT *to* POPE¹   1732/3

1741 La
                                                                Dublin, 1732–3.

I received yours with a few lines from the Doctor, and the account of
our losing Mr. Gay, upon which event I shall say nothing. I am only
concern'd that long living hath not hardened me: for even in this kingdom, and in a few days past, two persons of great merit whom I loved
very well, have dy'd in the prime of their years, but a little above thirty.
I would endeavour to comfort my self upon the loss of friends, as I do
upon the loss of mony; by turning to my account-book, and seeing
whether I have enough left for my support? but in the former case I
find I have not, any more than in the other; and I know not any man
who is in a greater likelyhood than my self, to die poor and friendless.
You are a much greater loser than me by his death, as being a more
intimate friend, and often his companion; which latter I could never
hope to be, except perhaps once more in my life for a piece of a summer.
I hope he hath left you the care of any writings he may have left, and
I wish, that with those already extant, they could be all published in a
fair edition under your inspection. Your poem on the Use of Riches
hath been just printed here,² and we have no objection but the obscurity of several passages by our ignorance in facts and persons, which
make us lose abundance of the Satyr. Had the printer given me notice,
I would have honestly printed the names at length, where I happened
to know them; and writ explanatory notes, which however would have
been but few, for my long absence hath made me ignorant of what
passes out of the scene where I am. I never had the least hint from you
about this work, any more than your former, upon Tast. We are told
here, that you are preparing other pieces of the same bulk to be

¹ The best detail for dating the letter is the recent appearance of Pope's Epistle to
Bathurst in Dublin. Since it was printed about the middle of January in London, a
prompt Dublin edition might fall within that month. This letter first appeared in 1741
Lab, and was reprinted in the Supplement to 1741 Dab.
² just printed here] just re-printed here *1741 Dab.*

inscrib'd to other friends, one (for instance) to my Lord Bolingbroke, another to Lord Oxford, and so on—Doctor Delany presents you his most humble service, he behaves himself very commendably, converses only with his former friends, makes no parade, but entertains them constantly at an elegant plentiful table, walks the streets as usual, by day-light, does many acts of charity and generosity, cultivates a country house two miles distant, and is one of those very few within my knowledge, on whom a great access of fortune hath made no manner of change.[1] And particularly he is often without mony, as he was before. We have got my Lord Orrery among us, being forc'd to continue here on the ill condition of his estate by the knavery of an Agent; he is a most worthy Gentleman, whom I hope you will be acquainted with. I am very much obliged by your favour to Mr. P—, which I desire may continue no longer than he shall deserve by his Modesty, a virtue I never knew him to want, but is hard for young men to keep, without abundance of ballast.[2] If you are acquainted with the Duchess of Queensbury, I desire you will present her my most humble service: I think she is a greater loser by the death of a friend than either of us. She seems a Lady of excellent sense and spirit: I had often Postscripts from her in our friends letters to me, and her part was sometimes longer than his, and they made up a great part of the little happiness I could have here. This was the more generous, because I never saw her since she was a girl of five years old, nor did I envy poor Mr. Gay for any thing so much as being a domestick to such a Lady. I desire you will never fail to send me a particular account of your health. I dare hardly enquire about Mrs. Pope, who I am told is but just among the living, and consequently a continual grief to you: she is sensible of your tenderness, which robs her of the only happiness she is capable of enjoying. And yet I pity you more than her; you cannot lengthen her days, and I beg she may not shorten yours.

POPE *to* MALLET[3] [1732/3?]

Sir John Murray

I am extremely troubled to find you so ill. I was taken so last night just as I calld at your door, & went directly to Bed, where I've continud

---

[1] He had recently married a fortune. See Swift to Gay, 12 Aug. 1732.

[2] This sentence, concerning Mr. Pilkington, was omitted in the Dublin reprint (1741 Dab). Is not the omission likely to be due to Swift alone? Faulkner and the average reader would feel no pain in reading the sentence. Swift would feel shame at having recommended Pilkington to Alderman Barber and others.

[3] Elwin suggests the year: but it is pure hypothesis. At this time Pope is staying perhaps in Dover Street with Lord Oxford or with Dr. Arbuthnot. Mallet is now tutor to Mrs. Knight's son, and she also lives in Dover Street. Lord Hervey, writing to Henry Fox (18 Jan. 1732/3: ed. Lord Ilchester), says, 'the whole world, high and low, rich and poor, are ill of this epidemical cold.'

most of this day, & am going again by the Doctors order. I am in great uneasiness to know better than I can by Messages, what your Case is? The first minute I can get abroad, it shall be to you. No man more sincerely wishes your health, or is more truly afflicted at your want of it than I.

Yours always, A. Pope

Address: To | Mr Mallet, at Mrs | Knight's.

POPE *to* JONATHAN RICHARDSON[1]   [1732-3]

Elwin–Courthope, ix. 501

Saturday.

I have continued ill ever since I wrote to you, nor once stirred out till the doctor obliged me to be removed hither to watch me more narrowly. I have been confined three days in town, still hoping daily to be able to get out to see you. In vain, I am still a prisoner. If it were any way reasonable or feasible to expect, what I can only wish, to see you here this evening, I should be very much pleased. But if that cannot be I will do my utmost towards you (though it be so long a way in my condition) in a few days. Dear sir, adieu. Yours, &c.

POPE *to* CARYLL   31 *January* 1732/3.

Add. 28618

Twittenham 31. Jan: 173⅔

I received your last with pleasure as indeed I do all yours, though my remissness sometimes in replying may make me seem too undeserving to receive them often.

You live daily in my thoughts, and sometimes in my prayers, if you will let a poet talk of prayers. Yet at least I have some title to *sermons*, which are next of kin to prayers. I find the last I made[2] had some good effect, and yet the preacher less railed at than usually those are who will be declaiming against popular or national vices. I shall redouble my blow very speedily.[3]

I made you no compliment as to your grandson, and I again desire to see whatever he writes that way. Your plan for his education is what (in my judgment) is a very right and reasonable one. And indeed you do me justice in thinking I am concerned he should make if not as good a man quite as his grandfather, yet such a one as he will not be ashamed of.

---

[1] This letter should be written during the illness of some days at Lord Oxford's house, during which Pope wrote the imitation of *The First Satire of the Second Book of Horace.*

[2] His Epistle to Lord Bathurst.

[3] Prophesying the appearance (15 Feb.) of his Imitation of Horace, Satire II, i, which proved a more offensive poem than did the Epistle to Bathurst.

I formerly mentioned to you a nephew of mine, bred an attorney but by nature and grace both an honest man,[1] which even that education hath not overcome. I am told there is a reform in the D. of N—k's stewards, or bailiffs, and if you [have] any means to recommend him to keep courts, &c., as one of our religion perhaps they might use him. I'm told Lord Stafford has a particular influence there; but I have little or no acquaintance either with the son (as he is) of my friend Mr Stafford,[2] or the daughter (as the duchess is) of my particular friend Ned Blunt.[3] Yet perhaps his being my nephew would not be a circumstance to either to reject him, if they were applied to, which I have more modesty than to do.

I shall fill this letter with requests: My next is that you'll favour me with a little venison, at the next seasonable time. I did not trouble you with the acceptance of the offer you lately made me of some, but now happen to have occasion of gratifying a friend or two by it.

I can only add I am now well, just recovered from a fever with the present distemper, and that my poor old woman has hitherto escaped all harm. God preserve you and all your family: and let them, and do you, dear sir, believe that no man is with more truth | Your faithful affect. servant | A. Pope.

POPE *to* ROBERT DODSLEY   5 *February* 1732/3

1803 (Swift's *Works*, ed. Nichols, xviii. 283)

Feb. 5, 1732–3

Sir,—I was very willing to read your piece,[4] and do freely tell you I like it, so far as my particular judgment goes. Whether it has action enough to please on the stage, I doubt; but the morality and satire ought to be relished by the reader. I will do more than you ask me; I will recommend it to Mr. Rich.[5] If he can join it to any play, with suitable representations, to make it an entertainment, I believe he will give you a benefit night; and I sincerely wish it may be turned any way to your advantage, or that I could shew you my friendship in any instance.

I am, &c. | A. Pope.

---

[1] See Pope to Caryll, 6 Dec. 1730.

[2] See Pope to Lansdowne, 21 Oct. 1713 and Pope to Caryll jr., 5 Dec. 1712.

[3] Mary Blount was married to Edward, 9th Duke of Norfolk. The passage throws doubt on the story that Pope had gone to school with a Duke of Norfolk, though Thomas the 8th Duke (d. 23 Dec. 1732) is a possibility. The death of the 8th Duke doubtless was causing 'the reform in the stewards'.

[4] Pope's reading and approval of Dodsley's *Toy Shop* is apparently their first connexion. Later, after the success of the play, Dodsley set up as bookseller and was often employed by Pope. Dodsley's first book, *A Muse in Livery*, was published a year before this letter was written.

[5] John Rich, manager of the Covent Garden theatre, where (partly because of Pope's warm recommendation) Dodsley's *Toy Shop* was acted with success beginning in Feb. 1734/5.

†POPE *to* SWIFT[1]   16 *February* 1732/3

1740

Feb. 16, 1732-3.

It is indeed impossible to speak on such a subject as the loss of Mr. Gay, to me an irreparable one. But I send you what I intend for the inscription on his tomb,[2] which the Duke of Queensbury will set up at Westminster. As to his writings, he left no Will, nor spoke a word of them, or anything else, during his short and præcipitate[3] illness, in which I attended him to his last breath. The Duke has acted more than the part of a brother to him, and it will be strange if the sisters do not leave his papers totally to his disposal, who will do the same that I would with them. He has managed the Comedy[4] (which our poor friend gave to the playhouse the week before his death) to the utmost advantage for his relations; and proposes to do the same with some Fables he left finished.

There is nothing of late which I think of more than mortality, and what you mention of collecting the best monuments we can of our friends, their own images in their writings: (for those are the best, when their minds are such as Mr. Gay's was, and as yours is.) I am preparing also for my own; and have nothing so much at heart, as to shew the silly world that men of Wit, or even Poets, may be the most moral of mankind. A few loose things sometimes fall from them, by which[5] censorious fools judge as ill of them, as possibly they can, for their own comfort: and indeed, when such unguarded and trifling *Jeux d'Esprit* have once got abroad, all that prudence or repentance can do, since they cannot be deny'd, is to put 'em fairly upon that foot; and teach the publick (as we have done in the preface to the four volumes of miscellanies) to distinguish betwixt our studies and our idlenesses, our works and our weaknesses: That was the whole end of the last Vol. of Miscellanies, without which our former declaration in that preface,[6] "That these volumes contain'd all that we had[7] ever

---

[1] Pope's revisions and Swift's for this letter have little significance except for the fact that they show clearly the two 'families' of texts that come from such revisions. They change the meaning hardly at all.

[2] Pope's epitaph was printed in June in *The Gentleman's Magazine*, which probably reprinted it from some unidentified newspaper. The monument was not 'opened' in the Abbey before September.   [3] his short and præcipitate] his præcipitate *1742 La*.

[4] Gay's *Achilles* had a good record of 11 performances in the first month, but it was bitterly attacked by some of the government writers. Lord Hervey in his letters disparages it.

[5] This word in Pope's quarto (1741 La) was misprinted *whieh*, and the error was corrected in the folio (1741 b)—an indication as to priority in impression.

[6] Prefixed to the third volume of the *Miscellanies* (1732) was 'The Booksellers Advertisement', which said that the volume 'contains the Remainder of those Miscellaneous Pieces, which were in some sort promised in the Preface to the former Volumes, or which have been written since. . . . The Reader may be assured no other Edition is either Genuine or Compleat, and that they are all the Things of this kind which will ever be Printed by the same Hands.'   [7] had] have *1741 Labc*; *1742 Lbc*.

offended in that way", would have been discredited. It went indeed to my heart, to omit what you called the Libel on Dr. D——[1] and the best panegyrick on myself,[2] that either my own times or any other could have afforded, or will ever afford to me. The book as you observe was printed in great haste; the cause whereof was, that the booksellers here were doing the same, in collecting your pieces, the corn with the chaff; I don't mean that any thing of[3] yours is chaff, but with other wit of Ireland which was so, and the whole in your name. I meant[4] principally to oblige a separation of[5] what you writ seriously from what you writ carelessly; and thought my own weeds might pass for a sort of wild flowers, when bundled up with them.

It was I that sent you those books into Ireland, and so I did my Epistle to Lord Bathurst even before it was publish'd, and another thing of mine, which is a Parody[6] from Horace, writ in two mornings.[7] I never took more care in my life of any poem[8] than of the former of these, nor less than of the latter: yet every friend has forc'd me to print it, tho' in truth my own single motive was about a score of lines[9] towards the latter end, which you will find out.

I have declined opening to you by letters the whole scheme of my present Work, expecting still to do it in a better manner in person: but you will see pretty soon, that the letter to Lord Bathurst is a part of it, and you will find a plain connexion between them, if you read them in the order just contrary to that they were publish'd in.[10] I imitate those cunning tradesmen, who show their best silks last: or, (to give you a truer idea, tho' it sounds too proudly) my works will in one respect be like the works of Nature, much more to be liked and understood when consider'd in the relation they bear with each other, than when ignorantly look'd upon one by one; and often, those parts which attract most at first sight, will appear to be not the most,[11] but the least considerable.

I am pleas'd and flatter'd by your expression of *Orna me*. The chief

---

[1] D——] Delany *1741 Dab*.

[2] This contradicts the attitude expressed to Fortescue in Pope's letter of 20 Feb. [1730] when Swift's poem first appeared.

[3] any thing of] any of *1742 La*.   [4] meant] mean *1741 Dab*.

[5] oblige . . . what] oblige them to separate what *1741 Labc*; *1742 Labc*.

[6] Sat. I. Lib. 2.—Footnote, 1740–2.

[7] Pope much later told Spence (*Anecdotes*, p. 297): 'When I had a fever, one winter in town, that confined me to my room for five or six days, Lord Bolingbroke, who came to see me, happened to take up a Horace that lay by on the table; and in turning it over, dipped on the first satire of the second book, which begins *Sunt quibus in satirâ*, *&c*. He observed, how well that would hit my case, if I were to imitate it in English. After he was gone, I read it over; translated it in a morning or two, and sent it to the press in a week or fortnight after. And this was the occasion of my imitating some other of the satires and epistles afterwards.'

[8] poem] thing *1741 L*; *1742 L*.

[9] a score of lines] twenty lines *1741 L*; *1742 L*.

[10] He is thinking of his four 'Moral Essays' which were published in an order opposite to that in which he intended to and did arrange them when they were collected.

[11] appear to be not] appear not *1741 Dab, Labc*; *1742 Lbc*.

pleasure this work can give me is, that I can in it, with propriety, decency, and justice, insert the name and character of every friend I have, and every man that deserves to be lov'd or adorn'd. But I smile at your applying that phrase to my visiting you in Ireland; a place where I might have some apprehension (from their extraordinary passion for poetry, and hospitality[1] in entertaining) of being *adorn'd* to death, and buried under the weight of garlands, like a Lady[2] I have read of somewhere or other. My mother lives (which is an answer to that point) and (I thank God) tho' her memory be in a manner gone, is yet awake and sensible to me, tho' scarce to any thing else; which doubles the reason of my attendance, and at the same time sweetens it.—I wish (beyond any other wish) you could pass a summer here; I might (too probably) return with you, unless you preferr'd to see France first, to which country I think you would have a strong invitation.—Lord Peterborow has narrowly escaped death, and yet keeps his chamber: he is perpetually speaking in the most affectionate manner of you: he has written you two letters which you never receiv'd, and by that has been discourag'd from writing more. I can well believe the post-office may do this, when some letters of his to me have met the same fate, and two of mine to him. Yet let not this discourage you from writing to me, or to him inclos'd in the common way, as I do to you: Innocent men need fear no detection of their thoughts; and for my part, I would give 'em free leave to send all I write to Curl, if most of what I write was not too silly.

I desire my sincere services to Dr. Delany, who I agree with you is a man every way esteemable. My Lord O.[3] is a most virtuous and good-natur'd Nobleman, whom I should be happy to know.[4] Lord B. receiv'd your letter thro' my hands; it is not to be told you how much he wishes for you. The whole list of persons to whom you sent your services return you theirs, with proper sense of the distinction—Your Lady friend is *Semper Eadem*, and I have written an Epistle to her on that qualification in a female character;[5] which is thought by my chief Critick in your absence to be my *Chef d'Œuvre*: but it cannot be printed perfectly, in an age so sore of satire, and so willing to misapply characters.

[1] hospitality in entertaining) of] hospitality) of *1741 L; 1742 L.*
[2] like a Lady] like one *1741 L; 1742 L.*
[3] Lord O.] Lord O—ry *1741 Dab.* Lord Orrery's acquaintance with Pope still had far to go. From Dublin (24 Feb. 1732/3) his lordship wrote to Mrs. Cæsar (Rousham MSS. G) of Pope: 'I must own that among the various misfortunes of my Life the Want of being better known to him, I reckon one of the greatest.' About this time Orrery wrote his lines 'To Mr. Pope', beginning 'Entom'd with Kings tho Gays cold ashes lye', and sent them to Mrs. Cæsar.   [4] to know.] to know better. *1741 Dab.*
[5] This quality—constancy of temper as contrasted with variability—is the compliment paid to Martha Blount at the expense of the rest of her sex in Pope's 'Epistle to a Lady, on the Characters of Women' (Moral Essay II). Bolingbroke was probably the chief critic, or possibly Arbuthnot.

As to my own health, it is as good as usual. I have lain ill seven days of a slight feaver (the complaint here) but recover'd by gentle sweats, and the care of Dr. Arbuthnot. The play Mr. Gay left succeeds very well; it is another original in its kind. Adieu. God preserve your life, your health, your limbs, your spirits, and your friendships!

POPE *to* JONATHAN RICHARDSON[1]   [18 *February* 1732/3]

Roscoe, 1824, i. 390

Sunday.

I thank you for your kind and facetious epistle, and particularly for your simile in it. But I must tell you it was not that idle poem which I meant my caution of, in my letter to your neighbour Cheselden. That was the work of two mornings, after my brain was heated by a fever. But the thing I apprehend is of another nature, viz. a copy of part of another work, which I have cause to fear may be got out underhand; but of how much, or what part, I know not. In that case pray conceal entirely your having any knowledge of its belonging, either wholly or partly, to me; it would prejudice me both in reputation and profit. My services attend your son and your neighbour. I want much to see you all; but though I was ten days together in town, I could not bring it about, unless I had sent for you to Lord Oxford's, while I lay sick, which I thought not proper even in your regard. Adieu, and all health attend you. I think I have made a panegyric of you all in one line, saying of myself that I am

To virtue only, and her friends, a friend.[2]

A. P.

POPE *to* FORTESCUE[3]   [18 *February* 1732/3]

1817 (Warner, p. 49)

Sunday, Feb. 1732–3.

I had written to you before, as well as sent; had I not hoped this day, or last night, to have seen you here. I am sorry for your complaints of ill health, and particularly of your eyes; pray be very careful not to increase your cold. I will infallibly, if I can't see you sooner, be with

---

[1] Most probably after composing his 'idle poem' in imitation of Horace's First Satire of Book Two Pope wrote to Cheselden speaking of it and of the danger of allowing any suspicion of his authorship of the *Essay on Man* to grow. Richardson has mistaken the poem for which concealment was desired. Pope's name was on the title-page of the Imitation. Possibly neither poem had appeared when Pope was writing, but he seems to be writing after the Imitation has appeared and before the first epistle of the *Essay on Man* is out; i.e. between the 15th and 20th of February. The 18th was Sunday.

[2] Quoted from l. 121 of his Imitation of Horace.

[3] The letter should date promptly after the publication (15 Feb.) of Pope's imitation of the First Satire of the Second Book.

you in the middle of the week. I am at all times desirous to meet you, and have this winter been often dissatisfied to do it so seldom. I wish you a judge,¹ that you may sleep and be quiet; *ut in otia tuta recedas,*² but *otium cum dignitate*: have you seen my imitation of Horace? I fancy it will make you smile; but though, when first I began it, I thought of you; before I came to end it, I considered it might be too ludicrous, to a man of your situation and grave acquaintance, to make you Trebatius, who was yet one of the most considerable lawyers of his time, and a particular friend of a poet. In both which circumstances I rejoice that you resemble him, but am chiefly pleased that you do it in the latter.

Dear Sir, adieu! and love me as I do you. | Your faithful and affectionate servant, | A. Pope.

Address: To Wm. Fortescue, Esq; in Bell-Yard, near Lincoln's Inn, London.

POPE *to* JONATHAN RICHARDSON³　　　[*February* 1732/3]

Roscoe, 1824, i. 388

Monday, 7 o'clock.

It was a sensible mortification that I could not find you and your son yesterday (the only time I have had to endeavour it this long time). I had a hundred things to talk to you of; and among the rest, of the Essay on Man, which I hear so much of. Pray, what is your opinion of it? I hear some cry it extremely up; others think it obscure in part; and some (of whom I am sure you are not one) have said it is mine. I think I could shew you some faults in it, and believe you can shew me more, though, upon the whole, it is allowed to have merit, and I think so myself. I am so uncertain when I can be so near you again as I wish, that I desire to hear from you. I am this morning setting out for the country. Adieu! and commend me sincerely to your good son. He deserves to be called so: and believe me to be your really affectionate friend.

¹ The wish is probably due to the unfounded rumour published in *The London Evening Post*, 6 Feb., that Fortescue might become a Judge of Common Pleas.

² Adapted from Horace, *Satires*, i. i. 31. The passage that follows indicates the perfectly sure conclusion that Pope's imitation was published without consultation with Fortescue, who was not identified as Trebatius in any of Pope's editions, but was first associated with the imitation by Warburton in 1751.

³ The first epistle of the *Essay on Man* appeared 20 Feb., and this letter should come a few days later. It seems to contradict earlier letters to Richardson (e.g. that of 2 Nov. 1732) which showed that Richardson was in the secret of Pope's authorship of the *Essay*. In the opinion of the present editor, however, this letter is written for Richardson to show to interested friends in order to conceal the authorship further.

THE EARL OF PETERBOROW *to* LADY MARY WORTLEY MONTAGU[1] [1732/3]

Egerton 1949

Madame,—I was very unwilling to have my name Made use of in an affair in which I had noe concern, and therfore would not engage my Self to speak to Mr Pope, but he coming to my house the moment you went away, I gave him as exact an account as I could of our conversation.

He said to me what I had taken the Liberty to say to you, that he wonderd how the Town could apply those Lines to any but some noted common woeman, that he should yet be more surprised if you should take them to your Self, He named to me fower remarkable poetesses & scribblers, Mrs Centlivre Mrs Haywood Mrs Manly & Mrs Been,[2] Ladies famous indeed in their generation, and some of them Esteemed to have given very unfortunate favours to their Friends, assuring me that Such only were the objects of his satire.

I hope this assurance will prevent your further mistake, and any ill consequences, upon so odd a Subject I have nothing more to add.

Your Ladys: | Most humble & obedient | servant | Peterborow

Address: For the Lady Mary Wortley

POPE *to* JONATHAN RICHARDSON   2 *March* [1732/3]

Elwin–Courthope, ix. 503

Twitnam, March 2.

I see that a glut of praise succeeds to a glut of reproach.[3] I am much overpaid this way now, as I was injured that way before. But you, Sir, kindly temper your praise with your rebuke. Indeed, I deserve the one as little as the other, for so far from neglecting one honest friend, that I may truly say I never thought of you more frequently than since I have been unable to see you. I am sorry, though we are true friends, that we agree in one thing, for my continued indispositions keep me in almost a continued inability of going to my friends. It is a serious truth that I went equally with an intent of seeing yourself and Mr. Chiselden. It was a warm impulse that carried me, when I had but three hours to do it in, from the waterside to Ormond Street[4] at two, being obliged

---

[1] More than once Pope persuaded a friend to sign a letter that he either dictated or at least shaped. Such seems to be the case in this terrifically caustic retort to Lady Mary's protests against ll. 83–84 of his recent imitation of Horace. Animosity had existed more or less hidden until Pope published 'The Capon's Tale' in the first volume of the *Miscellanies* (1728) and the outrageous couplet here in question. From this time on it will be open war.

[2] Mrs. Aphra Behn.

[3] Anonymity had made hostile critics kind, Pope thought, to his *Essay on Man*, Epistle I.

[4] Ormond Street, Queen Square, was where Richardson lived.

by too pressing business to return by five o'clock to St. James's. I was at the corner of the square on my way to your house past Mr. Chiselden's, when he met me and his dinner waiting. I knew it was too early for your dinner, and he told me you could hardly come to us, therefore you see it was no excuse; but I further assure you it was a real *complaint* I felt at my ill fortune, and an *inward concern* that I felt for it which I testified by that message.

Your very kind letter lay three days at Twitnam, while I was absent in the country near Windsor. I went to London then, and lay sick most part of a day. In the evening I resolved to go to you, but it rained so hard that I could not have a chair procured till near eight o'clock, which I thought too late to go from Dover Street to Bloomsbury and back again. This gave me more vexation than I can express, for I was compelled to return hither next morning by my mother's desire, whom I had been absent from almost seven days, and now this day I see her first, and am very sick, so truly answer you who writ to me in pain. I am sensible, and ever will be, of your kind regard and great partiality towards me. I am unfeignedly troubled for your uneasy distemper and rheumatism, and wish you as truly as any man alive ease of body and mind. I will pass a whole day with you after this week whenever you will. Excuse my bad writing; I can hardly see or think clearly, but I feel myself sincerely, dear sir, yours.

My services attend your amanuensis[1] and our friend Chiselden.

POPE *to* CARYLL   8 *March* 1732/3

Add. 28618

You would excuse my delay in answering yours if you knew how I have been employed. I'm now building a portico, in which I hope you will sit like Nestor on a stone at the gate, and converse delightfully with us, one of these days. Poetry has given place for the present, as it always does with me, to the beauties of nature and the pleasures of the spring advancing every day. I do not sing with birds; I love better to hear them. You may have seen my last piece of song, which has met with such a flood of favour that my ears need no more flattery for this twelvemonth. However, it was a slight thing the work of two days,[2] whereas that to Lord Bathurst was the work of two years by intervals. I have not forgot your questions in relation to the scrivener Sir J. Blunt,[3] and can assure [you] Morgan is a fictitious name. You'll smile

---

[1] Jonathan jr. doubtless is intended. He is thought to have served Pope also in transcribing the *Essay on Man*, &c.

[2] He speaks of his imitation of the First Satire of the Second Book of Horace.

[3] In his Epistle to Bathurst Blunt appears in ll. 103, 133, and Morgan in l. 61.

to hear that 1 or 2 good priests were gravelled at my saying in the last thing, *Term me what you will, papist or protestant, &c.*, not seeing so plain a meaning as that an honest man and a good Catholic might be indifferent what the world *called* him, while he knew his own *religion* and his own *integrity*. A man that *can* write in this age, *may*; but he really will find that he writes to fools: and it is now a most unreasonable demand to cry *qui legit, intelligat*.

The town is now very full of a new poem intitled *an Essay on Man*,[1] attributed, I think with reason, to a divine. It has merit in my opinion but not so much as they give it; at least it is incorrect and has some inaccuracies in the expressions; one or two of an unhappy kind, for they may cause the author's sense to be turned, contrary to what I think his intention a little unorthodoxically. Nothing is so plain as that he quits his proper subject, *this present world*, to insert his belief of *a future state* and yet there is an *If* instead of a *Since* that would overthrow his meaning and at the end he uses the Words *God*, the *Soul* of the *World*, which at first glance may be taken for heathenism, while his whole paragraph proves him quite Christian in his system, from *Man* up to *Seraphim*. I want to know your opinion of it after twice or thrice reading. I give you my thoughts very candidly of it, tho' I find there is a sort of faction to set up the author and his piece in opposition to me and my little things, which I confess are not of so much importance as to the subject, but I hope they conduce to morality in their way, which way is at least more generally to be understood and the seasoning of satire renders it more palatable to the generality. Adieu, &c. | A. Pope.

POPE *to* FORTESCUE[2]   8 *March* [1732/3]

Gabriel Wells (1938)

March 8th

Your most kind Letter was a Sensible pleasure to me: & the Friendship & Concern shown in it, to suggest what you thought might be agreable to a Person whom you know I would not disoblige, I take particularly kindly.[3] But the affair in question of any alteration is now at an end, by that Lady's having taken her own Satisfaction in an avowed Libell, so fulfilling the veracity of my prophecy.[4] There has

---

[1] Preserving his anonymity Pope tries to get a sincere and unbiased judgement from his friend. It is the same trick he played on the general public.

[2] The year, obviously correct, comes from Fortescue's endorsement.

[3] The person is probably Sir Robert Walpole, who was mentioned in l. 153 of Pope's Imitation of Horace. Pope was remarking, not that Sir Robert corrupted justice, but that anything Sir Robert approved could not be libellous or seditious. Fortescue has perhaps suggested a revision of the passage.

[4] On the day of Pope's letter to Fortescue advertisements were printed of *Verses address'd to the Imitator of the First Satire of the Second Book of Horace. By a Lady of Quality*. The Lady

been another thing, wherein Pigott is abused as my Learned Council,[1] written by some Irish attorney; & Curll has printed a Parody on my own words which he is proud of as his own production, saying, he will pay no more of his Authors but can write better himself.[2] The Town, since you went, has enterd much into the fashion of applauding the Essay on Man, & in many places it is Sett up as a Piece far excelling any thing of mine, & commended, I think more in opposition to Me, than in their real Judgment it deserves.

I congratulate with you for being got out of the Noise & Debate about the Excises, getting Money & Health at once, & doing Justice too: I think yours is much the better part. I must beg you to re-mind Mr Cruwys of Mr Bethel's affair, not to let slip this Lady-day in making the demand on the Premises in Wales, it is certainly now high time he should write to the attorney there.—Having done with all Law-matters, the rest of this paper should be filled with all Expressions of Esteem & friendship, if such Expressions could be of any use or grace after the Experience & Habit (the two strongest of things) of many years. Believe me you have the Essentials, & the Ceremonials therfore are layd aside. Such a practise, continued where it is needless, is like keeping up the Scaffolding after the Building is finishd; what helpd to raise it at first, will but disgrace it at last.

Adieu, & write at your leisure. Sit tibi cura mei,
Sit tibi cura tui.

Yours Ever, | A. Pope.

Address: To | William Fortescue Esqr at | his house in Bell yard near | Lincolns Inne | London
Postmark: 9/MR
Fortescue's endorsement: Mr Pope | Mar: 8. 1732/3.

†LEONARD WELSTED *to* POPE[3]   12 *March* 1732/3
1743 (*The Dunciad* 4to, p. xxiii)

ExTRACT

I must own, after the reception which the vilest and most immoral

was Lady Mary Wortley Montagu, and now that she has attacked, Pope will not soften remarks in the poem. Lady Mary was a friend and supporter of Walpole, and in this poem she is reacting to Pope's vicious couplet (ll. 83–84) in his imitation. His prophecy is realized: he is now 'libell'd by her hate'.

[1] Possibly *The Sequel of Mr. Pope's Law Case; or farther Advice thereon*, which was advertised for publication on 6 Mar.

[2] *The First Satire of the Second Book of Horace, imitated in a Dialogue between Mr. Pope and the Ordinary of Newgate. . . . By Mr. Burnet* was published by W. Mears on 2 Mar. It is reprinted by Curll in the second volume of *Mr. Pope's Literary Correspondence* (1735). Burnet may be a fiction for Curll. The poem is subscribed as from 'Bolt-Court, Fleet-street| 26 Feb. 1732/3'.

[3] This part of Welsted's letter is introduced among 'Testimonies of Authors' with the

ribaldry hath lately met with, I was surprised to see what I had long despaired, a performance deserving the name of a poet. Such, Sir, is your work. It is, indeed, above all commendation, and ought to have been published in an age and country more worthy of it. If my testimony be of weight any where, you are sure to have it in the amplest manner, &c. &c. &c.

*POPE to THE EARL OF BURLINGTON   [*March* 1732/3]

Chatsworth

My Lord,—The Zeal of my Portico has eaten me up, so that I cannot be from home to day; I sent yesterday & missed of you. I cannot proceed in my Stucco-ing, till I see your Lordship & have your directions about the Upper Cornish of my house, & the Moldings & members of the Entablature. I therefore beg you to throw away one hour upon me at Twitn'am as soon as is not inconvenient. I need not say how impudent your kindness has long made me, you see I think it extends to the smallest Trifles. I am with truth | My Lord | Your ever obligd Servant | A. Pope

Thursday.

Address: To the Rt. Honble. the Earl of Burlington.

POPE to FORTESCUE[1]   [18] *March* [1732/3]

Dr. Eric G. Millar

March [18. 1732/3]

I am sorry you partook of the Trouble of the Excise Bill, and as sorry I did not know of your Coming tho but for 2 days, for I would have come up just to see you. It had been very kind if you could have layn here in your way. But this is past, & may all the future be prosperous with you,[2] as I wish it! As to that Poem, which I do not, & must not owne,[3] I beg your absolute and inviolable Silence: You will see more

---

remark: 'Mr. LEONARD WELSTED thus wrote* to the unknown author, on the first publication of the said Essay' [on Man]. The asterisk pointed to a footnote that says: 'In a Letter under his hand, dated March 12, 1733.' Presumably the letter was written in Mar. 1733 after the publication of the first epistle only. The author would not have been unknown in Mar. 1734.

[1] In dating Pope wrote only 'March'. Fortescue superscribed the day and year upon receipt of the letter, both at the beginning and on the third blank page. He has evidently sent Pope a report on Mrs. Blount's affairs with Roberts and on Walpole's intimation about Pope's lines concerning Sir Robert's very good friend, Lady Mary. Fortescue as M.P. for Newport had been summoned to Parliament for the vote (2 a.m. on the 17th) on the celebrated Excise Bill. As a good Walpole man he voted for the Bill, and evidently planned to return at once to Devonshire.

[2] Pope alludes to reports of new honours (a judgeship?) for Fortescue.

[3] The *Essay on Man*. The second epistle appeared 29 Mar.

of it in another Week, & that too I shall keep private. It is so far from a mortification to do *any good thing* (if this be so & indeed I mean it so) & enjoy only one's own Consciousness of it, that I think it the highest Gratification: on the contrary, the *worst things* I do, are such as I would constantly owne, & stand the Censure of. It is an honest proceeding, and worthy a Guiltless Man. You may be certain I shall never reply to such a Libel as Lady Mary's. 'Tis a pleasure & a comfort at once to find, that with so much mind, as so much Malice must have to accuse or blacken my character, it can fix upon no one ill or immoral thing in my Life; & must content itself to say my Poetry is dull, & my Person ugly. I wish you would take an opportunity to represent to the Person¹ who spoke to you about that Lady, that Her Conduct no way deserves *Encouragement* from him, or any other Great persons: & that the Good name of a Private Subject ought to be as sacred even to the Highest, as His Behavior toward them is irreproachable, loyal, & respectfull.—What you writ of his Intimation on that head shall never pass my lips.

Mrs Bl.² is your faithfull Servant & much obliged to your Care. My Mother, I thank God, is fine & easy. I never had better health than of late, & hope I shall have long life, because I am much threaten'd. Adieu, and know me ever, for | Dear Sir | Your most Sincerely | affectionate Servant | A. Pope.

Address: To | William Fortescue, Esqr: | to be left at his house in | Bell Yard | Lincoln's Inne | London (To be sent forward)

Postmark: 19/MR

Endorsement (Fortescue's): Mr Pope. | Mar. 18. 1732/3

---

*POPE *to* MALLET   18 *March* [1732/3]

The Hyde Collection

I shall be in Town for a Week in 4 or 5 days, in the Enterval at Twitnam, building. It comes into my mind to desire you to postpone publishing your Poem (in which Tibbald is touched upon with so much justice, as your subject required) till after he has had a Benefit-Night for a Play of his call'd *Secret Love* or some such name;³ It may perhaps, else, be some prejudice to him.

I have not forgot J. Dennis; if you find occasion, pray Extend my

---

¹ Sir Robert Walpole, probably.
² Mrs. Martha Blount.
³ Mallet's *Of Verbal Criticism* ultimately appeared after the third night (6 Apr.) of Theobald's *Fatal Secret*. It was advertised in *The Daily Journal*, 3 Apr., as to appear the 9th. Theobald's play ran only three nights. Professor Knox Chandler first brought these facts to the editor's attention.

Debt to you by giving him a little more.[1] Adieu. Why won't you visit Lord B.[2] who wishes you would?

I am ever sincerely | Yours | A. Pope.

March 18.

POPE *to* CARYLL   20 *March* 1732/3

Add. 28618

March 20th 1732/3.

I never think I can hear from you too often, tho' I am frequently hindered from making the replies I would, or so soon as I would. Your last gave me a greater pleasure than any of yours have done a great while, for it conveyed to me the assurance that I shall see you here for some days. Pray remember this promise and (not charge your memory too long with it) come and perform it soon.

The poem you writ to me of[3] prevails much in the opinion of the world and is better relished than at first, insomuch that I hear we are in a week or two, to have the second part to the same tune. I can't but say I think there is merit in it; and I perceive the divines have no objection to it, tho' now 'tis agreed not [to] be written by one, Dr Croxall, Dr Secker, and some others having solemnly denied it.[4]

I have little to say to you in this letter being much employed today with workmen, and tomorrow I go for London for some time upon business but not poetical. I've made noise enough for one winter, tho' I've done another of Horace's Satires since I wrote to you last, and much in the same space of time as I did the former (tho' you don't believe when I speak truth).[5] The next time I'll compliment my own work better, and pretend it cost me more pains.—You will be received here when you come with proper dignity by a triumphal arch, under which you shall be led into my garden. I hope 'twill be finished in three weeks, and that you'll be the first man to pass thro' it. I beg my sincere services may be accepted by Mr Caryll and Mrs Caryll, the *seniores et juniores*, and by Mrs Cath: Caryll, to all whom I wish a happy Easter. My mother continues, I thank God, pretty easy. Adieu. Believe me with truth and at all times | Dear sir, Yours faithfully | A: Pope.

---

[1] Evidently, even before writing a Prologue for Dennis's benefit (in Dec. 1733), Pope was giving some small financial aid to Dennis, and doing it indirectly.

[2] Probably Bolingbroke. It might be Bathurst or Burlington, but not probably.

[3] The *Essay on Man*.

[4] Samuel Croxall, D.D., was known as a poet for his imitations of Spenser and for his *Fair Circassian* (1720). Thomas Secker (at this time M.D.; later D.D. and Archbishop of Canterbury) is not known as a poet. See *DNB*.

[5] Evidently the Second Satire of the Second Book, not published until July 1734. See Pope to Swift, 2[o] Apr. 1733.

POPE *to* THE EARL OF OXFORD [1733]

Longleat Portland Papers, xii

My Lord,—First to the First—I find here Two red Lead pencils, one of which I presume is for me, & therfore I have taken it away (for it writes well)[1] leaving on the Tables a gold ring, & seal, & a Silver Standish, untouch'd.

Secondly, I sate up last night till I fell asleep in hopes to see your Lordship, & am gone home with Lord Burlington, who inspects my Portico this day by appointment.[2]

Thirdly, I beg your Lordship to send, (by some Sober Man who can Swear upon occasion) the Letter to Curll,[3] (which I promisd Sir W. Wyndham to do, & now cannot, being to stay many days in the Country.) I shall think it a particular obligation. He must read the Contents, that he may testify it to be the same paper. Fourthly, I beg you to believe I am ever mindful of all your favours, where ever I am; & ever, with the sincerest Truth & respect, My Lord Yours.

Endorsement (by Lord Oxford): Mr. Pope.

E. P. *to* CURLL[4]   27 *March* 1733

1735 g
                                                    March 27, 1733.

Sir,—In pursuance to your Advertisement desiring such Accounts of Mr *Pope as his Deserts demand,* I send you these *Anecdotes,* the Truth of which I can testify (and will, if called upon) as having been his School-fellow myself at the time.

The fact is very remarkable, as it is a proof of that *natural spleen* which constitutes his *Temperament,* and from which he has never deviated in the whole course of his Life.

The last School he was put to, before the twelfth Year of his Age, was in *Devonshire-Street* near *Bloomsbury,* there I also was, and the

---

1 The parenthesis is written with a pencil.
2 In his last letter to Burlington (iii. 356) this appointment had been solicited.
3 Just what grievance, among many, Pope was concerned about at this moment is difficult to determine. The letter of E. P., which follows this, suggests that Pope was taking a high tone so that Curll would not suspect his identity with E. P. In the *Life of Mr. John Gay* (pub. 5 Feb.) Curll had advertised, 'Mr. Pope's life is preparing for the press', and such an announcement would annoy. Most probably, however, he is raising some objection to material in *Achilles Dissected,* issued with the imprint of W. Mears, but probably Curll himself is the actual publisher. There on page 9 (note) Sir William Wyndham is mentioned as one of Gay's friends who had completed (i.e. in Curll's idiom *mangled*) *Achilles.*
4 This letter is from Curll's 'Initial Correspondence: or, Anecdotes of the Life and Family of Mr. Pope', and is found in pp. 6–7 of his second volume of *Mr. Pope's Literary Correspondence* (1735). The information as to the poet's schooling is so completely wrong that one assumes that it is fabricated by Pope in a wilful desire to mislead Curll. Pope did not reprint this letter, and it should not be lightly used as a source for authentic anecdote.

late Duke of *Norfolk*, at the same time. It was kept by one Bromley, a *Popish Renegado*, who had been a Parson, and was one of King *James's* Converts in *Oxford*, some Years after that Prince's Abdication;[1] he kept *a little Seminary*, till upon an advantageous offer made him, he went a *Travelling-Tutor* to the present Lord *Gage*.

Mr *Alexander Pope* before he had been four Months at this School (or was able to construe *Tully's Offices*) employed his Muse in satirizing his Master. It was a Libel of at least one hundred Verses, which a Fellow-Student having given information of, was found in his pocket, and the young Satirist was soundly whipp'd, and kept a Prisoner to his Room seven days; whereupon his Father fetch'd him away, and I have been told, he never went to School more.

How much *past Correction* has wrought upon him, the World is Judge; and how much *present* Correction might, may be collected from this sample. I thought it a curious Fact, and therefore it is at your service, as one of the Ornaments of this excellent Person's Life. | Your's, &c. | E. P.

SWIFT *to* POPE[2]   [31 *March* 1733]

Longleat Portland Papers, xiii (Harleian transcripts)

I have been out of order for some weeks past with that giddiness which you have often heard me talk of, & once saw me in. It was not very violent, but lasted longer, and now I am pretty near as I was before; an ill walker when it is dusky; this hindred me from answering your long kind letter, that began with your Epitaph upon our deceased friend.[3] I have not seen in so few lines more good sence, or more proper to the Subject.[4] Yet I will tell you my remarks and submit them. The whole is intended for an Apostrophe to the dead person, which however doth not appear till the eighth line, Therefore as I checkt a little at the article *the* twice used in the second line, I imagined it might be changed into *thy* and then the Apostrophe will appear at first, and be clearer to common readers. My Lord Orrery your great admirer saith

---

[1] His Name was William Bromley, Son of Henry Bromley, of Holt in Worcestershire Esq; He was entered a Gentleman-Commoner of Christ-Church-College, *Oxon*, 1673. See *Wood's Athen. Oxon*, p. 1063. Vol. II. Edit. ult.—Footnote in 1735 g (Curll). Since this Bromley (not to be confused with the Tory Speaker and Secretary of State of the same name) was in Parliament from 1689 to 1702, he was hardly a renegado schoolmaster.

[2] The date is found embedded in the middle of the letter. The date of the postmark, subscribed together with the address by Lord Oxford himself at the end, was written into the transcript as an addition. Lord Oxford wrote in as superscription: 'Dean Swift to Mr. Pope.' This transcript furnishes good evidence that Oxford read proof on the transcripts against the original letter—a fact that augments confidence in the authenticity of the text.

[3] In an account book in the Forster Collection (No. 511) Swift records, 'giddy from 4th, very ill on 14th'.—Ball, iv. 412 n.

[4] In his Life of Pope Dr. Johnson gives this epitaph a far more caustic review than does Swift.

the word *mixed* suits not so properly the Heroes busts, as the dust of Kings. Perhaps My Lord may be too exact, yet you may please to consider it. The beginning of the last Line, *striking their aking bosoms.* Those two participles come so near, and sounding so like, I could wish altered, if it might be easily done. The Scripture expression upon our Saviour's death is that the People *smote their breasts.* You will pardon me, for since I have left off writing, I am sunk into a Critick. Some Gentlemen here, object against the expression in the second line, *A Child's Simplicity.* Not against the propriety but in complyance with the vulgar, who cannot distinguish *Simplicity* & Folly. And it is argued that your Epitaph quite contrary to your other writings, will have a hundred vulgar Readers, for one who is otherwise, I confess, I lay little weight upon this, although some friends of very good understanding, and who have a great honor for you, mentioned it to me. As to our poor friend, I think the D. of Qu. hath acted a very noble & generous part. But before he did it, I wish there had been so much cunning used as to have let the Sisters know, that he expected they would let him dispose of Mr Gay's Writings as himself, and other friends should advise, and I heartily wish His Grace had entirely Stifled that Comedy[1] if it were possible, than do an injury to our friend's reputation only to get a hundred or two pounds to a couple of (perhaps) insignificant women. It hath been printed here, and I am grieved to say, it is a very poor performance. I have often Chid Mr Gay for not varying his Schemes, but still adhering to those that he had exhausted; and I much doubt whether the posthumous Fables will prove equal to the first. I think it is incumbent upon you to see that nothing more be publish'd of his that will lessen his reputation, for the sake of adding a few pence to his Sisters, who have already got so much by his death. If the case were mine, my ashes would rise in judgment against you. I had very lately the great honor and happiness of a long letter from the Dutchess, which I have already answered; She is so very good as to promise the Continuance of her favour, and to desire a correspondence with me, which would be so useless to her otherwise than upon the accidental occasion it began that I cannot have the assurance to think of it.—As to Mortality, it hath never been out of my head eighteen minutes these eighteen years, neither do I value it a rush further than as it parts a man from his friends for ever, and that Share of it, I have Suffered already, and am likely to suffer as long as I live. I only apprehend some difficultyes in Settling my affairs, which without my fault, have been long embroyled, and the trouble of prudent settling my little fortune to a publick use. For the rest, I rely on God's mercy, and will do as little hurt, and as much good as I can in the scrap of life that may be left me. I am so much of your mind concerning the morality of Poets; that I know not whither

---

[1] *Achilles.*

virtue can possibly find a corner to retire, except in the Hearts of men of Genius and Learning, and what you call their Levityes have not the least tinture of impiety, but directly otherwise, tend to drive vice out of the world. The Libel on Dr D— gave great offence here, or at least Lord Allen did all he could that might anger the Parliament; but some people of the House of Commons, thinking the Kingdom owed the Author some   ,[1] and knowing that Lord Cart—liked the thing, made them drop it. However you will make it live and on your account it shall not be suffered to be forgotten. March. 31.[2] This day I received the two Poems to my self,[3] and one for Dr D— we are not obliged to you; for all your things came[4] over quickly, and are immediately printed, in tolerable wealdable volumes, not your monstrous twelvepenny folio. By compairing Kingdoms I find England just out weighs 24 Irild, for we get a shillings worth here for a halfpenny, only yours yeilds a penny. Your imitation of Horace the work of two mornings, is reconed here by the best Judges (and with submission we are not without them) to be worth 2 years of any Poets life except yours. Nor is there any objections against that to Lord Bathurst, but that some parts of it are not so obvious to midling Readers. That beast call'd Aler Burnet[5] I have read, and may you ever have such adversarys. But the other supposed to be writ by my Lady Mary &c. I have not yet seen, they say here it is certainly hers. Faulkener would not print it, nor do I know whether any body here will but there are some copies come from your side.—How can I judge of your Schemes at this distance. I heard you intended four or five Poems addressed to as many friends; and can easily believe they would together make a System with connexion, and a good moral for the conduct of life. But I want to be deep among all yours and your Dawly neighbors papers for a few months. And my present thought is to come over towards August, and pass the Winter there, and return (with you) hither in Spring, if my health, and embroylments will any way permit me. But, there must be some stipulations for my riding, with other necessary postulatums, and ultimatums. I drink less than usual, but to drink so little as you or my Lord Bol— is not to be expected; and yet I do not love wine, but take it purely as a medecine and I love Mault liquor,

1 Vacant space is left in the transcript so that, as usual, Lord Oxford may fill in a word which the scribe could not decipher. His Lordship failed to insert the word [gratitude?] though he got 'owed' (four words earlier) and 'wealdable' a half-dozen lines below.
2 This dates the concluding parts of the letter at least. Ball dates the letter *30 March*.
3 Apparently duplicate copies of the Epistle to Bathurst and the Imitation of the First Satire of the Second Book for Swift, and single copies for Dr. Delany. As yet he has seen no part of the *Essay on Man*.
4 An error for *come*?
5 Supposed by Swift to be the author of *Achilles Dissected*. That work is by 'Mr. Burnet' if one accepts the title-page evidence, but it is signed at the end 'Atex. Burnet,' which Swift evidently concludes to be a misprint for 'Alex or Ale[xande]r.'

but dare not touch a drop. All victuals are equal to my affections, yet I dare not meddle with strong meats, so that you and I are valetudinarians of a direct contrary kind. I am almost every second day on horseback for about a dozen Miles. For the rest, easy enough; only a most severe Critick, and only to my Lord Bol— and you. I know not whether my spirits with the addition of Six years weight, will support me to see France. Lady Suffolk stopt that journey, I thank her for it among the rest of her favors. There hath been a strong controversy betwixt me and Lady E. Germ.[1] on the Subject of Lady Suff:—sencerity with Regard to our deceased friend and my self; for you are out of the case, who ask nothing, and despise every thing that a Court hath to give. But I lately cut that dispute short, & by that means shall probably lose Lady E—'s favor.—I was always proud and pleas'd with Lord Peter—s letters, and should ne'er have let any of them gone unanswered; and I humbly acknowledge his favor in saying he had writ twice, for which I shall soon return him my thanks, as I now do my most humble service, I would inclose this to his Lordship if I knew where to direct to him, for though every body knows he *is*, yet is it hard to know where, because I think he had no house in town when I saw you last. Dr D— entertains his friends once a week in form; and as often as they please on other days. He sticks to his old set, without Parade, but great hospitality and bears a great addition of fortune as well as any man I have known. I never mention to him the singularityes of Opinions in his Books; and he is as easy a man in conversation as I have known. If Mr Pilkington continues to preserve that modesty and humility in his behaviour, which I have so often recommended to him, he will be happy to deserve your countenance and protection. I hope your Dawly neighbor continues his health, and Spirits, He laughs at my precepts of thrift, which I am sure you do not, nor ever will to a Virtue that brings ease & liberty. He is befathered worse than poor Wycherley,[2] and in that is a very expensive unthinking young man. I did not scruple sending Lord Orrery a copy of the Epitaph; he is absolutly the most hopefull young Gentleman I ever saw, and seems to excell in every Virtue, as if he only intended to cultivate any particular one. He is now in the Country battleing the most villanous agent (next to Waters)[3] that ever mined Lord or Commoner. Are the Verses to Patty a thing to see light?[4] Lord Peter, Masham, Bathurst, Oxford, Boling—Mr Poulteny, the Dr Mr Lewis

---

[1] Lady Elizabeth Germaine.

[2] Bolingbroke's father was then eighty-one and lived to be ninety.—Ball, iv. 416 n.

[3] For Peter Walter, frequent butt of satire by Pope, Fielding, and others. He was an unscrupulous attorney among other things. 'Waters' is Pope's spelling in his imitation of the First Satire of the Second Book, l. 89 and elsewhere. See Butt, p. 13 n.

[4] Pope's Epistle to a Lady [Martha Blount] 'Of the Characters of Women' appeared in February of 1735.

and Patty are to be presented as usual with my most Humble service as occasion offers. I have answered the D—s of Qu— letter.

Address:[1] For Alexander Pope Esqr, at | Twitenham, in | Middlesex | By way of | London.
Postmark: April 16. 1733.

POPE *to* FORTESCUE [*April* 1733]

1797 (Polwhele, i, 323)
Monday, April.

I was two nights in town, and aimed at seeing you on both; but the cursed attendance on the excise bill deprived me of it, and I grumble with the rest upon that score at it.[2] Your present life is labour, I hope your future will be in more repose, and that you may sleep either on the bench or off, just as you please. Twickenham will be as much at the service of my lord judge, as it was of my learned council; and I flatter myself in the imagination that your hours and days in general will be more mine, when they are more yours. Adieu! and keep my secret as long as it will keep:[3] I think myself so happy in being approved by you, and some few others, that I care not for the public a jot.

Address: To Wm. Fortescue, esq. in Bell-yard, near Lincoln's Inn, London.

*POPE *to* THE EARL OF BURLINGTON[4] [1733?]

Chatsworth

My Lord,—I find it out of my power to come to morrow & stay so long as my Inclinations prompt me & your Indulgence would allow, for I must meet a man of business at 12 a clock in Town. If your Lordship shall be at leisure to send for me to London, on Tuesday night, & will please to leave word at Burlington house at what hour I shall be there, I will not fail. I am My Lord (in spite of all Criticks, from the Courts of St. James's to the Garrets of Grubstreet) for ever | Your most obliged & most | faithfully-obstinate Servant, | A. Pope.
My sincerest Respects | to My Lady.

Address: To the Rt. Hon. the Earl of Burlington.

---

[1] The address and postmark are transcribed by Lord Oxford himself.
[2] Evidently Fortescue was unwillingly held in town until Walpole withdrew his Excise Bill, as he did on Wednesday, 11 Apr. The month in the superscription was probably added by Fortescue.
[3] Concerning the authorship of the *Essay on Man*.
[4] The letter can hardly be surely dated. The parenthesis in the last sentence seems to indicate that March or April of 1733 is possible. Other periods possible would be the beginning of 1732 when Pope was attacked for his *Of Taste* (though the Court of St. James's was less evidently concerned then) or after Nov. 1733 when Lord Hervey's *Epistle from a Nobleman to a Doctor of Divinity* appeared. See also the following letter, to Lord Oxford.

POPE *to* THE EARL OF OXFORD

Longleat Portland Papers, xii

April. 17. 1733.

My Lord,—I am just going with Lord Burlington to Chiswick, & beg your Lordship to send me King Henry's Prayerbook, unless you would keep it longer. I hope in a few days to see your Lordship again, I thank you for a thousand things & wish you a thousand blessings. Ever your Lordships | faithful Servant | A. Pope.

Address: To the E. of Oxford.
Endorsement: A. Pope Esqr. | April. 17: 1733

†POPE *to* SWIFT¹

2[o] *April* 1733

1740

April 2, 1733

You say truly, that death is only terrible to us as it separates us from those we love, but I really think those have the worst of it who are left by us, if we are² true friends. I have felt more (I fancy) in the loss of poor Mr. Gay,³ than I shall suffer in the thought of going away myself into a state that can feel none of this sort of losses. I wish'd vehemently to have seen him in a condition of living independent, and to have lived in perfect indolence the rest of our days together, the two most idle, most innocent, undesigning Poets of our age. I now as vehemently wish, you and I might walk into the grave together, by as slow steps as you please, but contentedly and chearfully: Whether that ever can be, or in what country, I know no more, than into what country we shall walk out of the grave. But it suffices me to know it will be exactly what region or state our Maker appoints, and that whatever *Is*, is *Right*. Our poor friend's papers are partly in my hands, and for as much as is so, I will take care to suppress things unworthy of him. As to the Epitaph, I am sorry you gave a copy, for it will certainly by that means come into print, and I would correct it more, unless you will do it for me (and that I shall like as well:) Upon the whole I earnestly wish your coming over hither, for this reason among many others, that your influence may be join'd with mine to suppress whatever we may judge proper of his papers. To be plunged in my Neighbours and my papers, will be your inevitable fate as soon as you come. That I am an Author whose characters are thought of some weight,

---

¹ Ball (iv. 424–5) was the first to see that since this letter answers that of Swift of 31 Mar. (postmarked in London, 16 Apr. 1733), Pope's date of 2 Apr. is impossible. Ball's emendation to 20 is perhaps correct; but Swift's answer to the present letter is dated 1 May.
² who . . . if we are] who are *1742 La.*
³ of poor Mr. Gay] of Mr. Gay *1741 Labc*; *1742 Labc.*

reat noise and bustle that the Court and Town make
any give: and I will not render them less important or interesting,[1] by sparing Vice and Folly, or by betraying the cause of Truth
and Virtue. I will take care they shall be such as no man can be angry
at but the persons I would have angry. You are sensible with what
decency and justice I paid homage to the Royal Family, at the same
time that I satirized false Courtiers, and Spies, &c. about 'em. I have
not the courage however to be such a Satyrist as you, but I would be
as much, or more, a Philosopher. You call your satires, Libels; I
would rather call my satires, Epistles: They will consist more of
morality than wit,[2] and grow graver, which you will call duller. I shall
leave it to my Antagonists to be witty (if they can) and content myself
to be useful, and in the right. Tell me your opinion as to Lady M—'s
or Lord H—'s[3] performance? they are certainly the Top wits of the
Court, and you may judge by that single piece what can be done against
me; for it was labour'd, corrected, præcommended and post-disapprov'd, so far as to be dis-own'd by themselves, after each had highly
cry'd it up for the others. I have met with some complaints, and heard
at a distance of some threats, occasion'd by my satires:[4] I sent fair
messages to acquaint them where I was to be found in town, and to
offer to call at their houses to satisfy them, and so it dropp'd. It is very
poor in any one to rail and threaten at a distance, and have nothing to
say to you when they see you.—I am glad you persist and abide by so
good a thing as that Poem, in which I am immortal for my Morality:
I never took any praise so kindly, and yet I think I deserve that praise
better than I do any other.—When does your Collection come out,
and what will it consist of?[5] I have but last week finished another of
my Epistles, in the order of the system; and this week[6] (*exercitandi
gratia*) I have translated, or rather parody'd, another of Horace's, in
which I introduce you advising me about my expences, house-keeping,
&c. But these things shall lye by, till you come to carp at 'em, and alter
rhymes, and grammar, and triplets, and cacaphonies of all kinds. Our
Parliament will sit till Midsummer, which I hope may be a motive

---

[1] or interesting] or less interesting *1741 Labc*; *1742 Labc*.
[2] than wit] that of wit *1741 Labc*; *1742 Labc*.
[3] *Verses addressed to the Imitator of the First Satire of the Second Book of Horace* appeared
8 Mar. in an edition with the indication on the title-page 'By a Lady'. The next day another
edition, printed for Roberts, appeared without indication of any author. It wrongly called
itself the more correct edition. The Dublin editions (1741 Dab) print *M—y's* and *H—y's*
in place of M— and H—.
[4] satires] verses *1741 Labc*; *1742 Labc*.
[5] No 'Collection' has before been mentioned in the extant correspondence. Swift's *Works*
(4 v) came out in 1735. See D. Nichol Smith, *Letters of Swift to Ford*, pp. 153–4, for the
first mention to Ford of this project. It had been mentioned to Motte, however.
[6] Pope, as has been remarked, is casual and unreliable in statements concerning time. In
a letter to Caryll, 20 Mar., he has already done this satire, the Second of the Second Book.
In its printed form Bethel becomes the Ofellus, but Swift speaks in ll. 161–4.

POPE *to* THE EARL OF OXFORD   17 *April* 1733

Longleat Portland Papers, xii

April. 17. 1733.

My Lord,—I am just going with Lord Burlington to Chiswick, & beg your Lordship to send me King Henry's Prayerbook, unless you would keep it longer. I hope in a few days to see your Lordship again, I thank you for a thousand things & wish you a thousand blessings.

Ever your Lordships | faithful Servant | A. Pope.

Address: To the E. of Oxford.
Endorsement: A. Pope Esqr. | April. 17: 1733

†POPE *to* SWIFT[1]   2[0] *April* 1733

1740

April 2, 1733

You say truly, that death is only terrible to us as it separates us from those we love, but I really think those have the worst of it who are left by us, if we are[2] true friends. I have felt more (I fancy) in the loss of poor Mr. Gay,[3] than I shall suffer in the thought of going away myself into a state that can feel none of this sort of losses. I wish'd vehemently to have seen him in a condition of living independent, and to have lived in perfect indolence the rest of our days together, the two most idle, most innocent, undesigning Poets of our age. I now as vehemently wish, you and I might walk into the grave together, by as slow steps as you please, but contentedly and chearfully: Whether that ever can be, or in what country, I know no more, than into what country we shall walk out of the grave. But it suffices me to know it will be exactly what region or state our Maker appoints, and that whatever *Is*, is *Right*. Our poor friend's papers are partly in my hands, and for as much as is so, I will take care to suppress things unworthy of him. As to the Epitaph, I am sorry you gave a copy, for it will certainly by that means come into print, and I would correct it more, unless you will do it for me (and that I shall like as well:) Upon the whole I earnestly wish your coming over hither, for this reason among many others, that your influence may be join'd with mine to suppress whatever we may judge proper of his papers. To be plunged in my Neighbours and my papers, will be your inevitable fate as soon as you come. That I am an Author whose characters are thought of some weight,

---

[1] Ball (iv. 424–5) was the first to see that since this letter answers that of Swift of 31 Mar. (postmarked in London, 16 Apr. 1733), Pope's date of 2 Apr. is impossible. Ball's emendation to 20 is perhaps correct; but Swift's answer to the present letter is dated 1 May.
[2] who . . . if we are] who are *1742 La*.
[3] of poor Mr. Gay] of Mr. Gay *1741 Labc*; *1742 Labc*.

appears from the great noise and bustle that the Court and Town make about any I give: and I will not render them less important or interesting,[1] by sparing Vice and Folly, or by betraying the cause of Truth and Virtue. I will take care they shall be such as no man can be angry at but the persons I would have angry. You are sensible with what decency and justice I paid homage to the Royal Family, at the same time that I satirized false Courtiers, and Spies, &c. about 'em. I have not the courage however to be such a Satyrist as you, but I would be as much, or more, a Philosopher. You call your satires, Libels; I would rather call my satires, Epistles: They will consist more of morality than wit,[2] and grow graver, which you will call duller. I shall leave it to my Antagonists to be witty (if they can) and content myself to be useful, and in the right. Tell me your opinion as to Lady M—'s or Lord H—'s[3] performance? they are certainly the Top wits of the Court, and you may judge by that single piece what can be done against me; for it was labour'd, corrected, præcommended and post-disapprov'd, so far as to be dis-own'd by themselves, after each had highly cry'd it up for the others. I have met with some complaints, and heard at a distance of some threats, occasion'd by my satires:[4] I sent fair messages to acquaint them where I was to be found in town, and to offer to call at their houses to satisfy them, and so it dropp'd. It is very poor in any one to rail and threaten at a distance, and have nothing to say to you when they see you.—I am glad you persist and abide by so good a thing as that Poem, in which I am immortal for my Morality: I never took any praise so kindly, and yet I think I deserve that praise better than I do any other.—When does your Collection come out, and what will it consist of?[5] I have but last week finished another of my Epistles, in the order of the system; and this week[6] (*exercitandi gratia*) I have translated, or rather parody'd, another of Horace's, in which I introduce you advising me about my expences, house-keeping, &c. But these things shall lye by, till you come to carp at 'em, and alter rhymes, and grammar, and triplets, and cacaphonies of all kinds. Our Parliament will sit till Midsummer, which I hope may be a motive

[1] or interesting] or less interesting *1741 Labc*; *1742 Labc.*

[2] than wit] that of wit *1741 Labc*; *1742 Labc.*

[3] *Verses addressed to the Imitator of the First Satire of the Second Book of Horace* appeared 8 Mar. in an edition with the indication on the title-page 'By a Lady'. The next day another edition, printed for Roberts, appeared without indication of any author. It wrongly called itself the more correct edition. The Dublin editions (1741 Dab) print *M—y's* and *H—y's* in place of M— and H—.

[4] satires] verses *1741 Labc*; *1742 Labc.*

[5] No 'Collection' has before been mentioned in the extant correspondence. Swift's *Works* (4 v) came out in 1735. See D. Nichol Smith, *Letters of Swift to Ford*, pp. 153–4, for the first mention to Ford of this project. It had been mentioned to Motte, however.

[6] Pope, as has been remarked, is casual and unreliable in statements concerning time. In a letter to Caryll, 20 Mar., he has already done this satire, the Second of the Second Book. In its printed form Bethel becomes the Ofellus, but Swift speaks in ll. 161–4.

to bring you rather in summer than so late as autumn: you use¹ to love what I hate, a hurry of politicks, &c. Courts I see not, Courtiers I know not, Kings I adore not, Queens I compliment not; so I am never like to be in fashion, nor in dependance. I heartily join with you in pitying our poor Lady² for her unhappiness, and should only pity her more, if she had more of what they at Court call Happiness. Come then, and perhaps we may go all together into France at the end of the season, and compare the Liberties of both kingdoms. Adieu. Believe me dear Sir, (with a thousand warm wishes, mix'd with short sighs) ever yours.

†SWIFT *to* POPE³   1 *May* 1733

1741 La

Dublin, May 1, 1733.

I answer your Letter the sooner because I have a particular reason for doing so. Some weeks ago came over a Poem call'd, *The Life and Character of Dr. S. written by Himself*,⁴ it was re-printed here, and is dedicated to you. It is grounded upon a Maxim in Rochefoucault, and the Dedication after a formal story says, that my manner of writing is to be found in every line. I believe I have told you, that I writ a year or two ago near five hundred lines upon the same Maxim in Roche-foucault, and was a long time about it, as that Impostor says in his Dedication, with many circumstances, all pure invention. I desire you to believe, and to tell my friends, that in this spurious piece there is not a single line, or bit of a line, or thought, any way resembling the genuine Copy, any more than it does Virgil's Aeneis, for I never gave a Copy of mine, nor lent it out of my sight. And although I shew'd it to all common acquaintance indifferently, and some of them, (especially one or two females) had got many lines by heart, here and there, and repeated them often; yet it happens that not one single line or thought is contained in this Imposture, although it appears that they who counterfeited me had heard of the true one. But even this trick shall not provoke me to print the true one, which indeed is not proper to be seen till I can be seen no more: I therefore desire you will undeceive

---

¹ use] us'd *1741 Labc; 1742 Labc.*   ² The Countess of Suffolk, probably.

³ This is one of the letters not included in the 1740 volume but added in Pope's published editions (1741 Labc, &c.) and reprinted by Faulkner (1741 Dab) in his Supplement. For a fuller text of this letter see vol. v, pp. 10–13.

⁴ The genuine verses, under this Title, were first printed by G. Faulkner in Dublin, 1739.—footnote in 1741 Dab. Since the dedication to Pope is signed L.M. and dated 'From my Chambers in the Inner Temple, Lond. Apr. 1. 1733', Swift either got a copy fari n advance of publication or else his 'some weeks ago' is implicitly exaggeration. On the matter of this obscure publication in London see Swift's *Poems* (ed. Williams), pp. 541–3. One may suspect that Mrs. Laetitia Pilkington was one of the 'females' who memorized parts of the poem and extemporized the rest for publication. Swift's protestations here are extreme, however.

my friends, and I will order an Advertisement to be printed here, and transmit it to England, that every body may know the delusion, and acquit me, as I am sure you must have done your self, if you have read any part of it, which is mean, and trivial, and full of that Cant that I most despise: I would sink to be a Vicar in Norfolk, rather than be charged with such a performance. Now I come to your Letter.

When I was of your age, I thought every day of death, but now every minute; and a continual giddy disorder more or less is a greater addition than that of my years. I cannot affirm that I pity our friend Gay, but I pity his friends, I pity you, and would at least equally pity myself, if I liv'd amongst you; because I should have seen him oftner than you did; who are a kind of Hermit, how great a noise soever you make by your Ill nature, in not letting the honest Villains of the times enjoy themselves in this world, which is their only happiness, and terrifying them with another. I should have added in my Libel, that of all men living you are the most happy in your Enemies and your Friends: And I will swear you have fifty times more Charity for mankind than I could ever pretend to.

Whether the production you mention came from the Lady or the Lord, I did not imagine that they were at least so bad versifyers. Therefore, *facit indignatio versus*,[1] is only to be apply'd when the indignation is against general Villany, and never operates when some sort of people write to defend themselves. I love to hear them reproach you for dulness; only I would be satisfy'd, since you are so dull, why are they so angry? give me a shilling, and I will ensure you, that posterity shall never know you had one single enemy, excepting those whose memory you have preserv'd.

I am sorry for the situation of Mr. Gays papers. You do not exert yourself as much as I could wish in this affair. I had rather the two sisters were hang'd than see his works swell'd by any loss of credit to his memory. I would be glad to see the most valuable printed by themselves, those which ought not to be seen burn'd immediately, and the others that have gone abroad printed separately like opuscula, or rather be stifled and forgotten. I thought your Epitaph was immediately to be ingrav'd, and therefore I made less scruple to give a Copy to Lord Orrery, who earnestly desir'd it, but to no body else; and he tells me, he gave only two, which he will recall. I have a short Epigram of his upon it, wherein I would correct a line, or two at most, and then I will send it you (with his permission.) I have nothing against yours, but the last line, *Striking their aching*,[2] the two participles, as they are so near,

---

[1] This motto appears in the title-page of *Verses addressed to the Imitator of . . . Horace* 'by a Lady'.

[2] For *aching* Pope substituted *pensive*. Swift had made the same criticism in his earlier letter of [31 Mar.].

seem to sound too like. I shall write to the Duchess, who hath lately honoured me with a very friendly letter, and I will tell her my opinion freely about our friend's papers. I want health, and my affairs are enlarged: but I will break through the latter, if the other mends. I can use a course of medicines, lame and giddy. My chief design next to seeing you is to be a severe Critick on you and your neighbour;[1] but first kill his father, that he may be able to maintain me in my own way of living, and particularly my horses. It cost me near 600*l.* for a wall to keep mine, and I never ride without two servants for fear of accidents; *hic vivimus ambitiosa paupertate.* You are both too poor for my acquaintance, but he much the poorer. With you I will find grass, and wine, and servants, but with him not.[2]—The Collection you speak of is this. A Printer[3] came to me to desire he might print my works (as he call'd them) in four volumes by subscription. I said I would give no leave, and should be sorry to see them printed here. He said they could not be printed in London, I answer'd, they could, if the Partners agreed. He said he "would be glad of my permission, but as he could print them without it, and was advis'd that it could do me no harm, and having been assur'd of numerous subscriptions, he hoped I would not be angry at his pursuing his own interest," &c.[4] Much of this discourse past, and he goes on with the matter, wherein I determine not to intermeddle, although it be much to my discontent; and I wish it could be done in England, rather than here, although I am grown pretty indifferent in every thing of that kind. This is the truth of the story.

My Vanity turns at present on being personated in your *Quae Virtus,*[5] &c. You will observe in this letter many marks of an ill head and a low spirit; but a Heart wholly turned to love you with the greatest Earnestness and Truth.

POPE *to* CARYLL   6 *May* 1733

Add. 28618

6. May. 1733.

The limits of this paper (and 'tis all I have just now) will save you the pains of reading much of my scrawl, but I would willingly express very strongly my thanks, & my desires of seeing you as you promise at the

---

[1] Lord Bolingbroke.
[2] This sentence is omitted in 1742 La, but not in 1742 Lbc.
[3] George Faulkner, Bookseller in Dublin,—footnote in 1742 La.
[4] The passage placed by Pope in quotation marks is one of a half-dozen or more so treated by him to call attention to the conditions under which the Swift–Pope correspondence was published. Pope explains this procedure in 'The Booksellers to the Reader' in 1741 Lab. Curll (1741 Lc) omits this prefatory statement.
[5] The Second Satire of the Second Book of Horace begins thus.

close of Whitsunweek or the beginning of the week after. I would give you the trouble of one line more to tell me which, and nothing of business or amusement shall, I assure you, prevent me enjoying a satisfaction I have so long desired. As to your God-daughter and my friend there's little hopes of seeing her; for they made the house at Petersham so uneasy last summer that 'twas agreed to put it off, tho' I should have thought to have kept that of 20ll. a year, and put off the London one of 45l. had been wiser, since a lodging for three months might have served as well there. But the elder sister is in eternal youth. I lament for poor Patty whose health is concerned as well as her quiet, and both which have been sacrificed to their humour these many years. I have often in my mind reflected on a saying in Scripture *those who love the wicked shall perish with them.* 'Tis pity it should ever be her case. It was she that sent you those pamphlets, and is always enquiring for any that may be worth your reading. She desired me to complain to you how very long it is since she heard from Mrs Caryll, and would have written to you, but that I undertook to say this for her, with her faithful respects and duty to you both. I long to see you. I'll say no more till I can say all, tho' all will be very short of my affection for you, who am entirely | Dear sir | Your most obliged and faith-|ful humble servant | A. Pope.

HILL *to* POPE   16 *May* 1733

1753 (Hill)

May 16, 1733.

I can assure you, with great truth and pleasure, that I never pass a day without thinking of you: And, but for this, I should be ashamed to remember, how long it is since I ought to have thanked you, for an imitation not to be imitated. I must own, there is a spirit, in the honest vivacity of that piece, that charmed me to the soul. In your other writings, I am pleased by the *poet*; I am, here, in love with the *man*:

I was, lately, looking among my papers, and met with the copy of some lines, I sent you, five or six years ago, from *Newcastle*, in one of my journeys to *Scotland.*—It was loosely, and negligently dressed; and, designing to let it be seen in the world, I have brushed off the dust of the road, and, I wish I could say, made it fit for your reception.

In a conversation, a year or two since, concerning the affairs of the stage, you told me, that there was a patent, in the hands of one of the *Davenants*, of which no use was made, and which you seem'd to think it easy to procure an assignment of.

Methinks, this must have been the *Killygrew patent*; for *that*, which was granted to Sir *William Davenant*, is the patent, under which Mr. *Rich* now acts.

I should be very much obliged to you, for an information, of what you know, concerning this patent; you shall shortly have my reason for this curiosity in, | Dear Sir, Yours, &c. | A. Hill.

POPE *to* HILL   22 *May* 1733

1751 (Hill)

Twickenham, May 22. 1733.

Sir,—Your very kind Letter came hither in my Absence, which occasion'd my Delay till now in acknowledging it. Your Partiality to me, both as a Poet, and as a Man, is great; the former I deserve not, but the latter I will never forfeit. It would be wronging your Modesty to say much of the Verses you inclose, but it would be wronging Sense and Poetry, not to say they are fine ones, and such as I could not forget, having once seen them.

I have almost forgot what I told you of the Patent; but at the Time I told it, I could not well be mistaken, having just then had the Account from Mr. *Davenant* the Envoy: Indeed I fansy it was only of his Ancestors Patent that he spoke (unless Sir *William Davenant* bought up *Killigrew*'s); I know no Way of coming to the Knowledge of this Affair, Mr. *Davenant* being now abroad, and I know not where. But if you would have me write about it, I will learn his Direction.

I am at all Times glad to hear of you, on any Occasion. I would willingly wait on you in the Park,[1] if I knew your Times: I have call'd twice or thrice there in vain, without being heard. I guess'd you were in the Country. My sincere good Wishes attend you; and your agreeable Family, as far as I have seen of it, I cannot but wish well to. I am, Dear Sir, | Your most affectionate | and faithful Servant, | A. Pope.

POPE *to* THE EARL OF OXFORD   25 *May* 1733

Longleat Portland Papers, xii

My Lord,—The Honour you did me in remembring (what every one here, & myself, forgot) my Birthday,[2] ought to make me happy & vain. And that Lady Margaret should be the person to record so inconsiderable a thing in her memory (if possible) would make me vainer. But all I can do, is to assure you all, that What ever was the Day of my Birth, the Whole Life is at the Service of your Lordship and your Family. I hope to wait on you in a few days, & to acknowledge This Favor in particular. My Mother has an urgent Desire to thank

---

[1] Hill lived in Petty France (now York Street) near St. James's Park.
[2] Pope was born on 21 May 1688.

my Lady Oxford & Lady Margaret in Person for this great honour
done her Son.

I am Sincerely & respectfully theirs, & | My Lord, | Your Ever
faithful | Servant | A. Pope.

Address: To the right Hon: the Earl | of Oxford.
Endorsement (by Lord Oxford): Friday morning. | may. 25 1733
Endorsement (by a secretary): Mr. Pope | May the 25th 1733

†POPE *to* SWIFT   28 *May* 1733

1740
                                                                      May 28, 1733
I have begun two or three letters to you by snatches, and been prevented from finishing them by a thousand avocations and dissipations.
I must first acknowledge the honour done me by Lord Orrery, whose
praises are that precious ointment Solomon speaks of, which can be
given only by men of Virtue: All other praise, whether from Poets or
Peers, is contemptible alike: and I am old enough and experienced
enough to know, that the only praises worth having, are those bestowed *by* Virtue *for* Virtue. My Poetry I abandon to the criticks, my
Morals I commit to the testimony of those who know me: and therefore I was more pleas'd with your Libel, than with any Verses I ever
receiv'd. I wish such a collection of your writings could be printed
here, as you mention going on in Ireland; I was surprized to receive
from the Printer that spurious piece call'd, The Life and character of
Dr. Swift, with a letter telling me the person who 'publish'd it had
assur'd him the Dedication to me was what I would not take ill, or
else he would not have printed it.' I can't tell who the man is, who
took so far upon him as to answer for my way of thinking; tho' had the
thing been genuine, I should have been greatly displeas'd at the publisher's part, in doing it without your knowledge.

I am as earnest as you can be, in doing my best to prevent the publishing of any thing unworthy of Mr. Gay; but I fear his friends
partiality. I wish you would come over. All the mysteries of my philosophical work shall then be clear'd to you, and you will not think of
me as you do of Dr. Y.[1] that[2] I am not merry enough, nor angry
enough: It will not want for Satire, but as for Anger I know it not;
or at least only that sort of which the Apostle speaks, "Be ye angry and
sin not."

My Neighbour's[3] writings have been metaphysical, and will next
be historical. It is certainly from him only, that a valuable History of

---

[1] Dr. Y] Dr. Young *1741 Dab*. See v. 11.
[2] think of me . . . that] think that *1741 Labc; 1742 Labc*.
[3] Bolingbroke.—footnote in 1741 Dab.

Europe in these latter times can be expected. Come, and quicken him; for age, indolence, and contempt of the world, grow upon men apace, and may often make the wisest indifferent whether posterity be any wiser than we. To a man in years, Health and Quiet become such rarities, and consequently so valuable, that he is apt to think of nothing more than of enjoying them whenever he can, for the remainder of life; and this I doubt not has caus'd so many great men to die without leaving a scrap to posterity.

I am sincerely troubled for the bad account you give of your own health. I wish every day to hear a better, as much as I do to enjoy my own, I faithfully assure you.[3]

POPE *to* CARYLL   *2 June* 1733

Add. 28618

2 June 1733.

'Tis purely to thank you for so very kind and distinguishing a mark of your favour and friendship to me as your last visit truly was, that I now write so soon. But it will be very long before I shall forget this and other proofs of my friend's humanity now experienced near thirty years. I am particularly impatient to hear that your journey did you no harm, especially since your lameness was so much upon you. I hope you found all your worthy family in as complete health as I wish them all. The company with whom I parted from you, drank your health together, and your good journey, that evening with much affection. Your god-daughter and [my friend] expressed equal concern that she could see you no longer. I stayed two days in town, and at my return found my poor mother much worse than you saw her. Indeed her weakness increases daily and the slightest accident would be fatal.[1] God grant her exit may be as easy as her life has been innocent, and then God send me such a life and such a death. Believe me, dear sir, with a sincere and true sense of your goodness, and ever praying for a due reward of it | Your most faithful, affectionate friend and real servant | A. Pope.

Sir Clement Cottrell[2] is here and sends you his unceremonious services.

---

[1] It seems probable that Mrs. Pope's state was such that she was unaware whether her son was at home or not—at least he seems to have been from home for a few days at a time more frequently during the first part of this year than had been the case. She died five days after this letter was written.

[2] Sir Clement, a Twickenham neighbour, was at Court the Master of Ceremonies; hence *unceremonious*, jocosely used.

[3] Pope omitted to print a postscript here added by Pulteney. See below, iii. 380.

POPE *to* FORTESCUE¹   7 *June* 1733

Arthur A. Houghton, Jr.

June 7. 1733²

It is indeed a Grief to mee which I cannot express, and which I should hate my own Heart if it did not feel, & yet wish no Friend I have ever should feel. All our Passions are Inconsistencies, & our very Reason is no better. But we are what we were Made to be.

Adieu, it will be a Comfort to me to see you on Saturday night Believe me truly Dear Sir | yours. | A. Pope

Address: To | Wm Fortescue Esq.

†POPE *to* JONATHAN RICHARDSON³   10 *June* 1733

1737

Twickenham, 10 June 1733

As I know, you and I mutually desire to see one another, I hoped that this day our wishes would have met, and brought you hither. And this for the very reason which possibly might hinder your coming, that my poor Mother is dead.⁴ I thank God, her death was as easy, as her life was innocent; and as it cost her not a groan, or even a sigh, there is yet upon her countenance such an expression of Tranquillity, nay almost of pleasure, that far from horrid,⁵ it is even amiable to behold it. It wou'd afford the finest Image of a Saint expir'd, that ever Painting drew; and it wou'd be the greatest obligation which even That obliging Art could ever bestow on a friend, if you cou'd come and sketch it for me.⁶ I am sure, if there be no very prevalent obstacle, you will leave any common business to do this: and I hope to see you this evening as late as you will, or to morrow morning as early, before this Winter-flower is faded. I will defer her interment till to morrow night. I know

¹ Printed from a transcript of the original made by Professor G. Tillotson. It was first printed by Rebecca Warner.

² Pope first wrote the date as Janʸ 7, but corrected it to June. The letter concerns the death of his mother, which had occurred on the 7th. She was buried on the night of the 11th (Monday) in Twickenham Church. According to *The Universal Spectator* (16 June 1733), 'The Supporters of her Pall were six of the poorest and oldest Women in the Parish, and six of the poorest and oldest Men to carry her Corpse; they all had Mourning except Gloves or Hatbands, which were not allow'd to the Minister, nor any Body to follow the Corpse.' The newspaper wrongly stated that she 'died very rich'. She was baptized on 18 June 1642; but her son thought she was 93 years old at the time of her death.

³ In his editions of 1737 Pope gave this letter the heading 'To Mr. —'. In 1739 and thereafter it was amplified to 'To Mr. Richardson'.

⁴ Mrs. Pope dyed the seventh of June, 1733, aged 93.—Pope, 1737–42. (Mrs. Pope was born in 1642.)

⁵ far from horrid] *omitted in 1742 e.*

⁶ The drawing was made, and is reproduced as frontispiece in Elwin–Courthope, vol. viii.

you love me, or I cou'd not have written this—I could not (at this time) have written at all.—Adieu! May you dye as happily! Your, &c.

POPE *to* CARYLL   25 *June* 1733

Add. 28618

25 June 1733.

I found you too true a prophet; but God's will be done. Reason and religion both tell me it is best; but affection will not be on their side, and I'm really more troubled than I would own. The very habitude of so many years, if there were little affection would have this effect, for men are creatures more of habit than principle. But in a word not [to] seem a better man than I am, my attendance upon her living was not virtue, but only duty, and my Melancholy for her dead, is not virtue but weakness. I thank God her life was innocent her death easy, and her state, I doubt not, happy. May yours and mine be just the same!

To see you at Ladyholt was the first thought I had upon this event, but as it is a great and new Æra of my life, and upon which the whole course of it will in a manner change, I must pause awhile to look about me. In the first place, I am acting like one that may die my self, and settling all that belongs to me, or may (thro' me) affect any others. I am paying all I owe, and disposing all my papers, &c., before I leave this place, to which I have no intentions to return a good while, it is become so melancholy to me.[1] I cannot therefore comply with so kind an invitation as you make me so soon, or if I did, it could be but 2 or 3 days or so. I rather think to come to you from Southampton in a month or less when I must be a few days with Lord Peterborough, than to make two journeys of what I may easily accomplish by one. Your god-daughter sends you her duty and service and wished to have had a longer and nearer conference with you, than that day she had here would afford. My sincere services attend you all. My health is but indifferent and that yours mends would be a piece of news always agreeable to him who is with due esteem | Dear sir | Your most affect. obliged friend and humble | servant | A. Pope.

---

[1] The letter is obviously written from Twickenham. Either its date is wrong or else Pope is exaggerating when he tells Bethel (letter of 9 Aug.), 'I was but four days at Twickenham since . . . .' William Pulteney had seen Caryll lame (cf. Pope to Caryll, 2 June 1733) at Pope's house (in May) and writes him on 14 July: 'I was very much concern'd to see you so Lame at Mr Pope's but hope you have now e're this quite recovered your strength. The Little Man is truly afflicted for the Loss of his Mother & tho' he has been for many years in dayly Expectation of her Death yet when the Blow comes it allways gives a shock to a good Natur'd Mind. He has for this reason quitted his house at Twittenham for some time, and gon to Lord Cobham's.'—Add. 28618, f. 118. See also Pope to Caryll, 27 Aug. 1733.

SWIFT *to* POPE¹   [*Summer of* 1733?]

1820 (Spence, p. 350)

[EXCERPT?]

Dear Pope, Though the little fellow that brings this be a justice of peace, and a member of our Irish House of Commons; yet he may not be altogether unworthy of your acquaintance.

POPE *to* FORTESCUE²   [? *July* 1733]

Professor C. B. Tinker

Friday

I have been hinderd by an accident of Ceremony, which could not be waved, from lying at your house last night or this. I must just look at my own home to morrow, & as it is Saturday, wish for your company. I am to be conveyd by a Party of your Friend, Miss Patty Blunt, who never having seen you of late, desires you will be of it. We go to pass some hours at Chiswick Gardens,³ & set out by water from Whitehall at 8 to morrow morn: thence I would attend you home. I could be glad you had leisure to do this, which would be a true pleasure to | Your ever obligd Friend & | faithful Servant | A. Pope.

A word in answer will find me at Lord Bathurst's.

Address: To | Wm Fortescue Esq. | in Bellyard, by | Lincolns Inn.
Endorsement: Mr Pope | 1733.

POPE *to* FORTESCUE⁴   [*July* 1733?]

1797 (Polwhele, i. 322)

Lady Gerard was to see Chiswick gardens, (as I imagined) and there-

¹ Spence identifies the 'little fellow' in the sentence that introduces this bit from an otherwise unknown letter. He observes: 'Doctor Swift gave Mr. Coote, a gentleman of very good character and fortune, a letter of recommendation to Mr. Pope, couched in the following terms.' In the early thirties Swift was frequently sending over Irish friends with letters of introduction to Pope, and since the Duchess of Queensberry (10 Nov. 1733; Ball, v. 41) thanks Swift for helping her to Mr. Coote's acquaintance, one may guess that he was in England, armed with such letters, in 1733. Ball (i. 281) gives an account of Coote, who had long been Swift's friend. Apparently he ceased to be a justice of the King's Bench upon the accession of George I. The letter of Swift to Pope was communicated to Spence by 'Mr. Jones, of Welwyn'. The Rev. J. Jones of Welwyn was a friend of Edward Young of *Night Thoughts* fame. See Spence, p. 455.

² The year comes from Fortescue's endorsement. The letter seems written during the time after Mrs. Pope's death when Pope might 'just look' at his villa, and go home for the night with Fortescue.   ³ Where Burlington's Palladian villa now stood.

⁴ This letter is placed on the hypothesis that it is written on Saturday after Pope had shown Martha Blount and her friend Lady Gerard Burlington's gardens. The ladies had to leave; but Pope stayed hoping in vain for the arrival of Fortescue and his sister. Pope is staying at Chiswick for the night, but will be home by noon tomorrow, unless Fortescue shows up at Chiswick by 10 a.m. The placing is obviously completely hypothetical.

fore forced to go from hence by five; it was a mortification to Mrs.
Blount to go, when there was a hope of seeing you and Mrs. Fortescue.
I can't get back to night for want of a vehicle, but will be at home by
eleven or twelve by water, ready to go with you to Jervas, unless you
all care to come and see Chiswick in the morning by ten, which if you
do not, I will set out on my voyage. Adieu! dear Sir.

Address: To Mr. Fortescue.

*POPE *to* FORTESCUE¹   [*July* 1733]

Harvard University

As soon as I got home, I found a Message from Lady Suffolk & Lord
Cobham, that they would make their Party of dining at my house next
Saturday, which cuts off my hopes of going with you to Chiswick;
but not of meeting you at Twitnam or Richmond, or any where, the
ensuing Week. Adieu. & let us meet the sooner the better. This
obliges me to be gone to morrow.
    I am Ever unfeignedly yours, | A. Pope

Thursday | night
Address: To | Wm Fortescue Esqr in | Bellyard, near | Lincolns-Inne.
Endorsement: Mr Pope | July 1733
Postmark: PENNY POST PAYD

‖SWIFT *to* POPE²   8 *July* 1733

1913 (Ball, v. 1–5)   Dublin, July 8, 1733

⌐I have been often prevented from answering your last kind letter by
my old disorder of giddiness and abundance of very impertinent business; and all my few hours of health and leisure I employ in riding or
walking. We are all here so fond of my Lord Orrery's good qualities,
that we think if he had leisure and inclination for verse, he would not
fail as to the want of a genius, and in all other points, I have not known
for his age a more valuable person. I therefore hope there will be a
friendship cultivated between you. As to the printing of my things
going on here, it is an evil I cannot prevent. I shall not be a penny the
richer. Some friends correct the errors, and now and then I look on

---

¹ Fortescue's endorsements are usually accurate, and consequently this letter must be
written on a Thursday (5, 12, 19, 26) in July.
² Most of this letter appears in Pope's own editions (1740–2). His extensive omissions
improved the tone of the letter perhaps, but since Ball first printed the entire text (from a
transcript of a transcript preserved at Welbeck Abbey), his text is here given. Apart from
omissions, indicated here by half-brackets, Pope's text follows that here given with hardly
a change. Of course Ball's text is modernized.

them for a minute or two. But all things except friendship and conversation are become perfectly indifferent to me, and yet I wish this collection could have been made on your side, and if I were younger, it would be some mortification to have it as it is.⌐

⌐Before I go further⌐ I must condole with you for the loss of Mrs. Pope, of whose death the papers have been full. But I would rather rejoice with you, because if any circumstances can make the death of a dear parent and friend a subject for joy, you have them all. She died in an extreme old age, without pain, under the care of the most dutiful son that I have ever known or heard of, which is a felicity not happening to one in a million. The worst effect of her death falls upon me, and so much the worse, because I expected, *aliquis damno usus in illo*,[1] that it would be followed by making me and this kingdom happy with your presence. But I am told, to my great misfortune, that a very convenient offer happening ⌐of a coach with one gentleman and his sister coming to Ireland from their elder brother,[2] your friend and neighbour,⌐ you waived the invitation pressed on you, alleging the fear you had of being killed here with eating and drinking; by which I find that you have given some credit to a notion of our great plenty and hospitality. It is true our meat and wine is cheaper[3] here, as it is[4] always in the poorest countries, because there is no money to pay for them. I believe there are not in this whole city three gentlemen out of employment, who ⌐do or⌐ are able to give entertainments once a month. Those who are in employments of Church or State, are three parts in four from England, and amount to little more than a dozen. Those indeed may once or twice invite their friends, or any person of distinction that makes a voyage hither. All my acquaintance tell me, they know not above three families where they can occasionally dine in a whole year. Dr. Delany is the only gentleman I know, who keeps one certain day in the week to entertain seven or eight friends at dinner, and to pass the evening, where there is nothing of excess, either in eating or drinking. Our old friend Southern,[5] who has just left us, was invited to dinner once or twice by a judge, a bishop, or a commissioner of the revenue, but most frequented a few particular friends, and chiefly the Doctor,[6] who is so easy in his fortune, and very hospitable.

⌐If you had ventured to come over you should have had a very convenient warm apartment more open then usual in great cities, with a

---

[1] Some advantage in that Loss.—Footnote in *1741 Dab.*

[2] In a letter to Mrs. Caesar (preserved at Rousham) Swift remarks (30 July 1733) that Pope soon after his mother's death 'waved the fairest opportunity of performing his promise two months ago, of coming over with ease, and in company of Dean Cottrell and his Sister. He said we should kill him with eating and drinking'. Dean Cottrell was younger brother to Pope's neighbour, Sir Clement.   [3] is cheaper] are cheaper *1741 Dab.*

[4] it is] they are *1741 Dab.*   [5] Thomas Southerne, the dramatist.
[6] Dr. Delany.

garden as large as your green plot that fronts the Thames, and another
about two hundred yards further, larger than your great garden and
with more air, but without any beauty. You should have small dinners
of what you liked, and good wine, and you eat and drink so little that
I could well afford it, considering how often you would be invited
either with me or without me.⌐ The conveniences of taking the air,
winter or summer, do far exceed those in London; for the two large
strands just at two edges of the town, are as firm and dry in winter, as
in summer. There are at least six or eight gentlemen of sense,[1] learning,
good humour and taste, able and desirous to please you, and orderly
females, some of the better sort, to take care of you. These were the
motives that I have frequently made use of to entice you hither; and
there would be no failure among the best people here, of any honours
that could be done you.

As to myself, I declare my health is so uncertain that I dare not
venture among you at present. I hate the thoughts of London, where
I am not rich enough to live otherwise than by shifting, which is now
too late. Neither can I have conveniences in the country for three
horses and two servants, and many others which I have here at hand.
I am one of the governors of all the hackney coaches, carts, and car-
riages, round this town, who dare not insult me like your rascally
wagoners or coachmen, but give me the way; nor is there one Lord or
squire for a hundred of yours, to turn me out of the road, or run over
me with their coaches and six. Thus, I make some advantage of the
public poverty, and to give you the reasons for what I once writ, why
I choose to be a freeman among slaves, rather than a slave among freemen. Then I walk the streets in peace without being justled, nor ever
without a thousand blessings from my friends the vulgar. I am Lord
Mayor of one hundred and twenty houses, I am absolute lord of the
greatest Cathedral in the kingdom, am at peace with the neighbouring
Princes, the Lord Mayor of the city and the Archbishop of Dublin;
only the latter, like the King of France, sometimes attempts encroach-
ments on my dominions,[2] as old Lewis did upon Lorraine. In the midst
of this raillery, I can tell you with seriousness, that these advantages
contribute to my ease, and therefore I value them. And in one part
of your letter relating to Lord Bolingbroke[3] and yourself, you agree
with me entirely, about the indifference, the love of quiet, the care of
health, etc., that grow upon men in years. And if you discover those
inclinations in my Lord and yourself, what can you expect from me,

----

¹ sense] understanding *1741 Dab.*

² The Liberty of St. Patrick's, which covered about five and a half acres ... was absolutely
independent of the Archbishop, as well as of the sheriff, and acknowledged no governor except
the Dean.—Ball. v. 4 n. (from Dean Bernard's *St. Patrick's Cathedral*, p. 26).

³ Bolingbroke] B— *1741 Labc; 1742 Labc.*

whose health is so precarious, and yet at your or his time of life, I could have leaped over the moon.

⌐I am very much pleased and honoured with three lines from Mr. Pulteney at the end of yours,¹ for which I desire to present him with my most humble service and acknowledgements. He never can be too much valued for saving England from beggary and slavery. Hath my Lord Bolingbroke yet learnt the art of minding the main chance? He hath often promised me his picture, but I never had the heart to mind him of it because I fear he could never afford the expense. Our friend Patty only affects shame, but laziness is at the bottom. She ought to come into this Catholic country, rather than be plundered by her mother and sister, and visit none but heretics, and hardly keep a whole gown out of four thousand pounds fortune. If you happen to see my Lord and Lady Masham, I desire with my humble service and thanks for their letter, that they may know I am yet ashamed to trouble them with an empty letter, but shall write to them by a private hand. My most humble service to my Lord Peterborough, Bathurst, Oxford, the Doctor, and Mr. Lewis when you see them.⌐

POPE *to* SPENCE²   [1733]

Elwin–Courthope, x. 131

If this finds you in good repair, after the concussion of the stage-coach, and before you are too strongly engaged in town, I shall be heartily glad to see you for as much as you can of this week. I shall be at home to-morrow, and so on and always, dear sir, yours.

†POPE *to* HUGH BETHEL³   9 *Aug.* 1733

1737
                                                                      Aug. 9, 1733.

You might well think me negligent or forgetful of you, if true friendship and sincere esteem were to be measured by common forms and compliments. The truth is, I could not write then, without saying something of my own condition, and of my loss of so old and so deserving a parent, which really wou'd have troubled you; or I must

---

¹ Pope's text as printed omitted the whole of this last paragraph. In 1733 Swift's praise of Pulteney's politics would be acceptable, but by 1740 the 'patriots' had cooled towards his obvious self-seeking.

² Elwin says the year is written on the original 'in another hand'. On the whole, the year seems improbable, but not impossible. Spence was abroad until July. This note hardly sounds like a welcome-home after a long absence on the Continent. Furthermore, Pope was not much at home this summer after the death of his mother. But he may have met Spence while in London, found him shattered by the journey from the landing to Town, and may have invited him to Twickenham after welcoming him to London.

³ In the editions of 1737 this letter has the heading 'To Mr. B—', but in editions of 1739–42 it is 'To Mr. Bethel'.

have kept a silence upon that head, which wou'd not have suited that freedom and sincere opening of the heart which is due to you from me. I am now pretty well; but my home is uneasy to me still, and I am therefore wandring about all this summer. I was but four days at Twickenham since the occasion that made it so melancholy.[1] I have been a fortnight in Essex, and am now at Dawley (whose master is your servant) and going to Cirencester to Lord Bathurst. I shall also see Southampton with Lord Peterborow. The Court and Twit'nam I shall forsake together. I wish I did not leave our friend,[2] who deserves more quiet and more health and happiness, than can be found in such a family. The rest of my acquaintance are tolerably happy in their various ways of life, whether court, country, or town; and Mr. Cleland is as well in the Park,[3] as if he were in Paradise. I heartily hope Yorkshire is the same to you; and that no evil, moral or physical, may come near you.

I have now but too much melancholy leisure, and no other care but to finish my Essay on Man: There will be in it one line[4] that may offend you, (I fear) and yet I will not alter or omit it, unless you come to town and prevent me before I print it, which will be in a fortnight in all probability. In plain truth, I will not deny my self the greatest pleasure I am capable of receiving, because another may have the modesty not to share it. It is all a poor poet can do, to bear testimony to the virtue he cannot reach; besides, that in this age, I have too few good examples not to lay hold on any I can find. You see what an interested man I am. | Adieu.

POPE *to* THE EARL OF OXFORD[5]   [16 *August* 1733]

Longleat Portland Papers, xii

Twickenham Aug. 16. 1733

My Lord,—The sooner we go, the better for me, but if you can lye here on Friday night, (tho' not on this night,) it will be the Easyer. If you cannot, I will be ready for you here to morrow morning, whether you come or not, by seven a clock; and so I will the next day also, take your choice—Believe me My Lord no man can be more Sincerely & respectfully | Your faithfull Servant, | & obliged Companion, in all ways, | A. Pope

Address: To the Earl of Oxford

Endorsement (by a secretary): | Mr Pope | Twickenham Augst 16. 1733.

---

[1] Pope must mean that he has not spent four consecutive days or perhaps four entire days at Twickenham since 7 June. He was back and forth, possibly spending many nights at Dawley or in town.   [2] Martha Blount.

[3] St. James's Park. Cleland had rooms in St. James's Palace.—Elwin.

[4] Epistle IV, l. 126, concerns the asthma of 'blameless Bethel'.

[5] The entire superscription is added by Lord Oxford. The 16th was a Thursday. No details of the projected journey are known. Presumably it was brief.

*POPE to THE EARL OF BURLINGTON   20 [August 1733]

Chatsworth

My Lord,—I trouble your Lordship with this, thro' the desire I have always to see your Lordship, joynd with that of my Friend Mr Fortescue, who wishes (to pay you his respects) an opportunity he has long sought for.[1] If Wednesday be a day you should chance to have at leisure, we would gladly do ourselves the pleasure of dining with you.

I am with all Esteem & affection, with my most humble Services to Lady B. | My Lord, | Your most faithful obligd Servant | A. Pope

Munday. the 20th.

POPE to THE EARL OF OXFORD[2]   [21 August 1733

Longleat Portland Papers, xii

Sunday the 21st | augt 1733

My Lord,—If I had not thought of returning[3] sooner, your Lordship had been troubled with a Remembrance of me before. My Thoughts often fly to you, & indeed I think my Body's following them of little consequence, it is so infirm & troublesome an one. I am never well enough when I am with those I value, to show them enough how I value them: or to injoy with them even those Hours they kindly allow me. I hope your self, my Lady, & Lady Margaret injoy all the health I sincerely wish, & I have nothing to add, but that next Week toward the End of it I hope to assure them how truly I am theirs, & Your Lordships, most faithfull & obliged humble Servant | A. Pope

I have seen Morley's Image at Halsted.[4]

Endorsement (by a secretary): Mr Pope Augst 21st 1733.

Address: To the Rt Hon. the Earl | of Oxford, in Dover street | Piccadilly | London

Postmark: 24/AV

[1] Fortescue can hardly be making Lord Burlington's acquaintance for the first time. The year, therefore, is altogether uncertain, but since in the summer of 1733 Pope and Fortescue had been disappointed once or twice in plans to visit Chiswick, and since Pope was at Twickenham between the 16th and 21st of August (the only month in 1733 on which the 20th was Monday), the letter is very tentatively placed as of 20 Aug. 1733.

[2] The date is an exasperating puzzle. Pope wrote simply 'Sunday the 21st.' Lord Oxford in the superscription added 'augt.' The secretary endorsed the full year on the cover of the letter, and inserted the year in the superscription. We have also the postmark, in which, to be sure, the month is blurred. In 1733, 21 Aug. was Tuesday. On the assumption that Pope is more likely to be wrong than the recipient of the letter, one discards either his 21 or his Sunday. Sunday the 19th might be a good bet except that the beginning of the letter sounds (but not surely) as if Pope had not been in touch with his lordship for some time. On the 16th they had planned a jaunt of some sort—which may not have come off. Of possible years only in 1726 was 21 Aug. a Sunday.   [3] Returning to London?

[4] Pope had been in Essex in July, and may have seen a son of Morley's resembling the father. Cf. Pope to Bathurst, 8 Oct. 1735, for the same use of 'image'. Morley died in 1732.

POPE *to* CARYLL   27 *August* 1733

Add. 28618

London. 27. Aug. 1733.

I was unwilling to write to you till I could doe it effectually, and make
you an offer of myself according to your desire. Your information that
I was at Lord Cobham's so long since was a mistaken one.[1] I was
detain'd about town on necessary business some time and stayed but
four days in all at Lord Cobham's. Few words are best: you shall be
troubled with me whenever you will, only give me some days' notice
before the day you name to send your chariot to Guilford and be exact
as to the hour and the inn. I write this in haste, or if I did not, could
not pretend to express the joy it will be to me to see you in your
domestic light, with all about you to whom I wish so well. I have a
small petition farther. If you can favour me with a piece of venison
before I come to you, pray do. Adieu, dear sir. God keep you. I am
ever most mindfully | Yours | A. Pope.

   Your god-daughter sends her duty, and thinks [it] long since she
heard of you.

†POPE *to* SWIFT   1 *September* 1733

1740

Sept. 1, 1733.

I have every day wish'd to write to you, to say a thousand things; and
yet I think I should not have writ to you now, if I was[2] not sick of
writing any thing, sick of myself, and (what is worse) sick of my
friends too. The world is become too busy for me, everybody so[3] concern'd for the publick, that all private enjoyments are lost, or dis-
relish'd. I write more to show you I am tired of this life, than to tell
you any thing relating to it. I live as I did, I think as I did, I love you
as I did: but all these are to no purpose: the world will not live, think,
or love, as I do. I am troubled for, and vexed at, all my friends by turns.
Here are some whom you love, and who love you; yet they receive no
proofs of that affection from you, and they give none of it to you.
There is a great gulph between! In earnest, I would go a thousand
miles by land to see you, but the sea I dread. My ailments are such,
that I really believe a sea-sickness, (considering the oppression of
cholical pains, and the great weakness of my breast) would kill me:
and if I did not die of that, I must of the excessive eating and drinking
of your hospitable town, and the excessive flattery of your most poetical
country. I hate to be cramm'd, either way: Let your hungry Poets and

---

[1] The report came from Pulteney. See note to Pope's letter to Caryll, 25 June.
[2] was] were *1741 Dab.*   [3] everybody so] everybody is so *1741 Labc; 1742 Labc.*

your rhyming Peers[1] digest it, I cannot. I like much better to be abused
and half starved, than to be so over-praised and over-fed. Drown Ireland! for having caught you, and for having kept you: I only reserve
a little charity for her, for knowing your value, and esteeming you:
you are the only Patriot I know, who is not hated for serving his
country. The man who drew your Character and printed it here, was
not much in the wrong in many things he said of you: yet he was a
very impertinent fellow, for saying them in words quite different from
those you had yourself employed before on the same subject: for surely
to alter your words is to prejudice them; and I have been told, that a
man himself can hardly say the same thing twice over with equal
happiness: Nature is so much a better thing than artifice. I have written
nothing this year: It is no affectation to tell you, my Mother's loss has
turned my frame of thinking. The habit of a whole life is a stronger
thing than all the reason in the world. I know I ought to be easy, and
to be free; but I am dejected, I am confined: my whole amusement is
in reviewing my past life, not in laying plans for my future. I wish you
cared as little for popular applause as I, as little for any nation in contra-
distinction to others, as I: and then I fancy, you that are not afraid of
the sea, you that are a stronger man at sixty than ever I was at twenty,
would come and see several people who are (at last) like the primitive
christians, of one soul and of one mind. The day is come, which I have
often wished, but never thought to see; when *every mortal that I esteem
is of the same sentiment in Politics and in Religion.*[2]

   Adieu. All you love, are yours, but all are busy, except (dear Sir)
your sincere friend.

POPE *to* CARYLL   4 *September* 1733
Add. 28618
                                                   4 Sept. 1733.
I am only able to say (I am so ill with the headache) that I will, God
willing, be at Guilford on Sunday night, or Munday[3] morn the 9th
instant at the Three Tuns. I cannot pretend to express how pleased
I shall be at Ladyholt; I only wish I may be in health enough to appear
as well pleased as I am, and that I may find and leave you in perfect
enjoyment of all you wish. My humble service attends you all, and
my thanks for the venison; all which I have seized upon, and so you
may send your god-daughter more; I have no farther demands of that
sort upon you, but a great many of your good will, and good prayers.
Adieu till Monday. | Dear sir | Your affect. and obliged servant |
A. Pope.

---

   [1] Peers] Poets *1742 Lbc.*   [2] An inexplicable remark!
   [3] The 9th fell on Sunday, but Pope evidently got to Ladyholt without trouble. See his
letter of 24 Sept. to Caryll.

†POPE *to* [MARTHA BLOUNT]¹   *7 September* 1733

1737
                                             Sept. 7, 1733.

You cannot think how melancholy this place makes me: every part of this wood puts into my mind poor Mr. Gay with whom I past once a great deal of pleasant time in it, and another friend who is near dead, and quite lost to us, Dr. Swift. I really can find no enjoyment in the place; the same sort of uneasiness as I find at Twitnam, whenever I pass near my Mother's room.

I've not yet writ to Mrs. G.² I think I should, but have nothing to say that will answer the character they consider me in, as a Wit: besides, my eyes grow very bad, (whatever is the cause of it) I'll put 'em out for no body but a friend; and I protest it brings tears into them almost to write to you, when I think of your state and mine. I long to write to Swift, but cannot. The greatest pain I know is to say things so very short of one's meaning, when the heart is full.

I feel the goings out of life fast enough, to have little appetite left to make compliments, at best useless, and for the most part unfelt, speeches. 'Tis but in a very narrow circle that friendship walks in this world, and I care not to tread out of it more than I needs must; knowing well, it is but to two or three (if quite so many) that any man's welfare, or memory, can be of consequence: The rest I believe I may forget, and be pretty certain they are already even, if not before-hand with me.

Life, after the first warm heats are over, is all downhill; and one almost wishes the journey's end, provided we were sure but to lye down easy, whenever the Night shall overtake us.

I dream'd all last night of — she has dwelt (a little more than perhaps is right) upon my spirits: I saw a very deserving gentleman in my travels, who has formerly, I have heard, had much the same misfortune; and (with all his good breeding and sense) still bears a cloud and melancholy cast that never can quite clear up, in all his behaviour and conversation. I know another, who I believe could promise and easily keep his word, never to laugh in his life. But one must do one's best, not be³ used by the world as that poor lady was by her sister; and not seem too good, for fear of being thought affected, or whimsical.

---

¹ In all Pope's editions this letter was printed without mention of Miss Blount as addressee, headed only 'To —.' Its date is almost certainly wrong. Since on the 4th Pope wrote to Caryll offering to meet his coach at Guildford on the 9th, but asking a reply, it is hardly probable that he was at Cirencester Park (from which this letter is certainly written) on the 7th. Pope says he longs to write to Swift but cannot, and yet he has written Swift a week back. Probably when editing the letter for printing Pope for the first time dated it, and gave it an approximate date. October would have been more plausible.
² This initial is replaced by an asterisk in 1737 e and thereafter.
³ not be] not to be *1739–42*.

It is a real truth, that to the last of my moments, the thought of you, and the best of my wishes for you, will attend you, told or untold: I could wish you had once the constancy and resolution to act for your self, whether before or after I leave you (the only way I ever shall leave you) you must determine: but reflect, that the first wou'd make me, as well as your self, happier; the latter could make you only so. Adieu.

HILL *to* POPE[1]   20 *September* 1733

1753 (Hill)

Richmond, Sept. 20, 1733.

I have, this moment, the honour of your Letter; and, like all other great pleasures in life, it brings me a mixture of delight and uneasiness.

The engagements, under which I receive it, give me a sensible mortification; for business, which has *naturally* no more, than a dull face, assumes, a *provoking* one, when it with-holds us from happiness.

Your obliging prophecy of my daughter's recovery, is in a fair way to be verified; but she will wonder, how, on this side death, she becomes intitled to a call of fellowship, with the saints, and the angels.

She and I might justly be proud, if we had qualities worth your praising; but the *rich* have a right to be liberal, and you bestow but your own, though you over-adorn us with your bounty.

I will say nothing superfluous, to so good a judge of expression, else my zeal, for your happiness, would be prompting me to wish you blessings, as if you possibly could be without them, and Lady D——[2] so near you. May she live to reckon birth-days, as numerous as the charms of her *mind*, and as shining as those of her *person*.

Though I have no room to wish *you* happier, I have an ambition to be made so *myself*; and for that reason, entreat her ladyship, and you, to submit to the mortification of dining, some day the beginning of next week, at *Westminster*; and, if you will be so good to name it, by the bearer, I will suffer nothing to mix with a delight, that must be lessened by addition, because it can find no equal. I am, with great respect, | Dear Sir, | Your most humble, | And most obedient Servant, | A. Hill.

---

[1] Hill as well as Pope could misdate letters when printing, and this seems probably a case. At least Hill shows no awareness that Pope is away from home. If we could date the illness of Urania (or was it Astrea or even Minerva?) Hill, the puzzle could be solved.

[2] Not identified. Could she be the Countess of the 5th Earl of Denbigh?

POPE *to* CARYLL   24 *September* 1733

Add. 28618

Bevis-Mount. 24. Sept. 1733.

I cannot let Mr Hebb[1] part from hence without charging him with my
real thanks and the expressions of that contentment I received in so
hearty and friendly a reception as I met with at Ladyholt. I truly
wished I could have stayed longer, but am now upon the wing either
for London or Cirencester. If I can get off from Lord Bathurst, it will
be for London where I have business at Michaelmas that ought to be
attended personally. If I must take the other journey, my return will
be very uncomfortable, unless I hasten thither, and I must try, tho'
inconveniently, to get some friend to do my drudgery in town, which
I fear will not be thoroughly done in such case. Upon the whole, I find
I am not yet a freeman. If a man be philosopher enough himself not
[to] be tied to the world, his friendships and charities will engage him
to it; which he neither can, nor ought to break thro', otherwise I think
there should be no man living more his own master than I, and if I
were so, no man would be more at your service, for I am very sincerely
ever | Dear sir | Your most faithful and obliged | Friend and servant |
A. Pope.

I desire Mrs Caryll, Mrs Cath. and the family at Compton[2] will
hold me their humble servant. You [have] by me the service of the
Lord and Lady of Mount-Bevis.

P. T. *to* CURLL[3]   11 *October* 1733

1735 *Narrative*

October the 11th, 1733.

Mr. Curll, Understanding you propose to write the *Life* of *Mr. Pope*,

---

[1] 'Mr. Hebb' must have accompanied Pope from Ladyholt, to which (or to its region)
he is now returning.

[2] Mr. Caryll's son, Edward, resided at Compton, a village in the immediate neighbourhood
of Ladyholt.—Elwin.

[3] This is printed by Pope in his *Narrative of the Method by which the Private Letters of
Mr. Pope Have been procur'd and publish'd by Edmund Curll*. This *Narrative* appeared about
10 June 1735, and Curll's 'Initial Correspondence' came out perhaps a month later. That
this letter comes from Pope is made probable by the details concerning his father and mother.
His father was a posthumous child, and his mother was one of seventeen children—details
which in 1733 could come only from the poet himself. The poet may have believed (wrongly)
in a family tie with the Popes who were Earls of Downe, but he probably knew he was
fabricating when he gave his uncle William the family estate and an Oxford education. See
Early Career, pp. 28–33. Pope would not mind lying to Curll! The letter has some bio-
graphical importance, but it is clearly designed as an answer to the wounding line in Lady
Mary's and Lord Hervey's *Verses . . . to the Imitator of . . . Horace*, 'Hard as thy heart,
and as thy birth obscure.'

Pope's text was derived from the letter that Curll sent to T. Cooper shortly after Pope
advertised in *The Daily Post-Boy* of 20 May 1735. Perhaps Curll sent Cooper a copy. The
text he prints in his 'Initial Correspondence' is dated 'Thursday Oct. 11, 1733', and instead

this is only to inform you, I can send you divers Memoirs which may be serviceable, if your Design be really to do him neither Injustice nor shew him Favour. I was well acquainted with his Father, and with the first part of his own Life, tho' since he has treated me as a Stranger. It is certain some late Pamphlets are not fair in respect to his Father, who was of the younger Branch of a Family in good repute in *Ireland*, and related to the Lords *Downe*, formerly of the same Name. He was (as he hath told Me himself, and he was [very different from his Son] a modest and plain honest Man) a Posthumous Son, and left little provided for, his elder Brother having what small Estate there was, who afterwards Study'd and dy'd at *Oxford*. He was put to a Merchant in *Flanders*, and acquir'd a moderate Fortune by Merchandize, which he quitted at the Revolution in very good Circumstances, and retired to *Windsor* Forest, where he purchased a small Estate, and took great Delight in Husbandry and Gardens. His Mother was one of seventeen Children of *W. Turnor* Esq; formerly of *Burfit Hall* in the —¹ Riding of Yorkshire. Two of her Brothers were killed in the Civil Wars. This is a true Account of Mr *Pope*'s Family and Parentage. Of his Manners I cannot give so good an one, yet as I would not wrong any Man, both ought to be True; and if such be your Design, I may serve you in it, not entering into any Thing in any wise Libellous. You may please to direct an Answer in the *Daily Advertiser* this Day-sennight in these Terms—*E. C. hath received a Letter, and will comply with P. T.* | Yours.

*POPE to HUGH BETHEL²   [1733?]

Egerton 1948

I am this minute got hither, weary, and busy in some papers which I can finish if I stay to night in my own Room. If you happen to be at leisure, pray come to me at Lord Oxfords up two pair of Stairs; if you are not, I'll come to you at all Events if this finds you. Dear Sir believe no man living more glad to see you, than | A. Pope.

Address: To Mr Bethel at | Sir Wm Codrington's in | Cleveland Court.

of 'W. Turnor' he offers as Mrs. Pope's father, 'William Turnor'. These variants indicate two texts probably, since Curll could not, if merely reprinting, supply Mr. Turner's Christian name. By 11 Oct. Pope had hardly returned from Bevis Mount or Cirencester.

¹ A curious dash. Worsborough, where Mrs. Pope was born, is in the West Riding.

² About the middle of Oct. 1733 Pope arrived, weary from rambling, at Lord Oxford's town house, where he was alone. (Hence possibly the task of the 'two pair of stairs', which might deter the asthmatic Bethel.) At this time Pope was as 'P.T.' first broaching to Curll the publication of his correspondence. Or possibly he was finishing the fourth epistle of the *Essay on Man*.

POPE *to* THE EARL OF OXFORD   20 *October* 1733

Harl. 7525

Oct. 20, 1733.

My Lord,—I am returned a week since from my Lord Peterborow, with whom I past 3 Weeks[1] as agreably and as healthfully as I ever did in my Life. I was not a little disappointed not to find your Lordship in London, tho considering the fine Weather and how late in the Season you enjoyed it, I ought not to lament an Absence which must both give you Health and Pleasure. Your House I found *totally* at my service, and took up my Choice (like a young, and ambitious man) in no Room of it but Lady Margaret's. How much might I say upon that Subject, were I a poet? But the misfortune of being what seldome consists with that Character, a bashful and backward man, keeps me silent. I shall be little in Town (if at all) till your Return, and in Truth, since I came home, I have had my health so ill, that I must in a manner live by myself; and think I must either lead such a life as I did at Southampton, which is inconsistent with a Town-Life, or lock my self up from all conversable Hours while I am in Town. I beg to hear a line of your Satisfactions and amusements, for of your State of health I am daily informed by your honest Porter: But the other he knows not, and I am not quite contented without it. That all Enjoyments may be yours, and all good Things attend your whole worthy Family, is the sincere prayer always of, | My Lord, | Your faithfullest Servant, | A. Pope.

Address: To the Rt Honble the | Earl of Oxford, at | Wimpole | Cambridge-shire |

Endorsement: Mr Pope Octr 20th 1733

Postmark: 20/OC

*POPE *to* THE COUNTESS OF BURLINGTON[2]

Chatsworth

20 *October* [1733]

Madam,—You have put me quite to Shame, by calling here yesterday. I was just sending to inquire of your Welfare: my own Health & Ease, I find to my sorrow, must be maintain'd by That which destroys both in most others, a Sedentary life: and this was the only time I had been

---

[1] This letter records the conclusion of Pope's rambles for the summer, which are difficult to determine. This letter (as well as those to Caryll of 4 and 24 Sept.) makes it clear that after reaching Ladyholt about 10 Sept. he spent three weeks at Bevis Mount, and some days in Lord Oxford's house in Dover Street. He seems to be writing from Twickenham.

[2] The year 1733 is more probable than most others that can be considered—which is all that can be said for it. The 20th was Saturday, and hence Pope's remark about 'next Sunday' is perhaps peculiar if he means 'tomorrow'.

from home since I last payd you my respects; one day excepted at London, when I called (at Mr. Kent's House in Piccadilly)¹ with a design to have repeated them, but he was gone half an hour too soon for me.

If your Ladyship shall be to be found, either at Chiswick or London, next Sunday, I shall do myself that Honour, or Pleasure shall I say? since I find it Both, to be | Madam | Your most obedient, obliged humble | Servt. | A. Pope.

Twitenham, | Oct. 20.

POPE *to* CARYLL   23 *October* 1733

Add. 28618

Twitnam. 23. Oct. 1733.

You will be so good as to excuse the delay of my answer to a letter whose expressions are kind beyond my merits, but not beyond my intentions, which are seriously and affectionately to serve you. I was in London when it came, for I left Lord Peterborough within two days after I gave my letter to Mr Hebbe² (to whom pray remember my service). I have not been so well since my return hither. Your caution about a servant I find pretty necessary, and I thank you for it. Here is a little pamphlet come out occasioned by your neighbour Norton's will,³ which I'll take the opportunity, to give your god-daughter, who can get it franked to you at present better than I, all my noble friends being gone out of town.

I must tell you that the hints you gave me, are not lost upon me; for I have left out of the character of the D. of Wharton (which I showed you) those lines you thought too hard.⁴ And I believe the author of the *Essay on Man* will end his poem in such manner as will satisfy your scruple. I think it impossible for him, with any congruity to his confined and strictly philosophical subject, to mention our Saviour directly; but he may magnify the Christian doctrine, as the perfection of all moral; nay, and even (I fancy) quote the very words of the gospel-precept, that includes all the law and the precepts, *Thou shalt love God above all things*, &c. And I conclude that will remove all possible occasion of scandal.

¹ A joke for Burlington House, in which Kent lived.
² If this statement means that Pope left Lord Peterborow on or about 26 Sept. (he gave Mr. Hebbe the letter to Caryll dated 24 Sept. on that day?), the statement seems to be untrue. Caryll might be jealous of a visit to Bevis Mount longer than that to Ladyholt.
³ Richard Norton of Southwick, in Hampshire, bequeathed his estate to the poor. The will was set aside.—Elwin. Throughout 1733 this will was of public interest. See *Gent. Mag.* iii (Feb.), 57–62, and 661 (Dec.).
⁴ The Duke is still mentioned in Pope's Epistle to Cobham, 'Of the Knowledge and Characters of Men', ll. 206–7. Doubtless other lines were omitted before publication in Jan. 1733/4.

My sincere services attend your Countess; I mean not your countess in gallantry, your neighbour's wife, but your true Countess, your own:[1] I hope she is as healthy as she is good. Mrs Cath: Caryll will oblige me in sending the fan (for which I've found a painter) to Lord Oxford's. My real service to Mr Ed: Caryll and his lady, not forgetting Mr Tooker,[2] whose friendship and acquaintance I was in great hopes of having renewed at Ladyholt. I am with true respect and affection | Dear sir | Yours always | A. Pope.

*POPE to FORTESCUE[3]   [*November* 1733]

Harvard University

I wished much to see you before Your present (and I know, to a good Father and good man, most Important Business) might wholly take you up, as doubtless it must this week. Your Family, where I have waited some time in hope of your return, seem to think you will not make that use of Twit'nam which would please me better than any I could make of it. I think to go thither to morrow, & wish'd to have prepared it for you, if not, I will go from thence in a few days to see & congratulate them on a Happiness which I hope will be lasting. Pray let me hear from you, | Dear Sir, | [Unsigned.]

Endorsement: Mr. Pope

VISCOUNT COBHAM to POPE[4]   1 *November* 1733

Egerton 1949

Stowe Novem the 1 1733

Tho I have not modesty enough not to be pleasd with your extra-ordinary compliment I have wit enough to know how little I deserve it   you know all mankind are putting themselves upon the world for more then they are worth and their friends are dayly helping the deceit, but I am afraid I shall not pass for an absolute Patriot   however I have the honour of haveing receivd a publick testimony of your esteem and friendship and am as proud of it as I coud be of any advantage which coud happen to me. as I remember when I saw the brouillion of this Epistle it was perplexd   You have now made it the contrary and I

---

[1] Living in England, Caryll did not use the Jacobite title inherited from his uncle, whom James II in exile had created Earl. It is most unusual for Pope to use the title.

[2] Possibly James Tooker of Woodhouse in the county of Southampton, a neighbour of Caryll's.—Elwin. See here v. 3.

[3] The approximate date is inferred from the interest in the marriage of Fortescue's daughter to John Spooner of Beachwood, which took place this month. See Pope's letter of 13 Nov.

[4] First printed by Ruffhead, p. 275. The letter concerns Pope's first Moral Essay, addressed to Lord Cobham, which, after further revisions, was published in Jan. 1733/4.

think it is the clearest and the cleanest of all you have wrote   dont you
think you have bestowd too many lines upon the old Letcher   the
instance it self is but ordinary and I think shoud be shortn'd or changd.
Thank you and believe me to be most sincerely Yours | Cobham

Address: For Mr Pope

HILL *to* POPE[1]   *7 November* 1733
1753 (Hill)
                                                      Nov. 7, 1733.

Sir,—Tho' I have, really, no skill in the *French*—and am (perhaps, for
that reason) not overfond of the language, yet, I read it with pleasure,
in respect to the *writers* of that nation; and have seldom been more
strongly delighted, than with the Tragedy of *Zaire*.

I had seen nothing of Mr. *Voltaire*'s before, except the *Henriade*;
and whether it was from my own *want of taste*, or the poem's *want of
fire*, I found it too cold, for an *epic* spirit; so conceiv'd but a moderate
opinion, as to the *dramatic* attempts of the same author:—But, genius
being limited, we act too rash, and unreasonable a part, when we judge
after so general a manner. Having been agreeably disappointed in
Zaire, it was due, as an atonement, that I should contribute, to widen
his applause, whom I had thought of, too narrowly.

I have, therefore, made this Tragedy speak *English*, and shall bring
it on the stage in a month, or two; where, though I have no interest
in its success, I should be vex'd to have it miscarry; because it is certainly, an excellent piece, and has not suffer'd, I hope, so much in the
translation, as to justify a cold reception at *London*, after having run
into the most general esteem, at *Paris*. I will do all, in my power, to
prepare the town to receive it, to which end I have given the *profits* to
a gentleman, whose *acquaintance* is too large for his *fortune*; and your
good taste and good nature, assure me of your willing concurrence, so
far, as not only to say of it, what it deserves, but, to say it at such times,
and in such manner, as you know best how to chuse; in order to give
your recommendation the intended good consequence.

Lord *Bolinbroke* was a patron of Mr. *Voltaire*, and can effectually,
advance the reception of his Play, among those who are most his
friends, and best able to support it, at its appearance. I have ventur'd,
to ask it in the author's behalf; and beg, you would convey the letter
and translation, to my Lord's hands, as soon as you please, after you
have read them.[2]

---

[1] Hill's *Zara* was performed at Drury Lane in Jan. 1735/6. For its earlier history see
D. Brewster, *Aaron Hill*, p. 141.

[2] Among the letters printed in Hill's *Works* (1753), i. 175–7, is a letter, also dated
7 Nov. 1733, to Lord Bolingbroke, bespeaking his interest in the translation, which Pope
will convey to his lordship.

I would desire you to excuse this trouble, if it were not to look, like a distrust of that delight, which, I know, it gives you when you have an opportunity put into your hands, to do a kind, or a generous action.

The last time I had the pleasure of seeing you, at *Westminster* you were observing among some rude beginnings of rock-work, which I am designing in my garden, a *little obelisk of Jersey Shells*, over a grotesque portico for *Pallas*, against the park-wall. You, then, express'd some thoughts of improving such a use of those shells, into a nobler obelisk, among your beauties, at *Twittenham*. Allow me to *bespeak* for *myself* against next spring, the permission of presenting you the shells, materials, and workmanship; that I may have the honour to plant in your gardens a probability of being, sometimes, remember'd by the master of that growing paradise. In the mean time, be so good to accept this smaller parcel, just enough, (if there is yet to come, of the season, half a week of dry weather without frost,) to embellish your *marine temple*, by inserting them, among the *Hollows*, between those large shells, which compose it: where being plac'd in oblique position, so as to lie open to the weather, they will enlighten the gravity, and catch a distant eye, with a kind of shining propriety.

I ought never to end a letter to you, without a wish for your perfect health; because it is impossible to think of you, without a pain from the reflection, that you *want* it too often, I am, | Yours, &c. | A. Hill.

VISCOUNT COBHAM *to* POPE[1]   8 *November* [1733]

Egerton 1949

Stowe Novem the 8

I like your Leachour better now 'tis shorter and the Glutton is a very good Epigram   but they are both appetites that from nature we indulg as well for her ends as our pleasure   a Cardinal in his way of pleasure would have been a better instance   What do you think of an old Lady dressing her silver locks with Pink and directing her Coffin to be lind with white quilted Satten trim'd with gold fringe or Councelour Vernon retiring to enjoy himself with five thousand a year which he had got and returning back to the Chancery to get a little more when he coud not speak so loud as to be heard or a judg turnd out coming again to the Barr   I mean that a passion or habit that has not a natural foundation falls in better with your Subject than any of our natural wants which in some degree we cannot avoid pursueing to the last and if a man has Spirits or appetite enough to take a bit of either kind at parting you may condemn him but you woud be proud to imitate him

I congratulate you upon the fine Weather   'tis a Strange thing that

---

[1] Printed by Ruffhead, p. 276. Pope has pleased by adopting at least some of Cobham's suggestions in revising his Epistle 'Of the Knowledge and Characters of Men'.

people of condition and men of parts must enjoy it in common with the rest of the world but now I think on't their pursuits are generally after points of so great importance that they do not enjoy it all   I wont trouble you any longer but with the assurance of What I hope you are perfectly convinc'd of that I am most sincerely   Yours |C

Address: For Mr Pope at his house | at Twitenham. | Middlesex
Postmark: 9/NO
Frank: Cobham

HILL *to* POPE   10 *November* 1733
1753 (Hill)

Nov. 10, 1733.

At my return home, after the Play,[1] I met with your letter, too late to enjoy the pleasure, it call'd me to, without trespassing upon the hour, made more improper too, by your being indisposed.

I hope to find you better, this morning, and if you will allow me to detain you, only long enough to receive your commands, at Lord *Bathurst*'s, will wait on you the moment my Servant comes back: for I think of you so often, and see you so seldom, that now you are so near, I would not lose you, if I could help it, who am, not fashionably, but faithfully, | Your most obedient | And devoted Servant, | A. Hill.

POPE *to* HILL[2]   13 *November* [1733]
1751 (Hill)

Twickenham, Nov. 13. 1732.

I writ to you a very hasty Letter, being warm'd in the Cause of an old Acquaintance, in which I was sure you would concur, I mean *John Dennis*, whose Circumstances were describ'd to me in the most moving Manner. I went next Day with the Lord to whom you directed your Letter and Play, which, at my Return home, I receiv'd but Yesterday. I thank you for your agreeable Present to my Grotto, for your more agreeable Letter, and your most excellent Translation of *Voltaire*, to whom you have preserv'd all the Beauty he had, and added the Nerves he wanted. This short Acknowledgment is all I can make just now;

---

[1] No play by Hill was being performed at this time. At both Drury Lane and the New Theatre in the Haymarket (the 'little' Haymarket) Mrs. Eliza Haywood's *Opera of Operas* (based on Fielding's *Tom Thumb*) was being performed. It seems to have annoyed Pope. At least four or five theatres were operating at this moment, and which Hill attended is unknown.
[2] In the *Collection* of 1751, where first printed, this letter is misdated 1732. It clearly is an answer to the letter of Hill of 7 Nov. The benefit arranged for Dennis at Drury Lane took place a month later. See *DNB*. The second sentence refers to the fact that Pope and Bolingbroke have gone to Dawley.

I am just taken up by Mr. *Thomson*, in the Perusal of a new Poem[1] he has brought me: I wish you were with us. The first Day I see *London*, I will wait on you, on many Accounts, but on none more than my being affectionately, and with true Esteem, dear Sir, | Yours, | A. Pope.

I desire Miss *Urania* will know me for her Servant.

POPE *to* FORTESCUE   13 *November* 1733

Amon G. Carter Foundation

Twit'nam. Nov. 13. | 1733

I fully hoped to have seen you e're now, but tho' I was in town two days & half, I could find no Evening; and am now unwilling to be there, till all the Bussle of the Wedding is over. In the meantime, I hope you'l secure Mrs Blount, by insuring Roberts life the moment he comes to town, if it were but for 2 or 3 months, or less, (if the mony be not actually paid sooner.) I've sent the Last Assurance, in case it can be any direction to the Next. I employ these few days in putting the last hand to my Essay, & I will then immediately print it. I meditate a fine edition of the whole, which I will soon have the pleasure to see in your Library, with an Inscription of the Love the author bears you sincerely. Dear Sir I am | always yours. A. Pope

I am told, that Miss Fortescue is perfectly well (I hope truly)

P. T. *to* CURLL[2]   15 *November* 1733

1735 Narrative

Nov. 15 1733.

Sir,—I troubled you with a Line sometime since, concerning your Design of the *Life* of Mr. *Pope,* to which I desir'd your Answer in the *Daily Advertiser* of *Thursday* the 10th[3] Instant *October.* I do not intend my self any other Profit in it, than that of doing Justice to, and on, that Person, upon whom, Sir, you have conferr'd some Care as well as Pains in the Course of your Life; and I intend him the like for his Conduct towards me. *A propos* to his Life, there have lately fall'n into my Hands a large Collection of his *Letters,* from the former Part of his Days to the Year 1727. which being more considerable than

---

[1] Unfortunately the records of Pope's friendship with the author of *The Seasons* are less abundant than with Mallet or Hill. Possibly the 'new poem' was a part of *Liberty?*

[2] On pages 18–19 of his *Narrative* after the letter to Curll of 11 Oct. comes the statement (which indicates that Pope was printing from the letter Curll had turned over to Cooper): 'On the backside of this Letter is endors'd in Curl's Hand, *Notice was accordingly given, as Desir'd, in the* Daily Advertiser *upon which was sent the following Letter.*' This present letter is thereupon printed. See iii. 461.

[3] This date is misprinted for 18th, which would be a proper Thursday. Curll's 'Initial Correspondence' prints *18th.* But no such notice appeared in the *Advertiser.*

any yet seen, and opening very many Scenes new to the World, will alone make a Perfect and the most authentick *Life* and *Memoirs* of him that could be. To shew you my Sincerity and determinate Resolution of assisting you herein, I will give you an Advertisement, which you may publish forthwith if you please, and on your so doing the Letters shall be sent you. They will make a Four or Five Sheet¹ Book, yet I expect no more than what will barely pay a Transcriber, that the Originals may be preserved in mine or your Hands to vouch the Truth of them. I am of Opinion these alone will contain his whole History (if you add to them what you formerly printed of those to *Henry Cromwell*, Esq; [*Here a part of the Letter is cut off, and the following Words indors'd by Curl*—But you must put out an Advertisement for—]² otherwise I shall not be justify'd to some People who have *Influence*, and on whom I have some *Dependance*; unless it seem to the Publick Eye as no entire Act of mine; but I may be justify'd and excus'd, if, after they see such a Collection is made by you, I acknowledge I sent some Letters to contribute thereto. They who know what hath pass'd betwixt Mr. *Pope* and me formerly, may otherwise think it dishonourable I should set such a thing a-foot. Therefore print the Advertisement I sent you, and you shall instantly hear from or see me. Adieu, T. P.³ *Here a Postscript is cut off.*

*POPE to THE COUNTESS OF BURLINGTON⁴

[*Late* 1733?]

Chatsworth

Twitenham. Wensday.

Madam,—Your Ladyship having (I hope) been edifyed by my Submission to my Critick & Friend, will I also hope add to the Catalogue of my Virtues, that of an unwillingness to trouble one who shows me

---

¹ For *Sheet* Curll (*Initial Correspondence*) prints *Shilling*, which makes better sense. The book sold for five shillings, and, with its irregular printing in half-sheets, &c., ran to the equivalent of over twenty sheets.

² The brackets are in Pope's text. Presumably Curll at this point cut off the prescribed form of the advertisement. In his 'Initial Correspondence' Curll repunctuates, without brackets or dash, and he omits the words that Pope places in italic type.

³ The inverted initials are a printer's error, which other editions correct. Pope's continuing text after this letter reads, 'There appears no other letter from P.T. till one of April the 4th. . . .'—a remark that makes the inversion evidently accidental. See iii. 461.

⁴ A wild guess is that Lady Burlington, who this year aided Pope as amanuensis, had some concern with Pope's 'Letter to a Noble Lord' (i.e. Lord Hervey), which is dated 'Nov. 30, 1733'. There is evidence that Lady Burlington, as a Lady in Waiting, did not care for the influential Vice-Chamberlain. On 6 Dec. Lord Hervey wrote to Stephen Fox concerning *The Epistle to a Doctor of Divinity*: 'I send you some verses, which you have already seen in manuscript, and which were printed without my knowledge. . . . Pope is in a most violent fury; and j'en suis ravi' (ed. Lord Ilchester, p. 183). On 31 Jan. 1733/4 he wrote to Henry Fox (ibid., p. 189): 'Pope has not written one word [in reply to Hervey] but a manuscript in prose never printed, which he has shown to several of his friends, but which I have never seen, and which, I have heard from those who did see it is very low and poor, ridiculing only my person, and my being vain of over-rated parts and the undeserved favour of a Court.'

so much goodness as you: This will appear in some measure by the inclosed: It will save you all further pains of transcribing this Trifle, & fall in with the rest of your Copy exactly, if written as here layd down. I shall do myself the honour of receiving it at your hands in a few days, & beg your Ladiship in the meantime to think me with Esteem & Obligation | Your most faithful humble Servant | A. Pope.

Address: To the Countess of Burlington.

*POPE to THE COUNTESS OF BURLINGTON[1]

Chatsworth

5 *December* [1733]

Decr 5th 1733.

Madam,—Your Ladyship will think I am extremely obliged to the Author of the Inclosed Paper; which I therfore send you, & beg the favor of you to tell me, What method of proving my Gratitude I am to take? Nothing ever was more applicable to the *Detractor*; I wish the same could be said of the *Poet*.

I impatiently long to pay my thanks to my Benefactress: to whom I can only wish (in the old-fashiond phrase) Health & Happiness: If God gives you the first, you can give yourself the other. If Lord Burlington will be troubled with me on Friday, I'll commit myself to his Horses, at whatever hour they'l come for me after twelve. I am Entirely his, and with the utmost regard, Madam, | Your Ladyships most | obliged Servant, | A. Pope.

Address: To the Right Honble the | Countess of Burlington | at | Chiswick.
Postmark: PENY POST PAYD.

POPE to THE EARL OF OXFORD

Harl. 7525

26 *December* 1733–
7 *January* 1733/4

Decr 26th 1733.

My Lord—I sincerely wish yourself Lady Oxford & Lady Margaret, the happyest New years to come. I have so many things to tell you, that I can tell you none, and therefore am inclined not to write at all.

---

[1] In November the pamphlet warfare had been renewed by the appearance of Hervey's *Epistle from a Nobleman from Hampton Court to a Doctor of Divinity*. The divine was Dr. Sherwin, Canon of Chichester and protégée of the Duke of Richmond. To these courtiers he was a stupid butt, and Hervey was indignant (or pretended to be) that Sherwin helped get some of Hervey's verses into the hands of printers. See Lord Ilchester's *Lord Hervey and his Friends*, pp. 177, 188–91, 300–1. Pope is probably sending to Lady Burlington verses by an ally, possibly *Tit for Tat; or Vice Versa. A small Poem in Answer to Vicey's Epistle to Parson Sh—n*, which was advertised on 4 Dec. in *The Daily Journal* for publication next week. Pope would receive an advance copy. 'Vicey' is a nickname for Vice-chamberlain Hervey. A small but indecent drawing preserved at Chatsworth among sketches possibly by William Kent concerns Vicey, Dr. Sh—n, and others.

Whatever I can say of my Zealous desires for your felicity is short of the truth; and as to the rest, it is too long a story to begin till I have the pleasure to meet your Lordship, and can at the same time make an end of it.

This I writ a week ago, and having nothing more material to say, was ashamd to send it. But seeing they can't tell me when you return to Town, I was resolvd not to let the Season pass without sending you all this Poor Wish at least. I hope my Lady Oxford is perfectly well, tho I heard she has not been so, notwithstanding your Porter has often told me all was well at Wimpole. Believe me to be with the truest Esteem and unalterable Sincerity, My Lord, | Your Lordship's most | obedient affection|ate, and obliged | Servant, | A. Pope.

Jan. 7. 1733

If Lord Dupplin be with you, I hope he will accept my humble Services.

The chief correspondents of this year were Fortescue—whose friendship was untroubled by the crises of '33 that estranged Pope from the Court—Lord Oxford, whose daughter in July was married to the Duke of Portland, Dr. Arbuthnot, whose health was sadly declining, and Caryll. Pope's publications for the year were brilliant, but apart from the *Epistle to Dr. Arbuthnot* they find little mention in the letters. At the beginning of the year several anonymous poets published in his defence against the somewhat scandalous Lord Hervey, but Pope was silent until 2 January 1734/5, when he published his *Epistle to Dr. Arbuthnot*. From July till October he was rambling to Stowe, Rousham, Cirencester, Bevis Mount, Bath, and then back home again. In general his health was not good except during his stay at Bevis Mount. Early in the year and again in December he was confined to his bed for some days.

POPE *to* TONSON, JR.¹   [1733/4]

(Facsimile)

Sir,—I desire you'l take these five Setts of the Odyssey, & do what you can with 'em.

I desire also you'l cause the Pacquet I send, to be bound together, as many in a Volume as are tyed together. Let the Octavo be made to match in colour & Size this which is already bound, & Letter it LIBELS, ON POPE &c. Vol. 2d

Pray Bind the duodecimos also in another vol. the same colour, Letterd CURL & COMPANY.

And Bind the Gulliveriana, & letter it (Same Colour) thus, LIBELS ON SWIFT & POPE.

In this you will oblige | Sir | Your Very faithful | Servant | A. Pope.

I don't know but soon we may have some better business together.

Pray send me Philips's Freethinkers. and the first or second Vol. of Blackmores Essays, in which is his piece of Heroic poetry.

One of these pamphlets is imperfect at the end, of which I desire you'l procure an entire one.

Address: To Mr. Tonson.

¹ The text is taken from a facsimile of the original found at the Huntington Library tipped into a copy of Pope's *Works*, vol. i (1871). The fascimile lacks the last sentence and the address, which are added from the text in *Gent. Mag.*, for 1836, p. 30.

The volumes here ordered to be bound are preserved in the British Museum (pressmark c. 116.61–4). Since the latest pamphlet included is dated 1733, one assumes that the binding was done currently—especially since Tonson is asked to find a perfect copy of one of the items.

POPE *to* CARYLL   1 *January* 1733/4

Add. 28618

New years day 1733-4

Many things have hindered you from hearing of me—among the rest
a willingness I had to give Mrs Cath: Caryll an account of her commission.[1] I have got it done and desire to know by what method it may
be conveyed safe to her hands.

You have heard of a poetical war begun upon me by Lord Harvey.[2]
but it is like to a war only on one side, for I shall not contend with
angels either of light or darkness. If my allies and volunteers will list
themselves against him, they may fight without their general, and (as
sometimes it hath happened in modern politics) of seconds, become
principals.

The *Essay upon Man* is a more serious thing; therefore it will be
sent you.[3] To the best of my judgment the author shews himself a
Christian at last in the assertion, that all *Earthy Happiness* as well as
Future Felicity depends upon the doctrine of the gospel, love of God
and man, and that the whole aim of our being is to attain happiness
here, and hereafter by the practice of universal charity to man, and
entire resignation to God. More *particular* than this he could not be
with any regard to the subject, or manner in which he treated it. I
shall be glad to know your opinion of his winding up.

I send you not the compliments but the sincere wishes of the season
and that the winter of your age may resemble this of the Year, than
which, surely, never was a gentler, a warmer and a finer. Your god-
daughter has a whole cargo of books for you. I have nothing to add
my self, but the assurance that I am truly | Dear sir | Yours A. Pope.

†POPE *to* SWIFT   6 *January* 1733/4

1740

Jan. 6, 1734.

I never think of you and can never write to you, now, without drawing many of those short sighs of which we have formerly talk'd: The
reflection both of the friends we have been depriv'd of by death, and
of those from whom we are separated almost as eternally by absence,
checks me to that degree, that it takes away in a manner the pleasure

---

[1] On this commission see Pope to Caryll, 28 Feb. 1733/4.

[2] By 'begun' Pope implies that Lord Hervey was the aggressor; Lord Hervey asserted
that Pope had begun the war. See Lord Ilchester's *Lord Hervey and his Friends*, p. 189.
During the first two months of 1734 the 'seconds' of the two principals were exceedingly
active.

[3] The fourth Epistle of the *Essay* had not yet appeared. Although generally assigned to
Pope by this time the poem was not yet by him acknowledged as his. Pope perhaps is sending
Caryll an advance copy of Epistle IV, which appeared later in January.

(which yet I feel very sensibly too) of thinking I am now conversing with you. You have been silent to me as to your works; whether those printed here are, or are not genuine? but one I am sure is yours;[1] and your method of concealing your self puts me in mind of the bird I have read of in India,[2] who hides his head in a hole, while all his feathers and tail stick out. You'll have immediately by several franks (even before 'tis here publish'd) my Epistle to Lord Cobham, part of my *Opus Magnum*,[3] and the last[4] Essay on Man, both which I conclude will be grateful to your bookseller on whom you please to bestow them so early. There is a Woman's war declar'd against me by a certain Lord *,[5] his weapons are the same which women and children use, a pin to scratch, and a squirt to bespatter. I writ a sort of answer, but was ashamed to enter the lists with him, and after shewing it to some people, suppress it: otherwise it was such as was worthy of him and worthy of me. ⌈He has been since very well answered by the Parish Bellman's repeating his Verses from door to door and printing them as his own in his paper.⌉[6]—I was three weeks this autumn with Lord Peterborow, who rejoices in your doings, and always speaks with the greatest affection of you. I need not tell you who else do the same, you may be sure almost all those whom I ever see, or desire to see. I wonder not that B——[7] paid you no sort of civility while he was in Ireland: he is too much a half-wit to love a whole-wit,[8] and too much half-honest, to esteem any entire merit. I hope and think he hates me too, and I will do my best to make him; he is so insupportably insolent in his civility to me when he meets me at one third place, that I must affront him to be rid of it. That strict neutrality as to publick parties, which I have constantly observ'd in all my writings, I think gives me the more title to attack such fools, that[9] slander and belye my character in private, to those who know me not. Yet even this is a liberty I will never take, unless at the same time they are Pests of private society, or mischievous members of the publick, that is to say, unless they are

---

[1] *On Poetry, a Rhapsody* appeared a week before Pope wrote this letter. Possibly Pope had already seen a copy of *An Epistle to a Lady, who desir'd the Author to make Verses on her in the Heroick Style*, for publishing which Wilford was arrested on 11 Jan., Gilliver on the 22d, and Mrs. Barber on the 30th.

[2] the bird . . . who] the Indian bird I have read of, who *1741 L; 1742 L*.

[3] The Epistle to Cobham appeared ten days later. It was a part of the great work detailed in Spence, p. 315.

[4] and the last Essay] and last the Essay *1742 Lbc*.

[5] The asterisk, standing for Hervey, was omitted in the London editions of 1741 and 1742.

[6] This sentence, found in the clandestine volume of 1740, was omitted in all succeeding texts. Is it possible that the *Bellman of St James's Verses for the Year 1734* (used and published at the beginning of the year) came from Pope's pen and for that reason were omitted from mention here? The verses were hardly more hostile to Hervey than several other 'answers' that Pope might have mentioned.

[7] B[ubb] Doddington, who had an Irish sinecure at this time.

[8] whole-wit] true-wit *1741 L; 1742 L*.   [9] that] as *1741 L; 1742 L*.

enemies to all men as well as to me.—Pray write to me when you can: If ever I can come to you, I will: if not, may providence be our friend and our guard thro' this simple world, where nothing is valuable, but sense and friendship. Adieu, dear Sir, may health attend your years, and then may more years be added to you.

P.S. I am just now told a very curious Lady intends to write to you about some poems said to be yours. Pray tell her, that you have not answered me on the same questions, and that I shall take it as a thing never to be forgiven from you, if you tell another what you have conceal'd from me.

POPE *to* JONATHAN RICHARDSON[1]   8 *January* [1733/4]

Elwin–Courthope, ix. 501

Tuesday, Jan. 8 [1732/3]

According to your kind request I will dedicate myself to you on Thursday morning from ten to one, and then dine with our friend Cheselden at two, whose hour better agrees with my stomach than yours. Adieu, and know me for your affectionate servant.

POPE *to* CARYLL   28 *February* [1733/4]

Add. 28618

Feb. 28.

I know 'tis long since I received yours, but really more of my time has been taken up here in town than you could almost credit, when you consider me as an unbusied and independent man: But a man that will be busy in his friend's concerns, and feels a part in the general concerns of mankind cannot have much leisure. And whosoever is linked by one relation, or other of society to half the town, and is (in one sense) a public person, tho' his heart and constitution both require him to be but a private one, such an one, I say, can hardly be an independent. If you wanted me you should hear more of me, but God forbid you should ever need so feeble a prop.

Your staircase, I think as you do, must be *in claro oscuro* with pillars and niches only painted. In order to which, if you'll send me a drawing of the feet and inches of each side with the outline and shape of the wall to be filled up I will make you a draught.

I hope the next coach or carrier will bring Mrs. C. Caryl's picture

---

[1] Elwin printed from 'Richardson's transcript'. Presumably the bracketed year 1732/3 is Elwin's choice. If Pope wrote correctly 'Tuesday Jan. 8', the year must be 1734, since the only years during Pope's acquaintance with Richardson and Cheselden on which the 8th was Tuesday were 1734 and 1740. In 1740 Pope was in Bath at this date. Nothing makes 1734 impossible, but of course Pope may have misdated the letter.

in safety:[1] I caused it to be carefully boxed up, and sent to Mr. Pigot's who promised it should be taken care of. I am forced to write this in the hurry of company, and steal from three ladies to do it. One is your god-daughter, who is ashamed of not writing too, but I leave her to speak for her self another day: by this post I am sure she cannot. Your candid opinion not only on the *Essay on Man*,[2] but its author pleases me truly. I think verily he is as honest, and as religious a man as myself, and one that never will forfeit justly, your kind character of him. It is not directly owned, and I do assure you never was, whilst you were kept in ignorance of it. Adieu, forgive me, and love me as becomes a Christian. I am Dear sir | Ever yours | A: Pope.

*POPE to THE EARL OF BURLINGTON

Chatsworth

[*March or April* 1734]

My Lord,—I had set out upon the Water to meet you at Chiswick, but found the Wind full in my teeth, & so chilling an East, that I could not proceed. Yet impatient I am at all times to see you, & at this have besides a strong Inclination to see the Bishop of Cloyne[3] before he departs. At all events, if you can, I beg your Lordship to send on your Coach hither & I'll be with you the moment it comes. I need not beg your Excuse for any thing, while I find my Heart truly yours, as It will ever be. | A. Pope

Twitnam: Friday, 9 aclock

Address: To the Rt. Hon. the Earl of Burlington. | at Chiswick.

POPE to FORTESCUE[4]

27 *March* 1734

Maggs Bros. Catalogue 140, November 1896

EXCERPT

Yet reflect that Riches can give neither Health nor Pleasure in any high degree; and that all we can have or enjoy in this world is Competence, Ease, and a good Concience. . . .[5]

---

[1] For Miss Catherine's commission see the letter of 1 Jan. 1733/4.

[2] The last Epistle of the *Essay* was on sale 24 Jan. of this year.

[3] Pope's friend, the philosopher George Berkeley, was notified of his elevation to the see of Cloyne 14 Jan. 1733/4. He left England about the middle or latter half of April, and did not return until 1752. Throughout February and early March Berkeley was confined by the gout.

[4] Offered for sale in the Maggs Bros. Catalogue No. 140 (Nov. 1896) and again in Catalogue 220 as lot 1072.

[5] Pope is paraphrasing lines 77–80 of his recently published Fourth Epistle of his *Essay on Man*.

POPE *to* THE EARL OF OXFORD[1]   [1734?]

Longleat Portland Papers, xii

Your Lordship gave me hopes that you would take up with a poor
Dinner at Twitnam in your Way to Bulstrode, some day this week.
I am just going thither, and beg to know the Day most convenient to
you. I am Ever | My Lord, | Your most sincerely- | -obliged humble
Servant | A. Pope.

Tuesday night.

Address: To the Rt. Hon. the | Earl of Oxford.

BOLINGBROKE *to* SWIFT   12 *April* 1734

Add. 4806

Reverend & Dear Sir,—I have received yours of the 16th of Feb;
very lately, but have not yet seen the person who brought it,[2] nor am
likely to see him, unless he finds me out in my Retreat: our friend Pope
is in Town, & to him I send this letter, for he tells me he can forward
it to you by the hands of one of our common friends. If I can do Mr
Faulkner any service, I shall certainly do it, because I shall catch att
any opportunity of pleasing you, but my help in a project of a subscription will, I fear, avail him little. I live much out of the world
and I do not blush to own that I am out of fashion in it. my wife, who
is extreamly obliged to you for your kind remembrance of her, & who
desires me to say all the fond things from her to you which I know
she thinks, enjoys a precarious health, easily shook, & sometimes interrupted by fits of severe pain, but upon the whole much better than it
has been these five years. I walk down hill easily & leisurely enough,
except when a strong disposition to the Jaundice that I have long
carried about me, gives me a shove. I guard against it as well as I can;
the censors say not as well as I might: too sedentary a life hurts me,
and yet I do not care to lead any other, for sauntering about my
grounds is not exercise. I say I will be very active this summer, & I
will try to keep my word. Riding is your panacea, and Bathurst is
younger than his sons by observing the same Regimen. if I can keep
where I am a few years longer I shall be satisfyed, for I have something, and not much to do, before I dye. I know by experience one
cannot serve the present age. about Posterity one may flatter oneself,
& I have a mind to write to the next age. you have seen I doubt not

---

   1 The marriage of Lady Margaret and the Duke of Portland was arranged early in 1734.
This letter might be written at any time either during the negotiation of the match or after
the wedding, provided Pope was at home and Oxford intending a visit to Bulstrode. Early
1734 is the first probable moment for it.
   2 George Faulkner, Swift's Dublin publisher, had come over hoping to enlist subscribers
for Swift's collected *Works*, which he was bringing out in four volumes.

the Ethic Epistles:[1] and tho' they go a little into metaphysicks I perswade myself you both understand and approve them. the first Book being finished, the others will soon follow for many of them are writ or crayoned out. what are you doing? good I am sure, but of what kind? pray Mr Dean be a little more cautious in your Recommendations. I took care a year ago to remove some obstacles that might have hindered the success of one of your Recommendations and I have heartily repented of it since. the fellow wants morals & as I hear Decency sometimes.[2] You have had accounts I presume which will not leave you att a loss to guess whom I mean. Is there then no hope left of seeing you once more in this Island? I often wish myself out of it, and I shall wish it so much more if it is impossible de voisiner, I know no English word to say the same thing, with you. Adieu Dear Sir, no man living preserves a higher esteem, or a more warm & sincere friendship for you than I do.

April the 12th 1734

Endorsement (by Swift): Ld Bolingbroke | May 14th 1734 | Ansd. May 25. 1734.

POPE *to* CARYLL[3]   *19 April* [1734]
Add. 28618

I was excessively out of humour to find that Mrs. Cath Caryll's picture was not come to your hands, which I sent glazed and boxed up full six weeks ago to Mr. Pigott's. Upon enquiry I have the satisfaction to hear it is safe there. I only directed it to your name, but the farther superscription to the carrier I did not add. Pray, therefore, enquire about it, as also a book[4] I shall send thither directed in like manner. I feared to open the case might endanger the glass in the hands of the servants, and therefore sent the book separate. As to my journey to Southampton, it is altogether uncertain as to the time, and my going thence will be as uncertain, because it is quite across the country to Cirencester. If it be possible for me to know, I will send, or come to you, unless the expedition be required in such haste (by the two most

---

[1] i.e. the *Essay on Man*.

[2] The reference is to the Rev. Matthew Pilkington, whom Swift had not merely recommended to the Lord Mayor as chaplain and to his other friends but had also allowed to act as agent in publishing various poems. Mrs. Barber had brought these poems to Pilkington, and *The London Evening Post*, 2 Feb. 1733/4, announces that 'On Wednesday Morning [30 January] Mrs. Mary Barber was taken up by two of his Majesty's Messengers', on the Information of the Rev. Mr. Pilkington, Chaplain to the late Ld. Mayor, on account of an *Epistle to a Lady* lately publish'd: She was examined yesterday in the Evening, and admitted to Bail.'

[3] At the top of this letter Caryll's scribe wrote the word 'Misplaced'. The letter is out of chronological order in the MS.

[4] The quarto (collected) edition of the *Essay on Man* was advertised in *The London Evening Post*, 20 Apr. 1734, as that day published.

impetuous men I know)[1] as to render it impracticable. In the mean time, a line from you will reach me here; whence I've no thoughts of stirring till the elections are over and the countrie's[2] quiet. You may therefore please to send me the draught of your staircase and lobby whenever it is convenient for you. It would be a great pleasure to me to contribute to the ornament of Ladyholt.

I truly congratulate you on the recovery of Mrs. Caryll. Your god-daughter and I often lament your condition in hers, knowing the just reasons you both have to love one another. She was twice or thrice beginning to write to you. Once indeed I hindered her, by giving her expectations of my daily hearing from you, and not doubting but you would send an account of what she most desired to know, your lady's health. And she told me that another time her brother prevented her, by requiring an immediate answer that post, to the most inconsiderate and unreasonable letter I ever saw; namely, desiring her to propose to a lawyer (of whom she had been forced to take up the money Mr. Blount owed her for near two years together for her daily subsistence) that he should lend her more till it was agreeable to his own conveniency or pleasure to pay her, and at the same time to dispute with her of a certain sum, which, thro' the length of time, he had forgot whether paid or no, and could produce no receipt for. In a word, he desired to let the account run on, and to let her run in debt, merely that he might keep her in debt, and then dispute the sum. I advised her to complain of this proceeding to you and some other relations, and endeavour to bring him to reason, first that way, before she obliged him to more punctuality the only way that insiderate[3] people will be compelled to do justice,—I mean by law. Whether she has or no, I know not, having not seen her for sometime.

My last employment has been to stucco over the rest of my palace, which you may now more truly style *Little Whitehall* than when last you saw it. I wish you would do me the same pleasure again. Next Monday the same company you parted with here, will be here again. And Sir Clement Cottrell shall drink your health. Mr. Pigott is much out of order. I wish good men were immortal, if it were only for example for others. But He who is the giver of all goodness, knows best, and ordains best | Adieu, | Yours ever | A. Pope.

Twittnam. 19. Apr. . . .

---

[1] Lords Peterborow and Bathurst.
[2] For *counties* or, more vaguely, *country districts*, as frequently in the idiom of Pope's day.
[3] The word is *ben trovato* for *inconsiderate* doubtless.

*POPE *to* FORTESCUE   [*May* 1734]

The Pierpont Morgan Library

Saturday

I have got up the Sum my Sister wants, which is, three hundred pounds, which I am to lend her upon the Security: I beg you to consult the writings, all which are what she carried you (the Deed) & which are in Mr Cruwys hands. You'l (I [doubt] not) take all possible care that [she] be secur'd in it. Pray let a proper writing be drawn between us, with what convenient speed you can (for the Money is wanted instantly) and let my Sister know how soon she may sign it, that it may be brought to Twitnam for me, for I would at the same time send her the Mony by the same Messenger. She can send her Son with it. I depend on seeing you on Saturday: all health attend you. I go to day or early to morrow. Yours ever, | A. Pope.

Address: To Wm Fortescue Esqr
Endorsement (by Fortescue): Mr Pope | May. 1734.

*ROBERT DODSLEY *to* POPE   8 *May* [1734]

Longleat Portland Papers, xii

May 8th 1734

Sir,—I beg you will be so good as to look over the Lines to Lady Mar: Harley,[1] & tell me whether you think I should be excus'd in presenting them to her Ladyship. If you think they would be favourably receiv'd, I should be glad (pardon my Freedome) that You would please to make any Alterations You think proper. As to the other,[2] I believe it will be my last Essay of the kind: if it is not too much trouble to You to read it over, I should be very glad of your Opinion of it. Your bearing with my Impertinence is an Instance of Goodness which I shall ever gratefully acknowledge.

     I am Sir | Your most Obedient Humble Servant | R. Dodsley

Address: To Alexander Pope Esqr

     [1] Pope evidently passed on this letter, with the enclosed verses, to Lord Oxford. The verses still are preserved with the letter, but they are not here printed. The year is added to the superscribed date in a later hand. The day and month are not surely in Dodsley's hand. The verses were promptly composed; for the marriage, though announced by the newspapers in May as speedily to be consummated, did not actually take place until July. Samuel Wesley of Westminster School published verses on the occasion, but Dodsley's undistinguished offering seems to have been unpublished.

     [2] 'The other' is hardly identifiable. In November of this year Dodsley published *An Epistle to Mr. Pope, Occasion'd by his Essay on Man*, which is probably *not* spoken of here.

POPE *to* MRS. KNIGHT[1]   [1734]

Elwin–Courthope, ix. 452

Saturday.

Dear Madam,—It was my intention to have returned to town this day to meet Mr. Mallet, but a good deal of indisposition obliged me to take a little physic to-night to enable me to live another day or two in London. If Lord Bolingbroke be in Dover Street, I wish Mr. M. would wait on him first and tell him of his journey. He would be sure to find me here to-morrow, but the first day I can I will be with you. I have nothing to add, but a very sincere assurance that I wish to be any way useful to you as being with truth, madam, your most obliged and faithful servant.

POPE *to* MALLET   [*May or June* 1734]

Sir John Murray

I am always obliged & pleased by your Letters; tho' I am too busy, too sick, or too lazy, often, to answer them regularly. Pray let it not discourage you. Indeed I have of late had a smaller share of Health than ever, & in hope of amending it, I shall ramble about the Kingdom, as you are to do, most part of the Summer. I wish it may so happen as we may meet in our progress. If you go to Down Amney, I go to Ciceter, if you go to Portsmouth, I shall be at Southampton, if you ramble near Oxford, I shall be at Stowe: in any of which places I can entertain you, a day or two. If I can, I will return from Stowe to Oxford, but this cannot be till July or August.

Pray tell Mr Harte I have given Gilliver his Poem to print,[2] but whether he would chuse to publish it now, or next winter, let himself judge. I undertook to correct the press, but find myself so bad a Reviser by what I see has escaped me in my last thing, that I believe he had best have it sent him to Oxford, & besides that may be but an amusement to his or Your Eyes which indeed is a Pain to mine, since the frequency of my last Headakes. You will order Gilliver accordingly, & upon the whole let Mr Harte give him directions. I fancy the Title of an *Essay on Reason* is the best, & am half of opinion, if no Name be set to it, the public will think it mine especially since in the Index, (annext to the large paper Edition of the Essay on Man) the Subject of the next Epistle is mentioned to be *of Human Reason* &c. But whether this may be an Inducement, or the Contrary, to Mr Harte, I know

---

[1] Elwin printed from a transcript from Stowe MSS. made by Peter Cunningham. The dating is completely hypothetical.

[2] The title-page of the Rev. Walter Harte's *Essay on Reason* is dated 1735. It does not bear Harte's name.

not: I like his poem so well (especially since his last alterations) that it would no way displease me.

What are You doing? or what are you writing? what ever it be, I wish it successful, and am always with Truth, Affection & Esteem | Dear Sir Yours | A. Pope.

POPE *to* FORTESCUE[1]   [*June* 1734]

Arthur A. Houghton, Jr.

The only day I had, I came hither, & was unlucky in missing you. I go away this moment, if you come on Saturday, Lady Suffolk dines with me, & you'l find her even after dinner, if you can't come sooner. On Sunday I shall be at home. Why can't you lye at Twitnam, Saturday night, I want to ask, & tell you, many things; some of business.

I hope Mr Cruwys has got the remainder of Mrs Blounts debt from her Brother, the whole 75*l*. which she has occasion enough for. Adieu, & Know me for | Yours ever faithfully | A. Pope.

Address: To Mr Fortescue.

*POPE *to* FORTESCUE[2]   [17 *June* 1734]

Sotheby sale, 4 December 1902, lot 502

Monday night.

I had been called for home on occasion of the fire in my neighbourhood, & just returned to town. I am gone for Stowe,[3] where I shall stay a week, and thence to Cirencester. I beg you to forward Mrs. Blount's business, as to the arrear, with what speed you can. . . . I am so unused to long journeys, that it is quite melancholy to me. Adieu once more,

---

[1] The year seems to be 1734 since Michael Blount is being pursued for his sister's income. It seems probable that the letter dates before Pope's summer rambles, and it should come before the letter here placed as [17 June 1734]. Lady Suffolk is preparing to retire from Court, as she does in August.

Pope is in town at the time of writing.

[2] The excerpt here given is from the sale catalogue. The date is arrived at from the mention of Mrs. Blount's arrears (see Pope to Caryll, 19 Apr.) and from the item in *The Daily Journal* on Saturday, 15 June 1734, which announces the loss by fire of the house in Twickenham occupied by M. de Chavigny, the French Ambassador. 'The house with its rich contents was entirely consumed.' The house was not close to Pope's villa, but since it belonged to the Earl of Denbigh, with whom and the Countess Pope had some friendship, Pope would be interested.

[3] Pope travelled in company with General Dormer and the Hon. George Berkeley, who in the following year married Lady Suffolk. Of the journey Berkeley writes to Lady Suffolk from Shotover, 19 June 1734, 'We performed our journey hither with great ease, only little Pope was very ill the whole day. . . . Pope grew better at supper, and of course very irregular, and laughed at me for the care I pretended to take of him' (*Suffolk Correspondence*, ii. 71). Shotover was where Col. Schutz lived.

and sometimes give me a line, which they will forward to me from Twickenham.

*POPE *to* JONATHAN RICHARDSON[1]   25 *June* [1734?]

Yale University

You might be certain I was either not in being, or not within the same Sphære, when you heard nothing & had no Commerce with me so long. I've been in Glostershire or Berkshire this good while. the Day before I set out on my journey I calld at your door. I hope to see you in less than a fortnight, & fix our Day; perhaps we may voyage together. Adieu. You are always to know me for | Your truly affectionate | Servant, | A. Pope.

Cirencester | June the 25.

I honour your Son, as he honours his Father.

Address: To | Mr Richardson, at his | house in Queen's Square | Bloomsbury. | London.

Postmark: 27/IV CIRENCESTER

Frank: Free | Bathurst

POPE *to* THE EARL OF OXFORD[2]   2 *July* [1734]

Longleat Portland Papers, xii

Cirencester July 2d | 1734

My Lord,—I have deferred giving your Lordship any account of myself, till I could send you a better, than my ill health for the first ten-days allowed me to do: And my letter will now have something in it more worthy your acceptance than my own Services, when I can assure you of those of my Lord Cobham & Lord Bathurst: who both of them drink your health, & wish with me all Prosperity to you & yours. I made your Compliments to Mr Dormer, with whom & the General[3] I past five days, partly at Rousham, partly at Stowe. My Lord Cobham hopes, we shall once more see that place together (tis I that have most reason to hope that) but he knows you were at present better imployed. Whether you have been at Wimpole, (as the news says), or not, whether Lady Margaret be marryd on Thursday (as the

---

[1] The year is difficult if one takes seriously the statement that Pope has been 'a good while' in Gloucestershire and Berkshire. There seems to be no year in which it can be so taken, and 1734 is otherwise plausible.

[2] The year in the superscription is in Lord Oxford's hand.

[3] General James Dormer was brother of 'Mr.' Robert Dormer of Rousham.

news says) or not.¹ I do most heartily wish you happy in all places, & Her happy at all times, & as many days as she lives. I could say a finer or a prettier thing, upon a Marriage, and so could my Lord Hervey, who yet cannot wish any body half so well as a Plainer Man can. But tis such a Lessening to a Good Heart to be hunting about for fine words, that I am content to say no more.

I am with all Sincerity & Respect, My Lady Oxford's & Your Lordships | Ever faithfull & obliged | humble Servant, | A. Pope.

Pray desire Lady Margaret to make my Excuses to Mrs Caesar² for writing no Verses on her Wedding.

Endorsement (by a secretary): Mr Pope | Cirencester July 2d 1734

BOLINGBROKE *to* SWIFT³   27 *June–*6 *July* 1734
Add. 4806

From my Farm June the 27th 1734

I thank you Mr Dean, or to use a name to me more sacred, I thank you my Friend, for your letter of the 23d of May, which came to me by the post: I answer it by the same conveyance, and provided the diligent Inspectors of private mens correspondence do not stop our letters, they have my leave to do what they will do without it, to open & read them. if they expect to find anything which may do us hurt, or them good, their disappointment will give me pleasure in the proportion I shall imagine it gives them pain. I should have another pleasure of higher Relish, if our Epistles were to be perused by Persons of higher Rank; and who knows, considering the mighty importance we are of, whether that may not happen? how would these Persons stare, to see such a thing as sincere, cordial friendship subsist inviolate, & grow and strengthen, from year to year, in spight of distance, absence, & mutual Inutility?

But enough on this. let us turn to other subjects. I have read in the golden verses of Pythagoras, or in some other collection of wise apothegms of the Ancients, that a man of business may talk of Philosophy, a man who has none may practice it. What do you think of this maxim? is it exact? I have a strange distrust of maxims. We make

¹ Lady Margaret was married to the Duke of Portland on Thursday, 11 July. Lord Hervey doubtless exercised his pretty wit on the marriage of the Princess Royal to the Prince of Orange, which, after delays, had taken place on 14 Mar. of this year. Some of his observations on the marriage, recorded in his *Memoirs*, are not pretty.

² Mrs. Caesar has evidently urged Pope to write an epithalamium for Lady Margaret's wedding. It is perhaps curious that the family of the second Earl of Oxford got so little attention in Pope's verse if one considers the close friendship and the usefulness to the poet of the Harleian Library.

³ Elwin printed only the last part of this letter, that concerning Pope. But the whole is so perfect an example of the common reasonings and fallacies of the period that it deserves currency. Ball (v. 75–79) prints the entire text.

as many observations as our time, our knowledge, & the other means we have, give us the opportunity of making on a "Physical matter". We find that they all correspond, and that one general proposition may be affirmed as the Result of them. This we affirm, and in consequence this becomes a maxim among our followers, if we have any. Thus the King of Siam affirmed that water was always in a fluid state, and I doubt not but the Talapoins, do they not call them so?, held this maxim. Neither He nor they had ever climbed the neighbouring mountains of Ava. their observations were confined to the burning climate they inhabited. 'Tis much the same in moral maxims, founded on observations of the conduct of men; for there are other moral maxims of universal truth, as there are moral dutys of eternal obligation. We see what the conduct is, and we guess what the motives are; of great numbers of men. But then we see often att too great a distance, or thro' a faulty medium, we guess with much uncertainty from a thousand Reasons concerning a thing as various, as changing, as inconsistent as the Heart of man, and even when we see right, & guess right, we build our maxims on a small number of observations (for such they are comparatively how numerous soever they may be taken by themselves) which our own age & our own country cheifly have presented to us.

You & I have known one man in particular,[1] who affected business he often hindered, & never did; who had the honour among some & the blame among others, of bringing about great Revolutions in his own Country & in the general affairs of Europe, and who was att the same time the idlest creature living; who was never more copious than in expressing, when that was the theme of the day, his indifference to power, and his contempt of what we commonly call Honours, such as Titles, Ribbonds, &c., who should, to have been consistent, have had this indifference, and have felt this contempt, since he neither knew how to use power, nor how to wear honours, and yet who was jealous of one & fond of the other, even to ridicule. This character seems singular enough, & yet I have known some resembling it very much in general, & many exactly like it in the strongest marks it bore. Now let us suppose that some Rochfoucault or other, some anthroponomical Sage, should discover a multitude of similar instances, & not stumble upon any one repugnant. You & I should not however receive for a maxim, that he who affects business never does it; nor this, that he who brings about great Revolutions is always idle; nor this that He who expresses indifference to power, & contempt of honours, is jealous of one, & fond of the others.

Proceed we now Dear Doctor to application. A man in business, and a man who is out of it, may equally talk of Philosophy. that is

[1] The first Earl of Oxford.

certain. The question is whether the man in business may not practice it as well as the man out of business. I think he may, perhaps in this sense, as easily; But sure I am he may in this sence, as usefully. if we look into the world, our part of it I mean, we shall find I believe few Philosophers in business, or out of business. The greatest part of the men I have seen in business, perhaps all of them, have been so far from acting on Philosophical principles, that is on principles of Reason and Virtue, that they have not acted even on the highest principles of vice. I have not known a man of real ambition, a man who sacrificed all his passions, or made them all subservient to that one. But I have known many whose vanity, and whose avarice mimicked ambition. The greatest part of men I have seen out of business have been so far from practicing Philosophy, that they have lived in the world arrant Triflers, or retiring from it, have fallen into stupid indolence, and deserved such an inscription as Seneca mentions in one of his letters to Lucilius, to have been put over the door of one Vattia, hic situs est Vattia.[1] But for all this I think that a man in business may practice Philosophy as austerely to himself, and more beneficially to mankind than a man out of it. [2]The Stoicks were an affected pedantical Sect; but I have always approved that Rule of the Portique, that a Philosopher was not to exempt himself from the dutys of society, neither in the community to which he particularly belonged, nor in the great community of Mankind. Mencius and his master Confucius were strange metaphysicians, but they were good moralists, and they divided their Doctrines into three parts, the dutys of Man as an individual, as a member of a family, and a member of a State. In short a man may be, many men have been, & some I believe are Philosophers in business. He that can ever be so out of it, can be so in it.

But it is impossible to talk so much of Philosophy, and forget to speak of Pope. He is actually rambling from one friends house to another. He is now att Cirencester, he came thither from my Lord Cobhams; he came to my Lord Cobhams from Mr Dormers; to Mr Dormers from London, to London from Chiswick; to Chiswick from my Farm, to my Farm from his own Garden, and he goes soon from Lord Bathursts to Lord Peterborows, after which he returns to my farm again. The Daemon of verse sticks close to him. He has been imitating the Satire of Horace which begins Ambubaiarum Collegia, Pharmacopolæ, &c.[3] and has chose rather to weaken the images than

---

[1] See Seneca, *Epistles*, lv, esp. 4. The passage and the mention of Vatia show how differently Bolingbroke regarded (or affected to regard) his own 'inutility'. See ii. 252.

[2] Here Bolingbroke takes up a new pen, and one assumes that the part of the letter dated, at the end, 6 July, began here.

[3] Horace, *Sermones*, i. ii. The imitation was published in Dec. 1734 as *Sober Advice from Horace*, etc., 'Imitated in the Manner of Mr. Pope'. Pope never quite admitted authorship, but he included it later (still 'Imitated in the Manner of') in his octavo *Works*.

to hurt chaste ears overmuch. he has sent it me, but I shall keep his secret, as he desires, & shall not I think return him the copy, for the Rogue has fixed a ridicule upon me, which some events of my life would seem perhaps to justify him in doing. I am glad you approve his moral essays. they will do more good than the sermons and writings of some who had a mind to find great fault with them, and if the doctrines taught, hinted att, and implyed in them, and the trains of consequences deducible from these doctrines were to be disputed in prose, I think he would have no reason to apprehend either the free thinkers on one hand, or the narrow Dogmatists on the other. Some very few things may be expressed a little hardly, but none are I believe, unintelligible. I will let him know your complaints of his silence, which I wonder att the more, because he has often spoke in such a manner as made me conclude you heard from him pretty regularly. Your compliments shall be payed likewise to the other friends you mention. You complain of the vast alteration which the last seven years have made in you, and do you beleive that they have not made proportionable alterations in us? Satisfy yourself they have. We all go the same road, and keep much the same Stages. Let this consideration therefore not hinder you from coming amongst us. You shall ride, walk, trifle, meddle, chide, & be as ill bred as you please, and the indulgence you receive on these heads you shall return on these or others. Adieu. Ile speak to you about Books next time I write, if I can recollect what I intended to say upon a passage in your letter, or if anything else worth saying comes into my head. Adieu my friend.

July the 6th.

Endorsement (by Swift): Ld Bo—ke | Rx about Jul. 20th | 1734

POPE *to* CARYLL   7 *July* 1734

Add. 28618

Cirencester. 7 July. 1734

I know 'tis long since I ought to have acknowledged the favour of your kind letter but I was got upon the ramble, and am like to be so for some time. I am at present with Lord Bathurst. When I shall approach nearer to you I know not, but if I possibly can will tell you, having a desire once more to pass some days at Ladyholt and settle your staircase plan, &c. At present Lord Peterborow is at London, and narrowly missed me here last week. My health I find too precarious to venture abroad as I used to do, the least accident giving me colds and headaches,[1] which last so damage my eyes that it is a sort of

---

[1] Pope's health was thought by his friends to be affected by his habits of eating. During this visit to Cirencester Lord Bathurst wrote to Lady Suffolk (*Suffolk Correspondence*, ii. 81) as follows: 'You do well to reprove him about his intemperance; for he makes himself

task to me to write a letter or to read half an hour. I am forced to make myself what amends I can by thinking, and I assure you not the least part of my thoughts is employed on my friends. I think not the less, nor study the less for writing but rarely, and in the like manner I think not the less on you and some few others for not writing to them so often as I gladly would.

You know your God-daughter always has a share in my concern and I am sorry to tell you her brother keeps her still out of what is quite necessary to her subsistence, and which is worse, knows he does so, for she represented the whole situation of her affairs to him. I wish he knew at least that others are acquainted with his hard and inconsiderate conduct towards her, which is all the service, I think, in your power in this case. I am almost angry at your frequent mention of that trifling thing I meant to desire Mrs. Catharine's acceptance of, but 'tis so little that I've never thought to pay for it yet. The painting cost me nothing, and you'll guess the frame could not be worth much. Pray therefore let me hear no more of it. I do always desire to hear of what I so sincerely wish, as your health and family's welfare, which intelligence if you send first to Twittenham, will from thence be sent after me, where're I am. I've nothing to add but what has been told you these 25 years at least with equal and constant truth, that I am | Yours &c. | A. P.

POPE *to* DR. ARBUTHNOT   15 *July* [1734]

The Royal College of Surgeons of England

Cirencester: July the 15th

The day after I saw you I left the Town, & was truly concerned to see you so much out of order. As my Journies were long, & continued, I bade my Servant send me an account of the state of your health from time to time; for which it is impossible but I must have all the Concern, which many years Friendship for you, grounded on a long Experience of yours for me, must imprint in any grateful or sensible mind. But finding Their accounts but uncertain, I was very uneasy; till Mrs P. Blount, who never neglects a Friend, ill, or absent, took the Care of inquiring at Your house very punctually about you, on her own account and also writ me word what she learn'd of you. I am very much troubled to find, you are so little recover'd as to be kept out of Town for some time;[1] I hope it will at least be to your advantage;

---

sick every meal at your most moderate and plain table in England. Yesterday I had a little piece of salmon just caught out of the Severn, and a fresh pike that was brought me from the other side of your house out of the Thames. He ate as much as he could of both, and insisted upon his moderation, because he made his dinner upon one dish.'

[1] In this his last illness Dr. Arbuthnot stayed much in Hampstead, where the air was supposedly less trying for asthmatic complaints.

and tho I know you are as fit to Dye as any Man, I think no man fitter to Live for that very reason, or more Wanted by those who are in this world, both as a Comfort, and as an Example, to them. I am glad that your Family are with you; and I do sincerely wish you had with you Every thing, & every Person else, that could be a Consolation to you. I would fain flatter myself, you enjoy more than I fear you do; If I could any way contribute to your Ease or Amusement, I would hasten my Return: but my Engagement to Lord Peterborow yet stands good, to pass some weeks at Southampton, where he expects me at the end of this month. Lord Bathurst, (with whom I now am) sends you his Services & best wishes: if you care for any Venison, he will send you Some whenever you please to order it, at any place in Town; It can come twice a week in one day from this place thither. If it be not much trouble to you pray dear Sir write me a Line: if it be, let your Daughter do it, just to acquaint me in what State you are. God preserve you! if Easy to yourself, Long to us! to no man more, than to, Dear Sir | Your faithful Friend, A. Pope.

Address: To Dr Arburthnott, in | Cork street in | Burlington Garden | Piccadilly | London.
Frank: Free | Bathurst
Postmarks: [   ]/IY [Cir]encester

†DR. ARBUTHNOT *to* POPE   17 *July* 1734

1735

Hampstead, July 17, 1734

I Little doubt of your kind Concern for me, nor of that of the Lady you mention. I have nothing to repay my Friends with at present, but prayers and good wishes. I have the satisfaction to find that I am as officiously serv'd by my Friends, as he that has thousands to leave in Legacies; besides the Assurance of their Sincerity. God Almighty has made my bodily distress as easy as a thing of that nature can be: I have found some relief, at least sometimes, from the Air of this Place. My Nights are bad, but many poor Creatures have worse.

As for you, my good Friend, I think since our first acquaintance there has[1] not been any[2] of those little Suspicions or Jealousies that often affect the sincerest Friendships; I am sure not on my side. I must be so sincere as to own, that tho' I could not help valuing you

---

[1] has] have *1747–42*.
[2] In replying (2 Aug.) Pope quotes this passage either from memory or (as has been thought) as it was actually written and not as printed after modification. In the August letter (which is still preserved) Pope quotes as 'your expression' . . . '*Scarcely* any of those suspicions or jealousies which affect the truest friendships'. Since there can be no question of the firmness and continuity of their friendship, the editing or misquotation is of slight importance.

for those Talents which the World prizes, yet they were not the Foundation of my Friendship: They were quite of another sort; nor shall I at present offend you by enumerating them: And I make it my Last Request, that you continue[1] that noble *Disdain* and *Abhorrence* of Vice,[2] which you seem naturally endu'd with, but still with a due regard to your own Safety; and study more to reform than chastise, tho' the one often cannot[3] be effected without the other.

Lord Bathurst I have always honour'd for every good Quality, that a Person of his Rank ought to have: Pray give my Respects and kindest Wishes to the Family. My Venison Stomach is gone, but I have those about me, and often with me, who will be very glad of his Present. If it is left at my house it will be transmitted safe to me.

A Recovery in my Case, and at my Age, is impossible; the kindest Wish of my Friends is *Euthanasia*.[4] Living or dying, I shall always be | Your most faithful Friend, | And humble Servant, | Jo. Arbuthnot.

*POPE to THE EARL OF BURLINGTON   25 *July* [1734]

Chatsworth

July the 25th.

My Lord,—I intended to have given you some account of myself and of my motions, but the best excuse is, that it is very hard for me to know either. I had a much stronger desire to hear of you, and be certify'd of your own, as well as Lady Burlington's welfare (which I believe are nearer a-kin than with most marryed people) but here too rose a great difficulty, I could not tell to what place I should request you to direct to me? But being now in a place I never thought of, and not to stay there but one day, I chuse this settled station to write in. It is one of the prettiest I ever saw, and one of the best Houses I ever was in, an admirable fine Library, a delicious Park, & extensive Plantations. It wants only a few Temples & ornaments of Building, which I am contriving, in defect of better architects (who are a Rare & uncommon Generation, not born in every Family) or rather to prevent a wild Goth, whom I think they call Kent, (from a Country which has ever been held no part of Christendome) I am told this man hath suggested an odd thing, which thro his Violence of Temper and Ungovernable Spirit of Dominion (natural to all Goths) he will infallibly erect; unless I lay a Temple in his way, which he will probably not venture to pull down, after what he has (doubtless) heard of the fate of his Countryman Brennus for sacrilege. However as I cannot get this done in a day, I fear the owner of this place (who is a man of

---

[1] you continue] you will continue *1737–42*.
[2] Again in his reply of 2 Aug. Pope misquotes—without change of the thought.
[3] one often cannot] one cannot *1737–42 octavos only*.
[4] Dr. Arbuthnot died in his house in Cork Street, London, on 27 Feb. 1734/5.

no Resolution & never Positive in any thing) may drop my design. Having said so much of this, it may be proper to tell your Lordship he is one who has the honour to be your Relation, my Lord Bruce,[1] and that I write this from Tottenham.

By a letter I received from Dr Clark,[2] I have the pleasure to hear my Lady Burlington is well: & that she did me the honour to enquire of me. She really has the same right so to do, as any one has to send a Hue & Cry after a stray and absented Servant, a Truant Schoolboy, or a Deserting Foot-Soldier: for the first of these I am to her, and shall never depart from the Character, tho unworthy; the second I am with respect to my Studies; and the third, as having neither Horse nor Coach. I think to morrow to follow the Impulse of my Spirit and walk towards Amesbury,[3] to humble myself before Inigo Jones, and to proceed for Southampton, till the first Coach I meet takes pity on me. (I guess it will be Lord Peterborow's.) In the meantime, Lord Bathurst's in which I came hither, and Lord Bruce's, may come after me, in case I meet no other.

What a Consolation is it, to any pious and resigned mind, to find Providence thus taking care of him! not to Care or have the least sollicitude for worldly ways or events, but to depend on That, which finds Food for the Sparrow, and a Couch for the Beasts of the Earth! I have set forth, on this long and painful Pilgrimage, without a good Coat to my back, Gloves to my hands, or entire Shooes to my feet; when lo! at Woodstock I got Gloves, at Stowe Slippers, at Cirencester Cloth, and a Peruke! How have I cause to bless my Lot, when I compare it with the Condition of King Stanislaus?[4] In two days I shall be at Lord Pets. at Southampton Deo volente, adjuvante, manuducente: There & Every where   My Lord, Faithfully yours.

‡POPE *to* DR. ARBUTHNOT[5]   26 *July* 1734

1737
                                               July 26, 1734.

I thank you for your letter, which has all those genuine marks of a

1 Lord Bruce was in his second marriage brother-in-law to Lord Burlington. His first wife had been a relative of Lady Burlington's.

2 Dr. Alured Clarke, prebend of Winchester and religious adviser (with Dr. Samuel Clarke and others) to the Queen, had evidently been at Court and reported to Pope on Lady Burlington's health. See *Memoirs of Viscountess Sundon*, ii. 261–4.

3 Amesbury, home of the Duke and Duchess of Queensberry, was designed by Inigo Jones and completed by his son-in-law John Webb. Burlington's devotion to the Palladian tradition of Jones was widely influential. See *Suffolk Correspondence*, ii. 107–8.

4 At this time France was at war with the Emperor in an attempt to indemnify King Stanislaus for his loss of the throne of Poland. Walpole, justifying a refusal to join allies against France, made his famous remark to Queen Caroline: 'Madam, there are fifty thousand men slain this year in Europe and not one Englishman.'

5 This letter was printed by Pope as his answer to the letter from the Doctor dated 17 July. The reply actually sent is probably that dated 2 Aug., which in some respects dupli-

good mind by which I have ever distinguish'd yours, and for which I have so long loved you. Our friendship has been constant; because it was grounded on good principles, and therefore not only uninterrupted by any Distrust, but by any Vanity, much less any Interest.

What you recommend to me with the solemnity of a Last Request, shall have its due weight with me. That disdain and indignation against Vice, is (I thank God) the only disdain and indignation I have: It is sincere, and it will be a lasting one. But sure it is as impossible to have a just abhorrence of Vice, without hating the Vicious, as to bear a true love for Virtue, without loving the Good. To reform and not to chastise, I am afraid is impossible, and that the best Precepts, as well as the best Laws, would prove of small use, if there were no Examples to inforce them. To attack Vices in the abstract, without touching Persons, may be safe fighting indeed, but it is fighting with Shadows. General propositions are obscure, misty, and uncertain, compar'd with plain, full, and home examples: Precepts only apply to our Reason, which in most men is but weak: Examples are pictures, and strike the Senses, nay raise the Passions, and call in those (the strongest and most general of all motives) to the aid of reformation. Every vicious man makes the case his own; and that is the only way by which such men can be affected, much less deterr'd. So that to chastise is to reform. The only sign by which I found my writings ever did any good, or had any weight, has been that they rais'd the anger of bad men. And my greatest comfort, and encouragement to proceed, has been to see, that those who have no shame, and no fear, of any thing else, have appear'd touch'd by my Satires.

As to your kind concern for my Safety, I can guess what occasions it at this time. Some Characters I have drawn are such, that if there be any who deserve 'em, 'tis evidently a service to mankind to point those men out: yet such as if all the world gave them, none I think will own they take to themselves. But if they should, those of whom all the world think in such a manner, must be men I cannot fear. Such in particular as have the meanness to do mischiefs in the dark, have seldom the courage to justify them in the face of day; the talents that make a Cheat or a Whisperer, are not the same that qualify a man for an Insulter; and as to private villany, it is not so safe to join in an Assassination, as in a Libel. I will consult my safety so far as I think becomes a prudent man; but not so far as to omit any thing which I

cates and discredits the authenticity of this present reply. Of course Pope accidentally or ineptly misdates letters frequently, but if his other letters at this time are properly dated, he was on 26 July *en route* from Tottenham to Amesbury (where he found the Queensberrys from home) and Southampton. It was not a day when he would have reached Peterborow's house in time or in a mood to write such a letter. The letter in fact seems an expanded and able rewriting of the first half of the letter of 2 Aug. It is most probably a 'forgery', but it is certainly Pope's best defence in prose of his satire, and as such is invaluable.

think becomes an honest one. As to personal attacks beyond the law, every man is liable to them: as for danger within the law, I am not guilty enough to fear any. For the good opinion of all the world, I know it is not to be had: for that of worthy men, I hope I shall not forfeit it: for that of the Great, or those in power, I may wish I had it, but if thro' misrepresentations (too common about persons in that station) I have it not, I shall be sorry, but not miserable in the want of it.

It is certain, much freer Satyrists than I have enjoy'd the encouragement and protection of the Princes under whom they lived. Augustus and Meccœnas made Horace their companion, tho' he had been in arms on the side of Brutus; and allow me to remark it was out of the suff'ring Party too, that they favour'd and distinguish'd Virgil. You will not suspect me of comparing my self with Virgil and Horace, nor even with another Court-favourite, Boileau: I have always been too modest to imagine my Panegyricks were Incense worthy of a Court; and that I hope will be thought the true reason why I have never offer'd any. I would only have observ'd, that it was under the greatest Princes and best Ministers, that moral Satyrists were most encouraged; and that then Poets exercised the same jurisdiction over the Follies, as Historians did over the Vices of men. It may also be worth considering, whether Augustus himself makes the greater figure, in the writings of the former, or of the latter? and whether Nero and Domitian do not appear as ridiculous for their false Taste and Affectation, in Persius and Juvenal, as odious for their bad Government in Tacitus and Suetonius? In the first of these reigns it was, that Horace was protected and caress'd; and in the latter that Lucan was put to death, and Juvenal banish'd.

I wou'd not have said so much, but to shew you my whole heart on this subject; and to convince you, I am deliberately bent to perform that Request which you make your last to me, and to perform it with Temper, Justice, and Resolution. As your Approbation, (being the testimony of a sound head and an honest heart) does greatly confirm me herein, I wish you may live to see the effect it may hereafter have upon me, in something more deserving of that approbation. But if it be the Will of God (which I know will also be yours) that we must separate, I hope it will be better for You than it can be for me. You are fitter to live, or to die, than any man I know. Adieu my dear friend! and may God preserve your life easy, or make your death happy.

POPE *to* MRS. RACKETT   28 *July* [1734]

Ushaw College

July 28.

Dear Sister,—Tho I have very little to say, I write this to tell you I am just arrived at Lord Peterborrow's at Southampton, to which place you may direct to me. I hope your fears are removed by this time, by some Letter from my Nephew Michael. pray let me know what you hear. When did my Cosen John set out? and are you all well? My Love to my Cos. Harry.[1]

I am better than I have been and upon the whole much in the old way. I am always ready to do you any service I can, and always desirous to know your welfare. I shall continue here these three weeks. Adieu and believe me ever | Your affectionate | Brother, | A. Pope.

Mrs. Robinson gives | her Service to you.

Address: To Mrs Racket at the green | Canister in New North street | near Red lion field | Bloomsbury | London
Frank: Peterborow
Postmark: 31/IY

MALLET *to* POPE[2]   2 *Aug.* [1734]

1857 (Carruthers, pp. 434–6)

Chester, 2nd August.

After a tedious ramble of six weeks through South and North Wales, I am just arrived at Chester; from whence I do myself the pleasure to send you some account of my travels. I wish it may not prove altogether uninteresting to you, since it is to me a real refreshment to converse with you even at this distance.

I have seen nature and human nature, both in their undress; and, to say truth, the latter especially is infinitely the better for a little culture. If the golden age was stocked chiefly with such animals, I heartily thank Heaven for having reserved me to these iron times.

The ordinary women in Wales are generally short and squat, ill-favoured and nasty. Their head-dress is a remnant of coarse blanket, and for their linen . . . they wear none, and they are all barefooted. But then they are wonderfully good-natured.

The parsons I have seen are beyond all description astonishing. One of them, who has a living of no less than 140*l.* a year, having been asked by his patron the day he was ordained priest, why we observe

---

[1] 'Cousins' may also be nephews: these are all names of Mrs. Rackett's sons.

[2] Carruthers probably got this letter from Mapledurham. At least Pope sent it to Miss Blount, as he says in a letter to Mrs. Knight, 1 Sept. [1734].

the 30th of January, answered seriously, On account of our Blessed Lady's Purification. Though the story is incredible, it is true. But then he kills more red game and hollas louder to a pack of hounds than any other man in the country. A second, whose face no Dutch painter could deform by a caricatura, had the impudence lately to attempt a rape on the body of his clerk, for, what is as odd as the rest, the clerk of this parish is a woman. The Squires are rather more admirable than they are in England, and distinguished by the same attributes— a gun on their shoulder, a leash of dogs at their heels, and three or four scoundrels for their bosom friends.

I saw nothing remarkable in South Wales except Tenby and Milford-Haven. Tenby is a little seaport town of a situation most delightfully romantic. It is built in form of a crescent on a very deep cleft, the sides of which towards the sea, are all overgrown with ivy, as the bottom is washed by the tide. In the rock which runs out farthest into the sea, are several natural arches of great height, and curiously adorned with all the variety of fretwork and shells. Here, indeed, to atone for the rest of her country-women, I met with the greatest beauty I ever saw, and yet this plebeian angel, this goddess of low degree, was doing the humble office of a jack, or in plain English, turning a spit. Milford-Haven is certainly a very noble harbour, and several hundred ships of burden may ride safe at anchor in its numerous bays and windings.

In this country I became acquainted with Sir Arthur Owen, Knight and Baronet, who, by his own authority, is Admiral of the haven and Viceroy of Pembrokeshire. He is for ever building and planting, and as he is his own gardener and architect his performances are uncommon. Orielton, his mansion-house, is an enormous pile, built, I cannot say in a false taste, for there is no shadow of any taste at all. It has a very little porch, reaching one story high, and removed as far from the middle as possible, which is just such another beauty as the nose to a human face would be within half an inch of the left ear. The ceilings of his rooms are inverted keels of ships, painted black and brown. The fortress is defended by twenty pieces of cannon, which are fired on all rejoicing days; for the knight is a passionate lover of the Court and of a great noise. As he walked over his grounds, he ever and anon turned his head to survey it from the several points of view, Heaven only can tell with what secret delight. You remember when Sancho was going to his government how he would be looking back every moment to steal a glance at his beloved Dapple, when the grooms had made him so fine with ribbons and Brussels lace. The plantations are all detached without regularity or design. They consist of about two acres each, and are each of them strongly confined within stone walls. One part of his garden is wonderful. It is a grove of near an acre and a half;

and here Sir Arthur desired me to mount my horse, as he did his, because, he said, it would take us an hour and a quarter to traverse it all: as, indeed, it did, for he rode two-and-thirty courses on it. You must know this grove is cut into thirty-two walks, to answer the number of points in the mariner's compass, with a tree in the centre which he calls the needle. Each of these walks may be about six foot in length, and near two in latitude. Our horses and we threaded every one of these, and this, he told me, was boxing the compass.

This letter has already run unto so great a length that I will say nothing of North Wales, but conclude at once with my best wishes for your health and happiness; and with assuring you that I am, in all places and on all occasions, dear sir, your most affectionate, humble servant, D. Mallet.

POPE *to* DR. ARBUTHNOT[1]   2 *August* [1734]

The Pierpont Morgan Library

Southampton. Augst 2d.

I was rejoiced to see your letter, and I hope it is no trouble to you to write: I would fain hope you grow better, that Life may be at least supportable, tho not quite healthy or happy. It is but justice that a man who never delighted to give Pain to others, should be compassionated when he feels any himself: and I dare say you have many friends who truly share with you, as I do. I can most sincerely say, in a Friendship of twenty years, I have found no one Reason of Complaint from you, and hope I have given you as little, abating common human failings. I am almost displeasd at your Expression "*Scarcely* any[2] of those suspicions or jealousyes which affect the truest friendships" for I know of *not one* on my part. I thank you dear Sir for making That your Request to me which I make my Pride, nay my Duty; "that I should continue my Disdain & abhorrence of Vice, & manifest it still in my writings."[2] I would indeed do it with more restrictions, & less personally; it is more agreeable to my nature, which those who know it not are greatly mistaken in: But General Satire in Times of General Vice has no force, & is no Punishment: People have ceas'd to be ashamed of it when so many are joind with them; and tis only by hunting One or two from the Herd that any Examples can be made. If a man writ all his Life against the Collective Body of the Banditti, or against Lawyers, would it do the least Good, or lessen the Body? But if some are hung up, or pilloryed, it may prevent others. And in my low Station, with no other Power than this, I hope to deter, if not to reform.

---

[1] This is evidently Pope's authentic reply to Arbuthnot's letter of 17 July. It is to be compared with the supposititious reply that he printed in 1737 under date of 26 July.

[2] Cf. the actual text of Arbuthnot under date of 17 July.

I left Lord Bathurst a week ago. I hope he has rememberd the Venison, as he promisd me at parting. My present Landlord gave me an account of your Condition, which he is really concerned at, as he is really a man of humanity, & (like all Men of true Courage) beneficent: He has often wishd you in This air, which is excellent, & our way of life quite Easy, & at liberty. I write this from the most beautiful Top of a Hill I ever saw, a little house that overlooks the Sea, Southampton, & the Isle of Wight; where I study, write, & have what Leisure I please.[1] Pray if it be not too uneasy to you, write to me now & then, or let some of your family acquaint me how you are? Is your Brother with you? If he is, let me be kindly rememberd to him, & to your Son & Daughters: I wish them sincerely well, & (what is the Best Wish I can form for them) I wish them the longer Life of so Good a Father.

Address: To | Dr Arburthnot in Cork-street, | Burlington buildings, in | Piccadilly | London.
Frank: Peterborow.
Postmark: 5/AV
Endorsement: From Pope.

POPE *to* THE EARL OF OXFORD   4 *August* 1734
Longleat Portland Papers, xii

Mount Bevis. Augst 4. 1734.

My Lord,—I arrived 3 days since at this place,[2] where we have had much agreable Talk of your Lordship & your Family. Tho I congratulated with your Lordship upon a Presumption of the Marriage, I can't but do it once more upon the Accomplishment. Yet I half condole with you the Loss of so lov'd a Companion, & so deserving to be lov'd, as Lady Margaret was: and now she is to be known by that name no more, if the Duke of Portland is not the happiest man in the world, the Devil must be in him: which is very contrary to the Character I have heard of his Grace. I hope She will find him, all the World says he is; & they will be the Richest Couple in England, whether they had any Money or not. I beg Lady Oxford to accept my Compliments, & Congratulation on this happy occasion. I really share in the Joy, tho not in the Show of it, by the Misfortune of my absence.

Believe me with my whole heart, My Lord | Your most faithfull, obligd, & affectionate Servant | A. Pope

Endorsement (by a secretary): Mr Pope Mount Bevis / Augst 4. 1734

---

[1] It would be in this environment that Pope put together his *Epistle to Dr. Arbuthnot*, and polished his *Sober Advice from Horace*.

[2] Clearly Pope has been at Peterborow's for over a week. He is habitually careless (untruthful?) in statements as to the lapse of days.

POPE *to* CARYLL [*c.* 5 *August* 1734]

Add. 28618

Bevis Mount.

Tho' Mr. Hebb[1] told me he thought you gone to Grinsted, I had attended his journey with a line or two, but he was gone away before I could get up. I've had but ill health since, and am sorry your own has hindered your journey, the rather because I fear my necessary return to Twittenham will not leave me time to pass a few days with you, as intended. If thro' any more lucky accident than I have reason to expect I should not be obliged to be gone so soon I will send a dispatch to Ladyholt, and accept of your conveyance halfway.

I lay hold of this opportunity to tell you I received a letter from your god-daughter three days ago[2] to ask me to send her some venison to Lady Gerrard's at Cheam in Surrey. Our coaches none of them go that way. Yours do; therefore pray send her some with a line or two directed beforehand to meet it at Kingston, and tell her I desired you; so she will see at once that she has *two friends*, a large portion as this world goes. Dear sir, believe me very desirous to wait on you, and, if possible, I will yet. My Lord Peterboro's being in London when I first proposed to get to him from Gloucester, made my whole time too uncertain to be able to fix a week for Ladyholt, which else I could have done. Adieu; my faithful service attends your family; so does my lord's and Mrs. Robinson's.[3] I am for ever yours (dear sir) | A. Pope.

POPE *to* MRS. KNIGHT 5 *August* 1734

Bowles (1806), x. 110–12

Southampton, Aug. 5, 1734.

Madam,—If I did not know you must take it for granted that I am always mindful of you, I should have been earlier in telling you such a piece of news. But the truth is, that all I ever think letters good for, is to convey to those who love one another the news of their welfare, and the knowledge that they continue in each other's memory. The first of these I heard by inquiries in London, which have been transmitted to me; and the last, I think so well both of you and myself, as to think unnecessary. I was very certain Mrs. Elliot's company would be an equivalent to you for all you could leave in town, and yours would be so to her. Indeed, I had a wish to make you a short visit

---

[1] Mr. Hebb was evidently a friend of Peterborow's and of Caryll's. See Pope to Caryll 24 Sept. and 23 Oct. 1733.

[2] Pope mentions this letter also in writing to Mrs. Knight 5 Aug.—a mention which helps to date this present letter.

[3] The former opera singer, whose secret marriage to Lord Peterborow was announced shortly before his death.

by surprize, and see this with my own eyes; but the account given me at Stowe (where I had but one week to stay, and given me after I had been half-jumbled to death, and just before I was to be jumbled again in the abominable stoney roads thereabouts) gave me a terror I could not overcome; especially when, chancing to see a clergyman who lives by you, and whose name I have forgot, he told me the way was farther and worse than ever my fears had imagined. I have been but in a poor state of health, ever since I set out from home; and can scarce say I have found rest till (where you would least expect it) under my Lord Peterborow. This place is beautiful beyond imagination, and as easy as it is beautiful. I wish you and Mrs. Elliot saw it. Here is a very good Catholic lady in the house, and she and I might pray together for you. One motive, which perhaps may one time or other draw you, is, that the Duchess of Montague is within ten miles of us, at Bewley, which, I'm told, is a fine situation on the sea, and I shall see it to-morrow: Lord Peterborow carries me thither. I had the satisfaction to hear this week from Mrs. Patty Blount, that you were well. She is got into Surrey to another Papist lady, and stays some time with her. I design to steer towards London before the end of this month. We expect here Mr. and Mrs. Poyntz.[1] What can I say to you? I wish you very happy. I wish Mr. Newsham all that you wish him to have, and to be. Where is he, and Mr. Mallet?[2] When shall you return to town? I desire you to be very kind to me, and very just to me; that is, to let me know you continue well, now, when I can no other way be sure of it, than by a line hither; and to believe me sincerely ever, with all esteem, Madam, | Your, etc.

I think I need not send Mrs. E. my services, for they will do her no good; but desire her prayers which may do me some.

*POPE *to* HUGH BETHEL   6 *August* [1734]

Egerton 1948

Southampton. Augst 6.

I think it long since I have asked you how you do? tho I have heard of you by two or three hands. I presume you are at Scarborow, in the Great World: I am in more Retirement than I have been many years, having past 2 months compleat[3] in the Country, part at Lord Bathursts by Cirencester, part here with Lord Peterborow, at Southampton. I think not of returning home till the end of the month. There is nothing about Town left at this time, except the Court, which I think the

---

[1] Stephen Poyntz, Esq., was governor to the royal Duke of Cumberland. Mrs. Poyntz, the Fair Circassian of Croxall's poem, was a niece of Peterborow's.

[2] Mallet was young Newsham's tutor.

[3] Pope had been from home almost exactly seven weeks.

worst thing about town. My health has been but bad, & especially my Eyes, which put me often in mind of yours. If I could but ride on Horseback, it would make me some amends: whereas to read is painful, & to talk wastes the spirits; which are all I can do, except write & study, which gives me the headake, & sometimes angers other people. Have you seen the last satire of Horace in which You are so ill treated?[1] I could not find any method of sending it to you. I should be very glad to hear, & shall make it my business to enquire of any that come from Scarborow, the true state of your health. Pray if Lord Cornbury be with you make him my Compliments, or if you are elsewhere, to Mr Moyser. I could not compass to see Lady Codrington[2] from Lord Bathurst's: it is full 20 miles, & the most rugged way imaginable. Mrs Blount is with my Lady Gerard in Surrey: her affairs go ill, and Robert's attorney acts in as shuffling a way as Roberts himself: not a Farthing to be gotten. Pray let me know at your leisure (by a line to Twitnam from whence they send anything to me) when you imagine you shall move towards London? I remember my debt to you, as I do all other your many & friendly obligations. You are sure at all times, dear Sir, of the sincerest affections and warmest wishes of | Yours most faithfully, | A. Pope

Lord Peterborow & Mrs Robinson send you their Services.

Address: To | Hugh Bethel Esq to be left | at Mrs Pecket's in the Shambles | in | Yorke | way of London
Frank: Peterborow
Postmark: 12/AV

POPE *to* MARTHA BLOUNT[3]   11 *August* [1734]

Francis Edwards Catalogue 464, lot 350

[Bevis Mount] Sunday, Aug. 11.

[The letter describes "an Adventure and Discovery, made by Lord Peterborow and me" last week. "He had a mind to a Sea Voyage, and I some curiosity to try if a sea-sickness would be supportable to me, in case I should ever run my country."]

[The voyage seems to have been a trip round the Isle of Wight, where Pope and his lordship landed. He gives a long account of how they explored Netley Abbey, lunched in the woods, sketched the ruins, and admired the views. He concludes by saying he hopes to go home by way of Mapledurham.]

---

1 In Pope's *Second Satire of the Second Book of Horace Paraphrased*, which was advertised for sale 3 July 1734 in *The Daily Post-Boy*, Horace's Ofellus becomes Bethel himself.
2 Bethel's sister, who lived at Dodington in Gloucestershire.
3 The excerpts come from Mr. Edwards's Catalogue. Unfortunately the entire letter has not been available for publication. It is one of Pope's best.

"This may be ye last time I shall see those scenes of my past life, where I have been so happy, & I look upon one of them in particular in this light, since it was there I first knew you. Adieu for this time."

Address: To Mrs. Martha Blount at Ldy. Gerard's at Cheam, near Croydon.

POPE *to* BUCKLEY   20 *August* [1734]

Sotheby Catalogue, 15 April 1918, lot 959

[This letter has not been seen or published. It is described as acknowledging the receipt of books and giving an account of Pope's visit to Lord Peterborow. In the catalogue the year assigned is [1735], but Pope in that year had not yet gone to Southampton.]

POPE *to* DR. ARBUTHNOT   25 *August* 1734

The Royal College of Surgeons of England

I am dissatisfied in hearing nothing further concerning your state of health, since my Letter to Miss Arbuthnot. I am bending homewards, tho it will be a fortnight first, but wish in the meantime to have just a line from you. Lord Peterborow's will be still the best direction, for he & I are to make some Excursions into Hamshire, but still our Letters will be sent after us. I am sorry to hear from Mrs Robinson of the danger of the little Boy,[1] but I hope 'tis over. You have no need to be afflicted by other Illnesses than your own. I have nothing to say more but that no Friend you have more warmly wishes your Recovery or your Ease, than I do. I took very kindly your Advice, concerning avoiding Ill-will from writing Satyr; & it has worked so much upon me (considering the *Time* & *State* you gave it in) that I determine to address to you one of my Epistles, written by piece-meal many years,[2] & which I have now made haste to put together; wherein the Question is stated, what were, & are, my Motives of writing, the Objections to them, & my answers. It pleases me much to take this occasion of testifying (to the public at least, if not to Posterity) my Obligations & Friendship for, & from, you, for so many years: That is all that's in it; for Compliments are fulsome & go for nothing.

I hope in God to find you better much than I left you. For my own part, I am rather better; and while I live, believe me, shall

---

[1] Presumably John Arbuthnot, nephew of Mrs. Robinson and the Doctor.—Elwin.

[2] The poem was made up of several fragments. A working MS. is preserved in the Huntington Library. It shows that the foundation of the poem existed (about 1730?) in a form running to about a hundred lines. Additions are interlined and scrawled in the margins.

always Esteem & Love you. Dear Sir, adieu. | Your truly affectionate | Friend & Servant | A. Pope

Southampton | Augst 25th 1734

Lord Peterborow & the Lady send you their Services. We drink your health daily.

SWIFT *to* THE EARL OF OXFORD[1]   30 *August* 1734

Portland MSS. Harley 1725-40

EXCERPT

I am glad to hear Mr Pope is grown a Rambler; because I hope it will be for his Health. I fear He hath quite forsaken me, for I have not heard from him many months. His Time hath indeed been better employd in his Moral Poems, which excell in their kind, and may be very usefull. In his last Translation out of Horace,[2] I could willingly have excused his placing me not in that Light which I would appear; and others are of my opinion, but it gives me not the least offence, because I am sure he had not the least ill Intention, and how much I have allways loved him, the World as well as Your Lordship is convinced.

POPE *to* THE EARL OF OXFORD   1 *September* 1734

Longleat Portland Papers, xii

Sept. 1st 1734.

My Lord,—If I had known where I was, or was to be, I would have acquainted your Lordship: Last week I thought it would have been at London at your house; This week I find it will be still at Bevis Mount, & that it will be a fortnight before I can hope to see you. I hope your Lordship will not be gone to Bath or elsewhere so soon. The good Lord, as well as Lady, of this house are very sensible of your Obliging Complements, and the Lord in particular has a request to your Lordship: If Dr Swift's Miscellanies are yet deliverd you from Dublin,[3] that you will please to send one Copy to him, by the Southampton Coach which goes out at certain days from the black Bear in

---

[1] The paragraph is printed from the original, deposited in the British Museum; the entire letter is printed in Ball, v. 84–87.

[2] *The Second Satire of the Second Book of Horace Paraphrased* (addressed to Hugh Bethel) appeared first in July of this year. Lines 161-4 are spoken by Swift, whose opinion they probably represent.

[3] *The London Evening Post,* 8 Oct. 1734, advertises, 'On Wednesday the 14th of November next will be deliver'd to the Subscribers, at George Faulkner's ... in York-street, Dublin, and no where else, *The Works of Jonathan Swift, D.D., D.S.P.D. In Four Volumes* ... Price bound a Guinea.'

Piccadilly. I am glad you writ him a long Letter, I ought to do the same, and speedily will. You cannot think how happy we are here; I wish, my Lord, you Saw it: If you did, you would be very well pleas'd, very well fed, and very Merry, if I am not very much mistaken: We have the best Sea fish & River fish in the world, much tranquillity, some Reading, no Politiques, admirable Melons, an excellent Bowling-green & Ninepin alley, Besides the amusement of a Witch in the parish. I have an incomparable Story to tell you on the last of these, but it would fill 2 sheets of paper. I have been at the Ruins of the finest Abbey & Castle[1] I ever saw, within five miles of this place, which I am surprised to find Camden take no notice of. I have nothing to add, but my Sincere Joy on the Settlement of Lady Margaret so much to your Satisfaction, as you are pleased to express, and my humblest Services to Lady Oxford. I am inviolably & entirely, | My Lord, | Your ever-obliged, faithfull, | humble Servant | A. Pope.

Address: To | the Rt Hon. the Earl of Oxford | and Mortimer, in Dover Street | Piccadilly: | London.

Postmarks: 2/SE SOUTHAMPTON

Endorsement (by a secretary): Mr Pope | Sepr 1st 1734

POPE *to* MRS. KNIGHT   1 *September* [1734]

Bowles (1806), x. 112-13

Sept. 1, 1734.

Dear Madam,—Idle as I am, no opportunity can offer that puts me in mind of you, but I comply with that mind, which is always yours. It therefore must tell you, by this gentleman,[2] how much I think of you; and that, if the body belonging to this mind were worth one farthing, it would follow it, and go to see you. But those wretched infirmities, which set it forward toward the blessings of another life, keep it back from doing what it likes in this. I am next week going from Southampton to London, where I shall impatiently expect you. I fancy you'll be as impatient to be in London, especially if Mrs. Elliot be not with you. I had the most entertaining letter imaginable from Mr. Mallet, from Wales.[3] I sent it to our friend Patty; and she (if she is not stupid) will keep it, to shew to you when we all meet. God send it, and the sooner the better. Believe me, without more words, yours. First, the Post told you so, when I had no other messenger; then Harte[4] had a line to tell you so, and now Mr. Newsham.

---

1 Pope mentions Beaulieu, here iii. 426, and Netley, iii. 427.
2 Mrs. Knight's son, James Newsham. See the last sentence of the letter.
3 See Mallet to Pope, 2 Aug. [1734].
4 Pope's protégé, the Rev. Walter Harte, later in this year became vicar of Gosfield, where Mrs. Knight lived.

POPE *to* DR. ARBUTHNOT   3 *September* [1734]

The Royal College of Surgeons of England

Sept. 3.

Your Letter is a great Consolation to me in bringing me the account
of the more tolerable State of your health. It is Ease I wish for you,
more than Life; and yet knowing how good an use you will make of
Life, I cannot but wish you that as long as it can be but as Supportable
to you, as it will be desireable to others, & to me in particular. I have
little to say to you; we have here little News or Company, and I am
glad of it because it has given me the time to finish the Poem I told
you of, which I hope may be the best Memorial I can leave, both of
my Friendship to you, & of my own Character being such as you
need not be ashamd of that Friendship. The apology is a bold one, but
True: and it is Truth and a clear Conscience that I think will set me
above all my Enemies, and make no Honest man repent of having
been my Friend.

I hope to see you in 9 or 10 days. Pray send a line to Twitnam to
inform me whether I shall come to you at Hampstead, or London?
My hearty Services to your family. The Lord and Lady of this place
are much yours. As you find benefit by riding, should you care to dine
or lye at Dawley, or at my house? Do whatever is most easy to you,
and believe me with all truth Dear Sir | Yours faithfully | A. Pope

I dine this day at Mr Conduits,[1] & will give them your Services.
I hear he is much recovered.

Address: To | Dr Arbuthnot, in Cork | Street, Burlington buildings, | near
Piccadilly | London
Postmark: 6/SE
Frank: Peterborow

†POPE *and* BOLINGBROKE *to* SWIFT[2]   15 *September* 1734
1740
Sept. 15, 1734.

I have ever thought you as sensible as any man I knew, of all the
delicacies of friendship, and yet I fear (from what Lord B.[3] tells me
you said in your last letter) that you did not quite understand the
reasons of my late silence. I assure you it proceeded wholly from the
tender kindness I bear you. When the heart is full, it is angry at all
words that cannot come up to it; and you are now the man in all the

---

[1] John Conduitt, who married Sir Isaac Newton's niece. See Pope to Conduit, 10 Nov. 1727.
[2] Pope has returned, as planned, from Bevis Mount (see his letters of 1 and 3 Sept.);
and now he and Bolingbroke plan to leave for Bath in three days. This seems to be the only
year in which Pope and Bolingbroke went to Bath together.
[3] B.] Bolingbroke *1741 Dab.*

world I am most troubled to write to, for you are the friend I have left whom I am most grieved about. Death has not done worse to me in separating poor Gay, or any other, than disease and absence in dividing us. I am afraid to know how you do, since most accounts I have give me pain for you, and I am unwilling to tell you the condition of my own health. If it were good, I would see you, and yet if I found you in that very condition of deafness, which made you fly from us while we were together, what comfort could we derive from it? In writing often I should find great relief, could we write freely; and yet when I have done so, you seem by not answering in a very long time, to feel either the same uneasiness as I do, or to abstain from some prudential reason. Yet I am sure, nothing that you and I wou'd say to each other, (tho' our whole souls were to be laid open to the clerks of the post-office) could hurt either of us so much, in the opinion of any honest man or good subject, as the intervening, officious, impertinence of those goers-between us, who in England pretend to intimacies with you, and in Ireland to intimacies with me. I cannot but receive any that call upon your name,[1] and in truth they take it in vain too often. I take all opportunities of justifying you against these friends, especially those who know all you think and write, and repeat your slighter verses.[2] It is generally on such little scraps that Witlings feed; and 'tis hard the world[3] should judge of our housekeeping from what we fling to our dogs, yet this is often the consequence. But they treat you still worse, mix their own with yours, and print[4] them to get money, and lay them at your door. This I am satisfied was the case in the Epistle to a Lady;[5] it was just the same hand (if I have any judgment in style) which printed your Life and Character before, which you so strongly dis-avow'd in your letters to Lord Carteret, myself and others. I was very well informed of another fact which convinced me yet more, that the[6] same person who gave this to be printed offer'd to a bookseller a piece in prose as yours, and as commissioned by you, which has since appear'd and been own'd to be his own.[7] I think (I say once more) that I know your hand, tho' you did not mine in the Essay on Man. I beg your pardon for not telling you, as I should had you been in England: but no secret can cross your Irish Sea, and every clerk in

---

[1] upon your name] upon me in your name *1741 L–1742 L*.

[2] Mrs. Pilkington and possibly Mrs. Barber memorized and repeated Swift's verses—and printed them perhaps!

[3] In 1741 La (the quarto) *world* comes at the end of a line (p. 146); *the* is omitted before it, but inserted at the end of the next following line, to read *to the our dogs*. Since this error is corrected in 1741 Lb (the folio), one infers that the imposition of type was first made for the quarto.   [4] yours, and print] yours, print *1741 L–1742 L*.

[5] See Pope to Swift, 6 Jan. 1734.   [6] more, that the] more, the *1741 L–1742 L*.

[7] Elwin, followed by Ball, thinks the pamphlet one concerning the will of Richard Norton, which left all to charity, but was set aside by the courts. The will is also mentioned in Pope to Caryll, 23 Oct. 1733. The name of the pamphlet is not given.

the post-office had known it. I fancy tho' you lost sight of me in the first of those Essays, you saw me in the second. The design of concealing myself was good, and had its full effect; I was thought a divine, a philosopher, and what not? and my doctrine had a sanction I could not have given to it. Whether I can proceed in the same grave march like Lucretius, or must descend to the gayeties of Horace, I know not, or whether I can do either? but be the future as it will, I shall collect all the past in one fair quarto this winter,[1] and send it to you, where you will find frequent mention of your self. I was glad you suffer'd your writings to be collected more compleatly than hitherto, in the volumes I daily expect from Ireland; I wish'd it had been in more pomp, but that will be done by others: yours are beauties, that can never be too finely drest, for they will ever be young. I have only one piece of mercy to beg of you; do not laugh at my gravity, but permit me to wear the beard of a philosopher, till I pull it off, and make a jest of it myself. 'Tis just what my Lord B.[2] is doing with Metaphysicks. I hope, you will live to see and stare at the learned figure he will make, on the same shelf with Locke and Malbranche.

You see how I talk to you (for this is not writing) if you like I should do so, why not tell me so? if it be the least pleasure to you, I will write once a week most gladly: but can you abstract the letters from the person who writes them, so far, as not to feel more vexation in the thought of our separation, and those misfortunes which occasion it, than satisfaction in the nothings he can express? If you can, really and from my heart, I cannot. I return again to melancholy. Pray however tell me, is it a satisfaction? that will make it one to me: and we will Think alike, as friends ought, and you shall hear from me punctually just when you will.

P. S.[3] Our friend who is just returned from a progress of three months, and is setting out in three days with me for the Bath, where he will stay till towards the middle of October, left this letter with me yesterday, and I cannot seal and dispatch it till I have scribled the remainder of this page full. He talks very pompously of my Metaphysicks, and places them in a very honourable station. It is true I have writ six letters and a half to him on subjects of that kind, and I propose a letter and an half more which would swell the whole up to a considerable volume. But he thinks me fonder of the Name of an author than I am. When he and you, and one or two other friends have seen them, *satis magnum Theatrum mihi estis*, I shall not have the itch of making them more publick.[4] I know how little regard you pay

---

[1] Pope's *Works*, vol. ii (quarto), appeared in Apr. 1735.   [2] B.] Bolingbroke *1741 Dab*.
[3] Above this postscript in 1741 Dab occurs the heading, 'P.S. by Lord Bolingbroke.'
[4] Bolingbroke's philosophical works were published by David Mallet after his lordship's death.

to Writings of this kind. But I imagine that if you can like any such, it must be those that strip Metaphysicks of all their bombast, keep within the sight of every well-constituted Eye, and never bewilder themselves, whilst they pretend to guide the reason of others. I writ to you a long letter sometime ago, and sent it by the post. Did it come to your hands? or did the inspectors of private correspondence stop it, to revenge themselves of the ill said of them in it? *vale & me ama.*

POPE *to* MARTHA BLOUNT[1]   [*17 September* 1734]

Mapledurham

Tuesday, the

I hope this will find you both setled in Peace & Joy at Bath; that your Court is numerous enough to keep a Court-&-Town-Lady in Spirits, and yet not so Importunate as to deprive you of Rest. Your Health nevertheless is my chief concern; which to Ladies or Gentlewomen, young, or advancing into Wisdome (but never above Pleasures) is a most Comfortable & necessary thing, with or without Admirers, even from Lady W—y to her great Grandaughter born last week.

I saw Dr Arbuthnot; who, was very cheerful. I past a whole day with him at Hampsted: he is at the Long room half the morning, & has Parties at Cards every night. Mrs Lepell,[2] & Mrs Saggioni the Singer, & his Son, & his two Daughters, are all with him. He told me he had given the best directions he could to yourself, & to Lady Suffolk seperately: that She ought to bleed, & you not; that it is his opinion the Waters will be of service to you, and that there can be no ill consequence if they should heat you, it could only bring out the Rash at worst, which he says might be the means to free your blood from it a long time.

I hope by this time the Pink colour Ribband in your Hat is pulld off, and the Pink colour Gown put on. I will not joke upon that, tho I did upon the ribband, because when people begin to sin, there may be hopes of amendment, but when the Whole Woman is become red as Scarlet, there's no good to be done.

Lady Suffolk has a strange power over me: She would not stir a days Journey either East or West for me, tho she had dying or languishing Friends on each Quarter who wanted & wishd to see her. But I am following her chariot wheels 3 days thro' Rocks & Waters, & shall be at her feet on Sunday night. I suppose she'l be at Cards, & receive me as coldly as if I were Archdeacon of the place. I hope I

---

[1] In Sept. 1734 Martha and Lady Suffolk were at Bath. On 15 Sept., in their letter to Swift, Pope and Bolingbroke are said to be leaving for Bath in three days. This letter seems to advise the ladies of their probable arrival on Sunday, 22 Sept. In 1734, 17 Sept. was a Tuesday, and thus fits Pope's fragmentary date.

[2] 'Mrs. Lepell' is probably the mother of Lady Hervey (*née* Mary Lepell). Her Ladyship has succeeded Lady Suffolk in the Queen's household.

shall be better with you, who will doubtless have been at Mass, (whither Mr Nash at my request shall carry you constantly when I come) and in a meek & christian-like way. I've no more to say to either of you, but that which we are all obliged to say even to our Enemies, the Lord have mercy on you! & have you in his *Keeping*.[1] adieu.

I intended you this by the last post, but it was too late; so that you'll hardly receive it sooner than we shall come. I was willing just to have told Lady Suffolk before, that one of my chief Motives was to see her in a place of Liberty & Health. & to advertise you Madam not to be discouraged if the Waters did heat you but to lose no time in them.

POPE to HUGH BETHEL   *28 September* [1734]

Egerton 1948

Bath. Sept. 28th

You will not expect my Letter from this date. But so it is that partly Fortune, partly Friendship have brought me hither, & extended my Rambles to four months. I just lookd upon Twitnam for three days with some Pleasure & some melancholy, and having kiss'd Bounce[2] (my only Friend now there) I came with Lord Bolingbroke to Bath. I can't say that any View of improving my own Health by the waters was my motive, but I hopd to find a pleasure in seeing that of a Friend of ours improve by them. Mrs Patty Blount came hither with Lady Suffolk,[3] & they live so regularly, that I think she will be the better, & the Doctor gives great hopes of it. I shewd her your last kind letter, and she is so sensible of your many repeated offers of kindness, that not only she but I, are incapable of expressing how much: I promise her to do it, but really I cannot. We want You, & nothing else, at present. All your Sisters are here. I saw Lady Cox at her house yesterday, & to day Sir William & my Lady[4] come to stay a fortnight. Sir William is the greatest Courtier we have, in his Devoirs to Princess Amelia, & Mrs Blount is to kiss her hand to morrow. Mr Cibber is here to celebrate her, and he writes his Verses now in such a manner that nobody can use them as they were wont to do, for nobody will wipe his breech with a pane of Glass.[5] This sort of news will not affect

---

[1] Between *Keeping* and *adieu* eight words have been illegibly overscored.

[2] Bounce was Pope's Great Dane.

[3] For a letter of Lady Hervey's to Lady Suffolk, 23 Sept. 1734, concerning Pope and Miss Blount, see *Suffolk Correspondence*, ii. 105–6. Pope's former friend, now wife of his enemy, Lord Hervey, here shares her husband's prejudices.

[4] The Codringtons.

[5] For Cibber's verses addressed to Beau Nash and inscribed on a window-pane at Bath see D. Senior, *The Life and Times of Colley Cibber* (1928), p. 123, and Ault's *New Light*, pp. 322–3, for Pope's verse retorts. This sentence of the letter was printed by Ruffhead, p. 390.

you so much as to know, that beyond my expectation the Waters pass
with me, & agree much better than formerly they did. While I was
at Lord Bathurst's I was by no means well, but much better at Lord
Peterborows, the difference of air was very sensible between the two
places. And that, together with the Quiet I enjoyed there for six
weeks, till your friend Mrs Cond.[1] came & put a Ferment into the
Country, was the Cause (I dare say) that I have been so well ever
since. Mrs Blount felt as sensible a change between the Flat Country
of Surrey where she had been with Lady Gerard & the clear air of
Hampshire, where they stay'd a few days only, in their way hither. I
have nothing to add but that we are both your faithful Servants, &
that Lord Bol. sends you his best Services. Here are several of your
friends with whom I can talk of you, Lord Lovel, Lord Burlington,
Lord Chesterfield & many others. My Services to Mr Moyser. No
man is with more sincerity Dear Sir Yours, than | A. Pope

*POPE to HUGH BETHEL   4 *October* [1734]

Egerton 1948

Bath: Oct. 4th

I did not write to you the same post that I receiv'd yours (which, tho
dated the 18th by means of my unexpected Journy to Bath, reach'd
me not till the 28th). It happen'd that Lord Lovel was here, so to
him I spoke first who freely consented, & the same day, viz: the 28th
I writ to the only Person I had any access by at this distance to the
Chancellor, his particular Friend Dr Rundle. You see his answer, & if
any thing can be done toward the Exchange,[2] acquaint me. You had,
I presume, a long letter from me three or four posts since, so that I can
add nothing, but that you'll direct your next to me, not hither, but to
Twickenham. The News in some publick papers that I was dangerously ill,[3] was groundless, but my usual Headakes afflict me, and this
day in particular, so that I can hardly write these few lines. Pray let
me hear from you, whether I can, or can not do anything in your
Service, for no man living is more warmly | Dear Sir | Yours, | A.
Pope.

[1] On the Conduitts see Pope to Arbuthnot, 3 Sept. 1734.
[2] The 'exchange', presumably ecclesiastical, involved in this letter is unidentified. Lord
Lovel (Thomas Coke, later Earl of Leicester) was a Walpole courtier and Dr. Rundle was a
protégé of Lord Talbot, Lord Chancellor. Rundle at this time was hoping to become Bishop
of Gloucester, but presently had to be content with a richer Irish see. Pope's letter to Rundle
is unknown. It was in 1734 that Lord Lovel began to build Holkham Hall, regarded as Kent's
architectural masterpiece. In Italy Coke (as he was then) became perhaps Kent's earliest
patron. They were thereafter friends.
[3] *The London Evening Post*, 28 Sept. 1734, announced, 'They write from Bath, that Mr.
Pope, the Famous Poet, lies dangerously ill there.'

POPE *to* CARYLL 15 *October* 1734

Add. 28618

Twitnam 15. Oct. 1734.

It is indeed, and I thought it so, long since I wrote to you, but I have been hurried about so much, and out of order so much, that I have neither had my time, nor my head my own. My heart is all that continues the same, and will ever belong to my friends.

As soon as I got home from Bevis-Mount (which was soon after I writ to you), I was persuaded to try the Bath waters, partly for my health, and partly I persuaded my self to attend several of my friends there, one of whom conveyed me thither and brought me back a week ago.[1] I saw there your god-daughter, whose brother I heard was expected there, and ought to be ashamed to see her. She went upon Dr. Arbuthnot's advice upon her complaints, and thought the waters agreed with them. But the power of going and being conveniently accomodated was owing wholly to my Lady Suffolk's friendship;[2] for indeed from her own family, she experiences none at all. They return to London at the end of the month. For my part I have not been so ill as to give any ground for the news of my danger, nor so well as to forget it may soon be my case in earnest: God prepare me for it. I am truly concerned that you are so persecuted by repeated fits of the gout. Poor Mr. Pigott (who was the first man I enquired after at my return), is in a very declining way: he will be a general loss.[3] I hope your lady is well: In this world, we live only upon the terms of compassionating, and lamenting one another by turns. It must be a better place where all tears are wiped away. I beg sometimes to hear from you, as I shall not fail to write to you who have long been, and shall be the little time we have to last, | Dear sir | Your sincerely obliged friend | and humble servant | A. Pope.

POPE *to* WILLIAM DUNCOMBE[4] 20 *October* 1734

1772 (Duncombe)

Twickenham, Oct. 20, 1734.

Sir,—I am obliged for the favour of yours. I have looked for the letter Mr. Hughes sent me, but cannot find it. I had a great regard for his

---

[1] Lord Bolingbroke.

[2] The Earl of Chesterfield was at Bath during Miss Blount's stay, and a letter from him to Lady Suffolk (2 Nov.) indicates that he and others were pleased with her company.

[3] Pigott died in 1737.

[4] This is the first of four letters printed by EC as if addressed to *John* Duncombe. In the existing MSS. and in the *Letters to Several Eminent Persons* (1772; 2nd ed. 1773) the Christian name of the addressee is not given; but internal evidence points to the fact that the other letters (and so this) were addressed to William Duncombe (see *DNB*) rather than to his brother John. The son of William, named John, published the letters in 1772.

merit, modesty, and softness of manners. He writ to me a few days before his death, concerning his play of the "Siege of Damascus," which is the only letter I can meet with.

I thank you for the part you are pleased to take, both in regard to my health (which has, I thank God, been as good as usual,) and to my reputation, my poetical welfare, which I resign as much to Providence as the other. But truly I had not the least thought of stealing applause by suppressing my name to that "essay": I wanted only to hear truth, and was more afraid of my partial friends than enemies. Besides, I really was humble and diffident enough, to distrust my own performance. All I can say of it is, that I know it to be an honest one.

I am, Sir, | Your most obedient humble servant, | A. Pope.

‖SWIFT *to* POPE[1]   1 *November* 1734

Longleat Portland Papers, xiii (Harleian transcripts)

Nov. 1st 1734.

I have yours with my Lord B.s[2] Postscript of Sept 15. It was long on it's way, & for some weeks after the date I was very ill with my two inveterate Disorders, Giddyness & deafness; the latter is pretty well off, but the other makes me totter towards Evenings, & much dispirits me. But I continue to ride & walk, both of which, although they be no cures, are at least Amusements. ⌈I have lost by those deseases much of my memory, which makes [me] commit many blunders, in my common Actions at home, by mistaking one thing for another; Particularly in writing, where I make a hundred literall errors, as you cannot but know, & as it is odds you will find in this paper.⌉[3] I did never imagine you to be either inconstant or to want right notions of Friendship; but I apprehended[4] your want of health; & it hath been a frequent wonder to me how you have been able to entertain the world so long, so frequently & so[5] happily under so many bodily disorders. My Lord B.[6] says you have been three months rambling, which is the best thing you can possibly do in a Summer Season; & when the winter recalls you we will for our own Interests leave you to your Speculations. God be thanked I have done with every thing & of[7] every kind that requires writing, except now & then a Letter, or, like a true old Man Scribbling trifles only fit for children or Schoolboys of the lowest Class at best, which three or four of us read & laugh at today, & burn to Morrow. Yet what is singular, I never am without some great works[8] in View, enough to take up forty years of the most

---

[1] Printed by Pope, 1740–2.   [2] B.s] Bolingbroke's *1741 Dab.*
[3] The passage is omitted in the London editions of 1741–2.
[4] apprehended] apprehend *1740–2*.
[5] frequently & so] frequently, so *London eds.*, *1741–2*.   [6] B.] Bolingbroke *1741 Dab.*
[7] thing & of] thing of *1741 Dab.*   [8] works] work *1740–2*.

vigorous healthy man: Although I am convinced that I shall never be
able to finish three Treatises,[1] that have layn by me severall years, &
want nothing but Correction. My Lord B.[2] sayd in his Postscript that
you would go to Bath in three days; We since heard that you were
dangerously ill there, & that the Newsmongers gave you over. But a
Gentleman of this Kingdom on his return from Bath ⌜(his name is
Towers)⌝[3] assured me he left you well, & so did some others whom I have
forgot. ⌜I am not scared from writing by any regard to the Post folks,
& wou'd be content to let them transcribe Copyes, provide they will
be so honest to Seal the Original & send it as directed. I cannot but
tell you that I am not so well able to write at night, both from my
disorder, & the weakness of my Eyes. And when I begin in a morning,
I am so pestered by impertinent People, & impertinent Business which
my Station exposeth me to, that the former part of the day is wholly
lost.⌝[3] I am sorry at my heart, that you are[4] pestered with People who
come in my name, & I profess to you, it is without my Knowledge.
I am confident I shall hardly ever have occasion again to recommend,
for my friends here are very few, & fixed to the free-hold, from whence
nothing but death will remove them⌜; I only except Dr Sheridan who
allways begs me to present his respects, & talks often of going to
England but I believe, considering many difficulties on his fortune will
never be able with any prudence to make such a Voyage. I have just
recalled the Money that was in the Duke of Qu—s hands;[5] which I
had set apart to maintain a Summer among you; but I found it in-
consistant with my present ill state of health to venture so far from a
convenient home. & by the great fall of my little Revenues: I was
under a necessity to supply my self with that money, till I cou'd recover some rents to support me. And I must now count upon worse &
worse every year, or rather every month I live.⌝[6] Surely I never
doubted about your Essay on Man, & I would lay any odds, that I
would never fayl to discover you in six lines, unless you had a mind
to write below or beside your self on purpose. I confess I did never
imagine you were so deep in Morals, or that so many new & excellent
Rules could be produced so advantageously & agreably[7] in that Science
from any one head. I confess in some few places I was forced to read
twice; I believe I told you before what the Duke of D—[8] said to me
on that occasion. How a Judge here who knows you, told the D—[9]
that on the first reading those Essays, he was much pleased, but found

---

[1] The three treatises would be *Polite Conversation* (1738), *Directions to Servants* (1745),
and the *History of the Four Last Years of Queen Anne* (1758).
[2] B.] Bolingbroke *1741 Dab.*   [3] Omitted in all texts of 1740–2.
[4] are] were *1741 Dab.*
[5] The money from the Miscellanies Swift had left in Gay's hands, and now the Duke of
Queensberry had it.
[6] Omitted in all editions of 1740–2.   [7] The Harleian transcript reads *agreeable*.
[8] D—] Dorset *1741 Dab.*   [9] the D—] him *1740–2.*

some lines a little dark; On the second most of them cleared up, & his pleasure increased; On the third he had no doubt remained, & then he admired the whole. My Lord B's[1] attempt of reducing Metaphysicks to intelligible sence & usefullness will be a glorious undertaking, & as I never knew him fayl in any thing he attempted, if he had the sole management, So I am confident he will succeed in this: I desire you will allow, that I write to you both at present, & so I shall while I live: It saves you[2] mony, & my time; And he being your *Genius*, no matter to which it is addressed. I am happy that what you write is printed in large letters; otherwise from[3] the weakness of my eyes, & thickness[4] of my hearing, I should lose the greatest pleasure that is left me. Pray command my Lord B— to follow that Example, if I live to read his Metaphysicks. Pray God bless you both. I had a Maloncholy account from the Doctor of his health. I will answer his Letter as soon as I can. I am ever entirely yours.

Address: To Alexander Pope Esqr | at Twitenham in | Middlesex | by London.

POPE *to* FORTESCUE[5]   *November* 1734

1797 (Polwhele, i. 324)
                                              Friday morning, Nov. 1734.

Your letter (by the negligence of our post, which often delivers 'em not here till ten o'clock) came too late for me to get any conveyance to town to-day. But certainly you have just as much authority as I, as a friend of Mrs. Blount, to determine in this affair, as to the quarter's rent: or if you scruple it, apply to her. You and I, I am sure, shall be of the same opinion of it. As to the bill of charges, I think that is out of the question of their rent and principal, and may be decided separately, but doubtless to be insisted on. I want to see you very much; shall you come this way on Saturday? For tho' I intended to be in town, I find I must take physic, being in a very ill way this week; tho' if I had found a coach to day, I had come; as I often have for my friends, when really I have been little able. Adieu! I am truly, dear Sir, yours, | A. Pope.

Have you lately seen lady Suffolk? she was ill when I left the town.

Address: To Wm. Fortescue, esq. in Bell-yard, near Lincoln's Inn. Speed.

---

[1] B's] Bolingbroke's *1741 Dab.*   [2] you] your *1740-2*.
[3] from] between *London editions of 1741-2*.
[4] & thickness] & the thickness *1740-2*.
[5] In 1734 the 1st of November was Friday, and that seems a possible date for this letter. See the letter to Fortescue here placed as of 5 Nov.

POPE *to* FORTESCUE[1]   5 [*November* 1734]

The Pierpont Morgan Library

Octr 5th

I should have told you, that if you have any occasion to direct to Mr Bethel it must be, at Bestwick near Beverley, Yorkshire. This I had told you last Saturday when I intended to have past the Evening with you, but one of my Fitts of Illness sent me to Bed at eight o'clock after a tiresome Day. I came to Twitnam, where I am in my Garden, amused and easy. This is a Scene where one finds no Disappointments; the Leaves of this year that are fallen, are sure to come on again the next: 'Tis far otherwise in the Great World, (I mean the Little World) of a Court &c. Get to be a Judge, the sooner the better, and go to Rest. Adieu. Believe me truly Yours. I think to see you at the end of the Week. In the meantime, if you have any thing Satisfactory from Eadnell or Roberts tell me, for my Friends Concerns are More than my own; or if you have not, at least tell me you are well, & when I may be securest to find you at home. I am | Most affectionately Yours, | A. Pope.

Address: To | Wm Fortescue Esq. in | Bellyard, by | Lincolns-Inne | London.
Endorsement (by Fortescue himself): Mr Pope | ~~Octr~~ Novr 5. 1734.

POPE *to* WILLIAM DUNCOMBE[2]   5 *November* [1734]

Add. 22488

Twit'nam. Nov. 5.

Sir,—I am extremely willing to bear any testimony to my Real Regard for Mr Hughes, & therfore what you mention of my Letter to his Brother[3] after his death, will be a greater instance of the Sincerity with which it was given: It is perfectly at your Service. The other relating to Spenser I think too trivial.—I thank you for the Tenderness with which you deal in this matter toward me, and I esteem you for that which you show to the memory of your Kinsman. I doubt

[1] Here an editor must prefer Fortescue's endorsement for date to Pope's clearly written 'Octr.' October of this year (and the year seems right) is impossible since Pope was still at Bath. It is notable that in his endorsing Fortescue copied Pope's 'Octr' first, and then crossed it out and corrected it to 'Novr'. On Friday (1 Nov.) Pope wrote to Fortescue in some hesitation about going to town. He found after all, one assumes, a coach and went. He was there on Saturday the 2nd, but too ill to see Fortescue in the evening, as this present letter explains.

[2] The condition of the holograph of this letter is interesting. Duncombe and his son prepared it for printing in the collection of *Letters* to and from John Hughes and others. He tore away the address but left the postmark. He wrote in the heading 'Mr. Pope to Mr. Duncombe'. In the first sentence he changed *to* to *of* (testimony to), and he heavily scored over and did not print (nor did EC) the sentence about Spenser. The year also is in Duncombe's hand. The holograph was evidently sent to the printer—a common practice in printing letters, and a practice which shows why holograph letters frequently do not survive printing.

[3] The brother was Jabez Hughes.

not but you will discharge it in a becoming manner, and am, | Sr. |
Your most obedient hum-|ble Servant | A. Pope.

Postmark: 5/NO

POPE *to* THE EARL OF OXFORD　　　10 *November* 1734

Longleat Portland Papers, xii

Twitenham. Nov. 10th 1734

My Lord,—I am angry at myself when I think how much a Stranger
I am become to you. Yet sincerely it is not my fault, but wholly
Fortune's; for within two days after I got home I went to London
in the Sole hope of finding your Lordship there, and then I tryd a
week after with no better success. I stayd 6 days complete, because
your Porter told me he expected you at a days warning. At last I return'd hither disconsolate, where I've been ever since. I had sent my
Complaints after you to Bulstrode, but in the daily hope of your return. I see it is hard for a good Parent & a good Child to part; it
must be the greatest of joys to you to see her happy, (as I doubt not
you do) and in the midst of that pleasure, I wonder not that your
Lordship should forget all meaner ones, especially the remembrance
of one of so little value, tho indeed full of so much affection & Esteem
for you, as he who will put you in mind of him by the name of A.
Pope.

I would tell the Duchess of Portland the same Story, if I had any
opportunity, of the miserable man that now sighs all alone in the
Upper Room in Dover street.

Address: To the Rt Hon. the | Earl of Oxford, at Bulstrode. | By Gerrards
　Cross | Bagg
Postmark: 12/NO

POPE *to* WILLIAM DUNCOMBE[1]　　　[23 *November* 1734]

The William Andrews Clark Library

Sir,—My Absence from home prevented my receiving your Two
Letters till this day. I would else have read your Tragedy willingly:
And I beg you not to take it amiss, that I return your present of the
Tickets, since it is not in my power to be there next week, thro'

---

[1] William Duncombe's tragedy, *Junius Brutus*, was acted at Drury Lane 25–30 Nov.
1734. Two different hands (apart from Pope's) are apparent in annotations of the original
letter for the press. One has added the subscribed date: Pope wrote only 'Saturday'. The
23rd was Saturday. Another hand has added a heading, 'Mr. Pope to Mr. Duncombe', and
has written in notes (now scored over) identifying the tragedy. The letter asking Pope to read
the tragedy is now unknown.

indispensable Obligations in the Country at some distance. I think your Prologue a good one, & I think of Players as I always thought of Players, & of the Son as I thought of the Father.¹ I sincerely wish you Success, & am, | Sir, | Your most obedient | humble Servant | A. Pope.

Saturday. [23 Novr 1734.]

POPE *to* FORTESCUE²   [13 *December* 1734]

The Wellcombe Historical Medical Library

Friday.

I fully intended to have dined with you yesterday, & the day before but the first of them I was taken in at Court, & yesterday & to day am so ill of a most troublesome Cold, which has brought down the Uvula of my mouth, that I cannot dine at all. Would you go to morrow to Twitenham, & could you spare your Coach, I would go gladly with you; if not, I must stay perforce till Sunday morning. I hope all your Fireside are well, & growing merrier & merrier as Christmass approaches. I shall have no Rest nor Joy till I get to my Mum³ again. Adieu dear Sir, | Yours, | A. Pope

Address: To | Wm Fortescue Esqr | in Bell Yard, near | Lincolns inn fields.
Endorsement (by Fortescue): Mr Pope | Decr 1734

POPE *to* FORTESCUE⁴   [?15 *December* 1734]

Professor F. W. Hilles

I was so far from being able yesterday to dine with you, that I kept my Bed all day, & to day have done the same till now at 2 a clock. If (as it is a leisure day with you) you can pass an hour here in the afternoon or evening, pray do; I think as soon as I get out, to go home, where I am more easy. My services to you all.

    Your ever affectio-|nate Friend & | Servant | A. Pope

Sunday.

Address: To | Wm Fortescue Esq in | Bellyard.
Endorsement (by Fortescue): Mr Pope. | Decr 1734

¹ Theophilus Cibber, son of Colley, was assuming the management of Drury Lane on 28 Nov. Cf. l. 60 of Pope's forthcoming *Epistle to Dr. Arbuthnot*. Duncombe's application to Pope might have been a case in point had it come earlier.
² In view of his other commitments on December Fridays Pope is pretty certainly writing here on the 13th.
³ Mum was a beer imported from Brunswick.
⁴ The date, like that of the preceding letter, comes from Pope's 'Sunday', Fortescue's endorsement, and the editor's hypotheses. Pope has not been able to get home, and he is perhaps alone (with the servants) at Lord Oxford's house. At least he is in town and wishes for company.

†POPE *to* SWIFT[1]

19 *December* 1734

1740

Twitenham, Decemb. 19, 1734.

I am truly sorry for any complaint you have, and it is in regard to the weakness of your eyes that I write (as well as print) in folio. You'll think (I know you will, for you have all the candor of a good understanding) that the thing which men of our age feel the most, is the friendship of our equals; and that therefore[2] whatever affects those who are stept a few years before us, cannot but sensibly affect us who are to follow. It troubles me to hear you complain of your memory, and if I am in any part of my constitution younger than you, it will be in my remembring every thing that has pleased me in you, longer than perhaps you will. The two summers we past together dwell always on my mind, like a vision which gave me a glympse of a better life and better company, than this world otherwise afforded.[3] I am now an individual, upon whom no other depends; and may go where I will, if the wretched carcase I am annex'd to did not hinder me. I rambled by very easy journies this year to Lord Bathurst and Lord Peterborow, who upon ev'ry occasion commemorate, love, and wish for you. I now pass my days between Dawley, London, and this place, not studious, nor idle, rather polishing old works than hewing out new. I redeem now and then a paper that hath been abandon'd several years;[4] and of this sort you'll soon see one, which I inscribe to our old friend Arbuthnot.

Thus far I had written, and thinking to finish my letter the same evening, was prevented by company, and the next morning found myself in a fever, highly disorder'd, and so continu'd in bed for five days, and in my chamber till now; but so well recover'd as to hope to go abroad to morrow, even by the advice of Dr. Arbuthnot. He himself, poor man, is much broke, tho' not worse than for these two last months he has been. He took extremely kindly[5] your letter. I wish to God we could once meet again, before that separation, which yet I would be glad to believe shall re-unite us: But he who made us, not for ours but his purposes, knows whether[6] it be for the better or the worse, that the affections of this life should, or should not continue into the other: and doubtless it is as it should be. Yet I am sure that while I am here, and the thing that I am, I shall[7] be imperfect without

---

[1] In 1742 La Pope or another changed the date to 13 Dec. As the second paragraph indicates, it may have been begun on that day. Only 1742 La has the 13th as date.

[2] and that therefore] and therefore *1742 La.*

[3] world otherwise afforded] world afforded *1742 La.*

[4] The Huntington Library and the Morgan Library have MSS. of the Epistle to Dr. Arbuthnot that indicate that in an early (1730?) form the poem consisted of a bit over a hundred lines, and had no connexion with Arbuthnot. The finished poem must have been in the press when Pope wrote to Swift.　　　　[5] extremely kindly] extremely kind *1741–2.*

[6] knows whether] knows only whether *1742 La.*　　　[7] am, I shall] am, shall *1741 Dab.*

the communication of such friends as you; you are to me like a limb lost, and buried in another country; tho' we seem quite divided, every accident makes me feel you were once a part of me. I always consider[1] you so much as a friend, that I forget you are an author, perhaps too much, but 'tis as[2] I would desire you would do to me. However, if I could inspirit[3] you to bestow correction upon those three Treatises which you say are so near compleated, I should think it a better work than any I can pretend to of my own. I am almost at the end of my Morals, as I've been, long ago, of my Wit; my system is a short one, and my circle narrow. Imagination has no limits, and that is a sphere in which you may move[4] on to eternity; but where one is confined to Truth (or to speak more like a human creature, to the appearances of Truth) we soon find the shortness of our Tether. Indeed by the help of a metaphysical chain of idæas, one may extend the circulation, go round and round for ever, without making any progress beyond the point to which Providence has pinn'd us: But this does not satisfy me, who would rather say a little to no purpose, than a great deal. Lord B.[5] is voluminous, but he is voluminous only to destroy volumes. I shall not live, I fear, to see that work printed, he is so taken up still (in spite of the monitory Hint given in the first line of my Essay) with particular Men, that he neglects mankind, and is still a creature of this world, not of the Universe: This World, which is a name we give to Europe, to England, to Ireland, to London, to Dublin, to the Court, to the Castle, and so diminishing, till it comes to our own affairs, and our own persons. When you write (either to him or to me, for we accept it as all one[6]) rebuke him for it, as a Divine if you like it, or as a Badineur, if you think that more effectual.

What I write will show you that my head is yet weak. I had written to you by that gentleman from the Bath,[7] but I did not know him, and every body that comes from Ireland pretends to be a friend of the Dean's. I am always glad to see any that are truly so, and therefore do not mistake any thing I said, so as to discourage your sending any such to me. Adieu.

POPE *to* THE EARL OF OXFORD   30 *December* 1734

Longleat Portland Papers, xii

My Lord,—Two things retarded my writing to your Lordship, the one was, that I must have told you what your Humanity would have

---

[1] consider] considered *1741 Dab.*   [2] 'tis as] 'tis as much as *1742 La.*
[3] inspirit] inspire *1741 Dab.*   [4] you may move] you move *1742 Lbc.*
[5] B.] Bolingbroke *1741 Dab.* (This remark would seem to date the continued composition of Bolingbroke's philosophical writings, and to indicate that they did not precede the *Essay on Man*.)   [6] as all one] all as one *1740; 1741 Dab.*
[7] Mr. Towers. See Swift to Pope, 1 Nov. 1734.

been displeasd to hear, that I continued ill, indeed was worse; the other, that I hoped to have had Interest enough with my negligent Bookseller to have procur'd a Copy of the Epistle to Dr A. to accompany my Letter. I doubt whether I shall do it yet?[1] One Obstacle would not be sufficient to hinder me of so great a Pleasure as is offerd me, that of paying my Respects to Bulstrode; but both Sickness, & this insupportable Weather, are too hard for me: My Spirit is ready, but my flesh is weak. I humbly beg the Duchess of Portland to beg the Duke to accept my thanks & Services;[2] Thro' her hands they may seem of some value. Your Lordship needs not be told, how much, & with what good reason, I am | My Lord, | Your ever obliged, ever | faithful Servant, | A. Pope.

Twit'nam: | Decr 30th 1734

I am Lord Duplin's humble Servant. I hope he will defend me from the imputation which all the Town I hear lay upon me, of having writ that impudent satire.[3]

Endorsement (by a secretary): Mr Pope | Twickenham Decr 30th 1734

POPE *to* CARYLL   31 *December* 1734

Add. 28618

Twitnam. 31 Decb 1734.

It is a truth that before I rose this day at twelve of the clock, I resolved to write to you by this night's post; and an hour after I had your kind letter brought me. Your guess indeed was right; I have been very ill, confined for some days, first to my bed, many more to my chamber in London, and as soon as I was able to get home, persecuted with a fresh cold, which brought all my maladies upon me at once. In such condition have I continued ten days more. The only reason I did not write to you for 3 weeks past, was that I could tell you only such ill news of myself as I knew would trouble you, and hoped daily to be able to give you better. If I can get rid of a night cough, which otherwise thro' long continuance will fall on my lungs, I shall do well enough. I heartily join in your prayers for your part as well as for mine; and I think it better to return those to you than the compli-

---

[1] The poem was on sale three days later, and normally there would have been advance copies for both Swift (letter of 19 Dec.) and for Lord Oxford.

[2] Evidently Pope has had a ducal invitation to Bulstrode, where Oxford still is.

[3] On 21 Dec. (*LEP*) was advertised as published *Sober Advice from Horace to the young Gentlemen about Town, as deliver'd in his second Sermon . . . Imitated in the Manner of Mr. Pope, together with the Text as restored by the Rev. Richard Bentley, D.D.* This was by Pope. See Bolingbroke to Swift, 6 July 1734. Pope concealed his authorship because of the indecency of the poem and the threats of Bentley's son to horsewhip the poet, if he was the author. See iii. 451.

ments of the season. However, you and all yours have them, into the bargain. Here is a piece of poetry from Horace come out, which I warn you not to take for mine, tho' some people are willing to fix it on me. In truth I should think it a very indecent Sermon,[1] after the *Essay on Man*. But in a week or so, you'll have a thing,[2] which is mine, and I hope not unworthy an honest man, in his own just vindication from slanders of all sorts, and slanderers of what rank or quality whatsoever. 'Tis the last thing, relating to my self, I will ever trouble the public with. Adieu; may you continue to think well of me; that is, to think me affectionately and mindfully | Dear sir | Yours | A. Pope.

Pray how is your own health?

[1] Pope uses his high skill in the art of genteel equivocation in this remark: he does not flatly deny authorship of his *Sober Advice*, but only a very thin partition divides the warning from a lie.

[2] *Epistle to Dr. Arbuthnot.* Pope's illness probably accounts for his ignorance of the fact that publication was two days off. Or is he ignorant?

Near the beginning of the year Pope published his *Epistle to Dr. Arbuthnot* and the last of his Moral Essays, *Of the Characters of Women*. Neither of these evoked immediate public attack, though Lady Mary protested to Dr. Arbuthnot. Actually Pope had silenced his two 'top' enemies, Lady Mary and Lord Hervey, whose avowed position as to Pope became much like that of Pope to Curll: inferior enemies were to be silently scorned. Just before publishing the two poems mentioned Pope brought out *Sober Advice from Horace*, which, though anonymous and loudly disowned, was still used against him. In April he published a second volume of *Works*, including poems printed since 1717; but the real event of 1735, of course, was the long-prepared publication of Pope's *Letters* in May, which caused interminable advertisements by and against Edmund Curll, whom Pope had tricked into publishing for him. The year was saddened by the deaths of Dr. Arbuthnot and Lord Peterborow, and the absence of Lord Bolingbroke in France was an additional, if milder, cause of sadness. During the year royalty was much concerned in constructing grottoes, gazebos, &c., &c. Pope's knowledge of these matters possibly served to increase his intimacy with the Prince of Wales, who in October did the poet the honour of a visit at his house in Twickenham.

LADY MARY WORTLEY MONTAGU *to* DR. ARBUTHNOT

The Royal College of Surgeons of England

3 *January* [1734/5]

Sir,—I have perus'd the last Lampoon of your ingenious Freind,[1] & am not surpriz'd you did not find me out under the name of Sapho, because there is nothing I ever heard in our Characters or circumstances to make a parallel, but as the Town (except you who know better) generally suppose Pope means me whenever he mentions that name, I cannot help taking Notice of the terrible malice he bears against the Lady signify'd by that name, which appears to be irritated by supposing her writer of the verses to the Imitator of Horace, now I can assure him they were wrote (without my knowledge) by a Gentleman of great merit, whom I very much esteem, who he will never guess, & who, if he did know he durst not attack;[2] but I own the design was so well meant, & so excellently executed that I cannot be sorry they were written; I wish you would advise poor Pope to

---

[1] Pope's *Epistle to Dr. Arbuthnot*, just published, mentions Sapho in ll. 101 and 369, but without especial malice. Lord Hervey came off far less well in this poem.

[2] The *Verses* were probably a product of the joint authorship of Lord Hervey and Lady Mary.

turn to some more honest livelihood than libelling, I know he will alledge in his excuse, that he must write to eat, & he is now grown sensible that nobody will buy his verses, except their curiosity is piqued to it, by what is said of their Acquaintance, but I think this method of Gain so exceeding vile that it admits of no excuse at all. Can any thing be more detestable than his abusing poor Moor scarce cold in his Grave,[1] when it is plain he kept back his Poem while he liv'd for fear he should beat him for it? this is shocking to me tho' of a man I never spoke to, & hardly knew by sight, but I am seriously concern'd at the worse scandal he has heap'd on Mr Congreve who was my Friend, & whom I am oblig'd to Justify because I can do it on my own knowledge, & which is yet farther bring wittness of it, from those who were then often with me, that he was so far from loveing Popes Rhyme, both that & his Conversation were perpetual jokes to him, exceeding despicable in his Opinion, & he has often made us laugh in talking of them being particularly pleasant on that subject.[2] as to Pope's being born of Honest Parents I verily beleive it,[3] & will add one praise to his mothers Character that (tho' I only knew her very old) she allways appear'd to me to have much better sense than himselfe. I desire Sir as a favour that you would shew this Letter to Pope & you will very much oblige Sir your humble Servant M W Montagu

Jan 3d.

POPE *to* FORTESCUE[4]   *January* 1734/5

1797 (Polwhele, i. 324)

Thursday, 1 o'clock, Jan. 1734–5.

I have been not only in and out of town so often, but so ridiculously employed (as I tell you at large) that I could not get one hour to see you. Pray tell me when I shall be sure of you at home? This day at any hour. Mrs. Blount has now disposed very well of her money, which a friend of ours will pay at 4 per cent. for from this day. Therefore, if you'l order it me, I'll take it for her forthwith, and bring you any proper receipt you shall send me. I write this from her house. Adieu! All happiness attend you, dear Sir, yours, | A. Pope.

Address: To Wm. Fortescue, esq. in Bell-yard.

---

[1] James Moore Smythe died in October of 1734. See *Ep. to Arbuthnot*, l. 385. Pope's animus harks back at least to Moore's *One Epistle to Mr. Pope* (1730), and Lady Mary is rather properly surprised at the mention of Moore.

[2] Lady Mary, in an obvious rage, is doubtless exaggerating.

[3] See Pope's defence of his parentage in his note to l. 381 of his *Epistle*.

[4] The date ('Thursday,' &c., apart) probably comes from Fortescue's endorsement. The 2nd was the earliest Thursday, and the beginning of the month might be a plausible time for financial arrangements, but Pope's ill health makes a later period in January more plausible.

POPE *to* FORTESCUE[1]   [*January* 1734/5]

Arthur A. Houghton, Jr.

Mrs Blounts Party with Mrs Knight to pay your Family a Visit is desired to be to morrow, if it suit with your Conveniency, & if so, they chuse to dine with you. The Evenings they are ingagd for all this week. I who know your Spirit of Hospitality, conclude you'l like the Dinner best. Adieu, & let them have your answer to night, or per bearer. Believe me ever with true affection | Dear Sir | Yours. | A. Pope.

Munday.

Address: To | Wm Fortescue Esq. in | Bellyard | Lincolns Inne
Endorsement (by Fortescue): Mr Pope | Jan. 1734/5

POPE *to* CARYLL   8 *February* 1734/5

Add. 28618

London 8. February 1734-5.

This letter has been deferred a fortnight from day to day, in the consideration of sending you with it the Epistle concerning the Characters of Women, for which you express (with your wonted partiality) some impatience. Unexpected accidents retarded its publication till now,[2] and now I fear 'twill not answer your expectation. The lady to whom it is addressed had the great modesty to insist on my suppressing her name.[3] So I must leave you with the rest of the world to guess at her. It is certain there are not many, who can justly claim the character. I know her to merit it, and so do, or should, all those that know her; yet the malice of a world which abounds not in good examples, would perhaps be glad she did not; for unless a lady be in some public station, it is nobody's vanity to be her friend; and few women are friends but out of vanity. Virtue in retirement is either not allowed or not seen.

I send you constantly whatever is mine. The ludicrous (or if you please) the obscene thing you desired me to send, I did not approve of, and therefore did not care to propagate by sending into the country at all. Whoever likes it so well as to think it mine, compliments me at my own expense. But there is another piece, which I may venture to send you, in a post or two, *An Essay on Reason*[4] of a serious kind, and the intention and doctrines of which I think you will not disapprove.

[1] 6 Jan. is the first Monday of 1734/5.   [2] It was published 8 Feb. 1734/5.
[3] Martha Blount, of course.
[4] By the Rev. Walter Harte. See Pope to Mallet, letter of May or June 1734. In Dec. 1734 Harte had become vicar of Gosfield, in the gift of Mrs. Knight.

I have nothing to add but my services and best wishes to all your family, and to tell you that your god-daughter is in pain that Mrs Caryll never writes to her. She well knows she does not deserve her favour and kindness less than she always did, and therefore is concerned at so long a silence.

My health is as usual: it has been worse, and I hope the advance of the spring will be to the benefit of both of us. For your welfare I sincerely pray, and am truly | Dear sir | Your obliged and most affectionate servant | A. Pope.

POPE *to* CARYLL   18 *February* 1734/5

Add. 28618

London 18 February 1734-5.

In great hurry I write this to thank you for your last, and answer you one or two questions of importance, indeed, since one concerns life, the other marriage. The story of Bentley is this in three words. He expressed a resentment as if I had injured his father in a thing I disowned. I told him if he was not satisfied in that, and if he required any other satisfaction, I would give it. After a three-weeks' hesitation, and messages, he gave it under his hand he did not, and confessed himself in the wrong.[1] Your other question about intending marriage made me laugh; for if that line meant any such thing, it must be over. 'Tis in the preterperfect tense, *Gave a Poet.*[2] 'Tis a new sort of father for marriage: he[3] gave me long ago to Belinda, as he did Homer to Achilles, and tis a mercy he has not given me to more ladies, but that I am almost as little inclined to celebrate that way, as the other. Dear Sir, Adieu; I have no time to explain to you upon a better subject, the *Essay on Reason*, which comes to you in three packets by this post. It was out of print, and I was forced to wait for a Second Edition. I am always | Your affectionate obliged servant | A. Pope.

*POPE *to* PHILIP MILLER[4]   19 *February* [1734/5?]

The Massachusetts Historical Society

Feb. 19th

Sir,—I make no scruple of giving you this trouble, since it is for a

---

[1] Pope's (disowned) poem, 'Sober Advice from Horace', advertised 'the Original Text, as restored by the Revd R. Bentley . . . And some Remarks on the Version'. The irony and indecency of some of the notes led Bentley's son to threaten Pope, who must have equivocated ingeniously to get out of the difficulty.

[2] Caryll had evidently hoped from the last line of the *Epistle on the Characters of Women* that a marriage between Pope and Martha Blount was a possibility.   [3] i.e. Phoebus.

[4] The year date is pencilled in on the original in a modern hand. Pope was in town at this time in 1734/5, and may have been staying (as he frequently did) with Lord Cornbury. The year might be any year after 1722 when Miller became foreman in the Chelsea Garden (*DNB*) and when Cornbury was in England.

particular Friend of mine, whose great Curiosity in Fruit has been terribly disappointed by the nursery men. It is that you will procure me some Cuttings of the Chaumontell, a French Pear, & of the Vingoleuse, & Epine d'Hyver. It is high time to graft them, I believe, & therfore beg you to help me to them as soon as possible. Be so good as to let each sort be marked with written labels, & the whole pack'd up in moistend Moss, or some proper Covering, & sent to me at Lord Cornbury's by Oxford Chapel; where I am to be found generally any morning before ten, if ever you have time to call on one who is Sincerely Sir, | Your obligd, & affectionate Servant | A. Pope

Address: To | Mr Miller at the Phy-|sic-Garden in | Chelsea.
Postmark: PENY POST PAYD

POPE *to* GEORGE ARBUTHNOT   1 *March* 1734/5
The Royal College of Surgeons of England
                                                    London, March 1st 1734.

It is a great Truth, that I can find no words to express the Share I bear in your present Grief, and Loss.[1] There can be but One happy of your whole Family at this hour: I doubt not He is so. But my Concern does not end in him, I really dread what may be the Situation of your Elder Sister in particular,[2] & it will be a great Satisfaction to me to know, that none of you are more afflicted than you ought to be. If there can be any thing, in which I can be, any way, of use or Service to you, on this melancholy occasion, pray freely command either my purse, or my faculties of any kind, to the utmost of their power. Believe it, you will oblige me, and think me to be Your Father's Friend belonging to You all.

Dear Sir I am Yours faithfully | A. Pope.

POPE *to* THE EARL OF OXFORD   3 *March* 1734/5
Longleat Portland Papers, xii
                                                    Twitnam. Mrch 3. | 1734/5.

My Lord,—I stay'd to the latest hour I could, to have bid your Lordship adieu, before I went. Many melancholy Circumstances, to me, have detain'd me of late from being so long & often happy as I hoped, in your Conversation: The death, & the sickness, of Friends, particularly.[3] My own Health is really bad, & I am harras'd out, both

---

[1] Dr. Arbuthnot died 27 Feb. His son George, to whom Pope now writes, became from this time a friend of Pope's, as did his sister Anne.
[2] Margaret Arbuthnot.
[3] The death of Arbuthnot, the incurable state of Lord Peterborow's health, and doubtless other illnesses were what depressed Pope.

in body & mind, by it. I beg your Lordship to give the Bearer my Waterman the bound Book of Copies of Letters, which I want to inspect for a day or two.¹ I fear it will be yet some days e're I can wait on you. My sincerest Services attend you ever, & my truest Affections, | A. Pope.

Address: To the Rt Hon. the Earl | of Oxford.
Endorsement: Mr Pope | Twitnam March 3. | 1734/5

POPE *to* FORTESCUE   22 *March* 1734/5

1797 (Polwhele, i. 324)

London, March 22, 1734–5.

I deferred this two or three posts to send you an answer from Dr. Mead, of the truth of what you heard. But he knows no example that can quite be depended on, of the pulvis A. curing, after any one began to rave, or otherwise than if taken very soon after the wound. I gave Mr. Bl.² the account, which will be paid as soon as you please, if your clerk have the receipts from the attornies, or if not, when you return. Mr. Bethel has been with Mr. C—s³ about it, who told him to defer it till you come. I've seen your family twice, once at Mr. Jervais's, and last night at home: they are all well, except a little cold which Miss Fortescue has, but was very merry. I hope you have this week seen Buckland with pleasure, and in a state of improvement; and that you will see Fallapit with the same. Twitnam is very cold these easterly winds; but I presume they don't blow in the happy regions of Devonshire. My garden, however, is in good condition, and promises fruits not too early. I am building a stone obelisk,⁴ making two new ovens and stoves, and a hot-house for anana's, of which I hope you will taste this year. The public news and votes tell you all the business of the season: it is generally thought the parliament will be up in the middle of April. Adieu! May success, health, and money attend you in all your circulations. I am faithfully and affectionately, dear Sir, yours, | A. Pope.

Address: To Wm. Fortescue, esq. in Bell-yard, Lincoln's Inn.

¹ It is not probable that Pope sent the Harleian transcripts of his letters to the press. He may have sent some revised originals, but pretty certainly the printed texts came from transcripts not preserved. It is quite possible that he was already reading proof on his letters—to be published 12 May.
² Possibly Michael Blount. See iii. 455.
³ Cruwys.
⁴ With an inscription to the memory of his mother.

*POPE to BUCKLEY   9 April 1735

The University of Texas

I hope you have by this time the present I orderd you, of All I am
worth, that is, *my Workes.*¹ It is a very poor return for your Thuanus,
or indeed for many friendly offices you have always been ready to do
me. It was meerly an Unwillingness to give you Trouble, that hinderd
my doing myself the Service of desiring your Assistance in printing this
book. As it is, it has cost me dear, & may dearer, if I am to depend on
my Bookseller for the Re-imbursement. If it lye in your way to help
me off with 150 of them, (which are not to be sold to the Trade at
less than 18s or to Gentlemen than a Guinea) it would be a Service
to me,² a Bookseller having had the Conscience to offer me 13s a
piece, & being modestly content to get 8s in the pound himself, after
I have done him many services. Another, quite a Stranger, has taken
100 at 17s but I want to part with the rest.

I lye at Lord Oxford's, where a line from you will find me. I make
you no apology, for I have a true Affection for you. | Dear Sir |
Your faithfull hum|ble Servant | A. Pope.

April 9th | 1735.

Address: To | Mr Buckley, at his house | in Little Britain, | London.
Postmark: 10/AP.

POPE to WILLIAM DUNCOMBE³   [6 May 1735]

Arthur A. Houghton, Jr.

                                    [Twit'nam, 6 May, | 1735]

Sir,—Many thanks for your kind present, in which I find several very
pleasing & very correct pieces of his,⁴ which were new to me. I beg
you to accept of the New Volume of my things just printed, which
will be delivered you by Mr Dodsley, the Author of the Toyshop,
who has just set up a Bookseller, and I doubt not, as he has more
Sense, so will have more Honesty, than most of that Profession. I am,
Sir, | Your most oblig'd hum-|ble Servant | A. Pope.

¹ Pope's *Works*, vol. ii, in quarto and folio were on sale now or (probably) later in April.
The volume contained the *Essay on Man*, the Moral Essays, and the satires and epistles
already published separately, &c.
² At this time Buckley was evidently a bookseller as well as a printer. Pope himself paid
the printer for this volume, and himself sold to booksellers. This had been his habit since
The Dunciad.
³ The superscribed dating is entirely in the hand of, presumably, the recipient of the letter.
At the top, in another hand (presumably that of the later editor of the letters, William's son,
John), is written 'Letter XCIV | Mr. Pope to Mr. Duncombe'.
⁴ The earlier of the two editorial hands has here inserted between the lines the annotation
'Mr Hughes'. Duncombe has sent Pope a copy of Hughes's *Poems* (1735).

POPE *to* CARYLL   12 *May* 1735
Add. 28618
                                        Twitnam 12. May 1735.

Many things conspired to make me silent of late. My constant attendance on a sick friend or two, my Lord Peterborow particularly who
lay very ill at a lodging at Kensington, where I generally past half my
time, and in business, and ill health the rest. But what makes me sick
of writing is the shameless industry of such fellows as Curle, and the
idle ostentation, or weak partiality of many of my correspondents, who
have shewn about my letters (which I never writ but in haste, and
generally against the grain, in mere civility), for almost all letters, are
impertinent farther than *si bene valeas, bene est, ego valeo* to such a
degree that a volume of 200, or more are printed by that rascal: But
he could never have injured me this way, had not my friends furnished
him with the occasion by keeping such wretched papers as they ought
to have burned.[1]

What I said to You on the *Essay on Reason* was true.[2] I think it a
piece much more worthy a serious man (that is of my self, for such I
am, and I hope you know me enough to think me so) than that idle
parody upon Horace, which some imputed to me. I was not sorry
many people took Mr Hart's poem for mine. It pleased me to see
they did him justice from that opinion, which otherwise perhaps they
had not done him.

You will see Mr Bl——. I dare say your god-daughter will think her
self obliged to you for thinking of doing her that good office; but it
would have been a little of the latest, had not a friend of hers (Mr.
Fortescue, the Prince's attorney general) supplied her with the money
a year ago. Either she must have been treated herself in the same way
that she has been (within this week) forced to treat Mr. Bl—— or her
friend must never have been repaid what he so generously lent her.
Mr Bl—— to my knowledge was informed of this by Mr Fortescue
himself above a twelvemonth ago, and to this hour he owes her a
year and a half's rent. This conduct is past *censure*, and past *shame*.
One ought only to despise and laugh at it. Therefore, pray lose not a
syllable upon him.

I want to make you a present of all I'm worth, the 2d (and perhaps
the last) volume of my *Works*, which are now become so voluminous,
as to outweigh their author. It is high time after the fumbling age of
forty is past, to abandon those ladies,[3] who else will quickly abandon
us. I am &c. | A. Pope.

---

1 Pope writes on the very day that Curll was first publishing Pope's letters—for Pope
himself. One need not wonder at Pope's daring in Caryll's lifetime to publish letters to Caryll
as if sent to other friends and not to Caryll. The best evidence to Caryll that the publication
was not authentic would be precisely such procedure.
   2 See Pope to Caryll, 8 Feb. 1734/5.   3 The Muses.

†SWIFT *to* POPE[1]   12 *May* 1735

1740

May 12, 1735.

Your letter was sent me yesterday by Mr. Stopford who landed the same day, but I have not yet seen him. As to my silence, God knows it is my great misfortune. My little domestick affairs are in great confusion by the villany of agents, and the miseries of this kingdom, where there is no mony to be had: nor am I unconcerned to see all things tending towards absolute power, in both nations (it is here in perfection already) although I shall not live to see it established. This condition of things, both publick and personal to myself, hath given me such a kind of despondency, that I am almost unqualified for any company, diversion, or amusement. The death of Mr. Gay and the Doctor, have been terrible wounds near my heart. Their living would have been a great comfort to me, although I should never have seen them; like a sum of mony in a bank from which I should receive at least annual interest, as I do from you, and have done from Lord Bolingbroke. To shew in how much ignorance I live, it is hardly a fortnight since I heard of the death of my dear friend my Lady[2] Masham, my constant friend in all changes of times. God forbid that I should expect you to make a voyage that would in the least affect your health: but in the mean time how unhappy am I, that my best friend should have perhaps the only kind of disorder for which a sea voyage is not in some degree a remedy. The old Duke of Ormond said, he would not change his dead son (Ossory) for the best living son in Europe. Neither would I change you my absent friend for the best friend round the Globe.

I have lately read a book imputed to Lord B.[3] called a Dissertation upon Parties.[4] I think it very masterly written.

Pray God reward you for your kind prayers: I believe your prayers will do me more good than those of all the Prelates in both kingdoms, or any Prelate in Europe except the Bishop of Marseilles.[5] And God preserve you for contributing more to mend the world, than the whole pack of (modern) Parsons in a lump. | I am ever entirely yours.

[1] For a fuller text of this letter, from the Portland Papers, see v. 13–16.
[2] She had died 6 Dec. 1734.   [3] B.] Bolingbroke, *1741 Dab.*
[4] Bolingbroke's *Dissertation upon Parties*, collected essays from *The Craftsman*, appeared as a volume at the end of February. It is perhaps Bolingbroke's most important work.
[5] When the Plague was raging in a most violent Manner in that City, in 1720, the Bishop went from House to House to visit the Sick, and sold all his Plate, &c. for the Relief of the Poor.—Footnote in *1741* Dab. (The footnote seems to be excellent evidence of Swift's editing of the clandestine volume for his Dublin readers.)

POPE *to* JONATHAN RICHARDSON   [1735?]

[A letter to Richardson, otherwise unknown, was offered for sale in the Catalogue of Thomas Thorpe in 1833 as lot 814. It introduces (according to the catalogue) a young gentleman about to set out for Rome and desirous first to see the collection of drawings formed by the two Richardsons. The following passage is quoted: 'He would be ashamed not to be able to give some account of the drawings; and not to say, also, he had seen you. If you can get him access to Sir Robert Walpole's pictures, it would be doubly obliging.' (Evidently Pope feels that an application from himself to Sir Robert might not be acceptable!)]

MALLET *to* POPE[1]   [1735]

1857 (Carruthers, pp. 436–7)

It seems strange that I should write less frequently to you than to my other friends, though I esteem and love you more than all of them. And yet it is true, for this only reason, that I have hardly met with anything in the course of my travels hitherto which I think deserves your attention; and the design of this letter is more to have news from you of Twitenham and of your own health, than to send you any accounts of Paris or Geneva. It is but a very poor compliment to assure you that the former will give me infinitely more satisfaction than you can receive from the latter.

I will say nothing of Paris, because, though I lived in it three weeks, I saw that great city—that metropolis of dress and debauchery—only, as it were, in a dream.

Geneva is a pretty town, but of no great extent. It is well fortified on all sides, and entertains a garrison of about seven hundred men, which, however, in case of an assault, would be found not near sufficient to man the walls. It is true that the little republic depends chiefly for its security on the mutual jealousy of the French king and the Duke of Savoy. The city is built on a rising ground in the middle of a fine plain, agreeably diversified with vineyards, meadows, and little villas. I need not tell you that the famous Leman lake is one of its greatest ornaments. Though everything looks green and gay in the valley before and behind us, where the spring is in full bloom, yet the tops of the high mountains which surround us in a double range at the distance of about a league and a half, are still white with snow, and even in this season afford a beautiful winter-piece.

As all public spectacles are forbidden, our amusements are few. These honest burghers lead a plain, uniform life, which, if it is not enlivened by many pleasures, is not ruffled by strong passions; a little commerce, a little love, and a very little gallantry, make up the business

[1] We do not know precisely when Mr. Newsham and Mallet, his tutor, went on the Grand Tour; but later letters make the summer of 1735 a certainty.

and ambition of the place. The whole town dines regularly at half an hour after twelve. About two they form themselves into parties, which they call societies, for cards, where, if a man is in an ill run of fortune, he may lose three or four shillings. This continues till six; and then all the little *beau monde* of Geneva appears either on the bastions of their fortifications or in a public walk which they call the Treille. The women simper at the men, and the men say silly things to the women, till half an hour after seven, when every one returns to his own home to supper and to bed.

The women (who are neither handsome nor ugly) dress disagreeably, though against their own inclination, for the mode is fixed by a reform of the commonwealth, which forbids them likewise to wear any gold or silver lace on their clothes. But that fashionable superfluity is indulged to strangers, because the inhabitants find their account in it. They do not paint, as the French women do, to a degree that at first very much shocks an English eye. In Paris a lady's quality may be guessed at by the quantity of red she lays on—the cheek of a duchess being in a higher state of colouring than that of a countess.

You see what valuable experience one gains by travelling! To be serious, I have learned by it to prize you more than ever, and to reckon as the greatest happiness of my life the friendship you have shown for, dear sir, your most affectionate, humble servant, | D. Mallet.

A NARRATIVE[1] OF THE METHOD BY WHICH THE PRIVATE LETTERS OF MR. POPE HAVE BEEN PRO-CUR'D AND PUBLISH'D BY EDMUND CURLL, BOOK-SELLER. NB. *The Original Papers, in* Curl's *own Hand, may be seen at* T. Cooper's. London. . . . MDCCXXXV.

It has been judg'd, that to clear an Affair which seem'd at first sight a little mysterious, and which, tho' it concern'd only one Gentleman, is of such a Conse-quence, as justly to alarm every Person in the Nation, would not only be acceptable as a *Curiosity*, but useful as a *Warning*, and perhaps flagrant enough as an *Example*, to induce the LEGISLATURE to prevent for the future, an Enormity so prejudicial to every private Subject, and so destructive of Society it self.

This will be made so plain by the ensuing Papers, that 'twill scarce be needful to attend them with any Reflections, more than what every Reader may make.

In the Year 1727, *Edmund Curl*, Bookseller, published a Collection of several private Letters of Mr. *Pope* to *Henry Cromwell* Esq; which he obtain'd in this Manner.

Mr. *Cromwell* was acquainted with one Mrs. *Thomas*, to whom he had the Indis-cretion to lend these Letters, and who falling into Misfortunes, seven Years after,

[1] This *Narrative*, inspired if not written by Pope, is placed here because the date of its publication is 12 June 1735 or thereabouts. It serves to annotate the letters and to illuminate the history of their publication.

sold them to Mr. *Curll*, without the Consent either of Mr. *Pope* or Mr. *Cromwell*, as appears from the following Letters.

[There follow the texts of three letters here found under their proper dates in 1727: E. Thomas to H. Cromwell, 27 June 1727; H. Cromwell to Pope, 6 July 1727; H. Cromwell to Pope, 1 August 1727. After these letters Pope's comment is as follows:]

This Treatment being extreamly disagreeable to Mr. *Pope*, he was advised to recal any Letters which might happen to be preserved by any of his Friends, particularly those written to Persons deceas'd, which would be most subject to such an Accident. Many of these were return'd him.

Some of his Friends advised him to print a Collection himself, to prevent a worse; but this he would by no means agree to. However, as some of the Letters served to revive several past Scenes of Friendship, and others to clear the Truth of *Facts* in which he had been misrepresented by the common Scribblers, he was induced to preserve a few of his own Letters, as well as of his Friends. These, as I have been told, he inserted in Two Books, some Originals, others Copies, with a few Notes and Extracts here and there added. In the same Books he caused to be copied some small Pieces in Verse and Prose, either of his own, or his Correspondents; which, tho' not finish'd enough for the Publick, were such as the Partiality of any Friend would be sorry to be depriv'd of.

To this Purpose, an Amanuensis or two were employ'd by Mr. *Pope*, when the Books were in the Country, and by the Earl of *Oxford*, when they were in Town.

It happen'd soon after, that the *Posthumous Works* of Mr. *Wycherly* were publish'd, in such a Manner, as could no way increase the Reputation of that Gentleman, who had been Mr. *Pope*'s first Correspondent and Friend; And several of these Letters so fully shew'd the State of that Case, that it was thought but a Justice to Mr. *Wycherly*'s Memory to print a few, to discredit that Imposition. These were accordingly transcrib'd for the Press from the Manuscript Books abovemention'd.

They were no sooner printed, but *Edmund Curl* look'd on these too as his Property; for a Copy is extant, which he corrected in order to another Impression, interlin'd, and added marginal Notes to, in his own Hand.

He then advertis'd anew the Letters to Mr. *Cromwell*, with *Additions*, and promis'd Incouragement to all Persons who should send him more.

This is a Practice frequent with Booksellers, to swell an Author's Works, in which they have some Property, with any Trash that can be got from any Hand; or where they have no such Works, to procure some. *Curl* has in the same manner since advertiz'd the *Letters* of Mr. *Prior*, and Mr. *Addison*. A Practice highly deserving some Check from the Legislature; since every such Advertisement, is really a *Watch-word* to every *Scoundrel* in the Nation, and to every *Domestick* of a Family, to get a Penny, by producing any Scrap of a Man's Writing, (of what Nature soever) or by picking his Master's Pocket of Letters and Papers.

A most flagrant Instance of this kind was the Advertisement of an intended Book, call'd *Gulliveriana Secunda*; where it was promis'd "that *any Thing*, which *any Body* should send as Mr. *Pope*'s or Dr. *Swift*'s, should be printed and inserted *as Theirs*."

By these honest means, Mr. *Curl* went on encreasing his Collection; and finding (as will be seen hereafter by No. 5.) a further Prospect of doing so, he retarded his

Edition of Mr. *Cromwell*'s Letters till the Twenty-Second of March 1734–5, and then sent Mr. *Pope* the following Letter, the first he ever receiv'd from him.

No. I.

Sir, | To convince you of my readiness to oblige you, the *Inclosed* is a Demonstration. You have, as he says disoblig'd a Gentleman, the initial Letters of whose Name are *P.T.* I have some other Papers in the same Hand relating to your *Family*, which I will show if you desire a Sight of them. Your Letters to Mr. *Cromwell* are out of Print, and I intend to Print them very beautifully in an *Octavo Volume*. I have more to say than is proper to write, and if you'll give me a Meeting, I will wait on you with Pleasure, and close all Differences betwixt you and yours | E. Curl.

Rose-Street 22 March 1735.

P.S. I expect the Civility of an Answer or Message.

The *Inclos'd* were two Scraps of Paper, suppos'd to be *P.T*'s (a feigned Hand) the first containing this Advertisement.

No. II.

Letters of *Alexander Pope* Esq; and several eminent Hands. From the Year 1705. to 1727. Containing a Critical, Philological, and Historical Correspondence between him and *Henry Cromwell* Esq; *William Wycherly* Esq; *William Walsh* Esq; *William Congreve* Esq; Sir *William Trumbull*; Sir *Richard Steele*; E. O—, Mr. *Addison*; M. *Craggs*; Mr. *Gay*; Dean *Swift*, &c. with several Letters to Ladies; to the Number of two Hundred. *N.B.* The Originals will be shewn at *Ed. Curl's* when the Book is Published.

The other Paper was a Scrap of some Letter in the same Hand, which exprest "a Dissatisfaction at *Curl* for not having printed his Advertisement"—What more cannot be seen, for the rest is cut off close to the Writing.

Mr. *Pope*'s Friends imagin'd that the whole Design of *E. Curl* was to get him but to look on the Edition of *Cromwel*'s Letters, and so to print it as *revis'd* by Mr. *Pope*, in the same manner as he sent an obscene Book to a *Reverend Bishop*, and then Advertis'd it as *corrected* and *revis'd* by him. Or if there was any such Proposal from *P.T. Curll* would not fail to embrace it, perhaps pay for the Copy with the very Mony he might draw from Mr. *P—* to suppress it, and say *P.T.* had kept another Copy. He therefore answer'd the only way he thought it safe to correspond with him, by a publick Advertisement in the *Daily Post-Boy*.

No. III.

Whereas *A.P.* hath received a Letter from *E.C.* Bookseller pretending that a Person, the initials of whose Name are *P.T.* hath offered the said *E.C.* to print a large Collection of Mr. *P.*'s Letters, to which *E.C.* requires an Answer, *A.P.* having never had, nor intending to have, any private Correspondence with the said *E.C.* gives it him in this Manner. That he knows no such Person as *P.T.* that he believes he hath no such Collection, and that he thinks the whole a Forgery, and shall not trouble himself at all about it.

Ed. Curl return'd an impertinent Answer in the same Paper the next Day, denying that he *endeavour'd to correspond with Mr. P.* and affirming that he wrote by

Direction, but declaring that he would *instantly print the said Collection.* In a few Days more he publish'd the *Advertisement of the Book* as above, with this Addition, "*E.C.* as before in the like Case, will be faithful."

He now talk'd of it every where, said "That *P.T.* was a LORD, or a PERSON of CONSEQUENCE, who printed the Book at a *great Expence,* and sought no Profit, but *Revenge* on Mr. *Pope who had offended him:*" particularly, "That some of the Letters would be such as both *Church* and *State would take Notice of;* but that *P.T.* would by no means be known in it, that he never would once be *seen* by him, but treated in a very *secret Manner.*" He told some Persons that sifted him in this Affair, "that he had convers'd only with his Agent, a Clergyman of the Name of *Smith,* who came, as he said, from *Southwark.*" With this Person it was that *Curl* transacted the Affair, who before all the Letters were delivered to *Curl,* insisted on the Letters of *P.T.* being return'd him, to secure him from all possibility of a Discovery, as appears from No. 12.

Mr. *Pope,* on hearing of this *Smith,* and finding when the Book came out, that several of the *Letters* could only have come from the *Manuscript*-Book beforemention'd, publish'd this Advertisement.

Whereas a Person who signs himself *P.T.* and another who writes himself *R. Smith* and passes for a Clergyman, have Transacted for some time past with *Edm. Curl,* and have in combination printed the *Private Letters* of Mr. Pope and his Correspondents [some of which could only be procured from his own Library, or that of a Noble Lord, and which have given a Pretence to the publishing others as his which are not so, as well as Interpolating those which are;] This is to advertise, that if either of the said Persons will discover the Whole of this Affair, he shall receive a Reward of *Twenty Guineas;* or if he can prove he hath acted by **Direction of any other* [*For Curl had said in his Advertisement, that he wrote to Mr. P. *By Direction,* and another of his drawing up of Mr. Pope's *Life* began thus, *By Direction.*——] he shall receive double that Sum.

Whether this Advertisement, or the future Quarrel of *Curl* and *Smith* about Profits produced what follow'd we cannot say, but in a few Days the ensuing Papers, being the whole Correspondence of *P.T.* and *Edm. Curl* were sent to the Publisher *T. Cooper,* which we shall here lay before the Reader.

They begin as high as

No. IV.

[Then follow the letters from P.T. of 11 October 1733 and of 15 November 1733; here printed under those dates given. See iii. 387 and 395.]

There appears no other Letter from *P.T.* till one of *April* the 4*th,* which must be in 1735, as it relates plainly to Mr. *Pope*'s Advertisement in Answer to *Curl*'s Letter to him of *March* 22*d.* which see above No. 3.

No. VI.

April 4.

I see an Advertisement in the Daily Advertisements, which I take to relate to Me. I did not expect you of all Men would have betray'd me to Squire *Pope;* but you and he both shall soon be convinc'd it was no *Forgery.* For since you would not comply with my Proposal to advertise, I have printed them at my own Expence, being advis'd that I could safely do so. I wou'd still give you the Preference, if you'll pay the Paper and Print, and allow me handsomely for the Copy. But I shall not trust you to meet and converse upon it [after the Suspicion I have of your Dealings with Master *P.*] unless I see my Advertisement of the Book printed first, within these Four or Five days. If you are afraid of Mr. *P.* and dare not set your Name to it, as I propos'd at first, I do not insist thereupon, so I be but conceal'd. By this I shall determine, and if you will not, another will. It makes a Five Shilling Book. I am | Your Servant, *P. T.*

No. VII.

On a Scrap of Paper torn from a Letter, the Direction crost out,

Sir, | I should not deal thus Cautiously or in the Dark with you, but that 'tis plain from your own Advertisement, that you have been Treating with Mr. *Pope.*

No. VIII.

On another Piece cut off,

I still give you, Sir, the Preference. If you will give me 3*l.* a Score for 650 [each Book containing 380 Pages 8*vo.*] and pay down 75*l.* of the same, the whole Impression shall be yours, and there are Letters enough remaining (if you require) to make another 30 Sheets 8*vo.* a Five Shillings Book. You need only Answer thus in the *Daily Post* or *Advertiser* in four Days—[*E.C.* will meet *P.T.* at the *Rose Tavern* by the Play-House at Seven in the Evening April 22*d.*] and one will come and show you the Sheets.

MR. CURL'S ANSWERS

No. IX.

29th April 1735

Sir, | I have not ever met with any thing more inconsistent than the several Proposals of your Letters. The First bearing Date *Oct.* 11*th* 1733. gives some Particulars of Mr. *Pope*'s *Life*, which I shall shortly make a publick Use of, in his Life now going to the Press.

The Second of your Letters of *Nov.* 15*th* 1733, informs me That if I would publish an Advertisement of a Collection of Mr. *Pope*'s Letters in your Custody, the Originals should be forthwith sent me, and for which you would expect no more than would pay for a Transcript of 'em.

In your Third Letter of the Fourth Instant, you groundlessly imagine I have attempted to betray you to Mr. *Pope*; say you have printed these Letters your self, and now want to be handsomely allow'd for the Copy, *viz.* 3 *l.* a Score, which is 2 *l.* more than they cost Printing; appoint a Meeting at the *Rose* on the 22*d.* Instant, where I was to see the Sheets, dealing thus, as you truly call it, in the Dark.

April 21, You put off this Meeting, fearing a Surprize from Mr. *Pope*. How should he know of this Appointment, unless you gave him Notice? I fear no such Besettings either of him or his Agents. That the paying of seventy-five Pounds would bring you to Town in a Fortnight, would I be so silly as to declare it. By your last Letter, of last Night, a Gentleman is to be at my Door, at Eight this Evening, who has full Commission from you.

You want seventy-five Pounds for a Person you would serve; That Sum I can easily pay, if I think the Purchase would be of any Service to me. But in one Word, Sir, I am engaged all this Evening, and shall not give my self any further Trouble about such jealous, groundless, and dark Negociations. An HONOURABLE and OPEN DEALING is what I have been always used to, and if you will come into such a Method, I will meet you any-where, or shall be glad to see you at my own House, otherwise apply to whom you please. | Yours, | E.C.

For P.T. or the Gentleman who comes from him at Eight this Evening.

This appears to be the first Time *Curl* had any personal Conference with *R. Smith* the Clergyman.

No. X.

To the Reverend Mr. ***

Sir, | I am ready to discharge the Expence of Paper, Print, and Copy-Money, and make the Copy my own, if we agree. But if I am to be your Agent, then I insist to be solely so, and will punctually pay every Week for what I sell to you.—

No. XI.

Answer to P.T.'s *of 3d of* May.

Sir, | You shall, as all I have ever had any Dealings with have, find a JUST and HONOURABLE Treatment from me. But consider, Sir, as the Publick, by your Means entirely, have been led into an Initial Correspondence betwixt *E.C.* and *P.T.* and betwixt *A.P.* and *E.C.* the Secret is still as recondite as that of the Free-Masons. *P.T.* are not, I dare say, the true Initials of your Name; or if they were, Mr. *Pope* has publickly declar'd, *That he Knows no such Person as* P.T. how then can any thing you have communicated to me, discover you, or expose you to his Resentment ?

I have had Letters from another Correspondent, who subscribes himself *E.P.* which I shall print as Vouchers, in Mr. *Pope*'s Life, as well as those from *P.T.* which, as I take it, were all sent me for that Purpose, or why were they sent at all ?

Your Friend was with me on *Wednesday* last, but I had not your last till this Morning, *Saturday 3d* of *May.* I am, Sir, Yours, E.C.

P.S. What you say appears by my Advertisement in relation to Mr. *Pope*, I faithfully told your Friend the Clergyman. I wrote to Mr. *Pope*, to acquaint him that I was going to print a new Edition of his Letters to Mr. *Cromwell*, and offer'd him the Revisal of the Sheets, hoping likewise, that it was now time to close all former Resentments, which, on HONOURABLE TERMS, I was ready to do. I told him likewise I had a large Collection of others of his Letters, which, *from your two Years Silence on that Head, I thought was neither unjust nor dishonourable.*

No. XII.

——I cannot send the *Letters [*P.T.'s *Letters to* Curl.] now, because I have them not all by me, but either this Evening or To-morrow, you shall not fail of them, for some of them are in a Scrutore of mine out of Town, and I have sent a Messenger for them, who will return about Three or Four this Afternoon. Be not uneasy, I NEVER BREAK MY WORD, and as HONOURABLE and JUST Treatment shall be shewn by me, I shall expect the same Return.

The Estimate and Letters you shall have together, but I desire the Bearer may bring me fifty more Books. Pray come to Night, if you can. | I am faithfully yours, | E. Curl.

For the Reverend Mr Smith | (*half an Hour past Ten*.)

Curl was now so elated with his Success, the Books in his Hands, and, as he thought, the Men too, that he raised the Style of his Advertisement, which he publish'd on the 12th of *May*, in these Words, in the *Daily Post-Boy*.

No. XIII.

This Day are published, and most beautifully printed, Price five Shillings, Mr. Pope's *Literary Correspondence* for thirty Years; from 1704 to 1734. Being a Collection of Letters, regularly digested, written by him to the Right Honourable the late Earl of Hallifax, Earl of Burlington, Secretary Craggs, Sir William Trumbull, Honourable J. C. General ****, Honourable Robert Digby, Esq; Honourable Edward Blount, Esq; Mr. Addison, Mr. Congreve, Mr. Wycherly, Mr. Walsh, Mr. Steele, Mr. Gay, Mr. Jarvas, Dr. Arbuthnot, Dean Berkeley, Dean Parnelle, &c. Also Letters from Mr. Pope to Mrs. Arabella Fermor, and many other Ladies. With the respective Answers of each Correspondent. Printed for E. Curl in Rose-street, Covent-Garden, and sold by all Booksellers. N.B. The *Original Manuscripts* (of which Affidavit is made) may be seen at Mr. Curl's House by all who desire it.

And immediately after he writes thus to *Smith*.

No. XIV.

12th May, 1735.

Sir, | Your Letter written at Two Afternoon on *Saturday*, I did not receive till past Ten at Night. The *Title* will be done to Day, and according to your Promise, I fully depend on the Books and MSS. To-morrow. I hope you have seen the *Post-Boy*, and *approve** [By this it appears, it was of *Curl*'s own drawing up, which he deny'd to the Lords.] *the* Manner *of the Advertisement*. I shall think every Hour a long Period of Time till I have more Books, and see you, being, Sir, | Sincerely yours, | E. Curll.

(*For the Reverend Mr.* Smith.)

But the Tables now began to turn. It happened that the *Booksellers Bill* (for so it was properly called, tho' entitled, *An Act for the better Encouragement of Learning*) came on this Day in the House of Lords. Some of their Lordships having seen an Advertisement of so *strange a Nature*, thought it very unfitting such a Bill should pass, without a *Clause* to prevent such an enormous *License* for the future. And the Earl of *I—y* having read it to the House, observed further, that as it pretended to publish several Letters to *Lords* with the *respective Answers of each Correspondent*, it was a *Breach of Privilege*, and contrary to a standing Order of the House. Whereupon it was order'd that the Gentleman Usher of the Black Rod do forthwith seize the Impression of the said Book, and that the said *E. Curl* with *J. Wilford*, for whom the *Daily Post-Boy* is printed, do attend the House To-morrow. And it was also order'd that the *Bill for the better Encouragement of Learning*, be read a second time on this Day Sevennight. By THIS INCIDENT THE BOOKSELLERS BILL WAS THROWN OUT.

May 13, 1735.

The Order made Yesterday upon Complaint of an Advertisement in the *Post-Boy*, of the Publication of a Book entitled *Mr. Pope's Literary Correspondence for thirty Years past*, being read, Mr. Wilford the Publisher, and Mr. E. Curl, were severally called in and examined, and being withdrawn,

Order'd, That the Matter of the said Complaint be refer'd to a Committee to meet To-morrow, and that E. Curl *do attend the said Committee. And that the Black Rod do attend with some of the said Books.*

May 14. P. T. writes to Curl, on the unexpected Incident of the Lords, to instruct him in his Answers to their Examination, and with the utmost Care to conceal himself, to this effect.

No. XV.

That he congratulates him on his Victory over the *Lords*, the *Pope* and the *Devil*; that the Lords could not touch a Hair of his Head, if he continued to behave boldly; that it would have a better Air in him to own the *Printing* as well as the *Publishing*, since he was no more punishable for one than for the other; that he should answer nothing more to their Interrogatories, than that he receiv'd the Letters from *different Hands*; that some of them he *bought*, others were *given him*, and that some of the *Originals he had*, and the rest he *should shortly have*. P.T. *tells him further*, That he shall soon take off the *Mask* he complains of; that he is not a MAN OF QUALITY (as he imagined) but *one conversant with such*, and was concern'd particularly with a noble Friend of Mr. *Pope*'s, in preparing for the Press the Letters of Mr. *Wycherly*; that he caused a Number over and above to be printed, having from that time conceived the Thought of publishing a Volume of *P*'s Letters, which he went on with, and order'd as nearly as possible, *to resemble That Impression*. But this was only *in ordine ad*, to another more material Volume, of his Correspondence with Bishop *Atterbury*, and the late Lord *Oxford* and *Bolingbroke*. And he confesses he made some *Alterations* in these Letters, with a *View* to those, which Mr. *Curl* shall certainly have, if he behaves as he directs, and every way conceals *P.T.*

We have not this original Letter, but we hope Mr. *Curl* will print it; if not, it can only be for this Reason, That as it preceded their Quarrel but one Day, it proves the Letters to Bishop *Atterbury*, Lord *Bollingbroke*, &c. cannot be in *Curl*'s Hands, tho' he has pretended to advertise them.

The next Day *Curl* answers him thus.

No. XVI.

Thursday 9 Manè, 15th May, 1735.

Dear Sir, | I am just again going to the Lords to finish *Pope*. I desire you to send me the Sheets to perfect the first fifty Books, and likewise the remaining three hundred Books, and pray be at the *Standard* Tavern this Evening, and I will pay you twenty pounds more. My Defence is right, I only told the Lords, I did not know from whence the Books came, and that my Wife receiv'd them. This was strict Truth, and prevented all further Enquiry. The *Lords declar'd* they had been made *Pope*'s *Tool*. I put my self upon this single Point, and insisted, as there was not any Peer's Letter in the Book, I had not been guilty of any Breach of Privilege. —Lord DELAWAR *will be in the Chair by Ten this Morning*, and the House will be up before Three.—I depend that the Books and the Imperfections will be sent, and believe of *P.T.* what I hope he believes of me.

For the Reverend Mr. Smith

The Book was this Day produc'd, and it appearing that, contrary to the Advertisement, there were no Letters of Lords contain'd in it, and consequently not falling under the Order of the House, the Books were re-deliver'd.

At the same time *Curl* produc'd, and shew'd to several of the Lords the *foregoing Letter* of *P.T.* which seems extraordinary, unless they had begun to quarrel about *Profits* before that Day. But after it, it is evident from the next Letter, that they had an Information of his Willingness to betray them, and so get the whole Impression to himself.

No. XVII.

To the Reverend Mr. Smith.

Rose Street past Three | *Friday* 16 *May* 1735.

Sir, | 1. I am falsly accus'd, 2. I value not any Man's Change of Temper; I will never change MY VERACITY for Falsehood, in owning a Fact of which I am Innocent. 3. I did not own the Books came from *across the Water*, nor ever *nam'd you*, all I said was, that the Books came *by Water*. 4. When the Books were seiz'd I sent my Son to convey a Letter to you, and as you told me every body knew you in *Southwark*, I bid him make a *strict Enquiry*, as I am sure you wou'd have done in such an Exigency. 5. Sir I HAVE ACTED JUSTLY in this Affair, and that is what I shall always think wisely. 6. I will be kept no longer in the Dark: *P.T.* is *Will o' the Wisp*; all the Books I have had are Imperfect; the First 50 had no Titles nor Prefaces, the Last 5 Bundles seiz'd by the Lords contain'd but 38 in each Bundle, which amounts to 190, and 50, is in all but 240 Books. 7. As to the Loss of a Future Copy, I despise it, nor will I be concern'd with any more such dark suspicious Dealers. But now Sir I'll tell you what I will do; when I have the Books perfected which I have already receiv'd, and the rest of the Impression I will pay you for them. But what do you call this Usage? First take a Note for a Month and then want it to be chang'd for one of Sir *Richard Hoare*'s—My Note is as good, for any Sum I give it, as the BANK, and shall be as punctually paid. I always say, *Gold is better than Paper*, and 20*l.* I will pay, if the Books are perfected to morrow Morning, and the rest sent, or to Night is the same thing to me. But if this dark converse goes on, I will Instantly *reprint the whole Book*, and as a Supplement to it, *all the Letters* P.T. *ever sent me*, of which I have *exact copies*; together with *all your Originals*, and give them in upon Oath to my Lord Chancellor. You talk of *Trust; P.T.* has not repos'd any in me, for he has my Mony and Notes for imperfect Books. Let me see, Sir, either *P.T.* or your self, or you'll find the *Scots* Proverb verify'd

Nemo me impune lacessit.

Your abus'd humble Servant, | E. Curl.

P.S. Lord — I attend this Day. Lord DELAWAR I SUP WITH TO NIGHT. Where *Pope* has one Lord, I have twenty.

Mr. *Curl*, just after, in the *London Post* or *Daily Advertiser*, printed this Advertisement.

No. XVIII.

Mr. *Pope's* Literary Correspondence &c. with a Supplement, of the *Initial Correspondence* of *P.T. E.P. R.S. &c.*
To which in two Days more his Correspondents return'd the following

No. XIX.

To manifest to the World the Insolence of *E. Curl*, we hereby declare that neither *P.T.* much less *R.S.* his Agent, ever did give, or could pretend to give any Title whatever in Mr. *Pope's* Letters to the said *E. Curl*, and he is hereby challeng'd to produce any Pretence to the Copy whatsoever,—We help'd the said *E. Curl* to the Letters, and join'd with him, on Condition he should pay a certain Sum for the Books *as he sold them*; accordingly the said *E. Curl* receiv'd 250 Books which he sold (Perfect and Imperfect) at 5 *shill.* each, and for all which he never paid more than 10 Guineas, and gave *Notes* for the rest which prov'd *not Negotionable.* Besides which, *P.T.* was perswaded by *R.S.* at the Instigation of *E. Curl*, to pay the Expence of the whole Impression, *viz.* 75*l.* no part whereof was repaid by the said *Curl.* Therefore every Bookseller will be indemnify'd every way from any possible Prosecution or Molestation of the said *E. Curl*, and whereas the said *E. Curl*, threatens to publish our Correspondence, and as much as in him lies, to *betray his Benefactors*, we shall also publish *his Letters to us*, which will open a Scene of Baseness and foul Dealing that will sufficiently show to Mankind his Character and Conduct. | *P.T. R.S.*

May 23*d.* 1735.

The Effect of this Quarrel has been the putting into our Hands all the Correspondence above; which having given the Reader, to make what Reflections he pleases on, we have nothing to add but our hearty Wishes, (in which we doubt not every honest Man will concur,) that the next *Sessions*, when the BOOKSELLERS BILL shall be again brought in, the Legislature will be pleas'd not to *extend* the *Privileges*, without at the same Time *restraining the Licence, of Booksellers.* Since in a Case so *notorious* as the printing a Gentleman's PRIVATE LETTERS, most Eminent, both *Printers* and *Booksellers*, conspired to assist the Pyracy both in printing and in vending the same.

P. S.

We are Inform'd, that notwithstanding the Pretences of *Edmund Curl*, the Original Letters of Mr. *Pope* with the Post-Marks upon them, remain still in the Books from whence they were copy'd, and that so many Omissions and Interpolations have been made in this Publication as to render it Impossible for Mr. *P.* to own them in the Condition they appear.

FINIS

THE EARL OF PETERBOROW *to* POPE   13 *June* 1735

The Historical Society of Pennsylvania

Sir,—I have Lead my Self out of Temptation, and brought my Self into the ways of Pennance, which the Lady[1] approves of, it has a good Catholick Sound   I have left the Mount to gett into the bottom, making Tryall of the Bath watters, hitherto I can make no judgement, if they prove not too hott, for severall of my Complaints they are very proper.

Some of my uneasy Symptomes are abated but I am weaker then I was, such Long continuance of pains are scarse to be resisted, however I submitt to directions, tho sometimes opprest with too much care & Kind persecution

I writte to you from Mr St Andrie's[2] but have not heard from you since I left Kensington, Mum agrees with me so well and as I am informed is so proper for our Complaints that I send you a Cask of itt, as the Lady does her Kind wishes | Sir | Your most affectionate Servant | Peterborow

June the 13th 1735.

Address: For Mr Pope

POPE *to* THE EARL OF OXFORD   17 *June* 1735

Longleat Portland Papers, xii

My Lord,—I was sorry to miss of you both morning & Evening, the last I was in town, when I hoped you would have fix'd some day, to make me happy this week at Twitnam. I wish it were the first you can give me, & make it as long an one as you can.

Since I saw you, I have learn'd of an Excellent Machine of Curl's (or rather, his Director's)[3] to ingraft a Lye upon, to make me seem more concern'd than I was in the affair of the Letters: It is so artfull

---

[1] Mrs. Robinson, about this time acknowledged as the wife of the Earl. She was a Catholic.

[2] Nathanael St. André, the royal anatomist, now somewhat discredited, was apparently (like Peterborow) in Bath at this time.

[3] The 'Director' of course was actually Pope himself. What the 'excellent machine' was is obscure; but Curll was threatening 'a whole reply to Cooper's half-narrative' (i.e. *Narrative of the Method* by which the letters got into print: pub. 10–12 June). He also advertised (*St. James's Eve. Post*, 3 June) 'the receipt of a packet of Bishop Atterbury's letters from Paris, to Mr. Pope', and in the *Post-Boy* (16 June) announced: 'Bishop Atterbury's Letters to Mr. Pope I am ready to shew any Gentleman, and the Original Letters under Mr. Pope's own Hand, which are to be in this Second Volume.' Pope probably well knew that much of this was false: Curll had received no packet of letters to or by Pope and as the event proved had no unpublished originals that concerned Pope. Already (12 June) Pope's man Cooper had advertised (*The Lond. Eve. Post*) a reward of £10 for a sight of any original letters in Curll's possession from Pope to Bolingbroke or Atterbury, or from them to him. Perhaps the 'machine' was the project of an 'authentic' edition, which Pope soon announced.

an one, that I long'd to tell it you: Not that I will enter into any Controversy with such a Dog, or make myself a publick antagonist to a T—m Tu—man. But I believe it will occasion a thing you won't be sorry for, relating to the Bish. of Rochester's Letters & Papers. I recollect that your Lordship has still in your custody the Brouillons of verses, & some Letters of Wycherley, I think in a red leather Cover with your arms upon it. I beg also that I may have it. Much I have to say to you, much I have to thank you for, much to wish & pray for you. My Lord, I am entirely & ever | Yours | A Pope.

¹~~July~~ June 17. | 1735.

Address: To the Rt Hon. the | Earl of Oxford. in | Dover Street
Endorsement (By a secretary): Mr Pope June 17. 1735.

POPE *to* FORTESCUE²   [?22 *June* 1735]
C. A. Stonehill (1935)

Since I left you, I am informed Curl has servd a Process upon Cooper, (the Publisher of the Letters which I told you I connived at, who Enterd them in the Hall-book) for what I know not? only I am told he put an advertisement into a news paper against Curll—I bid him send you the Process, that you may judge what is to be done in it; If any thing be necessary, pray acquaint me.

I send Mrs Blounts Receit, as you order'd. God prosper you, protect you, bless you! as I love you, & shall ever do: | Dear Sir, | write me a Line | of your health soon. | A. Pope.

Sunday | night

Address: To Wm Fortescue Esqr

POPE *to* THE EARL OF ORRERY³   12 *July* [1735]
The Pierpont Morgan Library

July the 12th

My Lord,—The Pleasure you gave me, in acquainting me of the

---

¹ For once Pope himself corrects a hasty misdating.

² To date the letter we need to know the date of Curll's process. Cooper's name first appears in advertisements of the rival edition of the Letters on 28 May: 'Printed and sold by the Booksellers . . . and to be had of T. Cooper.' Cooper's name appeared in imprints in June (edition 1735 e). Curll's process probably followed upon such imprints—thus making 22 June (Sunday) a plausible date for the letter.

³ This is Pope's first letter to John, 5th Earl of Orrery, who from this time will be an important link between Pope and Swift. Orrery preserved the letters in a bound volume now in the Morgan Library. This first letter is carefully labelled 'No. 1'—and the year date carefully cut out! There can be no doubt, however, of the year. In his *Remarks on Swift* Lord Orrery printed the first three sentences of the letter, and from the *Remarks* Elwin reprinted that passage under date of 12 July 1737 (EC vii. 360). From the original Elwin printed the whole letter under its proper date of 1735 (EC viii. 367–9). The original letter bears no year date.

Dean's better health, is one so truly great, as might content even your own Humanity: and whatever my sincere opinion & Respect of Your Lordship prompts me to wish from your hands, for myself, your Love for Him makes me as happy. Would to God my Weight added to yours, could turn his Inclinations to this side, that I might live to enjoy him here thro' Your means, & flatter myself 'twas partly thro' my own! But this I fear will never be the case, & I think it more probable His attraction will draw me on the other side which I protest nothing less than a probability of Dying at Sea, considering the Weak frame of my Breast, would have hinderd from, two years past. In short, whenever I think of him, 'tis with the vexation of all Impotent Passions, that carry us out of ourselves only to spoil our Quiet, & make us return to a Resignation, which is the most Melancholy of all Virtues. At this time I have need of it, for I am just losing (perhaps have this moment lost) my Lord Peterborrow. And Lord Bolingbroke whom I have loved longer than any man now living, is gone away.[1] And another, whom I had just begun to love, whose character I had some years esteemd, and whom I find I must love, if he & I live, for there's no helping it, (tho I'm weary of Loving & taking Leases when the Life is almost run out) another Lord I say, whose name I dare not tell you, is to stay a year in Ireland.[2] Well, the Dead & the Absent have my Memory, if not my Prayers, or Wishes strong enough to be calld so, that they may be happier than I can be till I joyn them.

I am greatly obliged to your Lordships Generosity in promising to contradict malicious Reports in my regard. I embrace 'em all with transport, while they procure me such Defenders as show I cannot be What Envy reports, for They are such as never could befriend an Ill man. I am not quite at the bottom of that Business, but very near it, & find a person whom I cannot think quite dishonest, has contributed to that suspicion by Exceeding a Commission which was given him, rather by my Friends than by myself. And what is the greatest mischief of all, is, that if he proves absolutely guilty, I must be merciful to him & screen him, or never know the Whole of it. This often happens when one is obliged to guard against Rogues, & many a Minister I dare say is wronged this very way in the opinion of half mankind.[3]

I am asham'd to write so fluently, & talk away to you as if I had the honor of having been familiar with you many years. But if I have not, my Lord, I wish I may be, and would prepare for it as fast as I can: If you can but bring over yourself & the Dean, it will be a greater Joy than I expect from this World. I beg to be known for one

---

[1] Bolingbroke left for France in May 1735.   [2] Lord Orrery himself.
[3] An interestingly disingenuous paragraph about the publication of the *Letters*.

who truly honours your Virtues, & must necessarily be | My Lord, |
Your most faithfull | & obedient Servant | A. Pope.

Endorsement: Mr Pope. | July 12th: 1735.

CURLL *to* POPE[1]　　　　　　　　　　　　　　12 *July* 1735

St. James's Evening Post, 12 July 1735

To the Author of the *St. James's Evening Post.*
Sir, Pray let me put a Letter under your Care, that it may go safe as
directed. | Yours, | E. Curll.

To Mr. POPE, | Sir,

We were very lately of one Mind; and, as you say, *Never had, nor
ever intended to have any* private *Correspondence with each other.* But,
as I assur'd you, I really was, *directed to write to you.*[2] What has been
the Consequence, the Town is now well acquainted with. A PUBLICK
Correspondence, in Justice to myself, I will hold with you, to convince
Mankind that you are not like *Achilles,* invulnerable.

Next *Monday,* the 14th Instant, I shall publish the SECOND VOLUME[3]
of your *Literary Correspondence;* and am ready to produce the Originals
(under your own Hand and Seal) therein contained.

Bishop Atterbury's Letters to you are, you well know, Genuine;
and some other Pieces of that great Man, which I had of his Son, &c.
together with his last Will, which fully proves he did not die a Papist.[4]

The *State-Letters* of Mr. Prior, Mr. Addison, and Mr. Harley,
open *some Scenes,* which, I dare say, *some People* had much rather
should have remain'd closed up, and been eternally forgotten[5]—But
as your Christian Prelate says,

　　　　　　——Reminiscitur Argos.

I flatter myself, that the *Literary Correspondence,* in this Volume
between King William III. and Lord Somers, will be grateful, in
your own Phrase, to all those who love King *George* II. *and his
Queen;* among whom I shall always reckon Sir *R. Walpole.*

[1] Not perhaps technically a letter, this advertisement is valuable as a link explaining other
letters. Advertisements of this sort had been almost daily occurrences since the middle of
May of this year.
[2] The italicized phrases quote the advertisement that Pope had inserted about the 1st
of April (so Curll tells us in *Lit. Corresp.* ii. 12) in *The Grub-street Journal, The Daily Journal,*
and *The Daily Post-Boy.* Curll in the Appendix I of his 'Initial Correspondence' reprints the
advertisement (p. 28). See iii. 460.
[3] Curll's advertisement gave Pope a bad week-end. See his letters following, dated the
13th.
[4] Curll here starts the rumour that Pope said the Bishop died a Catholic. It is highly
improbable that Pope would make such a statement.
[5] The rest of the letter enumerates the contents that Curll graciously is sheltering under
Pope's name!

A Person of Distinction, has sent me, for your Perusal the Religious Deistical-Remains of the late Mr. *LeNeve* Norroy King at Arms; think of 'em, Sir, as you please, but, this, I declare, I differ as widely in Opinion from him as I do from yourself. From Norfolk you are presented with *The Feast of Trimalchio*, and to his Entertainment you are heartily welcome as not being a Stranger.

I have made you my Patron, in sheltering the Contents, above recited, under your Name, and as you are well acquainted with the true Intent of these Kind of Compliments, I hope, Sir, you will not send me *empty away*.

I am, Sir, yours | till the next Opportunity, | E. Curll.

Rose street | July 12, 1735.

P.S. Your House, Sir, in a Curious Print I shall publish next Month; and your Picture from *Richardson* I intend for the Frontispiece of the Third Volume of your *Literary Correspondence*, which is now actually in the Press. | E. Curll.

*POPE *to* FORTESCUE   [?13 *July* 1735]

The Pierpont Morgan Library

I am extreme unlucky in not finding you neither yesterday nor this day when I rose early & got to your house the moment after you went out. Curl has reprinted my Letters with the addition of a great deal of Scandal of his own putting upon me, which he advertizes to be published to morrow.[1] I apprehend as it is just after the Term, an Injunction can't be got out against him. But this you know best, & pray tell me—Nevertheless as I understand, his pyrated book may be *seized* and *damaskd* & *made waste paper of*, by my authority, or by his who has Enterd them in the Hall book as his property, according to the Act of Queen Anne yet subsisting.[2] If so, I would by all means have T. Cooper & Gilliver who enterd it, search in the Printing houses, & at Curl's own Shop to morrow & destroy all they can. If, to this end, there be any Writing or Powers necessary from me to them, pray let it be sent to me by an Express Messenger to Twitnam, & I'll sign & return it with all speed. Or perhaps They alone who *Enter'd*, may be inabled to do it.

[1] Since Curll had advertised publication of his vol. ii for Monday the 14th, Pope should be writing on the 13th. Pope had little to worry about regarding the contents of the new volume, but he was always timid about his correspondence with Atterbury, and he did not yet know the contents of the volume.

[2] In *The St. James's Evening Post*, 3 June, Curll had cried 'pirate' to Cooper and the Booksellers. In *The Lond. Eve. Post*, 12 June, Cooper advertised his edition as 'enter'd in the Hall Book according to the Act of Queen Anne'.

Pray acquaint me if an Injunction can be had, besides, now the Term is past? I have tenfold reason, now, for doing all this, tho tis too long to tell you—I hope to see you on Saturday with Lady Suffolk. Dear Sir Yours always.

Curl certainly publishes to morrow, or I would not have troubled you so suddenly: I knew not of it till yesterday. Gilliver shall wait on you this afternoon for Instructions; if you can, pray write me a line I shall be at Lord Oxfords, till past ten.

Address: To Wm Fortescue Esq

POPE *to* BUCKLEY   [13 *July* 1735]

Collection of Marseille Holloway[1]

Twitenham, Sunday, the 13.

I am every day applying to you, as to one whose friendship is a thing secur'd to me at all Events. I know my self to have long born you so much, both of Esteem & Good will, that I will think you perceivd my Inclination toward you, & have as much toward me: Some of my most Considerate Friends are clear in the opinion, that I shou'd advertise what you see inclosed.[2] If you join in their opinion, do it in the Gazette forthwith: if you dissent from it, be so friendly to tell me your Sentiment. The Correspondence I had with the Bishop was entirely within the Limits the Law prescribed, & of a nature extremely innocent, in some degree so reputable to my own character as a Subject, that to divulge it, will confound my Detractors or Suspectors. A line from you will truly oblige | Dear Sir your very sincere Servant, A: Pope.

Address: To | Sam. Buckley, Esqr: | at his house in | Little Britain, | London.

[1] The collection formed by Mr. Holloway is now the property of his granddaughters Miss Gladys Burton and Mrs. Helen Marjorie Williams, who kindly have furnished the original text.

[2] The date is fixed by the facts that the 13th of July was a Sunday in 1735 and that the advertisement enclosed was inserted by Buckley (now Gazetteer) in *The London Gazette* for Tuesday, the 15th. The advertisement read: 'Whereas several Booksellers have printed several surreptitious and incorrect Editions of *Letters* as mine, some of them which are not so, and others interpolated; and whereas there are Daily Advertisements of *Second* and *Third Volumes* of more such *Letters*, particularly my Correspondence with the *late Bishop of Rochester*; I think myself under a Necessity to publish such of the said Letters as are genuine, with the Addition of some others of a Nature less insignificant; especially those which pass'd between the said *Bishop* and myself, or were any way relating to him: Which shall be printed with all convenient Speed. | A. Pope.'

Pope thus announced his intention of bringing out an authorized edition—which ultimately appeared in 1737.

POPE *to* CARYLL[1]   17 *July* 1735

Add. 28618

July. 17. 1735.

It is long ago that I sent you my *Works*, a huge large paper quarto, big enough to load your study. I hope I shall commit no more such excesses. Mr. Wright, to whom they were sent, I presume, has safely transmitted 'em to you. I have been in no very good health or humour of late, and less inclined to correspond than ever in my life; especially when I can tell a friend nothing that pleases me, I would not trouble him with [what] displeases me. I have been so much engaged in town, that I could not yet see your son and daughter near Twitnam, which I hope to do now, and my good friend Mr. Pigott. I have hardly seen another of yours who has been my neighbour for a week or so, Mrs. Patty; she is with the new married couple at Marble-hill for some days.[2] Mr. Berkeley seems very happy, and all his friends partake in his joy. Mr. Pulteney is here. I've just been at his house, but missed him. He has been ill of a fever. I am afraid you and I shall never meet again with Lord Peterborow. It was one of my projects this autumn; but Every year takes away something or other,[3] and when it takes away a friend, it hurts us indeed, especially those we have long known, who ought to know us best, and are inexcusable, I think, if they alter our opinions of us without sure grounds, and fair explanations. A general tenour of life and continued evenness of action ought to secure anyone from such changes, or suspicions as are mortal in friendship. As to little observances what this man said, or that man said, who writ last or not last, they should be left to women to quarrel about and men to laugh at. I intend ere long to take a little ramble and stay three weeks with a friend, whom I've known ten years without writing three letters to, and shall probably never write another to, yet esteem as much as any friend he has, I mean Lord Cobham. Believe me, therefore, unalterably, what I always was, | Dear sir | Your most affectionate faithful friend | and humble servant | A. Pope.

POPE *to* THE EARL OF OXFORD[4]   [21 *July* 1735]

Longleat Portland Papers, xii

Twitnam. Munday. | [July 1735]

My Lord,—It is with more Impatience than usual with one who has

---

[1] This is the last of Pope's letters to Caryll that have been preserved to us. Caryll died 6 Apr. 1736.

[2] The Countess of Suffolk (Mrs. Howard) had recently (26 June) married the Hon. George Berkeley, brother of the 2nd Earl of Berkeley.

[3] An allusion to Horace, *Ep.* ii. ii. 55, which in 1737 Pope effectively rendered.

[4] The day and month are inferred from the postmark; the year from the endorsement by a secretary. Pope's dating was simply 'Twitnam. Munday'.

been sick so often, that I complain of my frequent headakes of late; which have made me afraid of Town Hours so much, that I durst not stay a day or two there, purely to enjoy you a few hours in each. I am still in daily hopes of the Duchesses happy Hour,[1] both for her sake, your sake, & my own; since I have hopes, & (what you never broke) Promises, that I then shall see your Lordship an entire day here. I have much too to say to you, & advice to ask about a Book which you'l see advertised.[2] I beg a line to be more assured of your Lordships Lady Oxfords & the Duchesses welfare than I can by my drunken Messenger the Waterman. Believe me with the truest Esteem & sincere Obligation | My Lord | Your ever faithfull Servant | A. Pope.

Address: To | the Right Hon. the | Earl of Oxford, in | Dover street | Piccadilly | London.

Postmark: 22/IY

Endorsement: Mr Pope | Twitnam, Munday July 1735

CURLL *to* BROOME[3]   *22 July 1735*

Elwin–Courthope, viii. 168

Pope's Head, in Rose Street, Covent Garden, July 22, 1735.

Sir,—I doubt not but you have heard of the late affair, of which more than our country rings, between Mr. Pope and me, concerning the printing his letters. A friend of yours last week acquainted me how he evaded his contract[4] made with you and Mr. Fenton about the Odyssey. But that was no news, he being as well acquainted with the art of evasion as with the art of poetry. In short, sir, as all mankind admire his poetry, so they are now inclined to punish his perfidy, and the sight of papers sent me daily would surprise you. Two volumes of his literary correspondence are published, and a third is in the press, and if, in justice to yourself, and the memory of Mr. Fenton, you will send me any memorial, it shall be inserted; or if you have any letters which passed between you and Mr. Pope, they shall likewise be inserted, and acknowledged in whatever manner you please by, sir, your humble servant.

[1] The accouchement of the Duchess of Portland.

[2] The reference is perhaps to Pope's own advertisement in the *Gazette*. See his letter to Buckley, 13 [July], note 2.

[3] This letter is annotated by Broome: 'This letter I enclosed to Mr. Pope with the following letter' [of 4 Aug.].—Elwin. It brought about a reconciliation with Pope.

[4] There was, of course, no contract, and there can be little doubt that Broome and Fenton were better paid for their work on the *Odyssey* than for anything else that they ever wrote. Curll's remark, however, indicates the sort of gossip the dunces promoted—and Mr. Elwin accepted.

CURLL *to* THE PUBLIC¹   [26 *July* 1735]

Fog's Weekly Journal, 26 July 1735

From Pope's Head, | in Rose-street, | Covent-Garden, | July 26.

Mr. Pope having put me under a Necessity of using him as he deserves, I hereby declare, That the *First Volume* of his LETTERS which I publish'd on the 12th of May last, was sent me ready printed, by himself; and for *Six hundred* of which I contracted with his Agent *R. Smythe* who came to me in the Habit of a Clergyman. I paid the said *R. Smythe* half the Sum contracted for, and have his Receipt in full for *Three hundred Books*, tho' it has since, by him, been honestly own'd that he delivered me but *Two hundred and Forty Books*, and those all imperfect.² For this Treatment I shall have Recourse to a Legal Remedy. Mr. Pope in the Grub street Journal (a Libel wherein he has been concerned from its Original) the Daily Journal, and the Daily Post Boy, declared these Letters to be *Forgeries*, and complained of them to the House of Lords; which Falshood was detected before that most August Assembly; and upon my Acquittal, he publishes a very idle Narrative of a Robbery committed upon two Manuscripts, one in his Own, and the other in the Earl of *Oxford*'s Library.³ This Fallacy being likewise expos'd, he now Advertises *he shall with all convenient Speed* publish *some Letters* himself, particularly relating to his Correspondence with the Bishop of Rochester. But the Publick may be assur'd, that, if any Letters Mr. Pope himself, or any of his Tools, shall think fit to publish, are the same, or any Way interfere, with those I have publish'd, that the same shall be instantly reprinted by me.

The *Second Volume of Mr. Pope's Literary Correspondence*, contains the Remainder of his Own Letters to *Henry Cromwell* Esq; Bishop

¹ Not properly a letter, this advertisement gives the clearest account from Curll's point of view of what happened when the *Letters* were published on 12 May.

² They all lacked title-pages, and the 190 copies delivered to Curll in the afternoon of 12 May lacked the sheets containing the letters to Jervas, Digby, and Edward Blount. See Griffith, pp. 292 ff.

³ The advertisement in *The Daily Post-Boy*, 20 May 1735, which caused all these charges is as follows:

'WHEREAS a Person who signs himself P. T. and another who writes himself *R. Smith*, and passes for a Clergyman, have transacted for some time past with *Edm. Curll*, and have in Combination printed the *Private Letters* of Mr. *Pope* and his Correspondents (some of which could only be procured from his own Library, or that of a Noble Lord, and which have given a Pretence to the publishing others as his which are not so, as well as Interpolating those which are;) This is to advertise, that if either of the said Persons will apply to Mr. *Pope*, and discover the Whole of this Affair, he shall receive a Reward of *Twenty* Guineas; or if he can prove he hath acted by *Direction of any other*, and of what Person he shall receive double that Sum.'

The advertisement was printed in the three journals, and reprinted in the *Post-Boy* at least on 22 May. The promise of forty guineas must have agitated somewhat the mind of James Worsdale, the painter, who supposedly enacted the role of the Rev. R. Smythe.

Atterbury's Letters to Mr. Pope, and some other curious Pieces which I had of his Son. Also, Original Letters to, and from, Ld. Somers, Ld. Parker, Ld. Harrington, Judge Powys, Sir R. Steele, Mr. Prior, Mr. Addison, &c. with which I presume Mr. Pope has not any Thing to do.

The *Third Volume of Mr. Pope's Literary Correspondence*, I shall publish next Month, ORIGINALS being every Day sent me, some of them to a certain DUTCHESS, which I am ready to produce under *his own Hand*.

I know not what Honours Mr. Pope would have confer'd on him. 1st. I have hung up his *Head*, for my *Sign*. And 2dly. I have engraved a fine View of his House, Gardens, &c. from Mr. Riijsbrack's Painting,[1] which will shortly be publish'd. But if he aims at any farther Artifices, he never found himself more mistaken than he will, in trifling with me. | E. CURLL.

POPE *to* FORTESCUE[2]   2 *August* 1735

1817 (Warner, p. 51)

August 2, 1735.

I had sooner written to you, but that I wished to send you some account of my own and of your affairs in my letter. This day determines both; for we cannot find out who is the pirater of my works, therefore cannot move for an injunction, (though they are sold over all the town;) that injury I must sit down with, though the impression cost me above £200, as the case yet stands, there being above half the impression unsold. Curl is certainly in it, but we can get no proof. He has done me another injury, in propagating lies in Fog's Journal of Saturday last,[3] which I desire you to see, and consider if not matter for an information. One Mr. Gandy, an attorney, writes me word, Mr. Cruwys is too busy to attend my little affairs, and that you approve of his being employed for him. Now, as to your business, I write this from your house;[4] the windows will be done, and a stone chimney-

---

[1] These paintings, now unknown, would be by Peter Andreas Rysbrack, brother of Michael, the sculptor.—Mrs. M. I. Webb.

[2] Before writing this letter, 'Pope . . . with some of his pettifoggers threatened to bring an information' (so Curll tells us) against Fog's *Journal*. Consequently in the issue of 2 Aug. Fog's printer appended to Curll's current advertisement the following: 'N.B. There having been inserted in our Paper of Saturday last [26 July] a defamatory Advertisement signed, containing several Reflections on Mr. *Pope*, which we have since been inform'd from very good Hands are without Foundation, the Printer of this Paper is heartily sorry the same was inserted, and asks Pardon of Mr. *Pope* and the Publick.' This retraction 'not a little surprised' Mr. Curll when, after an absence from town, he learned of it.

[3] See the preceding 'letter', 'Curll to the Public'. Pope could not allow assertions of his complicity in publishing the letters to pass in silence.

[4] The Vineyard, Fortescue's house at Richmond.

piece up, by the end of next week. I will see all effected, and order the painting after. I have paid the fisherman.

I have exercised hospitality plentifully these twenty days, having entertained many of mine, and some of Lady S.'s,[1] friends. There is a greater court now at Marble hill than at Kensington, and God knows when it will end. Mrs. Blount is your hearty humble servant, and Lady S. returns you all compliments. Make mine to your whole family, when you write. I dine to-day with some of your friends, and shall give your services in the evening to Lord Hay.[2] The town has nothing worth your hearing or care; it is a wretched place to me, for there is not a friend in it. The news is supposed to be very authentic, that the Persians have killed sixty thousand Turks. I am sorry that the sixty thousand Turks are killed, and should be just as sorry if the sixty thousand Persians had been killed; almost as sorry as if they had been so many Christians.

Dear Sir, adieu! As soon as you get home, pray contrive (if you can) to send what letters you have been so partial to me as to keep, especially of an early date, before the year 1720. I may derive great service from seeing them in the chronological order; and I find my collection, such as it is, must be hastened, or will not be so effectual.[3] May all health and happiness follow you in your circuit, and, at the end of it, with repose to join them; and then, I think, you'll have all that is worth living for in this world; for as for fame, it is neither worth living for, or dying for. I am truly, dear Sir, | Your faithful friend, and affectionate servant, | A. Pope.

From the Vineyards, Aug. 2.

Pray, when you write to Mr. Cruwys, enquire if he has not forgot Mrs. Blount's arrear from her brother of £25, due last Lady-Day.

Address: To William Fortescue, Esq.

BROOME *to* POPE   4 *August* 1735

Elwin–Courthope, viii. 168

Aug. 4, 1735.

Sir,—I fancy you will not be sorry to see the enclosed.[4] I have there-

---

[1] The newly wed Countess of Suffolk.

[2] A misprint for *Ilay*. When Pope writes the name of his neighbour and friend, Lord Ilay, it looks exactly like *Hay*. Ilay was the agent in getting Curll brought before the House of Lords, 14–15 May, for advertising that letters to or from peers (privileged) were included in the volume of Pope's *Letters*.

[3] Various causes delayed Pope in this project for an authorized collection of his letters, as we shall see. Possibly Curll's threat to republish anything of the sort that Pope brought out may have been cause for an initial delay.

[4] The enclosed was Curll's letter here printed under its own date, 22 July 1735. Broome thus became reconciled to Pope.

fore taken the liberty to send it, and to assure you that I am incapable of complying with any such proposals. I look upon letters as a trust deposited in the hands of friends, which an honest man will not break, and a bad one cannot without dishonour. If any man has made use of my name against you, it was done without my consent or knowledge. Every man's name is in every man's power. I have never wrote a single line in my own cause, nor encouraged any person to write. This, perhaps, an enemy may ascribe to pride, a friend to a better principle. I am no way answerable for what Mr. Curll writes; but I confess I have complained to hear my veracity called in question with relation to the share I had in the Odyssey. I have always spoken truth in this point,[1] and assumed to myself no more than eight books of the verse translation. But this, though exactly true, has been ascribed, not to my veracity, but vanity. Yet I have borne this imputation without any public vindication. My own heart tells me I never stood in need of it, and was therefore too proud, or too good-natured, to use it. But adieu, henceforth, to all pretensions to poetry.[2] I am as willing as any man in England to have it forgot, and indeed the world seems pretty ready to oblige me. However, to be a bad poet is no sin; it may be a folly. If it be a sin, I have heartily repented of it, and whatever the critics may have done, I am sure heaven has forgiven it. I am out of the world, regardless of its praise or censure. Applause offered to me is like holding a nosegay to a dead man; it may be sweet, but he is insensible of it. I study to be quiet, and a man that would repose does it best in obscurity. I sincerely subscribe to the wish of the poet:

> Sic cum transierint mei
> Nullo cum strepitu dies
> Plebeius moriar senex.[3]

I have not returned any answer to Mr. Curll, I suppose you would not advise it. I hope you will excuse this trouble. It proceeds from a good intent, and from the sincere inclination I have, of approving myself, sir, your most obedient and most humble servant.[4]

---

[1] Unfortunately at the end of the *Odyssey*, v (1726), 285, 288, Broome had signed a statement that he translated three books of the epic. In his *Poems* (1727) he implied that more had been done (pp. 1, 3, 98, 194, &c.) and in his reprinted *Poems* (1739) he claimed as his share (truthfully at last) eight books.

[2] It was the failure to signalize his poetic abilities rather than failure in monetary reward that irked Broome. Even at this moment of alleged adieu to poetry he is negotiating with Lintot for a reprint of his *Poems*. See Lintot to Broome, 26 August; here iii. 489.

[3] Seneca, *Thyestes*, 398–400.

[4] Broome has written at the bottom of the page, 'To this letter I received the following from Mr. Pope:' and his next draft is headed, 'An answer to the foregoing letter of Mr. Pope,' but Pope's letter is not now among the Broome papers.—Elwin.

*POPE *to* GEORGE ARBUTHNOT   6 *August* 1735

Lieut.-Col. F. D. E. Fremantle[1]

Aug. 6. 1735

I never was more vexed than to miss you & Miss Anne yesterday. I was oblig'd to dine with Lady Suffolk, & left word I wd be at home after dinner, as I was. They tell me they prest you to stay, & I'm heartily sorry you did not. My hope was that you wd have past a few days here together & I know nothing that would have oblig'd & pleas'd me so much: As the Vacation is come, I hoped you could. I must go out of the Country to Lord Cobham's in ten days; & beg you will do so, before I goe. If you send me a line at any time 2 days before, nothing shall hinder my being wholly at your disposall for 2 or 3 days, after next Tuesday, when I must be abroad. If I come to town, you shall be sure to see me & to receive back your picture which I think I shall by that time have the copy of. I am sincerely pleas'd it was in my power to give you any thing so agreeable to you. I am always with true affection & Esteem Dear Sir | Yours, | A. Pope.

Address: To Mr Arbuthnot, in Cork street in Burlington buildings near Piccadilly, London

Postmark: PENY POST PAID

POPE *to* LORD BATHURST   6 *August* 1735

Cirencester

August. 6. 1735.

My Lord,—I impatiently hoped to see you here, as you promised me: but to day Mr Lyttleton tells me he doubts you will not come, & that it is possible you may leave London to morrow. He & Mr West being here,[2] I can't come to You, which otherwise I would. I never leave you but I wish to say a hundred things to you: & when you go away for any time, I feel my sense of the loss of you tenfold, as men do of the loss of Life, when near its End, tho they never knew how to make a right use, or possess a full Enjoyment of it. You cannot know, how much I love you, & how gratefully I recollect all the Good & Obligation I owe to you for so many years. I really depend on no man so much in all my little distresses, or wish to live & share with no man

---

[1] Transcribed for the editor by Professor G. H. Healey.

[2] George (later Lord) Lyttelton and Gilbert West (1703–56) were sons of sisters of Lord Cobham. We have no letters to West, who, however, was a close friend of Pope's. Pope left him in his will £5 to buy a ring and a reversion of £200 at the death of Martha Blount (who outlived him). Towards the end of August, when Pope was at Bevis Mount, he evidently lent his house to Martha Blount's friend Mrs. (Algernon) Greville, to whom Lyttelton addressed the four quatrains found among his poems, 'Verses, written at Mr. Pope's house, which he had lent to Mrs. Greville. In August 1735.'

so much in any Joys or pleasures. I think myself a poor unsupported, weak Individual, without you. I am afraid you do not love your self so well, I am su[re] not enough, nor according to your Deserts; from m[e,] from your Family, from your friends, from the Publick. Pray my Lord think seriously of your health, & consult with Dr Burton before you go.[1] This will be the greatest Kindness to me in the world, to keep yourself in it in what Vigour & Enjoyment you can, at least till I am out of it.

If it were not very inconvenient, I wish I could see you once—If not, God prosper & protect you Every where, & if it's possible, pray tell me if there be any prospect of our meeting at Stowe, or any where.

Pray can you find any thing about the Duchess of Buckinghams Letters, or does she know what they are, which that Rascal Curl has advertised?[2] I cannot conceive the least of 'em.

My faithful Services to Lady Bathurst. Why could you [not] come & dine in your way, here? I am quite troubled at your going so suddenly. I am for ever | My dear Lord Yours Entirely | A. Pope

pray write to me.

THE EARL OF ORRERY *to* POPE[3]   10 *August* 1735

Harvard University

Egmonte August 10th: 1735.

Sir,—Amidst a thousand vexations and troubles, to receive so kind a Letter from You, gave me a most sensible Pleasure. Be assur'd I shall always endeavour to deserve your Freindship: You shall have my Hand and Heart:—Sure my Fortune is beginning to change, and my most ardent Wishes are at length to be accomplish'd, for at the same time that you allow me the Liberty to enlist myself among your humble Servants, I am crown'd with Victory in all my Lawsuits. My Affairs here are taking such a Turn that I hope not only to be with You at the Expiration of a Twelve-Month, but to stay many Years in my native Country without taking a Journey to this empoverish'd & desolate Island.

I have lately pass'd a week at Corke with our mutual Freind *Dean Ward*:[4] His Acquaintance with me begun in Sorrow: He attended

---

[1] To Cirencester.

[2] Curll had the perfect recipes for annoying Pope. For vol. ii of his *Literary Correspondence* he advertised Pope's letters to Atterbury—which, it was implied, were treasonable. For vol. iii Curll advertised letters to 'a certain DUTCHESS', and thus worried Pope. Curll had one letter to the Duchess, that of 27 Jan. 1721/2.

[3] The text is from Orrery's letterbook among the Orrery Papers, vol. vii, into which Orrery himself transcribed many of his letters.

[4] The Rev. James Ward, Dean of Cloyne, had contributed small pieces to Lintot's *Poems on Several Occasions* (1717), supervised by Pope.

One of the best Women that ever liv'd, in her latest Moments,[1] and bless'd One of the purest Souls that Heaven has or will receive into it's Mansions. She was much fitter for the Place She is gone to, than for my Arms; and the Almighty Justice was doubly manifest in her Death, by punishing Me, and rewarding Her. But why do I mention this? I would have You partake of my Joys and not of my Afflictions: To make You some amends (for I know your Humanity will plunge you into the Torrent of my Woe) Lett me tell You that the Dean of St Patrick's is well. I have this day seen a Gentleman from Dublin who brought me a Letter from him.

In the Place where I am we live in a State of Ignorance many weeks together, and know nothing but how Beef & Butter sell by the Pound. It will be a most charitable Act in you, dear Sir, to enliven me a little by your Correspondence. I will be mighty reasonable in my Expectations, well knowing how much better You can employ your Time: but assure yourself of this Truth, that not even the Muses are more devoted to You than | your very faithfull & obedient Servant. | Orrery.

Address: To Alexander Pope Esq; at | Twickenham near Hampton Court: Middlesex.

*POPE to BUCKLEY   17 August 1735

The Athenaeum, 17 May 1884, p. 631.

I was glad to hear you got well home. I hope all health will attend you till we meet again which I fear will now not be till after my Rambles in the Country. I send you this very extraordinary answer of Tonson's to the Letter I sent him, & you saw.[2] I wish you'd tell me what I shall reply? My question surely was a very fair one; & I proposd to do him no sort of injury. I think the whole Race of Booksellers were created to set off one Man, who has to himself all the honour and probity of the Trade, and I'm mighty sorry he is a Bookseller no longer. I know nothing that can be done for the encouragement of Learning, but to oblige him to resume his first profession.

Adieu & believe me sincerely, Sir, | Your faithfull & affect: Servant, | A. Pope.

Twickenham, 17 Aug., 1735.

Address: To Sam. Buckley, Esq., in Little Britain, London.

[1] Henrietta, Countess of Orrery, had died at Corke, 22 Aug. 1732.

[2] The letter is now unknown. Presumably it concerned Pope's desire to collect his works in octavo. Lintot was already printing the early poems in this format, and Tonson owned the copy in the Pastorals and certain other things. It seems less probable that the difficulty concerned the fifth or sixth reprinting of Pope's edition of Shakespeare in this year.

POPE *to* THE EARL OF OXFORD   18 *August* [1735]

Longleat Portland Papers, xii

Munday. Aug. 18. | [1735.]

My Lord,—I was very unfortunate in your Lordships Excursion to Down hall last week, tho I hoped This Week would have repaired my Loss of the Day you was so good as to promise me, with my Lady, & who else you & she liked: Yet I am now justly grieved it was put off, because my Lord Peterborow has sent to summon me to what will be to me a Melancholy Scene, the Parting of him and his Friends at Southampton; he goes by the End of the month to France. I can not refuse this, which my mind forebodes will be the Last Office I shall pay him, & am to set out the first day I can. May I find You, my Lord, at my return, in such a State of health as to raise my spirits again, & bless God for the Friend he yet preserves to me in You. I am with a due sense of the Obligation, & with all Truth, | My Lord Ever Yours. | A. Pope.

Address: To the Rt. Hon. the | Earl of Oxford.
Endorsement (by a secretary): Mr Pope Augst 18. 1735.

POPE *to* LORD BATHURST   19 *August* 1735

Cirencester

Aug. 19th 1735.

My Lord,—I receiv'd your kind Letter the morning you left London. Every thing you write & every thing you say, & every thing you do, pleases or contents me. I am only sorry I am out of your hands, & out of your Sight: for I am never so safe as with you, or so happy. I hope in God you are in better health than I thought you when last we met, & that Exercise which generally mends you, has now that effect: Your Head & your Limbs are of so good a Make, that the more Active the Machine is made to play, the better it workes: With such weak ones as mine, the least extraordinary Motion puts 'em out of frame. My Body agrees better therfore with Rest than Motion, my Mind with Conversation than Study. But at present I am in the way that suits me least, I want the Conversation I most love, yours and Lord Bolingbrokes, & I am going to do the thing I am least able, take a Journey alone. My Lord Peterborow has desired me to see him once more at Southampton, before he parts, in all probability for ever, for France at the end of this month. I cannot refuse it, tho I've but just got up from a slight Fever. He writes me three lines, the last of which is. "If you can persuade Lord Bathurst to repay me my Visit, it will be the only trouble I may give him. pray do if you can." In the opinion that Riding is Physick & Strength at once to your Lordship, whereas to me it is Sickness & Pain, I hope this is not quite an Unreasonable Desire, that you would meet me there, after the 24. till the 30. which will be all the time I can stay: and to see the Last of an old Hero, the last Sparks of Such a Noble Flame, it will be a thing to dwell on our Memory & to talk of in our old age. I write this in great hurry, but the meer chance to see you makes me trouble you with this imperfect Letter for such it is when not full of expressions how great a part you deservedly have in my head & heart. Mrs Patty is yet here, & faithfully your Servant. I beg Lady Bathurst to believe me hers, & I am Eternally My dear Lord yours. | A Pope.

MALLET *to* POPE   19 *August* [1735]

The Gentleman's Magazine, iv. N.S. (1835), 374.

Openheim, Aug. 19th.
Hanover, Aug. 26th.

Tho' this letter comes to you from the banks of the Rhine, and in sight of two formidable armies, I write it with as much tranquillity as you will read it in your garden, or by the side of the Thames. This campaign has hitherto been as harmless as a campaign can be; Sporus might have made it without endangering his complexion, or B. his courage.

When we were introduced to the Marechal de Coigney, he told us, with great politeness, that if it depended on him, he would give us the pleasure of a — battle, or at least of a skirmish. Knowing us to be Englishmen, he concluded that we must take delight in the combats of our gladiators at Fig's Theatre,[1] and so would have given us an entertainment à L'Angloise.

That great general amuses himself, very innocently, with reading the memorable events of time in his almanack. The Count d'Eu and his brother the Prince of Dombes (who by the way is very like a late acquaintance of your's, John Bull of Sudbury) play on the fiddle. They are the first violins of the blood; and regaled us the other day with a concert, where they themselves were the chief performers, in a Lutheran church. This scene diverted me infinitely. While your greatest lords and finest ladies are obliged to pay, and afterwards to flatter, such things as Senesiny and Farinelli, and all for a song,—I, without the expense of one farthing or one ly,[2] have been fiddled to by two grandsons of Louis the Fourteenth! By this you will find that I have had the honor lately to be very much in what they call good company. And it is true. The Prince of Conti (who is handsomer than the whole family of the H—,[3] and no less gracious than he is handsome)

---

[1] James Figg, champion pugilist of his day, had an amphitheatre in Marylebone, in which prize-fights took place.
[2] An abbreviation for *liart?*   [3] Herveys? Hanoverians?

had the goodness to talk with me for seven, or, I believe it might be, eight minutes, of hounds and horses, wolves and wild boars. The Prince of Carignan, first prince of the House of Savoy, and director of the Opera in Paris, condescended to advise me concerning my travels.

May I never hope for the pleasure of hearing from you, that you are well, and have not forgot me? By saying just that and no more, you will give me the most agreeable piece of news that I can receive, or you yourself send. Believe me I am in no treaty with Curl, to furnish him any letters for his second volume; and if he has no more influence with the clerks of the Post-office than with me, yours will come very safe, as it will be most welcome to, dear Sir, your most affectionate, faithfull servant, | D. Mallet.

P.S. Mr. N—[1] is extremely your humble servant; and we beg leave to send, by you, a thousand good wishes to Mrs. B.[2] for the continuance of her good humour and good health.

*THE EARL OF PETERBOROW *to* POPE   20 *August* [1735]

The National Library of Scotland

Sir,—I have with me now a crowd of relations   they leave me on the six & Twenty   I goe in a fortnight to France but hope I shall see you att Bevis Mount before I goe   Whenever you apoint I will send my Coach for you to Farnham, I wish you could prevail with Ld Bathurst[3] to return my visit | Dear friend | Your most affectionate | servant | Peterborow

Aug the 20th.

Address: To Alexander Pope Esqr | at Twitnam in | Middlesex | by London.
    [*Not in Peterborow's hand*]
Endorsement: Lord Peterborow's Letters to Mr Pope.
Postmark: 21/AV
Stamped: MT

*POPE *to* JONATHAN RICHARDSON   22 *August* [1735]

The Huntington Library

This will show you I continue very willing to give you Testimonies under my hand of the Love I bear you & desire to see you. I was prevented unexpectedly from what I resolvd as firmly as I could to have past a day last week, with you and near you, by a Feverish Indisposition, & now I go directly to Southampton. I hope you shall be to be

---

[1] Newsham?   [2] Blount?
[3] Lord Peterborow's first letter begging for a farewell visit from Pope and Lord Bathurst has not come to light. Pope quoted from it in his letter to Bathurst, 19 Aug.

found in ten days or thereabouts in Town, or at Twitnam: pray send me a line thither to meet me at my return a week or a little more from this time, that we may pass a few friendly & philosophical hours together; which will be always a true Satisfaction to | Dear Sir | Yours most affectionately | & faithfully | A. Pope.

Augst 22d.

My hearty service to your Son, & to Mr Cheselden, always.

POPE *to* FORTESCUE   23 *August* 1735

Arthur A. Houghton, Jr.

                 Aug. 23d 1735.

I am summond unexpectedly to Southampton to take leave (I fear my last) of Lord Peterborow: from whence I return in a Week) he going for France at the months end. But I first took care of your House, the Window is done & the other brickd up: as to the back window, I think twill do as it is. The Painters have done, & next week the Up-holsterer sets up the Beds. I have not had one quiet day to possess my soul there in peace. I shall dye of Hospitality, which is a Fate becoming none but a Patriarch or a Parliament man in the Country. Those who think I live in a Study & make Poetry my business, are more mistaken than if they took me for a Prince of Topinambou. I love my particular Friends as much as if I knew no others, & I receive almost every body that comes near me as a Friend. This is too much, it dissipates me when I should be collected; for tho' I may be of some (not much) value to a few, yet divided among so many I must be good for nothing. Life becomes a mere Pas-time—when shall you & I sit by a Fireside, with-out a Brief or a Poem in our hands, & yet not idle, not thoughtless, but as Serious, and more so, than any Business ought to make us, except the great Business, that of enjoying a reasonable Being, & regarding its End. The sooner this is our case, the better: God deliver you from Law, me from Rhime! and give us leisure to attend what is more important. Believe me dear Sir, with all affection, but in great hurry (for my foot is in the Coach the moment my hand is off this paper.) | Entirely Yours. | A. Pope

May all happiness wait on Buckland & Fallapit.

Address: To Wm Fortescue Esqr | Fallow Pit | near | Totness | Devon: [This is written over Pope's address to Fortescue, which reads:] To Wm Fortescue Esqr | at Buckland Filleigh, near | Great Torrington | Devon.
Postmark: blurred [23/AV?]
Endorsement (Fortescue's hand): Mr Pope. | Augst 23 1735
Frank: [illegible]

S. E. *to* CURLL   23 *August* 1735

[A letter from this unknown set of initials was printed by Curll in his third volume
of *Mr. Pope's Literary Correspondence* (published about 23 September) to introduce
four letters allegedly from Pope to Martha Blount. Evidently Curll was desperate
for materials for this volume; for he knew the letters were not by Pope or to Miss
Blount. At the end of the fourth letter (vol. iii, p. xxviii) he puts at the bottom of
the page the following note: 'N.B. The WORKS of VOITURE, Translated from the
last Paris Edition, and Addressed by Mr. Pope to Miss Blount, in Two Volumes,
is Printed for Mr. Curll.' The four letters allegedly from Pope to Miss Blount were
in these volumes (a reissue of an earlier translation) printed properly as by Voiture.
The volumes were 'addressed by Mr. Pope to Miss Blount' since Curll printed in
his reissue Pope's 'To a Young Lady with the Works of Voiture'. The footnote
shows Curll knew what he was doing: he was annoying Pope and puffing his own
books. These letters are preserved in the Bodleian Library as Rawlinson MS 90.
With them is a letter from 'S. E.' dated 29 September, which indicates a desire to
keep the matter before the public. This was probably a part of an advertising scheme
by Curll. Pope had nothing at all to do with these letters, which Curll must have
known were by Voiture. They are certainly not in Pope's handwriting, disguised
or otherwise.]

POPE *to* MARTHA BLOUNT   25 *August* 1735
Mapledurham
                                                Tuesday.[1] Aug. 25. 1735.

Madam,—I found my Lord Peterborow on his Couch, where he
gave me an account of the excessive Sufferings he had past thro', with
a weak voice, but spirited. he talked of nothing but the great amendment of his condition, & of finishing the Buildings & Gardens for his
best friend[2] to injoy after him; that he had one care more, when he
went into France; which was, to give a true account to Posterity of
some Parts of History in Queen Anne's reign,[3] which Burnet had
scandalously represented; & of some others, to justify Her against the
Imputation of intending to bring in the Pretender, which (to his
knowledge) neither her Ministers Oxford & Bolingbroke, nor She,
had any design to do. He next told me, he had ended his domestic
affairs, thro' such difficulties from the Law, that gave him as much
Torment of mind, as his Distemper had done of Body, to do right to
the Person to whom he had Obligations beyond Expression. That he
had found it necessary not only to declare his Marriage to all his
relations, but (since the person who had marry'd them was dead) to
Re-marry her in the Church at Bristol, before Witnesses. The warmth
with which he spoke on these Subjects, made me think him much
recover'd, as well as his talking of his present State as a Heaven to

---

[1] Pope's misdating is deceptively precise: in 1735, 25 Aug. fell on a Monday!

[2] Mrs. Robinson, now his recognized wife. She had been introduced to his relatives as
such before Peterborow left London early this year. He had been operated on for the stone
at Bath, and had publicly remarried Mrs. Robinson presumably before the operation.

[3] Destroyed by Lady Peterborow after his death.

what was past. I lay in the next room to him, where I found he was awake, & calld for help most hours of the night, sometimes crying out for pain: In the morning he got up at nine, & was carryd into his Garden in a Chair: he fainted away twice there. He fell about 12 into a violent pang which made his limbs all shake & his teeth chatter, & for some time he lay cold as death. His Wound was drest (which is done constantly 4 times a day) & he grew gay, & Sate at dinner with ten people. After this, he was again in torment for a quarter of an hour; & as soon as the Pang was over, was carried again into the Garden to the Workmen, talk'd again of his History, & declaimd with great Spirit against the Meanness of the present Great men & Ministers, & the decay of Public Spirit & Honour. It is impossible to conceive how much his Heart is above his Condition: he is dying every other hour, and obstinate to do whatever he has a mind to. He has concerted no measures beforehand for his Journey, but to get a Yatcht in which he will Set sail, but no place fixed on to reside at, nor has he determin'd what place to land at, or provided any Accomodations for his going on land. He talks of getting toward Lyons, but undoubtedly he can never travel but to the Sea-shore. I pity the poor Woman who is to share in all he suffers, and who can in no one thing persuade him to Spare himself. I think he must be lost in the attempt; & attempt it he will.

He has with him, day after day, not only all his Relations, but every creature of the Town of Southampton that pleases. He lies on his Couch & receives them: tho he says little. When his Pains come, he desires them to walk out, but invites them to stay & dine or sup, &c. Sir Wilfred Lawson & his Lady,[1] Mrs Mordant & Col. Mordant, are here: Tomorrow come Mr Poyntz &c for 2 days only, & they all go away together. He says he will go at the months End, if he is alive. I believe I shall get home on Wensday night: I hope Lady Suffolk will not go sooner for Stowe, & if not, I'll go with her willingly. Nothing can be more affecting & melancholy to me than what I see here: yet he takes my Visit so kindly, that I should have lost One great pleasure had I not come. I have nothing more to say, as I have nothing in my mind but this present Object, which indeed is Extraordinary: This Man was never born to dye like other men, any more than to live like them.[2] I am Ever Yours.

Address: To Mrs Blount, at the Countess | of Suffolk's at Marble-Hill in | Twickenham. | Middlesex. Way of London
Frank: Free Wilfrid Lawson
Postmark: 27/AV

---

[1] Lady Lawson was the daughter of Peterborow's brother Harry; Sir Wilfred was M.P. for Cockermouth. Col. Mordaunt and Mrs. Poyntz were children of Peterborow's brother Lewis (by different mothers).

[2] There can be no doubt of the impressiveness of Peterborow's personality. Even Lord

LINTOT *to* BROOME 26 *August* 1735

Elwin–Courthope, viii. 170

From my Chambers over the Middle Temple Gate, Aug. 26, 1735.

Worthy Dr.,—What can be more agreeable to me than the accounts I have of the welfare of my friends in their autumn of life. No cares interrupt your studies, plenty and ease crown your days, a loving wife returns bliss for bliss. Your divinity and verse flow easily from you; no ill-natured satire rimples your affections to your friends. To them you were and are constantly, as the loadstone to the pole,—steady. It is your goodnature—born with you, and will die with you,—sets you in high esteem with all that know you. May you be universally known.

Mr. Holditch was so kind to leave your letter at my son's house. I looked over your volume of poems. They contain sixteen sheets and a half. If you publish a new edition, I suppose they will make more. Every printed sheet—number five hundred—will cost you thirty shillings. Working off the copper-plate and advertisements will add five pounds more to the account. How they will sell I know not.

I am again printing for Mr. Pope,—the first volume of his miscellaneous works, with notes, remarks, imitations, &c.,—I know not what. You will hear of me in the papers in November next.[1] Two volumes of Mr. Pope's letters, and letters to Mr. Pope, are printed. There is one letter of Mr. Pope's to Lord Burlington, giving an account of our journey together from Windsor Forest to Oxford,—a merry one. Dear Dr., adieu.

POPE *to* THE EARL OF OXFORD 27 *August* 1735

Longleat Portland Papers, xii

Aug. 27th 1735

My Lord,—As I am sure both yourself & Lady Oxford take part in your Concerns for my Lord & Lady Peterborow, I cannot be here without giving you some account of him. His Lordship (you will be certain) verifies the Saying of the Scripture, that his Spirit is prompt, tho the Body weak: but I find him not in so bad a way as I apprehended, & think it possible he may perform his intended Journey to France. He is indeed twice or thrice a day in pain, by the Effects of

---

Hervey characterized him as almost the last of the *vieille noblesse*. It is a pity that so little of the correspondence between his lordship and Pope has survived. Evidently the friendship was unusually close, since Pope was the only friend from outside the family circle to come from a distance for this final farewell. Peterborow died in Lisbon on 25 Oct., shortly after arriving there.

[1] The small octavo vol. i of Pope's *Works* (of which Lintot held the copyright?) appeared the middle of Jan. 1736. In *Notes & Queries*, 1 S. xi. 377, is printed Woodfall's bill to Lintot for printing 3,000 copies of the volume (paid 15 Dec. 1735). The cost for the volume of fourteen and a half sheets was two guineas a sheet.

the Wound & the necessary consequences of being dressed & prob'd so often, & has something of a Fever with it: But he eats & sleeps more tolerably than before, he is carried daily in his Chair into the Garden, & is moderately chearful, incompass'd with Company, & full of Conversation by fits. The Lady is indeed fully imployd, & has a thousand Cares to discharge; but I think Virtue can enable people to work miracles, above the natural Constitution, & surely God assists her, that she is so well as she is. I was sorry to be gone from Twitnam before I could see your Lordship, either there, or at your house: and I heard Lady Oxford was there. I hope to see you the moment I return, if I have but a day before I go for Stowe: I wish I had the same Company thither, I once (twice) had. My Stay will not be long, But my fear is, it will be longer than your Lordships in Town. Thus passes Day after Day, & we do with the Men we esteem, as we do with the Virtues we esteem, think we can reach them another Time, & So live & dye without the possession of them. I have nothing to add but that in all places & at all times I am mindfull of your Lordship, & wishing to approve myself what I truly am | My Lord | Your ever obliged, | & ever faithful humble Servant | A. Pope.

I suppose I need not tell you that Lord P. has ownd his Marriage to all his Relations here assembled, & that Lady Pet. desires my Lady Oxfords acceptance of her Sincere humble Services.

Address: To | the Rt Honble the Earl of | Oxford in Dover street | Piccadilly | London.

Postmark: 29/AV

Endorsement (by a secretary): Mr Pope Augst 27. 1735.

POPE *to* MRS. KNIGHT　　　　　　　　　　　　　　*29 August* 1735

Bowles (1806), x. 113–15

Southampton, Aug. 29, 1735.

Madam,— I must keep my old custom of giving my friends now and then, once or twice a year, my testimony in writing that I love and esteem them, and that they have a place in my memory when I have been longest absent from them. I have never any thing else to say, and it is all that friendship and good-will can, or ought to say: the rest is only matter of curiosity, which a newspaper can better gratify. I desire no more, Madam, from you, than to tell me just the thing that most concerns me, and therefore is not impertinent to ask, that you are well, and in a peaceful or happy state of mind or body. I hope Mrs. Elliot is with you, to contribute to yours, and increase her own happiness. It will not displease you to hear, that you are remembered at this distance, and in a place where you are not much acquainted:

but when you know that I am here, and that Mr. Poyntz is here, you will easily expect it should be so; and not wonder that your health and Mr. Newsham's are drank at Lord Peterborow's table. I am taking my leave (a melancholy office) of a friend I have long had a true regard for, and one of the most obliging turn, and the finest talents to make others easy and pleased, of any that I ever knew. There will not be many finer gentlemen left in the world, unless Mr. Newsham, and some other of the second generation, be very much bent upon it to rival him.

Pray let Mr. Harte know I am always his sincere well-wisher. I wish I were a day or two with you, to see how happy he is, besides making myself so. But Fate keeps me far from you: at Stowe will be my next stage, where, if I can be soon enough, I would meet my Lady Suffolk, who is to stay there but a few days. Mrs. Blount is yet with her, and not less your *sincere* servant (I can tell you, though perhaps she may not), than the finest lady in Christendom: nay, I take her to be as sincere as Lady S. herself, though she is now no courtier. I desire you to think of me as you used to do, which I am sensible is as well as I deserved, and I deserve just the same now, for I am just the same, that is, faithfully, Madam, | Your most obliged (why not affectionate) | humble servant.

Mrs. Elliot will believe me sincerely her servant, when I assure her so in all Christian truth, not in worldly compliment.

POPE *to* JOSEPH SPENCE[1]   [1 *September* 1735]

1820 (Spence, p. xxii)

Mr. Pope would be very glad to see Mr. Spence at the Cross Inn just now.

†SWIFT *to* POPE[2]   3 *September* 1735

1740

Sept. 3, 1735.

This letter will be delivered to you by Faulkner the printer, who goes over on his private affairs. This is an answer to yours of two months ago, which complains of that profligate fellow Curl.[3] I heartily wish

---

[1] This note serves to introduce the narrative of Spence's letter to his mother here given under date of 4 Sept. Pope is resting briefly in the Golden Cross Inn, Oxford.

[2] For a much longer text of this letter, found in the Portland Papers, see v. 16–18. Pope's excisions are most characteristic.

[3] Curll in his reprint of *Dean Swift's Literary Correspondence* (1741) comments in the following footnote (p. 197): 'Whatsoever Complaints, of Mr. *Pope*, these were, the Public are now fully convinced of their Falsehood, if in Relation to his *Letters*, for he printed them *Himself*, and sent them to me by his *Agent*, in the Masquerade of a Clergyman, of whom I purchased them. *E. C.*'

you were what they call disaffected, as I am. I may say as David did, I have sinned greatly, but what have these sheep done? You have given no offense to the Ministry, nor to the Lords, nor Commons, nor Queen, nor the next in Power. For you are a man of virtue, and therefore must abhor vice and all corruption, although your discretion holds the reins. You need not fear any consequence in the commerce that hath so long passed between us; although I neve destroyed one of your letters. But my Executors are men of honour and virtue, who have strict orders in my will to burn every letter left behind me.[1] Neither did our letters contain any Turns of Wit, or Fancy, or Politicks, or Satire, but mere innocent friendship; yet I am loth that any letters, from you and a very few other friends, should dye before me. I believe we neither of us ever leaned our head upon our left hand to study what we should write next; yet we have held a constant intercourse from your youth and my middle age, and from your middle age it must be continued till my death, which my bad state of health makes me expect ev'ry month. I have the ambition, and it is very earnest as well as in haste, to have one Epistle inscribed to me while I am alive, and you just in the time when wit and wisdom are in the height. I must once more repeat Cicero's desire to a friend; *Orna me.* A month ago were sent me over by a friend of mine, the works of one John[2] Hughes, Esq: They are in verse and prose. I never heard of the man in my life, yet I find your name as a subscriber too. He is too grave a Poet for me, and I think among the *mediocribus*[3] in prose as well as verse. I have the honour to know Dr. Rundle,[4] he is indeed worth all the rest you ever sent us, but that is saying nothing, for he answers your character; I have dined thrice in his company. He brought over a worthy clergyman of this kingdom as his chaplain, which was a very wise and popular action. His only fault is, that he drinks no wine, and I drink nothing else.

This kingdom is now absolutely starving, by the means of every Oppression that can be inflicted on mankind—shall I not visit for these things? saith the Lord. You advise me right, not to trouble myself about the world: But Oppression tortures me,[5] and I cannot live without meat and drink; nor get either without mony; and mony

---

[1] This sentence in all London editions of 1741–2 is placed in quotation marks to indicate its relevance to the history of the publication (1741) of the Swift–Pope letters. Swift's intention to burn letters hardly agrees with the statement of Faulkner (signed 'Dublin, March 25, 1767') printed in volume xiii (pp. v–vi) of Swift's *Works* (1772), who says that 'above thirty years ago' Swift offered Faulkner a chance to print his letters. 'Above thirty years ago' would be perhaps 1735. For one reason or another it was natural Pope should worry about Swift's *cache* of letters.

[2] of one John] of John *1741 L; 1742 L.*   [3] *mediocribus*] *mediocres 1741 Dab.*

[4] Recently made Bishop of Derry. The failure of the Court to give him the see of Gloucester had caused much feeling and pamphleteering.

[5] Here Swift's agony of despair seems more direct and sincere than in many of his published works.

is not to be had, except they will make me a Bishop, or a Judge, or a Colonel, or a Commissioner of the Revenues. | Adieu.

JOSEPH SPENCE *to his* MOTHER[1]   4 *September* 1735
The Huntington Library

Sept the 4th 1735

Dear Mother,—I have not seen honest Mr Duck yet, but have had the pleasure of another Visit that was wholly unexpected to me. Monday last after dinner, according to the good sauntering custom that I use here every day, I was got lolling at a Coffee House, half asleep & half reading something about Prince Eugene & the Armies on the Rhine, when a ragged boy of an Hostler came into me, with a little scrap of paper not half an inch broad, which contain'd just the following words; "Mr Pope would be very glad to see Mr Spence at the Cross-Inn, just now." You may imagine how pleasd I was; & that I hobbled thither as fast as my spindle shanks would carry me. There I found him quite fatigu'd to death, with a thin face lengthen'd at least two Inches beyond its usual appearance. He had been to take his last leave of Lord Peterborough: & came away in a Chariot of his Lordships, that holds only one person, for quick travelling. When he was got about 3 miles of Oxford, coming down a Hill in Bagly Wood, he saw 2 Gentlemen & a Lady setting as in distress by the way side. By them lay a chaise, overturn'd, & half broke to pieces; in the Fall of which the poor Lady had her Arm broke. Mr Pope had the goodness to stop; & to offer her his Chariot to carry her to Oxford, for help; & so walk'd the three mile, in the very midst of a close sultry day, to us; & came in, the most fatigu'd you can imagine. An Inn, tho' design'd for a place of Rest, is but ill suited to a man that's really tired; so I prevail'd on him to go to my Room; where I got him a little dinner, & where he enjoy'd himself for two or three hours; & sett out in the Evening, as he was obligd to do, for Col: Dormers; in his way to Lord Cobham's: which was to be the End of his fatiguing Journey: & so I think I have giv'n you a full History of all this affair.

CURLL *to* POPE[2]   15 *September* 1735
1735j

E. CURLL *ad* A. POPE
S. P. D.

That our Name and Fame may be equally transmitted to Posterity,

---

1 This narrative of Pope's arrival in Oxford on 1 Sept. speaks for itself. He was evidently hurrying to join friends at Stowe—very likely Miss Blount was to be there with Lady Suffolk.
2 Published in vol. iii of *Mr. Pope's Literary Correspondence*, pp. xiii–xvi. Its 'faithful (?) register of matters of fact' is worth study. Here Curll reasserts that Pope's *Letters* were

in this our *Literary Correspondence* most earnestly desiring; A faithful Register of Matters of Fact, will be the best Method for obtaining these desirable Ends.

Having given Notice in the *St. James's Evening-Post* of *Saturday July* 12th, that the SECOND *Volume* of *Literary Correspondence* would be published on *Monday* the 14th: You was pleased, in the *London Gazette*, of *Tuesday* the 15th to insert an Advertisement, which I shall here paraphrastically re-insert for the true Information of the Public, *viz.*

Whereas *several Booksellers* (Printers and Publishers, *viz.* L. *Gilliver, T. Cooper*, and *J. Watson) have printed several surreptitious and incorrect Editions of Letters as mine, some of which are not so,* (being written by those Persons to whom they are by *E. Curll* justly ascribed) *and others interpolated*; (by the Editor of those six hundred Copies sold by the Reverend Mr. *R. Smythe*, pursuant to the Direction of his Cousin *P. T.* (both Agents of mine) to the aforesaid *E. Curll) and whereas there are daily Advertisements of* SECOND *and* THIRD *Volumes of more such Letters, particularly my Correspondence with* (Dr. FRANCIS ATTERBURY) *the late Bishop of* Rochester; (the said SECOND and THIRD Volumes being now published) *I think myself under a Necessity to publish such of the said Letters as are genuine* (not hitherto published) *with the Addition of some others of a Nature less insignificant, especially those which passed between the said Bishop* (ATTERBURY) *and myself, or were any way relating to him, which shall be printed with all convenient Speed* (and which will likewise be faithfully re-printed by *E. Curll*, as a Supplement to the THREE VOLUMES of *Literary* Correspondence by him published and carried on with the universal Approbation of the Public.) | *A. Pope.*

This, Sir, must be understood to be the true Meaning of the foregoing Advertisement, and which shall be, by me, *literally* made good.

As to *R. Smythe*, whom you have been pleased to inform me, was only *a pretended Clergyman*[1] against, therefore, this nominal *R. Smythe*, exclusive of his Function, I have exhibited a Bill in *Chancery*, to hold him to his Contract of delivering to me six hundred printed Copies of the *First Volume* of your Letters, (printed by your own Direction to compleat your Correspondence with Mr. *Wycherley*, as *Lawton Gilliver* hath himself acknowledged, whom, with yourself, I have made Parties to my Bill against *R. Smythe*, not in the least doubting, but from such an equitable *Triumvirate* I shall obtain Justice.)

printed by Pope himself; and Curll now seems to know that the sheets of the Wycherley letters came from the *Posthumous Works*, vol. ii, published by Pope in 1729. On the chancery bill see Pope to Fortescue, 20 June 1735. The letter emphasizes, as did Pope in his *Narrative*, the need of legal clarification as to the status of private letters in copyright.

[1] Pope in his *Narrative of the Method* had once or twice betrayed an undue knowledge of the 'Rev.' R. Smythe.

For, with you, Sir,

> *Flatt'ry in ev'ry Shape I hold a Shame,*
> *And think a Lye in Verse or Prose the same.*[1]
> Bravo to God, and Coward unto Man,
> The Lyar is; *deny this Truth who can?*[2]

This *Vice*, Sir, is as *mean* as it is *base*; and as you have found, in all Debates between us, has been the Abhorrence of, | Your Humble Servant. | E. Curll.

Peckham, Sept. 15, 1735.

P.S. As I am pretty conversant with those Authors whose Works I print, in revising my old Friend Voiture for a new Edition; I find you have very politely pillaged his Letters:[3] Your *First*, To a *Lady* with a *Book* of *Drawings*, is evidently taken from *One* he *wrote* to *Madame Rambouillet*, in the Name of *Callot* the Engraver, presenting a Book of his Prints. Your *Second* is, I find, a Compliment to our Friend Parson *Broome*, and Mrs. *Betty Marriot* of *Sturston-Hall* in *Suffolk*. And *lastly*, the Compliments in those Letters of this Volume to Miss *B.* are transplanted from what Voiture wrote to *Madame Rambouillet*, M. *Vigean*, and to other Ladies of the Court of *France*.

BROOME *to* POPE   *22 September* 1735

Elwin–Courthope, viii. 171

Pulham, Sept. 22, 1735.

I find by experience that love and friendship are nearly allied. They kindle a divine flame in the heart which, like that of the Jewish altar, is never extinguished, though it may not always burn with equal warmth and brightness. In both those passions it is almost worth a little quarrelling, for the pleasure of the reconciliation.

I think it is about six years since I wrote to you.[4] I confess I looked upon you as a departed friend, and mourned for you as such. I was silent, but it was the silence of Dido, occasioned by a supposed hardship from a person I loved. It was not owing to any inconstancy or credulity, but to ocular demonstration.[5] I desire you to believe this

---

[1] Epistle to Dr. *Arbuthnot.*—Curll, 1735j. [Cf. ll. 338–9.]

[2] Dr. *South's* Character of the *Lyar.*—Curll, 1735j.

[3] Curll here refers to the first two among the 'Letters to Several Ladies', found in the 1735 *Letters*. See here under date of 1 Mar. 1705 and at the beginning of 1714. Curll's remarks are unwarrantably abusive. The two letters published by Pope show influence of Voiture but not plagiarism. On the four letters of Voiture published by Curll as from Pope to Miss Blount see S. E. to Curll, 23 Aug. 1735 (iii. 487).

[4] Broome means to say 'It is about six years since I stopped writing to you.' He had resumed writing 4 Aug. of this year (q.v.).

[5] Elwin thought the 'ocular demonstration' came from seeing letters from Pope to Fenton,

upon my own testimony. I know I speak in riddles, but to explain them *now* would be cowardice, perhaps dishonesty, though it be as easy for me to prove what I hint at, as to speak it. Adieu to all animosities. Let them sleep for ever. I am sure they shall never be awakened by me. With regard to myself they have been dead many years, and I shall not raise the ghost of a departed contest, to my own disturbance, or my neighbour's. As for all idle reports, they never found credit with me. They are to our advantage or disadvantage just as peevish persons happen to be out or in humour. Such men will ever be buzzing about their nothings, always indeed, like the fly, impertinently, but at worst more troublesomely than hurtfully. It is impossible to live without some slander in a world that delights to tell and hear it. Our care should be, not to deserve it. Of this nature was a falsehood I met, when last at Norwich. It was publicly affirmed[1] that you had claimed the notes upon the Odyssey—at least of twelve books, in a late advertisement before your Epistles. I have read those Epistles, but it was in the pirated edition, which has no such advertisement. I assured the company that you had too much honour and justice to assert such a falsehood; that you had large and fair flocks of your own, and were incapable of robbing me of my little ewe-lamb. No, I know you had rather enlarge than diminish my intellectual possessions. Such falsehoods rather create mirth than spleen. But it is a degree of weakness to repeat such weak stories.

I am now retired to my cell in Pulham for the winter, and like the bee, or rather the drone, shall take no more flights from it till the spring. If any disquiet comes abroad, I am well hid, and it will not easily find me. Yet, though I love quiet, I would not owe it to a lethargy. I must be a little active, though my activity prove no better than that of a child about bubbles and butterflies. You, I perceive, are of a stock to bear the gay blossoms of poetry in the decline of life. I am not of so vigorous a kind, and the little fruit I bear is like that of our gardens in this unseasonable autumn, not worth the gathering. You were my poetical sun, and since your influence has been intercepted by the intervention of some dark body, I have never thought

shown by Fenton's executors. That is possible. The reference may, however, be to the two passages from Broome's poems quoted in the Bathos. The reference to Broome in *The Dunciad* was explained away in the footnote, but ridicule of his poetry would be less readily forgiven —and the Bathos gave ocular demonstration of the ridicule.

[1] Broome's friends had grounds for their affirmation. In Pope's quarto *Works*, vol. ii (1735) 'The Author to the Reader' remarked: 'This Volume and the abovemention'd [that of 1717] contain whatsoever I have written and design'd for the press: except my Translation of the *Iliad* (with my Preface and Notes) of twelve books of the *Odyssey*, with the Postscript, (not the Notes) the Preface to *Shakespear*, and a few *Spectators* and *Guardians*.' The punctuation here is curious; but accidentally or suspiciously more curious is that to be seen in the octavo *Works*, vol. ii (Gilliver, 1735). The crucial passage reads there: 'except my Translation of the *Iliad*, with my Preface and Notes of twelve Books of the *Odyssey* with the Postscript, (not the Notes) the Preface to *Shakespear* and a few *Spectators* and *Guardians*'.

the soil worth cultivating, but resigned it up to sterility. I have indeed,
seen a tree bear as many crabs as an appletree, apples; but I am not
ambitious to produce trash plentifully, only to be more distasteful.
But I have hunted down the allegory, and it is time to release you,
to pursue nobler game of your own starting. I will only add, that I
am ready to do you justice with regard to the Odyssey, and that I am,
sincerely, your faithful and affectionate servant.

POPE *to* BROOME   2 *October* 1735

Elwin–Courthope, viii. 173

Twitenham, Oct. 2, 1735.

Your two very kind letters came not to hand till I returned hither,
three days since, from a long journey to Southampton, and thence to
Buckinghamshire. I would not else have delayed to renew assurances
of my real goodwill and friendship for you, which have never been
extinct in my breast, though cooled by accidents, or perhaps mistakes,
joined with ill offices which too many people are ready to do to those
they envy, or would displace from our affections. I sincerely embrace the
pleasures of reconciliation. To forgive and be forgiven is the tenderest
part of love or friendship; for none of us are without faults, none
without misconstructions. What you were told about the notes to the
Odyssey is utterly untrue. I expressly there claimed only twelve books
of the poem, "and not the notes."[1] Those are the words, as you will
see in my own edition, which I have a desire to send you, if you will
tell me by what carrier or to whose house. It is in quarto, to match
the first volume of my works, which you already have. Be not uneasy.
Indiscretion and credulity are the worst faults we have, and both proceed from open undesigning minds.

As to the justice you propose to do me, after so many public scandals
on that account, in relation to my conduct toward you about the
Odyssey, I think it will be sufficient to appeal to your own memory;
and I desire no more than that you will put down in a line to me that
there was no contract made about it, but that you trusted my friendship, and I made it good.[2] Recollect your circumstances and mine at
that time as to fame and to fortune. You will, I believe, think I did
you justice at least in both. I did what I could to elevate the one and
to increase the other. You may mention the sum of 500 *l.* if you will;
but do as you please. God forbid I should desire you to say anything

---

[1] See the note on this matter in the preceding letter.

[2] Pope wished something quotable, but Broome's statements embedded in his letter of 29
Oct. must have been satisfactory. Broome agrees that there never was a contract; that Pope's
aid advanced Broome's fame greatly, and that he was paid £500 for his labours, though his
fortune was such as to make payment not a major consideration.

beyond truth. It is certain I have been aspersed many lengths beyond
it. Let, therefore, your testimony to me only by a line express only
what your heart feels. I would rather be obliged to your friendship
than to any other motive.

I am sorry you speak in the style of a man absolutely retired, and
never to see this busy part of the scene. If you will, you may at any
time see, even here, a man as retired as yourself, and as much despising
that busy scene as your own noble patron does,[1] whom I honour now
more than I ever did. Pray, if you see him soon, tell him so. My
approbation can be of little or no consequence to him, but I am glad
of his happiness, and honour such men as can imitate him. I am, dear
Broome,—for I will use the old style, and forget the impertinence of
seven years[2] that intercepted it,—your faithful affectionate servant.

Sir Clement Cottrell sends you his service.

POPE *to* SPENCE   7 *October* [1735]

The Huntington Library

                                                   Twitenham Oct. 7th.

I heartily thank you for your very kind Letter, & kind Entertainment,[3] which gave me a greater pleasure than I almost ever receivd
in any Entertainment; it was so easy, & so warm an one. I left you all
with regrett: pray tell Mr Hay[4] so, & Mr Ayscough:[5] I conclude
Mr Murray is gone from you—You'l oblige me in sending those
Letters, not that I'll take from you any one Testimony of my Regard
& Love for you, which you think worth the keeping. You shall have
a fair account of 'em when you come this way: but the sooner I had
them the better, by a safe hand.—My health is pretty well restored,
which I know is the news you'l best like from this place; & the rest
is only to repeat that sincere Truth you have heard so often, & shall
hear while I live, that I am most affectionately Yours | A. Pope.

    Mr Spence

    [1] The noble patron was Lord Cornwallis. He had perhaps imitated his father-in-law,
Lord Townshend, who is said never to have reappeared in Parliament or visited London
after Townshend's differences with Walpole had forced him out of office in May 1730.
    [2] 'The impertinence of seven years' may have been due to the 'ill offices' of outsiders or
to the text of the Bathos.
    [3] Returning from Stowe, Pope had passed three pleasurable days in Oxford with Spence.
See his letter to Lord Bathurst, 8 Oct.
    [4] Probably Lord Dupplin's younger brother Robert. He became Archbishop of York in
1761.
    [5] Francis Ayscough (*DNB*) had been Lyttelton's tutor at Oxford; he married Lyttelton's
sister Anne, and in 1761 became Bishop of Bristol.

POPE *to* EDWARD CAVE¹   [*7 October* 1735]
BM Stowe 755

Sir,—You must excuse me that I decline to Erect myself into a
Judge.² I never went farther than to give an Opinion in these matters;
& that only to my private Friends: Who ask'd it of me Before Publication: After that, it is useless to Them, & an Arrogance in Me.

But as I am sensible of the Regard you shew me, & your promise
to make no other use of my Opinion than I give leave for: I insist
on your never naming me in this affair, & tell you, that I think there
is Merit in 4 or 5 of the Poems, & particularly in No. IV. the rather
as the Author says it is a *first attempt*.³

I think you have chosen your Judges well, & upon such a Subject,
Divines are the most Proper. I am | Sr. | Your obedient humble |
Servant. | A. P.

Address: To | Mr E. Cave, at St. John's Gate. | London.
Postmark: 7/OC
Endorsement: A. Pope Princeps Poetarum

POPE *to* LORD BATHURST   8 *October* 1735
Cirencester
Oct. 8th 1735

My Lord,—I am just got home after a long Train of Peregrinations,
which I wish had concluded at Cirencester, as they often have done.
I always found it a Place of Rest, where my Heart was at ease. But I
begin to perceive my self old (I believe you have perceivd me so before)
and dare hardly hope to enliven any Country Retreat so late in the
year, & so late in my life. The Abbè you have had with you I am told

¹ The date is from the postmark.
² In 1733 and 1734 Cave had offered prizes in poetical contests, the poems to be published
in his *Gentleman's Magazine*. For 1735 he had assigned to contestants the fairly inclusive
subject of *Life, Death, Judgment, Heaven and Hell*. The prize was £50, and the poems were
to be published together in an 'extraordinary' issue of the *Magazine* in July, and the prize
to be awarded by popular vote sent in by readers. Protests led Cave to choose as judges 'three
particular gentlemen of unexceptionable judgment' (*GM*, v. [227]). Pope here declines to
serve, but indicates confidentially an informal preference. The prize went, not to his 'number
IV' but to number VII, a poem by Moses Brown, one of Cave's chief poetical advisers.
Years later Thomas Marryat in a letter printed by Professor C. L. Carlson (*Philological
Quarterly*, xvii [1938], 117–18), says: '. . . no. vii, Mr. B's poem, the prize was adjudg'd
to and received by him, abnuente Pope, but the majority of the judges, (I think *all* but P.)
decided in his favour.' Evidently Cave disregarded Pope's injunction of never naming him.
The data for this note were assembled by Professor Agnes Sibley.
³ In his last line Pope's favourite (IV) speaks of his Muse, 'Who never knew to mount
in verse before' (*GM*, v. [1735], 407).

does wonders in the Vivacious way, & has not a little interrupted the sacred silence & deep Contemplation of those groves, where

> Cum uxore & cum natis,
> Dulcè ambulas in pratis, &c

But dull as I am, I wake a little at the thought of you, I dream of you still, & you are the object of my Dotings; like an old Woman that loves the man that had her Maidenhead: You animated my Youth, my Lord, Comfort my age!

> Let not th' insulting foe my fame pursue,
> But shade those Laurels that were raisd by You.[1]

Do not think this a florid Flamm, 'tis the serious Wish of my heart, to be lovd as much as you can, & protected by You. I feel the want of you in all my little distresses; if any other hurts me, I am like a Child that comes to complain to its best friend who has humourd it always; and if I play the fool, I want to complain to you against my self: I know you to be so much a better friend to me than myself. I think I am in an abandon'd state, if it is to be yet 2 months before you see the Town. Your Lordship is almost my only Prop. Two of those with whom my soul rested, & lean'd upon, are gone out of the Kingdom this Summer.[2] Every one that makes Life enjoyable to me is absent now. The greatest pleasure I can have will be to have some glympse open'd of your more speedy Return: of which if there be any prospect, pray give it me.

I wish'd for you at Lord Cobham's, as I did every where: I past 3 days at Oxford, where I saw your Image or my Lady's (I don't know which) very well pleasd with a playday which I procurd him.[3] I had a strong inclination to have gone to Ciceter from thence, but the Rains fell violently, & I was quite fatigued, so came home sick & sorrowfull. My health is now pretty tolerable, after a Complaint which weakened me much at Oxford & has been hereabouts Epidemicall. I was three days since surprised by a Favour of his R. Highness, an unexpected Visit of 4 or 5 hours.[4] I ought not to omit telling you that on sight of your picture, he spoke in high, just terms of you, & exprest great personal affection; I thought so very remarkably, that I

---

[1] The couplet is adapted from Dryden's 'Epistle to Congreve'; there the Laurels 'that descend to you' are mentioned.

[2] Bolingbroke and Peterborow.

[3] Henry, second son and eventual successor of Lord Bathurst, matriculated at Oxford in 1730; younger sons were too young to be there at this time.

[4] 'On Saturday Evening [the 4th] his Royal Highness the Prince of Wales did Mr. Pope the Honour o a Visit, at his House at Twickenham, and staid with him two or three Hours. His Royal Highness returned to Kensington by the Light of Flambeaux.'—*The General Evening Post*, 7 Oct. 1735.

found it the best Topic for me to make my Court to him. I have nothing to add, but that Mrs Lewis is recoverd of a Stroke of the dead palsy,[1] the Duchess of Queensberry stays all the winter abroad, Lady Suffolk is gone to Lady Betty Germaines[2] for a month, I know nothing of the Dutch, French, or the Emperour.[3] Mrs P. Blount is your ever faithful Servant. Curl has printed Letters of Mr Pope to Miss Blount, not one of which either I ever writ, or she ever receivd.[4] I hope in God something (but not any unpleasant thing) will bring your Lordship hither, where you will make a happy man at any time of | Your ever faithfull, ever | affectionate Servant | A. P.

Address: To the Right Honble the | Lord Bathurst, at | Cirencester. | Glo'ster-shire
Endorsement: Allen Bathurst

POPE *to* THE EARL OF ORRERY   8 *October* 1735

The Pierpont Morgan Library

My Lord,—I begin to be sick of conversing with Worthy men; they have so many Tendernesses, & such goodness of Nature, that they are eternally in affliction, for themselves, or for others; and I can't help feeling and bearing a part in it. Therfore you are the most Uneasy of all Correspondents. Your Lordship open'd a Grief to me in your last, which will hinder the Thought of You, which I always hoped to make a pleasure of, from being so. Pray my Lord, partake your Virtuous Sorrows with men of more Resignation, I mean of colder natures than I; who having lost a Mother, and four or five Friends I dearly loved, am broken to your hands, and melt with such Concerns as you express. I can only hope, my Lord, that the same Virtue that makes you so susceptible of feeling a Loss, will make you know Who inflicted it, & therfore how you ought to bear it.

I turn to the more pleasing side of your Letter, & congratulate you sincerely on the finishing your Lawsuit happily; Even the Justice of a Cause not always secures a Victory, and Knaves & Tricksters there are so much in their own Element, that they cannot but have the advantage of those who are less slippery. Honest Minds, like solid

---

[1] She died in 1736.
[2] Lady Betty, who was a wit and friend of Swift's, was now sister-in-law of our Countess, being the sister of Mr. Berkeley.
[3] i.e. of the wars going on on the Continent.
[4] Vol. iii of Curll's *Mr. Pope's Literary Correspondence* appeared late in September It contained the letters sent in by 'S. E.' See 23 Aug. The letters can be found as Nos. 14 13, 36, and 71 in the translation of Voiture's letters published in 1657 and republished by Curll about this time. His 'third edition' of them (1736) places them in Vol. i, pp. 81, 79, 118, and 236. See also Curll's letter to Pope of 15 Sept. of this year.

Bodies, are not so active & Versatile (if you'l pardon an adopted Phrase). You speak of my defending the Bishop's[1] character against Curl, I can hardly defend my own; *The Knaves will all agree to call you Knave*, as my Lord Rochester observ'd, and that is a terrible Majority. The most necessary Prudential Methods against the vilest of Slanderers, are complaind of & set forth by them, as Fraud & Injustice; To stop their practises is thought an Invasion of their Right, when they have so long exercisd them unpunishd by our Law, as if it really favourd only Rascals. I am therfore almost surprized your Lordship should find justice, against Attornies & Stewards especially. But you have lessened the pleasure I should take in this, by telling me it will yet be a twelvemonth before I must reap the fruits of your Tranquillity by your Settlement in England.

Your Lordship very well knows the things that make me most happy, by your choice of the News to tell me from Ireland: The Dean of St Patricks enjoying a tolerable state of health, is what, above all other, gives me comfort & satisfaction.

I think I should send you something, to entertain you, as I'm too conscious I have sayd nothing to do it: therfore inclose these fine verses of Lord Cornbury, which do me so much honour that I shall beg his leave to prefix them to a new Edition of my Poems, which will be the compleatest yet printed.[2] I would make you (my Lord) the like request as to those relating to Mr Gay, but that I fear the Occasion of them, being only a short Epitaph, it will be thought too Ostentatious in me.[3] I know you will not give any Copy of these, when I tell you, I've not yet spoke to him.[4]

I cannot but resume the Subject of our Friend, the Dean; It is what I do ten times every day of my life; His Memory is dearer to me than any living Friend's, & as melancholy as if he were dead. I seldome hear from him, and I seldome write to him: it tears out too much of my heart; & when I've said all I can, 'tis nothing, tis Impotence, 'tis one short Sigh! Pray my Lord see him as often as you can, love him you must. I almost wish I had never seen him. I hear his whole thoughts of late are turn'd to Charityes, & Provisions for the Helpless & Indigent. Ten such Clergymen would save a whole Nation; would save a whole Bench of Bishops. I beg your pardon My Lord, for writing thus carelessly: I will not compliment so worthy a Lord: I

[1] Atterbury's.

[2] Meaning the edition, now commencing in small octavo. No verses were prefixed to vol. ii (containing the *Essay on Man*) until the reprint of 1739, in which Cornbury's verses, signed (like the other commendatory poems) by his initial, stood first in a group of seven. Cornbury's fourteen lines, as printed later, were enclosed by Pope in this letter, and are still preserved in Pope's holograph, with the letter. They are not printed here.

[3] Lord Orrery had evidently sent or shown to Pope his four couplets praising Pope's Epitaph for Gay.

[4] Pope has not yet spoken to Lord Cornbury.

will esteem & love you, as far as your Condesending nature will permit
what your Goodness occasions.

I am My Lord | Your most obliged & | faithfull Servant | A. Pope.

Twitenham, Oct. 8th 1735.

I am Dean Ward's old humble Servant.

Endorsement: Mr Pope. 8r 8. 1735.

---

*POPE *to* LORD BATHURST¹   [*October* 1735?]

The Pierpont Morgan Library

I had written to your Lordship by the same post which brought me
yours: It shews a Sympathy which ought to be very pleasing to me,
that you think of me whenever I think of You. I can truly say I do
so every day of my life. My Letter of Lord Cobham I fear has been
mis-represented to you: It did justice to your Worth & acknowledged
my own Weakness. I only wish you would give me a fair Hearing
before Lord Cobham at Stowe at any time, & hear them in your turn;
for there's nothing I should more delight in than to get my friends
together upon *any argument*, I know them on both sides to be so reasonable, that You must needs concur. I begin to bless the Times, which
notwithstanding all we can complain of them for, have brought in a
manner all the sensible & honest to be of one mind.² It is better to
dispute about Poles & Tu[rks]³ than about Whig & Tory. You railly
me very agreeably, but your Conclusion, shewing the reason why you
prefer Poles, is a noble and great one: and I fully agree, that Such a
character is a better Monument than all that Wealth and Vainglory
can erect. I will be absolutely contented if you will but suffer me to
build one obelisque,⁴ and grave upon it that character of the Lord of
the place, & those Reasons why Posterity see no other Buildings.

I am very sensible of your kind Enquiries of my he[alth] a few
such Cotemporaries as You make it dearer to me & I wish it better
as much for their sakes almost as my own, that I might be a better
Companion to them. I have had for many years sufficient Experience

¹ This letter has been bound with letters to Lord Orrery, but it seems clearly to have been
written to Lord Bathurst, as the last paragraph indicates. The date is pretty certainly 1735,
and October seems plausible in view of Pope's recent visit to Lord Cobham, and the signing
in that month of the Treaty of Vienna.

² A treaty of peace may be said to bring men to be of one mind, but it is a curious remark.

³ The remarks here become facetious, but King Stanislaus would stand for the Poles, and
Prince Eugene had this summer made a considerable slaughter of Turks. There may, however,
be an allusion to an item in *The General Evening Post*, 23 Sept.: 'M. Ulrick, known at Court
by the Name of the *Young Turk*, hath obtained Leave to return to England, after an Exile
of about seven Years at Hanover.' Ulric had been mentioned years earlier in Pope's 'Court
Ballad'. He was favourite of King George I.

⁴ Lord Bathurst (14 Aug. 1736) wrote Pope that he was ready to erect an obelisk at
Pope's command.

of your Lordships attention to my welfare every way, & particularly
I am to reckon you the Guardian of my Fortune. In that Capacity,
I must tell you one of the greatest points I have left to wish to accomplish. 'Tis to have a Friend of mine join'd with some other, in an
annuity of 100ll. a year for your Lives. Your Lordship formerly gave
me some hope, you could accomodate such a thing, & purchase the
second life with the common proportion. The Money is now ready,
and I could be heartily glad, if you could.

As soon as Mr Bathurst[1] acquaints me what number of Scots cattle
he wants, they will be sent for: I beg your Lordship to tell him this,
with my humble Services. I intreat my Lady Bathurst to accept of the
same, & I am mightily pleased that she likes & enjoys my Seat:[2] may
she do so many Years!

POPE *to* SAMUEL WESLEY[3]   21 *October* [1735]

The Gentleman's Magazine, lvii. 589

Twitenham, Oct. 21.

Your letter had not been so long unanswered, but that I was not returned from a journey of some weeks when it arrived at this place.
You may depend on the money for the Earl of Peterborow, Mr.
Bethel, Dr. Swift, and Mr. Eckersall, which I will pay beforehand to
any one you shall direct; and I think you may set down Dr. Delany,
whom I will write to.[4] I desired my Lord Oxford some months since,
to tell you this: it was just upon my going to take a last leave of Lord
Peterborow, in so much hurry that I had not time to write; and my
Lord Oxford undertook to tell it you for me. I agree with you in the
opinion of Savage's strange performance,[5] which does not deserve the
benefit of the clergy. Mrs. Wesley has my sincere thanks for her good
wishes in favour of this wretched tabernacle my body; the soul that
is so unhappy as to inhabit it deserves her regard something better,
because it really harbours much good-will for her husband and herself;
no man being more truly, dear Sir, your affectionate and faithful ser-
vant, | Alexander Pope.

Address: To the Rev. Mr. Wesley, at Tiverton, Devon.

[1] Lord Bathurst in Apr. 1735 had given his estate of Riskins to his eldest son Benjamin
(d. 1767). His desire for Scots cattle may be a desire to restock the estate—or it may be some
sort of joke. Pope would hardly seem a normal agent in such a matter.

[2] 'Pope's Seat' was a stone construction in the Park at Cirencester.

[3] Samuel the Younger was son of Samuel (who was a schoolmate of Defoe) and was
elder brother to John and Charles, founders of Methodism. Formerly head usher in Westminster School, he is now master of the Tiverton grammar school.

[4] The reference is to subscriptions for Wesley's *Poems on Several Occasions*, published in
1736, and dedicated to Lord Oxford.

[5] Savage's *Progress of a Divine*, published in July 1735, did not win either friends or
admirers.

†SWIFT *to* POPE¹   21 *October* 1735
1741 La
                                              Oct. 21, 1735.
I answer'd your letter relating to Curl,² &c. I believe my letters have
escap'd being publish'd, because I writ nothing but Nature and Friendship, and particular incidents which could make no figure in writing.
I have observ'd that not only Voiture, but likewise Tully and Pliny
writ their letters for the publick view, more than for the sake of their
correspondents; and I am glad of it, on account of the Entertainment
they have given me. Balsac did the same thing, but with more stiffness,
and consequently less diverting. Now I must tell you that you are to
look upon me as one going very fast out of the world; but my flesh
and bones are to be carried to Holy-head, for I will not lie in a Country
of slaves. It pleaseth me to find that you begin to dislike things in spite
of your philosophy; your Muse cannot forbear her hints to that purpose. I cannot travel to see you; otherwise I solemnly protest I would
do it. I have an intention to pass this winter in the country with a
friend forty miles off,³ and to ride only ten miles a day, yet is my health
so uncertain that I fear it will not be in my power. I often ride a dozen
miles, but I come home to my own bed at night. My best way would
be to marry, for in that case any bed would be better than my own. I
found you a very young man, and I left you a middle aged one; you
knew me a middle aged man, and now I am an old one. Where is my
Lord —?⁴ methinks I am enquiring after a Tulip of last year—"You
need not apprehend any Curll's meddling with your letters to me; I
will not destroy them, but have ordered my Executors to do that
office."⁵ I have a thousand things more to say, *longævitas est garrula*
but I must remember I have other letters to write if I have time, which
I spend to tell you so; I am ever dearest Sir, Your, &c.

THE EARL OF ORRERY *to* POPE⁶   26 *October* 1735
Harvard University
                                        Corke October 26th: 1735.
I sitt down to answer your kind Letter the moment I have read It.
The Freindship of a valuable Man makes amends for all the slander
that the whole Tribe of Knaves and Fools can invent.—*Lord Corn-
bury's* Lines are very fine, and shine the brighter in my Eye for being

¹ This is the fourth in the series of letters first printed in the folio (London, 1741) and
reprinted in the supplement to Faulkner's octavo (1741 Da).
² Doubtless the answer was to an urgent request from Pope for the return of his letters
to Swift—a request recently made also to Bethel, Fortescue, Spence, and Broome.
³ i.e., with Sheridan.—Ball.
⁴ Bolingbroke.
⁵ Pope quotes this sentence as bearing on the history of the publication of the letters
⁶ The text is from Orrery's Letterbooks, vol. vii.

founded on an exact Truth. He is a young Nobleman with whose
Character I am well acquainted; but to whom I am not so personally
known as my Ambition desires: I know I make my Court to You by
entreating You to indulge me in my wishes, and lead me to his Freindship. The Verses shall certainly not be copied, but I will not promise
they shall not be imitated. As to the Trifle You was so good to accept
from me, Those Lines are not worthy so high a Place. Had I a little
Leisure, that is, would my Lawyers allow me a short breathing Time,
I would follow the example of my honour'd Preceptor dear Mr
Fenton,[1] in flinging in the Mite of my Freindship before your Works.
I rejoice to hear we are to have a new Edition of them.

The *Dean*[2] is my dulce Decus: All the moments I steal from Attorneys, Agents, and Sollicitors are pass'd, when I am at Dublin with him.
I propose to be there next month and to stay till the Spring.

And now lett me make you acquainted with the Gentleman, in
whose House I live, and who honours me with his Freindship. He is
a Man in whose breast All the Virtues Center: of great Learning, and
a sweetness of Temper scarce to be parallel'd: His Study has been
Physick: and tho' a young man He is at the Head of his Profession:
Buried at Corke his uncommon fine Qualities move in too narrow a
Sphere: nor will so valuable a Jewel shine in it's full Lustre, till he
goes to Dublin: To summ up all He is worthy of your Countenance.
We often read You together, with that sort of Pleasure which arises
from not only admiring the works, but the Author. Take him to your
Bosom, dear Sir, and be assur'd He will outstrip any Character I can
give him.— *Doctor Barry* is the Person I mean.[3]

Lett me ask you the plain English Question, How do you do? The
more I know You, the more I tremble for You. *Dean Ward's* best
wishes attend You. May Health and Happiness be your closest &
most constant Companions! Adieu, dear Sir; I am | most affectionately
Yours. | Orrery.

BROOME *to* POPE   29 *October* 1735

Elwin–Courthope, viii. 175

                                                          Oct. 29, 1735.

Dear Mr. Pope,—I am really ashamed of calling myself a man of
retirement. I am a perfect rambler. I have travelled over our two
counties with as much diligence as if I were to survey them. Truly I

---

[1] Possibly the fact that Fenton had been tutor to Orrery may have had some influence
on the equivocal nature of Orrery's attachment to Pope.

[2] Dean Swift.

[3] Sir Edward Barry, M.D. (created a baronet in 1775), is presumably here intended.
Boswell got a witticism out of Barry's theory of pulsation (*Life of Johnson*, ed. Hill-Powell,
iii. 34).

had almost forgot the world was so wide. I was called by a subpœna to Ipswich, where a debate arose as material as whether a word should be wrote with a great or little O. This important objection knocked the presentment dead at one blow. Very much edified, I started for Pulham. There I found my old friend Sir Edmund Bacon, of Garboldisham. He carried me off almost to Thetford, to sport upon the heath. At my return I found a summons to preach at Norwich. I complied: but am now your humble servant at Pulham. Thus have I lived the life of a courier, and in a literal sense the world has been my inn, and my life a journey. Now to your obliging letter. I have forgot we ever had any difference. It is true, though a wound is healed, it usually leaves a scar behind; but this is no blemish, unless it were contracted dishonourably. Adieu to all disputes. Let us make amends for seven years coldness by loving seven times more warmly and affectionately. I sincerely desire for the future,

Mihi

Fias recantatis amicus

Opprobriis, animumque reddas.[1]

Your request concerning the Odyssey is very reasonable, and in justice I ought, and therefore do declare that never any contract subsisted between us, and consequently no contract could be broken. You paid me 500*l.*—that is, 100*l.* for the notes, and 400*l.* for eight books of the verse translation, and Mr. Fenton in proportion for his four books.[2]

You desire me to recollect my circumstances as to fame and fortune at the time of the publication of the Odyssey. As to fame, I recollect with pleasure and acknowledge with gratitude, that you highly advanced it, *Quod placeo, si placeo, tuum est.* If I could invent stronger terms to express my sentiments I would use them, but every honest heart feels more than the tongue speaks.

As to fortune, Providence had, long before the publication of the Odyssey, blessed me abundantly. I have not possessed so little as 500*l.* annually near twenty years. I was so easy in my fortunes when you published the Iliad, that I was grown above taking any reward for my part of the annotations, and refused all lucrative acknowledgments. I speak not this out of vanity, but gratitude to a gracious God, who enabled me to make an aged father's declension easy, and to be the support of a distressed family. You are no stranger to this history.

---

[1] Horace, *Carmina*, i. xvi. 26–28.

[2] Broome omits mention of the subscription copies which came to him free—to the total value of 100*l.*, as Pope remarked in a note to *The Dunciad Variorum* (1729), Bk. III, l. 328. Accounts of the amount paid Fenton differ. See Spence, p. 326, and Ruffhead, p. 205. It would be natural for Broome to assume that Fenton was paid at the same rate as himself; but since Fenton had more prestige than Broome, it would be natural for Pope to pay him more.

Pray my service to Sir Clement Cottrell. I am happy to have a place in his memory. It is an honour to be lodged in a worthy mind; but I fear my name is the most insignificant image there—a fly in amber—a toy in a cabinet of curiosities. I shall always value my life the more while he expresses a concern for it. Yours affectionately.

POPE *to* FORTESCUE[1]   *November* 1735

1797 (Polwhele, i. 324)

Friday night, Nov. 1735.

I hope this finds you well arrived. I was put into more solicitude than I expected, for your health, by Dr. Hollings, who the other day told me you had been out of order, of which I knew nothing. I hope in God it is quite over. Give me a line when I may see you most at leisure. I think to be in town on Monday or Tuesday. The man whom Curl served with a process,[2] just before you went out of town, I suppose should have the assistance of an attorney, to appear for him the first day of term, to know what it is for? I am always impatient to see you, dear Sir, and always faithfully, yours, | A. Pope.

Address: To Wm. Fortescue, esq. in Bell-yard.

‡POPE *to* SWIFT[3]   [*November* 1735]

1740

To answer your question as to Mr. Hughes, I did just know him.[4] What he wanted as to genius he made up as an honest man: but he was of the class you think him.

I am glad you think of Dr. Rundle as I do. He will be an honour to the Bishops, and a disgrace to one Bishop,[5] two things you will like: But what you will like more particularly, he will be a friend and benefactor even to[6] your un-friended, un-benefited Nation; he will be a friend to human race, wherever he goes. Pray tell him my best wishes for his health and long life: I wish you and he came over together, or that I were with you. I never saw a man so seldom whom I liked so much as Dr. Rundle.

Lord Peterborow I went to take a last leave of, at his setting sail

---

[1] The dating is doubtless from Fortescue's endorsement.

[2] Curll's printed letter of 26 July (q.v.) threatened the law, and since Fortescue was leaving town early in August, Curll must have acted in July.

[3] This seems a peculiarly obvious example of conflating two letters. News of Lord Peterborow's death in Lisbon reached London about 12 Nov. In the third paragraph of this letter he is still alive; in the fourth Pope has already received his watch as a legacy. Ball prints the first two paragraphs separately under date of September and the remainder of the letter under date of December. Pope printed no date for the letter.

[4] Hughes, I did just know him. What] Hughes. What *1741 L*; *1742 L*.

[5] Gibson (Bishop of London) prevented Rundle's advancement in England.

[6] benefactor even to] benefactor to *1742 La*.

for Lisbon: No Body can be more wasted, no Soul can be more alive. Immediately after the severest operation of being cut into the bladder for a suppression of urine, he took coach, and got from Bristol to Southhampton. This is a man that will neither live nor die like any other mortal.

Poor Lord Peterborow! there is another string lost, that wou'd have help'd to draw you hither! He order'd on his death-bed his Watch to be given me (that which had accompanied him in all his travels) with this reason, "That I might have something to put me every day in mind of him." It was a present to him from the King of Sicily, whose arms and *Insignia* are graved on the inner-case; on the outer, I have put this inscription. *Victor Amadeus, Rex Sicilae, Dux Sabaudiae, &c. &c., Carolo Mordaunt, Comiti de Peterborow, D. D. Car. Mor. Com. de Pet. Alexandro Pope moriens legavit. 1735.*[1]

Pray write to me a little oftner: and if there be a thing left in the world that pleases you, tell it one who will partake of it. I hear with approbation and pleasure, that your present care is to relieve the most helpless of this world, those objects[2] which most want our compassion, tho' generally made the scorn of their fellow-creatures, such as are less innocent than they. You always think generously; and of all charities, this is the most disinterested, and least vain-glorious; done to such as never will thank you, or can praise you for it.

God bless you with ease, if not with pleasure; with a tolerable state of health, if not with its full enjoyment; with a resign'd temper of mind, if not a very chearful one. It is upon these terms I live myself tho' younger than you, and I repine not at my lot, could but the presence of a few that I love be added to these. Adieu.

POPE *to* MRS. CÆSAR   17 *November* 1735

Rousham

Twitenham, Novr. 17th 1735.

Madam,—Notwithstanding you expect I should write to you about nothing but Mum, I must disappoint you, by telling you I wish you better things than any I can send you. Your Temper is too good to need any thing to Compose your Spirits; & I only sincerely wish your Fortune and Happiness were equal to your Merit & Patience. I shall never forget your Zeal for your friends; & I am sure They owe you the same Warmth & Services, which it was always in your inclination to render them. I am, with sincerity, Madam, | Your obliged, & faithful Servant, | A. Pope

Address: To | Mrs Cæsar, in new | Bond street.

---

[1] A footnote in 1741 Dab translates the inscription.
[2] Idiots and Lunaticks.—Footnote in 1741 Dab.

POPE *to* BROOME 18 *November* 1735

Elwin–Courthope, viii. 177

Nov. 18, 1735.

I am glad to find by your letter that you are in spirits and health, and particularly that you are not fixed to the premises, nor plunged in retreat so much as you used to be; for this gives me a hope that we may one day meet again, and that you may once more be not unwilling to look at Twitnam as an old acquaintance, but more improved than the owner of it by so many years. Sir Clement will be as glad to see you as I, and I as glad to see you as ever I was in my life.

I thank you for what you say to me, and am quite content upon that head.[1] You do not tell me whether you sent a line to that scoundrel or not, and if you have not, I think it is better let alone, in your regard, on second thoughts; for I would not have him trifle with your name. It is a sort of disgrace to be but mentioned by him any way, though ever so indifferently; but to be commended by him is downright slander. If you have kept any letters of mine, I am sure they can be of little worth, and may be disagreeable ever to see in his or any other bookseller's hands; for there is little honesty in the profession, whenever the gain of a few shillings comes in their way. I should think it kind in you, and considerate toward me, if you would return them me.[2] None, I promise you, should ever see the light, unless I should find one or two not very contemptible, which might show the world my regard for you, and be a little monument that we were and are friends. I would add another instance of it, by changing that verse in the Dunciad thus:

> Hibernian politics, O Swift, thy fate,
> And Pope's, nine years to comment and translate.[3]

I have therefore sent you my second volume without that poem, till it is so altered in the next edition. It went by the carrier, directed as you prescribed, this week. Adieu, and may all felicity, mental and corporeal, attend you. I am, dear sir, your faithful and affectionate humble servant.

Perhaps you do not know the various fates of your acquaintance. Sir Harry Blount, who was married and separated from his wife, is now going to live with her again upon her submission, and at her desire.

---

[1] Pope did not, somewhat to one's surprise, publish Broome's statement in his later editions. Matters of hire are perhaps vulgar in parade; the affair was best served by silence in Pope's day.

[2] In his letter replying to this request (1 Dec.) Broome effectively declines.

[3] This change was made in later editions of *The Dunciad*, and the mention of Broome in the footnote excised.

POPE *to* MRS. KNIGHT   25 *November* 1735

Bowles (1806) x. 115–16

Twitenham, Nov. 25, 1735.

Madam,—You will not think my silence any evidence of my forgetting you, after what I have declared to you long ago. It is a pain to me to be writing things I cannot express, to friends I cannot see; for both my zeal for them, and my concern not to be nearer them, puts me into an uneasiness not to be told. I was much disappointed in not finding Mrs. Elliot: I was at her door the day before I left London, and the first day that I returned to it, which was the morning after she went. If a desire to be with you some days would transport me beyond such necessary business as my relations and friends find for me, I assure you my own business would not hinder my complying with it.

I have not, for I cannot forget what you mention in relation to Mr. Harte: one of the livings I can have no possible view of, knowing nothing towards the Duke of Rutland. The other, of Lord Essex, I'll speak to Lord Cornbury upon, who is but just returned from abroad. I've hopes of seeing him soon: but God knows, these are remote views.

To prove to you how little essential to friendship I hold letter-writing, after the experience of thirty years (for so long Mr. Curl tells you I kept a regular correspondence), I have not yet written to Mr. Mallet, whom I love and esteem greatly, nay whom I know to have as tender a heart, and that feels a friendly remembrance as long as any man. Pray send him the inclosed: 'tis all I can say, for (as I told you before) it makes me quite sick to be put upon the pikes, to be saying such things as can only be felt, not said. When do you come to town? The rascally *builders*, as you call them, do not deserve that name; they pull down more than they build up, and will keep you out of your house for ever, if you don't come and drive them out. Mrs. Patty loves you, and hopes no woman of quality can love you better; for then she would wish to be a woman of quality. I love you (modestly speaking), and I love Mrs. Elliot (Christianly speaking); so pray love and forgive him who is truly and morally hers, and, dear Madam, | Your, etc.

POPE *to* FORTESCUE[1]   *December* 1735

1797 (Polwhele, i. 322)

This is only to tell you, I love you not the less for not seeing you more. Ever since we dined in the park, I have been planting at home, have catched two colds on the neck of one another, but still plant on, being

---

[1] The date is probably from Fortescue's endorsement. In June 1736 Pope writes that he is rebuilding his temple—a temple unfortunate in all senses of the word.

resolved to finish this fine season. My alterations are what you would
not conceive. Besides my shell temple is fallen down; and yet I live!
Whether I shall see you before the end of the week, in town, I know
not. I dare not cross the water to lie abroad, with this cold upon me.
I hope you are well; I heartily love you, and wish you so. Adieu! |
A. Pope.

Dec. 1735.

BROOME *to* POPE   1 *December* 1735

Elwin–Courthope, viii. 179

Dec. 1, 1735.

Dear Mr. Pope,—If the value of letters depended upon the punctuality of the return, I should be the most estimable of all your correspondents; but this excellence is no more than that of the post-boy
who carries the letter, and usually with punctuality. When I open my
breast to you upon paper, it is but opening a toy shop which affords
only trifles. I remember a Spanish Governor in the West Indies, with
great gravity and solemnity, sent his whisker in pawn to a merchant
for many thousands of crowns. It was accepted as sufficient security.
If you can be as easily satisfied, you shall not want such pledges.

I do not wonder at your caution in recovering your letters, after
the late publication. Yet, after all, some few passages being retracted,
where is the mighty grievance? With the good they certainly do you
honour, and the worst that the ill-natured can say is what is no dishonour. You have, like our greatest beauties, shown there is such a
thing as an excellence in trifling agreeably. It is a Laelius or a Scipio
playing with pebbles,[1] and, in my opinion, the humane companion,
the dutiful and affectionate son, the compassionate and obliging friend,
appear so strongly almost in every page, that I assure you I had rather
be the owner of the writer's heart than of the head that has honoured
England with Homer, his Essays, Moral Epistles, &c. These gain you
honour with men, the other with heaven and angels.

I thank you for the obliging alteration intended in your poem. If
I were of your church, I should say it was a kind of releasement from
purgatory and from the company of condemned reprobate poets and
authors.

I have a desire to reprint my Miscellany, not out of any degree of
vanity, but merely to give them a more solemn interment, and to bury
my dead in a more decent monument. But Mr. Lintot lays me under
difficulties. He expects me to print them at my own expense, and then
he would be the vendor. If you can bring him to reason, I will thank

---

[1] An allusion to Dryden's description of Plutarch's methods in his *Life of Plutarch* (1683).

you for the obligation.[1] I desire no lucrative favours from him, but solely an opportunity of correcting my negligences.

I have taken the liberty to send you a poem on Death.[2] It has long laid by me. I beg you to read it with your usual patience. I know there are some things common in it, but no wonder when it is wrote on the commonest of all subjects, Death. I flatter myself that where I coincide with the sentiments of others I have done it at least equally poetically.

I hope once more to see you and Twickenham. I would not come to London for Lambeth, but a friend shall always command me. I have long given over all worldly aims. I protest knowing myself a mortal, I am ashamed, even in thought, to wish for any more earthly accessions; and for this best of reasons, because I know there is an immortality. But I will not preach; I will only pray that all happiness may attend you here and hereafter. I am ever yours.

POPE *to* JACOB TONSON, SR.   4 *December* 1735

Arthur A. Houghton, Jr.

Twitnam. Decr. 4. | 1735

I condole with you in the first place for the death of your Nephew,[3] between whom & me, a matter past a short time before, which gave me Concern,[4] as I believe it will You when I tell it you—I presume this occasion may have brought you to Town once more, and I hope it will not be without our seeing each other. Whether your Deafness will permit our Conversation to be on Equal terms, or whether I can only hear you, That will be a great pleasure to me, & I shall only be sorry to give you none on my part. Yet I think you love me well enough to find it some, meerly to be face to face. As soon as you can, pray write me a line, when, & where we shall pass a day & a night together. I can show you papers, if you can't hear me talk, & I can ask you Questions at least in writing, & I don't care how prolix you are in answering: I've often thought of writing to you, but I believe you may have read too many of my Letters of late, which is a favour you owe to Curll. I took very kindly the Paragraph in yours which your Nephew communicated to me. I am glad if any of my Writings

---

[1] Evidently Broome had confidence in Pope's influence and discounted the animosity to Lintot that Pope had frequently expressed in letters to Broome.

[2] First mentioned in Fenton to Broome, 3 Apr. 1728. It was printed in Broome's *Poems* (1739).

[3] *The London Evening Post*, 25 Nov. 1735, announced: 'Yesterday in the Afternoon died at Barnes in Surrey, aged about 52, Jacob Tonson, Jun. Esq; the greatest Bookseller in the World, reckon'd to have died worth 100,000*l*. Jacob Tonson, Sen. Esq; his Uncle, who belong'd to the memorable *Kit-Cat* Club is now living, aged about 80.'

[4] This 'concern' is obscure. See Pope to Buckley, 17 Aug. 1735 and note.

please you who have been used to so much better, and I am glad if
the Writer pleases you, who have known so many better. Let me be
what I will, I assure you I am very sincerely | Dear Sir | Your
Affectionate | Friend & humble | Servant | A. Pope.

Address: To Jacob Tonson, Senr Esq. | at Ledbury, | Herefordshire.
Postmark: 4/DE

UNDATABLE LETTERS

*POPE *to* THE EARL OF BURLINGTON[1]
Chatsworth

Friday.

My Lord,—Many things have hinderd my waiting on yourself & my Lady this week. I would be glad to do it on Saturday what hour you please, provided you don't both go to the Opera? if so, I beg to have your Coach on Sunday morning. Be pleasd to let the Bearer know if you would have the Puppy, in which case I will bring it with me & be its Foster-father. I am with great truth | My Ld. | Yours always. | A. Pope.

I have no paper to write on but this, & I don't care, now I have an amanuensis.

Address: To the Rt Hon. the | Earl of Burlington

*POPE *to* THE EARL OF BURLINGTON[2]
Chatsworth

Thursday.

My Lord,—If you happen to be at leisure enough to day to call on a poor distressed, undetermin'd Designer, whose works lie unfinishd for want of a little judgment (the case of many a man) pray come, & take me away with you if you please, for I can do nothing without you. I am with the truest Esteem, affection, & obligation | Your Lordships most faithful Servant | A. Pope.

*POPE *to* THE EARL OF BURLINGTON[3]
Chatsworth

Tuesday morning.

My Lord,—I was obliged after a very tiresome Days Indisposition on Saturday, to be in Bed before you went to Chiswick. I concluded, as

---

[1] Before the poem 'Bounce to Fop' appeared in April of 1736, Pope had given a puppy of Bounce's to Lord Burlington. In lines 59, 60 Bounce is made to say,

> 'My second (Child of Fortune!) waits
> At *Burlington*'s Palladian Gates.'

But how long before 1736 the puppy had enjoyed this eminence we do not know.

[2] Since Pope was an inveterate 'designer', one cannot place this letter. In 1732 he was adding a portico to his villa, and sought the aid of Burlington's taste; but obviously there are other possible periods.

[3] Bolingbroke was in England from September of 1729 to April of 1735. This is possibly the period of the letter. After 1735 Bolingbroke was much on the Continent, but he returned to England after 1735 more than once.

I heard nothing from your Lordship nor Lord Bolingbroke, that the Party was not made on Sunday concerning which I writ to him. Sir Clem. Cottrel & myself would gladly wait on you before your journey, either to day, or any (except to morrow) which might no way interrupt your other Engagements: His Servant who brings this, will convey your Commands to us. I am, with the sincerest Esteem, | My Lord | Your most faithfull obedient Servant, | A. Pope.

Address: To the Right Honble: the | Earl of Burlington.

*POPE to THE EARL OF BURLINGTON[1]

Chatsworth

Munday morning

My Lord,—After much Tribulation, I got home yesterday: & am confined by my Doctors directions to take physick this whole week at least, & not to walk abroad. There is nevertheless a Room in this little Tabernacle, that has no Close-tools, Basins, or Bottles in it: which if your Lordship will, at any idle hour, please to look into, as you pass by, it will be doing like yourself, that is, doing a very good naturd thing: as you have done many to | My Lord, Your ever-obliged faithfull | humble Servant | A. Pope.

Addressed: For the Rt. Honorable, the | Earl of Burlingtone [*sic*]

*POPE to THE EARL OF BURLINGTON

Chatsworth

My Lord,—It's so long since I've had the honour & pleasure of seeing you, tho I have twice or thrice seen your flying Horses & Chariots pass by my door, that I've some cause to fear you have quite forgot a man who (I faithfully assure your Lordship) can never forget to be yours. Not being satisfyd with having Applyed twice to your Ministers (the Porters at London & Chiswick) I in this manner Petition for Access to you, and beg to know if you shall lye at Chiswick on Friday or Saturday night? for to my shame be it spoken, my Days are not my own, & on Sunday or Munday I am to leave this Country. which I shou'd be grieved to do, without first putting you in mind, by bringing

---

[1] It is barely possible that the key word here is 'tabernacle'. Writing to Fortescue, 23 Aug. 1735, Pope had used the word of Fortescue's 'hermitage' at Richmond. He frequently echoes himself in such phrasing. He had about 1 Oct. returned from his summer ramble (Southampton, Oxford, Rousham, Stowe). Meanwhile Burlington had been in Yorkshire (*The Whitehall Evening Post*, 11 Oct. 1735), but he returned 4 Oct. apparently. If the letter dates from this period, Pope might well have mentioned his lordship's journey.

him into your sight, that there is yet in being, such an one as | My Lord | Your most obliged, & most faithfull Servant | A. Pope.

Twitenham, | Thursday.

*POPE *to* THE EARL OF BURLINGTON

Chatsworth

My Lord,—I hope the Servant told your Lordship I shd rejoice to see you any day after to morrow till Friday, when I am to set out for Lord Cobham's. I thank you for the salmon. Will you eat of it the day you come? & a Mutton Stake in the manner of that great Master, Signior Kent? I am sincerely & respectfully. | My Lord | Your most faithful Servant | A. Pope.

Address: To my Lord Burlington

*POPE *to* THE EARL OF BURLINGTON[1]

Chatsworth

> To the R. Hon. the E. of Burlington:
> The humble Petition of A. P. Gent.

My Lord

　　　Sheweth,

　　　　　That A Person in great distress, who should be with a Lawyer to morrow by 8, and with another by 10, in the morning, humbly Petitions you will let him follow his Necessary Business; and he will pass this whole Evening in Pleasure at Burlington house, in your Lordships Company (without Papists & disaffected persons) provided you let him go before you thither: and follow us as soon as ever you can.

　　　And your Petitioner shall humbly Pray &c.

*POPE *to* THE EARL OF BURLINGTON[2]

Chatsworth

> Burlington house, 7 aClock.
> Friday night.

My Lord,—I have wishd & wanted to see you, but the first moment

---

[1] In protecting his copyrights and, after 1729, in efforts to further his sister's interminable suit in chancery, Pope was often involved with lawyers.

[2] Even the tantalizing word 'congratulations' will not aid in dating this letter. Among the many occasions when congratulations would be appropriate were May 1729, when his lordship became one of His Majesty's Privy Council and Lord Lieutenant of the West Riding; June 1731, when he was made Captain of the Band of Gentlemen Pensioners; Aug. 1731, when he was made Captain of the Yeomen of the Guard; 27 Oct. 1731, when his daughter Charlotte was born; and 25 May 1737, when his claim to the Barony de Clifford was allowed. There must have been many other occasions as well.

I knew of your Return, I was waited for at dinner & could not stay
even to speak to your Lordship. I hoped to have been able to trouble
you at Chiswick with my Congratulations, to morrow, but that also
is put out of my power. If your Horses have nothing else to do but
to fetch me on Sunday morning (Mr Kent not imploying them) I
will call at Burlington house by eleven in the morning, & if I find
them there, commit myself to their discretion. I am much disappointed
to miss you so often, as yesterday, and again this afternoon. No man
is more | Your Lordships faithfull Servant. | A. Pope.

Address: The Earl of Burlington.

*POPE *to* THE EARL OF BURLINGTON[1]

Chatsworth

Saturday

My Lord,—I only beg leave (another would have said Humbly beg
leave) by this to put you in mind of the Ticket you were pleas'd to
give me hopes of. For all that I know the whole happiness of a Lady
depends upon it. I hope you'll let me know hers & my Fate to night,
by a decisive word in answer to this. I am with more Zeal & Sincerity
than can be cramm'd into this short paper | Your Lordships most
obliged | & faithful Servant | A. Pope.

*POPE *to* THE COUNTESS OF BURLINGTON

Sotheby, 13 Feb. 1928, lot 230

(Not Seen).

The catalogue prints:

"From Mr. Lyttelton's in Pall Mall"

"What I writ last night was in the sincerity of my heart. I have
no thoughts of going to Twitnam, but only to leave your Ladyship
my parting wishes."

*POPE *to* HUGH BETHEL

Egerton MS. 1948

I am just coming to Town, & send my Luggage to you intending to
lye (not dine, but sup) with you. I've sent a Chicken for that purpose
Adieu till then | Yours | A. Pope

[1] The 'ticket' may be a lottery ticket, issued to raise funds for building Westminster
Bridge—or Fulham Bridge; or it may be so simple a matter as an opera ticket! The *Gazette*
(26 June 1739) advertises the bridge lottery.

*POPE *to* HUGH BETHEL

Egerton MS. 1948

Twitnam, Tuesday Night

The weather is turnd so cold again with the Easterly wind, that I'll return & see you in Town on Thursday, rather than have you face it, in so much Dust[1] too. Therfore you may expect that Day | Your faithful Servant | Dear Sir | A. Pope after noon.

Address: To | Hugh Bethel Esq | Arlington Street.

POPE *to* HUGH BETHEL

Ruffhead, pp. 495–6

FRAGMENT

I am so aukward at writing letters, to such as expect me to write like a wit, that I take any course to avoid it. 'Tis to you only, and a few such plain honest men, I like to open myself with the same freedom, and as free from all disguises, not only of sentiment, but of style, as they themselves.

---

[1] The dust would be bad for Bethel's asthma. The address is that of Bethel's sister.

PRINTED IN
GREAT BRITAIN
AT THE
UNIVERSITY PRESS
OXFORD
BY
CHARLES BATEY
PRINTER
TO THE
UNIVERSITY